MW01231132

Collective Intelligence and E–Learning 2.0:
Implications of Web–Based Communities and Networking

Harrison Hao Yang
State University of New York at Oswego, USA

Steve Chi–Yin Yuen
University of Southern Mississippi, USA

INFORMATION SCIENCE REFERENCE

Hershey · New York

Director of Editorial Content:	Kristin Klinger
Senior Managing Editor:	Jamie Snavely
Assistant Managing Editor:	Michael Brehm
Publishing Assistant:	Sean Woznicki
Typesetter:	Michael Brehm
Cover Design:	Lisa Tosheff
Printed at:	Yurchak Printing Inc.

Published in the United States of America by
　　　　Information Science Reference (an imprint of IGI Global)
　　　　701 E. Chocolate Avenue
　　　　Hershey PA 17033
　　　　Tel: 717-533-8845
　　　　Fax: 717-533-8661
　　　　E-mail: cust@igi-global.com
　　　　Web site: http://www.igi-global.com/reference

Copyright © 2010 by IGI Global. All rights reserved. No part of this publication may be reproduced, stored or distributed in any form or by any means, electronic or mechanical, including photocopying, without written permission from the publisher.
　　　Product or company names used in this set are for identification purposes only. Inclusion of the names of the products or companies does not indicate a claim of ownership by IGI Global of the trademark or registered trademark.

Library of Congress Cataloging-in-Publication Data

Collective intelligence and e-learning 2.0 : implications of web-based
communities and networking / Harrison Hao Yang and Steve Chi-Yin Yuen,
editors.
　　　p. cm.
　Includes bibliographical references and index.
　Summary: "This book provides a useful reference to the latest advancements
in the area of educational technology and e-learning"--Provided by publisher.
　ISBN 978-1-60566-729-4 (hardcover : alk. paper) -- ISBN 978-1-60566-730-0
(ebook : alk. paper) 1. Distance education. 2. Web-based instruction. 3.
Educational Web sites. 4. Internet in education. 5. Online social networks.
6. Web 2.0. I. Yang, Harrison Hao, 1964- II. Yuen, Steve Chi-Yin, 1953-
　LC5803.C65C64182 2010
　371.35'8--dc22
　　　　　　　　　　　　　2009010521

British Cataloguing in Publication Data
A Cataloguing in Publication record for this book is available from the British Library.

All work contributed to this book is new, previously-unpublished material. The views expressed in this book are those of the authors, but not necessarily of the publisher.

List of Reviewers

J. Enrique Agudo, *University of Extremadura, Spain*
Luiz Fernando de Barros Campos, *Federal University of Minas Gerais, Brazil*
Leah Massar Bloom, *State University of New York Purchase College, USA*
Curtis J. Bonk, *Indiana University, USA*
Jeff Boyer, *University of Florida*
Cathy Cavanaugh, *University of Florida*
Chaka Chaka, *Walter Sisulu University for Technology and Science, South Africa*
Pearl Chen, *California State University, Los Angeles, USA*
Candace Chou, *University of St. Thomas, USA*
Clara Pereira Coutinho, *University of Minho, Portugal*
Katie Crenshaw, *University of Alabama at Birmingham, USA*
Elizabeth Downs, *Georgia Southern University, USA*
Michael Douma, *Institute for Dynamic Educational Advancement, USA*
Dimitrios Drogidis, *School Consultant of Primary Education, Greece*
Jianxia Du, *Mississippi State University, USA*
Carrie Eastman, *State University of New York Purchase College, USA*
Patricia Edwards, *University of Extremadura, Spain*
Deborah Everhart, *Georgetown University, USA*
Ann Dutton Ewbank, *Arizona State University, USA*
Teresa S. Foulger, *Arizona State University, USA*
Stephen W. Harmon, *Georgia State University, USA*
Richard Hartshorne, *University of North Carolina at Charlotte, USA*
Jeannine Hirtle, *University of Hawaii at Hilo, USA*
Morris S. Y. Jong, *The Chinese University of Hong Kong, Hong Kong*
Kathryn Kennedy, *University of Florida, USA*
Fong-Lok Lee, *The Chinese University of Hong Kong, Hong Kong*
Meng-Fen Grace Lin, *University of Hawaii, USA*
Yuliang Liu, *Southern Illinois University Edwardsville, USA*
Susanne Markgren, *State University of New York Purchase College, USA*
Paraskevi Mentzelou, *Alexander Technological Educational Institute of Thessaloniki, Greece*
F.R. "Fritz" Nordengren, *Des Moines University, USA*
Peter Reed, *Edge Hill University, UK*

Judi Repman, *Georgia Southern University, USA*
Mercedes Rico, *University of Extremadura, Spain*
Robin M. Roberts, *University of Nevada, USA*
Rajani Sadasivam, *University of Alabama at Birmingham, USA*
Junjie Shang, *Peking University, China*
Kaye Shelton, *Dallas Baptist University, USA*
Brian Smith, *Edge Hill University, UK*
Chareen Snelson, *Boise State University, USA*
Sharon Stoerger, *Indiana University, USA*
Daniel W. Surry, *University of South Alabama, USA*
Ann York, *Des Moines University, USA*
Chien Yu, *Mississippi State University, USA*
Ke Zhang, *Wayne State University*
Robert Zheng, *University of Utah, USA*
Cordelia Zinskie, *Georgia Southern University, USA*

Table of Contents

Section 1
From Web 2.0 to E-Learning 2.0 and Beyond

Section 2
Web 2.0 Technologies in E-Learning

Detailed Table of Contents

Section 1
From Web 2.0 to E-Learning 2.0 and Beyond

Section one "From Web 2.0 to E-Learning 2.0 and Beyond" introduces the theoretical aspect of e-learning 2.0 based on Web 2.0 technologies. The first part, consisting of six chapters, discusses new learning paradigms and the concept of e-learning 2.0, issues in designing and implementing e-learning 2.0, as well as the future of Web 2.0, e-learning 2.0, and university 2.0. Section one opens with a chapter by Downes who coined the term e-learning 2.0. Downes, in his chapter Learning Networks and Connective Knowledge, introduces his theoretical views on factors that may impact the future of e-learning. He discusses connectivisim theory, networked learning, connective knowledge, and network semantics that form e-learning 2.0. Ewbank and her colleagues review the capabilities of social networking tools and link those capabilities to recent legal and ethical controversies involving use of social networking tools. The third chapter in this part is from Repman, Zinskie, and Downs. They examine institutional factors that impede implementation of e-learning 2.0. Zheng's chapter presents a new instructional design model that specifically addresses the cognitive demands involved in Web 2.0 learning. Jones and Harmon discuss synchronous online learning environments (SOLEs) and their affordances for teaching and learning. Finally, Surry and Ensimger analyze many of the potential problems that could accompany university 2.0 and suggest a series of recommendations for university administrators.

Chapter 1

This chapter outlines some of the thinking behind new e-learning technology. Part of this thinking is centered around the theory of connectivism, which asserts that knowledge - and therefore the learning of knowledge - is distributive, that is, not located in any given place but rather consists of the network of connections formed from experience and interactions with a knowing community. And another part of this thinking is centered around the new, and the newly empowered, learner, the member of the Net generation, who is thinking and interacting in new ways. These trends combine to form what is sometimes called 'e-learning 2.0' - an approach to learning that is based on conversation and interaction, on sharing, creation and participation, on learning not as a separate activity, but rather, as embedded in meaningful activities such as games or workflows.

Chapter 2

This chapter reviews the capabilities of social networking tools and links those capabilities to recent legal and ethical controversies involving use of social networking tools such as Facebook and MySpace. A social cognitive moral framework is applied to explore and analyze the ethical issues present in these incidents. The chapter includes a description of current research with preservice students involving an intervention whereby students read and think about real cases where educators use social networking. Recommendations for applying institutional codes of conduct to ethical dilemmas involving online tools are discussed.

Chapter 3

As online learning continues to expand and evolve, new challenges emerge regarding the implementation of Web 2.0 tools and technologies in online pedagogy. The business model approach to online learning being embraced by many institutions may actually work against faculty who want to utilize Web 2.0 technologies to create e-learning 2.0 experiences for their students. Faculty and administrators need to recognize that differences in perspectives may significantly impact future directions of online courses and programs.

Chapter 4

With its ill-structured learning and rapid incrementation of information in a non-linear fashion, Web 2.0 learning poses enormous challenges to online instructional designers and teachers. The traditional ID models are deemed less fit for Web 2.0 learning due to their linear, well-structured design approach. This chapter proposes a new ID model that specifically addresses the cognitive demands involved in

Web 2.0 learning, promotes learning that focuses on metacognitive thinking and self-regulation, facilitates knowledge integration and construction of schemas-of-the-moment for ill-structured learning, and delivers an environment by connecting activities with behavior to form a dynamic learning environment in Web 2.0 application.

This chapter deals centrally with one emerging aspect of Web 2.0 for education, that of the increasing demand for real time and near real-time interaction among users. Whereas most online learning has, to date, taken place in an asynchronous format, there is a growing need for an ability to provide learning opportunities in a synchronous setting. This chapter discusses synchronous online learning environments (SOLEs) and the affordances they present for teaching and learning. Particularly it focuses on a capability of these environments known as ancillary communications. It discusses ancillary communications as an intentional instructional strategy and presents guidelines for its implementation.

University 2.0 offers amazing potential to fundamentally change the way higher education functions in the future. With this change will come the opportunity to improve educational quality, reach new learners, and create new organizational structures, but there will also be many potential problems. Many of the problems relate to the key issue of maintaining the vital human and social dimension of higher education in a rapidly changing, technology rich environment. This chapter describes many of the potential problems that will accompany university 2.0 and provides a series of recommended actions that university administrators can take to respond to the problems.

Section 2
Web 2.0 Technologies in E-Learning

Section two "Web 2.0 Technologies in E-Learning" discusses numerous Web 2.0 technologies and their uses in e-learning. Section two, consisting of ten chapters, discusses current research, case studies, as well as pedagogical approaches and strategies for using Web 2.0 technologies in e-learning environments. The first two chapters of Section two explore the use of Wiki in online learning, opening this part with Alden's chapter Use of Wikis to Support Collaboration among Online Students, in which he discusses the merits and challenges of using a Wiki to support the activities of students during group projects. Bonk, Lee, Kim, and Lin provide dozens of Wikibook collaboration ideas and suggestions from their cross-institutional study. Next, Snelson's chapter introduces Web-based video as a new type of educational motion picture, delves into the technical aspects of Web 2.0 video tools, describes instructional strategies that integrate Web-based video clips into e-learning, and examines barriers that could potentially inhibit its use. Everhart and Shelton's chapter provides effective pedagogical strategies for social bookmaking. The fifth chapter in this part is from Jong and his colleagues at the Chinese University of Hong Kong. The authors discuss the theoretical foundation and pedagogical implementation of VISOLE (Virtual Interactive Student-Oriented Learning Environment). The next three chapters explore the uses of Second Life® in online learning. Edwards and her colleagues address the application of e-learning in university degree programs based on the practical, intensive, and holistic aspects of Second Life®. Park and Baek introduce three educational uses of the Second Life® virtual world and provide empirical evidence of effective usage in an educational context. Stoerger discusses the theoretical perspectives, educational possibilities, and challenges of using Second Life® in teaching and learning. Following the three Second Life® chapters, Liu and McCombs discuss the uniqueness of podcasting technology in promoting e-learning, examine the educational efficacy of podcasting in e-learning, and provide podcasting best practice in e-learning design and delivery. Finally, Yuen and Yang's chapter discusses the potential uses of social networking in education and presents a case study where social networking is integrated into e-learning courses for the purposes of building a sense of community, improving communications and interactions, and promoting student-centered collaboration.

Chapter 7

Jay Alden, National Defense University, USA

This chapter discusses the merits and challenges of using a Wiki to support the activities of students during group projects. It shows the importance of student collaboration in online courses by fostering deeper learning, producing higher quality team products, and preparing students for today's collaborative workplace. The chapter focuses on the best practices of faculty from setting up the Wiki at the onset through the final phase of evaluating the group product and the individual contribution of individual team members. It also discusses a number of ways in which Wiki-supported collaborative activities can be introduced into online courses and the criteria for selecting particular Wiki products for an institution.

Chapter 8

Curtis J. Bonk, Indiana University, USA
Mimi Miyoung Lee, University of Houston, USA
Nari Kim, The University of Wisconsin Oshkosh, USA
Meng-Fen Grace Lin, University of Hawaii, USA

Wikibooks are part of the Web 2.0 which can provide a powerful force in changing, and improving education. However, creating successful Wikibooks in classes is not particularly easy. It is even difficult when it entails more than one institution or class. Cross-institutional and internationally designed Wikibooks present many instructional challenges and dilemmas to learners and instructors. In addition, there are collaboration issues, technology issues, knowledge construction and sense of community issues, and general issues related to the Wikibook technology and the Wikibook design process itself. In response, this chapter provides dozens of Wikibook collaboration ideas and suggestions.

Chapter 9

Since the creation of YouTubeTM in 2005, a video clip phenomenon has swept the Internet. Never before has it been so easy to locate, record, and distribute video online. This opens intriguing possibilities for teaching, learning, and course design for e-learning. This chapter introduces Web-based video as a new form of educational motion picture, delves into technical aspects of Web 2.0 video tools, describes instructional strategies that integrate Web-based video clips in e-learning, and examines barriers that could potentially inhibit its use. Future directions are also discussed.

Chapter 10

Collaborative research teaches students critical knowledge management skills, whether they are undergraduates learning the basics of Web research or advanced scholars defining their own knowledge domains. Instructors can benefit from practical examples and strategies to initiate social bookmarking activities. This chapter provides best practice examples for effective pedagogical applications of social bookmarking in undergraduate and graduate courses as well as insights into how these activities change the way students think and learn.

Chapter 11

VISOLE (Virtual Interactive Student-Oriented Learning Environment) is a constructivist pedagogical approach to empower computer game-based learning. This approach encompasses the creation of a near real-life online interactive world modeled upon a set of multi-disciplinary domains, in which each student plays a role in this "virtual world" and shapes its development. All missions, tasks and problems therein are generative and open-ended with neither prescribed strategies nor solutions. With sophisticated multi-player simulation contexts and teacher facilitation (scaffolding and debriefing), VISOLE provides opportunities for students to acquire both subject-specific knowledge and problem-solving skills through their near real-life gaming experience. This chapter aims to delineate the theoretical foundation and pedagogical implementation of VISOLE. Apart from that, the authors also introduce their game-pedagogy co-design strategy adopted in developing the first VISOLE instance—FARMTASIA.

This chapter addresses the application of e-learning in university degree programs based on exploiting the practical, intensive and holistic aspects of Second Life® (SL™). Although the specific framework dealt with is English as a foreign language, it seems feasible to assume that the learning processes are equally transferable to other disciplines. In light of the aforementioned premises, the outlook of e-learning 2.0 approaches require action research and shared experiences in order to back up or challenge the claims and expectations of the academic community concerned with best practices in education.

Chapter 13

This chapter offers practical ideas and cases for educational use of the Second Life® virtual world with Web 2.0 based technology. It introduces three cases and provides empirical evidence for effective usage within three educational contexts: (1) offering a field trip in virtual space, (2) switching gender roles in the Second Life® virtual world to understand opposite genders, and (3) Object-making and manipulation activities to improve spatial reasoning.

In an attempt to prepare students for work in the 21st century and to address the dropout crisis, educators are examining ways to integrate virtual worlds, including digital games, into the curriculum. This chapter begins by summarizing some of the theories that commonly frame the discussions about these worlds. Next an examination of the issues surrounding virtual worlds is presented. The concluding sections outline and describe the pedagogical mnemonic known as the "SECOND LIFE" model.

Chapter 15

Podcasting – as one of the Web 2.0 technologies - is one of the most flexible teaching and learning tool used today. It has been used increasingly in higher educational institutions. This chapter discusses the uniqueness of podcasting technology in promoting e-learning in following aspects: (1) podcasting addressing the needs of a dynamic e-learning environment, (2) research results indicating the educational efficacy of podcasting in e-learning, and (3) podcasting best practice in e-learning design and delivery.

Chapter 16

    Steve Chi-Yin Yuen, The University of Southern Mississippi, USA
    Harrison Hao Yang, State University of New York at Oswego, USA

This chapter provides an overview and development of sense of community and social networking; discusses the potential uses of social networking in education; and presents a case study that integrates social networking into two graduate courses for the purpose of building a sense of community, improving communications and interactions, and promoting student-centered collaboration. The construction of class social networking sites, the implementation of these networks, and their effects on the students' learning experience are examined. In addition, an analysis of feedback from students on the value of social networking in learning is included.

Foreword

For most of history, humans have made tools to extend the human body.

Since the development of writing, humanity has increasingly shifted to designing tools to extend the human mind. This shift has accelerated in the last century as the industrial age has waned and the so-called information age has grown in prominence. During this time, tools and methods have been developed to improve the capacity for people to *think together*.

In 1916, public relations pioneer Ivy Lee made the bold proclamation: "The people now rule. We have substituted for the divine right of kinds, the divine right of the multitude". Nowhere is the participatory power of the people more evident than online in sites such as YouTube, Wikipedia, blogs, podcasting, and social networking services. When seen from the perspective of higher education, open educational resources and open access journals promise a new information cycle, where the creation, dissemination, validation, sharing, and re-creation of information are available to all.

Yet, as is often the case, times of change also offer new beginnings. Uncertainty exists about how existing education systems will absorb and utilize new technologies and respond to the development of participative information creation evident in mainstream society. Power shifts are not readily absorbed by established segments of a society. As power flows from one system to another, the world appears to be unchanged: control, access, and information interaction are still supported the facade of previous systems. Newspapers and academic journals continue to publish in the same environment that produces blogs and open educational resources. The transition from individual genius to collaborative and collective genius is at a similar point – indications exist of a foundational change in social and information interactions, yet the curricular models of universities remains largely unchanged. Classroom teaching coexists with online learning. Traditional pedagogy reigns even as emerging social and networked pedagogies grow in prominence.

Imagine a future where learners have greater personal control in accessing experts, in joining groups of interest. A future where learner's education is not confined to one institution and where subject matter exploration is achieved through networks of experts and novices, rather than the one-educator model evident in classrooms today. Image a future where classrooms are not confined to physical space, but permit learners from around the world to share and create resources. A future where educational resources – text, videos, podcasts, simulations - are readily accessible by all learners. Imagine a future where technology plays a greater role in performing grunt cognition tasks of presenting patterns, relations, and connections between people and data, thereby permitting learners and academics to more readily consider implications of those patterns and connections. Imagine a future where the collective expertise of learners and educators is harnessed through social technologies.

The seed of this future has already been planted in many schools, universities and colleges, and the task now remains for administrators and educators to explore how our current education system can be transformed to embrace the potential of participatory pedagogy.

Many questions remain about collective intelligence and about how emerging technologies will impact traditional institutions. While Wikipedia demonstrates the ability for collectives to create content, questions of quality remain. What is the value of individual expertise? How are individuals to be related to the larger group. And, while many technologies for collective action already exist, what do we still need? Nascent tools for information and relationship visualizes offer a glimpse.

Collective Intelligence and E-Learning 2.0: Implications of Web-Based Communities and Networking tackles important outstanding questions about the foundation and extent of change impacting education. Learning networks, new literacies, emerging pedagogies, new institutional models, and more are considered. The methods and tools of collaborative information creation are prominent in our daily lives. It is important for educators to explore how to best implement these approaches in the service of teaching and learning.

Collective Intelligence and E-learning 2.0 addresses what will surely become one of the most important educational discussions of our generation: how does collective intelligence impact the current individualistic structure of education?

George Siemens
University of Manitoba
March, 2009

George Siemens *is a prominent writer, speaker, and researcher on learning, networks, technology and organizational effectiveness in digital environments. He is the author of Knowing Knowledge, an exploration of how the context and characteristics of knowledge have changed and what it means to organizations today, and the recently released Handbook of Emerging Technologies for Learning. Siemens is also Associate Director, Research and Development, with the Learning Technologies Centre at University of Manitoba. He is founder and President of Complexive Systems Inc. (www.complexive.com), a learning lab focused on helping organizations develop integrated learning structures to meet the needs of global strategy execution. He is an international speaker and consultant, detailing the changes universities, colleges, and corporations must make in order to address the challenges of an increasingly complex world. Siemens maintains www.elearnspace.org , www.connectivism.ca and www.knowingknowledge.com . Additional background information is available at www.elearnspace.org/about.htm.*

Preface

The Web is shifting from being a medium, in which information is transmitted and consumed, into being a platform, in which content is created, shared, remixed, repurposed, and exchanged. Learners become part of a global human network in which they can harness the collective intelligence of people in the world that could have never been possible previously. With the advent of Web 2.0, e-learning has the potential to become far more personal, social, and flexible. Consequently, e-learning 2.0 can capitalize on many sources of content aggregated together into learning experiences and utilize various tools including online references, courseware, knowledge management, collaboration, and search. *Collective Intelligence and E-Learning 2.0: Implications of Web-Based Communities and Networking* introduces theoretical aspects of e-learning 2.0 as well as disseminates cutting-edge research and first-hand practices regarding game-based simulation, podcasting, Second Life, social bookmarking, social networking, YouTube, Wiki, and so forth, on e-learning. In addition, instructional design models, strategies, and furture trends of e-learning are covered this book.

The book is written for broader audiences including educators, trainers, administrators, and researchers working in the area of e-learning or distance learning in various disciplines (e.g., educational fields, corporate training, instructional technology, computer science, library information science, information technology, and workforce development). The book can be used as a research reference, pedagogical guide, or educational resource in the area of Web 2.0 technologies and related applications applied to e-learning.

ORGANIZATION OF THE BOOK

Collective Intelligence and E-Learning 2.0: Implications of Web-Based Communities and Networking is designed to be used in a flexible manner, and it can adapt easily to suit a variety of educational technology related courses and needs by students, instructors, and administrators. The book includes a selection of chapters addressing current research, case studies, best practices, pedagogical approaches and strategies, related resources and projects related to e-learning 2.0. The book is organized into two sections, From Web 2.0 to E-Learning 2.0 and Beyond (chapters 1-6) and Web 2.0 Technologies in E-Learning (chapters 7-16). The book covers beyond theoretical insights of Web 2.0 and e-learning 2.0. It shares practical aspects of e-learning 2.0 and provides readers with a balance of research, theory, and applications on both innovative Web 2.0 technologies and future e-learning.

Chapter 1: Learning Networks and Connective Knowledge. This chapter introduces theoretical views on factors impacting the future of e-learning. It discusses connectivisim theory, networked learning, connective knowledge, and network semantics that form a new e-learning approach (e-learning 2.0).

Chapter 2: Conceptualizing Codes of Conduct in Social Networking Communities. This chapter reviews the capabilities of social networking tools and links those capabilities to recent legal and ethical controversies involving use of social networking tools such as Facebook and MySpace.

Chapter 3: Fulfilling the Promise: Addressing Institutional Factors that Impede the Implementation of E-Learning 2.0. As online learning continues to expand and evolve, new challenges emerge regarding the implementation of Web 2.0 tools and technologies in online pedagogy. This chapter examines institutional factors that impede implementation of e-learning 2.0. The business model approach to online learning being embraced by many institutions may actually work against faculty who want to utilize Web 2.0 technologies to create e-learning 2.0 experiences for their students.

Chapter 4: Designing Dynamic Learning Environment for Web 2.0 Application. This chapter presents a new instructional design model that specifically addresses the cognitive demands involved in Web 2.0 learning, promotes learning that focuses on metacognitive thinking and self-regulation, facilitates knowledge integration and construction of schemas-of-the-moment for ill-structured learning, and delivers a dynamic learning environment in Web 2.0 application.

Chapter 5: Instructional Strategies for Teaching in Synchronous Online Learning Environments (SOLE). This chapter discusses synchronous online learning environments (SOLEs) and their affordances for teaching and learning.

Chapter 6: University 2.0: Human, Social, and Societal Issues. Higher education is changing in important and profound ways. University 2.0 offers amazing potential to fundamentally change the way higher education functions in the future. This chapter describes many of the potential problems that will accompany university 2.0 and provides a series of recommended actions that university administrators can take to respond to the problems.

Chapter 7: Use of Wikis to Support Collaboration among Online Students. This chapter discusses the merits and challenges of using a Wiki to support the activities of students during group projects.

Chapter 8: Wikibook Transformations and Disruptions: Looking Back Twenty Years to Today. A Wikibook is a transformative and disruptive technology that is finding increasing use in schools and higher education institutions. This chapter describes the adoption of three Wikibooks in cross-institutional higher education settings and discusses collaboration issues, technology issues, knowledge construction and sense of community issues related to the Wikibook technology and the Wikibook design process.

Chapter 9: Web-Based Video for e-Learning: Tapping into the YouTube™ Phenomenon. The recent explosive growth of Web-based video has expanded the repository of free content that can be tapped into for e-learning. This chapter introduces Web-based video as a new form of educational motion picture, delves into technical aspects of Web 2.0 video tools, describes instructional strategies that integrate Web-based video clips in e-learning, and examines barriers that could potentially inhibit its use.

Chapter 10: From Information Literacy to Scholarly Identity: Effective Pedagogical Strategies for Social Bookmarking. This chapter provides best examples for effective pedagogical applications of social bookmarking and offers insights into how these activities change the way students think and learn.

Chapter 11: VISOLE: A Constructivist Pedagogical Approach to Game-Based Learning. VISOLE (Virtual Interactive Student-Oriented Learning Environment) is a constructivist pedagogical approach to empower computer game-based learning. This approach encompasses the creation of a near real-life online interactive world modeled upon a set of multi-disciplinary domains, in which each student plays a role in this "virtual world" and shapes its development. With sophisticated multi-player simulation contexts and teacher facilitation (scaffolding and debriefing), VISOLE provides opportunities for students to acquire both subject-specific knowledge and problem-solving skills through their near real-life gaming experience.

Chapter 12: Second Language E-Learning and Professional Training with Second Life®. *This chapter addresses the application of e-learning in university degree programs based on exploiting the practical, intensive, and holistic aspects of Second Life®.*

Chapter 13: Empirical Evidence and Practical Cases for Using Virtual Worlds in Educational Contexts. This chapter introduces three cases for educational uses of the Second Life® virtual world and provides empirical evidence for effective usage within the educational contexts.

Chapter 14: A Pedagogical Odyssey in Three-Dimensional Virtual Worlds: The Second Life® Model. This chapter discusses the theoretical perspectives, educational possibilities, as well as challenges of using virtual worlds in teaching and learning. In addition, it offers a pedagogical framework to support teaching and learning in virtual worlds - the Second Life® model.

Chapter 15: Podcasting: A Flexible E-Learning Tool. This chapter discusses the uniqueness of podcasting technology in promoting e-learning, examines educational efficacy of podcasting in e-learning, and provides podcasting best practice in e-learning design and delivery.

Chapter 16: Using Social Networking to Enhance Sense of Community in E-Learning Courses. This chapter provides an overview and development of sense of community and social networking, discusses the potential uses of social networking in education, and presents a case study that integrates social networking into e-learning courses for the purpose of building a sense of community, improving communications and interactions, and promoting student-centered collaboration.

Acknowledgment

Throughout this endeavor we have benefited from the advice, encouragement, and support of numerous individuals, including the contributing authors, thoughtful reviewers, supportive colleagues, and patient family members. Without the contributions of all of these people, this book would not been possible.

First, we would like to express our deepest thanks and sincere appreciation to the authors who contributed to this book. We believe the book includes the current works of some of the best practitioners/researchers in the e-learning field. They did an excellent job, and we are confident that you will feel the same way after you read the chapters. We have enjoyed working with all of the authors, for they have made our work interesting, enjoyable, and relatively painless.

Second, we are very grateful for the support provided by the reviewers. They have done outstanding work for providing us detailed comments and constructive suggestions of the chapters. Their comments and suggestions are helpful to us for making editorial decisions and also providing important feedback to the authors for improving and revising their chapters. Special thanks go to George Siemens for writing an insightful foreword for this book and Curtis Bonk for his stimulating suggestions and enthusiasm.

Finally, we would like to thank our families for their patience and encouragement. Both of our families have been a constant source of understanding, support, and encouragement. We dedicate this book to our spouses, Li Chen and Patrivan K. Yuen, and thank them both for love and support and for letting us disappear into the abyss for hours on end.

Harrison Hao Yang
State University of New York, USA

Steve Chi-Yin Yuen
University of Southern Mississippi, USA

Section 1
From Web 2.0 to E-Learning 2.0 and Beyond

Chapter 1
Learning Networks and Connective Knowledge

Stephen Downes
National Research Council, Canada

ABSTRACT

The purpose of this chapter is to outline some of the thinking behind new e-learning technology, including e-portfolios and personal learning environments. Part of this thinking is centered around the theory of connectivism, which asserts that knowledge - and therefore the learning of knowledge - is distributive, that is, not located in any given place (and therefore not 'transferred' or 'transacted' per se) but rather consists of the network of connections formed from experience and interactions with a knowing community. And another part of this thinking is centered around the new, and the newly empowered, learner, the member of the net generation, who is thinking and interacting in new ways. These trends combine to form what is sometimes called 'e-learning 2.0' - an approach to learning that is based on conversation and interaction, on sharing, creation and participation, on learning not as a separate activity, but rather, as embedded in meaningful activities such as games or workflows.

THE TRADITIONAL THEORY: COGNITIVISM

The dominant theory of online and distance learning may be characterized as conforming to a 'cognitivist' theory of knowledge and learning. Cognitivism is probably best thought of as a response to behaviourism. It provides an explicit description of the 'inner workings' of the mind that behaviourism ignores. It

is founded on the view that the behaviourist assertion that there are no mental events is in a certain sense implausible, if only by introspection. There is something that it is 'like' to have a belief, and this something seems clearly to be distinct from the mere assemblage of physical constituents. Searle in *Minds, Brains, and Programs* (1980) and Nagel in *What is it Like to Be a Bat* (1974) offer the most compelling versions of this argument.

In other words, cognitivists defend an approach that may be called 'folk psychology' (Ravenscroft,

DOI: 10.4018/978-1-60566-729-4.ch001

Copyright © 2010, IGI Global. Copying or distributing in print or electronic forms without written permission of IGI Global is prohibited.

2004). "In our everyday social interactions we both predict and explain behavior, and our explanations are couched in a mentalistic vocabulary which includes terms like 'belief' and 'desire'." The argument, in a nutshell, is that the claims of folk psychology are literally true, that there is, for example, an entity in the mind corresponding to the belief that 'Paris is the capital of France', and that this belief is, in fact, what might loosely be called 'brain writing' - or, more precisely, there is a one-to-one correspondence between a person's brain states and the sentence itself.

One branch of folk psychology, the language of thought theory, holds that things like beliefs are literally sentences in the brain, and that the materials for such sentences are innate. This is not as absurd as it sounds, and writers like Fodor offer a long and well-argued defense in works such as *The Language of Thought* (2005), *RePresentations* (1983) and *Psychosemantics* (1989). Intuitively, though, you can think of it this way: sculptors sometimes say 'the sculpture was already in the rock; I just found it'. And, quite literally, it makes no sense to say that the sculpture was not in the rock - where else would it be? The idea of 'shaping the mind' is the same sort of thing; it is a revealing of the potential that is latent in the mind, the pre-existing capacity to learn not only language but even sets of concepts and universal truths.

Where the Fodor approach intersects with learning theory is via communication theory, the idea that communication consists of information that flows through a channel (Griffin, 2002). When we join folk psychology with communications theory, we get the idea that there is something like mental content that is in some way transmitted from a sender to a receiver. That we send ideas or beliefs or desires thought his channel. Or at the very least, that we send linguistic or non-linguistic (audio music and video images, for example) *representations* of these mental entities.

In learning theory, the concept of transactional distance is based on this sort of analysis of communication (Moore, 1973). What that means is that there is exists a space (construed either physically or metaphorically) between two entities between which there exists a channel of communication. In one entity there exists a state, a mental state, which corresponds to a semantic state (in other words, a sentence), and in the process of communication, (aspects of) that state are transmitted from the first entity to the second. This transmission is known as a signal, and as writers like Schramm (1964, 1997) observe, the state transfer is made possible because it constitutes an experience (a mental state) shared between sender and receiver.

This signal, in physical form (such as, say, a book) may constitute an artifact; alternatively, it may be viewed as a medium. The physical analysis of learning, on this account, becomes possible because the physical state - the actual communicative entity - matches the mental state. Thus, the relative states in the sender and the receiver can be (putatively) observed and measured. For example, this approach allows Dretske, in *Knowledge and the Flow of Information* (1999), to explain communication from the perspective of information theory. The transfer of information, suggests Dretske, occurs when, as the result of a signal from an external entity, one's assessment of the total possible states of affairs in the world is reduced.

Moore's (1989, 1993) contribution to educational theory may be placed firmly within this framework. His view is that the effectiveness of communication is improved through interaction. Instead of viewing communication as a one-time event, in which information is sent from a sender and received by a receiver, the transfer of information is enabled through a series of communications, such that the receiver sends messages back to the sender, or to third parties. This is similar to the 'checksum' mechanism in computer communications, where the receiving computer sends back a string of bits to the sender in order to confirm that the message has been received correctly. Minimally, through this communication, a process of verification is enabled; one can easily infer more complex communications in which knowledge is actually generated, or constructed, by the receiver based on prompts and cues from the sender.

Again, though, notice the pattern here. What is happening is that information theorists, such as Dretske, along with educational theorists, such as Moore, are transferring the properties of a physical medium, in this case, the communication of content via electronic or other signals, to the realm of the mental. Transactional distance just is an application of a physical concept to a mental concept. And if you buy into this, you are bound to buy in to the rest of it, and most especially, that there is something we'll call 'mental content' which is an *isomorphism* between physical states of the brain and the semantical content transmitted to and received by students, who either in some way absorb or construct a mental state that is the same as the teacher's - a 'shared experience'.

THE EMERGENTIST ALTERNATIVE AND THE ARGUMENT AGAINST COGNITIVISM

The allure of a causal theory is also that there appears to be no alternative. If there is no causal connection between teacher and learner, then how can any learning take place, except through some sort of divine intervention? Once we have established and begun to describe the causal process through which information is transacted from teacher to learner, we have pretty much claimed the field; any further account along these lines is an enhancement, an embellishment, but certainly not something new.

There is, however, an alternative. We may contrast cognitivism, which is a *causal* theory of mind, with connectionism, which is an *emergentist* theory of mind. This is not to say that connectionism (Garson, 2007)) does away with causation altogether; it is not a 'hand of God' theory. It allows that there is a physical, causal connection between entities, and this is what

makes communication possible. But where it differs is, crucially: *the transfer of information does not reduce to this physical substrate*. Contrary to the communications-theoretical account, the new theory is a non-reductive theory. The contents of communications, such as sentences, *are not isomorphic* with some mental state.

Philosophically, there is substantial support for emergentist theories of knowledge (Malpas, 2005). Philosophers have come up with the concept of 'supervenience' to describe something that is not the same as (i.e., not reducible to) physical phenomena, but which are nonetheless dependent on them. Thus, collections of physical states may share the same non-physical state; this non-physical state may be described as a 'pattern', or variously, 'a mental state', 'information', a 'belief', or whatever. Knowledge (and other mental states, concepts, and the like) when represented in this way are 'distributed' - that is, there is no discrete entity that is (or could be) an 'instance' of that knowledge.

Computationally, the theory also enjoys support. It is based in one of two major approaches to artificial intelligence. When we think of AI, we usually think of programs and algorithms - the usual stuff of information, signals and channels in computer theory closely tied to associated concepts in communication theory. The 'General Problem Solver' of Newell and Simon (1963), for example, take a 'symbol processing' approach to computation in AI. This is similar to the Fodor theory, the idea that cognition is (essentially) reducible to a physical symbol set (and therefore instances of cognition and transaction) are governed by the same mechanism. Against this, however, and arguably superior, is the 'connectionist' approach to AI, as described above in the work of Minsky and Papert (1969) or Rumelhart and McClelland (1987).

Mathematically, there is additional support. The properties of networks, as distinct from (typical) causal systems are expressed as a branch of graph theory, the study of which has recently come into prominence because of the work of Watts (2004) and Buchanan (2002). These studies show not only how networks come to be structured as they are but also illustrate how something like, say, a concept can become a 'network phenomenon'. This mathematical description, note these authors, can be used to explain wide varieties of empirical phenomenal, from the synchronicity of crickets chirping to the development of trees and river systems.

What grounds this move to networks? On what basis is it proposed that we abandon the traditional conception of learning? In a nutshell, research in mental phenomena has been running in this direction. From early work, such as Marr's *Vision* (1982) and Kosslyn's *Image and Mind* (2002) through Churchland's *Neurophilosophy* (1986) to LeDoux's contemporary *The Synaptic Self* (2002), it is becoming increasingly evident that what we call 'mental contents' do not resemble sentences, much less physical objects, at all.

For example (and there are *many* we could choose from), consider O'Reilly on how the brain represents conceptual structures, as described in *Modeling Integration and Dissociation in Brain and Cognitive Development* (2006). He explicitly rejects the 'isomorphic' view of mental contents, and instead describes a network of distributed representations. "Instead of viewing brain areas as being specialized for specific representational content (e.g., color, shape, location, etc), areas are specialized for specific computational functions by virtue of having different neural parameters... This 'functionalist' perspective has been instantiated in a number of neural network models of different brain areas, including posterior (perceptual) neocortex, hippocampus, and the prefrontal cortex/basal ganglia system... many aspects of these areas work in the same way (and on the same representational content), and in many respects the system can be considered to function as one big undifferentiated whole. For example, any given memory is encoded in synapses distributed throughout the entire system, and all areas partici-

pate in some way in representing most memories." (¶ 5). In other words, what O'Reilly is proposing is a functionalist architecture over distributed representation. "*Functionalism* in the philosophy of mind is the doctrine that what makes something a mental state of a particular type does not depend on its internal constitution, but rather on the way it functions, or the role it plays, in the system of which it is a part." (Levin, 2004, ¶ 1). For example, when I say, "What makes something a learning object is how we *use* the learning object," I am asserting a functionalist approach to the definition of learning objects (people are so habituated to essentialist definitions that my definition does not even appear on lists of definitions of learning objects). It's like asking, what makes a person a 'bus driver'? Is it the colour of his blood? The nature of his muscles? A particular mental state? No - according to functionalism, what makes him a 'bus driver' is the fact that he drives buses. He performs that *function*. A *distributed representation* is one in which meaning is not captured by a single symbolic unit, but rather arises from the interaction of a set of units, normally in a network of some sort. As Churchland and Sejnowski (1992) noted, the concept of distributed representation is a product of joint developments in the neurosciences and in connectionist work on recognition tasks. Fundamentally, a distributed representation is one in which meaning is not captured by a single symbolic unit, but rather arises from the interaction of a set of units, normally in a network of some sort.

To illustrate this concept, I have been asking people to think of the concept 'Paris'. If 'Paris' were represented by a simple symbol set, we would all mean the same thing when we say 'Paris'. But in fact, we each mean a collection of different things and none of our collections is the same. Therefore, in our own minds, the concept 'Paris' is a loose association of a whole bunch of different things, and hence the concept 'Paris' exists in no particular place in our minds, but rather, is scattered throughout our minds.

O'Reilly (2006) indicates that human brains *are* like computers - but not like the computers as described above, with symbols and programs and all that, but like computers when they are connected together in a network. "The brain as a whole operates more like a social network than a digital computer... the computer-like features of the prefrontal cortex broaden the social networks, helping the brain become more flexible in processing novel and symbolic information." (¶ 6). Understanding 'where the car is parked' is like understanding how one kind of function applies on the brain's distributed representation, while understanding 'the best place to park the car' is like how a *different* function applies to the *same* distributed representation.

The analogy with the network of computers is a good one (and people who develop social network software are sometimes operating with these concepts of neural mechanisms specifically in mind). The actual social network itself - a set of distributed and interlinked entities, usually people, as represented by websites or pages - constitutes a type of distributed representation. A 'meme' - like, say, the *Friday Five* - is distributed across that network; it exists in no particular place.

Specific mental operations, therefore, are like thinking of functions applied to this social network. For example, if I were to want to find 'the most popular bloggers' I would need to apply a set of functions to that network. I would need to represent each entity as a 'linking' entity. I would need to cluster types of links (to eliminate self-referential links and spam). I would then need to apply my function (now my *own* view here, and possibly O'Reilly's, though I don't read it specifically in his article, is that to apply a function is to create *additional neural layers* that act as specialized filters - this would contrast with, say, Technorati, which polls each individual entity and then applies an *algorithm* to it).

This theory, stated simply, is that human thought amounts to patterns of interactions in neural networks. More precisely, patterns of input

phenomena - such as sensory perceptions - cause or create patterns of connections between neurons in the brain. These connections are associative - that is, connections between two neurons form when the two neurons are active at the same time, and weaken when they are inactive or active at different times. See, for example, Hebb's *The Organization of Behavior* (2002), which outlines what has come to be called 'Hebbian associationism'.

THE ARGUMENT AGAINST COGNITIVISM

As we examine the emergentist theory of mind we can arrive at five major implications of this approach for educational theorists:

- first, knowledge is subsymbolic. Mere possession of the words does not mean that there is knowledge; the possession of knowledge does not necessarily result in the possession of the words (and for much more on this, see Polanyi's (1974) discussion of 'tacit knowledge' in 'Personal Knowledge').
- second, knowledge is distributed. There is no specific 'mental entity' that corresponds to the belief that 'Paris is the capital of France'. What we call that 'knowledge' is (an indistinguishable) pattern of connections between neurons. See, for example, Geoffrey Hinton(1986), *Learning Distributed Representations of Concepts*.
- third, knowledge is interconnected. The same neuron that is a part of 'Paris is the capital of France' might also be a part of 'My dog is named Fred'. It is important to note that this is a non-symbolic interconnection - this is the basis for non-rational associations, such as are described in the article, *Where Belief is Born* (Jha, 2005)
- fourth, knowledge is personal. Your 'belief' that 'Paris is the capital of France' is

quite literally different from my belief that 'Paris is the capital of France'. If you think about it, this must be the case - otherwise Gestalt tests would be useless; we would all utter the same word when shown the same picture.

- fifth, what we call 'knowledge' (or 'belief', or 'memory') is an emergent phenomenon. Specifically, it is not 'in' the brain itself, or even 'in' the connections themselves, because there is no 'canonical' set of connections that corresponds with 'Paris is the capital of France'. It is, rather (and carefully stated), a recognition of a pattern in a set of neural events (if we are introspecting) or behavioural events (if we are observing). We infer to mental contents the same way we watch Donald Duck on TV - we think we see something, but that something is not actually there - it's just an organization of pixels.

This set of features constitutes a mechanism for evaluating whether a cognitivist theory or a connectivist theory is likely to be true. In my own mind (and in my own writing, as this was the subject of my first published paper, 'Why Equi Fails'), the mechanism can be summed in one empirical test: context sensitivity. If learning is context-sensitive then the 'language of thought' hypothesis fails, and the rest of folk psychology along with it. For the presumption of these theories is that, when you believe that 'Paris is the capital of France' and when I believe that 'Paris is the capital of France', that we believe the *same thing*, and that, importantly, *we share the same mental state*, and hence can be reasonably relied upon to demonstrate the same semantic information when prompted.

So I've concluded that 'language of thought' hypothesis could not possibly succeed, nor folk psychology either. Because it turns out that not only language but the whole range of phenomena associated with knowledge and learning are context-sensitive. Or so the philosophers say.

- Wittgenstein, in *Philosophical Investigations* (1973) and elsewhere, argues that meaning is context sensitive, that what we mean by a word depends on a community of speakers; there is no such thing as a 'private language', and hence, the meaning of a word cannot stand alone, fully self-contained, in the mind.

- Quine, in *Two Dogmas of Empiricism* (1951) and in *Word and Object* (1964), shows that observation itself is context-sensitive, that there is no knowable one-to-one matching between sense-phenomena and the words used to describe them; in 'On the Indeterminacy of Translation' he illustrates this with the famous 'gavagai' example: when a native speaker uses the word 'gavagai' there is no empirical way to know whether he means 'rabbit' or 'the physically incarnate manifestation of my ancestor'

- Hanson, in *Patterns of Discovery* (1958), argues, in my view successfully, that causal explanations are context-sensitive. 'What was the cause of the accident?' It depends on who you ask - the police officer will point to the speed, the urban planner will point to the road design, the driver will point to the visibility.

- Lakoff, in *Women, Fire and Dangerous Things* (1990), shows that categories are context sensitive (contra Saul Kripke); that what makes two things 'the same' varies from culture to culture, and indeed (as evidenced from some of his more recent political writings) from 'frame' to 'frame'.

- van Fraassen in *The Scientific Image* (1980) shows that explanations are context sensitive. 'Why are the roses growing here?' may be answered in a number of ways, depending on what alternative explanations are anticipated. 'Because someone planted them.' 'Because they were well fertilized.' 'Because the chlorophyll in the leaves converts the energy of the Sun into glucose' are all acceptable answers, the correct one of which depends on the presuppositions inherent in the question.

- Lewis (2001) and Stalnaker (1987) argue that the counterfactuals and modalities are context sensitive (though Lewis, if asked, would probably deny it). The truth of a sentence like 'brakeless trains are dangerous' depends, not on observation, but rather, on the construction of a 'possible world' that is relevantly similar (Stalnaker uses the word 'salience') to our own, but what counts as 'relevant' depends on the context in which the hypothetical is being considered.

If, as asserted above, what counts as knowledge of even basic things like the meanings of words and the cause of events is sensitive to context, then it seems clear that such knowledge is not a stand-along symbolic *representation* of that knowledge, since representations would not be, could not be, context sensitive. Rather, what is happening is that each person is experiencing a mental state that is at best seen as an *approximation* of what it is that is being said in words or experienced in nature, an approximation that is framed and indeed comprehensible only from which the rich set of world views, previous experiences and frames in which it embedded.

If this is the case, then the concepts of *what it is to know* and *what it is to teach* are very different from the traditional theories that dominate distance education today. Because if learning is not the transfer of mental contents – if there is, indeed, no such mental content that exists to be transported – then we need to ask, what is it that we are attempting to do when we attempt to teach and learn.

NETWORK SEMANTICS AND CONNECTIVE LEARNING

If we accept that something like the network theory of learning is true, then we are faced with a knowledge and learning environment very different from what we are used to. In the strictest sense, there is no semantics in network learning, because there is no *meaning* in network learning (and hence, the constructivist practice of 'making meaning' is literally meaningless).

Traditionally, what a sentence 'means' is the (truth of falsity of) the state of the world it represents. However, on a network theory of knowledge, there is no such state of the world to which this meaning can be affixed. This is not because there is no such state of the world. The world could most certainly exist, and there is no contradiction in saying that a person's neural states are caused by world events. However, it *does* mean that there is no *particular* state of the world that corresponds with (is isomorphic to) a particular mental state. This is because the mental state is embedded in a sea of context and presuppositions that are completely opaque to the state of the world.

How, then, do we express ourselves? How do we distinguish between true and false – what, indeed, does it even *mean* to say that something is true and false? The answer to these questions is going to be different for each of us. They will be embedded in a network of assumptions and beliefs about the nature of meaning, truth and falsity. In order to get at a response, therefore, it will be necessary to outline what may only loosely be called 'network semantics'.

We begin with the nature of a network itself. In any network, there will be three major elements:

- Entities, that is, the things that are connected that send and receive signals
- Connections, that is, the link or channel between entities (may be represented as physical or virtual)

- Signals, that is, the message sent between entities. Note that meaning is *not inherent* in signal and must be interpreted by the receiver

In an environment of this description, then, networks may vary according to a certain set of properties:

- Density, or how many other entities each entity is connected to
- Speed, or how quickly a message moves to an entity (can be measured in time or 'hops')
- Flow, or how much information an entity processes, which includes messages sent and received in addition to transfers of messages for other entities
- Plasticity, or, how frequently connections created, abandoned
- Degree of connectedness – is a function of density, speed, flow and plasticity

Given this description of networks, we can identify the essential elements of network semantics.

- First, *context*, that is, the localization of entities in a network. Each context is unique – entities see the network differently, experience the world differently. Context is required in order to interpret signals, that is, each signal means something different depending on the perspective of the entity receiving it.
- Second, *salience,* that is, the relevance or importance of a message. This amounts to the similarity between one pattern of connectivity and another. If a signal creates the activation of a set of connections that were previously activated, then this signal is salient. Meaning is created from context and messages via salience.
- Third, *emergence,* that is, the development

of patterns in the network. Emergence is a process of resonance or synchronicity, not creation. We do not *create* emergent phenomena. Rather emergence phenomena are more like commonalities in patterns of perception. It requires an interpretation to be recognized; this happens when a pattern becomes *salient* to a perceiver.

- Fourth, *memory* is the persistence of patterns of connectivity, and in particular, those patterns of connectivity that result from, and result in, salient signals or perceptions.

Given this background, what does it mean, then, to say that a sentence has semantical import? To say, similarly, that we 'know' something? As suggested above, most of us remain committed to something like a traditional (Tarski) semantics: we know something just in case what we know happens to be true. But of course, this fails to tell the whole story. The knowledge needs to be, in some way, in our mind (or in our society); it needs to be a 'belief'. And (so goes the argument) it needs to be in some way justified, through a process of verification, or at the very least, says Popper, through the absence of falsification.

Significant difficulties emerge when we try to articulate what it is that we know. Consider, for example, 'snow is white'. Sure, one could check some snow in order to determine that it is white, but only of one first understood what is meant by 'snow' and 'white' (not to mention, as Clinton taught us, 'is'). But as discussed above, that constitutes *the* meaning of, ay, 'snow', is far from clear. There is no such single entity. What it means is a matter of interpretation. So, for example, does enumerating what constitutes instance of snow. Does 'yellow snow' count? Does snow produced by artificial ice machines count?

From the discussion above, it should be clear that on the account being given here, to 'know' that 'snow is white' is to be *organized in a certain way* (one that is evidenced by uttering 'snow' when asked). To be organized in such a way as to have neural and mental structures corresponding to the words 'snow', 'is' and 'white', where those structures are such that the concept 'snow' is closely associated with (in certain contexts) the concept 'white' (obviously this is a gloss, since there is no real correspondence). Knowing that 'snow is white' is therefore being organized in *some* certain way, but not in *a specific* particular way (we couldn't examine one's neural organization and be able to say whether the person knows that snow is white).

What it means to 'know' then is based on organization and connectedness in the brain. What it is to 'know' is, if you will, a natural development that occurs in the mind when it is presented with certain sets of phenomena; other things being equal, present the learner with different phenomena and they will learn different things.

Whether something counts as 'knowledge' rather than, say, 'belief' or 'speculation', depends less on the state of the world, and more on the strength or degree of connectedness between the entities. To 'know' something is to not be able to not know. It's like finding Waldo, or looking at an abstract image. There may be a time when we don't know where Waldo is, or what the image represents, but once we have an interpretation, it is not possible to look without seeing Waldo, without seeing the image.

No wonder Dreyfus and Dreyfus (1986) talk about 'levels' of knowledge, up to and including an almost intuitive 'expert' knowledge. As a particular organization, a particular set of connections, between neural structures is strengthened, as this structure becomes embedded in more and more of our other concepts and other knowledge, it changes its nature, changing from something that needs to be triggered by cue or association (or mental effort) into something that is natural as other things we 'know' deeply, like how to breathe, and how to walk, structures entrenched through years, decades, or successful practice. Contrast this to a cognitivist model of knowledge, where once

justification is presented, something is 'known', and cannot later in life be 'more known'.

Connective semantics is therefore derived from what might be called connectivist 'pragmatics', that is, that actual *use* of networks in practice. In our particular circumstance we would examine how networks are used to support learning. The methodology employed is to look at multiple examples and to determine what patterns may be discerned. These patterns cannot be directly communicated. But instances of these patterns may be communicated, thus allowing readers to (more or less) 'get the idea'.

For example, in order to illustrate the observation that 'knowledge is distributed' I have frequently appealed to the story of the 747. In a nutshell, I ask, "who knows how to make a 747 fly from London to Toronto?" The short answer is that *nobody* knows how to do this – no one person could design a 747, manufacture the parts (including tires and aircraft engines), take it off, fly it properly, tend to the passengers, navigate, and land it successfully. The knowledge is *distributed* across a network of people, and the phenomenon of 'flying a 747' can exist at all only because of the connections between the constituent members of that network.

Or, another story: if knowledge is a network phenomenon, then, is it necessary for all the elements of a bit of knowledge to be stored in one's own mind? Karen Stephenson (1998) writes, "I store my knowledge in my friends." This assertion constitutes an explicit recognition that what we 'know' is embedded in our network of connections to each other, to resources, to the world. Siemens (2004) writes, "Self-organization on a personal level is a microprocess of the larger self-organizing knowledge constructs created within corporate or institutional environments. The capacity to form connections between sources of information, and thereby create useful information patterns, is required to learn in our knowledge economy." (¶ 17).

This approach to learning has been captured under the heading of 'connectivism'. In his paper of the same name, George Siemens articulates the major theses:

- Learning and knowledge rests in diversity of opinions.
- Learning is a process of connecting specialized nodes or information sources.
- Learning may reside in non-human appliances.
- Capacity to know more is more critical than what is currently known
- Nurturing and maintaining connections is needed to facilitate continual learning.
- Ability to see connections between fields, ideas, and concepts is a core skill.
- Currency (accurate, up-to-date knowledge) is the intent of all connectivist learning activities.
- Decision-making is in itself a learning process. Choosing what to learn and the meaning of incoming information is seen through the lens of a shifting reality. While there is a right answer now, it may be wrong tomorrow due to alterations in the information climate affecting the decision.

Is this the definitive statement of network learning? Probably not. But it is developed in the classic mold of network learning, through a process of immersion into the network and recognition of salient patterns. What sort of network? The following list is typical of what might be called 'network' practices online:

Practice: Content Authoring and Delivery
- Numerous content authoring systems on the web...
- Weblogs – Blogger, Wordpress, LiveJournal, Moveable Type, more
- Content Management Systems – Drupal, PostNuke, Plone, Scoop, and many more...
- Audio – Audacity – and audioblogs. com – and Podcasting

- Digital imagery and video – and let's not forget Flickr
- Collaborative authoring – Writely, Hula, the wiki

Practice: Organize, Syndicate Sequence, Deliver
- Aggregation of content metadata – RSS and Atom, OPML, FOAF, even DC and LOM
- Aggregators – NewsGator, Bloglines – Edu_RSS
- Aggregation services – Technorati, Blogdex, PubSub
- More coming – the Semantic Social Network

Practice: Identity and Authorization
- A raft of centralized (or Federated) approaches – from Microsoft Passport to Liberty to Shibboleth
- Also various locking and encryption systems
- But nobody wants these
- Distributed DRM – Creative Commons, ODRL...
- Distributed Identification management – Sxip, LID...

Practice: Chatting, Phoning, Conferencing
- Bulletin board systems and chat rooms, usually attached to the aforementioned content management systems such as Drupal, Plone, PostNuke, Scoop
- Your students use this, even if you don't: ICQ, AIM, YIM, and some even use MSN Messenger
- Audioconferencing? Skype...Or NetworkEducationWare...
- Videoconferencing? Built into AIM... and Skype

Web 1.0 Web 2.0
DoubleClick --> Google AdSense
Ofoto --> Flickr
Akamai --> BitTorrent
mp3.com --> Napster
Britannica Online --> Wikipedia
personal websites --> blogging
evite --> upcoming.org and EVDB
domain name speculation --> search engine optimization
page views --> cost per click
screen scraping --> web services
publishing --> participation
content management systems --> wikis
directories (taxonomy) --> tagging ("folksonomy")
stickiness --> syndication

THE MOVE TO 2.0

It is now ten years or so into the era of online learning. Schools, colleges and universities have now developed the internet infrastructure of their choice. Almost all have web pages, most have online courses, and many have synchronous online learning. The learning management system (LMS) has become a commodity business, educational software of all sorts abounds, and the phenomenon has spread around the globe.

Even so, it may be observed that most people online of school or college age are elsewhere. They may not be writing class essays, but they are writing blogs, perhaps one of the 50 million or more tracked by Technorati (2006). They are at MySpace, which counts some 86 million accounts (Kirkpatrick, 2006). They are recording videos, making YouTube even larger than MySpace. They are, in fact, engaged in the many networking activities described in the previous section. *Something* is going on.

On the web, what has happened has been described as the migration to something called *Web 2.0* (pronounced 'web two point oh'). The term, popularized by publisher O'Reilly (2005), describes the evolution of the web into the 'read-write' web. O'Reilly writes, "The central principle behind the success of the giants born in the Web 1.0 era who have survived to lead the Web 2.0 era appears to be this, that they have embraced the power of the web to harness collective intelligence."

As an example, he cites the difference between Netscape and Google. According to O'Reilly, Netscape saw the web as a software market. By releasing its popular browser for free and hence effectively controlling web standards, the company could gain a lock on the web server software market. Google, by contrast, never viewed the web as a place to ship product. Rather, it became a service, harnessing the collective linking behaviour of web users to create a more effective search engine.

The term 'Web 2.0', as has been widely noted, is a notoriously fuzzy term, difficult to nail down. O'Reilly (2005) offered one set of criteria to describe the difference:

This list is incomplete, of course, and as with any definition by example, ultimately unsatisfactory. Nonetheless, the definition may be characteristic of Web 2.0. "That the term has enjoyed such a constant morphing of meaning and interpretation is, in many ways, the clearest sign of its usefulness. This is the nature of the conceptual beast in the digital age, and one of the most telling examples of what Web 2.0 applications do: They replace the authoritative heft of traditional institutions with the surging wisdom of crowds." (Madden & Fox, 2006, p.2).

As the web surged toward 2.0 the educational community solidified its hold on the more traditional approach. The learning management system became central (and centralized, with Blackboard purchasing WebCT). Developers continue to emphasize content and software development, as Learning Object Metadata was standardized and IMS developed specifications for content packaging and learning design.

Even so, as traditional instructional software became entrenched, it became difficult not to notice the movement in the other direction. First was the exodus from commercial software in favour of open source systems such as Moodle, Sakai and LAMS. Others eschewed educational software altogether as a wave of educators began to look at the use of blogging and the wiki in their classes. A new, distributed, model of learning was emerging, which came to be characterized as e-learning 2.0 (Downes, 2005).

"What happens," I asked, "when online learning ceases to be like a medium, and becomes more like a platform? What happens when online learning software ceases to be a type of content-consumption tool, where learning is "delivered," and becomes more like a content-authoring tool, where learning is created?" The answer turns out to be a lot like Web 2.0: "The model of e-learning as being a type of content, produced by publishers, organized and structured into courses, and consumed by students, is turned on its head. Insofar as there is content, it is used rather than read— and is, in any case, more likely to be produced by students than courseware authors. And insofar as there is structure, it is more likely to resemble a language or a conversation rather than a book or a manual."

In the days since this shift was recognized a growing community of educators and developers has been gathering around a model of online learning typified by this diagram (Figure 1) authored by Wilson et al. (2006), and remixed by various others since then.

The 'future VLE' is now most commonly referred to as the 'Personal Learning Environment', or PLE. As described by Milligan (2006),

PLEs "would give the learner greater control over their learning experience (managing their resources, the work they have produced, the activities they participate in) and would constitute their own personal learning environment, which they could use to interact with institutional systems to access content, assessment, libraries and the like." (¶ 4).

The idea behind the personal learning environment is that the management of learning migrates from the institution to the learner. As the diagram shows, the PLE connects to a number of remote services, some that specialize in learning and some that do not. Access to learning becomes access to the resources and services offered by these remote services. The PLE allows the learner not only to consume learning resources, but to produce them as well. Learning therefore evolves from being a transfer of content and knowledge to the production of content and knowledge.

E-learning 2.0 promises a lot. ""Like the web itself, the early promise of e-learning - that of empowerment - has not been fully realized. The experience of e-learning for many has been no more than a hand-out published online, coupled with a simple multiple-choice quiz. Hardly inspiring, let alone empowering. But by using these new web services, e-learning has the potential to become far more personal, social and flexible." These technologies, in other words, would *empower* students in a way previous technologies didn't.

But the structure seems to deliver on the promise. As O'Hear (2006) writes, "The traditional approach to e-learning… tends to be structured around courses, timetables, and testing. That is an approach that is too often driven by the needs of the institution rather than the individual learner. In contrast, e-learning 2.0 takes a 'small pieces, loosely joined' approach that combines the use of discrete but complementary tools and web services - such as blogs, wikis, and other social software - to support the creation of ad-hoc learning communities." (¶ 2).

Figure 1. Future VLE

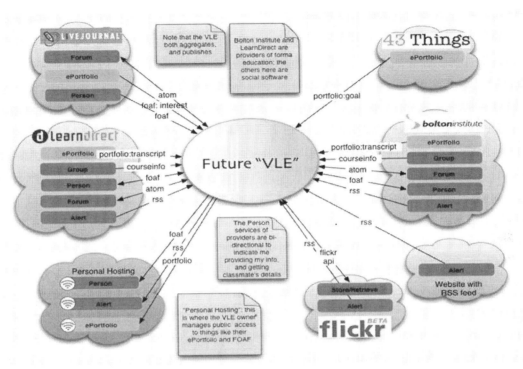

THE 2.0 ARCHITECTURE

The idea of e-learning 2.0 may appear elusive at first blush, but many of the ideas central to e-learning 2.0 may be evoked through a discussion of its fundamental architecture, which may be called 'learning networks'. The objective of a theory of learning networks is to describe the manner in which resources and services are organized in order to offer learning opportunities in a network environment. Learning networks is not therefore a pedagogical principle, but rather, a description of an environment intended to support a particular pedagogy.

I introduced learning networks formally in my Buntine Oration (2004):

If, as I suggested above, we describe learning objects using the metaphor of language, text, sentences and books, then the metaphor to describe the learning network as I've just described it is

the ecosystem, a collection of different entities related in a single environment that interact with each other in a complex network of affordances and dependencies, an environment where the individual entities are not joined or sequenced or packaged in any way, but rather, live, if you will, free, their nature defined as much by their interactions with each other as by any inherent property in themselves.

We don't present these learning objects, ordered, in a sequence, we present randomly, unordered. We don't present them in classrooms and schools, we present them to the environment, to where students find themselves, in their homes and in their workplaces. We don't present them at all, we contribute them to the conversation, and we become part of the conversation. They are not just text and tests; they are ourselves, our blog posts, our publications and speeches, our thoughts in real-time conversation. Sigmund Freud leaning on the lamp post, just when we need him. (p. 13).

This 'ecosystem' approach, realized in software, is based on a 'distributed' model of resources, as suggested by the PLE diagram. The difference between the traditional and decentralized approach may be observed in the following diagram (Figure 2):

It is interesting, and worth noting, that before the World Wide Web burst onto the scene, online access in general was typified by the centralized approach depicted in the upper figure. Users would dial up and log on to services such as CompuServe and Prodigy.

The World Wide Web, by contrast, is an example of a distributed environment. There is no single big server; resources and access are scattered around the world in the form of a network of connected web servers and internet service providers. Users do not log into a single service called 'The Web' but are also distributed, accessing through internet service providers. Even their software is distributed; their web browsers run locally, on their own machine, and function by connecting to online services and resources.

In an environment such as this, the nature of design changes. In a typical computer program, the design will be specified with an algorithm or flowchart. Software will be described as performing a specific process, with specified (and often controlled) inputs and outputs. In a distributed environment, however, the design is no longer defined as a type of process. Rather, designers

Figure 2. Centralized approach (above) and distributed approach (below)

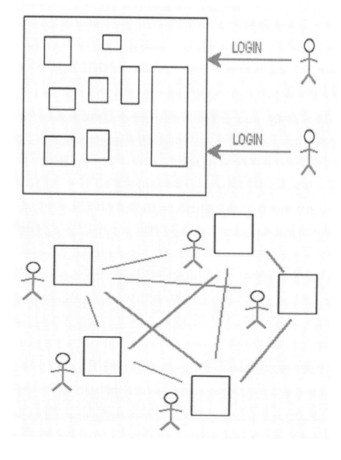

need to characterize the nature of the *connections* (Kraan, 2005) between the constituent entities.

What are the core principles (Kilkki, 2005) that will characterize such a description? The internet itself illustrates a sound set of principles, grounded by two major characteristics: simple services with realistic scope. "Simple service or simple devices with realistic scope are usually able to offer a superior user experience compared to a complex, multi–purpose service or device." Or as Weinberger (2002) describes the network: small pieces, loosely joined.

In practice, these principles may be realized in the following design principles. It is worth noting at this juncture that these principles are intended to describe not only networks but also network learning, to show how network learning differs from traditional learning. The idea is that each principle confers an advantage over non-network systems, and that the set, therefore, may be used as a means of evaluating new technology. This is a *tentative* set of principles, based on observation and pattern recognition. It is not a definitive list, and indeed, it is likely that there cannot be a definitive list.

1. Effective networks are *decentralized*. Centralized networks have a characteristic 'star' shape, where some entities have many connections while the vast majority have few. This is typical of, say a broadcast network or the method of a teacher in a classroom. Decentralized networks, by contrast, form a mesh. The weight of connections and the flow of information is distributed. This balanced load results in a more stable network, with no single point of failure.

2. Effective networks are *distributed*. Network entities reside in different physical locations. This reduces the risk of network failure. It also reduces need for major infrastructure, such as powerful servers, large bandwidth, and massive storage. Examples of distributed networks include peer-to-peer networks,

such as Kazaa, Gnutella and content syndication networks, such as RSS. The emphasis of such systems is on sharing, not copying; local copies, if they exist, are temporary.

3. Effective networks *disintermediated*. That is, they eliminate 'mediation', the barrier between source and receiver. Examples of disintermediation include the bypassing of editors, replacing peer review prior to publication with recommender systems subsequent to publication. Or of the replacement of traditional news media and broadcasters with networks of news bloggers. And, crucially, the removal of the intermediate teacher that stands between knowledge and the student. The idea is to, where possible, provide direct access to information and services. The purpose of mediation, if any, is to manage flow, not information, to reduce the volume of information, not the type of information.

4. In effective networks, content and services are *disaggregated*. Units of content should be as small as possible and content should not be 'bundled'. Instead, the organization and structure of content and services is created by the receiver. This allows the integration of new information and services with the old, of popular news and services with those in an individual's particular niche interests. This was the idea behind learning objects; the learning object was sometimes defined as the 'smallest possible unit of instruction' (Bath, 2003). The assembly of learning objects into pre-packaged 'courses' defeats this, however, obviating any advantage the disaggregating of content may have provided.

5. In an effective network, content and services are *dis-integrated*. That is to say, entities in a network are not 'components' of one another. For example, plug-ins or required software to be avoided. What this means in practice is that the structure of the message is logically distinct from the type of entity

sending or receiving it. The message is coded in a common 'language' where the code is open, not proprietary. So no particular software or device is needed to receive the code. This is the idea of standards, but where standards evolve rather than being created, and where they are adopted by agreement, not requirement.

6. An effective network is *democratic*. Entities in a network are autonomous; they have the freedom to negotiate connections with other entities, and they have the freedom to send and receive information. Diversity in a network is an asset, as it confers flexibility and adaptation. It also allows the network as a whole to represent more than just the part. Control of the entities in a network, therefore, should be impossible. Indeed, in an effective network, even where control seems desirable, it is not practical. This condition – which may be thought of as the *semantic* condition – is what distinguishes networks from groups (see below).

7. An effective network is *dynamic*. A network is a fluid, changing entity, because without change, growth and adaptation are not possible. This is sometimes described as the 'plasticity' of a network. It is through this process of change that new knowledge is discovered, where the creation of connections is a core function.

8. An effective network is *desegregated*. For example, in network learning, learning is not thought of as a Separate Domain. Hence, there is no need for learning-specific tools and processes. Learning is instead thought of as a part of living, of work, of play. The same tools we use to perform day-to-day activities are the tools we use to learn. Viewed more broadly, this condition amounts to seeing the network as infrastructure. Computing, communicating and learning are not something we 'go some place to do'. Instead, we think of network resources as similar to a utility,

like electricity, like water, like telephones. The network is everywhere.

It should be noted that though some indication of the justification for these methodological principles has been offered in the list above, along with some examples, this list is in essence *descriptive*. In other words, what is claimed here is that successful networks *in fact* adhere to these principles. The *why* of this is the subject of the next few sections.

THE SEMANTIC CONDITION

Knowledge is a network phenomenon. To 'know' something is to be organized in a certain way, to exhibit patterns of connectivity. To 'learn' is to acquire certain patterns. This is as true for a community as it is for an individual. But it should be self-evident that mere organization is not the *only* determinate of what constitutes, if you will, 'good' knowledge as opposed to 'bad' (or 'false') knowledge. Consider public knowledge. People form themselves into communities, develop common language and social bonds, and then proceed to invade Europe or commit mass suicide. Nor is personal knowledge any reliable counterbalance to this. People are as inclined to internalize the dysfunctional as the utile, the self-destructive as the empowering. Some types of knowledge (that is, some ways of being organized, whether socially or personally) are destructive and unstable.

These are examples of cascade phenomena. In social sciences the same phenomenon might be referred to as the bandwagon effect. Such phenomena exist in the natural world as well. The sweep of the plague through medieval society, the failure of one hydro plant after another, the bubbles in the stock market. Cascade phenomena occur when some event or property sweeps through the network. Cascade phenomena are in one sense difficult to explain and in another sense deceptively simple.

The sense in which they are simple to explain is mathematical. If a signal has more than an even chance of being propagated from one entity in the network to the next, and if the network is fully connected, then the signal will eventually propagate to every entity in the network. The speed at which this process occurs is a property of the connectivity of the network. In (certain) random and scale free networks, including hierarchal networks, it takes very few connections to jump from one side of the network to the other. Cascade phenomena sweep through densely connected networks very rapidly.

The sense in which they are hard to explain is related to the question of why they exist at all. Given the destructive nature of cascade phenomena, it would make more sense to leave entities in the network unconnected (much like Newton escaped the plague by isolating himself). Terminating all the connections would prevent cascade phenomena. However, it would also prevent any possibility of human knowledge, any possibility of a knowing society.

It is tempting to suppose that we could easily sure the excesses of cascading communities through a simple application of knowledge obtained through other domains, but in practice we gain no increased certainly or security. Nothing guarantees truth. We are as apt to be misled by the information given by our senses, for example, as by any wayward community. Descartes records simple examples, such as mirages, or the bending of a stick in water, to make the point. Today's science can point to much deeper scepticism. Perception itself consists of selective filtering and interpretation (pattern detection!). The mind supplies sensations that are not there. Even a cautiously aware and reflective perceiver can be misled.

Quantitative knowledge, the cathedral of the twentieth century, fares no better. Though errors in counting are rare, it is a fragile a process. *What* we count is as important as how we count, and on this, quantitative reasoning is silent. We

can measure grades, but are grades the measure of learning? We can measure economic growth, but is an increase in the circulation of money a measure of progress? We can easily mislead ourselves with statistics, as Huff (1993) shows, and in more esoteric realms, such as probability, our intuitions can be exactly wrong.

We compensate for these weaknesses by recognizing that a single point of view is insufficient; we distribute what constitutes an 'observation' through a process of description and verification. If one person says he saw a zombie, we take such a claim sceptically; if a hundred people say they saw zombies, we take it more seriously, and if a process is described whereby anyone who is interested can see a zombie for themselves, the observation is accepted. In other words, the veracity of our observations is not guaranteed by the observation, but by an observational *methodology*.

In quantitative reasoning, we take care to ensure that, in our measurements, we are measuring the same thing. Through processes such as double-blind experimentation, we additionally take care to ensure that our expectations do not influence the count. In statistical reasoning, we take care to ensure that we have a sufficiently random and representative sample, in order to ensure that we are measuring one phenomenon, and not a different, unexpected phenomenon. In both we employ what Carnap called the requirement of the total evidence: we peer at something from all angles, all viewpoints, and if everybody (or the preponderance of observers) conclude that it's a duck, then it's a duck.

Connective knowledge is supported through similar mechanisms. It is important to recognize that a structure of connections is, at its heart, *artificial*, an *interpretation* of any reality there may be, and moreover, that our observations of emergent phenomena themselves as fragile and questionable as observations and measurements - these days, maybe more so, because we do not have a sound science of network semantics.

In a network, a cascade phenomenon is akin to jumping to a conclusion about an observation. It is, in a sense, a rash and unthinking response to whatever phenomenon prompted it. This capacity is crucially dependent on the structure of the network. Just as a network with no connections has no capacity to generate knowledge, a fully connected network has no defense against jumping to conclusions. What is needed is to attain a middle point, where full connectivity is achieved, but where impulses in the network ebb and flow, where impulses generated by phenomena are checked against not one but a multitude of competing and even contradictory impulses.

This is what the human mind does naturally. It is constructed in such a way that no single impulse is able to overwhelm the network. A perception must be filtered through layers of intermediate (and (anthropomorphically) sceptical) neurons before forming a part of a concept. For every organization of neurons that achieves an active state, there are countless alternative organizations ready to be activated by the same, or slightly different, phenomena (think of how even a seed of doubt can destabilize your certainty about something).

Knowledge in the mind is not a matter of mere numbers of neurons being activated by a certain phenomenon; it is an ocean of competing and conflicting possible organizations, each ebbing and subsiding with any new input (or even upon reflection). In such a diverse and demanding environment only patterns of organization genuinely successful in some important manner achieve salience, and even fewer become so important we cannot let them go. In order therefore to successfully counterbalance the tendency toward a cascade phenomenon in the realm of public knowledge, the excesses made possible by an unrestrained scale-free network need to be counterbalanced through either one of two mechanisms: either a reduction in the number of connections afforded by the very few, or an increase in the density of the local network for individual entities. Either of these approaches

may be characterized under the same heading: the fostering of diversity.

The mechanism for attaining the reliability of connective knowledge is fundamentally the same as that of attaining reliability in other areas; the promotion of diversity, through the empowering of individual entities, and the reduction in the influence of well-connected entities, is essentially a way of creating extra sets of eyes within the network.

This leads to the statement of the semantic condition (Figure 3):

- First, *diversity*. Did the process involve the widest possible spectrum of points of view? Did people who interpret the matter one way, and from one set of background assumptions, interact with people who approach the matter from a different perspective?
- Second, and related, *autonomy*. Were the individual knowers contributing to the interaction of their own accord, according to their own knowledge, values and decisions, or were they acting at the behest of some external agency seeking to magnify a certain point of view through quantity rather than reason and reflection?
- Third, interactivity, or *connectedness*. Is the knowledge being produced the product of an interaction between the members, or is it a (mere) aggregation of the members' perspectives? A *different* type of knowledge is produced one way as opposed to the other. Just as the human mind does not determine what is seen in front of it by merely counting pixels, nor either does a process intended to create public knowledge.
- Fourth, and again related, *openness*. Is there a mechanism that allows a given perspective to be entered into the system, to be heard and interacted with by others?

Figure 3. The distinction between groups and networks

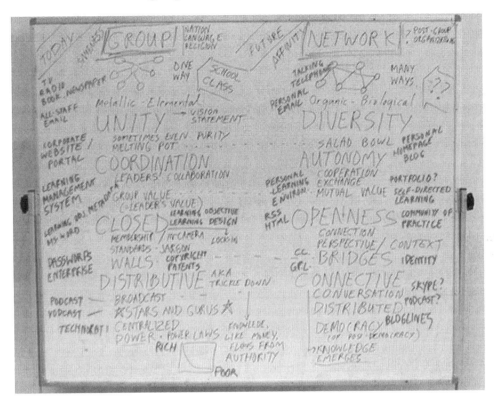

A NETWORK PEDAGOGY

The diagram in the previous section distinguishes between 'networks' and 'groups'. While it may be tempting to take this as a statement of some sort of ontology ('the world is divided into networks and groups, and these are their essential characteristics') it is better to think of the two categories as *frames* or *points of view* from with one may approach the creation of learning environments. After all, the same words may be used to describe the same entities at the same time, and this reflects not an error in categorization but rather the gestalt nature of the distinction. If the network theory applies to individual minds as well as to societies, then the network pedagogy I am proposing may be summarized as follows (and I *know* it's not original, or even substantial enough to be a theory properly So Called):

While this may not appear to amount to much on the theoretical side, it – in combination with the four elements of the semantic condition – amounts to a robust pedagogy.

In essence, on this theory, to learn is to immerse oneself in the network. It is to expose oneself to *actual* instances of the discipline being performed, where the practitioners of that discipline are (hopefully with some awareness) *modeling* good practice in that discipline. The student then, through a process of interaction with the practitioners, will begin to *practice* by replicating what has been modeled, with a process of *reflection* (the computer geeks would say: back propagation) providing guidance and correction.

Learning, in other words, occurs in communities, where the practice of learning is the participation in the community. A learning activity is, in essence, a *conversation* undertaken between the learner and other members of the community. This

Downes Educational Theory
A good student learns by practice, practice and reflection. A good teacher teaches by demonstration and modeling. The essence of being a good teacher is to be the sort of person you want your students to become. The most important learning outcome is a good and happy life.

conversation, in the web 2.0 era, consists not only of words but of images, video, multimedia and more. This conversation forms a rich tapestry of resources, dynamic and interconnected, created not only by experts but by all members of the community, including learners.

Probably the greatest misapplication of online community in online learning lies in the idea that a community is an adjunct to, or follows from, an online course. This is perhaps most clearly exemplified by the existence in itself of course discussions. It is common to see the discussion community created with the first class and disbanded with the last. The community owes its existence to the course, and ends when the course does. But the relation ought to be the other way around: that the course content (if any) ought to be subservient to the discussion, that the community is the primary unit of learning, and that the instruction and the learning resources are secondary, arising out of, and only because of, the community.

What needs to be understood is that learning environments are multi-disciplinary. That is, environments are not constructed in order to teach geometry or to teach philosophy. A learning environment is an emulation of some 'real world' application or discipline: managing a city, building a house, flying an airplane, setting a budget, solving a crime, for example. In the process of undertaking any of these activities, learning from a large number of disciplines is required.

These environments cut across disciplines. Students will not study algebra beginning with the first principles and progressing through the functions. They will learn the principles of algebra as needed, progressing more deeply into the subject

as the need for new knowledge is provoked by the demands of the simulation. Learning opportunities - either in the form of interaction with others, in the form of online learning resources (formerly known as learning objects), or in the form of interaction with mentors or instructors - will be embedded in the learning environment, sometimes presenting themselves spontaneously, sometimes presenting themselves on request.

The idea of context-sensitive learning is not new. It is already supported to a large degree in existing software; Microsoft's help system, for example, would be an example of this was the help pages designed to facilitate learning and understanding. Cross (2006) is talking about a similar thing when he talks about informal learning. In a similar manner, learners interacting with each other through a learning environment will access 'help' not only with the software but also with the subject matter they are dealing with. Learning will be available not in learning institutions but in any given environment in which they find themselves.

The Personal Learning Environment (PLE), which has attracted a lot of discussion in recent months, ought to be seen in this light. It is tempting to think of it as a content management device or as a file manager. But the heart of the concept of the PLE is that it is a tool that allows a learner (or anyone) to *engage* in a distributed environment consisting of a network of people, services and resources. It is not *just* Web 2.0, but it is certainly Web 2.0 in the sense that it is (in the broadest sense possible) a *read-write* application.

Attwell (2006) writes, "The promise of Personal Learning Environments could be to extend access to educational technology to everyone who wishes to organise their own learning. Furthermore the idea of the PLE purports to include and bring together all learning, including informal learning, workplace learning, learning from the home, learning driven by problem solving and learning motivated by personal interest as well as learning through engagement in formal educational programmes." (¶ 11).

The 'pedagogy' behind the PLE – if it could be still called that – is that it offers a portal to the world, through which learners can explore and create, according to their own interests and directions, interacting at all times with their friends and community. "New forms of learning are based on trying things and action, rather than on more abstract knowledge. 'Learning becomes as much social as cognitive, as much concrete as abstract, and becomes intertwined with judgment and exploration.'" And – crucially – *teaching* becomes the same thing as well. As I wrote in 2002, "Educators play the same sort of role in society as journalists. They are aggregators, assimilators, analysts and advisors. They are middle links in an ecosystem, or as Hiler puts it, parasites on information produced by others. And they are being impacted by alternative forms of learning in much the same way, for much the same reasons." (¶ 10).

POSTSCRIPT: THE NON-CAUSAL THEORY OF KNOWLEDGE

In recent years we have heard a great deal about evidence based educational policy. It is an appealing demand: the idea that educational policy and pedagogy ought to be informed by theory that is empirically supported. Such demands are typical of causal theories; following the methodology outlined theorists like Carl Hempel (www.iep.utm.edu/h/hempel.htm), they require an assessment of initial conditions, an intervention, and a measurement of observed difference, as predicted by a (causal) generalization.

In the earlier theory, there is a direct causal connection between states of affairs in the communicating entities; it is, therefore, a causal theory. But in the latter theory, there is no direct causal connection; it is what would be called (in the parlance of the new theory) an emergentist theory (that is, it is based on emergence, not causality). Calls for "evidence that show this claim is true" and "studies to substantiate this claim" are, like most Positivist and Positivist-inspired theories, reductive in nature; that is why, for example, we expect to find something like a reductive entity, 'the message', 'the information', 'the learning', and the like. They are also aggregationist; the presumption, for example, is that knowledge is cumulative, that it can be assembled through a series of transactions, or in more advanced theories, 'constructed' following a series of cues and prompts.

But what happens, first of all, if the entities we are 'measuring' don't exist?

Even if there are mental states, it may still be that our descriptions of them nonetheless commit some sort of category error. Saying that there are 'thoughts' and 'beliefs' that somehow reduce to physical instantiations of, well, *something* (a word, a brain state…) is a mistake. These concepts are relics of an age when we thought the mental came in neat little atomistic packages, just like the physical. They are an unfounded application of concepts like 'objects' and 'causation' to phenomena that defy such explanation; they are, in other words, relics of 'folk psychology'. Saying 'someone has a belief' is like saying that 'the Sun is rising' - it is literally untrue, and depends on a mistaken world view.

But even more significantly, what happens if we cannot 'measure' the phenomena in question at all?

On the network theory knowledge and learning are emergent phenomena, and it is necessary to highlight a critical point: emergent phenomena are not causal phenomena. That is (say) the picture of Richard Nixon does not 'cause' you to think of the disgraced former president. They require a perceiver, someone to *recognize* the pattern being displayed in the medium. And this recognition depends on a relevant (but not strictly defined) similarity between one's own mental state and the pattern being perceived. That's *why* perception (and language, etc), unlike strict causation, is context-sensitive.

And there is no means for a student to 'cause' (strictly speaking) recognition on the part of, say, an examiner, that he or she 'knows that Paris is the capital of France'. What is essential (and, I might add, ineliminable) is that the complex of this person's behaviours be recognized as displaying that knowledge. As Wittgenstein says, we recognize that a person believes the ice is safe by the manner in which he walks on the ice. And because this demonstration is non-causal, it depends on the mental state of the examiner, and worse, because (quite literally) we see what we want to see, the prior disposition of the examiner.

If this is the case, the very ideas of 'evidence' and 'proof' are turned on their heads. "Modeling the brain is not like a lot of science where you can go from one step to the next in a chain of reasoning, because you need to take into account so many levels of analysis... O'Reilly likens the process to weather modeling." (ScienceDaily, 2006, October 6, ¶ 12). This is a very important point, because it shows that traditional research methodology, and for that matter, traditional methods of testing and evaluation, as employed *widely* in the field of e-learning, will not be successful (are high school grades a predictor of college success? Are LSAT scores? Are college grades a predictor of life success?). This becomes even more relevant with the recent emphasis on 'evidence-based' methodology, such as the Campbell Collaboration (www. campbellcollaboration.org/) . This methodology, like much of the same type, recommends double-blind tests measuring the impacted of individual variables in controlled environments. The PISA samples are an example of this process in action (www.pisa.oecd.org).

The problem with this methodology is that if the brain (and hence learning) operates as described by O'Reilly (and there is ample evidence that it does) then concepts such as 'learning' are best understood as functions applied to a distributed representation, and hence, will operate in environments of numerous mutually dependent variables (the value of one variable impacts the value of a second, which impacts the value of a third, which in turn impacts the value of the first, and so on).

As I argue in papers like Public Policy, Research and Online Learning (2003) and Understanding PISA (2005) the traditional methodology fails in such environments. Holding one variable constant, for example, *impacts* the variable you are trying to measure. This is because you are not merely screening the impact of the second variable, you are screening the impact of the first variable on itself (as transferred through the second variable). This means you are *incorrectly* measuring the first variable.

Environments with numerous mutually dependent variables are known collectively as chaotic systems. Virtually all networks are chaotic systems. Classic examples of chaotic systems are the weather system and the ecology. In both cases, it is not possible to determine the long-term impact of a single variable. In both cases, trivial differences in initial conditions can result in significant long-term differences (the butterfly effect).

This was a significant difference between computation and neural networks. In computation (and computational methodology, including traditional causal science) we look for specific and predictable results. Make intervention X and get result Y. Neural network (and social network) theory does not offer this. Make intervention X today and get result Y. Make intervention X tomorrow (even on the same subject) and get result Z.

This does not mean that a 'science' of learning is impossible. Rather, it means that the science will be more like meteorology than like (classical) physics. It will be a science based on modeling and simulation, pattern recognition and interpretation, projection and uncertainty. One would think at first blush that this is *nothing* like computer science. But as the article takes pains to explain, it *is* like computer science - so long as we are studying *networks* of computers, like social networks.

Learning theorists will no longer be able to study learning from the detached pose of the empirical scientist. The days of the controlled study involving 24 students ought to end. Theorists will have to, like students, immerse themselves in their field, to encounter and engage in a myriad of connections, to immerse themselves, as McLuhan would say, as though in a warm bath. But it's a new world in here, and the water's fine.

REFERENCES

Attwell, G. (2006). *Personal learning environments*. Retrieved November 23, 2008, from http://www.knownet.com/writing/weblogs/Graham_Attwell/entries/6521819364

Bach, M. (2003). Critical view on a concept to present learning material using different didactical theories in a learning environment. In *Computers and advanced technology in education*.

Buchanan, M. (2002). *Nexus: Small worlds and the groundbreaking science of networks*. New York: W. W. Norton & Company.

Churchland, P. S. (1986). *Neurophilosophy: Toward a unified science of the mind-brain*. Cambridge, MA: MIT Press.

Churchland, P. S., & Sejnowski, T. J. (1992). Computation in the age of neuroscience. In D. Hillis (Ed.), *The new computation*. Cambridge, MA: MIT Press

Cross, J. (2006). *Informal learning: Rediscovering the natural pathways that inspire innovation and performance*. New York: Pfeiffer.

Downes, S. (2002). *Aggregators, assimilators, analysts and advisors*. Retrieved November 23, 2008, from http://www.downes.ca/cgi-bin/page.cgi?post=84

Downes, S. (2003). Public policy, research and online learning. *ACM Ubiquity Views, 4*(25). Retrieved November 23, 2008, from http://www.acm.org/ubiquity/views/v4i25_downes.html

Downes, S. (2004). The Buntine oration: Learning networks. *International Journal of Instructional Technology and Distance Learning, 1*(11), 3-14. Retrieved February 2, 2009, from http://www.itdl.org/Journal/Nov_04/Nov_04.pdf

Downes, S. (2005). *E-learning 2.0*. Retrieved November 23, 2008, from http://www.elearnmag.org/subpage.cfm?section=articles&article=29-1

Downes, S. (2005). Understanding PISA. *Turkish Online Journal of Distance Education-TOJDE, 6*(2). Retrieved November 23, 2008, from http://tojde.anadolu.edu.tr/tojde18/articles/article10.htm

Dretske, F. (1999). *Knowledge and the flow of information*. Stanford, CA: Center for the Study of Language and Inf.

Dreyfus, H., & Dreyfus, S. (1986). *Mind over machine: The power of human intuition and expertise in the era of the computer*. Oxford, UK: Blackwell.

Fodor, J. (1983). *RePresentations: Philosophical essays on the foundations of cognitive science*. Cambridge, MA: The MIT Press

Fodor, J. (1989). *Psychosemantics: The problem of meaning in the philosophy of mind*. Cambridge, MA: The MIT Press.

Fodor, J. (2005). *The language of thought*. Cambridge, MA: Harvard University Press

Garson, J. (2007). *Connectionism.* Retrieved November 17, 2008, from http://plato.stanford.edu/entries/connectionism/

Griffin, E. (2002). *A first look at communication theory* (5th ed.). New York: McGraw-Hill.

Hanson, N. R. (1958). *Patterns of discovery: An inquiry into the conceptual foundations of science.* Cambridge, UK: Cambridge University Press.

Hebb, D. O. (2002). *The organization of behavior: A neuropsychological theory.* Mahwah, NJ: Lawrence Erlbaum.

Hinton, G. E. (1986). Learning distributed representations of concepts. In *Proc. of the Ann. Conf. of the Cognitive Science Society, volume 1.*

Huff, D. (1993). *How to lie with statistics.* New York: W. W. Norton & Company.

Jha, A. (2005). *Where belief is born.* Retrieved November 20, 2008, from http://www.guardian.co.uk/science/2005/jun/30/psychology.neuroscience

Kirkpatrick, D. (2006). *Life in a connected world.* Retrieved November 20, 2008, from http://money.cnn.com/2006/06/23/technology/brainstormintro.fortune/index.htm

Kosslyn, S. M. (2002). *Image and mind* (Reprint ed.). Cambridge, MA: Harvard University Press.

Lakoff, G. (1990). *Women, fire, and dangerous things.* Chicago, IL: University Of Chicago Press.

LeDoux, J. (2002). *Synaptic self: How our brains become who we are.* New York: Viking Adult.

Levin, J. (2004). Functionlism. In *Stanford encyclopedia of philosophy.* Retrieved February 2, 2009 from http://plato.stanford.edu/entries/functionalism/

Lewis, D. K. (2001). *Counterfactuals* (2nd ed.). New York: Wiley-Blackwell.

Madden, M., & Fox, S. (2006). *Riding the waves of "Web 2.0": More than a buzzword, but still not easily defined.* Retrieved November 23, 2008, from http://www.pewinternet.org/pdfs/PIP_Web_2.0.pdf

Malpas, J. (2005). *Donald Davidson.* Retrieved November 17, 2008, from http://plato.stanford.edu/entries/davidson/

Marr, D. (1982). Vision. *Times.*

Milligan, C. (2006). *What is a PLE? The future or just another buzz word?* Retrieved November 23, 2008, from http://www.elearning.ac.uk/news_folder/ple%20event

Minsky, M., & Papert, S. (1969). *Perceptrons: An introduction to computational geometry.* Cambridge, MA: The MIT Press.

Moore, M. G. (1973). Towards a theory of independent learning and teaching. *The Journal of Higher Education, 44*(9), 661–679. doi:10.2307/1980599

Moore, M. G. (1989). Editorial: Three types of interaction. *American Journal of Distance Education, 4*(2), 1–6.

Moore, M. G. (1993). Three types of interaction. In K. Harry, M. John, & D. Keegan (Eds.), *Distance education: New perspective.* London: Routledge.

Nagel, T. (1974). What is it like to be a bat? [from http://www.clarku.edu/students/philosophyclub/docs/nagel.pdf]. *The Philosophical Review*, 435–450. Retrieved November 3, 2008. doi:10.2307/2183914

Newell, A., & Simon, H. A. (1963). GPS, a program that simulates human thought. In E. A. Feigenbaum & J. Feldman (Eds.), *Computers and thought* (pp. 279-293). New York: McGraw-Hill. Retrieved November 18, 2008, from http://www.math.grinnell.edu/~stone/events/scheme-workshop/gps.html

O'Hear, S. (2006). *E-learning 2.0: How Web technologies are shaping education.* Retrieved November 23, 2008, from http://www.readwrite-web.com/archives/e-learning_20.php

O'Reilly, R. C. (2006). *Part of human brain functions like a digital computer, professor says.* Retrieved February 2, 2009 from http://www.physorg.com/news79289076.html

O'Reilly, R. C. (2006). Modeling integration and dissociation in brain and cognitive development. In Y. Munakata & M. H. Johnson (Eds.), *Processes of change in brain and cognitive development: Attention and performance XXI.* New York: Oxford University Press. Retrieved February 2, 2009, from http://psych-www.colorado.edu/~oreilly/papers/OReillyIPap.pdf

O'Reilly, T. (2005). *What is Web 2.0: Design patterns and business models for the next generation of software.* Retrieved November 23, 2008, from http://www.oreillynet.com/pub/a/oreilly/tim/news/2005/09/30/what-is-web-20.html

Polanyi, M. (1974). *Personal knowledge: Towards a post-critical philosophy.* Chicago, IL: University Of Chicago Press.

Quine, W. V. O. (1951). Two dogmas of empiricism. [from http://www.ditext.com/quine/quine.html]. *The Philosophical Review, 60,* 20–43. Retrieved November 20, 2008. doi:10.2307/2181906

Quine, W. V. O. (1964). *Word and object.* Cambridge, MA: The MIT Press.

Ravenscroft, I. (2004). *Folk psychology as a theory.* Retrieved November 3, 2008, from http://plato.stanford.edu/entries/folkpsych-theory/

Rumelhart, D. E., & McClelland, J. L., & the PDP Research Group. (1987). *Parallel distributed processing: Foundations.* Cambridge, MA: The MIT Press.

Schramm, W. (1964). *Mass media and national development.* Stanford, CA: Stanford University Press.

Schramm, W. (1997). *The beginnings of communication study in America: A personal memoir.* Thousand Oaks, CA: Sage.

Scott, W., Oleg, L., Phil, B., Colin, M., Mark, J., & Paul, S. (2006). *Personal learning environments: Challenging the dominant design of educational systems.* Retrieved November 23, 2008, from http://hdl.handle.net/1820/727

Searle, J. R. (1980). Minds, brains, and programs. *Behavioral and Brain Sciences 3*(3), 417-457. Retrieved November 3, 2008, from http://www.bbsonline.org/Preprints/OldArchive/bbs.searle2.html

Siemens, G. (2004). *Connectivism: A learning theory for the digital age.* Retrieved November 23, 2008, from http://www.elearnspace.org/Articles/connectivism.htm

Stalnaker, R. C. (1987). *Inquiry.* Cambridge, MA: The MIT Press.

Stephenson, K. (1998). What knowledge tears apart, networks make whole. *Internal Communication Focus, 36.* Retrieved November 23, 2008, from http://www.netform.com/html/icf.pdf

Technorati. (2006). *State of the blogosphere.* Retrieved November 20, 2008, from http://www.sifry.com/alerts/archives/000436.html van Fraassen, B. C. (1980). *The scientific image.* New York: Oxford University Press.

University of Colorado at Boulder. (2006, October 6). Human brain region functions like digital computer. *ScienceDaily.* Retrieved November 23, 2008, from http://www.sciencedaily.com /releases/2006/10/061005222628.htm

Watts, D. J. (2004). *Six degrees: The science of a connected age*. New York: W. W. Norton & Company.

Weinberger, D. (2002). *Small pieces loosely joined.* Cambridge, MA: Perseus Books.

Wittgenstein, L. (1973). *Philosophical investigations* (3rd ed.). Upper Saddle River, NJ: Prentice Hall.

Chapter 2
Conceptualizing Codes of Conduct in Social Networking Communities

Ann Dutton Ewbank
Arizona State University, USA

Adam G. Kay
Dartmouth College, USA

Teresa S. Foulger
Arizona State University, USA

Heather L. Carter
Arizona State University, USA

ABSTRACT

This chapter reviews the capabilities of social networking tools and links those capabilities to recent legal and ethical controversies involving use of social networking tools such as Facebook and MySpace. A social cognitive moral framework is applied to explore and analyze the ethical issues present in these incidents. Three ethical vulnerabilities are identified in the use of social networking tools: 1) the medium provides a magnified forum for public humiliation or hazing, 2) a blurring of boundaries exists between private and public information on social networking sites, and 3) the medium merges individuals' professional and non-professional identities. Prevalent legal and social responses to these kinds of incidents are considered and implications are suggested for encouraging responsible use. The chapter includes a description of the authors' current research with preservice students involving an intervention whereby students read and think about real cases where educators use social networking. The intervention was created to improve students' critical thinking about the ethical issues involved. Recommendations for applying institutional codes of conduct to ethical dilemmas involving online tools are discussed.

DOI: 10.4018/978-1-60566-729-4.ch002

Copyright © 2010, IGI Global. Copying or distributing in print or electronic forms without written permission of IGI Global is prohibited.

INTRODUCTION

Social networking sites such as Facebook and MySpace have become ubiquitous. Whereas email was the electronic communication norm in the late twentieth century, social networking is rapidly replacing email as the most favored means of networking, connecting, and staying in touch. In fact, MySpace is the sixth most visited site on the Internet (Alexa, 2008) and Facebook is the world's largest and the fastest growing social networking site (Schonfeld, 2008). These tools are quite popular with teenagers, college-age students, and young professionals because they allow them to more easily stay connected. Using social networking sites, individuals can present themselves to others through an online identity that is tailored to their unique interests and desires, and participate in a variety of inter-connected communication networks - personal, professional, creative, or informative. However, when individuals create a personal space online, they also create a digital footprint—the kind of footprint that can be permanent. And when a trail of personal information is left behind in a searchable and open format, notions of public and private information are challenged and the potential for liabilities may be high. This is of particular importance to those who wish to convey a professional image. An online profile that may have seemed innocuous and private during one stage of life may haunt an individual at the point in their life when they transition from student to professional.

For educational institutions, the widespread popularity of social networking sites as a means of communication, provide in-roads for experimenting with ways to connect with clientele. While innovative educators are quick to embrace and harness the learning potential of Web 2.0 tools, an understanding of the ethical issues in these unusual forms of social interaction has been slower to develop. Undoubtedly there are value-added features, many of which are yet to be discovered; but some institutions are refusing to innovate with this powerful technology tool due to the risks involved.

In order to design and endorse effective use of these tools, educators need socially responsible models and guidelines. What are the ethical considerations required of online social networking, and how can educational organizations capitalize on this innovative means of communicating while promoting responsible use? This chapter will highlight legal and ethical controversies surrounding social networking sites, identify ethical vulnerabilities associated with using the online tools through a social cognitive moral framework, and discuss implications for promoting socially responsible use of social networking tools.

BACKGROUND

Our inquiries into this topic began when one of the authors of this chapter encountered a situation involving social networking in her preservice teacher education class. What started as a class assignment turned into a moral and ethical dilemma for the instructor when a student revealed his MySpace profile as a part of a larger class assignment. Students were to create a homepage and provide three links to sites that a future teacher might use in the classroom as part of a lesson plan. Many students chose to link to their MySpace profiles as part of the assignment, but one particular link captured the attention of the instructor who was not prepared for what she saw—a MySpace profile showing a bloody machete stabbed into a hand with the caption that read, "Twist the hand that forces you to write." Other images and words on the profile were equally disturbing. The personal icon used to identify the profile owner was an image of a cut wrist with directions on how to commit suicide. The instructor wondered why a student would turn in what seemed to be a private and personal site as part of a class assignment. Perhaps Web 2.0 and online social networking caused this student to think differently than the instructor about revealing private thoughts in such a public forum. Because technology users in the Web 2.0 environment can be both consumers and creators of information, similar scenarios are occurring often. At what point is the boundary crossed when sharing information about self and others via social networking tools? And who draws that line? The ability to communicate personal, informational, or editorial information en masse—at the click of a mouse—poses new and different ethical dilemmas not as prevalent in the pre-Web 2.0 world. And this issue is compounded by the fact that as users share authored information with others, they invite countless people into their personal space. Social networking creates a window into users' lives that is much more immediate, permanent, and impactful than ever before.

Social Networking Tools and Their Capabilities

Social networking sites are Websites designed to bring together groups of people in order to communicate around shared interests or activities (Wikipedia, 2008). Because meeting places are virtual, the idea that any two people can be connected through several intermediaries, commonly known as "six degrees of separation," is magnified and expanded (Leskovec & Horvitz, 2007). This kind of interconnectivity among individuals would be impossible without the Web. The online manifestation of social networking typically refers to a minimum of three networking capacities, first popularized by Friendster in 2002. This includes publicly displayed profiles, publicly accessible lists of friends, and virtual walls for comments or testimonials (boyd, 2008). In any of the myriad social networking sites created since Friendster, individuals can join a Web service, and then design a profile to showcase and highlight personal information, hobbies, employment and any other topics they wish to be shared. Upon becoming a member of an online social network,

the user can communicate with other members or groups, link their profile to others, and even invite those outside the social networking site to join the system and link to their profile. Thus, a network continually expands.

Revisiting the story of the student with the disturbing MySpace profile highlights the differences between in-person and online social networks. Prior to viewing the profile, the instructor had only the day-to-day interactions in the classroom to form an opinion of the student. The informal social network of this student was not revealed to the instructor prior to viewing the MySpace profile. However, it was the student's choice to share the public profile with the instructor, and when that happened the cloak over a previously invisible network was removed and a facet of this student's life that was markedly different than his in-class persona was revealed. The instructor had more information from which to form an opinion of the student, and could not help but think differently about the student from that day forth. However, the student was naively unaware of impact that his online profile had on interactions with the instructor.

More importantly though, with the lasting vision of a bloody hand, the instructor was in turmoil about the ethics behind what was brought to light. Unlike an incident in the classroom where a course of action would be clear, the most appropriate response to the personal information revealed through the online profile was not obvious to the instructor. Where did the instructor's authority end and the student's personal life begin? Was the instructor responsible for reporting the actions that took place outside of her classroom? Was the online information within or outside the classroom? How would this student interact with children during his field placement and in his future classroom? Was the profile indicative of a troubled individual or was it simply a manifestation of creative, albeit dark, expression? For these reasons, the instructor grappled with whether to report the student to campus authorities for the disturbing images and ideas relayed on his profile.

Legal Actions and Campus-Based Incidents

Professional or formal relationships may become tainted when people either purposefully or inadvertently share information about themselves via online social networking services, and some users fail to think about the consequences that may arise as a result. Furthermore, appropriate responses to online personal information by those in authority, such as instructors and supervisors, may not be clear.

In recent years, many campus-based incidents involving perceived student misuse of social networking sites have occurred in both K-12 and postsecondary institutions. For example, Elon University in North Carolina took disciplinary action against members of the baseball team after photos of players involved in hazing activities found their way onto a student's MySpace profile (Lindenberger, 2006). An academic institution's *in loco parentis* responsibilities are often interpreted by campus administrators as encompassing the cyberworld. Some universities including Penn State University and the University of California-Davis utilize information contained in social networking sites to investigate campus incidents of harassment, code of conduct violations, and criminal activity (Lipka, 2008).

Slightly different problems exist for younger students. K-12 students have been suspended or expelled for creating false and potentially libelous profiles of faculty or administrators. These suspensions have been met with an interesting reaction from parents; in some cases, parents have filed suit against the educational institution for impeding a student's right to free expression by nature of the discipline imposed for creating the profile (see Layshock v. Hermitage School District, 2007; Requa v. Kent School District, 2007; J.S. v. Blue Mountain School District, 2007; A.

B. v. State of Indiana, 2008). These claims of free speech violations have largely been unfounded by the courts. However, in some cases decisions have held a student's right to free expression in the form of an Internet parody if no significant disruption to the educational institution has occurred. Faculty have also filed suit or pressed criminal charges against students for harassing, defaming, or intimidating speech online (see Wisniewski vs. Board of Education, Weedsport Central School District, 2007; WSBTV.com, 2006).

And faculty sanctions for perceived misuse of social networking are becoming commonplace as well. Regulation of faculty conduct outside of professional duties is embedded in institutional codes and social norms, and many cases exist where faculty have claimed that sanctions or dismissals are unconstitutional (Fulmer, 2002). However, with the advent of online social networking, traditional tests of rights vs. duty may not apply. In a conventional sense, educational institutions realize the boundaries of faculty behavior to be regulated. But the transparency of online social networking has somewhat eroded those boundaries. For example, do faculty have the *right* to free expression online even if it conflicts with the values of the institution? Or do institutions have the *duty* to ensure that the values of the institution are upheld online as they are in the physical world?

One particularly striking example of this dilemma is the Tamara Hoover case. Hoover, a high school art teacher in the Austin (Texas) Independent School District, was fired when nude photographs were discovered on her MySpace profile and on her photo-sharing website, Flickr (May, 2006). Hoover was fired based on "conduct unbecoming a teacher," even though the photographs displayed could be interpreted as artistic and professional. Hoover agreed to a cash settlement from the school district, and now uses her MySpace profile to promote teachers' free speech rights (Hoover, 2007). The case has attracted national media attention.

The Hoover case is not an isolated incident. Many other cases of faculty sanctions over social networking have occurred in recent years (Crawford, 2007; Phillips, 2007; Vivanco, 2007). Do education administrators have the right to screen potential employees by "Googling" them, or to monitor employees' electronic communications without evidence of inappropriate contact with students (Wheeler, 2007)? These and other questions concerning ethical conduct within social networking sites have been met with a variety of responses from teacher preparation programs, school districts, and universities. Some have warned faculty not to use the sites at all (e-School News, 2007) and others have taken an educational approach, encouraging users to critically think about what they post online (The Pennsylvania State University, 2007). Given the ubiquity of online social networking communities among youth (boyd, 2008) as well as the potential of these powerful tools to provide communications that would not otherwise be possible, barring their use strikes the authors of this chapter as an educational disservice. To best calculate the risks that could be incurred in leveraging the power of these innovative tools, we believe a careful analysis of the potential ethical issues involved in interactions in online social networks is necessary.

APPLYING A MORAL FRAMEWORK

The events described above begin to illustrate the confusing social and ethical landscape of communications in this changing time, especially for educators who are obligated by their professional standards to serve as role models. To add to the complexity, the multiple players, including faculty, students, administrators, and parents, appear to have vastly different points of view about what is appropriate and inappropriate conduct. This is partly due to the multiple and often competing social and moral concerns present in these types of incidents. To both investigate the ethical points of view involved in judging these incidents and to uncover the ethical vulnerabilities inherent in this new medium, we have applied a socio-moral framework with a legacy of describing moral and non-moral features of complex social interactions. Specifically, social cognitive domain theory (Turiel, 1983; Turiel, 2002) is an appropriate starting point for understanding the complexities in online social networking.

First, the theory provides an analytical framework that differentiates moral from non-moral concerns in social interactions. Prior research applying this framework has demonstrated that people consistently think about moral (such as notions of harm, fairness, and rights), conventional (such as social roles, institutional organization, and matters of social efficiency), and personal matters (such as tastes and choices) in different ways (see Smetana, 2006 for a review). From early childhood, individuals actively distinguish between these domains and make judgments specific to domains about these distinct categories of social interaction. These insights are critical because many real-world social interactions are multi-faceted in the sense that multiple social domains are involved. Judgments and actions based on social interactions often involve weighing and coordinating various moral and non-moral concerns. For example, a judgment about whether a teacher should be disciplined for approaching parents with alarming information acquired from a student's online profile involves the consideration of multiple issues. There are concerns for the student's welfare (moral), the limits of teacher authority (conventional), and the student's right to privacy (moral) when choosing to post information in a public forum (personal).

Second, the framework allows for analytical investigation rather than a prescribed approach to how one should behave in ambiguous situations. There are conflicting perspectives about whether a teacher should be disciplined in such a situation; the authors of this chapter do not pretend to be certain about the right or ethical course of action in complicated, multi-faceted events. Our purpose is not to prescribe a set of moral actions that fit under a wide variation of circumstances, but instead to better understand the issues involved and also discover the ways people weigh those various issues in their thinking as online social networks continue to grow. To this end we conducted an investigation into student ethical decision-making in online social networking communities. This study has implications for how instructors might develop ways to allow students to ponder their ethical reasoning while engaging in the use of these tools.

Research within this framework can provide insights and useful points of comparison for our topic because of multiple studies of reasoning about two relevant social issues: developing concepts of role-related authority (Laupa, 1991; Laupa & Turiel, 1993; Laupa, 1995) and thinking about rights and privacy issues with the use of modern technologies (Friedman et al., 2006; Friedman, 1997). For example, when asked about the limits of educators' authority and responsibility over students, older students are more likely than younger students to limit their influences to the concrete boundaries of the school context (Laupa & Turiel, 1993). As classroom and school boundaries become progressively virtual, limits on educators' responsibilities and authority are unclear for students and staff alike. While reasoning about moral issues in technology, one study demonstrated that many students who believe in property and privacy rights in non-technological arenas condone piracy and hacking activities on computers (Friedman, 1997). Interviews with these students revealed that this apparent contradiction had to do with fundamental aspects of technology: the perceived distance between the actor and potential victims, the indirect nature of the harmful consequences, the invisibility of the act, and the lack of established consequences for such behavior online. Therefore, social cognitive

domain theory is a useful framework to guide an analysis of the kinds of issues that can arise in the use of social networking tools. It allows us to do so in a way that respects the complexity of these kinds of interactions. Finally, it enables us to connect directly with a body of research that informs investigations of the ways in which online social interaction might cultivate its own set of ethical vulnerabilities. For example, the studies highlighted above suggest at least three such vulnerabilities:

1. A magnified forum for public humiliation and hazing--Students might be more likely to engage in public humiliation through social networking tools because harmful consequences are not directly observed, in contrast to acts in physical public spaces such as the cafeteria or locker room. Furthermore, when hazing or humiliation is conducted online there is greater distance (and sometimes even anonymity) between the actor and the victim.
2. Privacy issues in public spaces--Online social networking has the power to re-frame the way we consider and apply traditional rights to privacy.
3. The merging of professional and non-professional identities--The classroom walls and school premises no longer frame the jurisdiction of the educational institution. How does this shift impact higher education? How can social networking tools be appropriately used by university programs, administrators, instructors, and students?

Using the social cognitive moral framework as a lens for analysis, these ethical vulnerabilities are described in detail in the following section.

ETHICAL VULNERABILITIES OF SOCIAL NETWORKING TOOLS REVEALED

A Magnified Forum for Public Humiliation and Hazing

It is not uncommon to see academic units represented on MySpace or Facebook, as they attempt to find ways to provide services and assistance to students who are familiar with online tools (Hermes, 2008). Additionally, academic units can use these spaces as an outreach tool for marketing (Berg, Berquam & Christoph, 2007; O'Hanlon, 2007). With this level of transparency it would be easy to witness students engaging in the kinds of online activities that could be characterized as public humiliation and hazing. Most university codes of conduct prohibit this sort of behavior. However, when the behavior is discovered online, questions may arise about whether academic officials should access online profiles at all. While conducting research recently on the feasibility of creating a presence for a university academic library in Facebook, one of the authors came across a student group called "Have you seen the homeless guy in the library?" The description of the group was, "He's always on the computers. He stinks really bad. And he has like 1,000's of plastic bags..." Updated in the *recent news* section of the page was a description of where he was sitting in the library that day as well as a Web site that he had viewed. There were seventeen students in this group (no doubt with various levels of engagement), creating and sustaining a public community with the sole purpose of ridiculing one specific human being.

Public humiliation is not a new phenomenon; but the power of the collective sentiment conveyed by this online "community" would be hard to fathom offline, as a group with a purpose such as this would take considerably more time and effort to create. But by accident this particular group became visible, and when the activity was reported to the library administration, the university student affairs department was alerted. The student affairs officer explained to the library representative that student issues involving online public humiliation and hazing are not uncommon, and that the department frequently engages in mediation to resolve disputes—student to student, student to instructor, and around potentially disturbing group behavior. The officer explained that she would talk to the students who had joined the Facebook group, and use the incident as a "teachable moment" to address ethical use of the social networking tool among the students.

More and more educational administrations are grappling with issues between and among students that have extended into online social networking. As these online forums become ubiquitous to the masses, they have developed into a natural extension of students' social and personal lives. In a recent survey the Pew Internet & American Life Project found that fifty-five percent of online teens (ages 12-17) have created a profile at a social networking site such as MySpace or Facebook (Lenhart, Madden, Macgill, & Smith, 2007). University students in particular frequent social networking sites. In fact, a recent survey of all first-year English students at the University of Illinois-Chicago (Hargittai, 2007), reported that 88% use social networking sites.

Incidents involving public humiliation or hazing such as the one that took place in the university library as described above, have become commonplace in both K-12 and institutions of higher learning. Through "cyberbullying," defined as "willful and repeated harm inflicted through the medium of electronic text," (Patchin & Hinduja, 2006, p.152) students and faculty can either become the targets or perpetrators of incidents that would be unacceptable in offline situations. Electronic humiliation and hazing of this nature can have lasting physical and psychological effects on the victims such as depression, insomnia, and anxiety disorders (Griffiths, 2002). In the interest of student and faculty welfare, educational institutions have responded to these incidents in a variety of ways. Some situations are minor and can easily be solved through mediation by administrators or student affairs professionals (Lipka, 2008) while others have warranted more serious disciplinary or even criminal action.

It is because of the sheer reach of electronic communication that the Internet and social networking have become a magnified forum for public humiliation and hazing. This activity occurs within all sectors of the educational spectrum. Almost one-third of teens who use the Internet say that they have been a victim of annoying or potentially threatening activities online, including others "outing" personal information via email, text messaging, or postings on social networking sites. Those who share personal identities and thoughts are more likely to be the targets of such activities (Lenhart, 2007). Additionally, in a recent survey conducted by the Teacher Support Network of Great Britain, 17% of K-12 teachers indicated that they had been a target of online humiliation or harassment (Woolcock, 2008). College-age students and faculty are not immune from online defamation of character. In a survey conducted at the University of New Hampshire 17% of students reported experiencing threatening online behavior, yet only 7% of those experiencing vicitmization reported it to campus authorities (Finn, 2004). Sites such as JuicyCampus.com and TheDirty. com, perhaps the most notorious Web sites aimed at college students, allow anyone to post humiliating or threatening messages and photos, some of which have cost students job opportunities and internships (O'Neil, 2008). Female law school students have reported sexual harassment and defamation on AutoAdmit.com, a message board about law school admissions (Nakashima, 2007). And Web sites like RateMyProfessors. com and RateMyTeachers.com allow students to be anonymous as they air their opinions about faculty, including rating an instructor's easiness and "hotness".

Such activity on social networking sites has led to several court cases over perceived defamation. For example, *Drews vs. Joint School District* (2006) described a situation where Casey Drews, a high school student, was the subject of rumors and gossip at school after a snapshot her mother took of Drews kissing a female friend was circulated on the Internet. Drews sued the school district for deliberately ignoring the harassment. Cases illustrating faculty harassment and defamation are evident as well. A Georgia teacher brought criminal charges against a high school student who created a fake MySpace profile about the teacher, claiming that the teacher "wrestled midgets and alligators" and stating that he liked "having a gay old time" (WSBTV.com, 2006). And a federal circuit court found that a student's distribution of a text message icon depicting a gun firing at a picture of his English teacher and the words "Kill Mr. Van der Molen" was threatening speech not protected by the First Amendment (Wisniewski vs. Board of Education, Weedsport Central School District, 2007).

Steve Dillon, director of student services at Carmel Clay Schools, states, "Kids look at the Internet as today's restroom wall. They need to learn that some things are not acceptable anywhere" (Carvin, 2006). If the Internet is a restroom wall, then it is a giant, unisex restroom open to all citizens. But unlike a restroom wall that can be painted over, the Internet can be a permanent archive of electronic communication. Localized or place-bound codes of conduct are clearly no longer adequate in a Web 2.0 environment. How do educational organizations come to terms that the school's four walls have been virtually obliterated, and craft appropriate responses in codes of conduct that protect the privacy and welfare of its students and faculty, while simultaneously honoring First Amendment rights?

Privacy Issues in Public Spaces

A number of recent controversies highlight our collective lack of clarity about how we can and should use personal information that is publicly available on the Web. English Education candidate Stacy Snyder of Millersville (Pennsylvania) University was denied her teaching certificate and given an English degree rather than an education degree after campus administrators discovered photos where she portrayed herself as a "drunken pirate" on her MySpace profile, even though she was of legal drinking age. The 27-year old filed a lawsuit against the university, and is asking for $75,000 in damages (Steiner, 2007). In another example (one which we have used to explore reasoning in our own research), a teacher revealed to students that she had a MySpace profile. The student consequently "friended" the teacher, giving the teacher access to the student's profile. In the process of exploring the student's profile, the teacher discovered information about activities such as underage drinking in which the student was engaged. Concerned about what she saw online about the student, the teacher contacted the parents. The parents contacted the school, outraged that the teacher was snooping into the student's personal life, and demanded that the teacher be disciplined. Scenarios such as these suggest that both producers and consumers of online information are unclear as to exactly what is public and exactly what is private.

Are producers aware of the extent to which their online disclosures are publicly accessible? Are consumers clear about producers' rights to privacy in this online community? Studies reveal that teens and adults alike underestimate who accesses their online submissions and how that information is used (Vièhas, 2005). The nature of online social interaction allows for such vulnerabilities to protecting privacy. Palen and Dourish (2003) suggest that this illusion is perpetuated, at least in part, because of our reliance on non-virtual strategies for monitoring privacy, and that

online interactions call for implications for better controlling privacy violations and for different ways of thinking about privacy rights in online environments.

According to this view, our mechanisms for managing privacy have traditionally been spatial and sensory: we know who our audience is (and can control it) because we can see, hear, and read traditional forms of communication. Online, these cues are distorted. Our audience is frequently unknown and underestimated (Vièhas, 2005) and the boundaries between personal and professional domains are often easily crossed. Lastly, information shared online is often available for access at future times and for future audiences. Not only do these attributes impact our abilities to regulate our intended audience, they also weaken our control over how that information is interpreted and used. In an attempt to understand and improve privacy management in information technology, computer scientists have engaged in analysis of the concept of privacy and an examination of privacy online (Palen & Dourish, 2003). Conceiving privacy as a *boundary regulation process* (Altman, 1977), Palen & Dourish identify three boundary negotiation processes as essential to the management of privacy in a networked world: disclosure, identity, and temporality.

Issues involving disclosure dominate recent social networking controversies, including the two scenarios above. Some would argue that both teacher and student should have known better than to reveal personal information in a public forum -- both should simply have avoided disclosing information. But Palen & Dourish argue that this view undermines the true social interactive nature online. Disclosure is essential to online interaction. Effectively negotiating private and public spaces involves selective decisions about what to disclose and what kind of persona to display. Problems arise, they argue, in how we control who is targeted by this public display and consequently how the display is interpreted.

There is also an inherent tension in our attempts to control how others see us online. When creating and publishing our virtual identities we choose to affiliate with certain groups, networks, each with their own set of identity markers, language conventions and patterns of interaction (Yates & Orlikowski, 1992). Likewise, we modify our ways of interacting based on our perceptions of the identities and affiliations of our audience. Online, these various identities can appear quite fragmented and disconnected, such that viewing one facet of an online persona out of context (such as the "drunken pirate") can lead to distortions and errors in judgments of the person's character and personality, largely outside of the individual's control. Assessments can be made and then applied to the hiring and firing decisions within a variety of professions. Central to protecting privacy is "the ability to discern who might be able to see one's action" (Palen & Dourish, 2003, p.4).

Lastly, our attempts to control the information we share have a temporal quality. That is, in any moment of information sharing, we typically respond to the results of past attempts at information sharing and anticipate future consequences of information sharing. Moments of information sharing are connected historically and logically. However, online these moments can be viewed out of sequence, preserved for future use, and even reorganized into alternative sequences. The photos, stories, and conversations uploaded during college may return to contribute a completely different image of responsibility than the one conveyed by the professional resumé uploaded ten years later.

This analysis has implications for both education and ethics. First, these lenses offer useful entry points for developing awareness and understanding of the vulnerabilities to privacy online for both those sharing and those interpreting information shared online. Second, the review suggests a way of thinking about privacy rights online. In contrast to those who believe that privacy rights are surrendered when information is made public,

this review suggests that rights to privacy might still be negotiated after information is publicly accessible. For example, individuals sharing the information might deserve the right to have that information understood in context or within its original logical sequence; that is, understood in a way which maintains the integrity of the sharer's initial intentions. There is some limited empirical evidence suggesting that people already do uphold privacy rights in public spaces (Friedman et al., 2006). In one study, when college students were asked to judge whether an installed video camera capturing video of them in a public place was an invasion of their privacy, the majority of students judged that it was. Furthermore, in this study, students' responses illustrated a complex construal of privacy issues in public. Judgments of privacy were mediated by a variety of factors such as the location of the camera, the perceived purpose of the video camera (safety vs. voyeurism), the audience viewing the footage, and the extent of disclosure about the video camera (from posted signs to informed consent). As new technologies continue to alter the nature of our social interactions in online communities, more studies are needed both to highlight the privacy vulnerabilities inherent in these types of social interaction and to capture the adaptive reasoning about privacy rights that are constructed through those experiences.

The Merging of Professional and Non-Professional Identities

Social networking tools can serve as both a rich resource and a potential liability. As with any powerful tool, there are far-reaching risks and potential disaster if use of the tool is not thoroughly calculated—but there are beneficial uses as well. Some online social networking tools go beyond a function of socialization to include professional communication functions. For example, Zinch. com helps students connect with the colleges and universities they are interested in attending.

After students register with Zinch, they complete a personal profile and prepare an online digital portfolio illustrating their talents. Profiles are automatically private to those other than approved admissions officers. Recruiters across the nation use the network to connect with students whose profiles are of interest to their institutions. A similar site, Cappex.com, has the added feature of a calculator that estimates students' chances for admission to their desired institution. These tools take admissions criteria beyond testing, basic academics, and letters of recommendation, to allow those in non-local areas to connect with learning institutions, and provide a convenient opportunity for individual students and admissions officers to connect.

Once schooling is out of the way and the job hunt begins or a promotion is imminent, students in some professions face the news that a background check, also known as a consumer report, is required. Background checks can be conveniently conducted during the hiring process through third party investigation services to verify any level of candidate qualifications from education records to drug tests and credit records. The Fair Credit Reporting Act mandates that a consumer report should be conducted within compliance of the law to prevent discriminatory actions (Federal Trade Commission, 2004). To assure their compliance, most often employers conduct screenings by contracting with consumer reporting agencies that have access to specialized information sources. But consumer reports can also reveal information about a candidate that is irrelevant, taken out of context, or even inaccurate. This leaves room for concern for some applicants who have not paid attention or were unaware of how their prior behavior could be interpreted by employment agencies.

An online search of a person's name could also be conducted to obtain as much information as possible about a candidate's level of qualification. An Internet search can reveal a candidate's Web site or portfolio, professional accomplishments and awards, and other pertinent information. But use of an Internet search during the hiring process could also pull up a candidate's social networking profile or other Internet-based information outside a normal background check. Voluntarily-disclosed information on profiles that are public may reveal an applicant's sexual orientation, political affiliation, age, and marital status, and an employer who allows consideration to these factors could be acting in violation of workplace-discrimination statutes. But, it appears that use of information from social networking sites such as "drunken, racy, or provocative photographs" in order to make a judgment about the candidate's suitability is perfectly legal (Byrnside, 2008).

These scenarios play out over and over during the hiring process. For example, a Boston marketing recruiter was screening applications and noted one of particular interest. A member of the interview team asked the recruiter if she had seen the applicant's MySpace page, which included pictures of the recent college graduate "Jell-o wrestling." Based on more relevant factors the applicant was not interviewed, but the MySpace page remained in the recruiter's memory (Aucoin, 2007). Here again, misimpressions about privacy could pose life-changing implications if conscious actions were not promoted. How many emerging professionals have lost jobs or been denied opportunities because of the blurred boundaries between professional life and private life? The liabilities associated with social networking are potentially staggering, for both employers and employees.

Also consider the fact that individuals can experience a sort of identity theft through social networking sites. Cicero (Illinois) Town President, Larry Dominick, had two MySpace profiles. City officials found the sites, which were "replete with photos and questionable comments about his sexuality and ethics." But both sites were created by imposters (Noel, 2008). Imposter profiles are so prevalent that MySpace now has protocol and a division within the company to address cyberbullying, underage users, and imposter profiles

(MySpace, 2008). Cicero attorneys are asking MySpace to identify the anonymous users who created the profiles, and Dominick is planning on suing.

When social networking sites are made public, everyone in the world, including colleagues, has the capability to view the content. No doubt, we make judgments about a person's character based on what we see. The merging of professional and non-professional identities has implications for those who choose to create and display personal profiles.

IMPLICATIONS FOR SOCIALLY RESPONSIBLE USE OF SOCIAL NETWORKING TOOLS

Given the prevalence of incidents surrounding social networking within educational institutions, there is a need to embed socially responsible usage principles in academic programs rich in technological innovation. We have begun to implement and study such interventions. As instructors in a teacher education program we (Foulger, Ewbank, Kay, Osborn Popp, & Carter, 2009) investigated the use of case-based coursework (Kim et al., 2006; Kolodner, 1993) for encouraging change in preservice teachers' reasoning about ethical issues in Web 2.0 tools. As we have grappled with ethical dilemmas around social networking at our own institution, we were curious about the ways in which new technologies might alter traditional forms of social interaction. These circumstances gave rise to the following questions that drove our research: a) What are preservice teachers' perspectives regarding a social networking scenario that involves multiple ethical dilemmas? And b) In what ways does case-based coursework change preservice teachers' reasoning about social networking? In this study we assessed the effectiveness of a case-based intervention with a group university freshman-level education class. They participated in a homework assignment that

was developed to help them better understand the features of social networking tools. It also helped them clarify their ethical positions about recent legal sanctions pertaining to the use of social networking tools by students and teachers.

Based on a review of the literature about case-based reasoning, we expected coursework that included case-based teaching about controversial social networking issues to (a) increase students' recognition and integration of multiple perspectives or viewpoints about the benefits and harms of teachers' use of social networking tools and (b) develop students' appreciation for the range of ethical vulnerabilities inherent in social networking media. Fifty students participated in a three-part assignment. First, they were asked to respond to online selections about the technological nature of social networking. Students then commented on cases where teachers used social networking tools for pedagogical purposes. Finally students responded to cases where teachers were disciplined or dismissed for inappropriate conduct as defined by educational institutions. Comparisons of perceptions before and after the assignment were examined to analyze the preservice teachers' reasoning about controversial social networking incidents. Some significant changes in student perceptions did occur, indicating that case-based coursework increases awareness of the ethical complexities embedded in social networking tools.

Several trends emerged from the analysis. The homework helped students develop more complex ethical reasoning to the scenarios posed and revealed a significant increase among students in the call for some form of teacher discipline. Additionally, the homework developed students' recognition of the complexities of social networking sites and the need to develop clearer protocols around their educational use. Finally, the assignment had an impact on students' understanding of the ethical vulnerabilities of social networking tools. A deeper exploration of one common set of responses revealed that the study participants grappled with the line between a teacher honoring a student's right to privacy and a teacher's responsibility of caring for the students' well-being.

It was apparent that the case-based coursework encouraged students to contemplate rights to privacy in a public online forum. This level of thought is important because of the unknown norms of social networking. Even though many students are immersed in technology every day, there is still room for education about social networking and professional ethics..

Future studies should include investigations about educator conduct and rights to privacy in online spaces. Those who are engaged in supporting future professionals should consider ways in which they can assist the development of thinking about these kinds of ethical dilemmas so that new professionals can anticipate and prevent potential problems, develop well-reasoned responses to ethical decisions, and participate in the construction of protocols that continue to harness the educational potential of social networking tools. Developing such awareness and protocols are initial steps toward encouraging responsible use of these tools.

THE FUTURE OF SOCIAL NETWORKING IN EDUCATION

News stories continue to surface about questionable social behaviors that occur online. Although some behave as though the faceless world of online communities is lawless territory and continue to test the waters, no firm legal precedents have been established to guide online codes of conduct.

Educational organizations have taken a variety of positions on this issue, some in response to real problems they have encountered, and some prompted by attempts to be proactive in light of the news events they hear. Lamar County School Board has taken a conservative position. Although no incidents led to the decision, the attorney of the southern Mississippi district recommended

adoption of a policy to lessen liabilities. Now communications between teachers and students through social networking sites or through texting are prohibited (Associated Press, 2008).

But Tomás Gonzales, Senior Assistant Dean at Syracuse University School of Law and a nationally recognized speaker in the legal issues concerning on-line communities, believes that educational organizations should embrace collaborative technologies and explore appropriate uses even in the midst of much negative press about the drawbacks of social networking (2008). He also claims that current codes of conduct about appropriate face-to-face behavior are probably sufficient for providing online guidance for students and administrators.

Codes of conduct in educational institutions should be examined to determine whether protocols for online behavior are embedded within existing policies. At a minimum, institutions should consider how their existing codes of conduct would be applied in the event of a dilemma involving social networking tools. Additionally, education programs that result in awareness of both proactive behaviors as well as potential situations to be avoided in social networking would benefit students and faculty alike.

CONCLUSION

We must recognize the limitations of our own experience and expertise. This applies to the use of many Web 2.0 tools, including online social networking. With the use of social networking tools, as with any powerful tool, come many vulnerabilities. As society becomes more technologically advanced, it has become the responsibility of educational institutions to support the use of the kinds of technologies that might prove to strengthen and support the learning process. However, it is also the responsibility of policymakers to assure participation in a safe learning environment. Ironically, news broadcasts have been mostly negative press about the pitfalls of social networking tools, and have not showcased innovative and pedagogical uses of Web 2.0 features. In order for any beneficial uses of such tools to be realized and refined, and then incorporated into learning environments, the fear and apprehension surrounding them must be set aside long enough for real innovation to occur.

We encourage institutions to first create a safe place for ideas to percolate by revisiting existing codes of conduct to assure their policy and procedures embrace the idea of virtual connectivity, and to publish guidelines for acceptable and appropriate uses of technology. By providing guidance to their members, institutions can encourage them to utilize online tools in a socially responsible manner, without squelching innovative uses of technology. Just as institutions use codes of conduct to ensure the safety and rights of each member on campus, they can utilize those same codes in the online extension. By conceptualizing online spaces as an integral part of institutions' physical and temporal community, codes of conduct can be applied in a manner that respects privacy and individual rights, while allowing innovation and security for all participants.

REFERENCES

A. B. v. State of Indiana, 885 N.E. 2d 1223 (Ind., 2008).

Alexa. (2008). Traffic rankings for MySpace. com. *Alexa.com.* Retrieved April 25, 2008 from http://www.alexa.com/data/details/traffic_details/myspace.com

Altman, I. (1977). Privacy regulation: Culturally universal or culturally specific? *The Journal of Social Issues, 33*(3), 66–84.

Associated Press. (2008). Mississippi school district bars teacher-student texting. *Yahoo News.* retrieved August 13, 2008 from http://news.yahoo.com/s/ap/20080721/ap_on_bi_ge/text_ban

Aucoin, D. (2007). MySpace or the workplace? *Boston Globe.* Retrieved April 25, 2008 from http://www.boston.com/news/globe/living/articles/2007/05/29/myspace_vs_workplace/

Berg, J., Berquam, L., & Christoph, K. (2007). Social networking technologies: A "poke" for campus services. *EDUCAUSE Review, 42*(2), 32–44.

Boyd, D. (2008). Why youth (heart) social network sites: The role of networked publics in teenage social life. In D. Buckingham (Ed.), *Youth, identity, and digital media.* Cambridge, MA: The MIT Press.

Byrnside, I. (2008). Six clicks of separation: The legal ramifications of employers using social networking sites to research applicants. *Vanderbilt Journal of Entertainment and Technology Law, 445.*

Carvin, A. (2006, October 10). Is MySpace your space as well? *Learning.now.* Retrieved July 21, 2008 from http://www.pbs.org/teachers/learning.now/2006/10/is_myspace_your_space_as_well.html

Crawford, J. (2007, January 25). Teacher fired over MySpace page. January 25, 2007. *Tallahassee.com.* Retrieved December 3, 2007 from http://tallahassee.com/legacy/special/blogs/2007/01/teacher-fired-over-myspace-page_25.html

Drews vs. Joint School District, Not Reported in F.Supp.2d, 2006 WL 1308565 (D. Idaho).

E-School News Staff. (2007). Teachers warned about MySpace profiles. *e-School News.* Retrieved July 17, 2008 from http://www.eschoolnews.com/news/top-news/related-top-news/?i=50557;_hbguid=49a1babb-b469-4a85-a273-292a0514d91d

Federal Trade Commission. (2004). *The fair credit reporting act.* Retrieved August 13, 2008 from http://www.ftc.gov/os/statutes/031224fcra.pdf

Finn, J. (2004). A survey of online harassment at a university campus. *Journal of Interpersonal Violence, 19*(4), 468–483. doi:10.1177/0886260503262083

Foulger, T., Ewbank, A., & Kay, A. Osborn Popp, S., & Carter, H. (2009). Moral spaces in MySpace: Preservice teachers' perspectives about ethical issues in social networking. *Journal of Research Technology in Education, 42*(1), 1-28.

Friedman, B. (1997). Social judgments and technological innovation: Adolescents' understanding of property, privacy, and electronic information. *Computers in Human Behavior, 13*(3), 327–351. doi:10.1016/S0747-5632(97)00013-7

Friedman, B., Kahn, P. H. Jr, Hagman, J., Severson, R. L., & Gill, B. (2006). The watcher and the watched: Social judgments about privacy in a public place. *Human-Computer Interaction, 21*(2), 235–272. doi:10.1207/s15327051hci2102_3

Fulmer, J. (2002). Dismissing the 'immoral' teacher for conduct outside the workplace-do current laws protect the interests of both school authorities and teachers? *Journal of Law and Education, 31*, 271–290.

Gonzales, T. (2008). *Facebook, Myspace, and online communities: What your college must know* (CD recording). Retrieved August 28, 2008 from https://www.higheredhero.com/audio/main.asp?G=2&E=1317&I=1

Griffiths, M. (2002). Occupational health issues concerning Internet use in the workplace. *Work and Stress, 16*(4), 283–286. doi:10.1080/0267837031000071438

Hargittai, E. (2007). Whose space? Differences among users and non-users of social network sites. *Journal of Computer-Mediated Communication, 13*(1), 14.

Hermes, J. (2008). Colleges create Facebook-style social networks to reach alumni. *The Chronicle of Higher Education, 54*(33), A18.

Hoover, T. (2008). *MySpace profile*. Retrieved August 26, 2008 from http://myspace.com/mshoover.

J.S. v. Blue Mountain School District, 2007 WL 954245 (M.D.Pa.).

Kim, S., Phillips, W. R., Pinsky, L., Brock, D., Phillips, K., & Keary, J. (2006). A conceptual framework for developing teaching cases: A review and synthesis of the literature across disciplines. *Medical Education, 40*, 867–876. doi:10.1111/j.1365-2929.2006.02544.x

Kolodner, J. (1993). *Case-based reasoning*. San Mateo, CA: Morgan Kaufmann.

Laupa, M. (1991). Children's reasoning about three authority attributes: Adult status, knowledge, and social position. *Developmental Psychology, 27*(2), 321–329. doi:10.1037/0012-1649.27.2.321

Laupa, M. (1995). Children's reasoning about authority in home and school contexts. *Social Development, 4*(1), 1–16. doi:10.1111/j.1467-9507.1995.tb00047.x

Laupa, M., & Turiel, E. (1993). Children's concepts of authority and social contexts. *Journal of Educational Psychology, 85*(1), 191–197. doi:10.1037/0022-0663.85.1.191

Layshock v. Hermitage School District, 496 F.Supp.2d 587 (W.D.Pa., 2007).

Lenhart, A. (2007). Cyberbullying and online teens. *Pew Internet & American Life Project.* Retrieved July 21, 2008 from http://www.pewInternet.org/pdfs/PIP%20Cyberbullying%20Memo.pdf

Lenhart, A., Madden, M., Macgill, A., & Smith, A. (2007). Teens and social media. *Pew Internet & American Life Project.* Retrieved July 18, 2008 from http://www.pewInternet.org/pdfs/PIP_Teens_Social_Media_Final.pdf

Leskovec, J., & Horvitz, E. (2007). *Planetary-scale views on an instant-messaging network* (Microsoft Research Technical Report MSR-TR-2006-186). Retrieved August 26, 2008 from http://arxiv.org/PS_cache/arxiv/pdf/0803/0803.0939v1.pdf

Lindenberger, M. (2006). Questions of conduct. *Diverse Issues in Higher Education, 23*(21), 36–37.

Lipka, S. (2008). The digital limits of "in loco parentis." . *The Chronicle of Higher Education, 54*(26), 1.

May, M. (2006, June 23). Hoover: Caught in the flash. *Austin Chronicle.* Retrieved December 3, 2007 from http://www.austinchronicle.com/gyrobase/Issue/story?oid=oid%3A378611

Myspace.com. (2008). Myspace.com safety and security. *Myspace.com.* Retrieved August 26, 2008 from http://www.myspace.com/safety

Nakashima, E. (2007, March 7). Harsh words die hard on the Web. *Washingtonpost.com.* Retrieved July 21, 2008 from http://www.washingtonpost.com/wp-dyn/content/article/2007/03/06/AR2007030602705.html

Noel, J. (2008, May 17). Cicero town president wants MySpace poser's identity revealed. *Chicagotribune.com.* Retrieved August 13, 2008 from http://www.chicagotribune.com/news/local/chi-myspaceimposters_bdmay18,0,3460074.story?page=1

O'Hanlon, C. (2007). If you can't beat 'em, join 'em. *T.H.E. Journal, 34*(8), 39–40, 42, 44.

O'Neil, R. (2008). It's not easy to stand up to cyberbullies, but we must. *The Chronicle of Higher Education, 54*(44), A23.

Palen, L., & Dourish, P. (2003). Unpacking "privacy" for a networked world. In *Proceedings of the ACM Conference on Human Factors in Computing Systems CHI 2003,* Fort Lauderdale, FL (pp. 129-136). New York: ACM.

Patchin, J., & Hinduja, S. (2006). Bullies move beyond the schoolyard: A preliminary look at cyberbullying. *Youth Violence and Juvenile Justice, 4*(2), 148–169. doi:10.1177/1541204006286288

Phillips, G. (2007, June 6). Teacher's blog draws probe from the system. *Southern Maryland Newspapers Online.* Retrieved December 3, 2007 from http://www.somdnews.com/stories/060607/rectop180341_32082.shtml

Requa v. Kent School District, 492 F.Supp.2d 1272 (W.D.Wash., 2007).

Schonefeld, E. (2008). Facebook is not only the world's largest social network, it is also the fastest growing. *Techcrunch.com.* Retrieved August 13, 2008 from http://www.techcrunch.com/2008/08/12/facebook-is-not-only-the-worlds-largest-social-network-it-is-also-the-fastest-growing/

Smetana, J. G. (2006). *Social-cognitive domain theory: Consistencies and variations in children's moral and social judgments.* Mahwah, NJ: Lawrence Erlbaum Associates.

Steiner, E. (2007, May 1). MySpace photo costs teacher education degree. *Washington Post.com.* Retrieved April 25, 2008 from http://blog.washingtonpost.com/offbeat/2007/05/myspace_photo_costs_teacher_ed.html

The Pennsylvania State University. (2007). *Student teaching handbook: The Pennsylvania State University college of education.* Retrieved July 17, 2008 from http://www.ed.psu.edu/pre-service/things%20to%20update/2007-2008%20ST_HANDBOOK_August%202007.pdf

Turiel, E. (1983). *The development of social knowledge: Morality and convention.* Cambridge, UK: Cambridge University Press.

Turiel, E. (2002). *The culture of morality: Social development, context, and conflict.* New York: Cambridge University Press.

Viégas, F. B. (2005). Bloggers' expectations of privacy and accountability: An initial survey. *Journal of Computer-Mediated Communication, 10*(3). doi:.doi:10.1111/j.1083-6101.2005. tb00260.x

Vivanco, H. (2007, March 29). Teacher still posting on MySpace. *Inland Valley Daily Bulletin.* Retrieved on December 3, 2007 from http://www. dailybulletin.com/news/ci_5553720

Wheeler, T. (2007). Personnel pitfalls in the cyberworld. *School Administrator, 64*(9), 22–24.

Wikipedia. (2008). *Social networking.* Retrieved August 13, 2008 from http://en.wikipedia. org/wiki/Social_networking

Wisniewski v. Board of Education, Weedsport Central School District, 494 F. 3d 34, (2nd Cir. 2007).

Woolcock, N. (2008). Soaring number of teachers say they are 'cyberbully' vicitms. *The Times.* Retrieved July 21, 2008 from http://www. timesonline.co.uk/tol/life_and_style/education/ article3213130.ece

WSBTV.com. (2006, May 16). Student faces criminal charges for teacher jokes. *WSBTV.com.* Retrieved July 21, 2008 from http://www.wsbtv. com/education/9223824/detail.html

Yates, J., & Orlikowski, W. J. (1992). Genres of organizational communication: A structurational approach to studying communication and media. *Academy of Management Review, 17*(2), 299–326. doi:10.2307/258774

Chapter 3

Fulfilling the Promise:
Addressing Institutional Factors that Impede the Implementation of E-Learning 2.0

Judi Repman
Georgia Southern University, USA

Cordelia Zinskie
Georgia Southern University, USA

Elizabeth Downs
Georgia Southern University, USA

ABSTRACT

As online learning continues to expand and evolve, new challenges emerge regarding the implementation of Web 2.0 tools and technologies in online pedagogy. The business model approach to online learning being embraced by many institutions may actually work against faculty who want to utilize Web 2.0 technologies to create e-learning 2.0 experiences for their students. Faculty and administrators need to recognize that differences in perspectives may significantly impact future directions of online courses and programs.

INTRODUCTION

Online learning is changing the postsecondary landscape (Cox, 2005). The 2008 *Horizon Report*, a collaboration between the New Media Consortium and the EDUCAUSE Learning Initiative, identified several ways that technology is impacting higher education including the growing use of Web 2.0 and social networking, the evolution of how we collaborate and communicate, access and portability of content, and the continual widening of the gap between students and faculty regarding their perceptions of technology. These trends also portend some of the challenges that exist with regard to e-learning and specifically to the incorporation of Web 2.0 technologies into online instruction.

Online learning by itself has proven to be a significant force in the reform of higher education as a result of increased access to courses and degree programs to students anytime/anywhere (Beldarrain, 2006). This rapid growth is challenging traditional

DOI: 10.4018/978-1-60566-729-4.ch003

Copyright © 2010, IGI Global. Copying or distributing in print or electronic forms without written permission of IGI Global is prohibited.

instruction in higher education with the movement from teaching-centered to learning-centered and synchronous to asynchronous (Hartman, Dziuban, & Moskal, 2007). Course instructors must assume a different, broader role as the model of instructor as the center of the classroom is no longer effective in all situations (Grush, 2008; Levy, 2003).

As e-learning continues to expand and evolve, new challenges emerge at the institutional level regarding implementation of Web 2.0 tools and technologies in online pedagogy. One such challenge is the growth of the business model of online learning which emphasizes control and efficiency, with less value placed on the innovation, creativity, and sense of community that comes with the use of Web 2.0 technologies. This chapter explores our belief that the growth of the business model of online learning may hinder or prevent the widespread development of E-Learning 2.0 communities.

The objectives of this chapter include the following:

- Briefly define the potential of Web 2.0 technologies to create E-Learning 2.0 communities of practice;
- Summarize key factors related to the business model with regard to online learning in higher education;
- Describe and discuss the disconnect between the "business model" approach and the use of Web 2.0 technologies within the online learning enterprise; and
- Suggest a series of action steps for faculty and university administrators to ensure that campus online learning initiatives avoid "swapp[ing] the little red schoolhouses for the little online boxes we call course management systems" (Gary Brown, as quoted in Grush, 2008, p. 20).

BACKGROUND

Definition of Terms Used

The literature related to online learning frequently uses terms such as online learning, distance learning, and e-learning synonymously. For the purposes of this chapter, we are defining online learning as the widely used model that centers around the use of a course management system for synchronous and asynchronous communication between faculty and students. In the context of this chapter distance learning refers to the broader historical span of the field, dating back to correspondence courses and interactive television courses. We use the term e-learning 2.0 to indicate a newer model of online learning that incorporates the use of learner-centered Web 2.0 tools and technologies (blogs, wikis, social networking, folksonomies, etc.) as additions to or replacements for course management systems. Finally, the discussion presented in this chapter focuses on learning delivered entirely online, not on the use of online tools to support face-to-face instruction or on blended classes which substitute online technologies for parts of a face-to-face course.

The Growth of Web 2.0 Technologies

Web 2.0 tools including blogs, wikis, podcasts, and folksonomies provide opportunities for knowledge building and collaboration for higher education in the 21st century, and these tools are learner-centered, affordable, and accessible (McGee & Diaz, 2007). It is easy to document the growth of Web 2.0 technologies. The blog index Technorati estimates 175,000 new blogs are created daily ("Welcome to Technorati", n.d.) while the social networking site Facebook reports 100 million active users. Facebook statistics indicate that the fastest growing group user is adults over age 25 ("Facebook statistics", 2008). The use of these technologies within higher education in general and e-learning in specific is the subject of considerable discussion.

In its *Horizon Report* the New Media Consortium (2008) annually outlines cutting edge technologies (grassroots video, data mashups, collaboration webs, mobile broadband, social operating systems, and social intelligence are described in the 2008 edition) and identifies key trends that will impact higher education. The 2008 *Report* describes the following trends:

- The growing use of Web 2.0 and social networking—combined with collective intelligence and mass amateurization—is gradually but inexorably changing the practice of scholarship;
- The way we work, collaborate, and communicate is evolving as boundaries become more fluid and globalization increases;
- Access to—and portability of—content is increasing as smaller, more powerful devices are introduced; and
- The gap between students' perception of technology and that of the faculty continues to widen. (pp. 6-7)

The power of Web 2.0 technologies in education is twofold. First, the individual's role changes from that of a passive recipient/consumer of information into the role of an active creator of content (Prensky, 2008; Richardson, 2007). The second aspect, which is equally important, is in the ease of connectivity and collaboration that the tools facilitate (McGee & Diaz, 2007; Richardson, 2006). The use of these tools has become pervasive, although that use is often outside of educational settings (Prensky, 2008; Villano, 2008).

Online Learning and Web 2.0 Technologies

Online learning requires faculty to assume the role of facilitator as compared to the traditional role of

transmitter of knowledge (Guri-Rosenblit, (2005); these faculty serve as "intermediaries between students and knowledge" (Beaudoin, 2006, p. 6). Grush noted that today's students want ownership and authority over their learning and are able to create their own personal learning environments. Thompson (2007) posed an important question: "Will administration and faculty react against these students, or will they respond thoughtfully to a new student body that is accustomed to the Web 2.0 environment?" (¶9).

The literature related to online learning provides abundant examples of faculty use of Web 2.0 tools to create innovative online learning experiences (see Boettcher, 2008, McGee & Diaz, 2007, and Villano, 2008 for examples and discussion). At the same time, many faculty who teach online recognize the digital divide that exists between their own understanding and use of technology and that of their students (Abel, 2007; Prensky, 2001, 2005, 2008). Furthermore, there is a lack of research on faculty development regarding online teaching (McQuiggan, 2007) and online course development.

Many institutions of higher education use a commercial or institutionally-developed course management system for instructional delivery. Course management systems usually include tools such as text, audio and video chat, e-mail, Instant Messaging (IM) and threaded discussion boards to facilitate student-faculty and student-student interactions. These tools can be used synchronously or asynchronously to provide instruction and support learning. Unlike Web 2.0 tools, course management system tools are used within the closed context of the system (Dalsgaard, 2006; Grush, 2008; Wilson, Parrish, Balasubramanian, & Switzer, 2007). Craig (2007) questioned whether it is possible to use the traditional course management system mandated by institutions and still provide a digital learning environment designed to "foster innovation and collaboration" (p. 157), as most course management systems are focused on administrative support (e.g., grading, attendance) rather than integration of innovative tools for creative and collaborative learning activities (Hiltz & Turoff, 2005; Papastergiou, 2006; Wilson et al., 2007).

Although we have little evidence of the impact of Web 2.0 tools on student learning (Moore, Fowler, & Watson, 2007; Villano, 2008), the combination of Web 2.0 tools with existing models for online learning offers significant potential for a socially constructed learning environment. When participation in knowledge building is available to anyone/anywhere, the opportunities for learning and collaboration also multiply. While Beldarrain (2006) asserted that "the ever-evolving nature of technology will continue to push distance educators to use new tools to create learning environments that will indeed prepare students to be life-long learners, who can problem solve through collaboration with global partners" (p. 150), the impact of the use of these technologies on higher education reform is unknown (Wilson et al., 2007).

The Business Model of Online Learning

The growth of online learning at all levels of education is also easy to document (Beaudoin, 2006). The Sloan Consortium regularly surveys colleges and universities across the United States about their involvement in online learning. In 2007, the results of five years of surveys showed online enrollments growing by 9.7% annually, which contrasts with a 1.5% growth rate in overall higher education enrollment. The survey also found that most institutions involved in online learning expect continued growth, particularly since the presidents of these institutions foresee increasing student demand for online course offerings (Allen & Seaman, 2007).

Because of increased competition for students in today's online world, higher education is being forced to rethink how things have always been done (Thompson, 2007). Thompson also noted

that although higher education does not handle change to tradition very well, there is a willingness to experiment with new business models. Institutions of higher education are now using terminology once reserved for the corporate world such as market, targets of opportunity, revenue streams, business plans, return on investment, revenue distribution and generation, cost management, and product development (Lorenzo, 2006; Miller & Schiffman, 2006; Schiffman, Vignare, & Geith, 2007).

Beaudoin (2006) noted that institutions operating more like for-profit institutions will thrive in the competitive marketplace. Online learning will be a key component of the business strategic plans of these thriving institutions. The increased pressure for all universities to do more with less often results in growth in online programs to offset rising costs (Mackintosh, 2006). Although Guri-Rosenblit proposed in 2005 that institutions with the greatest resources are less likely to have online instruction, Lorenzo (2006) noted that well respected institutions have now developed business models for online education. Efficiency and access have been noted in several studies (e.g., Schiffman et al., 2007) as the primary rationale for an increased presence of online programs at higher education institutions. The competing forces of efficiency/control and innovation/creativity created by the implementation of the business model have been described as centralized versus decentralized (Otte & Benke, 2006) and conservative versus progressive (Wilson et al., 2007).

Many faculty view online learning as a way for administration to cut costs and increase student enrollment (Eynon, 2008). The business approach, i.e., "higher education as big business," has engendered considerable faculty "pushback" to online learning initiatives (Carlson & Fleisher, 2002; Hartman et al., 2007), a limiting factor for the implementation of e-learning 2.0 on campuses. Carlson and Fleisher also noted that faculty believe that the "treating of the student body as customers has lessened the rigor of the curricula and teaching methods" (p. 1098). In contrast, administrators participating in a study conducted by Vignare, Geith and Schiffman (2006) perceived that faculty are slowing down the process by calling for quality without a real understanding of online learning. In such cases, faculty discussion of online learning focuses on a definition of quality that only encompasses face-to-face or perhaps hybrid/ blended classes. The underlying belief is that a quality program can only exist when students and faculty are physically present in the same place at the same time.

Under the business model for online learning, the traditional practice of individual faculty creating and delivering courses often gives way to faculty creating courses for others to deliver, a typical corporate training model (Vignare et al., 2006). The design of online courses may follow an institutional template as uniformity in the delivery of online instruction is seen as efficient. This model allows an institution to shift delivery of instruction from full-time to part-time faculty similar to the operation of many for-profit institutions (Natriello, 2005). Natriello questioned whether university faculty would continue to have a role in instruction under the business model. Smith and Mitry (2008) emphasized that "only full-time faculty can stop avarice disguised as better, cost-effective practices" (p. 150).

ISSUES RELATED TO ACHIEVING E-LEARNING 2.0 IN HIGHER EDUCATION

As noted by Samarawickrema and Stacey (2007), "understanding enabling and impeding factors to technology adoption in a higher education setting is not possible without understanding the power and politics related to the setting" (p. 320). At Georgia Southern University, our College of Education is experiencing growth in online learning that exceeds the national average as reported in

the Sloan Consortium surveys. As faculty members and administrators we have been involved in distance learning in a variety of formats for many years but until recently online learning has not been a campus or university system priority. Our campus faces three realities resulting in a new focus on online learning. The first reality consists of financial challenges that have led to a closer examination of the potential of online learning to increase enrollment (and therefore revenue). The second reality for us is geographic. We are not located in the population center of our state and the pool of learners willing to drive to campus is limited. The final reality is one faced by all institutions of higher education. Today's students have many more options available. We simply are no longer the only game in town. As we engaged in discussion of these issues on our own campus and at the university system level, we were struck by the disconnect between faculty excitement about new learning tools and the desire of administrators to control design and delivery of online instruction to enhance its potential as a revenue stream.

As described in the previous section summarizing the background and literature related to both Web 2.0 and the business model for online learning, there is a distinct tension between the personalized, collaborative, participatory communities being developed in the world that exists outside of most higher education classes and the activities, resources, and instructional approaches that are frequently employed in online learning. As Otte and Benke (2006) noted, "there is no more powerful disincentive than the sense that online instruction is an external imposition and a threat to the faculty prerogatives" (p. 30). This section focuses on five issues where the plans of campus administrators to build the online learning enterprise intersect with the ideals of faculty actually charged with designing and teaching those classes.

Institutional Goals and Policies Regarding Online Learning

"Colleges that want to have an effective [online] program need to consider all aspects of providing an education, which are much more than simply putting classes online." (Levy, 2003, Conclusion section, ¶2). A connection between online learning and institutional goals is critical to successful implementation of online learning on a campus; without this, online learning can challenge the mission and values of the institution (Hartman et al., 2007; Mackintosh, 2006). Mackintosh noted that it is very important to integrate online learning into the strategic plan and vision of the institution to avoid the perception of online learning as something that "just happened to" the university.

Administrators must take the lead in the progress and growth of online instruction, but they should not get too far ahead without faculty input and involvement as vision and plans should involve all stakeholders, i.e., avoid the "top-down" approach (Hartman et al., 2007; Otte & Benke, 2006). Too often a lack of meaningful dialogue about online learning results in lack of faculty "buy-in" to this new approach to teaching and learning (Smith & Mitry, 2008). Otte and Benke noted that ownership is needed for transformation; a disconnect between the mission for online learning and the institution as a whole limits transformation (Miller & Schiffman, 2006).

"It is clear that the ultimate potential of online technology to enrich higher education resides less in the technology itself than in the practices and discourses that it prompts individually and institutionally" (Larreamendy-Joerns & Leinhardt, 2006, p. 597). Panda and Mishra (2007) noted that institutional policies should be developed on online learning that address not only design and implementation but evaluation and reflection, for institutional policy can play an important role in the adoption and effective use of online learning. Policies must consider faculty workload and compensation, curriculum, professional develop-

ment and support, intellectual property rights, and assessment (Hartman et al., 2007; Levy, 2003; Wang, 2006).

Cox (2005) stated that many faculty feel that the "institutional imperative to provide online education has taken precedence over most considerations of teaching and learning quality" (p. 1779). This institutional imperative may occur without any discussion of the development of metrics or assessments to ensure program quality, despite the fact that those metrics may be in place for traditional campus-based programs. To date, there has been a lack of assessment data for online courses; without data, how can one evaluate and improve the quality of these courses? Hartman et al. (2007) noted that assessment can assuage those with questions about quality regarding online learning. One problem that exists is the lack of a common definition of what is quality in this setting; stakeholders should work together to determine the attributes needed to produce quality online courses (Kidney, Cummings, & Boehm, 2007). Planning for inclusion of these quality standards in online programs should be part of the online program planning and implementation process.

Faculty Attitudes Toward Online Learning

Many faculty members began teaching online due to top-down mandates, student demands, and imperatives to increase enrollment (Samarawickrema & Stacey, 2007). For many faculty, their only experience with online learning is uploading their text-based course materials into a course management system (Haber & Mills, 2008), most of which do not integrate Web 2.0 tools. Several researchers (Eynon, 2008; Mackintosh, 2006) noted that a transition to online instruction does not always lead to a transformation of the teaching and learning process. A study by Haber and Mills found that online learning consisted of processing text and other course materials with no groundbreaking components of e-learning incorporated into the course. Another study of online learning by Cox (2005) found that the instructional approach for the online course did not differ from traditional face-to-face instruction.

Barriers to faculty developing and/or transforming their online courses include lack of skills, time, and support (Panda & Mishra, 2007) as well as a lack of recognition of online learning efforts in the traditional faculty reward structure (Grush, 2008; McGee & Diaz, 2007). Similarly, a study conducted by Hiltz, Kim, and Shea (2007) regarding teaching online listed the motivators for faculty as flexible schedule and more personal interaction with students and the de-motivators for online instruction as more work, inadequate compensation, lack of support, and lack of appropriate policies. Incorporation of additional elements such as Web 2.0 tools into online instruction is time-consuming, and faculty often see no motivation or reward to change their teaching and learning practices.

McGee and Diaz (2007) noted that rapidly changing technology can be a demotivator for faculty. Faculty often lack the skills to create an effective online experience (Eynon, 2008; Smith & Mitry, 2008) or the imagination to integrate technology into teaching and learning (Grush, 2008). Professional development of faculty is key to enhancing the online learning experience for both faculty and students (Otte & Benke, 2006; Panda & Mishra, 2007). One problem noted by Cox (2005) is that sometimes professional development is offered by technology personnel who know nothing about teaching and learning. Research findings of Gibson, Harris and Colaric (2008) stated that perceived usefulness was the best predictor of acceptance of online teaching technology.

However, according to Panda and Mishra (2007), faculty are not aware of positive things that can be accomplished with online learning. Some faculty do not believe that students can have a sound pedagogical experience in the online environment; they feel that instructional integrity and quality are at risk (Cox, 2005). Cox stated that

some faculty see an emphasis on information, not education, and on the convenience for students. Without appropriate institutional support or an administrative guarantee that quality is valued, the full potential of online learning may not be achieved. Natriello (2005) summarized this dilemma as follows: "In general, the current barriers to faculty involvement in distance learning may be the result of the unsettled nature of pedagogy for distance learning efforts. It is difficult to move to something new when the patterns of behavior required for success are not fully established." (p. 1891).

The Digital Divide between Faculty and Students

"Engage me or enrage me: What today's learners demand" is the title of an article written by Marc Prensky (2005). Prensky (2001) is usually credited with developing the widely used terminology digital native/digital immigrant to describe the difference between our students who grew up connected to the network via a wide range of technologies and those of us beyond the age of 25 or 30 who grew up using technologies like typewriters and telephones.

Current college faculty are either "Baby Boomers" (born between 1946 and 1964) or "Gen X'ers" (born between 1965 and 1982) and, as such, bring distinct generational characteristics into the higher education classroom. The current college students are termed the "Net Generation" (born between 1983 and 1991) and have meaningful differences from their professors (Oblinger & Oblinger, 2005). The Net Generation is used to having many options and selecting what they want or need. Net Generation learners use more graphics and expect fast-paced learning and a quick response (Oblinger & Oblinger, 2005). These students have a completely different way of thinking about technology – to the degree that these digital natives indeed do not "think" about technology.

Conversely, most faculty, digital immigrants, are constantly in a learning cycle to stay current with new technology and emerging applications. They spend precious professional time developing the technology skills needed to implement various tools in online courses. Oblinger and Hawkins (2006) noted that while early adopters of online teaching possessed needed technology skills, many current online instructors lack the requisite skills and do not understand that the course is more than content. Blin and Munro (2008) concurred that the lack of transformation seen in online teaching practices is associated with lack of instructor competency and suggested that training alone is not sufficient to rectify this situation. A challenge that deepens the digital divide is that universities are handicapped by tradition and "are not the best environments to promote innovation in technology, certainly not for instructional purposes" (Beaudoin, 2006, p. 9). Blin and Munro stated that the cultural context of the institution must change regarding teaching practices. Craig (2007) noted that faculty must become familiar with Web 2.0 tools and must reflect continually on the changing nature of the e-learning environment in an effort to engage this "Net Generation".

Reliance on Course Management Systems

One impetus behind the research and discussion presented in this chapter was Wilson et al.'s article published in 2007 that identified the use of course management systems as a potentially conservative force in the distance learning revolution. Wilson and his co-authors made a strong case that the use of course management systems is a key factor in the technologizing of instruction, likening their use to a production system where institutions take "raw material (unskilled, unknowledgeable students), processing those students, and outputting graduates with the knowledge and skill they need" (p. 336).

Larreamendy-Joerns and Leinhardt (2006) noted that online education "may fail to go the distance if technological solutions and pedagogical perspectives are imposed at the expense of diversity and variation" (p. 597). In our university system the use of a specific course management system is expected and even required in some of our online learning initiatives. Faculty are presented with a pre-defined course template, designed to incorporate a variety of what are considered best practices in online education. The tools used in the course template are the tools available within the course management system, including both synchronous and asynchronous communication, quizzes, and assessments. It often seems that the intent of a course management system is to duplicate the face-to-face instructional experience (Natriello, 2005). Craig (2007) asserted that institutions use course management systems to manage and formalize the learning environment; however, he questioned whether these systems would meet the needs of students who are used to creating their own content.

Yet as Dede (2008) and Boettcher (2008) pointed out, Web 2.0 technologies go beyond a slight change in perspective about the way that learning and education "work". Dede asserted that we are at a point where we have technologies available that call into question the nature of the educational enterprise and the role of the faculty member. Using the terminology of Classical knowledge and Web 2.0 knowledge, he further stated that proponents of Web 2.0 knowledge are questioning fundamental beliefs related to knowledge, expertise and learning. In contrast, Classical education proponents follow a model where "the content and skills that experts feel that every person should know are presented as factual "truth" compiled in curriculum standards and assessed with high-stakes tests" (Dede, 2008, p. 80). Achieving the goals implicit in a Web 2.0 knowledge world goes far beyond the "little online boxes" (Grush, 2008, p. 20) of course management systems (Boettcher, 2008; Mabrito & Medley,

2008; McLoughlin & Lee, 2008). In an e-learning 2.0 paradigm, communities of students become creators of knowledge for their communities and beyond. Creation of an e-learning 2.0 community requires tools with very different functions than tools included in most course management systems (Boettcher, 2008; Dede, 2008; McLoughlin & Lee, 2008; Papastergiou, 2006).

Papastergiou (2006) completed an extensive review of the course management system literature. One of her research questions focused on the use of CMS to support innovative instructional approaches. Although only limited research has been done in this area, she did find examples of CMS being used to support collaborative, constructivist learning environments while at the same time noting that "the design process of a CMS [does] have an impact on the instructional approaches that can be implemented through it as well as on its expandability" (p. 606).

It should also be noted that the use of open source learning management systems such as Moodle and Sakai frequently support a very different approach to e-learning. Wiley (2006) labels this the "empowering nature of open source software" (heading following ¶4). A course titled "Connectivism and Connected Knowledge" is currently being taught online using a wide range of Web 2.0 tools including the open source learning management system, Moodle (http://ltc.umanitoba.ca/connectivism/). The innate flexibility of open source course management systems is frequently highlighted as a major advantage over commercial course management systems (Sclater, 2008).

Administrators and many faculty might be justifiably reluctant to stop using current commercial course management systems. These systems do allow faculty who are inexperienced with the use of any technology (much less Web 2.0 technologies) to design, develop and deliver online courses with a manageable learning curve. Faculty and technology support staff have spent untold hours building repositories of instructional materials using course management systems and removing that support

system would be challenging, at least in the short term. Some institutions and individuals have begun to modify course management systems to include more Web 2.0 tools while others are working to develop new course management systems based on a more learner-centered instructional paradigm (Boettcher, 2008; Papastergiou, 2006). Administrators will need to consider policy issues such as intellectual property, copyright, privacy, and archiving of learning products if instruction leaves the boundaries of course management systems for the Web (Boettcher, 2008; McLoughlin & Lee, 2008).

The Rapidly Changing Nature of Web 2.0 Technologies

The *Horizon Report* (New Media Consortium, 2008) makes interesting reading on many levels, not the least of which is the attempt of the authors to read into the future and predict which new technologies will have staying power. The authors group technologies based on their time-to-adoption. In 2008, technologies with a one year or less time to adoption include grassroots video (YouTube) and collaboration webs (Google Apps). The two to three year adoption technologies include mobile broadband and data mashups while the four to five year technologies are collective intelligence (Wikipedia, Google's Page Rank) and social operating systems (Yahoo Life!). The authors of the *Report* define the time-to-adoption horizon as the time during which the technology will be adopted for widespread use in a learning-focused organization. This prediction is based on the growth of use of the technology in the world outside of education. The *Report* is still simply a prediction which begs the question of where an individual or an institution should start in terms of using any of the technologies described. It also places higher education in the position of catching up to technologies being used for non-instructional purposes by the general public.

Readers of the EDUCAUSE Learning Initiative's "*7 Things You Should Know About. . . .*" find a similar range of cutting-edge Web 2.0 tools discussed within the context of their use in higher education. Current topics addressed in this series include Google Apps, Flickr, Ustream, and geolocation (available online at http://www.educause.e du/7ThingsYouShouldKnowAboutSeries/7495). Like *The Horizon Report*, the *7 Things* series is designed to both raise awareness of new tools as well as suggest the potential use of those tools in teaching and learning. Blogs such as The NOSE (http://tatler.typepad.com/nose/emerging_tech-nologies/), Stephen's Web (http://www.downes.ca/), and The Wired Campus blog (http://chronicle.com/wiredcampus/) provide details about the use of emerging technologies in education in general as well as within e-learning environments.

The 2008 *Horizon Report* includes a section on megatrends, which notes that "we have seen many of the technologies and practices highlighted in this series converge, morph, and shift over the years" (p. 7). Faculty may be reluctant to devote the time and effort required to develop learning experiences based on such rapidly changing technologies. Another delay in the time to implement a technology is the recommendation that faculty become immersed in using the technologies prior to adopting them for instructional purposes (Mabrito & Medley, 2008). And while faculty members in many institutions struggle to keep abreast of Web 2.0 technologies (and we count ourselves in that group), discussion of Web 3.0 has already become prevalent. Web 3.0, also known as the intelligent web or the semantic web, promises to once again revolutionize the way we use the web in our everyday lives (Web 3.0, 2008). As noted in the earlier discussion about faculty attitudes toward online learning, faculty already believe that online learning is more time consuming than face-to-face instruction. Having to master tools that "converge, morph, and shift" without warning could challenge even the most enthusiastic online instructor. As much as our students seem

to demand use of new tools for collaboration and knowledge construction (New Media Consortium, 2008; Prensky, 2008; Thompson, 2007) they probably would be frustrated and unhappy if the Web 2.0 technology they were using for a project changed radically during the middle of a semester (or even worse, vanished or became a fee-based product).

ACTION STEPS TO MOVE THE E-LEARNING 2.0 AGENDA FORWARD

Ensure that the Institutional Vision and Mission Support E-Learning 2.0

This action step encompasses several important concepts. The changing nature of teaching and learning (summarized earlier in this chapter) must be part of the dialog related to the institution's mission and vision. Faculty and administrators need to be aware of the discussion that technology is transforming the way that today's students learn. The institutional vision and mission also need to address the use of Web 2.0 technologies as part of this new teaching and learning environment. Research on the adoption of innovations has consistently found that the initial stage of adoption is awareness (Rogers, 1995).

Providing regular information about the tools themselves along with examples of their use is an action step that should not be skipped. Our regular department meetings end with brief descriptions and demonstrations of a variety of instructional technologies, including Web 2.0 tools such as online surveys, blogs, and wikis. Simply because you have had one demonstration of the wiki concept does not mean that you should not revisit the topic. The capabilities of all Web 2.0 tools change frequently and the faculty audience also changes in its receptivity to new ideas. Sharing articles, web sites, blogs and other sources of information is another way to build awareness.

Sending teams of faculty members to conferences and workshops focusing on Web 2.0 technologies could be another awareness strategy. While it is nice to reward faculty who have been early adopters, diffusion of innovation research stresses the important of identifying the opinion leaders in your institution and getting them beyond the awareness phase (Rogers, 1995). To complete the cycle, it then becomes important for participants in these efforts to have a voice in the regular review of mission and vision statements. In an e-learning 2.0 world, the alignment of mission and vision with the realities of teaching and learning become critical.

Model the Use of the Tools

The truism that "we teach the way we were taught" holds true when it comes to Web 2.0 technologies, except in the case of these new tools it goes beyond that. Can you recall how long it took you to build the ATM/online banking habit? Yet if you drive by your local bank, you will see plenty of people lined up inside or at the drive-through window to do their banking business. Perhaps a better example is the airline industry. Can you recall when there were actually airline employees at a counter who would check in you and your bags for a flight? Now it is all about the self-service kiosk. Our ingrained patterns of behavior changed because technology was available to allow those tasks to be accomplished in a new way. You do not need a travel agent when you can go online, book your ticket, choose your seat, and check in the day before your flight. As faculty and administrators, it is important to take advantage of opportunities to model the use of Web 2.0 tools to complete those familiar tasks. Once a faculty committee has seen how Google Apps could be used to collaborate on a schedule or a document they will find it much easier to see how student groups could use Google Apps for a class project. Like the airline self-service kiosk, when individuals are forced to use new tools to do something they need to

do they will usually figure it out. Modeling the use of the tools may become another additional responsibility for early adopters of Web 2.0 but the payoff could be great.

Address Institutional Support

One of the ironies of this discussion of e-learning 2.0 is that Web 2.0 tools, which are used so seamlessly by digital natives, cannot be easily integrated into instructional programs without extensive institutional support (Mabrito & Medley, 2008). Most campuses have offices or centers devoted to pedagogy and instruction that provide a variety of services to faculty in the form of training, workshops, resources libraries, and consultant services. Other centers or offices may be devoted to technology support services. In a Web 2.0 world, these functions cannot be separated. Much of the literature providing the framework for this chapter supports the assertion that we are moving into a Knowledge 2.0 or Pedagogy 2.0 world where technology and instruction are so intertwined that they cannot be addressed apart from each other (Dede, 2008; Mabrito & Medley, 2008; McLoughlin & Lee, 2008). As faculty examine their beliefs about pedagogy, administrators must examine how these centers function to support new instructional approaches.

Who will have control over the online programs? Miller and Schiffman (2006) asserted that when online programs are housed in continuing education, access is the goal with the expectation to recover costs of operations. In contrast, institutions with online programs under the control of academic units seem to have the goal to improve quality in teaching. Otte and Benke (2006) suggested that an appropriate compromise would be for institutions to centralize resources with means and methods of instruction controlled by instructors.

Wallace (2007) questioned how academic policies work in an online world. If a faculty member is asked to provide a policy in writing, does an electronic version count? Should traditional office hours still be required for full-time faculty teaching solely online? What about the development of student conduct codes addressing online behavior? How is faculty performance evaluated in an online course? Should the criteria differ from a face-to-face course evaluation? Craig (2007) addressed the tradition of timelines in academia. Should learning be contained within the traditional academic calendar, e.g., a semester-long course? Another major issue is the development of an assessment plan for evaluating the quality of online courses.

Beyond support for pedagogy and technology, institutional support is critical in terms of policies related to such topics as intellectual freedom, copyright, privacy issues, and intellectual property. Faculty course creation is typically work-for-hire, which means that the institution "owns" course content. In a model where students become the creators of knowledge, who "owns" that intellectual property? In a world of mashups, what institutional policies need to be revisited to ensure that current copyright laws are followed? How are copies of student "work" retained in cases where grades might be challenged? What are the boundaries of intellectual freedom for both students and faculty members in the blogosphere where opinions and products developed as part of class requirements are accessible to anyone with an Internet connection? Can a faculty member require the use of a social networking site like Facebook for instructional purposes? While high speed/broadband Internet access is widely available, there are still parts of the United States (including rural southeast Georgia) where access is an issue. Does the institution have an obligation/responsibility to students in this case?

Just as the nation's copyright laws have failed to keep pace with changes in technology, so have campus institutional support systems. Institutional support structures needed to support students who come to campus are quite different from support for online learners. The rapid growth of online courses and programs often happens prior to a discussion of critical institutional support questions. When these discussions are held, faculty members experienced with e-learning 2.0 need to be at the table.

Revisit the Faculty Reward System

The institution needs to revisit the faculty reward system to show the value of innovative online course development. While early adopters were offered release time or stipends for online course development, there is a lack of compensation for today's online faculty (Oblinger & Hawkins, 2006). Most faculty add online course development efforts on top of an already heavy workload. In many higher education institutions, there are increased expectations for scholarship and obtaining external funds. Time constraints may force faculty members to make a choice about where they will focus their professional efforts. This is a particularly critical (from the faculty perspective) support issue related to tenure and promotion. Craig (2007) noted that success for faculty at tenure and promotion time is still measured by print publications while success in the web environment is measured by the creation of tools and products that can be used and shared by others.

Returning to the business model, another type of faculty reward that must be considered is revenue sharing. It is a common practice to charge an e-tuition rate for online courses/programs. Who will benefit from the revenue generated by these courses? Individual faculty? Departments? Colleges? All of the above? Is it fair for funds being generated by faculty teaching online to be shared with other faculty? It is essential for institutions to develop a plan prior to funds disbursement, and faculty input is key in this planning effort.

Openly Acknowledge the Challenges and Issues Related to E-Learning 2.0

On many campuses, migrating courses from face-to-face to an online environment is not a choice, it is a requirement. When things formerly seen as optional become required, it may be tempting to try to convince faculty that development and delivery of quality online courses is easy. After all, our students use online and digital technologies constantly and often use them simultaneously. Faculty early adopters of online learning who have found ways to integrate Web 2.0 technologies into their classes might share their excitement and enthusiasm without realizing that many faculty members have limited technology skills and simply are not aware of how Web 2.0 technologies can transform pedagogy. Mabrito and Medley (2008) asserted that the Net Generation is actually developing an entirely new learning style which directly results from their constant interaction with the digital world. This shift leads to implications for classrooms (i.e. learning spaces) and for pedagogy. Mabrito and Medley's recommendations include having faculty participate in these learning spaces before trying to develop pedagogical strategies appropriate for those students. Again, for many faculty members this involves a significant commitment of time and effort that must be added to an already full workload.

Faculty members may also be reluctant to acknowledge that they "don't get it." In the Classical model of higher education (Dede, 2008) faculty see themselves as content experts and in the traditional and familiar face-to-face classroom they also believe that they understand how to create effective learning environments. In the world of Web 2.0, all of the familiarity that scaffolds our actions is gone. In addition, while there is a growing body of literature sharing excitement about anecdotal use of Web 2.0 tools in instruction, there is little formal research that faculty can use to guide their actions. Recommendations are often made to make modifications and adjustments to widely used

models of instructional design but will that really work in a time when epistemology is experiencing Dede's (2008) "seismic shift?"

CONCLUSION

Technologies with the potential to transform the environment of e-learning already exist. The challenges facing higher education include evolving from a traditional culture to a future-thinking philosophy in which technology continues to change the way we think about teaching. The technology will continue to develop, and students will continue to immerse all aspects of their lives in digital experiences. Educators cannot become inconsequential participants in this changing culture.

The support of campus administration for e-learning 2.0, which may require business model approaches to be modified or abandoned, is a critical issue to be addressed. The tension created by the opposing forces of the business model and integration of Web 2.0 may hinder universities from seizing the opportunity to lead educational reform in our global learning communities.

Faculty need to bring new technology opportunities to the table as administrators plan future directions for e-learning. Institutions need to determine a strategy that allows faculty to creatively implement Web 2.0 to improve and enhance instruction for today's learning communities. Faculty need to support colleagues who are at the forefront of restructuring their online environments to adapt to technology opportunities. Support for faculty should include incentives for technology pioneers as well as rewards for all faculty who devote time to explore possibilities available to create future learning experiences.

Although we have little evidence of the impact of Web 2.0 tools on student learning (Moore et al., 2007; Villano, 2008), the combination of Web 2.0 tools with existing models for online learning offers significant potential for e-learning

2.0. When participation in knowledge building is available to anyone/anywhere the opportunities for learning and collaboration also multiply. While Beldarrain (2006) asserts that "the ever-evolving nature of technology will continue to push distance educators to use new tools to create learning environments that will indeed prepare students to be life-long learners, who can problem solve through collaboration with global partners" (p. 150), the impact of the use of these technologies on higher education reform is unknown (Dede, 2008; Natriello, 2005; Wilson et al., 2007).

Higher education is not an institution comfortable with change. Given the history and tradition of higher education, the challenge of technology implementation may continue to be a game of catch up. Failure to keep abreast of these constant changes will define the preparedness of higher education to be relevant in the lives of 21st century students.

REFERENCES

Abel, R. (2007). Innovation, adoption, and learning impact creating the future of IT. *EDUCAUSE Review, 42*(2), 12–30.

Allen, E. I., & Seaman, J. (2007). *Online nation: Five years of growth in online learning.* Needham, MA: Sloan Consortium. Retrieved from http://sloanconsortium.org/publications/survey/pdf/online_nation.pdf

Beaudoin, M. F. (2006). The impact of distance education on the academy in the digital age. In M. F. Beaudoin (Ed.), *Perspectives on higher education in the digital age* (pp. 1-20). Hauppauge, NY: Nova Science Publishers.

Beldarrain, Y. (2006). Distance education trends: Integrating new technologies to foster student interaction and collaboration. *Distance Education, 27*(2), 139–153. doi:10.1080/01587910600789498

Blin, F., & Munro, M. (2008). Why hasn't technology disrupted academics' teaching practices? Understanding resistance to change through the lens of activity theory. *Computers & Education, 50*, 475–490. doi:10.1016/j.compedu.2007.09.017

Boettcher, J. V. (2008). 'Socializing' the CMS. *Campus Technology, 21*(11), 20–23.

Carlson, P. M., & Fleisher, M. S. (2002). Setting realities in higher education: Today's business model threatens our academic excellence. *International Journal of Public Administration, 25*(9/10), 1097–1111. doi:10.1081/PAD-120006127

Cox, R. D. (2005). Online education as institutional myth: Rituals and realities at community colleges. *Teachers College Record, 107*(8), 1754–1787. doi:10.1111/j.1467-9620.2005.00541.x

Craig, E. M. (2007). Changing paradigms: Managed learning environments and Web 2.0. *Campus-wide Information Systems, 24*(3), 152-161. Retrieved from http://www.emeraldinsight.com/1065-0741.htm

Dalsgaard, C. (2006). Social software: E-learning beyond learning management systems. *European Journal of Open, Distance and E-Learning.* Retrieved from http://www.eurodl.org/materials/contrib/2006/Christian_Dalsgaard.htm

Dede, C. (2008). New horizons: A seismic shift in epistemology. *EDUCAUSE Review, 43*(3), 80–81.

Eynon, R. (2008). The use of the World Wide Web in learning and teaching in higher education: Reality and rhetoric. *Innovations in Education and Teaching International, 45*(1), 15–23. doi:10.1080/14703290701757401

Facebook statistics. (2008). Retrieved August 15, 2008 from http://www.facebook.com/press/info.php?statistics

Gibson, S. G., Harris, M. L., & Colaric, S. M. (2008). Technology acceptance in an academic context: Faculty acceptance of online education. *Journal of Education for Business, 83*(6), 355–359. doi:10.3200/JOEB.83.6.355-359

Grush, M. (2008). The future of Web 2.0. *Campus Technology, 21*(7), 20–23.

Guri-Rosenblit, S. (2005). Eight paradoxes in the implementation process of e-learning in higher education. *Higher Education Policy, 18*, 5–29. doi:10.1057/palgrave.hep.8300069

Haber, J., & Mills, M. (2008). Perceptions of barriers concerning effective online teaching and policies: Florida community college faculty. *Community College Journal of Research and Practice, 32*, 266–283. doi:10.1080/10668920701884505

Hartman, J., Dziuban, C., & Moskal, P. (2007). Strategic initiatives in the online environment: Opportunities and challenges. *Horizon, 15*(3), 157–168. doi:10.1108/10748120710825040

Hiltz, S. R., Kim, E., & Shea, P. (2007). Faculty motivators and de-motivators for teaching online: Results of focus group interviews at one university. In *Proceedings of the 40th Hawaii International Conference on System Sciences*. Retrieved from http://doi.ieeecomputersociety.org/10.1109/HICSS.2007.226

Hiltz, S. R., & Turoff, M. (2005). Education goes digital: The evolution of online learning and the revolution in higher education. *Communications of the ACM, 48*(10), 60–64. doi:10.1145/1089107.1089139

Kidney, G., Cummings, L., & Boehm, A. (2007). Toward a quality assurance approach to e-learning courses. *International Journal on E-Learning, 6*(1), 17–30.

Larreamendy, J., & Leinhardt, G. (2006). Going the distance with online education. *Review of Educational Research, 76*, 567–606. doi:10.3102/00346543076004567

Levy, S. (2003). Six factors to consider when planning online distance learning programs in higher education. *Online Journal of Distance Learning Administration, 6*(2). Retrieved August 25, 2008, from http://www.westga.edu/~distance/ojdla/spring61/levy61.htm

Lorenzo, G. (2006). Business models for online education. *Educational Pathways, 10*(2), 69–95.

Mabrito, M., & Medley, R. (2008). Why Professor Johnny can't read: Understanding the Nt generation's texts. *Innovate, 4*(6). Retrieved from http://www.innovateonline.info/index.php?view-article&id=510

Mackintosh, W. (2006). Modelling alternatives for tomorrow's university: Has the future already happened? In M. F. Beaudoin (Ed.), *Perspectives on higher education in the digital age* (pp. 1-20). Hauppauge, NY: Nova Science Publishers.

McGee, P., & Diaz, V. (2007). Wikis and podcasts and blogs! Oh, my! What is a faculty member supposed to do? *EDUCAUSE Review, 42*(5), 28–40.

McLoughlin, C., & Lee, M. J. W. (2008). Future learning landscapes: Transforming pedagogy through social software. *Innovate, 4*(5). Retrieved from http://www.innovateonline.info/index.php?view=article&id=539

McQuiggan, C. A. (2007). The role of faculty development in online teaching's potential to question teaching beliefs and assumptions. *Online Journal of Distance Learning Administration, 10*(3). Available online at http://www.westga.edu/~distance/ojdla/fall103/mcquiggan103.htm

Miller, G. E., & Schiffman, S. (2006). ALN business models and the transformation of higher education. *Journal of Asynchronous Learning Networks, 10*(2), 15–21.

Moore, A. H., Fowler, S. B., & Watson, C. E. (2007). Active learning and technology: Designing change for faculty, students, and institutions. *EDUCAUSE Review, 42*(5), 43–60.

Natriello, G. (2005). Modest changes, revolutionary possibilities: Distance learning and the future of education. *Teachers College Record, 107,* 1885–1904. doi:10.1111/j.1467-9620.2005.00545.x

New Media Consortium & EDUCAUSE Learning Initiative. (2008). *The horizon report.* Retrieved from http://www.nmc.org/pdf/2008-Horizon-Report.pdf

Oblinger, D. G., & Hawkins, B. L. (2006). The myth about online course development. *EDUCAUSE Review, 41*(1), 14–15.

Oblinger, D. G., & Oblinger, J. L. (2005). Is it age or IT: First steps toward understanding the Net generation. In D. G. Oblinger & J. L. Oblinger (Eds.), *Educating the Net generation.* Retrieved August 26, 2008, from http://www.educause.edu/books/educatingthenetgen/5989

Otte, G., & Benke, M. (2006). Online learning: New models for leadership and organization in higher education. *Journal of Asynchronous Learning Networks, 10*(2), 23–31.

Panda, S., & Mishra, S. (2007). E-learning in a mega open university: Faculty attitude, barriers and motivators. *Educational Media International, 44*(4), 323–338. doi:10.1080/09523980701680854

Papastergiou, M. (2006). Course management systems as tools for the creation of online learning environments: Evaluation from a social constructivist perspective and implications for their design. *International Journal on E-Learning, 5,* 593–622.

Prensky, M. (2001). Digital natives, digital immigrants. *On the Horizon, 9*(5). Retrieved from http://www.marcprensky.com/writing/Prensky%20-%20Digital%20Natives,%20Digital%20Immigrants%20-%20Part1.pdf

Prensky, M. (2005). "Engage me or engage me": What today's learners demand. *EDUCAUSE Review, 40*(5), 60–64.

Prensky, M. (2008). Turning on the lights. *Educational Leadership, 65*(6), 40–45.

Richardson, W. (2006). *Blogs, wikis, podcasts, and other powerful Web tools for classrooms.* Thousand Oaks, CA: Corwin Press.

Richardson, W. (2007, March). The seven C's of learning. *District administration.* Retrieved from http://www.districtadministration.com.

Rogers, E. M. (1995). *Diffusion of innovations* (4th ed.). New York: The Free Press.

Samarawickrema, G., & Stacey, E. (2007). Adopting Web-based learning and teaching: A case study in higher education. *Distance Education, 28*(3), 313–333. doi:10.1080/01587910701611344

Schiffman, S., Vignare, K., & Geith, C. (2007). Why do higher-education institutions pursue online education? *Journal of Asynchronous Learning Networks, 11*(2), 61–71.

Sclater, N. (2008, July 6). *Are open source VLEs/LMSs taking off in UK universities?* Retrieved from http://sclater.com/blog/?p=114

Smith, D. E., & Mitry, D. J. (2008). Investigation of higher education: The real costs and quality of online programs. *Journal of Education for Business, 83*(3), 147–152. doi:10.3200/JOEB.83.3.147-152

Thompson, J. (2007). Is education 1.0 ready for Web 2.0 students? *Innovate, 3*(4). Retrieved from http://www.innovateonline.info/index.php?view-article&id=393

Vignare, K., Geith, C., & Schiffman, S. (2006). *Business models for online learning: An exploratory survey.* Retrieved August 25, 2008, from http://www.sloan-c.org/publications/jaln/v10n2/pdf/v10n2_5vignare.pdf

Villano, M. (2008). Wikis, blogs, & more, oh my! *Campus Technology, 21*(8), 42–50.

Wallace, L. (2007). Online teaching and university policy: Investigating the disconnect. *Journal of Distance Education, 22*(1). Retrieved August 26, 2008, from http://www.jofde.ca/index.php/jde/article/viewArticle/58/494

Wang, Q. (2006). Quality assurance: Best practices for assessing online programs. *International Journal on E-Learning, 5*(2), 265–274.

Web 3.0. (2008, August 25). In *Wikipedia, the free encyclopedia*. Retrieved August 25, 2008, from http://en.wikipedia.org/w/index.php?title=Web_3.0&oldid=234152612

Welcome to Technorati. (n.d.). Retrieved from http://technorati.com/about/

Wiley, D. (2006). Open source, openness, and higher education. *Innovate, 3*(1). Retrieved from http://www.innovateonline.info/index.php?view-article&id-354.

Wilson, B. G., Parrish, P., Balasubramanian, N., & Switzer, S. (2007). Contrasting forces affecting the practice of distance education. In R. Luppicini (Ed.), *Online learning communities* (pp. 333-346). Charlotte, NC: IAP-Information Age Publishing.

Chapter 4
Designing Dynamic Learning Environment for Web 2.0 Application

Robert Z. Zheng
University of Utah, USA

ABSTRACT

The growth of online resources and the advancement of Web 2.0 technology are changing the instructional landscape and have significantly impacted the practices in education. With its ill-structured learning and rapid incrementation of information in a non-linear fashion, Web 2.0 learning poses enormous challenges to online instructional designers and teachers. The traditional ID models are deemed less fit for Web 2.0 learning due to their linear, well-structured design approach. This chapter proposes a new ID model that specifically addresses the cognitive demands involved in Web 2.0 learning, promotes learning that focuses on metacognitive thinking and self-regulation, facilitates knowledge integration and construction of schemas-of-the-moment for ill-structured learning, and delivers an environment by connecting activities with behavior to form a dynamic learning environment in Web 2.0 application.

INTRODUCTION

The presence of new technology like Web 2.0 application has dramatically changed the instructional landscape in education (Brewer & Milam, 2006; Ellison & Wu, 2008; Glass & Spiegelman, 2007). Many universities, including K-12 schools, are already exploring the instructional use of Web 2.0 technologies such as blogs, wikis, iPods, podcasting, text messaging, and other social software like distributed classification systems (Glogoff, 2005; Ferris & Wilder, 2006). One of the challenges to use Web 2.0 application in education is to effectively design and develop instruction that prepares learners for discovery, change, and creativity in a highly complex and challenging learning environment.

Research shows that as technology has increasingly become a key component in teaching and learning, the amount of effort and enthusiasm that goes into the development and implementation of new technology often fails to yield desired results (Oliver & Herrington, 2003). This is due partly to

DOI: 10.4018/978-1-60566-729-4.ch004

Copyright © 2010, IGI Global. Copying or distributing in print or electronic forms without written permission of IGI Global is prohibited.

poor implementation of technology in learning and partly to a lack of effective instructional models and strategies that support such implementation. Current instructional design (ID) models are only moderately successful in taking advantage of the new online medium (Irlbeck, Kays, Jones, & Sims, 2006) because the existing models are characterized by a linear implementation procedure which suits well for well-structured learning but is less appropriate for complex, ill-structured learning (DeSchryver & Spiro, 2008), thereby omitting the most effective and innovative options for successful and creative online learning like Web 2.0 technologies. The inconsistency between existing ID models and practices has impeded the successful integration of new web technologies like blogs, podcasting, wikis, etc. into teaching and learning. Hence the need for a new ID framework that addresses the complexity in Web 2.0 learning. The chapter starts with a discussion of the characteristics of Web 2.0 learning and relevant cognitive demands associated with such learning, followed by a review of ID models which includes the traditional ID models, non-linear system instructional design (SID) models, and emergent e-learning ID models. Finally, a new ID framework is proposed for designing nonlinear, ill-structured learning in Web 2.0 application.

WEB 2.0 LEARNING AND COGNITIVE DEMANDS

Akbulut and Kiyici (2007) describe Web 2.0 technology as the second generation web services which provide a new learning platform for online collaboration and sharing among web users. These services enact a perceived transition from static and isolated information chunks as represented by the learning model of the first generation web services to self-generated and open communication where the authority is decentralized allowing end-users to use the web space as a conversation field (Collis & Moonen, 2008). Whereas the first

generation web services are characterized by a search for information coupled with well structured instructional strategies like WebQuests to facilitate learners' knowledge acquisition (Zheng, 2007), Web 2.0 learning reflects a participatory, collaborative, and dynamic approach with which knowledge is created through the collective efforts of participants (Rogers, Liddle, Chan, Doxey, & Isom, 2007). In this section the discussion will primarily focus on the idiosyncratic features of Web 2.0 learning and cognitive demands associated with such learning.

Characteristics of Web 2.0 Application

The traditional Web technology which is also known as the first generation Web technology reflects a one-to-many model in which the content was designed and developed by an individual, a team, a company, an institute or an organization (Breeding, 2006; Kesim & Agaoglu, 2007). The primary purpose was for readers to consume the information. For example, many of the early Websites were text-based serving as an information pamphlet for the business and industry, or as didactic lecture notes in education (Andrews, 1999). With the advent of the second generation WWW, namely Web 2.0 technology, information as well as knowledge are no longer distributed by an individual, a team, a company, an institute, or an organization. Rather, they are distributed and created by users within the cyber community. The new Web 2.0 technology is characterized by shared ownership, simultaneous traversals of multiple knowledge spaces, and social negotiation (DeSchryver & Spiro, 2008; Kesim & Agaoglu, 2007; Wang & Hsua, 2008). A discussion of each of those characteristics follows.

Shared Ownership

Differing from the first generation WWW, Web 2.0 technology is designed to create a forum for everyone in online community. One of the characteristics of Web 2.0 is that knowledge is created collectively by a group of participants who share the same interest in the topic (Wang & Hsua, 2008). For example, participants who are interested in photography may form an online discussion group called the blog to discuss various issues related to photography. Thus, the content is no long pre-crafted by a specific author. Instead, it is contributed by whoever is involved in the online community and has a shared ownership among the group members who contribute to the well-being of the blog. Wang and Hsua (2008) point out that the shared ownership in Web 2.0 application has an instructional significance in that it facilitates collaboration among learners which "can be an ideal forum for social constructivist learning" (p. 82).

Simultaneous Traversals of Multiple Knowledge Spaces

With Web 2.0 technology, learners are exposed to multiple knowledge spaces in a single learning environment (e.g., blog, wikis, etc.) in contrast to accessing information through separate websites which people typically do with the first generation WWW (Breeding, 2006). The fact that the learner is able to simultaneously access information across multiple knowledge domains within a single learning environment makes Web 2.0 application a popular form for both teaching and learning. Kim (2008) studied the differences between traditional computer-mediated communication (CMC) application and Web 2.0 application and concluded that the Web 2.0 application has a great potential for learning because it promotes critical thinking skills such as analysis, synthesis and evaluation. Wassell and Crouch (2008) have drawn similar conclusions by pointing out that the Web 2.0 application such as blogs, wikis, etc. enables learners to focus on a particular topic while accessing wide range of

knowledge domains at the same time. This unique feature of Web 2.0 application enhances learners' ability to categorize and synthesize information, and therefore empowers them to become more informed in an ill-structured environment like Web 2.0 learning.

Social Negotiation

Web 2.0 technology is characterized by a constructivist, collaborative social learning environment in which knowledge is shared through multiple ownership among online contributors (Wang & Hsua, 2008). Because of its shared ownership, the content in Web 2.0 is created collectively by the online community. However, some educators are concerned about the authenticity of the knowledge created (Xie, Ke, & Sharma, 2008; Young, 2008). Yet, those concerns become mitigated with the unique features in Web 2.0 application that underscore the process of social negotiation in knowledge construction.

With instant feedback and synchronous and asynchronous responses, Web 2.0 technology provides learners with a conversation space for elaborating ideas and thoughts and corroborating facts and findings. The learner can challenge previous statements by going back to the archived messages and then propose new ideas based on his/her findings. This process of elaboration, corroboration and refinement represents a social negotiation process among web users whose opinions are critiqued, corrected and finally transformed into concepts acknowledged and accepted by the online community (Sorensen, Takle, & Moser, 2006; Trentin, 2008). Zheng, Flygare, Dahl, and Hoffman (in press) noted that social negotiation represents an important aspect in Web 2.0 learning where learners become dynamically engaged in the process of knowledge construction and creation.

Cognitive Demands in Web 2.0 Learning

Learners who learn with Web 2.0 can benefit from collaborating with others, engaging in online discussions to deepen understanding and develop critical thinking skills for learning (Ellison & Wu, 2008; Glass & Spiegelman, 2007; Rogers et al., 2007). Notwithstanding the benefits that Web 2.0 has brought to its users, there are some challenges the users must face as they engage in Web 2.0 learning (DeSchryver & Spiro, 2008; Lee, 2004). They include cognitive overload, selection/use of appropriate cognitive strategies, and integration of information across multiple domains. A discussion of each of the above cognitive demands follows.

Cognitive Load

The concept of cognitive load was first introduced by Sweller and his colleagues (Sweller, 1988; Sweller & Chandler 1991, 1994) who found that certain materials were more difficult to learn than others. Sweller and his colleagues (Sweller, 2006; Sweller, van Merrienboer & Paas, 1998; van Merrienboer & Sweller, 2005) identified three types of cognitive loads: intrinsic, extraneous and germane load. While the first two types of cognitive load pose threats to effective learning, the latter is considered to be effective, in that it elicits "mindful engagement" in learning. In Web 2.0 learning high intrinsic or extraneous cognitive load may occur due to the demand to synchronize information across multiple knowledge spaces (Lee, 2004). Thus, the challenge to instructional designers is to create a cognitively effective learning environment that reduces intrinsic and extraneous cognitive load by optimizing "mindful effort" in learning. For example, Sweller (1988) found that the goal free design helps reduce the amount of cognitive load associated with complex learning. By extrapolating the previous findings to Web 2.0 application, it can be reasonably assumed that implementing

the goal free strategy would reduce learners' cognitive load in an open-ended, ill-structured learning environment – a theoretical assumption that undergirds the proposed ID framework that will be discussed later in this chapter.

Selection/use of Appropriate Cognitive Strategies

The second cognitive demand is associated with the selection and use of appropriate cognitive strategies. Characterized by an ill-structured, nonlinear learning environment, Web 2.0 application underscores a *schemas-of-the-moment* in learning as opposed to *schema construction and automation* in well-structured learning (DeSchryver & Spiro, 2008). For example, online blogging requires learners to quickly synthesize the existing information while responding to a continuing influx of new information. Obviously, cognitive strategies as defined in well-structured learning become less useful in this ill-structured learning environment. Instead, strategies in tantamount with cognitive demands in ill-structured learning are needed (Shin, Jonassen, & McGee, 2003). Because of the complexity and irregularity (i.e., ill-structured) pertaining to Web 2.0 learning, selecting and using cognitive strategies to construct open and flexible knowledge structures for situation specific application remain one of the challenges for learners.

Integration of Information Across Multiple Domains

The third cognitive demand is related to the integration of information across multiple domains. In Web 2.0 learning, learners are exposed to kaleidoscopic presentation of information that imposes a high cognitive demand in terms of information integration (DeSchryver & Spiro, 2008). Rogers et al. (2007) identify areas of challenges when making connections among different domains. The challenges include (a) connecting between fields, ideas, and concepts, (b) maintaining connections among specialized nodes or information sources, (c) synthesizing diverse opinions, and (d) harnessing collective intelligence. Notably, the challenges identified by Rogers et al. are similar to those faced by the learners in Web 2.0 application where the abilities to connect between fields, ideas, and concepts; maintain connections among specialized nodes or information sources; and so forth are essential for the success of Web 2.0 learning. Failure to develop and maintain these abilities can significantly impede learners' learning in a Web 2.0 environment.

Taken together, the high cognitive demands involved in Web 2.0 learning have posed challenges to educators and instructional designers who have perceived an increasing incongruency between existing instructional design models and new Web 2.0 technology (Akbulut & Kiyici, 2007; Maloney, 2007; Rogers et al., 2007). The ill-structured nature of Web 2.0 learning renders traditional ID models less applicable to learning that demands high cognitive flexibility and metacognitive thinking. Many educators and instructional designers thus question the stereotyped approach in applying traditional ID models to the fast evolving e-learning where ill-structured, rather than well-structured, learning is emphasized (Irlbeck et al., 2006).

EXISTING MODELS OF INSTRUCTIONAL DESIGN

This section presents a review of ID models and their relevance to the design of Web 2.0 learning. Three types of ID models are discussed. They include early ID models, non-linear SID models, and recent emergent e-learning ID models.

Early Instructional Design Models

The early efforts of instructional design were represented by the ADDIE (Analyze, Design, Develop, Implement, Evaluate) model which provided the foundation for later system instructional design (SID) models such as Dick, Carey and Carey's (2005) system design model. Early ID models tended to have their premise based on behavioral principles. They were characterized by a linear design process in which components are streamlined to reflect a hierarchical structure in learning. Early ID models were designed for goal oriented, well-structured learning (Andrews & Goodson, 1980). The problem with this type of instructional design is that learning is considered to be stereotyped, cookie-cut behaviors with little variation and changes. It leaves little room for learning that requires a nonlinear, ill-structured thinking like Web 2.0 application.

The SID models in the late 80s and early 90s emphasized human information processing in learning. The SID models were influenced by Gagne's (1965) conditions of learning theory which identifies five outcomes related to human learning: psychomotor skills, verbal information, intellectual skills, cognitive strategies, and attitudes. Despite of their obvious improvement over the early ID models, the SID models were designed for well-structured, goal directed learning. They followed a *linear* system design process (see Gagne's (1965) nine events of instruction and Dick, Carey and Carey's (2005) ten steps of system instructional design) that pre-determines the sequence of instruction. Some critics argued that the rigidity of linear SID models may limit what the instructor can teach and what learners can actually learn (Mashhadi, 1998). New philosophy like constructivism changed the mentality in instructional design. As a result, new instructional design models were proposed that allowed instructors to choose the instructional event(s) they deemed the most important based on their assessment of the instructional and learning situations (Morrison, Ross, & Kemp, 2004).

Non-linear SID Models

Like linear SID models, the non-linear SID model contains similar critical design components including needs assessment, learner assessment, goals and objectives, instructional materials, instructional strategies, instructional assessment and evaluation, and so forth. Unlike the linear SID models, the non-linear SID model is not confined to a specific sequence of instructional design process where the events of instruction are organized based on the logic between the events. For example, in Morrison et al.'s (2004) ID model, the instructional designer can select any instructional event(s) (e.g., learner assessment, task analysis, or identification of instructional objectives) as a specific starting point. These instructional events are concurrently examined in a larger environment that is supported by planning, implementation, revision, formative and summative evaluations, and so on. The strength of non-linear SID model is that it allows the instructional designer to (a) choose one or several instructional events simultaneously in the design, (b) relate instructional event(s) to implementation and evaluation, (c) support the planning, implementation, and management of the instruction with adequate services, and (d) implement the instructional design from a holistic perspective.

As demonstrated, non-linear SID is descriptive. It does not prescribe the steps that the instructional designer must follow. Instead, the model presents a holistic relationship among the components in the design process by asking the *big-picture* questions: What is the problem we are asked to solve? Will instruction solve the problem? What is the purpose of the planned instruction? and Is an instructional intervention the best solution? These questions guide the designer to determine exactly which instructional event to choose. Obviously, the non-linear SID gives instructional designers more latitude in design, specifically by allowing them to put in perspective simultaneously the interrelationship among various design

components in the design process – a process advocated by early E-Learning instructional designers like Gunawardena, Ortegano-Layne, Carabajal, Frechette, Lindemann, and Jennings (2006). Nonetheless, like linear SID models, the non-linear SID model shows its limitation when being applied to ill-structured learning because both emphasize *priori* instructional goals and objectives as the primary instructional component in the instructional design.

Emergent Instructional Design Models in E-Learning

In the wake of the wide application of the Internet, the Web has become more popular for educational instruction. Educators and instructional designers resort to traditional ID models to design and develop Web-based courses to meet the increasing societal needs. Irlbeck et al. (2006) point out that "existing instructional design models … provide a foundation but not a relevance to complex and dynamic models for online learning environment" (p. 176). Recently, new approaches have emerged to address issues unique to online learning. The following models represent, among many emergent e-learning ID models, instructional approaches that focus on learner-centered, social learning in a Web-based environment.

WisCom Design Model

The WisCom design model was created by Gunawardena et al in 2006. The word "WisCom" stands for wisdom community. The model drew from Vygotsky's (1978) socio-constructivism and Wertsch's (1991) sociocultural philosophy of learning. It was grounded in the theory of distributed cognition (Hutchins, 1991; Pea, 1993; Salomon, 1993) by advocating authentic contexts in learning where cognitive capability is distributed across groups of peers to do an activity (Brown, Collins, & Guguid, 1989). The core of the WisCom design model is to create an authentic learning environment in which collective wisdom is created among the community members who initiate reflection-in-action (Schon, 1983), social negotiation (Vygotsky, 1978; Wertsch, 1991), and knowledge creation through the stages of (a) building WidCom communities, (b) mentoring and learner support, (c) knowledge innovation, and (d) transformational learning. By implementing the model, the designer will be able to foster: shared identity; shared goals and missions; opportunities for critical reflection, dialogue, emergence, change, and transformation; exchange of diverse views and multiple perspectives; space for social interaction; and care for the common good of the members, all of which are critical for successful online learning. The model is distinguished by its power of exteriorizing the process of learning and facilitating scholarly inquiry in online learning. It encourages learners to become reflective thinkers and to acquire collaborative thinking skills that transcend the single disciplinary context. Despite its improvement over the ID or SID models previously mentioned, the *WisCom* design model focuses on the existing content as a starting point where knowledge is consumed by learners (first generation WWW). It lacks a mechanism that promotes self-generated and open communication which Collis and Moonen (2008) describes as decentralized authority that allows end-users to use the web space as a conversation field for knowledge creation and construction, a feature known to Web 2.0 application.

The "T5" Design Model

The "T5" design model was developed by Salter, Richards, & Carey (2004) to provide a framework for effective online instruction. The design model emphasizes five critical components in online learning: Tasks, Tools, Tutorials, Topics, and Teamwork. The model takes an object oriented approach in which learning objects are used and reused to create the content. In order to optimize the effects of learning content, several mechanisms are created which include (a) a reflective thinking on learning process and roles, (b) feedback to learning deliverables and tasks, and (c) online supports for collaborative work. As with other online learning models, the "T5" design model adopts reflection-in-action approach to provide feedback to on-going learning activities and tasks. The model purports to provide a pedagogical gateway to online learning. It is designed to help faculty and other educational professionals to effectively integrate learning management system (LMS) into their teaching, promote development and delivery of courses with a collaborative-constructivist approach to learning, and support creative and innovative thinking in an ill-structured online learning environment. Similar to the *WisCom* design model, the "T5" design model emphasizes the existing content as the basis for online learning. It fails to include the component in its design where end-users can use the web space as a conversation field for knowledge creation and construction.

Three-Phase Design (3PD) Model

The 3PD model (Irlbeck et al., 2006) focuses on the creation of functional course delivery components, evaluation and improvement activities, and scaffolding in learning. The framework of 3PD model is manifested through three discrete phases: first, establishing environments for fully functional online teaching and learning components; second, modifying the components based on feedback from the teacher, learners, and others; third, monitoring and maintaining the quality of the online learning environments. In this model, the design proceeds from the bottom-up rather than from top-down, allowing for global behavior. The model is learner-oriented in that learners are given the options to choose learning elements. The role of teacher in this model is defined as a facilitator who provides feedback, and acts as part of the collective. More importantly, the model institutes a variety of interactions by creating effective communication paths which help shape learning experiences without predefined orders. Although the 3PD model takes a more interactive approach in its design by focusing on the relationship between learners' behavior and related components in online learning, there is a lack of systematic approach to coordinate various components of learning in the design process. For example, it is not clear how bottom-up behaviors are measured, and how the feedback from teachers, learners and others is negotiated to form a collective wisdom for learning which is highly emphasized in Web 2.0 application.

In short, the emergent online ID models manifest a new trend in design in that these models take an object oriented approach which is more flexible and provides larger interactive learning space as compared to that of hierarchical design approach in traditional ID models. Additionally, they are characterized by a learner-centered, social learning process in which feedback, reflection-in-action, and metacognitive skills are highlighted. All in all, the emergent online ID models have demonstrated characteristics that fit uniquely with online learning environment.

Existing ID Models and Web 2.0 Learning

As mentioned earlier, Web 2.0 learning is characterized by its shared ownership, social negotiation, and simultaneous traversals of multiple knowledge domains. It is learner-centered and learner-initiated, featuring a nonlinear, ill-structured learning environment which imposes high cognitive demands on learners in terms of cognitive load, selection/use of appropriate strategies, and integration of information across multiple domains.

The traditional ID models, including linear and nonlinear SID models, seem less applicable for Web 2.0 learning because they are goal oriented and marked by a linear, hierarchical design approach. The non-linear ID models, albeit their nonlinear nature, are goal specific and lack flexibility for ill-structured learning where unexpected outcomes

are typically found. The emergent e-learning ID models address some aspects of Web 2.0 learning. However, there is a lack of systematic approach to coordinate various components of learning in the design process. For example, in Irlbeck et al.'s (2006) 3PD model it is not clear how bottom-up behaviors are measured, and how the feedback from teachers, learners and others is negotiated to form a collective wisdom for learning.

AN INSTRUCTIONAL DESIGN FRAMEWORK FOR WEB 2.0 APPLICATION

In this section the author proposes an instructional design framework for Web 2.0 learning. A discussion of the theoretical bases of the proposed ID framework will be presented, followed by a description of the framework and its implementation.

Theoretical Bases

The proposed framework is informed by several theories including emergence theory (Johnson, 2001), functional contextualism (Fox, 2006), and literature in individual differences (Anastasi, 1965; Buss & Poley, 1976; Tyler, 1974), metacognition (Reeve & Brown, 1984), and self-regulation (Zimmerman, 2008).

Emergence theory emerges from the study of the complex natural and social phenomena where dissimilar organized occurrences such as slime moulds, ant colonies, and human cities have exhibited similar results. These results, along with studies from molecular biology and computer science were drawn together by Johnson (2001) into the picture of a new scientific perspective called "emergence." The key to understanding this new perspective, according to Johnson, lies in the understanding that simple interactions of the elements in a system – without any central top-down control – can lead to the emergence of highly complex, intelligent behavior. This theory has been used to explain the complex phenomena in Web 2.0 learning. In Web 2.0 learning we already see various types of emergent systems in use, such as blogs which allow the system to govern itself and learn from itself in a dynamic way.

As indicated, emergence theory aligns well with the philosophy that underscores ill-structured and constructivist learning. While the theory provides an ideal for constructivist, ill-structured design, it is not without problems. It is difficult to measure the learning outlined by the emergence theory. Winn (2006) commented on some of the problems with descriptive measurement commonly employed by constructivist researchers:

We cannot build useful theory without establishing causal relationships among phenomena. And we cannot establish causal relations just through observation. Without being able to establish through experiments, with a high level of certainty, that Factor A or Context B causes Behavior C, we will not be able to build theory, which successfully predicts learning outcomes, that we so desperately need. (p. 56)

Beware of the lack of theoretical clarity in a significant amount of constructivist writing and the ambiguity in measuring the outcome in constructivist learning, Fox (2006) proposes a framework for constructivist instructional design by blending behaviorist positivism with constructivist learning, which results in a goal oriented constructivist instructional design approach. Such approach provides a behavior-in-context that "predicts and influences events with precision, scope, and depth using empirically based concepts and rules" (Fox, 2006, p. 11). However, functional contextualism focuses on *priori* goals and objectives in well-structured learning. In web 2.0 application like blogs, MySpace, YouTube, etc. where goals or objectives are often not specified, functional contextualism appears to be less congruent with such learning. The author thus proposes a modified

version of functional contextualism by suggesting a design that emphasizes *posteri* goals and objectives. That is, instead of specifying the goals and objectives at the beginning of the design, the designer incorporates a mechanism to have the goals and objectives formulated after the initial open-ended learning. The goals and objectives thus formulated will provide guidance to the next phase activities while still allowing open-ended learning to occur. This modified version of functional contextualism provides the learner with the opportunity to construct and create new knowledge in an ill-structured learning environment while receiving support to shape their learning content with clear targets.

The proposed framework is also informed by the research in individual differences, metacognition, and self regulation. Research suggests that individual differences can influence learners' learning (Anastasi, 1965; Buss & Poley, 1976; Tyler, 1974). Zheng et al (in press) studied college students' communication pattern in an online environment and found that learners' online communication is significantly correlated with their individual differences. Metacognition is believed to be another factor that significantly influences learners' learning (Reeve & Brown, 1984). In a study that investigated secondary students' (N = 32) problem-solving vs. text-studying skills, van der Stel and Veenman (2008) detected a significant relation between intellectual ability and metacognitive skills as predictors of learning performance in young students. Further, research suggests that learners' metacognitive skills are correlated with their individual differences in learning (Metallidou & Platsidou, 2008). Metallidou and Platsidou investigated the psychometric properties of Kolb's LSI-1985 in a Greek sample of pre-service and in-service teachers (N = 338) and found the participants' learning styles were correlated with their metacognitive knowledge about the frequency of using various problem-solving strategies. They proposed that teaching should take into consideration the roles of individual differences and metacognitive skills in learning.

Self-regulation has long been recognized as an important factor in learning (Muis, 2008; Zimmerman, 2008). Torrance, Fidalgo, and Garcia (2007) found that learners' self-regulation can significantly predict their academic performance. Muis (2008) concurred with Torrance et al.'s findings by identifying the role of self-regulation in math problem solving. Johnson and Liber (2008) argued that self-regulation is one of the issues that strike at the heart of current debates about the education and more deeply, the human condition in the modern world.

Instructional Design Framework for Web 2.0 Learning

Drawn from the above theories and literature, a new ID framework is proposed for designing and developing Web 2.0 learning. The framework is characterized by (a) learner-centered approach, (b) interactive social communication, and (c) dynamic learning in Web 2.0 application.

Learner-Centered Approach

The design is guided by a learner-centered approach which takes into consideration learners' cognitive and metacognitive abilities, e.g., information processing ability, cognitive skill management, and self-regulation, in the process of learning. Informed by the findings in cognitive load studies, the learner-centered approach in the proposed framework specifically underscores a design process in Web 2.0 application in which learners are able to access simultaneously multiple knowledge spaces without being cognitively overloaded. For example, the concepts of distributed cognition (Hutchins, 1991; Pea, 1993; Salomon, 1993) and goal free design (Sweller, 1988) are implemented at the core of the proposed framework that focuses on learners' behavior, where knowledge is assimilated, distributed and at the same time contributed collectively by the learners. This approach aligns with Web 2.0 learning which highlights open-ended, ill-structured learning and in which skills like metacognition, self-regulation, and social negotiation are highlighted.

Interactive Social Communication

Based on a revised version of functional contextualism, the design incorporates an interactive social communication process in which learners initiate the learning process through an open-ended discussion. The discussion is further guided by a social negotiation for exchanging opinions, elaborating thoughts, and corroborating facts and findings. The social negotiation process guides the initial discussion and leads to a more elaborate, refined discussion with collectively negotiated goals and objectives, that is, *posteri* goals and objectives for online learning. An important component in social negotiation is the feedback mechanism, through which the learners critique, correct and transform individual ideas and concepts into socially acceptable norms.

The interactive social communication in the proposed framework is influenced by early works including Morrison et al.'s (2004) non-linear ID design and Gunawardena et al.'s (2006) WisCom design model. However, it differs from the previous ID models in that it accentuates an open-ended, dynamic learning process through interactive social communication. It can be reasonably argued that such approach would better fit the learning mode in Web 2.0 application (e.g., blogs, wikis, podcasting, etc.) because interactive social communication is essential to learning that is open-ended and ill-structured and in which knowledge is created through social negotiation.

Dynamic Learning

The framework is characterized by a dynamic learning environment that includes (a) evolving activities accompanied by behavior that reflects a changing learning process; (b) schemas-of-the-moment for ill-structured learning; and (c) collaboration among online learners. First, the activity in Web 2.0 learning is defined as a continuum from lower level complex learning to higher level complex learning. The concept of complex learning is explained by the number of element interactivity in learning (Sweller & Chandler, 1991, 1994). For instance, in low complex learning the learner is exposed to one subject domain or fewer element interactivity whereas in high complex learning the learner is required to deal with multiple subject domains or more element interactivity. The change from lower complex learning to high complex learning is achieved by a concomitant change in behavior, that is, learners' abilities to socially negotiate with other learners, execute metacognitive thinking skills, and self-regulate in order to adjust to new learning demands. Next, due to the ill-structured nature of learning in Web 2.0 application, learners largely rely on *schemas-of-the-moment* to deal with emergent issues and solve ill-structured problems (DeSchryver & Spiro, 2008). Learners develop schemas-of-the-moment by accessing multiple knowledge spaces in learning. The information gleaned is refined through socially negotiated goals and objectives to facilitate deep learning. Finally, the dynamic learning is promoted by collaboration among learners and instructor. Differing from the traditional ID models which define instructor-learner relationship as didactic stable working relationship, this framework assumes the instructor-learner relationship to be of a collective and immersive type in that the instructor may provide instructional guidance at the beginning but quickly becomes merged into the collective body of learning community.

During the entire process of Web 2.0 learning, the emphasis is made on the connection between behavior and activities. As learning evolves from lower level complex learning to higher level complex learning, learners adjust their self-regulation and metacognitive thinking skills to the changing activi-

ties in online learning. Figure 1 shows the dynamic learning environment for Web 2.0 application.

IMPLEMENTATION OF THE FRAMEWORK

In this section the implementation for the framework is proposed. Undoubtedly, the effectiveness of such implementation can only be substantiated when it is carried out in real learning environment. Therefore, instead of focusing on the operational aspects of the implementation, the following discussion attempts to present the implementation of the framework from a conceptual perspective. In other words, readers should take this as a guideline to the implementation of the framework rather than actual steps of the implementation.

Activity vs. Behavior

The implementation is pivoted around the relationship between activity and behavior. The designer must determine a starting point along the continuum of complex learning by putting learners' behavior in perspective. In other words, what behavior should be involved in carrying out the learning activity identified? And what criteria (e.g., level of efficacy) should be applied to the outcomes of such behavior?

Initiate an Open-Ended Learning Environment

Next, for complex learning to occur, an open-ended learning must be initiated. The open-ended learning should be further refined by incorporating *posteri* goals and objectives to effect learning at a deeper level. This initiation of the open-ended stage is accomplished by including in place the mechanism of social negotiation where learners and the instructor collaborate on an equal footing in exploring, corroborating, negotiating concepts and principles, constructing and creating new

Figure 1. Instructional design framework for Web 2.0 learning

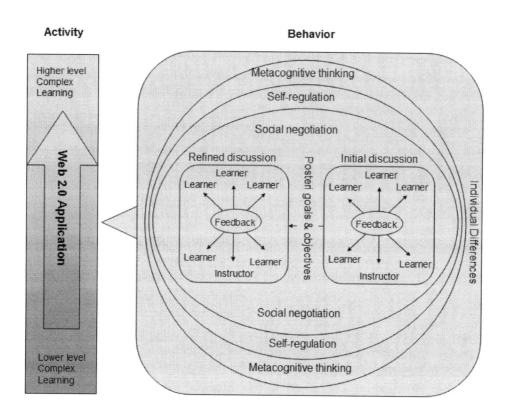

knowledge. It should be noted that the initiation stage requires the consideration of several factors such as learner-learner and learner-instructor interactions, cognitive demands, selection and use of cognitive strategies, simultaneous traversals of multiple knowledge spaces, and so forth. Such consideration enables the designer to enact a process that optimizes learners' engagement and reduces downtime in learning (Snelbecker, Miller, & Zheng, 2007).

Promote Metacognitive Thinking and Self-Regulation

Finally, the initiation of open-ended learning is culminated in the design that promotes metacognition and self-regulation. Ill-structured learning like Web 2.0 application requires considerable self-regulation and metacognitive monitoring on the part of learners to develop cognitive strategies that handle the irregularity and complexity in learning (Kauffman, 2004). Promoting self-regulation and metacognitive monitoring enhances learners' critical thinking and improves their performance in ill-structured learning like Web 2.0 application. Of all the factors considered, individual differences are perhaps most influential and could have a direct bearing on learning. The instructional design in Web 2.0 application should thus put individual differences in perspective when designing activities pertinent to creative and constructivist learning in Web 2.0 application.

Figure 1 delineates the behavior and supporting components at a specific learning point. As learning progresses along the continuum of activity, more complex behavior (e.g., high level metacognitive thinking) and related supporting components (e.g., *posteri* goals and objectives for higher level complex learning) should be designated to support higher level complex learning activities.

DISCUSSION

The proposed framework suggests a new perspective in regard to the design and development of Web 2.0 learning. Differing from the traditional ID design models, the framework proposes that instructional design for online learning, especially Web 2.0 learning, should take into consideration the ill-structured, non-linear nature of learning. As such, the framework includes a level of flexibility for activities and learning behavior with respect to learners' cognitive and metacognitive abilities, individual differences, and self-regulation in learning. It allows complex and deep learning to emerge through a social negotiation process. The framework takes a holistic approach in design by examining concurrently various components in Web 2.0 learning.

As a new instructional design approach, the proposed framework is specifically designed to reduce cognitive demands related to cognitive load, selection of appropriate cognitive strategies, and information integration in Web 2.0 learning. Firstly, the social learning mechanism like social negotiation and feedback enables the load of learning to be distributed among group members, hence reducing the cognitive load involved in Web 2.0 learning. Secondly, the collaboration among learners creates a supporting environment for metacognitive thinking and self-regulation. Learners are able to reflect on their actions and select appropriate strategies for learning and self-adjustment. Finally, by supporting *schemas-of-the-moment* in learning, the framework enables learners to make association among various chunks of knowledge and therefore enhance their abilities to integrate information across multiple knowledge domains.

FUTURE TRENDS

As with other instructional design models, the proposed framework needs to be empirically tested to verify its underlying theoretical constructs and assumptions. Future research is needed to examine the function of the social mechanism in promoting metacognitive thinking and self-regulation. Further, investigation should be conducted to understand the relationship between activities and learning behavior in terms of cognitive demands, knowledge construction, and motivation in learning. It is suggested that research in the future should focus on the efficacy of behavior and supporting components (e.g., posteri goals and objectives) and the resultant impact on learners' ability to succeed in an ill-structured learning, especially in the situation that evolves from lower complex to higher complex learning.

Research in the future should focus on measurement scheme that clearly identifies the performance and outcomes related to Web 2.0 learning. Such measurement scheme should clearly explain the relationship between behavior and activity described in the framework and would help scale up the complex learning such as social blogging in Web 2.0 application.

CONCLUSION

The growth of online resources and the advancement of Web 2.0 technology are changing the information landscape and impacting teaching and learning. With its ill-structured learning and rapid incrementation of information in a non-linear fashion, Web 2.0 learning poses enormous challenges to online instructional designers and teachers. The traditional ID models are deemed less fit for Web 2.0 learning due to their linear, well-structured design approach. This chapter proposes a new ID model that specifically addresses the cognitive demands involved in Web 2.0 learning, promotes learning that focuses on metacognitive thinking and self-regulation, facilitates knowledge integration and construction of schemas-of-the-moment for ill-structured learning, and delivers an environment by connecting activities with behavior to form a dynamic learning environment in Web 2.0 application. Unlike traditional ID models which spell out every design procedure in the process of learning, the proposed framework identifies the structural components in Web 2.0 learning, i.e., activities, behavior, and supporting components for behavior and allows the learning process to form its own direction and let the complex learning emerge through social negotiation.

It should be pointed out that the proposed framework should not be interpreted as the only design approach for Web 2.0 learning. Instead, it provides an alternative view to traditional design models and calls for the need of studying the dynamic relationship between various components in Web 2.0 learning. The activities, behavior, and supporting components thus identified help instructional designers and educators to refocus on the dynamics of learning in the design process rather than imposing the design as a priori on the dynamics of learning.

REFERENCES

Akbulut, Y., & Kiyici, M. (2007). Instructional use of Weblogs. *Turkish Online Journal of Distance Education, 8*(3), 6–15.

Anastasi, A. (1965). *Individual differences.* New York: Wiley.

Andrews, A. S. (1999). When is a threat "truly" a threat lacking first amendment protection? A proposed true threats test to safeguard free speech rights in the age of the Internet. *The UCLA Online Institute for Cyberspace Law and Policy.* Retrieved on May 19, 2008 from http://www.gseis.ucla.edu/iclp/aandrews2.htm

Andrews, D. H., & Goodson, L. A. (1980). A comparative analysis of models of instructional design. *Journal of Instructional Development, 3*(4), 2–14. doi:10.1007/BF02904348

Breeding, M. (2006). Web 2.0? Let's get to Web 1.0 first. *Computers in Libraries, 26*(5), 30–33.

Brewer, S., & Milam, P. (2006, June). New technologies-like blogs and Wikis-are taking their place in the school media center. *School Library Journal, •••,* 46–50.

Brown, J. S., Collins, A., & Guguid, P. (1989). Situated cognition and the culture of learning. *Educational Researcher, 18*(1), 32–42.

Buss, A. R., & Poley, W. (1976). *Individual differences: Traits and factors.* New York: Gardner Press.

Collis, B., & Moonen, J. (2008). Web 2.0 tools and processes in higher education: Quality perspectives. *Educational Media International, 45*(2), 93–106. doi:10.1080/09523980802107179

DeSchryver, M., & Spiro, R. (2008). New forms of deep learning on the Web: Meeting the challenge of cognitive load in conditions of unfettered exploration in online multimedia environments. In R. Zheng (Ed.), *Cognitive effects of multimedia learning* (pp. 134-152). Hershey, PA: IGI Global Publishing.

Dick, W., Carey, L., & Carey, J. O. (2005). *The systematic design of instruction* (6th ed.). Boston, MA: Pearson/Allyn & Bacon.

Ellison, N. B., & Wu, Y. H. (2008). Blogging in the classroom: A preliminary exploration of student attitudes and impact on comprehension. *Journal of Educational Multimedia and Hypermedia, 17*(1), 99–122.

Ferris, S. P., & Wilder, H. (2006). Uses and potentials of Wikis in the classroom. *Innovate, 2*(5). Retrieved May 23, 2008, from http://www.innovateonline.info/index.php?view=article&id=258

Fox, E. J. (2006). Constructing a pragmatic science of learning and instruction with functional contextualism. *Educational Technology Research and Development, 54*(1), 5–36. doi:10.1007/s11423-006-6491-5

Gagne, R. (1965). *The conditions of learning.* New York: Holt, Rinehart and Winston.

Glass, R., & Spiegelman, M. (2007). Incorporating blogs into the syllabus: Making their space a learning space. *Journal of Educational Technology Systems, 36*(2), 145–155. doi:10.2190/ET.36.2.c

Glogoff, S. (2005). Instructional blogging: Promoting interactivity, student-centered learning, and peer input. *Innovate, 1*(5). Retrieved May 23, 2008, from http://www.innovateonline.info/index.php?view=article&id=126

Gunawardena, C. N., Ortegano-Layne, L., Carabajal, K., Frechette, C., Lindemann, K., & Jennings, B. (2006). New model, new strategies: Instructional design for building online wisdom communities. *Distance Education, 27*(2), 217–232. doi:10.1080/01587910600789613

Hutchins, E. (1991). The social organization of distributed cognition. In L.B. Resnick, J.M. Levine, & S.D. Teasley (Eds.), *Perspectives on socially shared cognition* (pp. 283-306). Pittsburgh, PA: Learning Research and Development Center, University of Pittsburgh, American Psychological Association.

Irlbeck, S., Kays, E., Jones, D., & Sims, R. (2006). The Phoenix rising: Emergent models of instructional design. *Distance Education, 27*(2), 171–185. doi:10.1080/01587910600789514

Johnson, E. (2001). *Emergence: The connected lives of ants, brains, and software.* New York: Simon & Schuster.

Johnson, M., & Liber, O. (2008). The personal learning environment and the human condition: From theory to teaching practice. *Interactive Learning Environments, 16*(1), 3–15. doi:10.1080/10494820701772652

Kauffman, D. F. (2004). Self-regulated learning in Web-based environments: instructional tools designed to facilitate cognitive strategy use, metacognitive processing, and motivational beliefs. *Journal of Educational Computing Research, 30*(1), 139–161. doi:10.2190/AX2D-Y9VM-V7PX-0TAD

Kesim, E., & Agaoglu, E. (2007). A paradigm shift in distance education: Web 2.0 and social software. *Turkish Online Journal of Distance Education, 8*(3), 66–75.

Kim, H. N. (2008). The phenomenon of blogs and theoretical model of blog use in educational contexts. *Computers & Education, 51*(3), 1342–1352. doi:10.1016/j.compedu.2007.12.005

Lee, Y. J. (2004). The effect of creating external representations on the efficiency of Web search. *Interactive Learning Environments, 12*(3), 227–250. doi:10.1080/10494820512331383439

Maloney, E. J. (2007, January). What Web 2.0 can teach us about learning. *The Chronicle of Higher Education, 53*(18), B26.

Mashhadi, A. (1998). *Instructional design for the 21st century: Towards a new conceptual framework.* Paper presented at the International Conference on Computers in Education, Beijing, China. (ERIC Document Reproduction Service No. ED429583)

Metallidou, P., & Platsidou, M. (2008). Kolb's learning style inventory-1985: Validity issues and relations with metacognitive knowledge about problem-solving strategies. *Learning and Individual Differences, 18*(1), 114–119. doi:10.1016/j.lindif.2007.11.001

Morrison, G., Ross, S., & Kemp, J. (2004). *Designing effective instruction* (4th ed.). Hoboken, NJ: John Wiley.

Muis, K. R. (2008). Epistemic profiles and self-regulated learning: examining relations in the context of mathematics problem solving. *Contemporary Educational Psychology, 33*(2), 177–208. doi:10.1016/j.cedpsych.2006.10.012

Oliver, R., & Herrington, J. (2003). Exploring technology-mediate learning from a pedagogical perspective. *Interactive Learning Environments, 11*(2), 111–126. doi:10.1076/ilee.11.2.111.14136

Pea, R. (1993). Practices of distributed intelligence and design for education. In G. Salomon (Ed.), *Distributed cognition: Psychological and educational considerations* (pp. 47-86). Cambridge, MA: Cambridge University Press.

Reeve, R. A., & Brown, A. L. (1984). *Metacognition reconsidered: Implications for intervention research.* Cambridge, MA: Bolt Beranek and Newman.

Rogers, P. C., Liddle, S. W., Chan, P., Doxey, A., & Isom, B. (2007). Web 2.0 learning platform: Harnessing collective intelligence. *Turkish Online Journal of Distance Education, 8*(3), 16–33.

Salomon, G. (1993). No distribution without individual's cognition: A dynamic interactional view. In G. Salomon (Ed.), *Distributed cognition: Psychological and educational considerations* (pp. 111-138). Cambridge, MA: Cambridge University Press.

Salter, D., Richards, L., & Carey, T. (2004). The "T5" design model: An instructional model and learning environment to support the integration of online and campus-based courses. *Educational Media International, 41*(3), 207–218. doi:10.1080/09523980410001680824

Schon, D. A. (1983). *The reflective practitioner: How professional think in action.* New York: Basic Books.

Shin, N., Jonassen, D. H., & McGee, S. (2003). Predictors of well-structured and ill-structured problem solving in an astronomy simulation. *Journal of Research in Science Teaching, 40*(1), 6–33. doi:10.1002/tea.10058

Snelbecker, G., Miller, S., & Zheng, R. (2007). Functional relevance and online instructional design. In R. Zheng & S. P. Ferris (Eds.), *Understanding online instructional modeling: Theories and practices* (pp. 1-17). Hershey, PA: IGI Global.

Sorensen, E. K., Takle, E. S., & Moser, H. M. (2006). Knowledge-building quality in online communities of practice: Focusing on learning dialogue. *Studies in Continuing Education, 28*(3), 241–257. doi:10.1080/01580370600947470

Sweller, J. (1988). Cognitive load during problem solving: Effects on learning. *Cognitive Science, 12*, 257–285.

Sweller, J. (2006). How the human cognitive system deals with complexity. In J. Elen & R.E. Clark (Eds.), *Handling complexity in learning environments: Theory and research* (pp. 13-25). Amsterdam: Elsevier.

Sweller, J., & Chandler, P. (1991). Evidence for cognitive load theory. *Cognition and Instruction, 8*(4), 351–362. doi:10.1207/s1532690xci0804_5

Sweller, J., & Chandler, P. (1994). Why some material is difficult to learn. *Cognition and Instruction, 12*(3), 185–233. doi:10.1207/s1532690xci1203_1

Sweller, J., van Merrienboer, J. J. G., & Paas, F. (1998). Cognitive architecture and instructional design. *Educational Psychology Review, 10*(3), 251–296. doi:10.1023/A:1022193728205

Torrance, M., Fidalgo, R., & Garcia, J. (2007). The teachability and effectiveness of cognitive self-regulation in sixth-grade writers. *Learning and Instruction, 17*(3), 265–285. doi:10.1016/j.learninstruc.2007.02.003

Trentin, G. (2008). Learning and knowledge sharing within online communities of professionals: An approach to the evaluation of virtual community environments. *Educational Technology, 48*(3), 32–38.

Tyler, L. E. (1974). *Individual differences: Abilities and motivational directions.* New York: Appleton-Century-Crofts.

van der Stel, M., & Veenman, M. V. J. (2008). Relation between intellectual ability and metacognitive skillfulness as predictors of learning performance of young students performing tasks in different domains. *Learning and Individual Differences, 18*(1), 128–134. doi:10.1016/j.lindif.2007.08.003

van Merrienboer, J. J. G., & Sweller, J. (2005). Cognitive load theory and complex learning: Recent developments and future directions. *Educational Psychology Review, 17*(2), 147–177. doi:10.1007/s10648-005-3951-0

Vygotsky, L. S. (1978). *Mind in society: The development of higher psychological process.* Cambridge, MA: Harvard University Press.

Wang, S. K., & Hsua, H. Y. (2008). Reflections on using blogs to expand in-class discussion. *TechTrends, 52*(3), 81–85. doi:10.1007/s11528-008-0160-y

Wassell, B., & Crouch, C. (2008). Fostering critical engagement in preservice teachers: Incorporating Weblogs into multicultural education. *Journal of Technology and Teacher Education, 16*(2), 211–232.

Wertsch, J. V. (1991). *Voices of the mind: A sociocultural approach to mediated action.* Cambridge, MA: Harvard University Press.

Winn, W. (2006). Functional contextualism in context: A reply to Fox. *Educational Technology Research and Development, 54*(1), 55–59. doi:10.1007/s11423-006-6495-1

Xie, Y., Ke, F., & Sharma, P. (2008). The effect of peer feedback for blogging on college students' reflective learning processes. *The Internet and Higher Education, 11*(1), 18–25. doi:10.1016/j.iheduc.2007.11.001

Young, J. R. (2008, February). Blog comments vs. peer review: Which way makes a book better? *The Chronicle of Higher Education, 54*(21), A20.

Zheng, R. (2007). Understanding the underlying constructs of Webquests. In T. Kidd & H. Song (Eds.), *Handbook of research on instructional systems and technology* (pp. 752-767). Hershey, PA: IGI Global.

Zheng, R., Flygare, J. A., Dahl, L. B., & Hoffman, R. (in press). The impact of individual differences on social communication pattern in online learning. In C. Mourlas, N. Tsianos, & P. Germanakos (Eds.), *Cognitive and emotional processes in Web-based education: Integrating human factors and personalization.* Hershey, PA: IGI Global.

Zimmerman, B. J. (2008). Investigating self-regulation and motivation: Historical background, methodological developments, and future prospects. *American Educational Research Journal, 45*(1), 166–183. doi:10.3102/0002831207312909

Chapter 5
Instructional Strategies for Teaching in Synchronous Online Learning Environments (SOLE)

Marshall G. Jones
Winthrop University, USA

Stephen W. Harmon
Georgia State University, USA

ABSTRACT

This chapter deals centrally with one emerging aspect of Web 2.0 for education, that of the increasing demand for real time and near real-time interaction among users. Whereas most online learning has, to date, taken place in an asynchronous format, there is a growing need for an ability to provide learning opportunities in a synchronous setting. This chapter discusses synchronous online learning environments (SOLEs) and the affordances they present for teaching and learning. Particularly it focuses on a capability of these environments known as ancillary communications. It discusses ancillary communications as an intentional instructional strategy and presents guidelines for its implementation. And, in the spirit of Web 2.0, this chapter was written using the Web 2.0 application Google Docs.

INTRODUCTION

Internet-based classes appear to dominate the landscape of distance education today. Online classes are common place in most colleges and universities and are becoming more common in high schools as well. While pioneering courses were offered through techniques using email, Internet Relay Chat (IRC) or bulletin boards, today's courses are almost all managed by portal systems such as WebCT™, Blackboard's CourseInfo™, or Elluminate™ to name but a few. These systems share many communication features such as bulletin boards, email, chat, whiteboards and assignment drop boxes. As technology advances and bandwidth improves, we see changes in these environments. Today's systems offer audio and video communication tools as well as traditional text based communication. These new tools provide us with a unique opportunity. No longer is an online environment constrained to text for synchronous meetings and packaged media for asynchronous meetings. The environment now affords unique opportunities for communication

DOI: 10.4018/978-1-60566-729-4.ch005

Copyright © 2010, IGI Global. Copying or distributing in print or electronic forms without written permission of IGI Global is prohibited.

patterns that are usually reserved for face-to-face classes, mainly the ability to talk and listen.

Moreover, with the addition of audio and video we are able to add new channels of information to the online environment. Historically there has been much research done on multiple-channel communication and cue summation. Moore, Burton, and Myers (2004) provide an exhaustive review of the literature on both. At the risk of oversimplifying this review, we can say that on the positive side multiple-channels of information may provide greater enrichment in learning. On the negative side it may lead to cognitive overload for learners.

We have studied the use of these communication tools for a number of years (Harmon & Jones, 1999, 2001; Jones & Harmon, 2002, 2006) and found that the implementation of multiple communication channels in an online environment (e.g. audio, text, or whiteboards) may be used to provide redundancy of information and enrichment of material, (in the manner of traditional multiple-channels or cue summation). However, these channels can be used another way as well. They may be used as either a primary communication mode or a supporting communication mode, such as chat supporting audio, or audio supporting whiteboards, or audio supporting chats. When these tools are present, students will use them. We have found that they will certainly use them for personal discussions, such as an updated version of passing notes in class. This can, obviously, be distracting and can cause lack of attention to learning and hinder the ability of an individual learner to focus on class materials. However, when used in a purposeful manner these multiple channels may create increased learner focus and more efficient communication. Moreover, the use of multiple channels of communication may provide instructors a powerful physical manifestation of constructivist learning.

In traditional positivist learning environments the primary instructional communication occurs between the teacher and the students. In constructivist learning environments the primary instructional communication may occur between the instructor and students or between students and students. In either environment the instructional emphasis of the communication is almost wholly on one or the other. We argue that potential learning benefits may accrue if we place more emphasis on the communications that are occurring in a learning environment simultaneously with, but outside the focus of the primary communications. We call the exchange of information in support of learning that occurs synchronously with, but is physically and semantically separate from a primary communication mode *Ancillary Communication*.

RESEARCH FOUNDATIONS FOR ANCILLARY COMMUNICATION

Ancillary Communication as an intentional instructional strategy is based on our ongoing study of an online course we teach on the topic of online learning (Harmon & Jones, 1999, 2001; Jones & Harmon, 2002, 2006). It follows, then, that the design of the course has influenced the development of our definition of Ancillary Communication. To that end, we offer some of the guiding literature we use in designing and refining our course. Our course is based on the discussions of constructivist learning (Jonassen, 1999), situated cognition (Brown, Collins & Duguid, 1989) and anchored instruction (Bransford et al, 1990; Cognition and Technology Group, 1990). The class was set up to be experiential and to create a learning environment that is driven by the learner (Papert, 1980; Wilson & Ryder, 1996; Greening, 1998). Analysis of early offerings of the class (Harmon & Jones, 2001) indicated that students were unprepared for the responsibility of this type experience initially and typically floundered during the early portion of the semester. Today the course employs a pedagogical shift approach, with a more positivist perspective and instructor delivered content early in the semester, to a more constructivist perspective with student generated content and instructor guidance later in the semester. This shift allows the students to quickly gain confidence in the online environment and master the fundamental knowledge and skills they will need to succeed later on, while still affording them the benefits usually conferred by a student-centered learning environment (i.e. greater motivation and enhanced transfer) (Land, S. & Hannafin, M., 2001). This is particularly important since motivation has been found to be a key component for successful online learning (Kawachi, 2003).

This work draws heavily upon a taxonomy of web-based instruction developed by Harmon and Jones (1999), research focusing on analyzing learner interaction in online classes (Harmon & Jones, 2001; Jones & Harmon, 2006) and discourse patterns in online discussions (Mcklin, Harmon, Jones & Evans, 2002). Additionally it is related to the foundational research in communications theory (Schramm, 1961; Shannon & Weaver, 1964) and multiple-channel communication and cue summation (Moore, Burton, & Myers, 2004).

WEB 2.0, LEARNING, AND ANCILLARY COMMUNICATION

For centuries the teacher was seen as the center of epistemological authority in the classroom. Information entered the classroom largely, if not solely through the teacher. Either he or she directly imparted information to the students, or vetted content provided by others such as textbooks and readings. As other avenues of information dissemination evolved, the teacher's hold on learners began to weaken. The rise of constructivism acknowledged that different learners created knowledge in different ways. The Internet gave learners access to far more information than ever before. Savvy teachers realized this and began changing the way they taught. The well known

aphorism "sage on the stage" gave way to the now well-known aphorism "guide on the side." In the earliest applications of the Internet in the classroom this was often manifested by teachers facilitating learners' exploration of content instead of providing them with vetted content. But even this exploration of multiple and varying perspectives that exist on the Internet had its limitations. And the most significant limitation was that most of that content still originated from a limited number of sources and the students themselves had little opportunity to engage with or add to the content that they were discovering on the Internet. Despite the increased access to information, the overall model of Internet use in teaching and learning was still remarkably similar to traditional classroom learning: learners were still seen as information consumers. This circumstance was reflected in the practice of many Internet service providers who allotted customers substantially more bandwidth for downloading than for uploading (Moran, 2007). The major difference that the Internet made in learning and instruction is that the teacher was now no longer able to vet all of the information coming in to the classroom. Students were still consumers of information.

With the rise of what has been called Web 2.0 the paradigm of students as consumers of information has begun to change. We are still in the nascent stages of Web 2.0 in education, but already we are beginning to see the impact (Alexander, 2006). Web 2.0 is centered on the concept of user generated content. Instead of the majority of Internet users being consumers of information coming from a limited number of sources, Web 2.0 is currently in a state where there is increased parity between consumption and production of information by users. Just as desktop publishing software and laser printers allowed everyone to have the equivalent of his or her own printing press in the 1990's, the tool sets and protocols of Web 2.0 allow everyone to have not only his or her own publishing company, but rather, if you prefer, his or her own broadcast network.

When applied to education, the user-created content aspect of Web 2.0 has been referred to as Learning 2.0 (Brown & Adler, 2008). In an educational setting this changes the traditional model of students as consumers of information to one where students are producers of information. The content creation and collaboration tools of Web 2.0 give students the ability to interact and form communities of practice (Wenger, 1998; Alexander, 2006) like never before. This, in turn, opens up a range of instructional and learning strategies that have not been easily accessible in the classroom. These strategies have the potential to achieve real advances in education and training. According to Brown & Adler (2008),

The most profound impact of the Internet, an impact that has yet to be fully realized, is its ability to support and expand the various aspects of social learning. What do we mean by 'social learning?' Perhaps the simplest way to explain this concept is to note that social learning is based on the premise that our understanding of content is socially constructed through conversations about that content and through grounded interactions, especially with others, around problems or actions. The focus is not so much on what we are learning but on how we are learning. (Brown & Adler, 2008, p.2)

That is the heart of Learning 2.0, the promise of Web 2.0 for education, and the compelling rationale for Ancillary Communication as an instructional strategy. Besides just sounding like a good idea, there is a sound theoretical underpinning for this concept. On the surface, the notion of students creating content may not seem like a good idea. Students, almost by definition, are novices in whatever content they are studying. If they already knew the content there would be no need for them to learn it. But, if they do not know the content, how can they create it? Presumably their fellow students will be learning from the content they create. This seems like it could lead

to the widespread adoption of fallacies and fact. Imagine a student of brain-surgery making up his or her own content and other brain-surgery students adopting it in practice. Most of us would decide to choose another group of surgeons or forgo the operation entirely if our brain-surgeons were trained this way. Where then, is the benefit in student-generated content?

As noted above, it is the act of generating the content that has value. Papert (1991) advocated a similar notion in his work on *constructionism*. Constructionism is the idea that students learn by building something in a public context. There is still a roll for the teacher, only it is not as a disseminator of knowledge, but as a quality control agent, who insures that the knowledge created is consistent with current and generally accepted thought on the topic, or in the case of some states, with whatever the state standards happen to say is accurate. The fact that students create this concept in collaboration also resonates with the social constructivism theory of Vygotsky (1978). Reality is a shared social construct. It is, in effect, whatever we agree it is. The earth may not be flat but the world is, if you get our drift. Vygotsky held that we learn by creating this reality and negotiating meaning. There is perhaps no better example of this than the Web 2.0 space, Wikipedia. In Wikipedia users come together to negotiate the official entry for any given topic. One has only to follow the discussions that occur behind the main entry page to see that in most cases the negotiation of meaning that occurs typically results in all participants coming away with a richer, more nuanced understanding of the topic.

While most Web 2.0, and therefore Learning 2.0 tools, are asynchronous, there is a growing trend for more real-time interaction. The growth of social networking services like Twitter and Spoink, and of instant messaging services like AOL's AIM or Windows Live Messenger point to a desire on the part of users for more synchronous interaction. While education has traditionally been synchronous (face to face classes), elearning has traditionally been asynchronous (content modules and bulletin board based discussions). The tools did not exist, or were not readily accessible to allow for synchronous online teaching and learning. In the last few years, however, that has changed. Today a wide variety of platforms exist that allow us to take advantage of what we know about synchronous instruction, combine it with what we have learned about asynchronous instruction, and create new learning environments online. The trick is figuring out how to use this new capability in ways that maximize its effectiveness. We have been attempting to do just that.

TEACHING AND LEARNING WITH SOLE

Since 1998 we have been preparing professional educators for work with online learning by teaching an online class on the subject of online learning. Two sections taught at two different universities are joined together to study the theories behind online learning and to experience an online class from a variety of different perspectives. This recursive opportunity appealed to us and seemed to present an exciting challenge and advantage: we could provide learners with a realistic way to study online learning in an online environment and we could study the environment to contribute to the body of knowledge in the field on online learning.

The goal of the class was to provide students with both a realistic web-based course and experience in designing, developing, using, and evaluating realistic web-based courses. It was designed to be a multi-site distance education class with half the class in one location, and half the class in another distant location thus creating a realistic distance education environment. Since the topic and the delivery mechanism were essentially the same, it seemed that situated cognition (Brown, Collins & Duguid, 1989) and anchored instruction (Bransford et al, 1990; Cognition and Technology

Group, 1990), might apply to the design of this particular course.

To study the class we used qualitative methodologies such as interviews, observations, and document analysis. Data is generated through public and private chats, bulletin boards, emails, transcripts of team meetings, formal and informal interviews (both online and face to face) and an analysis of student projects. A single class tends to generate an enormous amount of data (a typical course offering can be in excess of 4,000 printed pages of data from bulletin board postings and chat logs and over 30 hours of recorded class interactions). This data was analyzed using constant comparative analysis (Glaser & Strauss, 1967). During subsequent offerings of the class we were able to identify specific phenomenon to study and were able to combine constant comparative analysis with analytic induction (Patton, 1990). Research results, including more details on data collection and analysis on many of these course offerings may be found at Harmon and Jones (1999, 2001) and Jones and Harmon (2002, 2006).

ANCILLARY COMMUNICATION

Historically the class has been offered through a portal system such as WebCT™ or CourseInfo™. Consequently our communication tools were bulletin boards, email, and drop boxes for asynchronous meetings and IRC for synchronous meetings. During 2004 we added a course system called Elluminate™ which provided two way audio communications between students and students, faculty and students, and faculty and faculty. The system provided space for posting packaged PowerPoint™ presentations and also provided the ability to break students into small groups in the synchronous meetings and provide them with audio tools and whiteboard space for group work during class meetings. As instructors we were able to see all communications in the class, even those that were "private" to the students. Students were given problems during class, such as doing the front end analysis for a web-site for a client, in a small group and then brought back together with the larger class to present their findings. Student interactions and discourse using these tools and strategies were analyzed both at the small group level and the whole class level. Initially we found that these tools were not technically difficult for people to use, but that students were not clear on *why* they should use them and *how* they could be best used. Through the use of recursive data analysis we began to develop strategies to use these new tools. What we found was that they were best used when one communication tool or mode was used to support the other.

During a typical course interaction, such as a student presentation, a dominant mode might arise. For example, a small group's white board (a visual mode) might be perceived to be the dominant mode. To support this, students may explain it using an ancillary mode, such as the audio functions, (a verbal - audio mode) while taking questions from faculty and other students through another ancillary mode, the chat window (a verbal - text mode). The dominant and Ancillary Communication modes might change without notice, but participants in the system were able to recognize and adapt to this almost immediately. They were then able to use Ancillary Communication modes to support the dominant mode. Consequently, audio was used to support whiteboards and vice versa depending on which mode was perceived to be dominant. At no point was one mode stated to be dominant. The class appeared to be able to develop and instantly manifest a shared understanding of which mode is dominant and which mode is ancillary.

But what we found most interesting was that people were not confused by the tools or by what sounds like a barrage of information. They were actually engaged by the communication and able to make sense out of multiple streams of information coming at them at one time. Evidence of this is found both in their test scores and in the quality

and quantity of their interactions. Consequently, data from the study suggests initially that this is more than enrichment or cue summation, especially since the Ancillary Communications often varied widely from the content being discussed in the primary channel. These communication tools are seen by participants as being interconnected in one sense, but separate in another. Therefore their mutual support of each other makes them unique and allows us to focus on their use as an intentional instructional strategy.

LEARNER INTERACTIONS IN A SOLE

Generally, we found that students in the course interact in a manner consistent with the types of interaction noted by Miltiadou & Savenye (2003). Learner-content interactions occur when students in the course work directly with course materials. These types of interactions are perhaps the most common when viewed from the perspective of time on task, both in traditional and online environments. Reading a text book or website, researching a paper, or working through a tutorial would all be examples of learner content interaction. This type of interaction can occur concurrently with Ancillary Communications and frequently does so in our classes.

Learner-instructor interactions occur when the student works directly with the instructor. These types of interactions are also very common in both traditional and online classes, but may frequently be characterized by a greater flow of information in pedagogical approaches that view the instructor as content provider. Interestingly, direct learner-instructor interactions may be less common in the type of eLearning environments that have come to dominate education with the advent of course management systems (CMS). While in traditional CMS learner-instructor interaction typically occurs both on bulletin boards and in chat rooms, there is also a greater prevalence of stand alone instruction in which there is little or no direct learner-instructor interaction.

In SOLE's however, we found there to be copious and intense learner-instructor interaction. Indeed, we found the level of learner-instructor interaction to frequently exceed that which is found in a face-to-face environment. We have noted four sub-categories of learner-instructor interaction in this environment.

1. In the first sub-category the instructor is communicating with the entire class at once through audio and visual channels. This sub-category interaction may be most easily thought of as an instructor presenting a lecture via PowerPoint. Note though, that while this is the easiest way to characterize the interaction, it is also a bit misleading since pure lecture is a technique we try to employ rarely, preferring instead a more interactive form of discourse.

2. The second sub-category of learner-instructor interaction occurs when the instructor is communicating with the class as a whole through the chat window. This type of interaction is a central component of the discussion of Ancillary Communication we are presenting.

3. The third sub-category of learner-instructor interaction occurs with the instructor communicating with an individual student or a small group of students privately in the chat window. By privately we mean that the communication is not seen by the class as a whole, only by the intended recipients.

4. The fourth type of sub-category is what we refer to as a pseudo-private communication, in which the instructor communicates with the class as a whole via the chat window, but does so as a private communication. This means that each recipient may think that the communication was intended only for him or her even though in fact the entire class got the same communication.

The third type of interaction noted by Miltiadou & Savenye (2003) is learner-learner interaction. This occurs when learners communicate directly with each other. This type of interaction may occur in traditional classrooms, particularly those that are set up along constructivist lines, or may occur perhaps surreptitiously in a classroom set up with a direct instruction format. In a traditional online classroom, this type of interaction may occur more often than in a traditional face to face classroom, particularly with student interaction that might occur on a discussion board, or in a chat room. We observed that like learner-instructor interaction, there are sub-categories for this type of interaction in the virtual classroom. These include, learners communicating with the class as a whole via audio and visual channels; learners communicating with the class as a whole via the chat window; and learners communicating with other individual or small groups of learner's via private chat. Note that in both the learner-instructor, and the learner-learner sub-categories we suppose that there could be an additional category of accidental communications, in which either the learner or the instructor sends a private message that was supposed to the public, or more commonly, a public message that was intended to be private. For the purposes of this chapter we will not consider these unintentional communications.

The fourth type of interaction noted by Miltiadou & Savenye (2003) is learner-interface interaction. Unlike the other three types of interaction which may have learning as their primary purpose, learner-interface interaction has as its primary purpose the enabling of the other types of interactions. While it may be possible to design online learning environments in which the interface itself is intended as a mechanism to enhance instruction and learning, we know of no course management system or virtual classroom environment in which this is the case.

AFFORDANCES OF ANCILLARY COMMUNICATION

It has been well documented in the literature that media do not themselves influence learning (Clark, 1994). It makes no difference whether instruction is delivered via a book, or a film strip, via a computer or via a television. In study after study it has been shown that it is not a medium itself that makes a difference in learning outcomes, it is the instructional strategy that is employed. If that is the case, then why should we use one medium instead of another? Why use a rather expensive medium, such as a computer, instead of a relatively inexpensive medium, such as a newspaper? The answer is because different media have different capabilities for delivering instruction. Televisions can do things that newspapers can't and computers can do things that neither televisions nor newspapers can. The key to using technology successfully in instruction is to identify the unique capabilities of the technology and employ them in ways that are most advantageous to their strengths and least prone to their weaknesses. Another term used in discussing the capability of media is the term affordances. An affordance is a potential for action that exists in a given object or technology (Gibson, 1977; Norman 1988). Different media afford us the ability to do different things. Text affords us the ability to rapidly peruse a lot of information in a highly abstract form. Video affords us the ability to fairly rapidly evoke strong emotional response in viewers. If we are to improve education overall we must be able to determine the affordances of new technologies and create effective instructional strategies that use them. Synchronous online learning environments afford us new capabilities that did not exist or would be difficult to implement in a traditional classroom. One of these capabilities, or affordances, is Ancillary Communication.

Ancillary Communication can be difficult to implement. This may be due to its relative infancy as an instructional strategy or to the fact that it requires facility with online tools, such as reading and responding to chat messages quickly while still maintaining the flow of a verbal discussion. Imagine sitting in front of your computer and speaking to your class room of twenty students while they all ask questions at once. To read and process all of this information takes patience and practice. It is a skill that a growing number of students implement quite effortlessly in daily communication, but one that has not been commonly used instructionally. We have worked almost exclusively in a multi-instructor environment which has made it somewhat easier. While one of us speaks, the other can manage the questions from the students. Instructors new to SOLEs and Ancillary Communication may want to get some help to implement them. Using a team teaching approach or a graduate or teaching assistant should prove beneficial.

It is also possible to designate individual students in a class to serve as teaching assistants during the class to help with the management of the environment. This rotating assistant arrangement can both solve the problem of dealing with potential information overload and also increase student engagement. Additionally it has the added benefit that students seem to be sympathetic to their peers working as teaching assistants, thus creating a greater level of collegiality in the classroom. Groups of students may work as assistants during the class to actually present course material by themselves or with the instructor, thus creating a unique constructivist environment.

Ancillary Communication harnesses the increased facility students have with both experiential cognition (Norman, 1988) and online tools to provide greater focus on learning goals and instructional tasks. We find that students use video game like speed to ask and answer questions in class. Ancillary Communication appears to be a way for us to harness this new set of skills students bring to class based on their non-academic use of Instant Messaging and "Googling" for answers during a discussion. But let us be clear:

we found that students were using this quick reaction and quick response in instructionally meaningful ways.

Because Ancillary Communication can be so intense, we recommend blending the synchronous online class with an asynchronous component as well. This allows instructors to balance the fast paced experiential cognition of the environment with more reflective cognition activities (Norman, 1988). For both students and instructors in our graduate level course, two hours appears to be the maximum amount of time one can spend in a SOLE using Ancillary Communication without losing focus or becoming overly fatigued. Our examination of Ancillary Communication has yielded the following affordances. Below we discuss the development of our understanding of how these affordances can be used.

Community and Shared Experience

The addition of audio to an online classroom appeared to provide a greater sense of community and shared experience with the students and the instructors. Because so many classes are built, traditionally, on a model of teacher talking and students listening, the addition of audio to an online class made it fell "like a real class," as one participant put it. Having the ability to hear the professor and your fellow students talking lessened the sense of isolation in the online classroom. Students reported feeling more connected and indeed a greater sense of collegiality was noted in course offerings using audio than in offerings in the past. We have always required weekly synchronous meetings, historically in text only chat rooms. And while meeting regularly has more of a "real class" feel than a completely asynchronous class, the addition of audio appeared to be the variable for increased community building. Examples of community building are included in other findings below.

Shared Work Space

The use of whiteboards as a shared work space on which to think as a group provided richer interactions between students than text chats alone. In previous offerings of the class it was possible to break students into small groups to have them do small group discussions. We have recommended the use of smaller chat communities as a method of increasing student interactions in the past (Jones & Harmon 2002). But the addition of a shared workspace increased the amount of interaction. For example as students worked on the problem of creating motivational strategies for a piece of online instruction in a chat window they could write down what they thought. When they returned to present their work to the entire class they could tell people what they did through the use of text in a chat window. But the addition of the white board gave them someplace to hold the information while they discussed it. It also provided them with something tangible to refer to during their presentations. We like to think of it as the digital equivalent of a student generated flip chart. The result was greater engagement in small group work and more concrete representations of abstract thoughts during in class presentations.

Chat Window Summaries

The use of chat windows to summarize what the speaker is saying grew naturally out of the environment. The novelty effect of using a microphone for live audio was significant initially, to be sure. Both instructors and the students relished the idea of being able to talk instead of type during synchronous meetings. The way the system works, only one person was able to talk at a time. Students are given microphone "privileges" by the instructor, but only one person can talk at a time. During one presentation, while one instructor spoke, the other instructor began to summarize what the other was saying in the chat window because a student was having problems with audio. What was unexpected was that students who had audio found the summaries not to be distracting, but helpful. The instructor who was typing in the chat window could not provide a full transcript of the audio, so he would shorten and summarize and at times add more detail or a different perspective than that being presented by the speaker. Watching the instructor do this seemed to provide the students permission to do much the same thing.

Students began to use the chat window to ask questions while the instructor spoke, and the instructors used the questions to shape the direction of their comments. While the instructors modeled this technique originally, the students were coming to the same conclusion at the same time. While the novelty effect of using audio initially made the audio the "best" way of communicating, or the primary communication mode, if you will, the use of chat as a way to supplement audio or to communicate when the microphone was not available elevated the use of text chats in the eyes of the students. Soon the use of chats became not just a secondary mode of communication but actually rivaled the use of audio. In a current course offering students seemed to prefer the use of chatting to the use of audio as a way of making their thoughts heard. We suspicion that one reason that text based communication is so popular for students today is because of their familiarity and facility with online communication tools such as IM and mobile phone based text chats.

Increase in Collegiality

Ancillary Communication through the use of the chats provided people with the ability to comment at will, make jokes, and generally increased the collegiality of the class from past offerings. If a presenter, either a professor or a student, made a joke, or a malapropism, the chat window would light up with people commenting that they were "LOL" (laughing out loud) or "ROFL" (rolling on the floor laughing). Students used the private

messaging feature to pass notes to each other and to discuss things off topic, to be sure, but they also used the private messaging feature to ask each other questions that were on topic. Because students and professors were able to comment at will while someone was speaking it created an atmosphere that was not only conducive for sharing information, but it actually demanded that people share information. The use of the chat windows increased engagement, and this engagement in turn increased the quantity and quality of the communication.

The collegiality seemed to help in the building of community as well. If you are a regular reader and commenter of a blog you have witnessed this type of collegiality. And as people got to know each other better, both personally and academically, the level of trust and collegiality increased.

Manifesting Understanding

The use of chat windows for Ancillary Communication allowed students to manifest their cognitive processes instantly. This thinking out loud, if you will, provided the instructors in an online class with a tool that is often cited as a benefit of face to face instruction but typically not found in face to face classes. In a face to face class, instructors often talk about being able to "see the eyes" of their students. This lets a teacher know that person is on task or "gets it," if you will. Because one mode of communication is happening through audio, the ancillary mode of chat provides a remarkable opportunity to get instant feedback from the learners. And because the learner must write what they are thinking it leaves little doubt as to whether they "get it" or not. Additionally Ancillary Communication allowed the students to explore aspects of the course content not covered in the primary instructional communication mode, and thus potentially enhanced their motivation and understanding. Students were able to use the ancillary mode of communication to make comments that contributed to their private understanding of

Table 1. Methods of ancillary communication

1. Agree-disagree
2. Elaborate
3. Diverge
4. Scaffolding
5. Reiterate
6. Emphasis
7. Show relevance of
8. Social Engineering

the material in a public way. Because of this their private thoughts became public and these public thoughts helped provide other learners with examples the professors were not able to provide. Faculty soon began to use private and public communication intentionally as a way to further the benefits of Ancillary Communication.

METHODS OF ANCILLARY COMMUNICATION

Using Ancillary Communication in an online environment can be made more concrete through the application of one or more method as listed in Table 1 and discussed in the narrative below.

While there are many potential methods emerging from our work in employing Ancillary Communication in synchronous online learning, we will review eight of these that we have used and refined in our own work. We note at the outset that our circumstances may be a bit uncommon in that we are fortunate to have two instructors present in the classroom at the same time. The methods of Ancillary Communication we employ typically take the form of one instructor being responsible for the primary communication which is occurring in audio and visual channels, and the other instructor responsible for the Ancillary Communication which occurs in the chat window. It is possible to use students in the role of ancillary or primary instructor as well. For example, during student presentations or student led discussions the instructor of record can play the role of ancillary instructor. And with proper planning, students can serve in a predetermined ancillary role while the instructor of record serves as the primary instructor.

Agree-Disagree

Description: In the first method the ancillary instructor either agrees or disagrees with what the primary instructor is saying via the audio channel. The intention is to either affirm the content, and thus add weight to it, or to stimulate discussion and more critical thought by disagreeing with the primary instructor.

Example and Discussion: We found that it is often startling for the students to see two instructors disagree with each other in front of the class. In our environment we have two authority figures who are disagreeing with each other, and this is a powerful statement in a class. The disagreement forces students to think more deeply about the content and to come to some resolution as to their own perspective. We began using this method after we noticed that students frequently view a communication from the instructor as the final word on a subject. We found that, particularly on discussion boards, one of the quickest ways to end a discussion is to have one of the instructors offer an opinion on the matter. In a single instructor classroom you can still provide for disagreement with some preparation and planning. It is possible to have a student play the disagreement role as well. While this often happens organically in classes, you can also prepare for it by "planting" a student. This technique requires that that student is well prepared to play their role convincingly, but it also opens the door for other students to disagree with the professor during a synchronous class meeting. We found in practice that we typically disagree little with each other. Therefore in order to use this technique it is necessary for one of us to play devil's advocate, but do so in a manner that is convincing to the students.

Elaborate

Description: In this technique the ancillary instructor elaborates on the primary instructor's point. Providing further information in a chat window while a primary instructor speaks, the ancillary instructor is both adding to the depth of the discussion and at times adding details that may have been left out of the initial presentation.

Example and Discussion: Consistent with Reigeluth's elaboration theory of instruction (Reigeluth & Stein, 1983), we found it helpful to provide elaboration on both a macro and micro level. That is to say, the ancillary instructor offers comments that place the primary instructor's point in a broad context. For example, in a discussion on the problems related to the perception of rigor and quality in online learning, the ancillary instructor may broaden the discussion by adding a discussion on pre-Internet distance education classes in order to provide context to online learning. Providing learners with greater detail in this manner is intended to provide macro level support for learners. Of course there are also times when it is important to zoom in for a more micro focus on a particular aspect of the primary instructor's point. For example, in a discussion on the affordance of particular media types in online learning, an ancillary instructor may provide details on the advantages of a media type, such as digital audio files, in the chat window while the primary instructor is discussing how they work.

Diverge

Description: Discussions are presented by the ancillary instructor in a manner that has the initial appearance of being unrelated to the primary instructor's main content object. Ultimately, the divergence is reconnected to the initial point, but the divergence creates a memorable, unique manifestation of the primary instructor's main content object.

Example and Discussion: This technique, drawn from work in creativity theory, consists of having the ancillary instructor offer comments that may initially not seem related to the primary instructor's comments. We find this technique to be most helpful when we are trying to get students to think about unfamiliar concepts in a new way. For example, in our class there is a classic and long running joke about sardines causing chickenpox. The story goes that after eating sardines as a child, the instructor got the chickenpox. The instructor goes on to tell the class, in a long winded, often hilarious story, how he made the faulty causal relationship that eating sardines causes chicken pox and how the mention of sardines can still make him scratch at phantom pox. This seemingly unrelated story is told during a discussion of semantic network theory, illustrating how learners can make their own connections between seemingly disparate pieces of information. It has both the effect of providing a memorable example and providing an initial impression that the instructor may have lost the thread of the discussion in an almost embarrassing manner. But it works. It is a difficult technique to employ skillfully. With too much divergence the students may become confused and lose track of the main content object. However, we have achieved good results by having the ancillary instructor begin the divergence and, after some time for reflection, the primary instructor show the relevance of the divergence to the main content object. It is also a technique that can be employed in a single instructor classroom by having the instructor diverge intentionally, making sure, of course, that they make it back to the main point.

Scaffolding

Description: Scaffolding in SOLE is similar to scaffolding in traditional classrooms. A teacher may begin by providing support to the student by demonstrating a technique or modeling a process. The instructor then begins to shift the responsibility to the learner to do the entire procedure themselves.

Example and Discussion: If an instructor can show up for class with five different, unique, and relevant examples of a difficult concept, then anyone in the class can learn the new concept. The key is providing examples that are relevant to a wide array of learners and learning styles. The problem is that most of us have only one really good example, and when the learners don't understand it we simply repeat the same example again, only louder and slower. Scaffolding is an attempt to help provide support for learners who may be having problems understanding an example. In this technique while the primary instructor presents a difficult concept the ancillary instructor assists the class in comprehending the topic by providing both the subordinate skills necessary to comprehend the topic, and relevant examples and non examples that may assist in understanding. The ancillary instructor may also answer individual student's questions either publicly or privately depending on how relevant they seem to the class as a whole.

Reiterate

Description: This brief technique occurs when the ancillary instructor reiterates a point the primary instructor is making. We use it mainly for emphasis and to increase focus on particularly important points. In reiteration, we typically try to use the exact language that was used by the primary instructor.

Example and Discussion: One way to do this is to prepare a detailed outline of the presentation in a class. While the primary instructor talks about the topic, the ancillary instructor is literally copying from the outline and pasting into the chat window. This is particularly useful when dealing with definitions or complicated descriptions. It is a technique, when used judiciously, which can help people who may need to see and hear what is going on at the same time. It is also a

technique that can be used quite easily with a student assistant during class, or even by a single instructor. The addition of an ancillary instructor may mean that you can combine reiteration with scaffolding to meet many learning needs in a single class session.

Emphasis

Description: Another technique we use frequently is to either emphasize or occasionally de-emphasize points the primary instructor has made. In this technique an ancillary instructor may emphasize a point made by a primary instructor or a student in a discussion. By highlighting a useful comment or suggestion in the chat window the ancillary instructor can draw attention to salient points that may help the entire class.

Example and Discussion: Unlike reiteration emphasis typically does not use the same language as the primary instructor. Additionally the emphasis may be applied to a student comment as easily as it may be applied to a primary instructor's comment. It may take the form of approbation such as "Good point; that's very important." De-emphasis occurs less frequently but is used when students may have a tendency to place too much importance on a particular point.

Relevance

Description: The ancillary instructor makes explicit the reasons why the learners should know and be able to use the content under discussion. (Note that "because it's on a test" is not a generally acceptable reason.)

Example and Discussion: If you have ever been a student in a classroom you have at some point in your educational career been deeply involved in a lesson and found yourself wondering "what's the point?" While hopefully there typically is a point, it is sometimes difficult for learners, particularly those in the beginning stages of learning a particular content, to understand the relevance of the topic under study. (Over three decades later, one of the authors is still struggling to find the relevance of some of his high school calculus classes.) We frequently find it helpful for the ancillary instructor to make explicit the relevance of the content. Even more helpful is for the ancillary instructor to guide the class in providing their own examples of the relevance of the content during the primary instruction. We have considered, but not yet attempted, having the ancillary instructor work through all phases of Keller's (1987) ARCS model at appropriate points in a lesson.

Social Engineering

Description: Social engineering involves modifying the emotional state of the class to best fit the instructional purposes of the lesson. It is not as Machiavellian as it sounds.

Example and Discussion: In this category we include any attempt by the ancillary instructor to help set the tone or mood of the class. This might include adding humor to the content, building confidence in the learners (as in the manner of emphasis), or perhaps creating tension in the class (as in the manner of agree-disagree). In other words, social engineering involves modifying the emotional state of the class to best fit the instructional purposes of the lesson. One example of how we do this is when we are discussing rules for course interactions in an online class. We will send a private message to everyone in the class telling them that they are not participating enough. Everyone gets the same message at once, and it has the desired effect of creating mass confusion. The chat window will be scrolling by too quickly to read as people race to make sure they are participating enough. We intentionally try to overwhelm them in order to make the point that there probably should be some rules. We then engage them in the process of writing those rules for the class. The exercise provides a common experience for everyone to reference throughout the class.

CONCLUSION

We can expect new communications technologies and increases in bandwidth to be upon us quickly. While the time shifting capability of asynchronous instruction ensures that it will remain in use for the perceivable future, it also appears that the growing ubiquity of computing resources will increase the demand for more synchronous online learning opportunities. Rapid growth in real time or near real time communications technologies seems to indicate a preference among Internet users for immediate feedback and interaction. New and emerging technologies continue to make this interaction not only feasible, but also inexpensive and easy. If we are to take advantage of the affordances of this technology then we need to be experimenting with it, and applying what we already know about teaching and learning to its use for instruction. We propose that purposefully including Ancillary Communications as an instructional strategy in online courses may enhance retention and transfer of content, and increase student motivation and instructor feedback.

Much has been written about teaching in asynchronous online classrooms (Schank, 2007; Denigris & Witchel, 2000). This paper seeks to add to the nascent but growing body of research on synchronous online learning tools and strategies (Foreman, 2003; Cheng-Chang, 2005). The need for strategies that deal specifically with synchronous online learning is great. Students in these classes may bring with them both online communication skills and needs that are foreign to many instructors. The tools are easy enough to learn, but strategies to use them effectively in SOLEs should be developed, analyzed and disseminated. Indeed, in a SOLE it is not only possible but quite simple to present one's PowerPoints and lecture, allowing for the occasional student question, and thus perpetuate the much maligned lecture format through another generation of technology. While this approach would be easy, it misses the opportunity to take advantage of the truly significant affordances of synchronous online learning environments. And perhaps worse, it opens the door for critics of instructional technologies to point out how ineffective they can be. Ancillary Communication in SOLEs gives us one opportunity to avoid that fate.

REFERENCES

Alexander, B. (2006). Web 2.0: A new wave of innovation for teaching and learning? *EDUCAUSE Review, 41*(2), 32–44.

Bransford, J. D., Sherwood, R. D., Hasselbring, T. S., Kinzer, C. K., & Williams, S. M. (Eds.). (1990). *Anchored instruction: Why we need it and how technology can help.* Hillsdale, NJ: Lawrence Erlbaum.

Brown, J. S., & Adler, R. P. (2008). Minds on fire: Open education, the long tail, and learning 2.0. *EDUCAUSE Review, 43*(1), 16–32.

Brown, J. S., Collins, A., & Duguid, P. (1989). Situated cognition and the culture of learning. *Educational Researcher, 18*(1), 32–42.

Cheng-Chang, S. P., & Sullivan, M. (2005). Promoting synchronous interaction in an elearning environment. *T.H.E. Journal,* (September). Retrieved from http://www.thejournal.com/articles/17377

Clark, R. (1994). Media will never influence learning. *Educational Technology Research and Development, 42*(2), 21–29. doi:10.1007/BF02299088

Cognition and Technology Group at Vanderbilt. (1990). Anchored instruction and its relationship to situated cognition. *Educational Researcher, 19*(6), 2–10.

DeNigris, J., & Witchel, A. (2000). *How to teach and train online.* Needham Heights, MA: Pearson.

Foreman, J. (2003). Distance learning and synchronous interaction. *The Technology Source,* (July/August). Retrieved from http://ts.mivu.org/default.asp?show=article&id=1034

Gibson, J. J. (1977). The theory of affordances. In R. Shaw & J. Bransford (Eds.), *Perceiving, acting, and knowing.* Hillsdale, NJ: Erlbaum.

Glaser, B. G., & Strauss, A. L. (1967). *The discovery of grounded theory: Strategies for qualitative research.* New York: Aldine.

Greening, A. (1998). WWW support of student learning: A case study. *Australian Journal of Educational Technology, 14*(1), 49–59.

Harmon, S. W., & Jones, M. G. (1999). The five levels of Web use in education: Factors to consider in planning an online course. *Educational Technology, 39*(6), 28–32.

Harmon, S. W., & Jones, M. G. (2001). An analysis of situated Web-based instruction. *Educational Media International, 38*(4), 271–280. doi:10.1080/09523980110105123

Jonassen, D. H. (1999). Designing constructivist learning environments. In C. M. Reigeluth (Ed.), *Instructional design theories and models: Their current state of the art* (2nd ed.). Mahwah, NJ: Lawrence Erlbaum Associates.

Jones, M. G., & Harmon, S. W. (2002). What professors need to know about technology to assess online student learning. *New Directions for Teaching and Learning, Fall*(91), 19-30.

Jones, M. G., & Harmon, S. W. (2006). Ancillary communication as an intentional instructional strategy in online learning environments. In M. Simonson & M. Crawford (Eds.), *Proceedings of the 2006 international conference of the Association of Educational Communications and Technology* (Vol. 2, pp. 194-199).

Kawachi, P. (2003). Initiating intrinsic motivation in online education: Review of the current state of the art. *Interactive Learning Environments, 11*(1), 59–82. doi:10.1076/ilee.11.1.59.13685

Keller, J. M. (1987). The systematic process of motivational design. *Performance and Instruction, 26*(9/10), 1–8.

Land, S., & Hannafin, M. (2001). Student-centered learning environments. In D. Jonassen & S. Land (Eds.), *Theoretical foundations of learning environments* (pp. 1-23). Mahwah, NJ: Lawrence Erlbaum Associates.

Mcklin, T., Harmon, S. W., Jones, M. G., & Evans, W. (2002). Cognitive engagement in Web-based learning: A content analysis of student's online discussions. In M. Crawford & M. Simonson (Eds.), *Proceedings of the 2001 international conference of the Association of Educational Communications and Technology* (Vol. 1, pp. 272-277).

Miltiadou, M., & Savenye, W. C. (2003). Applying social cognitive constructs of motivation to enhance student success in online distance education. *Educational Technology Review, 11*(1), 78–95.

Moore, D. M., Burton, J. K., & Myers, R. J. (2004). Multiple-channel communication: The theoretical and research foundations of multimedia. In D. H. Jonassen (Ed.), *Handbook of research on educational communications and technology* (2nd ed.) (pp. 981-1005). Mahwah, NJ: Lawrence Erlbaum Associates.

Moran, J. (2007). *Battling the upstream bottleneck of broadband connections: How fast does your data swim upstream?* Retrieved August 29, 2008, from http://cws.internet.com/article/3541-.htm

Norman, D. (1988). *The design of everyday things.* New York: Doubleday.

Papert, S. (1980). *Mindstorms.* New York: Basic Books.

Papert, S. A., & Harel, I. (1991). *Constructionism.* Norword, NJ: Ablex Publishing

Patton, M. Q. (1990). *Qualitative evaluation and research.* Beverly Hills, CA: Sage.

Reigeluth, C. M., & Stein, F. S. (1983). The elaboration theory of instruction In W. Schramm (Ed.), *The process and effects of mass communication* (pp. 5-6). Urbana, IL: The University of Illinois Press.

Schank, R. C. (2007). The story-centered curriculum. *eLearn, 4*(April).

Shannon, C. F., & Weaver, W. (1964). *The mathematical theory of communication.* Urbana, IL: The University of Illinois Press. Torrance, E. P. (1985). *Creative motivation scale: Norms technical manual.* Bensenville, IL: Scholastic Testing Service.

Vygotsky, L. S. (1978). *Mind in society.* Cambridge, MA: Harvard University Press.

Wenger, E. (1998). *Communities of practice: Learning, meaning, and identity.* Cambridge, UK: Cambridge University Press.

Wilson, B., & Ryder, M. (1996). Dynamic learning communities: An alternative to designed instructional systems. In M. Crawford & M. Simonson (Eds.), *Proceedings of the 1996 international conference of the Association of Educational Communications and Technology.*

Chapter 6
University 2.0:
Human, Social, and Societal Issues

Daniel W. Surry
University of South Alabama, USA

David C. Ensminger
Loyola University Chicago, USA

ABSTRACT

Higher education is changing in important and profound ways. New technologies are enabling universities to reach new students and create innovative learning environments. Technology is also allowing students to interact, collaborate, and create customized learning experiences in ways that were previously impossible. University 2.0 offers amazing potential to fundamentally change the way higher education functions in the future. With this change will come the opportunity to improve educational quality, reach new learners, and create new organizational structures, but there will also be many potential problems. Many of the problems relate to the key issue of maintaining the vital human and social dimension of higher education in a rapidly changing, technology rich environment. This chapter describes many of the potential problems that will accompany university 2.0 and provides a series of recommended actions that university administrators can take to respond to the problems.

INTRODUCTION

The history of the modern university can arguably be traced back to any one of a number of important dates and events. While there is no single widely accepted date for the birth of the modern university, perhaps the most important event occurred in the mid-12th century when the modern concept of academic freedom was formalized at the University of

DOI: 10.4018/978-1-60566-729-4.ch006

Bologna (Watson, 2005). In the nearly 1,000 years since then, change has come slowly to higher education. Certainly, many innovations, both technical and social, have changed the way universities function over the centuries. Technology in some form has affected the university experience of most faculty and students for many years (Burbules & Callister, 2000). However, despite occasional change, the modern university has remained fundamentally the same since its inception. As a general rule, the university has always been seen as a "place" occupied

Copyright © 2010, IGI Global. Copying or distributing in print or electronic forms without written permission of IGI Global is prohibited.

by a well defined and relatively unchanging group of faculty who interacted with students in a more or less standard manner. A professor or a student from the University of Bologna in the mid-12th century would likely have felt very comfortable and familiar at most universities well into the 20th century. That, however, is no longer the case.

Recent advances in technology have led to radical changes in the way colleges and universities operate. Technology now allows students to take classes without ever setting foot on campus or ever meeting their instructors in person. Once major factors in a student's decision about which college to attend or degree to pursue, geographic and time constraints have now been eliminated, or at least reduced, for most students. Perhaps as important as the reduction of geographic and time concerns, online learning has made possible an amazing number of pedagogical changes (Pursula, Warsta, & Laaksonen, 2005). University students in online courses can receive information, interact with the material, communicate with the instructor, cooperate with each other, and demonstrate mastery of course content in ways that are impossible, or at least not often attempted, in traditional courses. The use of blogs, wikis, and other types of communication, social networking, and collaboration software has changed the way students work, has created new teaching challenges and opportunities, and will be a major factor driving innovation in higher education in the future (Rantanen, 2007). These tools have the potential to fundamentally alter the university experience and create an entirely new conceptual model of higher education. This new conceptual model of higher education, freed from the limits of geography and time, and based on technologically advanced, student driven innovations in communication and collaboration, is commonly referred to in the literature (e.g., Barnes & Tynam, 2007) as "University 2.0".

Most people would agree that technology has already begun to bring about significant changes to higher education and that the ever expanding power of technology will likely mean that col-

leges and universities will continue to change at an increasingly rapid rate in the future. This change will have both positive and negative effects on higher education. The potential benefits of technology to colleges and universities have been well documented, but the potential negative effects are less well understood. These negative effects could include loss of institutional and cultural identity, reduced educational quality (Smith & Mitry, 2008), worsening of class and regional divisions, an overemphasis on curricular areas that most lend themselves to online or technical modes of delivery, commoditization of higher education (Rowley & Sherman, 2004), alienation of older, less technologically adept students, and problems related to faculty workload (Oh, 2003). As Volti (2006) writes, "technology does not yield it benefits without extracting a cost" (p. 18). University administrators and political leaders will have to carefully consider not only the potential benefits of University 2.0 but also the potential costs, both fiscal and human, in order to ensure that higher education reaches its greatest potential in the future.

In this chapter, we will discuss five ideas that can help to guide university administrators and policy makers in making appropriate decisions about the future of higher education. First, we will discuss the theory of Technological Determinism (Ellul, 1967). We will provide a discussion of Ellul's framework of determinism including specific examples of how the theory is relevant to University 2.0. Second, we will discuss the theory of Social Construction of Technology. Often considered the polar opposite of determinism, social construction views all technologies as being contextualized within a social system and, as a result, largely shaped by social issues. Many social issues are driving developments in University 2.0 including economic conditions, the rise of global economies, the evolution of knowledge workers, and the breakdown of traditional family and community structures. By discussing University 2.0 using the analytical lenses of both determinism and social construction, we hope this chapter will describe the current situation accurately and holistically. Third, we will discuss theories related to the implementation of innovations. Any new technology or system must overcome a daunting array of implementation challenges in order to be successful. A number of writers (e.g., Ely, 1999; Surry, 2002) have described factors that enable or inhibit the successful implementation of innovations. In this chapter, we will use these theories to develop recommendations that higher education administrators can use to facilitate the successful utilization of various aspects of University 2.0. Finally, we will discuss a methodology for understanding the ultimate impact of University 2.0 on our society (Kirkpatrick, 1994). The purpose of this discussion is to emphasize the need to consider the intended impact of University 2.0 and develop a realistic plan for measuring that impact prior to the widespread use of University 2.0.

This chapter has three main objectives. The first objective is to provide an overview of the current state of research and theory related to the social aspects of technological development, especially those most relevant to the concept of University 2.0. The second objective is to inform university administrators and others interested in University 2.0 about common problems related to the implementation and utilization of innovative technological systems and suggest strategies for fostering the effective implementation of various elements of University 2.0 The third objective is to recommend a series of steps that universities can take to ensure technological advances are compatible with the essential human, societal, and personal goals of higher education.

BACKGROUND

Technology is a fascinating topic. There is a large and rich body of literature related to all aspects of technology including its design, development, use, and evaluation. One of the most fascinating and popular areas of the technology literature deals with the relationship between technology and people. There is an ongoing debate about whether technology is a tool that societies develop and use for specific purposes or if technology has moved beyond human control and taken on a life of its own. Understanding the different positions in this debate can provide valuable insights into the possible impact of University 2.0 on the future of higher education.

Technological determinism is one position in the debate about the relationship between technology and society. In its simplest definition, technological determinism is the philosophical stance that technology is the driving force in the modern world. A key tenet of determinism is that technology has transcended direct human control and become an autonomous force. Jacques Ellul is one of the most commonly cited writers on the topic of technological determinism. Ellul (1967) described a broad framework of interrelated factors that allowed technology to become an autonomous force. For example, Ellul analyzed the period of the Industrial Revolution in the mid-18th century to understand the conditions that led to the rise of autonomous technology. He concluded that the precipitating conditions were a long period of technological maturation, rapid population growth, suitable economic conditions, social plasticity, and clear technological intention. Of these, Ellul's concept of social plasticity is perhaps the most intriguing. He defines social plasticity as a breakdown of existing social groups and structures, social norms, and traditions. This breakdown of existing structures made it easier for people to abandon their customary roles, relocate to cities, and work in factories.

Ellul (1967) also described the five essential characteristics of modern technology that contributed to the rise of determinism. These characteristics are automation of technical choice, self-augmentation, monism, linkage to other technologies and technical universalism. Automation of technical choice, monism, and technical universalism are the most relevant to our discussion of University 2.0. Ellul believed that as technology became more powerful and prevalent, decisions about technology came to be framed in increasingly technical terms and, as a result, the human and social dimensions of those decisions came to be seen as less important. Through this process, technical considerations gradually supplanted human considerations as the central focus of technological development and use. Ellul's concept of monism is that as technology becomes more powerful and interconnected, it becomes increasingly difficult and less useful to analyze technologies as separate and discrete artifacts. Ellul believed the impact of modern technology could only be fully understood by considering it as a holistic, interconnected, pervasive, and monolithic force. Technical universalism is defined as the homogenizing effect that technology has on people, cultures, and nations. According to Ellul, as technology becomes more powerful and available, people tend to adapt their activities, organizations, languages, preferences, skills, and routines to the technology. For example, the widespread use of automobiles around the world caused people from very different cultures to develop similar views about personal transportation, the organization of modern cities, social status, dating and courtship practices, and acceptable levels of air quality, among many other things.

A final piece of Ellul's (1967) concept of technological determinism is his view about the conjunction of the state and technology. Ellul believed that as technology became more powerful, the state sought to assume authority over the use, direction, and development of technology. The first reason for this was the rapid expansion of technology into areas not previously considered state functions. As new technologies allowed ordinary citizens to, for example, publish ideas, travel abroad, and develop new products, the state became threatened with the loss of control or reduced revenue. As a result, the state sought to ensure the use of technology was regulated and monitored. Another reason for the conjunction of the state and technology is the large expense often associated with the development and implementation of technology. Finally, Ellul suggested the changing nature of the state helped to create an autonomous technology. Ellul believed that technology was seen as an essential tool by the state in its transition from less formal and decentralized structures to more formalized, highly bureaucratic, and authoritarian structures.

While technological determinism provides an interesting perspective to help understand the relationship between technology and people, it is not the only, or even the currently prevailing perspective. Another interesting and widely held perspective is the theory of Social Construction of Technology (SCOT). Often considered the polar opposite of determinism, SCOT views any technology as a tool that is designed, developed, and used within a social system and, as a result, largely shaped by social issues. Under this view, technologies are seen as tools that societies develop to further their goals. Every technology is viewed as a tool that can be used in a positive or negative manner. In a simple example, a knife is a tool that can be used for positive or negative purposes depending upon the intentions of the person using the knife. In the same manner, any technology can be seen as furthering either positive or negative societal purposes, depending on the intentions of the society using the technology.

Proponents of social construction typically point to two main advantages the theory has over technological determinism. First, they claim that studying technology from the perspective of SCOT requires one to have a broad and non-linear view of technology (Pinch & Bijker, 2003). Technological development is not seen as a simple or straight forward process, but as the result of a complex set of dynamic human, societal, political, and economic conditions. As second advantage is that SCOT views users not as passive recipients of technology, but as active agents who shape the design and use of technology (Oudshoorn & Pinch, 2005).

Technological determinism and social construction of technology offer extremely different and essentially incompatible perspectives about the relationship between technology and societies. The theory of Co-construction of Technology (e.g., Edwards, 2003), however, represents a middle ground. Co-construction theory views technology and society as each influencing the other in important ways. Human intelligence and societal goals are constantly designing, developing, modifying, and repurposing technology. Technology, in turn, shapes human desires, alters social structures, creates new opportunities, and allows for innovative solutions. According to co-construction theory, it is overly simplistic to view technology as either the driving force in modern life or as merely a tool that societies employ to meet their goals. Technology and societies are seen as constantly interacting, alternately competing and cooperating, to shape the future.

Technological determinism, social construction, and co-construction are three important perspectives about the relationship between humans and technology. Each theory offers unique and interesting insights. In order to fully understand the possible impact of University 2.0 on the future of higher education, administrators and policy makers should carefully consider each of these perspectives. Before discussing the implications of these three perspectives on the future of higher education, we will briefly mention two other important topics that can help to inform the discussion about the relationship between technology and people – implementation and evaluation.

Adoption, the initial decision to begin use of an innovation, has historically been seen as the key stage in the innovation process. However, in recent years, there has been a trend to move from an emphasis on adoption to an emphasis on implementation (Surry & Ely, 2006).

Implementation refers to the process of fostering the effective use of an innovation within an organization or social system after adoption. Even with careful planning, many innovations fail to be widely or effectively used. A large number of variables affect the implementation process. These variables include the organization in which the innovation is being used, the personal characteristics of the people using the innovation, and the characteristics of the innovation itself. Implementing any innovation is a difficult and frustrating task. Even relatively small scale and superficial innovations often require a great deal of planning and commitment in order to be successfully introduced into an organization. An innovation as broad and profound as University 2.0 will require intense planning and massive resources to ensure that it is successfully implemented.

There are many theories about how to foster the successful implementation of an innovation. For example, Ely (1999) developed a list of eight conditions that facilitate the implementation of educational technology innovations. These conditions are dissatisfaction with the status quo, skills and knowledge, time, resources, rewards and incentives, participation, commitment, and leadership. Organizations can use these conditions to anticipate potential problems and design effective implementation plans. Unfortunately, the relative importance of the conditions varies widely from organization to organization and for different types of innovations (Ensminger, 2005; Surry, Porter & Jackson, 2005). Therefore, organizations must carefully analyze each implementation situation and develop implementation plans that account for the conditions that are most important to each unique situation.

A theory of implementation specific to higher education states that there are seven factors that can either serve as enablers or barriers to implementation (Surry, 2002). These factors are resources, infrastructure, people, policies, learning, evaluation, and support. This theory emphasizes the importance of maintaining a focus on learning outcomes in higher education innovation. Universities must ensure that learning does not become secondary to other potential benefits of technology such as financial gains brought about by greater access to students, flexible scheduling, and reduced demands on the physical plant (Surry). The theory is also notable for its emphasis on providing not only technical support but also pedagogical support to faculty and students. Pedagogical support is intended to help people take full advantage of innovative learning opportunities and overcome obstacles to teaching and learning brought about by a new or unfamiliar learning environment.

Even if University 2.0 is successfully implemented, how will we know if its ultimate impact has been positive or negative? University administrators and public officials should try to answer this crucial question before University 2.0 is widely implemented. Determining what would constitute positive or negative impact now will ensure that decisions about the direction of University 2.0 are based on specific, agreed up criteria.

Kirkpatrick's (1994) evaluation model provides a framework that can be used to determine the criteria by which University 2.0 can be judged. Kirkpatrick's evaluation model includes four levels. These levels are reaction, learning, transfer, and impact. Reaction refers to the positive or negative perceptions that people have in regard to a training program. Learning refers to the extent that learners are able to master the objectives at the end of instruction. Transfer refers to the extent that learners are able to apply skills and knowledge gained during instruction in the work environment. Impact refers to the ways that the instruction changed the overall organization.

Determining the ultimate impact of any training program is by far the most important goal. However, it is also the most difficult. Perhaps the most common method for determining impact is to calculate the return on investment of training. It is often extremely difficult, however, to accurately link a training program with specific cost savings or revenue increases. In addition, Kirkpatrick's level four should include not only financial factors but any factors which impact organizational performance (Dick & Johnson, 2007). In addition to fiscal outcomes, many organizations consider

learning outcomes and performance change (Burgess & Russell, 2003). It is also common for organizations to include intangible outcomes, such as increased employee satisfaction, in their calculation of impact.

Determining the impact of training programs and other interventions can be even more difficult in higher education than in business settings. Reasons for this include the decentralized nature of most universities, long time delays between instruction and application of skills in a work environment, the difficulty in attributing specific outcomes to specific instructional interventions, and the complex overlap of revenue sources and expenses that is common to many universities. In addition, many evaluation projects in higher education do not employ rigorous evaluation methods (Alexander, 1999). As a result, universities often base their determination of impact on superficial, incomplete, or extraneous factors. Determining the impact of innovative instructional programs, such as e-learning, on society as a whole is even more difficult. Because of the difficulty in measuring the impact of e-learning and other innovative instructional options, this level of evaluation is often ignored in higher education (Derouin, Fritzsche, & Salas, 2005).

In this section, we have provided a brief overview of several ideas that provide a broad background of key issues related to University 2.0. We began with a discussion of various philosophical perspectives about the relationship between technology and society. We then discussed two theories of implementation specific to educational settings. Finally, we discussed evaluation, specifically Kirkpatrick's (1994) concept of impact. In the following section, we will discuss how each of these ideas can inform important issues that university administrators and policy makers will have to confront related to University 2.0 and the future of higher education.

BALANCING THE HUMAN
AND TECHNICAL ASPECTS
OF UNIVERSITY 2.0

As we have seen in the previous section, technology and people are always interacting and influencing each other. But this is not just an abstract or pedantic idea. The interaction of technology and people has a profound and tangible impact on our world. Advances in technology shape the way people live, alter the way people think about the world, and influence the behavior of individuals, organizations, and entire nations. People, in turn, are constantly developing new technologies, using existing technologies in creative ways, and choosing, rationally or irrationally, between competing technologies. All of these activities occur every day and impact our lives in subtle and profound ways.

The development and use of University 2.0 is a classic example of the ongoing tension between people and technology. Technology now offers powerful tools for reinventing higher education. These tools are forcing changes in the way universities operate, requiring administrators to rethink long held ideas, allowing faculty to structure lessons in different ways, and changing the expectations of students about how a college class should be organized. However, as with any innovation, University 2.0 presents a number of serious issues that have to be addressed. In this section we will discuss issues and potential problems that are inherent with University 2.0.

University 2.0: Issues
and Challenges

Finding the proper balance between technological considerations and human considerations is the most compelling issue that university administrators will have to address related to University 2.0. The theories discussed earlier in this chapter offer valuable insights into many of the key points relevant to this issue.

By looking at the development and use of University 2.0 through the analytical lens of technological determinism, we can highlight potential problem areas. For example, each of Ellul's (1967) characteristics of modern technology can also be seen as a characteristic of University 2.0. Universities are justifiably excited about the opportunities afforded by innovative online learning environments. However, the same power that makes these opportunities possible can also force important decisions about the future direction of higher education to be made based on technical criteria and not on human or societal criteria. There is a danger that important ethical and philosophical issues related to the goal of education or the role of a university in modern society will be ignored in an attempt to maximize the potential benefits of technology. There is also the danger that technologies related to University 2.0 will become so large, interconnected, and pervasive that they form into a monolithic structure that is beyond the ability of any organization or policy making body to fully understand or control. If this were to happen, universities would face the possibility that educational and curricular decisions would be made without any meaningful oversight or regulation. University 2.0 could result in all of the educational and curricular components of the university becoming autonomous. A final concern related to Ellul's characteristics of modern technology is technical universalism. As University 2.0 becomes more widespread and reaches more people around the world, there will be a natural tendency for universities and other education providers to develop courses on topics that are widely needed and to organize those courses in a standardized manner. As a result, the courses will gradually become more and more similar and education will become a generic, homogenized commodity. University 2.0 may lead to a stagnant educational experience that is devoid of divergent philosophies, economically untenable course offerings, or culturally unique experiences.

Ellul's (1967) conditions that led to rise of determinism during the Industrial Revolution are also directly analogous to the current discussion of University 2.0. Of particular interest is Ellul's concept of social plasticity – the breakdown of traditional social structures that contributed to the rise of technological determinism. Social plasticity is a serious potential problem related to University 2.0. As students take more courses online and combine courses from various providers to create tailored plans of study, they will naturally lose the sense of identity and affiliation with any one university that has long been a hallmark of the university experience. Students who take all of their courses online will likely not avail themselves to the human, social, and communal aspects of the traditional university such as social and civic clubs, intramural and intercollegiate sports, fraternities and sororities, and other extracurricular activities. These students will also not benefit from the informal acculturation, intellectual growth, and social development gained by interacting closely with a peer group over time. The long range impact on universities brought about by this type of hyper social plasticity is impossible to predict. It is likely, however, that essential university functions related to alumni affairs, development, counseling, housing, recruitment, and transcript control will be fundamentally altered. The long range impact on the personal development of students, especially younger, more traditional students, is likely to be even more unpredictable and profound.

Ellul's (1967) discussion of the conjunction of state and technology is another part of his framework of determinism that is relevant to University 2.0. As University 2.0 allows for greater access to a variety of educational opportunities, states will come to have less control over the education of their citizens. In addition, states could also begin to lose revenue to both private competition and other states. When this happens, there will be a natural tendency for the states to try to regain control over the technologies associated with higher education. In some cases there will also likely be attempts, both sincere and sinister, by states to control access of their citizens to unap-

proved educational opportunities. Increased state control over technology and expanded regulation of educational opportunities for its citizens present potentially serious threats to not only the innovative applications of technology that make University 2.0 possible, but also to core university values such as academic freedom, tenure, privacy, diversity, and equal access to education. In addition, the large costs associated with an increased state role in the development, maintenance, and control of University 2.0 may result in increased tuition and fees for students and higher taxes for individuals and businesses. Finally, increased state control could also lead to an overemphasis on fields of study that are most compatible with the prevailing political, social, and economic climate of the state.

The theory of Social Construction of Technology also raises important issues related to the development and use of University 2.0. From the social construction perspective, technological advance is seen as the result of a complex and recursive interaction between diverse social forces including human creativity, individual desires, social norms, and economic activity. This complex interaction of forces requires university administrators and policy makers to carefully consider all of the forces which are influencing the move towards University 2.0. Decisions about University 2.0 and the future of higher education should be made in a collaborative environment that includes members of all stakeholder groups both within and outside the university. The potential benefits and possible risks of University 2.0 should be discussed from multiple viewpoints in consultation with experts from a variety of fields. Unilateral decisions made by a small group of high level university administrators should be rejected as inherently flawed because they do no include the broad, multidisciplinary input required by the complexity of University 2.0.

Social construction theory also sees any technology as a tool that societies employ to achieve their goals. From this perspective, technology can be used to achieve positive or negative societal goals. If we accept this perspective, we must then assume responsibility for ensuring that University 2.0 is used in ways that are compatible with our shared vision for higher education and society as a whole. This will necessitate an ongoing conversation about the role of the university, the meaning of education, the fundamental values of our society, and the goals we hope to achieve through the use of University 2.0. Without this conversation, there is a danger that University 2.0 will achieve unimportant, secondary, amoral, or counterproductive goals. Without being linked to the attainment of specific, desirable societal goals, University 2.0 will never achieve its greatest potential to improve higher education and could result in irreparable damage to higher education. Another danger highlighted by social construction theory is the possibility that groups that do not have the best interests of higher education, or are even hostile to higher education, will define the goals and dictate the development and direction of University 2.0. For example, corporations that have as their primary focus the sale of hardware and software to support University 2.0 will likely push its development without carefully considering the broader human and societal implications.

Research into the implementation of innovations (e.g., Ely 1999; Ensminger, 2005; Surry, Porter & Jackson, 2005) also points out several important issues that are relevant to University 2.0. The first important issue is that implementation is often considered more important and more difficult than adoption. It is not enough for universities to make a decision to adopt University 2.0. After the initial adoption decision, universities have a responsibility to foster the ongoing use and continued development of University 2.0. If higher education administrators do not anticipate problems with the implementation of University 2.0 and actively work to overcome those problems, there could be several serious consequences. These could include lack of widespread utilization, inconsistent instructional quality, wasted time

and resources, reduced access to educational opportunities by traditionally underserved groups, increased frustration and "burn out" by faculty, and the inability to adequately manage or monitor the system.

A second important issue related to implementation is the need to account for the diverse set of factors that affect implementation. The interaction of these factors makes each implementation situation unique. It will be impossible to implement University 2.0 the same way at every university. Every university will have to analyze the factors which are most important to their situation and develop plans to meet their unique needs. Using Ely's (1999) conditions of implementation, it is likely that skills and knowledge, time, participation, and leadership will be the most important conditions relevant to the implementation of University 2.0. Faculty and students will require the skills and knowledge needed to not only use University 2.0 initially, but to stay current with new technologies that will emerge. Faculty and students will also need time to understand how to teach and learn in an innovative, technology rich online environment. University administrators should not expect quick and widespread acceptance of all elements of University 2.0. Participation and faculty governance are greatly valued in higher education. Implementing University 2.0 without first developing a consensus for change among faculty, staff, and students will likely result in incomplete or delayed implementation. However, there are numerous problems associated with fostering participation. For example, faculty often have reward structures related to tenure and promotion that are incompatible with many elements of University 2.0. This could force significant changes to the ways that universities hire faculty, award tenure, grant promotion, and structure faculty work requirements. It is not difficult to envision that University 2.0 will require a fundamental change in the relationship between universities and faculty.

Even if these policy issues can be overcome and University 2.0 is adopted and widely implemented, there will still be a need for university administrators to provide day to day leadership to overcome obstacles and problems that will arise. In addition, University 2.0 will likely require universities to constantly upgrade their infrastructure to keep pace with the changing demands of technology. This, in turn, will require universities to continually explore ways to increase revenue or reduce costs in order to have sufficient funds to devote to infrastructure improvements.

Determining the impact of University 2.0 may be the most difficult task for university administrators now and in the future. Because determining impact is so difficult, there is a danger that universities will judge the impact too narrowly or base decisions about impact on inadequate, inappropriate, or incomplete information. There is also the danger that university administrators and policy makers will substitute a reaction level or learning level evaluation for a true evaluation of impact. Even if students and faculty have positive perceptions of University 2.0 and student learning outcomes are comparable to outcomes in traditional classrooms, that would not necessarily mean that University 2.0 has had a positive impact on higher education or society as a whole. Further, it is unlikely we will ever be able to adequately measure the impact of University 2.0 without first developing clear goals and expectations and establishing the criteria by which attainment of those goals and expectations can be measured.

Solutions and Recommendations

As we have seen, there are many issues and potential problems related to the development and use of University 2.0. However, there are also a number of steps that university administrators and policy makers can take to address the issues and respond to the problems. For example, Surry (2008) recommended six steps that university administrators can take to respond to technologi-

cal determinism in higher education. These six steps are to increase awareness, take individual responsibility, provide for meaningful choice, push decisions down the hierarchy, reduce social plasticity, and establish formalized oversight. Of these, the two most relevant to University 2.0 are to push decisions down the hierarchy and reduce social plasticity. If decisions are made by a small group of high level university administrators and policy makers, it will be impossible to identify, understand, and account for all of the complex social, economic, and political forces that shape the development and use of University 2.0. In addition, it is essential to include a broad and diverse group of stakeholders in the decision making process in order to increase participation, foster a sense of ownership, anticipate potential problems, better serve traditionally underrepresented groups, and take advantage of emerging opportunities.

Reducing the high levels of social plasticity that will undoubtedly accompany the widespread use of University 2.0 is also extremely important. This can be done by creating opportunities for students to experience meaningful and ongoing social interactions with other students and the university as a whole. Just as University 2.0 will allow for innovative approaches to teaching and learning, it can also allow for innovative approaches in social development. For example, universities could develop virtual fraternities and sororities, social clubs, student groups, alumni associations, and other extracurricular activities to approximate the traditional university experience. Universities could also require or encourage students to spend at least some time on campus in traditional courses or create specific course requirements that foster meaningful interaction with other students, faculty, and the university. This can be done, for example, by integrating into the curriculum at least some university and community service activities that require students to interact with peers and community members both inside and outside of the online environment.

The theory of Social Construction of Technology also provides a framework for ensuring that the human elements of University 2.0 are valued and protected. As mentioned earlier, two dangers of University 2.0 are that the technology will be used to accomplish goals that are not compatible with core societal values and beliefs and that the development and use of University 2.0 will be driven by groups with motives that are not necessarily in line with the aims of higher education. To ensure that University 2.0 is used in ways that are compatible with a society's values and goals, it is important to first understand what those values and goals are and the role of the university in furthering those values and goals. Certainly, one core goal of any society is to develop educated citizens. There is no reason to think University 2.0 will not be able to provide well designed and effective instruction to future generations of students. But can University 2.0 do more and, if so, what more should it do? There will have to be an ongoing discussion of these key questions by all groups with a stake in the future of higher education if we expect University 2.0 to ever be used in appropriate ways. To ensure that the development and use of University 2.0 are not driven by groups with motives incompatible with the goals of higher education, it is crucial for universities to be aware of the competing motives of different groups and to take a leading role in promoting University 2.0. Universities should not be passive recipients of technology or allow new technologies to dictate the future direction of higher education. Instead, universities, working alone or in partnerships, should seek to carefully understand the potential advantages and disadvantages of new technologies and proactively integrate the most promising technologies into the university's long range plan.

Other recommendations for university administrators can be based on research into the implementation of innovations. It will be important for university administrators to remember that implementation is a long and difficult process.

They should remember that deciding to adopt University 2.0 is a relatively simple decision, but fostering its effective and widespread use will be much more difficult. In addition, administrators should be aware that implementation is a highly contextualized process. No simple, widely applicable implementation strategy will be available for University 2.0. Administrators should analyze the unique factors that are most likely to enable or inhibit the implementation of University 2.0 at their institutions and develop a plan to account for those localized factors. While each university will have a different plan, each plan will likely include methods for establishing participation of all stakeholder groups, upgrading and maintaining infrastructure, allowing for sufficient time, improving the required skills and knowledge of its faculty, staff, and students, and identifying and adapting institutional policies that are incompatible with the implementation of University 2.0.

One extremely important implementation challenge that all universities will likely face is how to effectively manage the ways University 2.0 is changing the relationship between the university and its faculty. Much has been written about the changing relationship between a university and it students brought about by powerful new technologies, but little has been written about the changing nature of the faculty/university relationship. Faculty play a key role in any higher education implementation situation and this will certainly be the case with the implementation of University 2.0. In order for University 2.0 to be widely implemented, faculty will have to develop new types of courses, master new technologies, adapt existing instructional methods, alter assessment practices, communicate with students in new ways, and recruit and advise students differently. In short, the job of a typical university professor will have to change dramatically if University 2.0 is to be successful. As a result, existing university policies related to faculty retention, tenure, and promotion will have to modified. In all likelihood, this would require universities to develop a plan for changing faculty reward structures from emphasizing research to at least including the development of technology skills (Guri-Rosenblit, 2001). Also, as technology allows for faculty to teach courses for multiple universities and to live far away from a university's campus, other policies related to faculty recruitment, outside income, office hours, health benefits, retirement, sabbatical leaves, travel, and service requirements will also have to be modified. Any university would be well served to begin planning for these fundamental changes in the faculty/university relationship immediately.

The literature related to evaluation is another key resource university administrators can use to guide developments in University 2.0. The main lesson university administrators and policy makers should take from the evaluation literature is that determining impact is the most important level of the evaluation process. To do this, universities will need to reach a consensus about the intended impact of University 2.0 on higher education and society as a whole. If nothing else, administrators and policy makers will have to be aware of the difficulty in evaluating impact and devote the time and resources necessary to adequately judge the impact of University 2.0. They will also have to avoid the temptation to substitute information related to the reaction, learning, or transfer levels for a true evaluation of impact. More research is needed to determine the criteria by which University 2.0's impact should be evaluated and to develop tools for gathering, analyzing, and disseminating the data needed to make that determination.

The recommendations provided in this section represent only a small sample of the types of activities universities will have to undertake in order to ensure that the human and societal aspects of University 2.0 are addressed. It is impossible to identify all of the ways University 2.0 will affect the future of higher education or provide an exhaustive list of steps that universities can take to ensure that they are prepared for the widespread use of University 2.0. Every university will have to continually monitor technological developments related to University 2.0 and engage in ongoing institutional analysis and planning. This will, of course, require a massive and ongoing commitment of time and resources, but not doing so could result in dire consequences for even the best and most established universities.

FUTURE RESEARCH DIRECTIONS

There are several trends that will affect the future direction of University 2.0. These trends relate to both student expectations and potential problems brought on by the constantly changing nature of technology. Perhaps the most important trend affecting the future of University 2.0 is the constantly evolving and expanding nature of student expectations related to technology. As students become more technologically literate at younger ages, they will demand increasingly sophisticated educational experiences (Patten, 2007). This will require universities to continually upgrade their course offerings to ensure they are engaging and relevant to a population of learners that will have increasingly sophisticated technological skills. In addition, both faculty and students will have to stay continually up to date on technology. Because technology is constantly evolving, there will always be a tension between learners who are more technologically literate and students and faculty in need of newer skills. And, since the rate of technological change is likely to increase in the future, the timeframe that one's technological skills can be said to be current will become increasingly short. As a result, universities will have to place greater emphasis on continually upgrading the technological skills of its faculty and students.

Another trend that is important to the future is the need to identify and account for learners who are not being effectively served by University 2.0. Non-users and former users of any technology can provide valuable information that may increase utilization or improve performance (Wyatt, 2005). No matter how widely implemented University 2.0 becomes, there will always be learners who are not adequately served by the system. These undeserved learners will be made up of people who have never used University 2.0 (non-users) and those who used the system but then discontinued use (former users). Included in these groups will be people who do not have access to sufficiently advanced technological tools or skills, those whose learning styles might not be compatible with the prevailing pedagogical methods, those who have special needs, and those interested in courses of study that do not lend themselves to a technology rich online environment. Higher education has a moral obligation to account for these non-users and former users. Therefore, universities will have to develop methods for identifying non-users and former users, determining their needs, and putting into place structures, both technologically advanced and traditional, by which those needs can be met.

The future of higher education is not static. Just as we are today discussing University 2.0, it is likely that we will soon be discussing University 3.0, 4.0, and so on. Higher education will likely never again experience a 1,000 year period of relative stability like the one discussed at the beginning of this chapter. Managing this change will require a long term and substantive commitment from university administrators (Löfström & Nevgi, 2007). The trend will be for university administrators to assume a more active role in the change management process and become skilled change agents. The most effective university administrators in the future will be those who understand the change process, anticipate problems and opportunities, are comfortable working in a changing environment, embrace participation and decentralized decision making processes, and are able to stay current with technology.

Change is always a difficult process. Any change brings about numerous problems and issues. Moving to University 2.0 will be a major challenge and there will be a many problems. These problems will continue throughout the entire life cycle of University 2.0. However with careful planning and continued monitoring, many of the potential problems can be anticipated and addressed.

CONCLUSION

Technology is changing the way we live and work. It is difficult to think of any aspect of our lives that is not being impacted by technology. Higher education, perhaps for the first time in 1,000 years, is also being fundamentally transformed by the power of technology. New technologies are offering universities the potential to create exciting new forms of education, to develop new models of interaction, and to bring exciting learning experiences to a new generation of technologically sophisticated learners. There is certainly much to be optimistic about in regard to University 2.0. However, there are also many potential problems.

Technology forces society to constantly reconsider its values and often choose between contradictory value systems (Mesthene, 2003). The increased development and expanded use of University 2.0 will force higher education, and society in general, to reconsider their values in a fundamental and systematic manner and to make difficult decisions between widely contradictory value systems. Higher education may be forced to choose between providing technologically advanced learning opportunities or providing learning opportunities that are profoundly human, intimate, and personal. Society may be forced to choose between having a higher education system that produces graduates who can perform well in a highly technical, decentralized, rapidly changing environments or one that produces graduates who are thoughtful, social, reflective, and imaginative. None of the choices that University 2.0 confronts us with are easy, simple, or without danger. However, by understanding the important human, social, and societal issues that are raised by the power and potential of University 2.0, we will be able to make intelligent decisions about which choices are best now and in the future.

REFERENCES

Alexander, S. (1999). An evaluation of innovative projects involving communication and information technology in higher education. *Higher Education Research & Development, 18*(2), 173–183. doi:10.1080/0729436990180202

Barnes, C., & Tynan, B. (2007). The adventures of Miranda in the brave new world: Learning in a Web 2.0 millennium. ALT-J . *Research in Learning Technology, 15*(3), 189–200.

Burbules, N. C., & Callister, T. A. Jr. (2000). Universities in transition: The promise and the challenge of new technologies. *Teachers College Record, 102*(2), 273–295. doi:10.1111/0161-4681.00056

Burgess, J. R. D., & Russell, J. E. A. (2003). The effectiveness of distance learning initiatives in organizations. *Journal of Vocational Behavior, 63*, 289–303. doi:10.1016/S0001-8791(03)00045-9

Derouin, R. E., Fritzsche, B. A., & Salas, E. (2005). E-learning in organizations. *Journal of Management, 31*, 920–940. doi:10.1177/0149206305279815

Dick, W., & Johnson, R. B. (2007). Evaluation in instructional design: The impact of Kirkpatrick's four-level model. In R. A. Reiser & J. V. Dempsey (Eds.), Trends and issues in instructional design and technology (2nd ed.) (pp. 94-103). Upper Saddle River, NJ: Pearson Educational.

Edwards, P. N. (2003). Infrastructure and modernity: Force, time, and social organization in the history of sociotechnical systems. In T.J. Misa, P. Brey, & A. Feenberg (Eds.), Modernity and technology (pp. 185-226). Cambridge, MA: MIT Press.

Ellul, J. (1967). The technological society. New York: Knopf

Ely, D. P. (1999). Conditions that facilitate the implementation of educational technology innovations. *Educational Technology, 34*(6), 23–27.

Ensminger, D. C. (2005). The conditions that facilitate the implementation of technology and process innovations: A comparison of K-12, higher education, and business/industry using the implementation profile inventory (DAI-A 66/02).

Guri-Rosenblit, S. (2001). Virtual universities: Current models and future trends. *Higher Education in Europe, 26*(4), 487–499. doi:10.1080/03797720220141807

Kirkpatrick, D. L. (1994). Evaluating training programs: The four levels. San Francisco: Berrett-Koehler.

Löfström, E., & Nevgi, A. (2007). From strategic planning to meaningful learning: Diverse perspectives on the development of Web-based teaching and learning in higher education. *British Journal of Educational Technology, 38*(2), 312–324. doi:10.1111/j.1467-8535.2006.00625.x

Mesthene, E. G. (2003). The role of technology in modern society. In E. Katz, A. Light, & W. Thompson (Eds.), Controlling technology: Contemporary issues (2nd ed.) (pp. 117-138). Amherst, NY: Prometheus Books.

Oh, C. H. (2003). Information communication technology and the new university: A view on elearning. *THE ANNALS, 585*, 134–153. doi:10.1177/0002716202238572

Oudshoorn, N., & Pinch, T. (2005). Introduction: How users and non-users matter. In N. Oudshoorn & T. Pinch (Eds.), How users matter: The co-construction of users and technology (pp. 1-25). Cambridge, MA: The MIT Press.

Patten, L. (2007). Successful integration of WebCT into a small business school. Developments in Business Simulation and Experiential Learning, 34.

Pinch, T. J., & Bijker, W. E. (2003). The social construction of facts and artifacts. In R. C. Scharff & V. Dusek (Eds.), The philosophy of technology: The technological condition: An anthology (pp. 221-232). Malden, MA: Blackwell.

Pursula, M., Warsta, M., & Laaksonen, I. (2005). Virtual university – a vehicle for development, cooperation and internationalisation in teaching and learning. *European Journal of Engineering Education, 30*(4), 439–446. doi:10.1080/03043790500213201

Rantanen, T. (2007). University 2.0: Enhancing communication and collaboration in universities. Helsinki, Finalnd: Helsinki University of Technology.

Rowley, D. J., & Sherman, H. (2004). Academic planning: The heart and soul of the academic strategic plan. Lanham, MD: University Press of America.

Smith, D. E., & Mitry, D. J. (2008). Investigation of higher education: The real costs and quality of online programs. *Journal of Education for Business, 83*(3), 147–152. doi:10.3200/JOEB.83.3.147-152

Surry, D. W. (2002, April). A model for integrating instructional technology into higher education. Paper presented at the meeting of the American Educational Research Association (AERA), New Orleans, LA.

Surry, D. W. (2008). Technology and the future of higher education: An Ellulian perspective. In J. Luca & E. R. Weippl (Eds.), Proceedings of the ED-MEDIA 2008-World Conference on Educational Multimedia, Hypermedia & Telecommunications (pp. 4901-4906). Chesapeake, VA: Association for Advancement of Computing in Education.

Surry, D. W., & Ely, D. P. (2006). Adoption, diffusion, implementation, and institutionalization of educational innovations. In R. Reiser & J. V. Dempsey (Eds.), Trends & issues in instructional design and technology (2nd ed.) (pp. 104-111). Upper Saddle River, NJ: Prentice-Hall.

Surry, D. W., Porter, B., & Jackson, M. K. (2005, April). A comparison of technology implementation factors for three adopter groups. Presentation at the annual meeting of the American Educational Research Association, Montreal, Quebec, Canada.

Volti, R. (2006). Society and technological change (5th ed.). New York: Worth.

Watson, P. (2005). Ideas: A history of thought and invention from fire to Freud. New York: HarperCollins.

Wyatt, S. (2005). Non-users also matter. In N. Oudshoorn & T. Pinch (Eds.), How users matter: The co-construction of users and technology (pp. 67-79). Cambridge, MA: The MIT Press.

Section 2
Web 2.0 Technologies in E-Learning

Chapter 7
Use of Wikis to Support Collaboration among Online Students

Jay Alden
National Defense University, USA

ABSTRACT

The emergence of Web 2.0 technologies with its emphasis on social networking has presented an opportunity for academic institutions to take advantage of new tools to support educational courses. One of these tools is a Wiki. This chapter discusses the merits and challenges of using a Wiki to support the activities of students during group projects. It shows the importance of student collaboration in online courses by fostering deeper learning, producing higher quality team products, and preparing students for today's collaborative workplace. The chapter focuses on the best practices of faculty from setting up the Wiki at the onset through the final phase of evaluating the group product and the individual contribution of individual team members. It also discusses a number of ways in which Wiki-supported collaborative activities can be introduced into online courses and the criteria for selecting particular Wiki products for an institution.

INTRODUCTION

Since its inception, online education has been a solitary endeavor for students working on course assignments. Their link to classmates distributed around the country and the world has often been limited to discussion forums, a useful but somewhat awkward device for working collaboratively. Online discussion forums by themselves seem a poor substitute for in-residence students working interactively across a table constructing a team response to a group assignment on flip-chart paper. The distinction between collaboration in the classroom and collaboration online has been narrowing with the recent advent of social networking software. The purpose of this chapter is to show how one of these social networking software applications – a *wiki* – can be introduced into an online course in order to better support collaboration among geographically dispersed students. More specifically,

DOI: 10.4018/978-1-60566-729-4.ch007

Copyright © 2010, IGI Global. Copying or distributing in print or electronic forms without written permission of IGI Global is prohibited.

its objective is to enable faculty and administrators to understand how student collaboration can facilitate deep learning into an online course and to decide if and how a wiki can support collaboration among distributed students.

BACKGROUND

Why Student Collaboration?

Some, maybe even many, students express an intense dislike for working collaboratively on class assignments, especially in online courses (Payne and Monk-Turner, 2006). "It takes more time than doing it alone" they say, and they loathe having to make up for the burden of *slackers* on the team. "It is just not fair" they claim "that we all get the same grade even though our individual contributions are quite unequal." In spite of these misgivings, several good reasons exist for requiring collaboration among students in online classes. In fact, in graduate-level education, collaborative activities appear virtually required.

First and foremost, collaborative activities tend to foster *deep* learning. That is, the drive towards the consensus necessary to produce a single collective response to the group assignment demands multifaceted exploration and interaction among students. According to Warren Houghton,

...deep learning involves the critical analysis of new ideas, linking them to already known concepts and principles, and leads to understanding and long-term retention of concepts so that they can be used for problem solving in unfamiliar contexts. Deep learning promotes understanding and application for life. In contrast, surface learning is the tacit acceptance of information and memorization as isolated and unlinked facts. It leads to superficial retention of material for examinations and does not promote understanding or long-term retention of knowledge and information. (Houghton, 2004, p.9)

Experience suggests that superficial and uncritical acceptance of information does not typically occur in a group activity. New ideas are challenged for their underlying meanings and are perhaps modified to fit better into the cognitive structure of collective understandings. The dialog in group activities aids students in investigating the underlying causal factors explaining phenomena rather than merely reporting the surface issues of who did what to whom. It should be noted that deep learning does not automatically happen merely when students are assigned to groups (Johnson, Johnson, and Rogers, 1998, p.31). A study by Vaughan (2008) determined that collaborative tools support deep approaches to learning "... only when the teaching strategies and assignments for a course are intentionally designed to facilitate and assess peer collaboration and self-reflection" (p.2863). Moreover, the students must be motivated both internally and externally to want more than just a passing grade from the course and to have access to a well structured base of knowledge related to the assignment. With these tenets of effective course design in place, the components of "activity" and especially "interactivity" with peers inherent in collaborative group assignments greatly facilitate deep learning.

A second benefit for collaboration among students online is that the group response to the assignment is usually better than any of the individual student responses. Collaboration taps into the notion of the "Wisdom of Crowds." According to James Surowiecki (2004), for certain types of problems, the solution posed by a group of reasonably informed and engaged people is almost invariably better than any single expert's answer. Think back to the *Who Wants to be a Millionaire* game show that was so popular on television several years ago. When the contestant was stymied by a question, he or she could call on any of three lifelines – reducing the four choices to just two, calling on an expert by telephone, or asking for a poll of the audience. The first lifeline tends to produce the correct answer fifty percent of the time (sort of a flip of the coin); the expert provided the correct answer a respectable two-thirds of the time; while the majority response of the audience - composed of a variety of people with diverse knowledge on the topic - was correct over ninety percent of the time. Of course, groups in online courses are not typically assigned the task of solving a problem where there is a single correct answer (i.e., a *cognition* problem) as in the Millionaire game. But, the concept of the wisdom of crowds has been shown to apply equally to problems that require aspects of *coordination* and *cooperation*. That is, the concept applies to problems where individuals have to figure out how to take a shared course of action and to do so in a way that yields mutual advantage among individual team members. These requirements precisely fit the type assignment that is the norm for group projects in online courses.

The idea that the group response to a problem will be better than any of the individual team member solutions also depends upon the characteristics of the team and the way it functions. Surowiecki (p.10) suggests that the following criteria distinguish the wise crowd from the irrational mob:

- Diversity: Team members are not all cut from the same mold. They have different opinions and perspectives.
- Independence: Team members are not easily intimidated by the opinions of their teammates. They can voice their disagreement.
- Decentralization: Team members can draw upon different sources of specialized information.
- Aggregation: A mechanism exists for individual team members to share their local knowledge and come to a collective decision.

Collaborative projects in online courses tend to satisfy these conditions so that the team response should lead to a product superior to one than if the members of the teams were to work totally independent of each other. By being exposed to the *wisdom* of the group, they learn more than if they had been assigned to work on the task individually.

Lastly, collaborative projects prepare students for the Information Age workplace. The world of work has changed radically in the last decade or two. Rigid hierarchical organizational structures and an attitude of "if you want something done right, do it yourself" do not seem to fit today's business environment. There may actually be more activity going on in the white space between boxes in the organizational chart than in the vertical connecting lines (Rummler & Basche, 1995). After all, so much more information is available now than there used to be, the information is a great deal more complex, and it is distributed among many more people. It is a rare occurrence in the workplace where bosses know more about the units' business specialization than the people working for them. Business activities typically require major contributions from technical specialists in a variety of organizational departments (Tapscott & Williams, 2007). Also, great pressure exists nowadays to obtain firsthand input from customers and users and maybe even involve them in decision making. Suppliers as well are often tied tightly into the organization's knowledge base and are frequently consulted in planning activities. Further complicating the Information Age environment are the many partnerships that organizations enter into in order to gain competitive advantage. No, this is not your father's workplace. Collaboration is now the name of the game. *Committees, project teams, cross-functional teams,* and *communities of practice* are all part of today's business lexicon. And, they are often accomplished, at least in part, with online tools.

Whatever the particular content of the course and whether or not students perceive the value of group projects at the onset, collaboration in online courses helps prepare them to succeed in the Information Age workplace. And, the process of collaboration leads to deeper learning by online students as well as team products that are a cut above the work of any one individual.

What is a Wiki?

A *wiki* is a type of social networking software that has evolved over the last several years. It has the potential for being an excellent tool to support the collaboration activities during student group projects in online courses. A wiki offers a shared online workspace where team members can contribute their individual pieces to a common document: editing, removing, or adding to what is already there. Even though each member can modify the document, all previous unedited versions are available and can be restored if deemed necessary. And, the direct contributions by each team member are clearly visible. The final agreed-upon product in the wiki is the collective response of the online team to the assigned task.

As an example, suppose five graduate students in an online business class are assigned the task of creating a set of five strategic goals for a hypothetical organization whose strategic direction (i.e., *mission* and *vision*) and competitive situation have been defined. Their final submission should offer the statement of these five goals and the justification for their inclusion in the organization's strategic plan.

- Phase 1 – Brainstorming Goals: Working under the guidance of a designated student team leader, each team member begins populating the shared workspace in the wiki with a variety of potential strategic goals. This phase of the task is comparable to brainstorming. The team collectively produces a total of twenty plus goals with some apparent duplication.
- Phase 2 – Eliminating Duplication: Using a separate discussion forum as a messaging medium, the team leader assigns individual team members the responsibility of combining particular overlapping goals to eliminate the duplication. The students revise the shared wiki page individually to reflect the combining of the goals assigned to them, resulting in 14 unique goals. Since the team members are working on separate goals, there is little chance for any conflicts arising in this phase.

- Phase 3 – Editing Goal Statements: The team leader then asks the team members to review all the goals against the given standards for effectively written strategic goals (e.g., *broad in scope and dealing with high-level issues relevant to the organization's strategy for success*) and to assure that a critical goal has not been inadvertently eliminated. They are asked to rewrite any deficient goals directly on the wiki page and to post comments with their rational for change. Although such a review and rewrite activity typically leads to a better product in a harmonious manner, there is potential for two or more students to disagree strongly as to the optimum wording of a goal. The disagreement may manifest itself as a series of alternate revisions or dueling comments. Matt Marshall (2006) coined the term "wiki war" to describe situations of this sort. The group should have prepared a team work plan in advance that would spell out how such conflicts would be resolved. For example, perhaps the designated team leader will choose the final wording of the goal as he or she sees fit after reading the comments posted. Or the team leader might ask the team members not involved in the conflict to comment or to vote. One way or another, the activity should result in a set of complete goals that are well stated. We'll assume that the team now has a set of 14 unique and well-stated strategic goals for the hypothetical organization displayed on the wiki page.

- Phase 4 - Choosing Final Goals: The original task assignment was to create a set of *five* strategic goals, so it is now necessary for the team to reduce the 14 goals it had developed to a set of only the five highest priority goals. The team leader creates a new wiki page for each of the 14 proposed goals and, using the discussion forum, asks the team members to choose the five strategic goals they would prefer to retain and to post their rationale for assigning high priority to those particular goals. Let us say six goals are eliminated for further consideration since they were not promoted by any team member. The team leader polls the team on the remaining eight goals; a list of the five strategic goals with the highest number of votes is the result (the team leader breaks any ties).

- Phase 5 – Justifying Selected Goals: The last requirement of the group task is to prepare the justification for the five selected strategic goals. The team leader assigns each team member to one of the five goals for the purpose of combining the statements of rationale offered by the team members in the previous phase into a single coherent justification for inclusion of that goal in the strategic plan. The team members are then requested to visit the page of each goal and either indicate their acceptance of the statement of justification as a comment or make revisions. The team member assigned to each particular goal, who receives an email notification when his or her goal justification statement has been modified, has the final say so as to the final wording of the statement of justification and may choose to re-edit the statement or to revert to the previous wording.

- Phase 6 – Submitting the Final Response: The team leader then collects all five strategic goals and justifications from the five wiki pages and posts them as the final submission to the assigned group task.

This team project might have been completed more quickly by simply having each team member create and justify a single strategic goal that is combined into the final submission. But, by developing the response in a collaborative way using a wiki, the final submission is likely to be a much higher quality product with a deeper understanding of the concept of "strategic goals" by the students. And, they will be better prepared for the kind of work they will be doing in the Information Age workplace.

To accommodate collaboration of this type among students, a wiki software application typically offers the capabilities described in Table 1.

The best known wiki is Wikipedia (http://en.wikipedia.org/wiki/Main_Page). This site serves as an encyclopedia that is created, updated and self-managed by users. Wikipedia exemplifies all of the wiki capabilities listed above, but because of the immense volume of content, untold numbers of users, and the public nature of the site, some of these capabilities are not self-evident from a casual visit. A wiki used in support of a class collaboration project in an online course, on the other hand, embodies most if not all of these capabilities in a highly transparent fashion.

USING WIKIS

To What Kinds of Student Collaboration Might a Wiki be Applied?

A wiki can be applied to a variety of group activities in online courses to enhance learning. Some involve collaboration among the entire class and others among small teams of students:

- Student Team Projects: A wiki can support the collaboration activities during student team project assignments - projects in which small groups of students collaborate

Table 1. Wiki capabilities

Online Shared Workspace	Members of the student teams can each access the online pages and modify them. If one team member is in the process of editing a page, other team members may be blocked from opening the same page or a second version of the modified page is generated.
Automatic Index Creation	Each time a new page is created by the team leader or team member, the wiki automatically adds the title of the page to the index used to navigate around the workspace.
Workspace History	A view of all previous pages showing their date of creation, the author, and the specific highlighted changes is available to all team members via an historical index page.
Page Restoration	Designated members of the team have the ability to restore a previous page version in order to eliminate what is believed to be an inappropriate page modification.
Commenting	Team members can insert viewable comments and, perhaps, ratings on information posted by other team members.
Posting Notification	Team members may subscribe to a service that notifies them by email when a page they've identified has been modified by another team member.
Administrative Control	The faculty member can assign the level of authorization to different users as to their ability to edit, remove content or pages, or to restore previous versions of edited pages

to produce a product, conduct a case study, or answer open-ended questions posed by the instructor. The wiki can be used as a tool for both planning for the team and the creation of the final project product.

- Discussion Summary: A team of students may be directed to summarize a weekly discussion conducted in an online forum for use by the remainder of the class. Each week a different team is assigned the task of summarizing the weekly online discussion. The wiki could be used to make draft notes and reflections by individual team members, and to collaboratively construct the final summary document. The summary is then made available to all other students in the class for their review and comments.
- Course FAQ: A wiki can be used to create a "Frequently Asked Questions" page for the course. In this case, students would post questions concerning the conduct of the course and both students and the instructor can furnish and edit answers.
- Course Glossary: Borrowing the approach used with *Wikipedia*, students in a class can collectively construct a glossary of

technical terms associated with a course. That is, students can offer definitions, examples, explanations, links to relevant research and references for a set of technical terms suggested by the faculty or the students.

- Knowledge Repository: An annotated bibliography of online resources for the course can be maintained in a wiki with both students and faculty able to add to and revise the contents. The posted information might include the title, an active link to the website containing the reference material, and a brief description of the contents of the document or website. Students might then be asked to post ratings and evaluative comments of the material.

What are the Role Responsibilities of the Instructor?

The faculty member plays a vital role in assuring that the group project using a wiki runs smoothly and, in fact, leads to deep learning. Without the planning, ongoing monitoring, and occasional prompting by the instructor, the student group project can easily change from the initial promise of an exciting learning adventure using a wiki to a forlorn burden (Webber, 2005). The role of the faculty member can be organized into seven critical responsibilities:

Set-up Wiki Software

The wiki software has to be configured so that the teams of students have the appropriate access and authority to use the wiki for its intended purpose. Typically, this involves naming the wiki page, providing a description that will appear next to the name, choosing the options by which it will operate (e.g., will it automatically link to the course's online grade book), assigning the particular students who can access the wiki pages, and defining what responsibilities each or all students will have (e.g., editing pages, commenting on postings by others, creating new pages, purging existing pages, reverting to previous pages and thereby eliminating edited pages considered inappropriate). Of course, different software products employ different means for setting up the wiki, but they invariably use a simple-to-use interactive worksheet where the instructors make their selections by checking off boxes and entering titles into formatted workspaces. In cases where the wiki has been institutionalized into academic programs, much of the set-up may be accomplished by the technology support group when the online course is initially created.

Create Framework for Wiki Pages

It would be tempting to create a wiki composed of a blank page and turn it over to the students to use as they will. Perhaps, when the use of a wiki is as familiar to students as preparing a document on a word processor, this would be possible and maybe even advantageous. But, that time seems quite a ways off. A blank wiki page represents a formidable challenge to most students at this

time. Instead, it is strongly recommended that the instructor prepare an initial welcoming page for students to view when accessing the wiki and any templates (i.e., formatted task pages) deemed necessary for student teams to complete the assigned task.

Here is an example from one of the online courses conducted by the author – the course deals with measuring organizational performance. One of the weekly units involving a team project covers the topic of *sampling*. More specifically, the case requires that a sampling plan be developed to allow the military commissary system to demonstrate their ability save their customers money on a "selected market basket of food items when compared to prices at supermarkets in the private sector." The team assignment at the completion of the unit's instruction is shown in Figure 1.

To help facilitate the use of the wiki, a template for the response was provided on the team's wiki page as shown in Figure 2.

In this way, the teams would merely submit their responses by checking off boxes and entering text into the form. They could then concentrate their deliberations on the week's content on sampling, rather than on formatting a wiki page.

Develop Instructions for Students

Written instructions should be provided to the students the first time they are directed to use a wiki in a team project. The instructions can indicate such information as how the wiki will be used in the course, how they can access it, and what kinds of activities they are expected to perform using the wiki. Exhibit 1 shows sample instructions used in one of the author's courses. These instructions exclude directions for operations such as accessing the wiki, logging in, posting comments, and editing pages which also must be provided to students.

Figure 1. Sampling team assignment

> **Team Assignments:** As with the previous team activities, the class has been divided into three teams, each being assigned the following need for sampling in this exercise. One member of the team has been assigned the role of "Team Leader" for this exercise.
>
> | RED TEAM | BLUE TEAM | GREEN TEAM |
> |---|---|---|
> | Which of the hundreds of commissaries around the world will be checked in the price comparison? | Which of the many private sector supermarkets in the vicinity of the selected commissaries will be used for comparison? | Which of the thousands of commissary products will form the "market basket" for price comparison? |
>
> Each team is assigned the task of describing and justifying a sampling methodology for one of the sampling requirements above, including the selection of the appropriate sample size.

Encourage Editing of Other Students' Entries

Some students are reluctant to modify a classmate's submission to the wiki even if they believe the modification would improve the product being developed. They are apparently concerned about alienating the feelings of the originator's writing or cultural influencers might make some students uncomfortable deleting the works by others (Pfeil, Zaphiris, and Ang, 2006). The alternatives to rewriting a section are to post the suggested change as either (1) an addition to the section on the wiki beneath the original material, or (2) a suggestion for change in the Comment section of the wiki pointing out the item to which the suggestion applies. Both these approaches are more awkward than merely rewriting the original item by incorporating the suggested improvements directly into the wiki and replacing the previous submission. The

Figure 2. Pre-prepared template for Wiki page

WEEK 7 TEAM PROJECT
Commissary Price Comparison Case
Red Team
Which of the hundreds of commissaries around the world will be checked?

ACCESSIBLE POPULATION	SAMPLING TECHNIQUE	RATIONALE FOR SAMPLING TECHNIQUE
	[ ] Cluster [ ] Convenient [ ] Judgment [ ] Random [ ] Stratified [ ] Systematic	

SELECTION OF SAMPLE SIZE	DESCRIPTION OF SAMPLING METHODOLOGY

Exhibit 1. Written instructions on use of the Wiki

Here is how the Wiki is expected to be used in the class for team projects:

1. Each team will have a workspace for each project that only team members (and I) can access. Teams cannot access each other's team's workspace - they are private. You can access your team's workspace by clicking on "Group Wiki" in the course menu and choosing "View" under your team's name.

2. I will set up a template for the deliverable product in each workspace.

3. Each team will also have the usual *Group Discussion Board* capability that is part of the Group section of the online learning system. This discussion board should be used for communication among team members including such messages as the assignment of tasks by the designated team leader, the schedule of activities during the week, and suggestions for how the team project should be conducted.

4. The wiki workspace is used for the actual construction of the team's final deliverable. As part of the team leader's task instructions to the team, he or she will describe what elements of the template should be completed by each team member (different team members may have responsibility for different elements or all team members may be expected to contribute to the same element).

5. The team leader and each team member have the ability to add to, remove, or modify any of the content existing in the workspace. New sub-pages can also be added to each project workspace if that capability can help in the development of the final project deliverable. Any person with access to the workspace can also restore (revert to) an earlier version of the workspace page from the history file if a newer version is deemed inappropriate.

6. From a project management perspective, the responsibility for removing content and reverting to previous versions of a page should lie solely with the designated team leader. However, any team leader for a particular project may delegate that capability to team members if he or she deems such action appropriate.

7. It is hoped that everyone will adopt an experimental perspective on the use of the wiki and attempt innovative actions permitted by the software even though they are not covered in these instructions.

8. It is recommended that the *Group Wiki* be used directly for submission and improvement of the responses to the assignment and that the *Group Discussion Board* in the "Groups" area be used for messaging concerning project administration.

9. When the project deliverable has reached what is believed to be its final version as determined by the team leader, he or she should request comments from the team members that indicate their agreement or disagreement with the final draft response. Team member comments can be made either in the *Group's Discussion Board* or using the "Comment" feature of the *Group Wiki*, at the discretion of the team leader.

10. Based on the team member's comments, the team leader can modify the draft as he or she sees fit, copy it from the Group Wiki, and post it as the team's submission to the *Posting Assignment* area of the Discussion Board for all class members to view.

---

instructor should post an announcement or send personal email messages encouraging students to overwrite previous postings if they believe that the project deliverable would benefit by doing so. Schweitzer (2008) believes that incentives such as extra grading points ought to be offered for students to edit each other's work. One way or another, the idea should be promoted that everyone in the team develop a "thick skin" and not be defensive if a classmate modifies a section that he or she submitted. All team members must recognize that the shared goal is to produce a superior final product using a collaborative effort - everyone owns the team's final submission. Students should be reminded that if their submissions are changed by teammates and they believe that the modifications made the team's product worse, they may again rewrite the material, building on the teammates' apparent concerns and perhaps posting comments to help explain the change they feel necessary. In the unlikely event that a point of disagreement between two or more classmates deteriorates into a wiki war among the parties, the team leader has the responsibility to mediate or make the final decision.

Plan in Advance for Dispute Resolution

Online team projects share some challenges with face-to-face team projects and add some opportunities for additional disputes. According to Millis (2006), team projects often involve "hitchhikers" (i.e., students who fail to carry their weight and have to be prodded for contributions of any kind) and "workhorses" (i.e., overachievers who contribute frequently and voluminously, more than is requested and perhaps even more than is desired). Such different and opposing working styles often come into conflict with each other and with the more moderate members of the team. Working in a virtual environment offers other challenges for communication during academic team projects.

Without having eye contact with the originator of a proposal, it is easy to be candid, less civil, and maybe even rude, when expressing an opinion of someone else's contribution (Follett, 2008). Other opportunities for disputes arise in online team projects involving wikis, especially in the case where one student overwrites the contribution of another.

Student teams should be made to face the possibility of clashes arising in their teams before the group projects even begin. At the very least, they should be directed to references that offer guidance on preventing disputes and resolving them if they should occur. Northeastern University's College of Business Administration offers such a reference in their "Surviving the Group Project: A Note on Working in Teams" (Wertheim, n.d.). The instructor can offer his or her own tips on managing team projects and perhaps open a discussion forum or even a wiki on eliciting student suggestions for preventing and resolving disputes. Some universities require that student teams prepare a plan for working as a group including their own process for conflict management. Exhibit 2 shows the plan developed by one team in a course taught by the author.

Incidentally, a wiki is a useful tool for the development of such working plans.

Monitor Use of Wiki during the Course

Experience indicates that in the vast majority of cases, a student team's use of a wiki is smooth and effective. The teams are self-governing and require little or no intervention by the instructor. The instructor gives the team assignment at the start of the project and reviews the final team product when it is completed. The team leaders have things in hand during the project. But of course there are exceptions, especially during the initial team projects in a course. Some of these problems are common to student team projects in general, independent of whether or not a wiki is used:

- Time is getting short and the team is struggling with the assignment and does not seem to have any idea what to do.
- Right from the onset, the team has embarked on a path that is likely to be unfulfilling.
- A heated argument breaks out among members of the team, and the team leader

Exhibit 2. Team Conflict Management Plan

Team Conflict Management Plan

As conflicts are inevitable in the team development process, we, as members of Team APEX shall resort to the following guidelines and procedures to provide resolution when conflicts arise:

Any conflict shall be handled in a constructive way and the project leader shall assist and direct the disputing parties to:

　　1. Identify the key issues and their position without making any accusations;
　　2. Lay out the advantages and disadvantages of each party's position on the issue;
　　3. Look for other alternative options that will satisfy both parties interest and fulfillment the team's needs;
　　4. Request other member's opinions and views; and
　　5. Find the point of balance and work out a mutual decision between parties.

However, if a mutual decision cannot be reached, the team leader shall seek assistance from faculty members to act as mediator to help the parties to reach an agreement.

Every member should keep in mind that the purpose of team assignments is to give us the chance of learning and developing management skills in a cooperative and reciprocal setting while achieving a common team goal. Therefore, we should refrain ourselves from and to avoid unnecessary conflicts and disputes that would hinder or delay the team's progress. The followings are some suggestions and rules that have been provided by members of Team APEX to assist the team in the avoidance of unnecessary conflicts and disputes:

　　1. Be certain that any suggestions and solutions are practical and achievable;
　　2. Encourage and welcome different ideas and opinions;
　　3. Be positive and sincere with your words;
　　4. Be conscious about your own part of problem; and
　　5. Before giving your own point of view, try to listen and understand others first.

is either unable to deal with the issue or is a participant in the dispute.

Other potential team problems may be directly related to the required use of a wiki. For example, the lack of fluency with a wiki or the fear of having to rewrite a colleague's contribution might result in the wiki workspace remaining bare of content. All the team's contributions may occur within the confines of the more familiar threaded discussion forum, as clumsy as that might be. In some cases, team leaders might reserve the right to themselves to post content to the wiki, with other team members restricted to merely suggesting content and posting comments in the discussion forum. And, occasionally, a wiki war might break out among two or more team members that is unresolved by the self-governance capability of the team.

At the very least, the instructor should regularly monitor each team's wiki workspace for signs of potential problems. If some are found, the tough question to answer is whether or not to intercede. Sometimes the best reaction to a problem is no reaction; let the team handle it themselves (Follett, 2008). Often, all that is necessary is a personal email message or telephone call to the team leader, noting the potential problem and asking if assistance is required. If help is requested, then appropriate guidance should be offered to help steer team activities towards the fruitful use of the wiki for collaboration. If the team leader is at the heart of the problem or a party to a dispute, more assertive action may be required to defuse the situation. Intervention into team projects is a touchy issue and instructors have to learn to step back without stepping out of the picture entirely.

Evaluate Collaborative Effort

Since group projects typically represent an extensive amount of effort by students in a class, general agreement exists among faculty that the team effort should be assessed, graded, and feedback provided. With some exceptions (Cohen,

1994), there is further accord that grading ought to represent both (1) the quality of the product developed jointly by the team as well as (2) the degree of participation and quality of contribution by each individual student involved in the group process. Different faculty and institutions might stress the relative weight of the common product and the individual contribution dissimilarly in the assessment, but both components are typically factored into each student's grade. The assessment of the team's final product tends to fall within the typical task requirements of most faculty. In virtually all ways related to assessment, a paper produced by a group is indistinguishable from a paper authored by an individual student. Faculty members are quite experienced in the application of stated project requirements or criteria and the use of grading rubrics to assign a score to the final group product. On the other hand, the assessment of each team member's contribution to the final group product poses special challenges to the course instructor.

The individual members of student teams typically contribute to the group project in a variety of ways. They post comments to discussion boards, send email messages, submit documents they've created, and take part in team chat sessions. They might participate in telephone conversations or teleconferences or even meet face-to-face with team members who are located in the same general vicinity. It is arduous for the faculty member to track down the sum total of contributions by individual students in order to assign a grade to their involvement in team deliberations. Possibly because of this difficulty, many faculty members rely on "peer assessment" to provide the portion of the group project grade relating to individual contribution. In peer assessment, each student team member is asked to evaluate the contribution of the other team members to the final group product (McCoy, 2006). The assessment, often anonymous, may be in the form of a ranking or graded score on such factors as taking responsibility, contributing ideas, and completing tasks, accompanied by justifying comments. The composite score from all team members for each student is factored into the group project grade for each individual member of the team. Some faculty members have qualms with the fairness of peer assessment. They feel that students are not trained to rate people's performance and that the grades they assign may consider factors irrelevant to team contribution and might even be determined by collusion among some team members (Ohland, Layton, Loughry, and Yuhasz, 2005).

The historical index feature of all wiki applications may enable a lower weighting of peer evaluation or possibly its elimination in the assessment of an individual's contribution to the group effort. This feature allows the instructor to view exactly what each team member contributed to the group project. The page history file provides access to each version of the wiki page with the modification highlighted in color and the name of the person listed who made the change as well as the day and time that the revision took place. The faculty member can conveniently determine the quantity and quality of contributions by each team member and rate that performance accordingly. Most faculty members are adept at rating student performance fairly and accurately, given direct access to their contributions. Moreover, just the knowledge that faculty will have easy access to their contributions may serve as an incentive for students to participate more actively and with higher quality contributions

By What Criteria Should the Wiki Software Product be Chosen?

Currently one hundred or so software products are available on the market that have the term "wiki" in their names or can serve the functions of a wiki. Which one is best for a particular institution? Several criteria might be used in the selection process.

Technical Performance Features and Cost

If the choice is to be made purely on the basis of *features* and *cost*, the decision is not exceptionally difficult. Virtually all wiki software products offer common wiki functions that enable the basic essence of online collaboration:

- Page Creation & Revision: The ability to enter or revise textual content on a shared workspace using a typical text editor.
- Page Index: Automatic creation of an index of page titles that have been created with built-in links to those pages.
- Page History: A means of viewing previous versions of the pages with indications of when the edits took place, the user who made the change, the specific changes that were made, and the ability to restore that previous page as the visible page on the wiki.

Higher-end wiki products offer some additional features that may not be found on the lower cost offerings:

- Hyperlinking: The ability to easily insert links to other Wiki pages and pages available on the Web.
- Multimedia: The ability to insert graphical images, video clips, and audio files into the page.
- Attachments: The ability to upload and insert existing documents into a page.
- Email Notification: A subscription service in which users are notified by email when a wiki page they have identified has been modified by another user.
- Access Control: The assignment of different levels of authorization to different users as to the ability to edit or remove content or pages or to restore previous versions of edited pages.

- Commenting: The ability to insert viewable comments by users on information posted by other users.

The institution must first decide on the wiki features it deems critical for its application and the available budget for purchasing the software product. Several online tools are available to help shrink the number of potential wiki software offerings to a manageable set based on available features and cost. These tools include Wikipedia's *Comparison of wiki software* (n.d.) and WikiMatrix's *Compare them all* (n.d.). Wikipedia offers a large updated table listing differences among approximately 50 wiki software products on factors such as *owner, release dates, cost, technical parameters, target audience, features,* and *installation requirements.* It should be noted that Wikipedia's tool is the creation of users so that the authenticity of the data is likely but not assured. WikiMatrix is an interactive website that enables users to choose or compare Wikis from among approximately 100 Wiki software products. Users can make use of a built-in wizard as an aid in the selection of a specific wiki software product that meets their particular needs. Or, users can choose two of the available wiki software products for a side-by-side comparison on *features, hosting and system requirements, security arrangements, usability,* and other technical parameters. The website also offers a link to a discussion forum devoted to wikis where questions can be asked and comments made within a community of people interested in this collaborative software capability.

Institutional Integration Issues

The choice of a particular wiki software product may very well involve factors beyond it purchase price and features. Two different institutions might have the same budget and need for the same wiki features for its collaborative application, but one product might suit one institution better than the other institution and offer significantly lower life-cycle costs than another product. The ease of integration of the wiki functionality into the culture and technology infrastructure of the institution ought to be of critical concern in the choice of software.

- Usability for Target Audience and Available Support Services: Because of the programmatic thrust of its academic offerings, students in some institutions or departments might have more experience or greater aptitude with new software products. They therefore could be more skillful at some advanced wiki features and require less technical support. The WikiMatrix tool described above gives some indication of the ease of use of the various products based on available features (e.g., *WYSIWYG Editing*), but an actual trial of a product with targeted users would be worthwhile. The availability and cost of technical support services such as a 24/7 toll-free number call assistance should also be considered, especially if the student body or faculty of the institution tend to be hesitant in adopting technology innovations.

- Integration with Existing Course Management System: The course management system used to deliver online courses at the institution might be home grown or purchased from a commercial software vendor (e.g., BlackBoard). In either case, a wiki capability may or may not be embedded in the course management system. And, even if a wiki is available as part of the course management system, its array of features might not be as rich as a wiki software product acquired as a stand-alone application. In spite of this drawback, heavy weight in the decision process might be awarded the criterion of *course management system integration.* That is, a wiki that has a similar look and feel to the software used to deliver the online courses greatly assists adoption of its collaborative features. A wiki with these characteristics gives the appearance of being merely an extension of the course management system rather an entirely new software product to learn. If the course management system does not incorporate a wiki, then consideration should be given to commercial software applications that can be readily customized to offer colors, layout, button shapes, and branding similar to the appearance of the current online course displays.

- Hosting: Most commercial suppliers of wiki software offer institutions the option of hosting the application on either the vendor's servers or those of the institution. For some institutions, hosting is a critical criterion in the decision process. Hosting by the vendor probably has a higher life-cycle cost of ownership than the outright purchase of a software license by the institution that will host the software itself; however, vendor hosting may offer benefits that institutions with relatively small and unsophisticated information technology support units are unable to provide. These benefits include assurances for secure and private interactions during collaborative activities as well as the systematic and frequent back-up of data files. Because hosted services specialize in this line of business, they tend to offer fewer and less lengthy outages and may have the ability to switch to a back-up server if the primary server shuts down for any reason. The extra cost associated with remote hosting of the wiki might also lead to more timely updates of the software and more reliable support services for users. Each institution has to consider the cost-benefits of outright purchase of the wiki software versus paying the vendor to host the service.

FUTURE TRENDS

According to Bill Venners (2003), Ward Cunningham created the first modern wiki, named *WikiWikiWeb*, in 1995. After more than a decade, wikis are just beginning to appear in academia, typically in support of student team projects. Using Gartner's Hype Cycle curve (Linden and Fenn, 2003), the author would position the use of wikis in education on the upward slope approaching the "Peak of Inflated Expectations" (see Figure 3). That is, wikis are currently receiving positive hype from articles dealing with a limited number of first-generation academic applications that need extensive customization to work effectively. The use of wikis in education has yet to receive much negative press describing the likely failures by the second round of adaptors. But, criticism will almost certainly occur as faculty lacking the enthusiasm and technical aptitude of the early adaptors attempt to implement wikis in their online classrooms. They will find putting the current generation of wikis into practice challenging.

Passing through the "Trough of Disillusionment" phase of the Hype Cycle to begin rising on the "Slope of Enlightenment" will require a number of modifications to the wiki software. First and foremost, a wiki must become an integral component of each institution's course management system. A stand-alone wiki capability with a different look and feel than the standard online learning application and separated from administrative functions like the course address book and class assignment utilities is daunting to both students and faculty. A wiki should become the primary *collaboration* module of the course management system and seem as common to users as the course discussion board. Second, the built-in facilities for editing, commenting on, and viewing previous page versions need to become integrated and make use of a more user-friendly graphical interface. In most current wiki configurations, these three functions tend to be accomplished in entirely different ways, complicating the mastery

Figure 3. Gartner's Hype Cycle

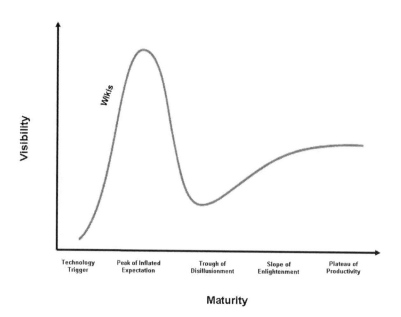

by users. Last, to speed up the collaborative efforts among multiple users, it would be helpful if changes to the common workspace were made immediately available on students' mobile display devices such as cell phones and personal digital assistants so that they could respond quickly if they wish. All of these modifications are quite likely to occur within the next few years as social networking tools become more universal.

CONCLUSION

Current wiki software exists as stand-alone applications having some features similar to a word processor and other features offering unique capabilities for collaboration among distributed users. As such, it now represents a challenge for academic institutions to choose a particular wiki product and configure it for use in their online courses. Tight resources would have to be diverted to this particular emerging technology. Early adopters on the faculty must be willing to share their experiences and enthusiasm with their

colleagues. It is tempting to just wait the few years necessary for this software capability to evolve further and become more integrated with the institution's course management system. Yet, besides offering a challenge, the current standing of wiki software also offers an opportunity for far-thinking academic institutions. These institutions are embracing the quickly evolving world of Web 2.0 with its emphasis on social networking. They see how such new capabilities as offered by a wiki can transform their online programs in ways unheard of just a few years ago. Their students, no matter how far removed from each other, can more readily collaborate on joint efforts. Yes, they still cannot read body language and facial expressions as can residential student teams sitting around a conference table (at least until video conferences or animated avatars are added to the mix), but they have the benefit of collaborating in group projects on their own schedule from any location while contributing relevant dynamic media resources that exist on the Web. These insightful institutions are taking advantage of state-of-the-art wiki software to build more opportunities for student collaboration into their courses. By doing so, their students acquire deeper learning of the subject matter, produce a higher quality product that they can be proud of, and are being prepared to work effectively in today's collaborative-based workplace. By not waiting for the next generation of wiki software to emerge, these far-thinking institutions are working their way through the "trough of disillusionment" in the Hype Cycle into the "slope of enlightenment" so that they can be the leaders in the "plateau of productivity" when the time comes in the next few years.

The views expressed in this article are those of the authors and do not reflect the official policy or position of the National Defense University, the Department of Defense, or the U.S. Government.

REFERENCES

Cohen, E. G. (1994). *Designing groupwork: Strategies for the heterogeneous classroom.* New York: Teachers College Press.

Compare them all. (n.d.). Retrieved June 30, 2008 from http://www.wikimatrix.org/

Comparison of Wiki software. (n.d.). Retrieved June 30, 2008 http://en.wikipedia.org/wiki/Comparison_of_wiki_software

Follett, J. (2008). *The rules of digital engagement.* Retrieved June 23, 2008, from http://alistapart.com/articles/rulesofdigitalengagement

Houghton, W. (2004). *Learning and teaching theory for engineering academics.* Retrieved October 23, 2008, from http://www.engsc.ac.uk/downloads/resources/theory.pdf

Johnson, D. W., Johnson, R. T., & Smith, K. A. (1998). Cooperative learning returns to college: What evidence is there that it works? *Change,* (July/August): 27–35.

Linden, A., & Fenn, J. (2003). *Strategic analysis report R-20-1971: Understanding Gartner's hype cycles.* Stamford, CT: Gartner Inc.

Marshall, M. (2005). *Wiki war born out of deal with Walt Disney.* Retrieved October 23, 2008, from http://www.mickeynews.com/News/DisplayPressRelease.asp_Q_id_E_1195Wiki

McCoy, S. (2006). Evaluating group projects: A Web-based assessment. In *Proceedings of the 2006 Midwest Instruction and Computing Symposium.* Retrieved June 27, 2008, from http://www.mic-symposium.org/mics_2006/papers/McCoy.pdf

Millis, B. J. (2006). *Using new technologies to support cooperative learning, collaborative services, and unique resources.* Retrieved June 23, 2008, from http://www.tltgroup.org/resources/rmillis3.html

Ohland, M. W., Layton, R. A., Loughry, M. L., & Yuhasz, A. G. (2005). Effects of behavioral anchors on peer evaluation reliability. *Journal of Engineering Education,* (July). 319-326.

Payne, B. K., & Monk-Turner, E. (2006). *Students' perceptions of group projects: The role of race, age, and slacking.* Retrieved October 22, 2008, from http://findarticles.com/p/articles/mi_m0FCR/is_/ai_n26844266?tag=artBody;col1

Pfeil, U., Zaphiris, P., & Ang, C. S. (2006). Cultural differences in collaborative authoring of Wikipedia. *Journal of Computer-Mediated Communication, 12*(1), article 5. Retrieved October 23, 2008, from http://jcmc.indiana.edu/vol12/issue1/pfeil.html

Rummler, G., & Brache, A. (1995). *Improving performance: How to manage the white space in the organization chart.* San Francisco: Jossey-Bass.

Schweitzer, H. (2008). Extending the online classroom with Wikis. In *Proceedings of the 2008 Conference of the Society for Information Technology & Teacher Education* (pp. 2826-2830).

Surowiecki, J. (2004). *The wisdom of crowds.* New York: Doubleday.

Tapscott, D., & Williams, A. D. (2007, March 26). The Wiki workplace. *BusinessWeek.* Retrieved May 30, 2008, from http://www.businessweek.com/innovate/content/mar2007/id20070326_237620.htm?chan=search

Vaughan, N. D. (2008). Supporting deep approaches to learning through the use of Wikis and weblogs. In *Proceedings of the 2008 Conference of the Society for Information Technology & Teacher Education* (pp. 2857-2864).

Venners, B. (2003). *Exploring with Wiki: A conversation with Ward Cunningham, part I.* Retrieved July 2, 2008, from http://www.artima.com/intv/wiki.html

Webber, C. (2005). *Making collaboration work.* Retrieved June 16, 2008, from http://www.projectsatwork.com/content/articles/222381.cfm

Wertheim, E. (n.d.). *Surviving the group project: A note on working in teams.* Retrieved June 23, 2008, from http://web.cba.neu.edu/~ewertheim/teams/ovrvw2.htm

Chapter 8
Wikibook Transformations and Disruptions:
Looking Back Twenty Years to Today

Curtis J. Bonk
Indiana University, USA

Mimi Miyoung Lee
University of Houston, USA

Nari Kim
The University of Wisconsin Oshkosh, USA

Meng-Fen Grace Lin
University of Hawaii, USA

ABSTRACT

A Wikibook is a transformative and disruptive technology that is finding increasing use in schools and higher education institutions. This new form of technology is inexpensive, accessible, and fairly responsive to the user. When engaged in a Wikibook project in an academic setting, learners are granted power to control the content and process of learning. Wikibooks are part of the Web 2.0 which can provide a powerful force in changing, and improving education. However, the authors' multiple attempts to build Wikibooks in their own classes reveal that creating a successful Wikibook is not particularly easy. It is even more difficult when it entails more than one institution or class. Cross-institutional and internationally designed Wikibooks present many instructional challenges and dilemmas to learners and instructors. In addition, there are collaboration issues, technology issues, knowledge construction and sense of community issues, and general issues related to the Wikibook technology and the Wikibook design process itself. In response, in this chapter, the authors provide dozens of Wikibook collaboration ideas and suggestions based on our experiences.

DOI: 10.4018/978-1-60566-729-4.ch008

Copyright © 2010, IGI Global. Copying or distributing in print or electronic forms without written permission of IGI Global is prohibited.

INTRODUCTION

Imagine a Web page that anyone with access to the Internet can edit, not just read (Evans, 2006). Now imagine if that editing process extended well beyond that page to an entire chapter or book. If successful, you have envisioned the birth of the wikibook. A wikibook is one of many so-called Web 2.0 technologies that are now finding their ways into K-12 and college classrooms. Wikis are collaborative writing spaces wherein a learner can perpetually tinker with ideas as well as remold and share them.

Clearly Wikibooks are empowering tools for education. With such devices at their fingertips, learners take control over their own learning situations. They might develop the theme or title of the wikibook and coordinate the entire process of assembling one. They might take on the role of writer who collaborates with others in building a product that is shareable. When done, they might decide to take on roles of editors or proofreaders of the wikibook. At the same time, they might provide help or resources as needed, including assistance with references, copyright clearance, page layout, and cover design.

A central aspect of the wikibook is that anyone can determine where, what, when, and how much to contribute. During writing, the learner is no longer just finding a perspective for a teacher or for herself, but for an unknown and potentially gigantic audience. There is a sense of contributing to the greater good of humankind. Along these same lines, there is a generative spirit and process that is exhibited in a wikibook project. Learners participate in their own learning as opposed to be given a preset learning agenda or set of learning items to review and practice until perfection. When individuals can contribute to the knowledge building process instead of passively consuming prepackaged knowledge and information, they engage more deeply with the content and assume control over their own learning. In a word, learners are empowered. It is in such situations that passion-based learning is possible (Brown, 2006). When passion is present, depth in learning often occurs as one seeks more knowledge that is later shared in the wikibook.

And that may be the most important factor of all--the wikibook is shared. If made public, a wikibook is an open educational resource for reading, discussing, and still further sharing among any member of this planet. Suppose it is a book on introductory algebra. Such a text could be translated into other languages and shared further still. Given that most introductory concepts in algebra do not change much, once created, that book could be reused for years or even decades. A student in Cameroon could enjoy and learn from it as much, if not more, than one in Canada, Korea, or Chile. Of course, the examples and problems should be localized for each culture and setting.

As indicated, a wikibook is part of the Web 2.0 where learners contribute to learning rather than being handed it in a textbook or a set of lecture notes. As opposed to the casual browsing that typified the initial incarnation of the Web, the Web 2.0 or "read-write Web" is no longer a device to be used for passive reception of information or for accessing and perusing content. When learners are put in charge of their own learning, it is nothing less than a revolution in human learning. Revolutions, however, are rarely won easily.

Wikibooks as a Disruptive Technology

A revolution in education? Yes! In fact, Christenson, Horn, and Johnson (2008) argue that the types of disruptive technologies that have found their way in business management practices will soon "disrupt" education. As they insightfully point out, disruption brought on by new technologies is rarely abrupt. The disruptive technology or innovation must obtain a series of minor improvements first. Often, they are more affordable, accessible, and responsive to learner and teacher needs than existing systems or resources. In addition, they do not attack the system directly but find ways around it. With such a set of features in place, the technology tool or innovation can take root often without the interference of mainstream educational establishments and bureaucracies. That is definitely the state of wikibooks today. They hold immense potential to shake the very foundations of education as well as the associated textbook publishing industry, but many enhancements must be made related to the tools and the collaborative environments in which they are used. When this happens, dramatic changes in educational settings could occur.

Christenson and his colleagues, in fact, predict momentous changes in textbook industry in the coming decades with increasing reliance on online materials that are individualized to learner needs. Wikis are one way to provide access to such materials. They break instructors out of millennia of reliance on prepackaged or prebuilt content. Authority-driven content is eschewed in favor of user-generated content. With technology tools such as wikis and e-books, monolithic structures in the publishing industry are finally giving way to something new. As they point out, customization of content at the individual learner level is beyond what is possible in the traditional publishing industry. Technology has the potential to change that. In fact, online technologies can place free or inexpensive learning content in the hands of billions of learners when and where they ask for it.

Technology-based solutions to the high costs of textbooks are mounting. As an example, the Global Text Project (Garrobo, 2007), which began as a small project in one graduate class at the University of Georgia in 2004, is now helping design many free textbooks for those in developing countries. The alternative book formats of the Global Text Project include CDs, DVDs, wikibooks, and html documents. Non-profits are not the only ones making such choices available. Companies like Flat World Knowledge are providing content freely available online in wikis, PDF format, and other innovative means. At the same time, university presses such as Yale University Press and MIT Press are offering some of their books as free PDF copies or html documents. Yale University Press is also experimenting with wiki-based books and other novel book ideas such as allowing the readers to electronically comment on the online book.

Wikibooks are just one of many such technologies that can transform educational practices in K-12 schools, higher education, and training environments. Technologies such as blogs also give learners the power to craft and share their ideas in textual formats with hyperlinks among common themes or elements of multiple blog posts or Web resources. In addition, podcasts allow learners to vocalize their ideas to the world listening community. And they can be replayed many months or years later.

At the root level, then, wikibooks, and the myriad other technologies made available for learning today, have the potential to dramatically change education. It is important now to experiment with different types of wikibooks across educational settings. As this occurs, educators will better understand how they might be successfully deployed.

The Climate of 2008

This year 2008 was marked by myriad politicians and their followers arguing for far reaching change. Such calls for transformative change, however, were not restricted to legislative offices and government agencies. Across educational settings, too, transformation was in the air. It seemed that everyone was focused on it; almost as if it was a necessity for schools and institutions of higher learning. Much of these pleas and pronouncements arose from concerns that youth were dropping out of schools and colleges due to dull curricula and a lack of meaningful and engaging activities (Cassner-Lotto & Wright Benner, 2006). From such perspectives, there was a deep disconnect between what learners preferred in terms of tasks assigned, resources to accomplish those tasks, and the assessment of that work. Unfortunately, this concern was arising at a time when the skills and competencies needed to be successful in the working world of adults were rising. As repeatedly pointed out, students desperately need critical thinking, collaboration, leadership, evaluation, creativity, and problem solving skills (Cassner-Lotto & Wright Benner, 2006). From such reports, it is clear that students are not workforce ready.

Such criticisms are not entirely unfounded. At the same time, there are numerous reports on how schools and universities do not accommodate the experiences, needs, and preferences of different generations of students (Dede, 2005; Dziuban, Moskal, & Hartman 2005; Oblinger, 2008). Timely studies from the Pew Internet & American Life Report indicate that today learners arrive on college campuses with more technology savvyness and expectations than preceding generations (Lenhart & Fox 2006; Lenhart, Madden, & Hitlin, 2005). In response, technologies such as those brought about by the Web 2.0 are often seen as transformational in shifting learning situations from passive to more interactive and engaging learning climates. Those promoting the Web 2.0 and other online learning technologies argue that they can foster new ways to collaborate and share ideas with peers and instructors (Alexander, 2006; Downes, 2005). Further fueling this learning environment transformation, mobile technologies such as the iPhone, the iPod, text messaging, and Twitter bring a new sense of connectedness to learners and learning (Dye, 2006; Young, 2008a, 2008b). As a result, instructors are repeatedly asked to embed technology in their instruction, foster student collaboration and knowledge building, and provide more options, choice, and autonomy for their learners. In a word, they are being asked to transform their teaching practices.

Reflections Twenty Years Back

This intensity in which schools and institutions of higher learning have been asked to transform has been inching upward each year for the past two decades. Think back a couple of decades to the late 1980s for a moment. It was a time of change in educational research from cognitive views of learning to those espousing situated learning and social constructivism. A technical report in 1988, "*Cognitive apprenticeship, situated cognition, and social interaction*" from Brown, Collins, and Duguid (1988) issued through the offices of Bolt, Beranek, and Newman, got the rumbling started. That was exactly twenty years ago. The following year, the stir hit a more fevered pitch when John Seely Brown gave a keynote talk at the American Educational Research Association Conference in San Francisco entitled "Situated Cognition—A View of Learning" (Brown, 1989) to a packed audience while simultaneously publishing a paper in the prestigious Educational Researcher (Brown, Collins, & Duguid, 1989).

Many educational researchers have yet to recover from the sea change in educational research and practices brought about by that one article and associated speech. Such ideas have their roots in theories developed decades, and perhaps even centuries, ago. In fact, most other learning-related researchers in the 1980s and 1990s cited Lev Vygotsky (1978, 1986) and John Dewey (1884, 1910, 1916) to theoretically ground their work. From these perspectives, learning should be socially interactive and involve doing or building something tangible. In addition, learners must have a voice. Their work must have some personal meaning as well as value to the community. From Dewey's perspective, passion for learning can be fostered with projects directly in the community (Dewey, 1897). But like many today, he ran into enormous barriers including curricula that were out-of-date, textbook-driven learning, and an overreliance on tests that required simple memorization and recitation. Students were likely as bored then as they are now where information is deposited in awaiting minds for later use at some unknown time period. What Brown and company provided was life to ideas from Dewey and others related to learning in a social context.

While the work by Brown and his colleagues (e.g., Collins, Brown, & Newman, 1989) some twenty years back was definitely not the only such effort in the area at that time (see also Brown & Palincsar, 1989; Langer & Applebee, 1987; Scardamalia & Bereiter, 1986, and many others), it helped focus educational researchers on the importance of context in education as well as the apprenticeship process for learning new skills or competencies. As an example, at about the same time, Roland Tharp and Ronald Gallimore authored a book called *Rousing minds to life* (Tharp & Gallimore, 1988) which outlined ways in which instructors could assist in the learning process instead of simply assessing it. An effective instructor is aware of the task and activities and forms of instruction available that can be employed to push or scaffold learners to new cognitive heights (Gallimore & Tharp, 1990). The seven dependable techniques for assisting in learning that they outlined were similar to Collins (1990) but also argued for feedback, contingency management, instructing, questioning, cognitive structuring, and task structuring (Bonk & Kim, 1998; Tharp, 1993).

Since the 1988 report of Brown et al. and work by Tharp and Gallimore, there has been much other scholarship that has added dimensions to the importance of context and building a culture of learning. Work from Lave and Wenger (1991) outlined what a legitimate peripheral participation process looked like while Wenger more richly described communities of practice (Wenger, 1998). For twenty years there have been inroads into understanding the social aspects of learning. We know more about the role of dialogue in providing scaffolded instruction (Palincsar, 1986), informal learning (Cross, 2007), how learning communities as well as communities of practice

are formed (Wenger, 1988), the various ways in which apprenticeship learning might unfold, and the types of tasks that better engage learners in meaningful instruction.

Back to Reality Again

In early 2008, Brown and his colleague, Richard Adler, published an article in EDUCAUSE Review, "Minds on fire: Open education, the long tail, and learning 2.0" (Brown & Adler, 2008), related to participatory learning. As Brown noted in his December 2006 invited address at MIT (Brown, 2006), we have entered a participatory learning culture wherein the emphasis is on engaging learners in building, tinkering, remixing, and sharing. Students can now create, remix, and share information online. So, too, can their instructors. Brown and Adler contend that in our flatter learning world filled with multiple careers and job skill changes, such learning opportunities are vital. More importantly, with the range of content providers and experts now found online and the ease in which one can access them in the Web 2.0, we are in a continual apprenticeship. But the myriad learning demands of this century can no longer be met with the building of more physical campuses. Digital learning participation is now a key factor for learning of anyone at any age.

A recently popular video on YouTube (Wesch, 2007) from Kansas State Professor Michael Wesch illustrates Web 2.0 technology in less than 5 minutes. This particular video demonstrates that with a world filled with wikis for online collaboration as well as a new blog every second, we are the Web. Platforms such as Wikibooks not only permit joint editing, they also allow for easy monitoring of progress, expert modeling, and peer critiques. Job aids or scaffolded supports can be embedded in a wiki environment to support and extend the learning possibilities. Learners interact with other learners whenever they want. In effect, Wikis, when effectively created, provide the apprenticeship and situated learning possibilities that Brown et al. discussed two decades ago and Vygotsky long before that. And, as John Dewey would have hoped, they are the spaces for creating and then displaying projects for the community. It is the evolving and dynamic nature of a wikibook that links it to sociocultural theory.

Sociocultural theory is not the only theoretical linkage. Most adult learning theorists (e.g., Knowles, 1984; Rogers, 1983) and distance learning experts (e.g., Moore, 1989; Wedemeyer, 1981) argue that the more choices and self-directed learning opportunities you provide to learners, especially adult learners, the greater the chance for learning-related success. From their vantage point, learning must be meaningful, interactive, and reflective. Activities chosen should foster higher self-esteem, internal motivation, and goal driven opportunities. In addition, learning should be open, genuine, inviting, respectful, active, collaborative, and student driven. As emphasized by adult learning expert Jack Mezirow (1991), when these principles are in place, learning is transformed. We believe there are opportunities for such a transformation when employing wikibook projects. With thoughtfully integrated, they can be a disruptive force in education.

BACKGROUND

Series of Wikibook Research Projects

Wikibook Class Project #1

In the spring of 2006, we embarked on the first of three cross-institutional wikibook projects. The lessons were immediate. In offering students the option of writing a chapter in a wikibook across classes at the University of Houston and Indiana University (both Bloomington and Indianapolis campuses), we had only a couple of students who participated. These students were enrolled in courses related to sociocultural aspects of learn-

ing and instruction, especially those involving technology. Surveys about the use of wikibooks were collected from 14 of the students, of which 4 were also interviewed. We used their feedback to enhance the wikibook activity during the following year.

Wikibook Class Project #2

In the fall of 2007, we decided to embed a wikibook project in our courses on learning theories and instructional design. There were two classes—one at the University of Houston and one at Indiana University at Bloomington. Unlike the previous year, this time we made wikibook activities required. Based on feedback from previous students, we designed extensive structures and supports for wikibook activities.

This was a three-part experience which the students knew as "Wikibook Online Work" (WOW) (Bonk, Lee, Kim, & Lin, 2008). Across these two classes, 22 students initially critiqued an existing wikibook on learning theories ("Emerging Perspectives on Learning, Teaching, and Technology"). This wikibook had been designed by students from Professor Michael Orey's classes at the University of Georgia. Houston and Bloomington students were paired up across sites to provide feedback to each other on their respective wikibook critiques. The critiques were posted to Wikispaces and linked back to the original online articles as a means of sharing. The second phase of this experience involved students editing an existing wikibook on learning theories or learning theorists posted by students from Dale Fowler's classes at Indiana Wesleyan University. A job aid or help guide was provided for students.

The first two stages were deemed important in exposing students to wikibooks and the power of the Web 2.0. The third leg of this activity was for students to write chapters of a book that we had initiated at the Wikibooks Website entitled, "The Practice of Learning Theories" (The POLT; see Figure 1). Based on prior student complaints

Figure 1. Digital book cover for the second wikibook project, "The Practice of Learning Theories" (The POLT).

about time dilemmas and coordination of cross-institutional peer reviews, in this phase, we decided that students would receive feedback within their respective institution rather than across them. Again, they were sent a job aid to help with the posting of their chapters. Nevertheless, most students needed our help to do this. Students who did not want their writing posted to a public site were given the option to share with their instructors only. These students wrote 23 chapters for 9 different sections of the POLT. Students also completed an end of semester survey about their wikibook experiences.

The WOW work was definitely unique. It may have been the first time that students critiqued a wikibook, edited a wikibook, and then designed their own wikibook in a single class. Such a procedure emphasizes process and task-based approaches to learning. It also demonstrates the power of wikis and the Web 2.0 as well as the variety of activities that can be designed around them. At the end of the semester, students across

the two sites engaged in a videoconference to share their projects and to celebrate the creation of the POLT wikibook (see Figure 2). Students were given special certificates for completing their wikibook project. Feedback from these students about the use of certificates was extremely positive.

Some students from the POLT project were excited about using wikibooks in their own future teaching. One student, Terry, who spent much time on Native American reservations stated:

I've worked with Native American students and I believe Wikibooks would be a wonderful way for them to display their classroom art collections. I know that all students would benefit from using Wikibooks, but if teachers on the Navajo Nation had the ability to use Wikibooks they could create innovative ways of displaying their works for all to see. Students who had the means to work on projects at home or in dorm settings can access their classroom Wikibook and edit and update

Figure 2. Final class videoconference between students at the University of Houston and Indiana University celebrating the completion of The POLT wikibook.

their works at anytime. Wikibooks could also be created based on their tradition oral stories, ensuring they are preserved for future generations. Also, the wonderful thing about Wikibooks is that you have the ability to put these types of text in their native and translated languages.

Even off the reservations, Wikibooks could be used to create student portfolios, classroom portfolios and other types of alternative assessments. I honestly think that this is just the tip of the "wiki-iceberg" if you will in how it could be applied to a classroom setting anywhere in the world.

As indicated, with this one course experience, Terry had many keen insights into the potential benefits of wikibooks as a resource for cultural and societal preservation and education. The wikibook activity had him thinking well beyond traditional textbooks opportunities.

Wikibook Class Project #3

The third wikibook project was the most ambitious. It involved collaboration across five institutions in four countries (Bonk et al., 2008). These organizations included Indiana University at Bloomington (IUB), Indiana State University (ISU), Beijing Normal University (BNU) in China, the Open University of Malaysia (OUM), and National Chiao Tung University in Hsinchu, Taiwan. While there were many cultural differences, this Wikibook project was conducted in English. This decision placed those in Taiwan, Malaysia, and China at somewhat of a disadvantage. Nonetheless, in many ways, this larger project was the most transformative and interesting, and perhaps the most disruptive.

There was much less structure in this third wikibook project than in the second one. While it was not a chaotic experience, students were given more choice on what and where to contribute. In fact, they brainstormed the wikibook topics and sections at the beginning of the semester in their

Figure 3. Digital book cover for the third wikibook project, "The Web 2.0 and Emerging Learning Technologies" (The WELT).

respective classes. After that, they ranked and grouped the different topic ideas from all those that were offered across the five classes. Those rated the highest, were placed in the wikibook and organized by sections or themes. Students then worked on their respective wikibook chapters during the semester. The duration and timing of the activity, however, varied by location depending on instructor and student preferences as well as university course timetables. Those in Asian universities, for instance, started and ended later than their American counterparts. The resulting book was titled "The Web 2.0 and Emerging Technologies" or "The WELT" (see Figure 3).

Instead of pre-assigning partners across sites as we had done previously, in the WELT project, students could decide to edit or add to anyone's wikibook chapter. In effect, this was a more open learning process than the previous two projects. Though many were at times nervous about how to complete the task, the students seemed to appreciate this more open atmosphere.

Students from these five universities contributed 29 chapters in the six sections of the WELT.

When completed, we surveyed 33 students across the 5 sites about their experiences. In addition, the instructors were email interviewed about their experiences. They reported many challenges as well as successes. Some of their comments are detailed below.

As we were watching the WELT project unfold, we noticed that the five instructors employed vastly different teaching approaches and philosophies to complete the wikibook activity. Interestingly, their approaches led to different degrees of success. For instance, one instructor, Faye, used careful planning and treated each step as a task to complete early. Her extensive planning benefitted the project in immense ways. Not surprisingly, Faye's class was the first to start and first to end the project. However, there was minimal collaboration of her students with those at the other four universities in the project. It is likely that her class completed their work too early for intense interaction and collaboration to occur. In the end, her class experienced mixed levels of success. As Faye put it:

Students followed the schedule and completed their projects on time. Students discussed their chapter outlines in class and when their first drafts were done, students did peer critiquing to help improve each other's chapter writing. Students liked those class activities because they learned from other students' presentations and class discussion on how to improve their chapters.

While her class was generally highly successful in producing chapters for the WELT, Faye also noted that some students did not like having their names removed from their wikibook chapters or others editing their works. As she stated:

(1) some students did not like other people's editing. They believed that their writing was better; and (2) they were not very happy when they names were removed from the site. They spent time on the project and would like to see their names with their chapters.

A second instructor, Cheryl, provided extensive scaffolding and support for her students who lacked English language skills. She recommended greater emphasis on orientation sessions to familiarize students with the wikibook task and associated tools. As someone who had recently moved to a new country, Cheryl was only teaching this one course at the time and, therefore, could spend an extensive amount of time helping her students. As she said, "I tried to stay online more than 6-8 hours a day, in order to chat with my students via MSN, or provide instant feedbacks to their emails or online discussions." Now that is some commitment!

Cheryl helped her students in many ways. As an example, six of her nine students required a writing workshop to improve their English skills. She also matched up one experienced doctoral student with every two new master's students to provide senior level support for their projects. Cheryl's efforts led to much success and satisfaction among her students despite them not having

high levels of English skills. She had the most available time and definitely provided it. Despite her best efforts, she felt her students were at somewhat of a disadvantage compared to other classes. For instance, as the following quote indicates, Cheryl sensed some inequalities in terms of the cross-institutional collaborations.

Some cultural issues and unequal collaborations – Asian students usually are shy of expressing themselves in the public. Besides, because of their language barriers, I observed some of my students tended to agree on what their American peers had commented, especially with those master students of limited English competencies.

A third instructor, Marvin, led much of the WELT wikibook efforts, including writing the introduction to this wikibook. However, his students tended to only collaborate within his class and not with those at other institutions. As with Faye's class, he encountered problems in coordinating interactions across courses in different countries since they started and ended their semesters on different days. To facilitate the wikibook process as well as engage his students, Marvin provided immediate feedback to his students on their wikibook chapters. However, his feedback approaches changed during the semester. For instance, he provided feedback on student midterm papers using track changes features in Microsoft Word. For their final chapters, however, he made his changes right in the WELT wikibook. With Marvin's extensive guidance and careful task structuring, student work was well written and there was a relatively high level of success.

As a result of his efforts, Marvin's students were highly involved in the WELT project. In addition to the wikibook activities, in Marvin's course, all assigned articles were freely available online. Marvin, in fact, had incorporated many reading options each week. With such an approach, his students were no longer required to read mandated textbooks created by traditional publishers. At the same time, they were designing a book of their own. His class, therefore, was an example of extreme disruption in the educational process (Christensen et al., 2008). Whether extensive transformative learning occurred is more difficult to determine.

A fourth instructor, Sunny, who was relatively young, loved to experiment with new technologies. Throughout the semester, she sent Marvin links to many of the Web tools and resources she was using. Sunny assigned her students to work on the topic of personalized learning environments (PLE) in the WELT even though the concept was new to her culture. As she noted, "As for the concept of "PLE," most students cannot make connection to their practices; most of us get the concept from the literature, not from practice. They cannot deeply feel the existence of PLE from their practice." Besides the dilemma of being assigned a topic which is not well known in their culture, Sunny's students were not used to constructivist activities. They also lacked access to the wikibook and would often have to rely on a proxy server to connect to the project.

Again, we would label her class as having modest success. Part of the problem, once again, was the timing of the posting of the wikibook chapters. As with two other classes, her students posted their chapters after the semester had ended for others. Nonetheless, her students seemed to revel in the project.

The fifth instructor, Careen, was not involved much in the project and made the assignment optional. Unlike the other instructors, Careen did not demonstrate the wikibook or require students to be involved in it. Furthering limiting the involvement of her class was the fact that some of her students experienced access problems. Nevertheless, a couple of her students enthusiastically contributed to the Wikibook. Still, unlike the other instructors, this project did not seem to match her course content that semester.

While the project was generally successful, all five instructors raised many serious issues and concerns. Some of these related to wikibook technology and associated tools and features such as editing control and collaboration features. Some problems related to inadequate Internet access or problems accessing the wikibook. At the same time, a couple of instructors noted problems that stemmed from insufficient student backgrounds with such a student-centered and hands-on mode of instruction. And they all found it difficult to coordinate such extensive cross-institutional collaboration. Still the project was a success for most students and classrooms.

Students also sent notes about the motivational benefits of the program. One student from Taiwan stated that "I believe every one of us has got a better understanding, real experiences of wikis and a lot of fun." In the end, the WELT was a success, though, like the other two wikibook projects we have attempted, it was fraught with many challenges and frustrations.

At the time of this writing, we are still adding to the POLT and the WELT in our classes. In fact, as indicated, since the POLT and WELT are publicly available, anyone is welcome to contribute them. For those who are interested in doing so, Web links to all of the resources mentioned in this chapter, including these two wikibooks, are provided at the end of this chapter.

Across this series of wikibook experiences and research, we were interested in determining the degree of support or scaffolding required for students to take advantage of the Web 2.0 and participate in their own learning. Just how might their interactions and collaborations be encouraged and supported? Will they take ownership over the project and be energized by the opportunities to generate learning? Will receptive learning practices really give way to student-centered, participatory ones? To be honest, we have encountered a plethora of challenges and issues as well as success stories. We detail many of these below.

Twenty Tensions of Cross-Institutional Wikibook Projects

As indicated, there were many tensions felt when developing a cross-institutional wikibook. There were problems in designing, coordinating, and completing wikibook activities. For instance, wikibooks do not have sophisticated tools for peer-to-peer and instructor-to-instructor collaboration. As a result, such projects were more difficult than expected. Based on our research as well as our practical experiences, we have much advice or tips for others wishing to design similar projects. Listed in Table 1 is a summary of some of these tensions along with ideas and suggestions related to resolving or addressing them. These are organized into five categories of concerns: (1) instructional issues; (2) collaboration issues; (3) technology issues; (4) knowledge construction and sense of community issues; and (5) wikibook issues.

Instructional Issues

As indicated, Wikibooks are a form of disruptive technology in education (Christensen et al., 2008). Given that most college instructors were not trained to teach with them, if they had any training at all, many of the challenges instructors face with when incorporating wikis and wikibooks in their classes are instructional in nature. First, there is always an inherent risk in attempting something new as well as the associated time requirements. While global education is increasingly important, the time required to coordinate and monitor it as well as the high risk of failure may not be worth the effort.

If one remains convinced of the benefits, testing any new technology is always an important first step. This is especially true of a wiki. To lessen the potential risk, an instructor who has used wikis in the past might archive prior semester work as examples. He might also solicit testimonials from students who helped with previous wikibooks projects. Those coordinating the project might design job aids for instructors related to how to facilitate the wikibook process. At the same time, instructors can make available job aids for students as well as take them to a computer lab for brief training in wikibook creation and editing.

There are also issues related to the degree of control over the wikibook task. Each wikibook situation we have encountered is unique. The amount of support will depend on the type of course, number of students, student familiarity with wikibooks, and many other factors. Based on our experience, it seems that larger numbers of participants in a wikibook project might allow for more open-ended structures than when only a dozen or two students are involved. The more students, the greater the choice and flexibility that might be granted, though more general guidance sheets and additional progress reports may be required. This advice is tentative at best; you will have to see what works best in your situation.

Global education projects also require more coordination and leadership skills among one or more instructors involved in the project. Those involved need to plan their schedules early and make available all necessary contact information. Written commitments may be needed as to what each instructor and class will contribute to the project. They might also come to tentative and clear agreements about assessment practices prior to commencement of the project. Instructors must also decide whether factual knowledge is important and how such knowledge should be assessed in a wikibook activity.

A final instructional issue worth pointing out relates to motivational rewards. Students seem to appreciate recognitions and rewards such as certificates for their wikibook work. Such extrinsic reward practices seem counter to the ideals of participatory and passion-based learning. However, these same students are enrolled in college courses with associated scores, grades, and assessments. It is difficult to overcome such inherent structures in one course activity.

Table 1. Cross-institutional wikibook collaboration issues, tensions, and suggestions.

Cross-Institutional Wikibook Issues	Wikibook Tensions	Wikibook Collaboration Ideas and Suggestions
I. I. Instructional Issues	**1.** Experimentation and risk versus actual impact of learning and requirements related to change.	• Modeling from others. • Create job aids and help sheets. • Train students in wikibook editing and creation. • Archive prior wikibook projects. • Evaluate wikibook efforts. • Share wikibook efforts with colleagues.
	2. Global education deemed important versus time and effort to coordinate.	• Designate contacts and coordinator. • Plan schedules. • Check calendars. • Obtain testimonials from previous students.
	3. Technologies offer new benefits versus frustrating to learn nuances of the technology.	• Test the technologies. • Write to other instructors who have been successful in their wikibook projects and ask about the technologies that they found useful. • Ask students what they already use or are familiar with.
	4. Open-ended learning versus instructor or designer guided.	• Guided learning probably better for first exposure. • The larger the number of participants, the more open-ended the design might be.
	5. Inclusiveness of anyone who wants to be involved versus the reality of coordinating schedules.	• Check schedules. • Get written commitment from other instructors, not just verbal agreements. • Communicate updates or changes related to the wikibook project as they occur. • Share emails and create a distribution list of key participants.
	6. Intrinsically valued experience versus valuing external rewards.	• Experiment with reward structures. • When more participants considering using peer interaction and peer learning as the primary incentive. • Ask current wikibook students what motivates them. Ask former ones what worked.
	7. How learning is assessed versus the excitement of building a product that has no identifiable learning markers.	• Be clear on assessment policies. • Identify exemplary work. • Consider grading reflection papers and group processes.
	8. Factual knowledge versus spontaneous learning and unexpected outcomes.	• Showcase former students who have sent "thank you" emails or notices to you that they have attempted a wikibook in their own classes. • Evaluate the wikibook project after the semester or project ends.
	9. The facilitation skills and activities required versus time available and prior experience.	• Create instructor guides on facilitating a wikibook. • Create wikibook checklists or prompt sheets for instructors. • Embed peer and expert feedback.
II. Collaboration Issues	**10.** Collaboration deemed beneficial versus additional requirements, time, stress, etc.	• Find balance—perhaps experiment with different wikibook collaboration structures and determine what works and what does not work. • Start with a small project and just two classes or institutions.
	11. Intentions of project inclusiveness versus the stress or hesitancy of writing in a second or nonnative language.	• Give non-native speakers wikibook guide sheets and orientation sessions. • Offer praise for small steps completed successfully. • Provide special help sessions for non-native speakers; such special assistance might include a partner who is more experienced but from the same culture. • Provide student testimonials. • Be flexible in terms of time. • Experiment with different language options.

continued on following page

Table 1. continued

Cross-Institutional Wikibook Issues	Wikibook Tensions	Wikibook Collaboration Ideas and Suggestions
III. Technology Issues	**12.** Experimenting with new technologies versus overwhelming students and instructors.	• Try out just 1 or 2 new technologies or technology related activities each semester. • Have a training or demonstration session on wikis and wikibooks. • Create online resources with help text or job aids. Share these with colleagues. • Perhaps have students experiment with editing a wikibook.
	13. Use latest emerging tools for sharing versus using what one has access to or familiarity with (which is always changing); i.e., international participants will not all have the same technologies available.	• Make sure all classes and instructors can implement the technologies used in the wikibook project. • Gain commitment and confirmation early from other instructors and participants.
IV. Knowledge Construction/ Sense of Community Issues	**14.** Constructivist ideals versus previous life experiences of reception learning.	• Scaffold students through editing or critiquing a wikibook before building their own. • Assign peer editing activities of wikibook content early in the course. • Have students discuss and reflect on their learning during the wikibook project.
	15. Learning community goals versus the reality of a 15 week class.	• Consider extending the wikibook project over more than one semester. • Assign some wikibook tasks early in the semester. • Invite students back in later semesters as mentors and experts.
	16. Transformative learning versus bounded course with grades.	• Have a class discussion on the topic of transformative learning. • Assign individual or group reflection activities or debates on the content of the wikibook chapters. • Debrief when and where possible and also reflect on principles and strategies that students found more effective or transformative.
V. Wikibook Issues	**17.** Getting paper done versus abiding by academic and wikibook rules.	• Establish deadlines and structures for the wikibook. • Require peer feedback on multiple drafts of wikibook chapters and assign points for it. • Test out procedures in a computer lab. • Show students the copyright pages or forms in the Wikibooks Website. • Discuss copyright issues and ethics.
	18. Individual ownership versus group or no ownership.	• Hold class discussions on the topic of learning ownership. • Read articles on wikibooks. • Assign students to edit a Wikipedia page or some other wiki. • Create a brief questionnaire asking students about learning ownership related to the wikibook project.
	19. Instructor control versus student control.	• Maintain reflection journal or blog on such issues. • Discuss what worked in prior semesters with students. • Find a happy medium. • Simply ask students how much structure they would like.
	20. Wikibook chapter generated is permanently available online to share versus just doing this for a grade and do not want work up there forever unless it is high quality.	• Give students options of not posting their wikibook chapter when they are done. • Make wikibook password protected or restrict access in some way. • Celebrate success.

Collaboration Issues

Besides instructional issues, a second area of concern and tension relates to collaboration. As all instructors know, collaboration of any type requires additional time and skill. This adds to instructional planning and preparation requirements and, of course, to the associated stress of the wikibook project. Our advice is to start small. Do not attempt a major global wikibook project until you have experimented in a smaller forum first. Some students may also be quite hesitant to write in a second or nonnative language. There are many tactics that can help. Among them are orientation sessions, guide sheets, praise, and prior student testimonials. As seen in Cheryl's class, newer students might also be matched with someone with more experience but who is from the same culture. In addition to lowering any lingering assignment anxiety, such people can provide timely mentoring and advice. Nonnative English students might also be allowed greater flexibility in completing the assignment. Finally, as we saw with the WELT, special help sessions or writing workshops can overcome hesitation surrounding collaborative writing of wikibook chapters or modules.

Technology Issues

A third area to consider concerns the technology involved. Do not simply assign a wikibook project because it sounds novel or interesting. Our advice is to avoid adopting more than one or two new technologies per semester. Test out the technology first and thoughtfully integrate it into your curriculum. As already stated, training resources and orientation events will help prepare your students for such events. During these training sessions, consider having students experiment with browsing or editing a wikibook prior to creating their own. And if you are attempting a cross-institutional wikibook, make sure that the technologies are accessible and understandable by all parties.

Knowledge Construction and Sense of Community Issues

The fourth area of concern we witnessed in our three wikibook projects relates to student familiarity with constructing knowledge and feeling a sense of community within such constructivist practices. Students from Asian countries might not be used to student-led forms of instruction. A wikibook pushes this to the extreme. Hence, they will need additional modeling, scaffolding, reassurance, and peer support. Such students might also discuss and reflect on their learning from the wikibook project during different phases of it. A related difficulty you might face is attempting to create a more constructivist activity and associated learning community in a bounded 15 week course. This issue requires serious planning on the part of instructors. To address this issue, wikibook activities might be assigned early in the semester, while invitations might also be offered for continuing in the project after the semester has ended. As seen with Terry in the POLT wikibook project, reflection, discussion, and debriefing activities awaken students to the potentially transformative aspects of such activities.

Wikibook Issues

Finally, there are a slew of technology issues related to wikibooks themselves. Given the open ended nature of a wikibook, students typically need structures related to due dates, collaborative partners, and what and how to edit content. Sometimes the instructor predetermines the content categories; other times, these are left up to the students. As a form of publishing, wikibooks require that the contributors obey copyright laws. The steps and procedures to abide by copyright laws may require more time and skill than a traditional course paper. At the same time, students should also be aware that as with most wiki-related projects, they do not maintain rights to the content generated. Reading articles on wikibooks or assigning students to edit an existing wikibook may help them better understand this issue. Keep in mind that some wikibooks might be public, while others are private or password protected. Students may not want their chapters permanently posted if the wikibook is public. Ask them. Allowing students to choose whether to post their work online or not will dramatically reduce any sense of tension and simultaneously help empower the students.

FUTURE DIRECTIONS

There are many possible next steps for us. The most obvious is to work on extending and improving the quality of the existing wikibooks: the POLT and the WELT. We welcome collaborative partners and interested parties who wish to enhance one or both books. We may also attempt a wikibook with earlier due dates so that more interaction and knowledge negotiation can occur around the wikibook which is produced, rather than having the wikibook due at the end of the semester with little time for reflection, discussion, and extension. A simple issue such as deciding on a common date the task is due should significantly impact the transformational potential of the class wikibook.

There are myriad future directions for wikibooks. Some Wikibookians we have interviewed feel that they could eventually replace textbooks. If that happens, then wikibooks will quickly become known as a disruptive and potentially transformative technology. Others believe that they are just too complex today for this to happen. In any event, greater understanding of the potential of wikibooks is needed. At the same time, a more refined set of tools for collaborative writing and interaction is required to make such disruptive and perhaps even revolutionary or transformative changes in education possible.

CONCLUSION

In these days of increasing focus on achievement test scores, the educational opportunities made possible by transformative and participatory technologies like wikis are not always apparent. However, transformed learning has been a goal of many educators for decades. John Seely Brown's (1989) invited address at AERA nearly two decades ago in San Francisco recognized the importance of situated cognition and creating cultures of learning. As the more recent article from Brown and Adler (2008) makes evident, such ideas have enormous implications for the world of wikis, blogs, social networking, and virtual worlds today. Learners can now participate more readily in their own learning process. Still, as we found in our three wikibook projects, participatory, and hence, transformational, learning is not easy. One must overcome many obstacles and tensions. Disruptions definitely happen but transformations and learning revolutions will require more sophisticated tools and better understanding of how to use them.

We remain optimistic. As shown in the three-phase wikibook-related work of the POLT and the final product of the WELT, students do engage in significant knowledge construction in well designed and thought out wikibook projects. As indicated, however, it takes much scaffolding, monitoring, modeling, and planning. Even with such supports, sufficient time is necessary for rich and engaging interactions to occur within a wikibook. To just say you can do a wikibook, as in our first wikibook project experience, will likely result in failure. We hope that our experiences can shed light on what works and does not so as to spring to life wikibooks at other educational institutions or settings which transform the learning process by empowering and engaging learners. Perhaps the next step for those exploring emerging technologies in the Web 2.0 will be to better understand the steps, phases, and procedures leading to disruptive and transformative learning experiences with such tools and resources. And perhaps you will be among those leading the charge.

ACKNOWLEDGMENT

We thank all the participants of this study as well as the support personal at the Wikibooks website. We also thank Suthiporn Sajjapanroj who helped us collect data in the first portion of this study.

CHAPTER WEB RESOURCES

Emerging Perspectives on Learning, Teaching, and Technology (wikibook): http://projects.coe.uga.edu/epltt/index.php?title=Main_Page

Flat World Knowledge: http://www.flatworld-knowledge.com/minisite/

Global Text Project: http://globaltext.terry.uga.edu/

Learning Theories (wikibook): http://en.wikibooks.org/wiki/Learning_Theories

Learning Theorists (wikibook): http://en.wikibooks.org/wiki/Learning_Theorists

MIT Press: http://mitpress.mit.edu/main/home/default.asp

The Practice of Learning Theories (The POLT) (wikibook): http://en.wikibooks.org/wiki/The_Practice_of_Learning_Theories

The Web 2.0 and Emerging Technologies (The WELT) (wikibook): http://en.wikibooks.org/wiki/Web_2.0_and_Emerging_Learning_Technologies

Wikibook Online Work (WOW): http://wow-iu-uh.wikispaces.com/

Wikibooks Website: http://en.wikibooks.org/wiki/Main_Page

Yale University Press: http://yalepress.yale.edu/yupbooks/home.asp

REFERENCES

Alexander, B. (2006, March/April). Web 2.0: A new wave of innovation for teaching and learning? *EDUCAUSE Review, 41*(2), 32-44. Retrieved July 9, 2007, from http://www.educause.edu/apps/er/erm06/erm0621.asp

Bonk, C. J., & Kim, K. A. (1998). Extending sociocultural theory to adult learning. In M. C. Smith & T. Pourchot (Eds.), *Adult learning and development: Perspectives from educational psychology* (pp. 67-88). Mahwah, NJ: Lawrence Erlbaum Associates.

Bonk, C. J., Lee, M., Kim, N., & Lin, G. (2008, March). *The tensions of transformation in cross-institutional Wikibook projects: Looking back twenty years to today.* Paper presented at the American Educational Research Association 2008 Annual Meeting, New York, NY.

Brown, A. L., & Palincsar, A. S. (1989). Guided, cooperative learning and individual knowledge acquisition. In L. Resnick (Ed.), *Cognition and instruction: Issues and agendas* (pp. 393-451). Hillsdale, NJ: Erlbaum.

Brown, J. S. (1989, March 29). Situated cognition---a view of learning [keynote address]. In *Proceedings of the Annual American Education Research Association Conference*, San Francisco, California.

Brown, J. S. (2006, December 1). *Relearning learning—applying the long tail to learning.* Retrieved February 9, 2007, from http://www.mitworld.mit.edu/video/419

Brown, J. S., & Adler, R. P. (2008, January/February). Minds on fire: Open education, the long tail, and learning 2.0. *EDUCAUSE Review, 43*(1), 16-32. Retrieved February 23, 2008, from http://connect.educause.edu/Library/EDUCAUSE+Review/MindsonFireOpenEducationt/45823

Brown, J. S., Collins, A., & Duguid, P. (1988). *Cognitive apprenticeship, situated cognition, and social interaction* (Tech. Rep. No. 6886). Bolt, Beranek, and Newman, Inc.

Brown, J. S., Collins, A., & Duguid, P. (1989). Situated cognition and the culture of learning. *Educational Researcher, 18*(1), 32–41.

Cassner-Lotto, J., & Wright Benner, M. (2006). *Report: Are they really ready to work?: Employers perspectives on the basic knowledge and applied skills of new entrants to the 21st century U.S. workforce.* Retrieved June 21, 2007, from http://www.21stcenturyskills.org/documents/FINAL_REPORT_PDF9-29-06.pdf

Christenson, C. M., Horn, M. B., & Johnson, C. W. (2008). *Disrupting class: How disruptive innovation will change the way the world learns.* New York: McGraw-Hill.

Collins, A. (1990). Cognitive apprenticeship and instructional technology. In L. Idol & B. F. Jones (Eds.), *Educational values and cognitive instruction: Implications for reform.* Hillsdale, NJ: Lawrence Erlbaum Associates.

Collins, A., Brown, J. S., & Newman, S. (1989). Cognitive apprenticeship: Teaching the crafts of reading, writing, and mathematics. In L. Resnick, (Ed.), *Knowing, learning, and instruction: Essays in honor of Robert Glaser* (pp. 453-494). Hillsdale, NJ: Erlbaum.

Cross, J. (2007). *Informal learning: Rediscovering natural pathways that inspire innovation and performance.* San Francisco, CA: Pfeiffer Publishing.

Dede, C. (2005). Planning for neomillennial learning styles: Implications for investments in technology and faculty. In D. G. Oblinger & J. L. Oblinger (Eds.), *Educating the Net generation.* Retrieved November 20, 2006, from http://www.educause.edu/content.asp?page_id=6069&bhcp=1

Dewey, J. (1884, January). The new psychology. *Andover Review, 2,* 278-289. Retrieved May 30, 2008, from http://psychclassics.yorku.ca/Dewey/newpsych.htm

Dewey, J. (1897, January). My pedagogic creed. *School Journal, 54,* 77-80. Retrieved May 30, 2008, from http://dewey.pragmatism.org/creed.htm

Dewey, J. (1910). *How we think.* Boston, MA: D. C. Heath.

Dewey, J. (1916). *Democracy and education: An introduction to the philosophy of education.* New York: Macmillan.

Downes, S. (2005, October). E-learning 2.0. *E-Learn Magazine.* Retrieved October 26, 2006, from http://elearnmag.org/subpage.cfm?section=articles&article=29-1

Dye, S. (2006, May 15). Text messages to help students study by phone. *The New Zealand Herald.* Retrieved August 22, 2006, from http://subs.nzherald.co.nz/topic/story.cfm?c_id=186&objectid=10381845

Dziuban, C. D., Moskal, P. D., & Hartman, J. (2005). Higher education, blended learning, and the generations: Knowledge is power--no more. In J. Bourne & J. C. Moore (Eds.), *Elements of quality online education: Engaging communities.* Needham, MA: Sloan Center for Online Education.

Evans, P. (2006, January/February). The Wiki factor. *BizEd,* 28-32. Retrieved February 11, 2007, from http://www.aacsb.edu/publications/Archives/JanFeb06/p28-33.pdf

Gallimore, R., & Tharp, R. (1990). Teaching mind in society: Teaching, schooling, and literate *discourse*. In L. C. Moll (Ed.), *Vygotsky in education: Instructional implications of sociohistorical psychology* (pp. 175-205). New York: Cambridge University Press.

Garrobo, A. (2007). No borders: Global text project digitizes third world. *Redandblack.com*. Retrieved January 30, 2007, from http://www.redandblack.com/news/2007/01/30/

Knowles, M. (1984). *Andragogy in action*. San Francisco: Jossey-Bass.

Langer, J. A., & Applebee, A. A. (1987). *How writing shapes thinking*. Urbana, IL: National Council of Teachers of English.

Lave, J., & Wenger, E. (1991). *Situated learning: Legitimate peripheral participation*. New York: Cambridge University Press.

Lenhart, A., & Fox, S. (2006, July 19). *Bloggers: Portrait of America's new storytellers*. Washington, DC: Pew Internet & American Life Report. Retrieved on July 9, 2007, from http://www.pewinternet.org/pdfs/PIP%20Bloggers%20Report%20July%2019%202006.pdf

Lenhart, A., Madden, M., & Hitlin, P. (2005). *Teens and technology: Youth are leading the transition to a fully wired and mobile nation*. Washington, DC: Pew Internet & American Life Report. Retrieved on November 3rd, 2006 from http://www.pewinternet.org/pdfs/PIP_Teens_Tech_July2005web.pdf

Mezirow, J. (1991). *Transformative dimensions of adult learning*. San Francisco, CA: Jossey-Bass.

Moore, M. G. (1989). Editorial: Three types of interaction. *American Journal of Distance Education, 3*(2), 1–6.

Oblinger, D. G. (2008). Growing up with Google: What it means to education. *Becta: Emerging technologies for learning, 3*, 10-29. Retrieved April 10, 2008, from http://partners.becta.org.uk/upload-dir/downloads/page_documents/research/emerging_technologies08_chapter1.pdf

Palincsar, A. S. (1986). The role of dialogue in providing scaffolded instruction. *Educational Psychologist, 21*(1 & 2), 73–98. doi:10.1207/s15326985ep2101&2_5

Rogers, C. R. (1983). *Freedom to learn for the 80s*. Columbus, OH: Charles E. Merrill Publishing Company.

Scardamalia, M., & Bereiter, C. (1986). Research on written composition. In M. C. Wittrock (Ed.), *Handbook of research on teaching*. (3rd ed., pp. 778-803). New York: Macmillan Education Ltd.

Tharp, R. (1993). Institutional and social context of educational reform: Practice and reform. In E. A. Forman, N. Minnick, & C. A. Stone (Eds.), *Contexts for learning: Sociocultural dynamics in children's development* (pp. 269-282). New York: Oxford University Press.

Tharp, R., & Gallimore, R. (1988). *Rousing minds to life: Teaching, learning, and schooling in social context*. New York: Cambridge University Press.

Vygotsky, L. (1986). *Thought and language* (rev. ed.). Cambridge, MA: MIT Press.

Vygotsky, L. S. (1978). *Mind in society*. Cambridge, MA: Harvard University Press.

Wedemeyer, C. A. (1981). *Learning at the back door: Reflections on non-traditional learning in the lifespan*. Madison, WI: University of Wisconsin Press.

Wenger, E. (1998). *Communities of practice: Learning, meaning, and identity*. Cambridge, UK: Cambridge University Press.

Wesch, M. (2007). *Web 2.0...the machine is us/ing us* [Video file]. Video posted to http://www.youtube.com/watch?v=6gmP4nk0EOE

Young, J. R. (2008a, February 28). Abilene U. to give iPhones or iPods to all freshman. *Chronicle of Higher Education*. Retrieved February 28, 2008, from http://chronicle.com/wiredcampus/article/2782/university-to-give-iphones-or-ipods-to-all-incoming-freshmen?utm_source=at&utm_medium=en

Young, J. R. (2008b, February 29). Forget e-mail: New messaging service has students and professors atwitter. *Chronicle of Higher Education*, A15. Retrieved February 26, 2008, from http://chronicle.com/free/v54/i25/25a01501.htm

Chapter 9
Web–Based Video for e–Learning:
Tapping into the YouTube™ Phenomenon

Chareen Snelson
Boise State University, USA

ABSTRACT

The recent explosive growth of Web-based video has expanded the repository of free content that can be tapped into for e-learning. Millions of video clips are now available online and more are uploaded each day. Since the creation of YouTube™ in 2005, a video clip phenomenon has swept the Internet. Never before has it been so easy to locate, record, and distribute video online. This opens intriguing possibilities for teaching, learning, and course design for e-learning. This chapter introduces Web-based video as a new form of educational motion picture, delves into technical aspects of Web 2.0 video tools, describes instructional strategies that integrate Web-based video clips in e-learning, and examines barriers that could potentially inhibit its use. Future directions are also discussed.

INTRODUCTION: THE YOUTUBE PHENOMENON

Since the invention of YouTube™ (http://www.youtube.com) in 2005, video has spread rapidly on the Web. These days online video is so common that it seems to turn up everywhere. Video is embedded or linked from Web pages featuring nearly every imaginable type of content including news, travel, fitness, education, and more. YouTube has sparked a phenomenon of online video viewing, sharing, and production that now extends well beyond the confines of its website. Dozens of video-sharing sites, with features similar to YouTube, have appeared online in recent years and this trend continues. While many of these sites were designed for the general user, others with a more specialized focus have begun to emerge including several oriented toward academic fields. Examples include video sites for science or scientific research such as LabAction (http://www.labaction.com) and SciVee™ (http://www.scivee.tv) Video-sharing sites designed for educators include TeacherTube® (http://www.teachertube.com) and SchoolTube® (http://www.schooltube.com)

DOI: 10.4018/978-1-60566-729-4.ch009

Copyright © 2010, IGI Global. Copying or distributing in print or electronic forms without written permission of IGI Global is prohibited.

As the number of video-sharing sites grows so does the amount of free video content available for instant access through the Internet. On YouTube alone, the number of video clips has skyrocketed into the millions and more clips are uploaded every day (USA Today, 2006). In fact, every minute more than ten hours of video content is uploaded to YouTube (YouTube, 2008). The result is a growing repository of media that can be tapped into for e-learning.

Web-based video has attracted a sizable viewing audience of Internet users as well. A report from the *Pew Internet & American Life Project* (Madden, 2007) indicates that many Internet users are regularly watching video online. This is corroborated by Internet marketing statistics which reveal that online video viewing is on the rise (e-Marketer, 2008). A form of video clip culture, characterized by frequent consumption of short video segments, has emerged on the Web with YouTube ranking among the top ten online video destinations (Comscore, 2007; Nielsen, 2008).

Web 2.0 video-sharing technologies are beginning to play an important role in educational institutions. *The Horizon Report* for 2008, co-published by the New Media Consortium and the EDUCAUSE Learning Initiative, predicts that adoption of video-sharing technologies by educational institutions will become widespread within one year or less. Already, a large number of universities have established YouTube channels that they populate with video clips of school news, lectures, or other events. Examples include the UC Berkeley channel (http://www.youtube.com/user/ucberkeley) and the Stanford University channel (http://www.youtube.com/user/stanforduniversity.)

The massive quantity of free online video content combined with the widespread availability of Web 2.0 video tools brings new opportunities to integrate multimedia into e-learning environments. This chapter introduces Web-based video as a new form of educational motion picture, delves into technical aspects of Web 2.0 video tools,

describes instructional strategies that integrate Web-based video clips in online education, and examines barriers that could potentially inhibit its use. Future directions are also discussed.

WEB-BASED VIDEO: THE NEW EDUCATIONAL MOTION PICTURE

Fundamental Attributes of Motion Picture Technologies

The term *Web-based video* is used in this chapter to describe digital video that is distributed through the Internet and accessed with computers. At its fundamental core, Web-based video is simply another form of motion picture technology. Video is composed of a sequence of moving images and may or may not include a sound track. This basic description includes any form of image sequence that plays across a timeline, including animation, image slideshows, and video recordings of real-world people and places. The elemental nature of film and video as an image sequence has remained a constant since the creation of motion picture technologies in the late 1800s. At that time, inventors such as Thomas Edison were busy crafting devices that would record and play motion picture film. The Edison Manufacturing Company recorded a large number of films in a homemade studio called the Black Maria (Dickson & Dickson, 1970). A few of these films can be found on YouTube by typing the name "Thomas Edison" into the search form. However, a more complete collection of digitized Edison films is located at the Library of Congress American Memory website (http://memory.loc.gov/ammem/edhtml/edmvhm.html.) These films provide a glimpse back to the earliest days of motion pictures.

Motion Pictures in the Schools

Early in the twentieth century, the motion picture began to appear in U.S. public schools. According to Saettler (2004) the first use of educational film occurred in 1910 in the Rochester, New York school system. Silent films were the available technology of the time and were considered by some to be a technological wonder. One of the earliest teaching manuals for classroom film described in glowing terms how film could bring the miracles and wonders of nature into the classroom (Ellis & Thornborough, 1923). A similar sentiment was echoed by Greene (1926) who wrote that, "The films furnished a wealth of new scenes, inaccessible actualities, new experiences that were instantly comprehensible; motion pictures broadened horizons swiftly and enjoyably; and thus inevitably started the world to thinking about the power of the picture" (p. 123). Others, who were less enthusiastic, warned that the benefits of educational film were unfounded and based on unproven psychological principles (Castro, 1922). Related concerns were articulated in recent years by Clark and Feldon (2005) who described several principles of multimedia learning that are commonly believed to be true, yet are not adequately supported by research. Questions about the effect of media on learning and the interplay between media and instructional method have been researched and written about for decades. Much of the discussion has manifested as an ongoing argument called the "media effects debate" (Clark, 1983, 1994; Kozma, 1994; Nathan & Robinson, 2001).

Technical Capabilities of Media that Support Learning

The complex issue of how media might impact learning is compounded by the technical parameters governing what it can actually do. Each form of media has different capabilities that support or inhibit how it can be used for instruction. As an example, consider the attributes of silent film, which was the first form of educational motion picture. This was a medium that supported presentations of visual motion sequences, without a synchronous audio track. It was visual and silent, but adequate for some instructional events. For example, a time-lapse video showing a flower bud opening in moments rather than days would be sufficient on its own without the inclusion of sounds from the surrounding environment. Alternatively, if a teacher wished to teach a science lesson on lightning, he or she could play a film showing the lightning strike. Unfortunately, the sound of the slightly delayed thunder could not be included in silent film. Thus, an incomplete representation of the natural phenomenon is constrained by the limitations of the technology used to present it. This further illustrates the complicated interplay between media and method. The media might support some methods, but not others and vice versa.

The technical capabilities of film began to expand in the late 1920s when the sound film became available. Brunstetter (1937) described how the sound film surpassed earlier forms of visual aids, including silent film, because motion could be coupled with its associated sound. One of the intrinsic benefits of synchronized sound was described by Brunstetter as *continuity of thought*, whereby "Scenes and sequences are linked together for the orderly exposition of ideas or the chronological development of narration" (1937, p. 3). Brunstetter described continuity of thought as an advantage of sound film that was logically evident. In the early days of sound film there was little in the way of theory or research to support this assertion. However, decades later Paivio's (1990) dual coding theory proposed the presence of separate channels for processing of visual and verbal information in the human mind. Related multimedia learning research on the modality effect revealed that the simultaneous presentation of visual and auditory information can reduce cognitive load and improve learning under certain conditions (Low & Sweller, 2005; Mayer, 2001).

Technological Advancements and Obsolescence

The fundamental combination of visual and auditory information that was introduced in the sound film has endured through decades of technological advancements. In general, prerecorded motion pictures involve the dual technologies of media and media players. The evolution of motion picture technology has produced several iterations of media and player systems. The film reel and projector was the dominant technology used in schools for several decades from the early 1900s through the 1950s (Saettler, 2004). In the 1960s schools began to switch over to videotape and the older film reels and projectors began to vanish (Winslow, 1970). During the 1980s and 1990s, a series of videodisc formats emerged, including the 12 inch interactive videodisc, compact disc, and DVD. Investment costs for players and media were imposed on schools and libraries when switching to newer formats. It was never certain how long the latest video media and player hardware would last before becoming obsolete. While writing about library acquisitions of media technologies, Dick (1999) noted that "In an age of increasingly rapid technological obsolescence, the anticipated shelf life of any new video format—rather than its inherent superiority—probably figures into its widespread adoption" (p. 51).

The problem of technological obsolescence due to continually changing media formats and players is minimized with Web-based video. The technology on YouTube is designed for the general Internet user to access and view through a standard Web browser. Authoring capabilities are also starting to become browser-based, which further diminishes issues of cost and obsolescence for video technologies. The technical capabilities of Web 2.0 video tools are becoming increasingly sophisticated, making them a valuable tool for e-learning designers and practitioners. Because of this, it is beneficial to gain at least a basic understanding of the tools and their capabilities. This facilitates the process of matching Web 2.0 tools to instructional methods that are supported by the existing technical capabilities. The next section provides an overview of the technical capabilities commonly found on YouTube, which is the largest video-sharing service online. Since similar features are found on many of the other video-sharing sites, knowledge of YouTube is generally transferable to other Web 2.0 video tools.

TECHNICAL CAPABILITIES OF WEB 2.0 VIDEO TOOLS

Flash Video Format

Web 2.0 video tools typically work through Web pages and browser software such as Internet Explorer®, Firefox®, and Safari®. There are some video services that require users to download and install a player on their computers (e.g. iTunes®). However, the discussion here will focus on those tools that allow users to work directly through the browser to view, manage, and upload video content. This is how YouTube works. Each video on the YouTube site is embedded in its own Web page for viewing directly from the browser window. Videos on YouTube, and most other video-sharing sites, are encoded as Flash® video, which is free and nearly ubiquitous. Marketing statistics published on the Adobe® website indicate that Flash has been installed on nearly 99% of all Internet-enabled computers (Adobe Systems Inc., 2008). Updates and installations are simple to perform through a few mouse clicks at the download site located at http://www.adobe.com/products/flashplayer/. The Flash player is not only common, but cross platform as well. This minimizes the need to install multiple players to open proprietary video formats such as Windows Media® Player, QuickTime®, and Real Player® media. For online educators, who have little control over the diverse array of computer systems students use to access their courses, this is a valuable technical attribute. It means that students should be able to view online videos without experiencing excessive technical difficulties.

Recording and Producing Video for YouTube

The process of recording, editing, and producing video for YouTube is relatively straightforward. This is due in part to the growing array of easy to use video cameras and software tools designed for the everyday user. These days, many cell phones and digital cameras have the capability to record short video clips in addition to static photos. Inexpensive portable video cameras, such as the Flip camera (http://www.theflip.com), make it easier than ever to record, capture, and edit video clips suitable for online video-sharing. Built-in webcams are now standard equipment on many laptop computers and low cost plug-and-play webcams are available for any computer with a USB port. Webcams can be used to record video directly into YouTube through the Quick Capture feature on the YouTube site. Alternatively, video can be saved or transferred to the hard drive of a computer where it can be edited using free software that comes bundled with the operating system. For example, Windows® computers typically come with Movie Maker software and Macintosh® computers come with iMovie®. YouTube will accept videos that are produced using either of these programs. Browser-based editing is also beginning to appear, which means that users may soon be able to do nearly all video production through the browser. An example is Adobe® Premiere® Express (http://www.adobe.com/products/premiereexpress.) This software makes it possible for users to edit video directly in the Web browser and then host it on the PhotoBucket (http://photobucket.com) media sharing site. Over time, more services like this may become available.

Tools Available with a YouTube Account

All video-sharing sites require users to create an account before they can use features beyond simple searching and viewing. After YouTube became an independent subsidiary of Google, Inc. it became possible to establish a YouTube account through an existing Google account (Google Press Center, 2006). Those with accounts can establish their own YouTube channel, which is a Web page that can be customized and populated with playlists, subscriptions to other channels, and uploaded videos. At the present time, account holders may upload any number of videos. However there is a limitation on length of approximately 10 minutes and file size of 1GB. This may change in the future since the technology is continually evolving. Currently, when a video is uploaded it is converted to Flash format and a player, Web page, and HTML embed code are automatically generated for the video as shown in Figure 1 (Fahs, 2008).

After logging into a YouTube account, videos may be collected and organized into playlists, quicklists, or favorites on the personal YouTube channel. Playlists add the advantage of providing a way to share a collection of videos using a link to the playlist, or with an embeddable player. An example of a playlist of is shown in Figure 2.

Custom players may be created from playlists or favorites to produce an interactive and navigable collection. Once established they can be updated to change the appearance or content dynamically. A screenshot of a custom player is shown in Figure 3. Users can watch the videos in sequential order, progress ahead or back using the arrows, or navigate by clicking on the desired selection in the navigation panel.

Basic usage statistics indicating number of views for each video clip, dates of viewing, demographics of users, and country of origin are available through the YouTube Insight tool shown in Figure 4. This can be valuable for an instructor or researcher who is interested in usage

Figure 1. YouTube video page

Figure 2. A YouTube playlist

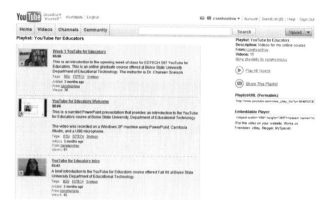

data for video content he or she has uploaded to YouTube.

After a video has been uploaded to YouTube, there are additional tools that can be used for editing. The screenshot in Figure 5 shows several of these. The *Info & Settings* tool enables changes to the video title, description, or tags to be made.

The *Audio Swap* tool provides a way to select a music track from a list within YouTube and use it as background music for a video. The *Annotations* tool makes it possible to add notes, speech bubbles, or clickable hotspots that can be linked to another YouTube video, channel, or search result. (For examples see: http://uk.youtube.com/t/

Figure 3. Custom video player created in YouTube

Figure 4. YouTube insight usage tracking data

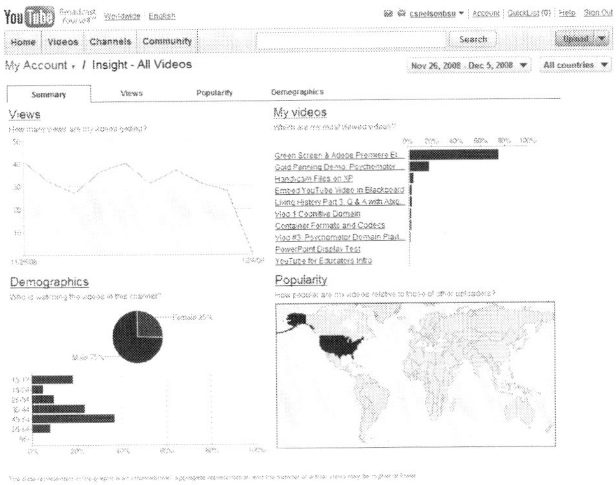

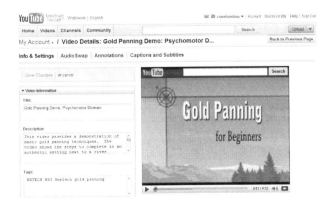

annotations_about). The *Captions and Subtitles* tool allows a closed caption file to be added to the video for accessibility.

Online Distribution of Video

Web-based videos are easily distributed online through hyperlinks, HTML embed code, or through a set of share options that allow video to be posted to MySpace® (http://www.myspace.com/), Facebook® (http://www.facebook.com/), personal blogs, or social bookmarking sites such as Del.icio.us® (http://del.icio.us/) or Digg™ (http://digg.com/.) The hyperlink to the video page can be pasted into other Web pages or electronic course documents for students to click and open just like any other Web page. Each video on YouTube typically comes with a piece of HTML embed code that can be copied and pasted into the HTML of a website, blog, or online discussion forum. Unless the person who uploaded the YouTube video has disabled embedding, this code is located in a box near the word "embed" on each video's Web page to the right of the video player as illustrated in Figure 6. The code contains a link that points to the video and the player appears directly where the code is pasted. The video looks like it is part of the Web page even though the actual video

Figure 5. Editing tools in YouTube

Figure 6. The HTML embed code for YouTube videos

file streams from YouTube and is not physically copied over to a new site. Once the code has been pasted, the player is embedded in the page and only needs to be clicked to play the video.

Downloading and Related Copyright Issues

The ability to download the actual video clip file varies from one video-sharing site to another. At the time of this writing, Google Video™ (http://video.google.com/) and Metacafe® (http://www.metacafe.com/) serve as examples of video-sharing services that do provide a mechanism for downloading. However, YouTube does not currently provide a download button or tool that will allow users to capture a copy of the video file to save on a computer hard drive or portable device. Many third party options are available to capture, download, and convert video files from YouTube and other similar services. A Google® search will turn up a considerable selection of software tools and how-to articles explaining how to download videos from YouTube. There are even videos on YouTube explaining how to download YouTube videos. However, caution is advised for two reasons. First, the YouTube terms of use at http://youtube.com/t/terms prohibits the use of technologies other than their own player to access video. Second, copyright and fair use issues are problematic, subject to change, and full of unclear

rules about the current online video distribution phenomenon. However, some information specific to online video is available. The Center for Social Media website at http://www.centerforsocialmedia.org is a good starting point for information related to fair use of online video.

Copyright applies to both downloading and uploading video, meaning of course that copyrighted video should not be uploaded or downloaded. Many video clips have been removed from YouTube due to copyright violations. Some of these have been tracked as part of a research project conducted by MIT Free Culture on the YouTomb website at http://youtomb.mit.edu/. In order to combat the problem, YouTube recently added a new video identification tool, which is a technology designed to help detect copyright violations. Through this tool content developers can attach a type of digital fingerprint to video content which can be detected through YouTube. This provides better control over copyright protected content on the YouTube website (YouTube Help Center, 2008).

Searching for Video Online

It is possible to avoid downloading or uploading video altogether if simple search and online sharing are all that is needed. Nearly all video-sharing sites offer a search tool and many have advanced search features. It should be noted that when users upload videos to YouTube, they type their own title, description, video category, and search tags for their video. This can sometimes lead to unexpected search results. It may be necessary to use multiple synonyms to locate clips of interest. The panel of related videos on each YouTube video page can also help identify content of interest on a particular topic.

It is typical to be able to search for, view, and share video clips from most video-sharing services. However, those tools work only within the service they are contained in. For example, when searching YouTube for a video clip about polar bears all results will be YouTube videos related to polar bears. Fortunately, there are other video search tools available that enable users to search across multiple video-sharing sites. A few examples of these are Blinx (http://www.blinkx.com), Google Video™ (http://video.google.com), Searchforvideo (http://www.searchforvideo.com), and TubeSurf (http://tubesurf.com) Specialty video search tools have also begun to appear online. EduTube (http://www.edutube.org) is a search tool designed specifically for educational video search. EduTube allows users to search for video by category, video type, duration, and educational level. Another search tool, called MeFeedia™ (http://mefeedia.com), provides a way for users to create channels where they can aggregate playlists of video clips from multiple video-sharing sites. Tools such as these expand the search coverage and increase the chances of finding useful video content.

Collaboration Tools

Within video-sharing sites there exists the potential for collaborative activities suitable for online instruction. The use of these tools may require that all participants have accounts with the service, however. As an example, YouTube has a contact list feature that works much like an internal message system. It allows videos to be shared with other YouTube users for either public or private viewing. If all of the students in an online course possess accounts on YouTube it is possible to share video clips privately with those students only. Comments and video responses can also be posted by YouTube members to respond to posted videos. YouTube Groups provides another mechanism for a community of YouTube members to post video and have asynchronous discussions based on a topic or interest. An example of an educational group on YouTube is the K12 Education group (http://www.youtube.com/group/K12.) Synchronous real-time collaboration is also possible through the YouTube Streams tool (http://www.youtube.com/streams_main.) With streams, a group of students can share and discuss YouTube videos in real time.

A summary of some of the technical capabilities of YouTube that online educators may find valuable are listed in Table 1. Many of these features are available on other video-sharing sites. The next section of this chapter explores instructional strategies that are possible given the existing technical attributes of YouTube and many other video-sharing services.

INTEGRATING WEB-BASED VIDEO: INSTRUCTIONAL STRATEGIES FOR E-LEARNING

YouTube as an Educational Tool

The literature about YouTube as an educational tool is scant at the present time. However, a selection of proposed educational strategies for YouTube video has begun to appear. Strategies for general classroom integration of YouTube videos include critical analysis and debate of video speeches posted by political candidates, evaluation of science experiment videos, presentation of art and music performances, student-generated videos to replace PowerPoint presentations, examples of real-world math concepts, and student plays recorded and posted online (Tamim, Shaikh, &

Table 1. Technical capabilities of YouTube conducive to online education

Locate Video	Basic and advanced search
Watch Video	Flash player embedded in Web page
Share and Distribute Video	E-mail or paste link in course documents, copy and paste HTML embed code, use social bookmarking tools
Collect and Organize Video	Personalized channel, favorites, quick list, playlist, subscriptions, custom players
Video Production	Video upload, quick capture, annotations
Collaboration	Contact list, comment tools, groups, live streams

Bethel, 2007). Strategies proposed for online education include the use of Web-based video for visualizing concepts, depiction of real world and historical events, vicarious experience through virtual field trips, video case analysis in online discussions or WebQuests, and motivational or human perspective videos (Snelson, 2008a, 2008b). Integration strategies have also been proposed for specific content areas as well. Rees (2008) explained how YouTube and other primary source video sites serve as valuable repositories of video clips for the history classroom. Historical video clips can be used to illustrate events, attitudes, and lifestyles of the past. YouTube videos are also being considered for use in medical education. Skiba (2007) described YouTube content that might be valuable in nursing education. McNeilly (2008) suggests that there is potential benefit in the use of YouTube video vignettes depicting psychiatric conditions within the field of behavioral science medical education.

Representational Attributes of Video for Learning

Although there is a small handful of published suggestions pertaining to integration strategies for YouTube, there is currently little direct theory or research to guide e-learning practitioners. Information must be extrapolated from related sources such as the educational film and video literature that spans back about one century. Since YouTube is essentially a hosting and distribution

system for video, this literature serves as a baseline of information to build on. There are research-based principles of multimedia learning that can be applied to Web-based video. The way people learn from multimedia presentations is likely to maintain some level of consistency across learning contexts. This assertion is based on the fundamental nature of video as a representation that combines a visual motion image sequence with a sound track, consistent with the visual-verbal information channels proposed by dual coding theory (Paivio, 1990). As video plays, the eyes and ears simultaneously channel dual streams of information together into working memory thus limiting competition for limited visual resources. This implies enhanced information processing efficiency while learning from video presentations, which are a form of multimedia. According to Mayer (2001), "The rationale for multimedia presentations—that is, presenting material in words and pictures—is that it takes advantage of the full capacity of humans for processing information" (p. 4). Depending on how it is designed, multimedia has the capacity to present information in an efficient form that minimizes cognitive load (Mayer & Moreno, 2003). In other words, video can be used to make learning easier under some conditions such as when illustrating how a bicycle pump works using animation and audio narration (Mayer, 2001).

As a dynamic form of representation, video has the capacity to effectively illustrate ideas, events, and processes. The intrinsic representational value

Table 2. Educational uses for representational attributes of motion pictures

Strategy	Example
Motion Sequence	Demonstrate the sequence of movements in a yoga stretch.
Draw Attention to Details	Use an animated diagram with moving arrows to illustrate blood flow through the human body.
Replay Real-World Events, People, or Performances	Show the Tacoma Narrows Bridge collapse, see a speech by President Kennedy, watch Luciano Pavarotti sing.
Visit Dangerous or Faraway Places	Use video in a virtual field trip to a volcano or the Moon.
Change the Speed of Natural Phenomena	Slow the speed of a water drop splashing to reveal the details or speed up the process of a flower blooming.
View the Very Small	Watch video of cell division or see the swimming motion of microscopic pond life.

of the educational motion picture has contributed to its longevity in education. Video can represent motion sequences; draw attention to details; replay real-world events, speeches, or performances; enable vicarious visits to dangerous or faraway places; change the speed of natural phenomena, or show scenes of microscopic life. These attributes span across all forms of motion picture technology available since late 1920s when sound films began to appear. Specific examples illustrating common educational uses for the representational attributes of motion pictures are listed in Table 2.

Interactive Video

The YouTube phenomenon extends the traditional instructional uses for video by providing greater ease of distribution and enhanced opportunities for interactivity. All videos on YouTube have basic interactivity in the YouTube video player, which is common to most video-sharing services. Multimedia with basic interactivity, where users have control over the pace of the presentation, has been associated with learning gains (Mayer & Chandler, 2001). Greater levels of interactivity that permit users to jump directly to video sections pertaining to specific informational needs have also been associated with learning gains (Zhang, Zhou, Briggs, & Nunamaker, 2006). The hypermedia environment of Web-based video supports both basic and branched interactivity. Basic

interactivity is provided through the player with its controls for stop, play, and rewind. Branching interactivity can be constructed through custom players, playlists, and annotation links placed directly on each video to enable users to jump to other videos. For example, a video documentary of the Oregon Trail could contain links to other videos showing stops along the way. Branching stories or training scenarios can also be created so that learners explore different video segments to correspond with the choices they click along the way. Collaboration among students working through this type of branching scenario can be facilitated through the comments or messaging system in YouTube. This is consistent with constructivist concepts of learning, where learners construct knowledge based on interpretation of their experiences in both individual and social learning environments (Jonassen, 1999). Social construction of knowledge aligns closely to the participatory culture of Web 2.0 learning environments (Brown & Adler, 2008).

Video for Online Discussions

Within the online course, video-sharing can serve as an alternative to text-based discussions. This works through the use of webcams, which students can use to record video logs, or vlogs, of thoughts and ideas about the discussion topic. The vlog posts are easily uploaded to YouTube for distribution to classmates and the instructor. An asynchronous video conversation occurs when video responses are made to reply to other student or instructor vlog posts. Vlogs can be shared directly through YouTube or by pasting the HTML embed code into the discussion board posts within a course management system. Other types of video-enhanced discussions can be centered on existing YouTube videos that match course content. News videos are easy to find online and can be used to introduce critical current event topics that depict scenes and people who are involved in the event. Web-based video can also be used to explore broad themes such as bias, diversity, human behavior, or media literacy. Critical thinking can be introduced by asking students to critique and analyze the quality or accuracy of information presented in YouTube videos. Students may also locate and contribute videos on a given topic for further discussion.

Tips for Getting Started with YouTube

Educators can find considerable value in Web-based video. It is free, easy to distribute, and integrates an audiovisual element to the text-based virtual classroom. Although video is something most educators are familiar with, they may experience some disorientation when first exploring the Web 2.0 video environment. Those who are new to the array of YouTube-like video sites may find themselves overwhelmed and not sure where to begin. The suggestions described above provide some direction and ideas. However, the applications of Web-based video may vary considerably across the content areas. The following strategies are useful when first exploring what Web-based video, YouTube, and the other services have to offer.

- Begin with a video search to see if there is any content available for the specific need. Try sites such as YouTube and also video search engines such as EduTube, TubeSurf,

and Blinx (described earlier). Use multiple synonyms as search phrases.

- If video for a specific topic is not located, then try a broader or more generic theme. Is there a common thematic thread that weaves through the topic such as equity, diverse human perspective, prosperity, activism, motion, or travel?
- Browse the video categories listed on each site. Videos are organized by genre such as comedy, education, and news. On YouTube the genres are found by clicking the *Videos* link near the top of the screen at the YouTube site.
- Create an account with YouTube (or other service) and collect links to videos that match course content. Prepare playlists with more video than needed in case a clip is taken offline.
- When possible, develop original content that meets course needs. Post it on YouTube (or elsewhere) for easy distribution on the Web.

While the tips and strategies just described provide direction toward successful integration of Web-based video in e-learning, it should be noted that there are also some potential barriers. The next section describes some of the most common issues that might surface when working with video on YouTube and the rest of the video sites now available.

ADDRESSING BARRIERS TO THE INTEGRATION OF WEB-BASED VIDEO

Concerns about Academic Value

One barrier that might be encountered when integrating Web-based video is a form of bias against video-sharing sites containing user-generated content. The academic value of what is considered

Table 3. Examples of YouTube channels containing educational content

Name of YouTube Channel	Website Address
Computer History Museum	http://www.youtube.com/user/ComputerHistory
Massachusetts Institute of Technology	http://www.youtube.com/user/MIT
National Geographic	http://www.youtube.com/user/NationalGeographic
Nobel Prize	http://www.youtube.com/user/thenobelprize
Public Broadcasting System	http://www.youtube.com/user/PBS
ScienCentral News	http://www.youtube.com/user/sciencentral
TED Talks	http://www.youtube.com/user/TEDtalksDirector
UChannel	http://www.youtube.com/user/uchannel

by some to be an entertainment service may not be readily apparent. There have also been instances of inappropriate or illegal behavior on YouTube. Examples include the recent videotaped beating of a teenage girl (Schoetz, Canning, & Brady, 2008) and embarrassing videos of teachers that were secretly recorded on cell phone cameras and posted on YouTube (Carr, 2007). While the presence of poor behavior and entertainment video give pause, nevertheless there are many educational gems to be found on sites like YouTube. They are not always obvious at first glance and some open-minded exploration is often necessary. The presence of good educational content should help to alleviate the concerns of skeptics. Several examples of educational YouTube channels are listed in Table 3. There are many more to be found online while searching for appropriate video content.

Additional evidence of educational and academic value of YouTube is found in the emergence of innovative research and practice. One example is the work of Kansas State University professor Michael Wesch, whose research in digital ethnography extends into YouTube (See: http://www.youtube.com/user/mwesch.) His video, *Web 2.0...The Machine is Us/ing Us* (http://www.youtube.com/watch?v=6gmP4nk0EOE) released on YouTube on January 31, 2007 has been viewed more than 6 million times. A more recent video called *An anthropological introduction to YouTube* (http://www.youtube.com/watch?v=TPAO-lZ4_hU),

was presented at the Library of Congress on June 23, 2008. This 55 minute presentation includes over 40 minutes of video prepared by Wesch and his students. This work highlights the academic credibility that can be found on YouTube.

Concerns about Quality

Concerns about the use of YouTube for e-learning may involve issues pertaining to quality. This is understandable given that video-sharing sites contain a mixture of content created by a range of amateur and professional developers. There are at least two logical dimensions where quality can suffer in Web-based video: 1) content, and 2) audiovisual display. In other words, the information in the video should be educationally valuable and it should be clearly seen and heard (if sound is included.) Of course, the educational value of video is subjective and will vary depending on instructional goals. In some respects almost anything can be educational depending on the purpose for which it will be used. For example, a video that includes erroneous information may not be suitable for introducing students to a new concept, but it could be used for the alternative purpose of initiating discussion of common misconceptions on the topic.

The quality of the audiovisual display is sometimes problematic on video-sharing sites such as YouTube. If the content is good, but it cannot be

Figure 7. Text distortion in small font sizes

clearly seen or heard then it may be rendered use-less for instruction. There are a number of reasons underlying poor audiovisual display ranging from production techniques to compression strategies. A video that starts out fuzzy, shaky, and full of audio static will only get worse when uploaded to YouTube. When video is uploaded to YouTube it is resized, compressed, and converted to Flash® video (Fahs, 2008). The result can be fuzzy or distorted, thus reducing the visual quality to the extent that important details become difficult to discern. This issue is particularly evident with on-screen text. Software tutorials created with screen recording software may be usable until after they are uploaded to YouTube simply because the text is unreadable. This is also a problem for PowerPoint slides that have text printed on them as illustrated in Figure 7.

Fortunately, there are some strategies that can help the video developer work around the screen resolution problem. The following tips are useful when working with video containing text.

- Use captions: Screen recordings of soft-ware tutorials can be enhanced with cap-tions in large text to help explain menus or icons containing fuzzy text.
- Zoom in on the text: Video editing or re-cording software that enables zooming in on the screen is also a good strategy. This will increase the size of the text and keep it readable after the video has been uploaded.

Part of the screen may be invisible when zooming in, however. Zoom back out to maintain perspective.

- Use large font and limit text: With PowerPoint slides it is better to stick with large font and limit text to key words or phrases. A lot of text or small font will like-ly end up unreadable.
- Use text caption, subtitle, or annotation tools. YouTube provides the annotation tool that can be used to add text after the video has been uploaded. Subtitles may be added to videos using tools such as dot-SUB (http://dotsub.com/)

At the present time, many of the Web-based video sites produce low resolution video clips. However, there is some movement toward high definition video for the Web. Vimeo (http://www.vimeo.com/hd) currently offers a service that sup-ports 1280 by 720 HD (high definition) video and YouTube recently switched to a widescreen high definition format. HD improves visual clarity of video considerably over the lower quality videos commonly found online today. Of course, the original video recording must be high quality to begin with. This is not always the case with por-table video recorders such as those found in cell phones or digital cameras. Mobile video clips can be enhanced, however. An online service called FixMyMovie (http://www.fixmymovie.com/splash/) provides a place where users upload their videos which were recorded on lower resolution mobile devices. After upload the video is processed and the resolution is enhanced. The fixed movie can then be shared directly from the site or downloaded to the user's computer hard drive.

Broadband and Web-Filtering Barriers

Barriers to the effective use of online video include broadband and computer limitations, particularly in U.S. public K-12 schools. This is not necessarily a problem of Internet availability because nearly all U.S. schools have access to the Internet (Wells, Lewis, & Greene, 2006). The problems are more along the lines of limited access to computers, lack of technical assistance, and lack of training, which inhibit opportunities to use online resources. A recent survey of teachers and support professionals indicates that the number of computers available for student use in individual classrooms is inadequate for effective instruction (National Education Association & American Federation of Teachers, 2008). Without adequate equipment, technical support, and teacher training the potential benefits gained with access to extensive online video resources are beyond reach. Even when computers with Internet access are available, broadband limitations can inhibit access to online video, one minute of which requires ten times the bandwidth of voice (Kleeman, 2007). A report from the Communication Workers of America (2008) indicates that high speed Internet access in the U.S. lags far behind other industrialized nations such as Japan and South Korea. Although broadband access is growing, access continues to vary. The online course developer should consider broadband availability when integrating video that will be delivered on the Internet.

Broadband is not the only potential barrier to Web-based video into a classroom. Access restrictions due to Web filtering are likely to occur in public K-12 U.S. schools as well. In order to receive financial support for Internet service under the E-Rate program, schools and libraries must demonstrate compliance to the Children's Internet Protection Act (CIPA). Technology protection measures are required to block access by minors to inappropriate or obscene content, secure safety when using e-mail, chat rooms, or online communications, prevent unauthorized hacking or unlawful online activity, protect against unauthorized disclosure and dissemination of personal information, and restrict access to material harmful to minors (U.S. Department of Education, National Center for Education Statistics, 2003; Universal Service Administration Company, 2008). This means that online video-sharing services, which may contain obscene content, will most likely be blocked at institutions supported under the E-Rate program.

Some control over offensive video content is managed by YouTube through a reporting mechanism in which the online community flags inappropriate videos. However, any video can end up on the site for a short period of time until it is reported and removed. In a school where access to YouTube is restricted, teachers have no access to the good content that is available, because the bad content forces the entire site to be blocked. This has led some educators to resort to the use of download tools which capture of video files that can be watched independently of the YouTube site (Dyck, 2007). As noted earlier in this chapter, video download from YouTube remains a questionable practice due to the uncertain legality of video downloads using third party software. A safer choice may be to locate a video site that is not blocked, although this will limit the amount of available content to select from.

Video Unavailable when Needed

Those who are not involved with K-12 public schools may have little to be concerned about with respect to filtering software. However, there is another potential barrier to be aware of when working with Web-based video for any audience of learners. Online content that is created and maintained by others can be removed from the Internet at any time. Hosting services can also go out of business or shut down for maintenance making content unavailable or temporarily inaccessible. Some video content seems to stay online for a long time, but there is always the chance that the wonderful video located today will be gone tomorrow. Because of this, it is essential to plan for the possibility that the video may vanish before it can be used in the classroom. Playlists of similar videos can be created in advance for this purpose. Sometimes, the same video will be uploaded onto more than one YouTube channel. When this occurs, each copy can be added to the playlist for backup.

Continually Changing Technologies

The potential disappearance of video is compounded by the continually changing technologies found on Web 2.0 services, including YouTube. In some ways it is like working with a moving target of evolving features. Something that works a certain way this week may change next week. This is the nature of the YouTube phenomenon and Web 2.0 in general. Some features such as video upload, play, and sharing remain consistent since they are core essential features. Other tools such as the *YouTube Remixer*, which allows users to edit video through the Web browser, have been known to be available for awhile and then go offline for repair. Features that appear on the YouTube TestTube site (http://www.youtube.com/testtube) are experimental and may be more likely to change. These can be used successfully within e-learning as long as alternative options are prepared in advance just in case. In some ways, it seems to require a sense of adventure to tap into the YouTube phenomenon. It can be a marvelous adventure, however.

FUTURE DIRECTIONS

The YouTube phenomenon, characterized by video viewing, sharing, and production has gained considerable momentum in a just a few years time. There is much to offer e-learning in terms of tools and content, yet there is little direct guidance to be found. A starting point for uncovering best practice strategies for e-learning is to build from what is already known about educational video. To expand on this prior knowledge, a series of case studies that explore how YouTube is used within authentic practice across the disciplines is needed. Formative and summative evaluations conducted as part of these studies will yield evidence of additional benefits or barriers within e-learning. Design-based research, characterized by repeated cycles of design, implementation and analysis may also be applicable to uncover the impact of YouTube within the context where it will be used for instruction (The Design Based Research Collective, 2003; Snelson, 2006). Experimental studies should be conducted with care to avoid the problems associated with media comparison studies, which have a history of producing results of no significant difference (Warnick & Burbules, 2007).

There is a need both now and in the future to clearly define the role of video-sharing and Web-based video content as a component of digital curriculum in both online and face-to-face education. Despite some continued skepticism (Tahmincioglu, 2008), online learning is now considered to be mainstream and enrollments continue to grow (Allen & Seaman, 2007). The expansion of online education implies a need for digital instructional content that can be accessed on the Internet. The need for digital curriculum has also begun to spread to face-to-face education as well. Some K-12 schools have already begun experimenting with laptop computers and digital content to replace traditional textbooks (Associated Press, 2005). Electronic textbooks are becoming widely available for higher education (Guess, 2008) albeit with concerns about affordability, printability, and accessibility (Allen, 2008). Computer-based digital content enables and supports integration of rich multimedia content including video. The millions of video clips, accessed for free on the Web, provide a repository of content that educators can tap into as part of the digital curriculum.

Much of the free content now on the Web is stored on sites like YouTube, which were designed for general public video-sharing purposes. Access problems due to Web filtering and confusion over the legality of video download add to the complexity of the problem. As Web filtering software becomes more sophisticated it may become feasible to open limited doorways of access for teachers allowing them to avoid resorting to questionable download solutions. The development of progressive school policy that supports reasonable use of YouTube content is also essential to guide the process of accessing the wealth of free video available to educators.

As more and more educators turn to video-sharing services there is increased need to clarify copyright and fair use laws to better inform those who create, upload, or download Web-based video. At the present time the rules are unclear, full of legal verbiage, and fail to clearly guide educators. As Web 2.0 evolves, the laws governing fair use and copyright may also need to evolve to address the use and distribution of online content including video. Fortunately, some informational resources are being produced to provide guidance (Aufderheide & Jaszi, 2008; Jaszi & Aufderheide, 2008). It is essential that all who are involved with the use or production of online video become as well informed as possible about copyright and fair use.

Web 2.0 video tools are an exciting addition to the suite of interactive, browser-based services. At some point in the future, the need to purchase software for desktop and laptop computers may be reduced or eliminated. It is conceivable that most software needs may eventually be handled through the browser. Video editing on the Web is still in its infancy, but work is underway to produce tools for this purpose. It is an excellent time to tap into the YouTube phenomenon for e-learning and ride the wave into the future.

REFERENCES

Adobe Systems, Inc. (2008). *Flash player penetration.* Retrieved July 12, 2008, from http://www.adobe.com/products/player_census/flashplayer/

Allen, I. E., & Seaman, J. (2007). *Online nation: Five years of growth in online learning.* Retrieved August 5, 2008, from http://www.sloan-c.org/publications/survey/pdf/online_nation.pdf

Allen, N. (2008). *Course correction: How digital textbooks are off track and how to set them straight.* Needham, MA: Sloan Consortium. Retrieved November 1, 2008, from http://www.maketextbooksaffordable.org/course_correction.pdf

Associated Press. (2005, July 11). *Arizona school won't use textbooks: Vail's new Empire High to be all-wireless, all-laptop.* Retrieved August 5, 2008, from http://www.msnbc.msn.com/id/8540381/

Aufderheide, P., & Jaszi, P. (2008). *Recut, reframe, recycle: Quoting copyrighted material in user-generated video.* Washington, DC: Center for Social Media. Retrieved July 19, 2008 from http://www.centerforsocialmedia.org/resources/publications/recut_reframe_recycle

Brown, J. S., & Adler, R. P. (2008). Minds on fire: Open education, the long tail, and learning 2.0. *EDUCAUSE Review, 43*(1), 16-32. Retrieved November 1, 2008 from http://connect.educause.edu/Library/EDUCAUSE+Review/MindsonFireOpenEducationt/45823?time=1225579636

Brunstetter, M. R. (1937). *How to use educational sound film.* Chicago, IL: The University of Chicago Press. Retrieved June 11, 2008, from http://www.archive.org/details/howtouseeducatio00brunrich

Carr, N. (2007, October). YouTube creates cyber nightmare for teachers. *eSchool News, 10,* 41.

Castro, M. (1922). Some psychological and pedagogical aspects of visual education. *The Educational Screen, 1*(3), 6-9. Retrieved June 6, 2008, from http://www.archive.org/details/educationalscree01chicrich

Clark, R. E. (1983). Reconsidering research on learning from media. *Review of Educational Research, 53*(4), 445–459.

Clark, R. E. (1994). Media will never influence learning. *Educational Technology Research and Development, 42*(2), 21–29. doi:10.1007/BF02299088

Clark, R. E., & Feldon, D. E. (2005). Five common but questionable principles of multimedia learning. In R. E. Mayer (Ed.), *The Cambridge handbook of multimedia learning* (pp. 97-115). New York: Cambridge University Press.

Communication Workers of America. (2008). *Speed matters: A report on Internet speeds in all 50 states.* Retrieved August 23, 2008, from http://www.speedmatters.org/document-library/source-materials/cwa_report_on_internet_speeds_2008.pdf

Comscore. (2007). *YouTube continues to lead U.S. online video market with 28 percent market share.* Retrieved October, 6, 2008, from http://www.comscore.com/press/release.asp?press=1929

Dick, J. T. (1999). DVD the next big (digital) thing? *Library Journal, 124*(9), 50–51.

Dickson, W. K. L., & Dickson, A. (1970). *History of the kinetograph, kinetoscope & kinetophonograph.* New York: Arno Press & The New York Times.

Dyck, B. (2007). *Using YouTube in the classroom.* Retrieved August 3, 2008, from http://www.education-world.com/a_tech/columnists/dyck/dyck016.shtml

e-Marketer. (2008). *Online video viewing still rising.* Retrieved May 29, 2008, from http://www.emarketer.com/Article.aspx?id=1006291&src=article_head_sitesearch

Ellis, D. C., & Thornborough, L. (1923). *Motion pictures in education: A practical handbook for users of visual aids.* New York: Thomas Y. Crowell Company. Retrieved June 4, 2008, from http://www.archive.org/details/motionpicturesin00ellirich

Fahs, C. (2008). *How to do everything with YouTube.* New York: McGraw-Hill.

Google Press Center. (2006). *Google to acquire YouTube for $1.65 billion in stock.* Retrieved May 29, 2008, from http://www.google.com/press/pressrel/google_youtube.html

Greene, N. L. (1926). Motion pictures in the classroom. *The Annals of the American Academy of Political and Social Science, 128,* 122–130. doi:10.1177/000271622612800120

Guess, A. (2008, August 26). Next steps for e-texts. *Inside Higher Ed.* Retrieved November 1, 2008 from http://www.insidehighered.com/news/2008/08/26/etextbooks

Jaszi, P., & Aufderheide, P. (2008). *Code of best practices in fair use for online video.* Washington, DC: Center for Social Media. Retrieved August 10, 2008 from http://www.centerforsocialmedia.org/resources/publications/fair_use_in_online_video/

Jonassen, D. (1999). Designing constructivist learning environments. In C. M. Reigeluth (Ed.), *Instructional-design theories and models: A new paradigm of instructional theory* (Vol. 2, pp. 215-239). Mahwah, NJ: Lawrence Erlbaum Associates, Inc.

Kleeman, M. (2007). *Point of disconnect: Internet traffic and the US communications infrastructure.* San Diego, CA: University of California. Retrieved November 1, 2008, from http://cpe.ucsd.edu/assets/013/6535.pdf

Kozma, R. B. (1994). Will media influence learning? Reframing the debate. *Educational Technology Research and Development, 42*(2), 7–19. doi:10.1007/BF02299087

Low, R., & Sweller, J. (2005). The modality principle in multimedia learning. In R. E. Mayer (Ed.), *The Cambridge handbook of multimedia learning* (pp. 147-158). New York: Cambridge University Press.

Madden, M. (2007). *Online video.* Washington, DC: Pew Internet & American Life Project. Retrieved from http://www.pewinternet.org/PPF/r/219/report_display.asp

Mayer, R. E. (2001). *Multimedia learning.* New York: Cambridge University Press.

Mayer, R. E., & Chandler, P. (2001). When learning is just a click away: Does simple user interaction foster deeper understanding of multimedia messages? *Journal of Educational Psychology, 93*(2), 390–397. doi:10.1037/0022-0663.93.2.390

Mayer, R. E., & Moreno, R. (2003). Nine ways to reduce cognitive load in multimedia learning. *Educational Psychologist, 38*(1), 43–52. doi:10.1207/S15326985EP3801_6

McNeilly, D. P. (2008). YouTube and the emerging worlds of video-sharing for behavioral science education. *Annals of Behavioral Science and Medical Education, 14*(1), 25–30.

Nathan, M., & Robinson, C. (2001). Considerations of learning and learning research: Revisiting the "media effects" debate. *Journal of Interactive Learning Research, 12*(1), 69–88.

National Education Association & American Federation of Teachers. (2008). *Access, adequacy, and equity in education technology: Results of a survey of America's teachers and support professionals on technology in public schools and classrooms.* Washington, DC: National Education Association. Retrieved June 11, 2008, from http://www.nea.org/research/images/08gainsandgapsedtech.pdf

New Media Consortium & EDUCAUSE Learning Initiative. (2008). *The horizon report: 2008 edition.* Retrieved May 18, 2008, from http://www.nmc.org/publications/2008-horizon-report

Nielsen Online. (2008). *The video generation: Kids and teens consuming more online video content than adults at home.* Retrieved October, 6, 2008, from http://www.nielsen-netratings.com/pr/pr_080609.pdf

Paivio, A. (1990). *Mental representations: A dual coding approach* (Vol. 9). New York: Oxford University Press.

Rees, J. (2008). Teaching history with YouTube. *Perspectives on History, 46*(5). Retrieved June 11, 2008, from http://www.historians.org/Perspectives/issues/2008/0805/0805tec2.cfm

Saettler, P. (2004). *The evolution of American educational technology.* Greenwich, CT: Information Age Publishing.

Schoetz, D., Canning, A., & Brady, J. (2008). Teens in video beating case charged as adults. *ABC News.* Retrieved August 1, 2008, from http://abcnews.go.com/GMA/Story?id=4609528&page=1

Skiba, D. J. (2007). Nursing education 2.0: YouTube. *Nursing Education Perspectives, 28*(2), 100–102.

Snelson, C. (2006). Virtual design based research. *Academic Exchange Quarterly, 10*(4), 107–110.

Snelson, C. (2008a). Web-based video in education: Possibilities and pitfalls. In *Proceedings of the Technology, Colleges & Community Worldwide Online Conference* (pp. 214-221). Retrieved August 23, 2008, from http://etec.hawaii.edu/proceedings/2008/Snelson2008.pdf

Snelson, C. (2008b). YouTube and beyond: Integrating Web-based video into online education. In K. McFerrin, R. Weber, R. Carlsen, & D. A. Willis (Eds.), *Proceedings of Society for Information Technology and Teacher Education International Conference 2008* (pp. 732-737). Chesapeake, VA: AACE.

Tahmincioglu, E. (2008, September 7). Online colleges earning respect to a degree: Many hiring managers still skeptical, but distance learning hard to ignore. *MSNBC*. Retrieved November 1, 2008 from http://www.msnbc.msn.com/id/26458424/

Tamim, R., Shaikh, K., & Bethel, E. (2007). EDyoutube: Why not? In G. Richards (Ed.), *Proceedings of World Conference on E-Learning in Corporate, Government, Healthcare, and Higher Education 2007* (pp. 1302-1307). Chesapeake, VA: AACE.

The Design Based Research Collective. (2003). Design-based research: An emerging paradigm for educational inquiry. *Educational Researcher, 32*(1), 5–8. doi:10.3102/0013189X032001005

Today, U. S. A. (2006, July 16). *YouTube serves up 100 million videos a day*. Retrieved May 29, 2008, from http://www.usatoday.com/tech/news/2006-07-16-youtube-views_x.htm

Universal Service Administration Company. (2008). *Step 10: Children's Internet Protection Act (CIPA)*. Retrieved June 11, 2008, from http://www.usac.org/sl/applicants/step10/cipa.aspx

U.S. Department of Education, National Center for Education Statistics. (2003). Web-related legal issues and policies. In *Weaving a secure Web around education: A guide to technology standards and security*. Retrieved from http://nces.ed.gov/pubs2003/secureweb/ch_3.asp#H9

Warnick, B. R., & Burbules, N. C. (2007). Media comparison studies: Problems and possibilities. *Teachers College Record, 109*(11), 2483–2510.

Wells, J., Lewis, L., & Greene, B. (2006). *Internet access in U.S. public schools and classrooms: 1994-2005* (No. NCES 2007-020). Washington, DC: U.S. Department of Education, National Center for Education Statistics. Retrieved November 4, 2008, from http://nces.ed.gov/pubsearch/pubsinfo.asp?pubid=2007020

Winslow, K. (1970). *The adoption and distribution of videotape materials for educational use*. Washington, DC: Academy for Educational Development, Inc. (Eric Document Reproduction Service No. ED039716)

YouTube. (2008). *YouTube fact sheet: Overview and features*. Retrieved October, 08, 2008 from http://www.youtube.com/t/fact_sheet

YouTube Help Center. (2008). *What is YouTube's video identification tool?* Retrieved July 30, 2008, from http://www.google.com/support/youtube/bin/answer.py?answer=83766&topic=13656

Zhang, D., Zhou, L., Briggs, R. O., & Nunamaker, J. F. (2006). Instructional video in e-learning: Assessing the impact of interactive video on learning effectiveness. *Information & Management, 43*(1), 15–27. doi:10.1016/j.im.2005.01.004

Chapter 10
From Information Literacy to Scholarly Identity:
Effective Pedagogical Strategies for Social Bookmarking

Deborah Everhart
Georgetown University, USA

Kaye Shelton
Dallas Baptist University, USA

ABSTRACT

Collaborative research teaches students critical knowledge management skills, whether they are undergraduates learning the basics of Web research or advanced scholars defining their own knowledge domains. Instructors can benefit from practical examples and strategies to initiate social bookmarking activities. This chapter provides best practice examples for effective pedagogical applications of social bookmarking in undergraduate and graduate courses as well as insights into how these activities change the way students think and learn.

INTRODUCTION

Collecting and organizing references to scholarly resources has always been one of the staples of academic work. As more and more resources are available online, saving or bookmarking links to websites has become part of this practice. Earlier Web technologies allowed users to aggregate and categorize their own bookmarks, but this was an individual activity and did not provide an easy method for sharing the resources and their categorization with others. Today, "Web 2.0 tools harness the collective intelligence of the Web, and by tapping into that intelligence, make the services better and more powerful" (Gordon-Murnane, 2006, p. 29). Because of the collaborative and social characteristics of Web 2.0 tools, the practice of collecting references to scholarly resources has advanced into social bookmarking, which is defined as "the practice of saving bookmarks to a public web site and 'tagging' them with keywords" (Lomas, 2005). Websites such as Blackboard Scholar, Delicious, Connotea, Diigo, Furl, CiteULike, and many others not only allow users to save and store bookmarks, but also provide methods for classifying or add-

DOI: 10.4018/978-1-60566-729-4.ch010

Copyright © 2010, IGI Global. Copying or distributing in print or electronic forms without written permission of IGI Global is prohibited.

ing "tags" along with annotated descriptions for future identification and retrieval. Because social bookmarking websites are public, visitors may search the sites by the identifying tags that others have already provided. This is particularly useful when trying to share online resources for scholarly collaboration.

The 2007 Horizon Report includes social bookmarking in "user-created content" with a time-to-adoption horizon of one year or less. However, the Report also states that "we face a significant challenge as we seek to marshal these techniques in the service of education" (The New Media, 2007, p. 9). There has been much talk about social bookmarking, particularly its use in research communities for collaboratively finding and tagging Web resources so that they can be searched and reused. But how is social bookmarking being used effectively in teaching? What are the best pedagogical practices? Can the needs of many different kinds of learners who have various levels of research skills be met with the same technology?

Research shows that students learn more when they are actively engaged and have a sense of ownership over the course materials and their own learning processes. Yet instructors are generally reluctant to give up control of course content, and they often lack the skills to effectively integrate social learning activities and collaborative, dynamic content generation into their teaching environments. Social bookmarking can provide a bridge for this gap (both generational and technical) by offering an easy-to-use, engaging tool for managing Web-based resources on course topics, with minimal implementation costs or barriers. An added bonus is that social bookmarking overlaps with instructors' research motivations (many are probably already using this technology in their own research communities), appealing to instructors' desires to include their own scholarly worlds in their teaching. The outcome can be dynamic course resource management and the opportunity for students to learn valuable information analysis

and research skills while collaboratively contributing to a body of learning materials. This vision will become a reality more readily if instructors have good examples and pedagogical strategies that are applicable to courses and students at different levels.

This chapter provides real-world examples that demonstrate different pedagogical models for social bookmarking. The examples demonstrate the use of social bookmarking in undergraduate and graduate courses. They are applicable in community college and university courses, hybrid and fully online courses, and in many different disciplines. Each example includes assessment of student engagement, information literacy, research abilities, and the quality of students' bibliographies and knowledge management skills. Instructors who use these strategies in their own courses are more likely to have a positive experience with social bookmarking and cross the bridge to pedagogical innovations and expanding active learning opportunities for their students.

BACKGROUND

Social bookmarking has recently emerged within the scholarly literature and is primarily found within three areas: social bookmarking usage, tagging and folksonomy, and educational uses. The majority of references to social bookmarking identify usage and typical practice and are often provided by librarians interested in how users are tagging resources (i.e., Hargadon, 2007; Richardson, 2007; Trexler, 2007). Gordon-Murnane (2006) examined several Web 2.0 tools and identified various features of social bookmarking: "keeping found things found, sharing collaboration, vertical search, discovery/serendipity, and portability/mobility (multiple access points)" (p. 29). She further identified noticeable strengths such as community creation, searchable tags and folksonomies, and tagged content with mobility. Weaknesses considered were the lack of a standard set of keywords, tags lacking standard structure and/or hierarchical relationships, and tags used incorrectly or too personally. Furthermore, Kamel, Boulous and Wheeler (2007) found that within health care education, the collaborative tagging may be poorly organized and inefficient.

The classification of resources with user-generated tags has drawn interest from scholars primarily directed toward a comparison between taxonomy (formal classification) and folksonomy (informal classification) (i.e., MacGregror & McCulloch, 2006; Noruzi, 2007). With further analysis, Golder and Huberman (2006) were able to determine that most user-generated tags achieve stable meaning despite the randomness of how tags are employed without a formal classification scheme.

Muir (2005) recommended social bookmarking for the following educational uses: websites for student research or projects; book recommendations; professional research; listing books for later reading; placing web links in a school web page; students using the identified resources both at home and at school; sharing current reading topics; and website collections tagged by school topic. Berger (2007) added the following educational uses: the support of discovery/exploration processes for students, the creation of collaborative environments, and anytime/anywhere learning that integrates with newer technologies such as RSS feeds and blogging. In spite of these possible applications, it appears instructors have just recently begun using social bookmarking pedagogically (Watwood, 2007).

Taxonomies and Folksonomies

When considering social bookmarking, some instructors may be concerned about the use of folksonomies, or user generated tags, rather than taxonomies. This is not a pure dichotomy, however. Students need to learn a controlled vocabulary in order to communicate effectively in a disciplinary field. Once they know the terms, their meanings,

and the relationships among terms, they should be able to apply this vocabulary in a variety of ways and contexts. A disciplinary taxonomy, "a subject-based classification that arranges terms in a controlled vocabulary into a hierarchy" (Garshol, 2004), provides a professional structure for classifying and finding resources (Macgregor & McCulloch, 2006). "Folksonomy," a term coined by Thomas Vander Wal to describe collaborative informal categorization of materials (Vander Wal, 2007), typically provides a more informal context for tagging and finding resources. Both provide learning opportunities for students to develop their understanding of a disciplinary vocabulary while also finding their own voices.

The differences between taxonomies and folksonomies are tied to the level of professionals that produce them and the level of control in their production and dissemination. The more tightly controlled a taxonomy, such as the Library of Congress Subject Headings, the more stable it is for professional classification of resources and reliable retrieval of resources. Less controlled folksonomies allow more freedom and provide less professional classification, resulting in less reliable tagging and retrieval, but at the same time offering the benefits of social sense-making (Golder and Huberman, 2006) and rapid evolution.

Taxonomies cost more to produce and generally are not intuitive to use until one has some training. Professionals, often highly-trained librarians, create taxonomies and apply meta-data when cataloguing academic resources so that researchers can use a controlled vocabulary to search for resources and understand the clearly-defined relationships among them. Researchers then invest in learning the taxonomies and the methodologies of controlled searches. The pay-off is that controlled searches of cataloged materials, when accurately defined, yield results that are highly relevant.

Folksonomies, on the other hand, cost almost nothing to produce; anyone can tag materials without learning a controlled vocabulary (Macgregor

& McCulloch, 2006). The trade-off is that consumers of those resources incur a perpetual cost in searching and discovery. Grammatical variations, misunderstandings of terminology, misspellings, and a lack of hierarchical or otherwise logical organization among tags all contribute to search results that are inaccurate, irrelevant, and/or not appropriately inclusive.

Nonetheless, both taxonomies and folksonomies have appropriate pedagogical uses. In fact, one could argue that the more skilled students become in using disciplinary taxonomies, the more likely they are to make professional, accurate contributions to folksonomies, blurring the differences between the two. Using folksonomies in a scholarly context, such as in a course or with groups of users in an academic field, provides many of the benefits of using professional classification combined with the benefits of scholarly collaboration, knowledge-sharing, and creative generation of new knowledge. A taxonomy represents the known field of research; a well-formulated folksonomy offers the opportunity of expanding the field of disciplinary knowledge. Students who learn how to use taxonomies effectively are well-positioned to take the next step toward expanding knowledge in their areas of expertise.

Therefore teaching social bookmarking in parallel with teaching disciplinary taxonomies offers opportunities beyond those of a specific course or learning objective. The examples below explain how to achieve these benefits through a careful combination of taxonomic study and folksonomic exploration that develops not only students' classification skills, but also their scholarly communication skills.

Effective Uses of Social Bookmarking at Different Levels of Learning

Students go through stages of development and levels of interaction with a discipline that can be roughly divided into lower-level undergraduate,

upper-level undergraduate, and graduate students. From the perspective of disciplinary taxonomies and folksonomies and their use in social bookmarking and research, these levels of learners can be characterized as follows:

- Lower-level undergraduates need to learn the basic vocabulary of a discipline and how to apply it to analysis of scholarly resources. These learners typically have deficiencies in information literacy and basic research skills. They also have very limited experience in scholarly collaboration.
- Upper-level undergraduates have mastered basic disciplinary vocabulary but need to develop a thorough understanding of the taxonomies of a discipline and how to apply them accurately to analysis of scholarly resources. These learners need to be able to explore specific sub-topics in the discipline, articulate their own areas of focus, and position their own research in an existing body of knowledge. They generally have some experience in scholarly collaboration and benefit from activities that help them build communities of expertise with their peers.
- Graduate students have mastered the taxonomies of a discipline and how to apply them to research but need to find their own scholarly niches and be socialized into the profession. These learners should be encouraged to explore under-developed areas of specialization and discover where and how they can contribute new knowledge to the field. They are generally proficient in informal scholarly collaboration, but they need to learn how to communicate effectively with professionals in the discipline and collaborate with peers on joint projects and research.

For purposes of the examples below, these levels correspond to the students' capabilities and learning needs in a particular discipline, not necessarily corresponding to their actual educational level. For example, upper-level undergraduates may take courses in unfamiliar disciplines and therefore need to learn the basic vocabulary of a discipline, even though their research skills are more advanced in their major field of study.

Each of the sections below focuses on one of these levels of learning. Each section characterizes relevant research and collaboration learning needs at that level, states learning objectives that address these needs, refers to traditional pedagogical methods of meeting these learning objectives, and provides examples of how social bookmarking activities can be applied and assessed. All of these sections focus on the interactions learners have with academic resources in the discipline and how the "social" aspects of social bookmarking can be used to build and reinforce scholarly communities.

Lower-Level Undergraduates: Challenging the "Net Gen" to Go Beyond Shallow Searches

Lower-level undergraduates usually have not developed a vocabulary for understanding and articulating the subject matter they are studying. Worse yet, they may come into a course with an incorrect or overly informal understanding of the material and its disciplinary context. A key learning objective therefore is the assimilation of a controlled vocabulary that allows the student to speak and write accurately about the disciplinary subject matter. Vocabulary learning objectives go beyond simple memorization of glossary terms; they also include an understanding of the relationships among the terms, the ability to visualize their hierarchies and levels of abstraction, and the ability to apply them to disciplinary resources. By the end of an introductory course, students are generally expected to pass a test or writing assignment in which they can effectively

differentiate and articulate key concepts by using a controlled vocabulary.

An even greater challenge for lower-level undergraduates is overcoming their deficiencies in information literacy. The ease of searching the web to find just about anything masks the difficulty of finding the right thing for the right purpose at the right time. Inexperienced students too easily equate "search" with "research." Therefore the ability to discern the appropriateness of resources for academic purposes is a key learning objective. Along with the objective of learning a controlled vocabulary, students need to learn how to apply appropriate terms to classify and characterize the resources they are using, including materials that they themselves have discovered. To demonstrate these skills, students are generally required to research and find appropriate disciplinary resources, accurately describe the contents of these materials, and formulate their own arguments based on their findings.

In light of these learning objectives, among others, social bookmarking can be applied to both individual and collaborative learning activities. Instructors can provide a controlled vocabulary of tags that represent key terminology in the discipline. Students individually and/or collectively can tag resources to apply the terminology as they are learning it, in context.

Example: Individual Research Project

Students are provided with a list of disciplinary terms and their definitions. They are also given a "starter" bibliography that is a set of bookmarks in a social bookmarking system that have already been accurately tagged with some of these terms. Students search and find additional resources to add to the set of bookmarks and they tag them with the disciplinary terms. They also write useful descriptions of the resources. During this process, instructors coach them on the validity of the resources, the usefulness of their descriptions, and the accuracy of their tagging. When a suitable volume of resources have been accumulated, the student writes a short research paper assimilating key concepts from the materials and making their own argumentative points.

This project is assessed by grading the final artifact, the student's argumentative writing, including their accurate application of the disciplinary terminology and concepts. This project can also be given a "process" grade that specifically evaluates their collection of bookmarks and provides feedback on how the appropriate tagging of these resources (or not) contributed to the success of their argumentative writing.

This project can be made more flexible (although that does not make it easier) by allowing the student to apply not only the fixed set of terms, but also their own tags.

Example: Group Treasure Hunt

Students are divided into small groups and all groups are provided with the same list of disciplinary terms and their definitions. The groups are given a fixed amount of time to find and accurately tag resources that are relevant to these terms and the subject matter of the course. The groups keep their bookmarks "hidden" or "private" during the hunt. When the time is up, the instructor assesses the quality and quantity of resources collected by each group.

For additional learning opportunities, the groups then make their bookmarks available to everyone in the class. This leads to interesting discoveries and discussion of overlapping bookmarks and tags among the groups, clusters of resources that are much richer now that more resources are combined, and informative analysis of the relative success and accuracy of different tagging approaches. Students discuss not only the value of the resources, but also how they found them and why they tagged them the way they did. This activity can be made more flexible (although that does not make it easier) by allowing the groups to

apply not only the controlled vocabulary, but also their own tags. It may also be combined with a writing project wherein the students use what they have learned from the group tagging and apply it in an argumentative written analysis of a chosen subset of the resources.

Example: Collaborative Evaluation of Resources

An online class discussion forum is set up with threads on different topics related to the course content, and the instructor seeds each thread with a few links to resources to be evaluated. These should include both valuable and questionable resources. Students are given a "scorecard" that the instructor or library have written as guidelines for assessing the scholarly value of online resources. The students are also given a "starter" set of vocabulary for tagging and instructions for the activity.

Students participate in the discussion threads and comment on the scholarly value of the resources, using the criteria outlined in the scorecard. They also add to the discussion thread resources they have discovered on the given topic. The students come to consensus about whether the resources are appropriate to add to the class bookmarks and if so, how they should be tagged and described. They then add the valuable resources to the set of class bookmarks. These become a reliable set of resources that everyone in the class can use in their research.

Alternatively, the students work together in groups, where the discussion forum is divided into topic areas that are assigned to specific groups. These groups are responsible for evaluating and adding to the resources on their own topics, and they are also expected to achieve enough expertise in these areas that they can present their findings to the rest of the class.

This activity can optionally be done in a social bookmarking context that already includes bookmarks from students who were in the course in a prior term. The pre-existing set of student-produced resources adds another dimension to the current students' analysis, in that they are not only freshly evaluating new resources, but also discussing the strengths and weaknesses of decisions made by other students, comparing their own work to that of their peers. If the social bookmarking context includes ratings or comments, others' prior opinions and the number of people who have added each bookmark also become factors to consider. In this situation, instructors can use the "teaching moment" to explain that opinions are not the same as structured evaluation, cautioning the students against assuming that "popular" bookmarks are academically valuable. While these additional variables make the learning experience more authentic, lower-level undergraduates may not be well-equipped to process the "noise," especially if this is their first academic social bookmarking exercise.

In all of these variations, students are assessed on the quality and quantity of their contributions to the resource evaluation discussions and the set of class bookmarks. This can also be factored into a general class participation and/or group grade. The activity can be time-bound or continue throughout the term.

Pedagogical Value

These lower-level undergraduate social bookmarking activities can be used to teach information literacy and collaborative evaluation of resources. Students develop a contextual, practical understanding of the disciplinary vocabulary and how to apply it to analysis of resources. Class and group discussions, with guidance from the instructor, provide students with the opportunity to articulate what they are learning and try out their ideas in a low-stakes environment where they can quickly and immediately learn from their mistakes through peer and instructor feedback. Their understanding of the vocabulary and how it applies to resources evolves through trial, error,

feedback, and gradual refinement. Therefore these exercises can be even more effective if applied frequently throughout the term.

Since lower-level undergraduates are generally new to the discipline and are probably sorely lacking in information literacy skills, these exercises tend to work best if they are heavily scaffolded. The instructor can start with the most narrowly structured of the exercises, using only instructor-provided vocabulary, seeded sets of resources, very explicit instructions, and a short time-frame. Based on the results of this approach, the instructor can make the exercises more flexible and allow more creativity. If this strategy is frankly explained to students, they will be less likely to see the activities as tedium and more likely to recognize the value of the scaffolding as it helps them succeed in a more controlled activity and then take what they have learned and apply it in the next activity.

The social aspect of these activities also contributes to students' enthusiasm and desire to do well. Students take pride in knowing that their bookmarks will be used by other students in the class and perhaps those who take the course next time. They feel empowered by the fact that they are helping to build the class resources, and they develop a sense of responsibility to their peers knowing that they need to accurately identify and describe valuable, appropriate resources. These peer pressures help them understand at least the most basic values of scholarly communities.

Upper-Level Undergraduates: Advancing Students in their Disciplinary Taxonomies

Upper-level undergraduates are expected to have mastered a set of disciplinary vocabulary, but they generally need more development in their understanding and skill for applying a taxonomy. A key learning objective therefore is assimilation of a full disciplinary taxonomy and the ability to use it accurately in research. Achievement of this objective gives students a structured way of visualizing and articulating the different facets of the discipline and the position of their own research projects within that structure.

Research learning objectives related to the disciplinary taxonomy go beyond simply the ability to formulate accurate searches; they also include the ability to refine and re-shape searches to explore specific sub-topics, articulate the student's area of focus, and effectively use appropriate resources to support the student's research agenda. By the end of an upper-level course, a student is generally expected to complete a research project or paper in which they articulate a well-supported argument that is accurately positioned in a survey of the field.

In the process of their research projects or papers, students also learn that even the "simple" ability to formulate an accurate search is nuanced; they must navigate the relative merits of hierarchical taxonomies vs. free-form terms, folksonomies, and flat organization of resources. Web searches and even simple keyword searches of scholarly databases give the illusion of easy finding tools, but how do students determine the value of what they have found? As students' research skills evolve, they need to learn how to drill into hierarchical taxonomies without losing their way, use controlled vocabulary to combine or differentiate specific subject areas, and select resources to review and analyze based on the meta-data professionals have applied to those resources.

For students to attain research goals beyond the mastery of taxonomies and professional meta-data, they need to learn how to channel their intellectual curiosity and creativity into the creation of their own extensions to professional taxonomies and meta-data. Learning objectives designed to capitalize on research creativity encourage students to find gaps in the taxonomies, discover resources that have not yet been professionally cataloged, explore folksonomies, and participate in scholarly online discussions that are constantly reshaping the disciplines.

Example: Individual Research Project

In an upper-level undergraduate course geared toward majors in a discipline, the instructor builds a scaffolding of tags that parallel the standardized, library-produced taxonomy for the course topics. If it is not clear that students already understand the taxonomy, the instructor also sets up multiple-attempt self-tests that the students can take as many times as they need to until they can successfully answer questions about the taxonomy. This strategy allows students who have mastered the taxonomy to move forward with their research as soon as they are ready.

As they research and formulate their arguments, students tag resources with the standard disciplinary taxonomy tags. They also use their own personal tags to help organize their work, such as "to read" and "supplemental." For each resource, they write their own scholarly annotated description. As an interim deliverable in this project, the instructor may assess the student's collection of resources, which can be presented as a annotated bibliography with accurate disciplinary labels (tags). This interim assessment is a good point at which to intervene if the student has not mastered the research skills necessary to succeed in the project.

Note that even though not all resources are online, virtually any resource can be represented with a URL and therefore added to a bookmarks collection. Hard-copy books and other non-electronic resources have library reference URLs. A local library reference may be more immediately useful to the student than a standard URL, such as the Library of Congress Control Number Permalink, but the instructor should provide guidelines on how to reference non-electronic resources. This information can be provided with other bibliographical requirements, including whether or not the student needs to use a social bookmarking system that accurately tracks full citation information.

As students progress in their research projects, they are learning to use the standard taxonomy to achieve their research goals. Optionally, they may be sharing resources with others in the class and forming their own study groups for collaborative tagging and analysis of resources. When students have mastered an appropriate set of materials, they produce their project findings or research papers. This project is assessed by grading the final artifact, the student's argumentative writing, accurate use of the disciplinary vocabulary, and correct positioning within the disciplinary taxonomy.

Example: Group Searches and Evaluation of Findings

The instructor sets up discussion forums as spaces for the students to work together and discuss their findings. Students organize themselves into small groups based on similar research interests and topics in which they are developing expertise. With the help of the instructor, they build a framework of tags based on the areas of the disciplinary taxonomy they are researching. They then use library databases to search for resources in these areas. They find strong correlations and exact matches between their tags and the library subject headings because they started with a controlled vocabulary. The students discuss the relevance

Figure 1. Applying the standard taxonomy of a specific discipline (© 2008, Blackboard Inc. Used with permission.)

of the resources to their research topics and each student bookmarks the resources that are directly relevant to their own work. They collaborate on writing the scholarly annotations for the resources, with each student adapting what the group does to their own needs. Each student may also choose to add personal tags for their own reference.

To compare taxonomies to folksonomies, the groups go to a scholarly social bookmarking system and search for tags that are the same or similar to the controlled vocabulary they've been using. They discuss why the similar tags are not exact matches and gain an understanding of the value of controlled vocabulary. They then explore tags that are related to their controlled vocabulary. There are a variety of ways to do this, including browsing the way other scholars have tagged resources the student has already reviewed and tagged, or looking at the tag clouds of scholars who have included the same resources in their own collections (i.e., browse tags starting from the resources, or browse tags starting from the users). They will probably find other resources or other ways of approaching the topic that they had not yet considered. This can lead to a discussion of the value of folksonomies and scholarly communities.

To compare taxonomies and folksonomies to raw searching, the groups use a web search engine to search for terms from their controlled vocabulary. The tens of thousands of results returned immediately demonstrate the value of professional filtering of resources by librarians and other scholars. The students discuss whether or not the resources they've already collected are given higher relevance in the search results. They also discuss whether or not there are additional resources that are valuable in search results. The students should notice that they need to apply more effort to screening and reviewing the validity of the resources discovered in this open context. This should lead to a useful discussion of the trade-offs; more up-front work learning and applying a controlled vocabulary to a professionally organized

library database, or quicker search results but more challenges involved in screening them.

Depending on the skill level of the students, the instructor may need to participate heavily in the groups' discussions to help them apply the taxonomy and accurately review resources. To make this exercise immediately relevant to the students' learning goals, this activity can be part of the process of the students' research project or papers. It can be assessed as a stand-alone activity, as part of class participation, or as part of the students' research projects/papers, in each case evaluating not only the resulting set of annotated, classified resources, but also the quality of the discussion insights that lead to these sets of resources.

Pedagogical Value

These upper-level undergraduate social bookmarking activities can be used to teach the disciplinary taxonomy and how it is applied to evaluation of resources. Students develop a contextual, practical understanding of taxonomies and how they are immediately useful for their own research.

It is not uncommon for upper-level undergraduates to suffer from a lack of information literacy, and therefore exercises that are scaffolded to help them understand the differences between using taxonomic vs. raw searches help address this issue in the context of research that is relevant to upper-level courses. Students then also benefit from understanding the trade-offs between investing time in learning research skills and how to use scholarly databases vs. the effort and risk of analyzing vastly variable raw search results.

Group discussions accompanying online research provide students with opportunities to share their ideas and learn from their peers. Students may be more comfortable asking a "stupid question" in the context of a small group discussion rather than asking the instructor. If the students working together in groups are focusing on a similar set of topics, each group becomes a peer community of experts in their topic areas. The more time and effort they apply to their shared research and analysis, the greater the benefits not only for their individual learning goals, but also for their sense of responsibility to their peers. And as students explore the resources collected by other scholars online, they broaden their understanding of scholarly communities and can begin to imagine themselves as professionals participating in these communities.

Students' understanding of disciplinary taxonomies and how to apply them to resources and their own research topics evolves as their collections of resources grow and are refined. Their sense of peer community grows as they work together in groups over time. Therefore it is useful to structure these activities as long-term components of the class to allow time for maturation.

Graduate Students: Encouraging Advanced Students to Extend Disciplinary Taxonomies

By graduate school, students are expected to have mastered their disciplinary taxonomies and be adept at applying them to research projects large and small. They have the analysis skills needed to select research strategies, efficiently and effectively collect organized sets of annotated resources, and apply these materials in their own arguments. If they are lacking in these skills, the learning objectives in a research methods class should be aimed at addressing these fundamentals.

Beyond the nuts and bolts of graduate-level research, graduate school is an opportunity for delving into the knowledge communities of the discipline. Part of the purpose of graduate school is to socialize students and build both their aptitude and their ability to collaborate and contribute new knowledge in their chosen disciplines and professions. The tendency of some graduate programs in some professions may be toward scholarly isolation and competition, but this is counter to increasingly prevalent trends toward the social

production of knowledge. Therefore key learning objectives for graduate students are the ability to communicate effectively with peers in the discipline and the ability to collaborate with peers on joint projects and research.

Socialization into the profession combined with a thorough understanding of prior work in the field are necessary pre-requisites for graduate students to visualize where and how they can contribute new knowledge. Without effective research skills, graduate students cannot know whether or not they are well-read in a topic area, and this is particularly true in disciplines where the field of knowledge changes quickly. Therefore graduate learning objectives also include the ability to accurately survey a topic area and position one's own argument in light of other scholars' work.

Example: Individual Research Project

A graduate research project is designed to require students to articulate the field of knowledge on a selected topic and formulate a new argument in that context. Students are challenged to define a topic area, explain the limitations of prior work, understand the current issues that are relevant to this topic, and make an argument that moves research forward. This would be a useful exercise in the early stages of a graduate program, to help students realize how to find a research niche before they start their thesis or dissertation.

Graduate students might start the project with a prior collection of their own disciplinary bookmarks. If they do, they can explore that set of resources for logical starting points. Whether they are starting from scratch or not, students need to define the taxonomic areas that are relevant for this project. They search for relevant resources in these areas using the controlled vocabulary of the taxonomy, analysing the resources for applicability, and adding them to an existing collection if they have one or building a collection if they do not.

To find relevant resources that are not strictly identified according to the taxonomy, students explore the bookmarks of other scholars in the field, browsing the way other scholars have tagged resources the student has already reviewed and tagged, or looking at the tag clouds of scholars who have included the same resources in their own collections (i.e., browse tags starting from the resources, or browse tags starting from the users). These strategies lead to additional resources or other ways of approaching the topic that they had not yet considered. Resources discovered in this way may also be more recent than library-catalogued resources, which may in some cases be several years out of date by the time they get catalogued.

Students by this point have tagged a collection of resources according to a controlled vocabulary,

but they also have adopted the tags of other scholars and applied their own. By studying their own tag clouds and those of their peers, they can begin to analyze not only the resources themselves, but also the patterns of interrelationships among the resources. They should be able to identify gaps in the research, and they need to determine whether these are gaps that should be filled in by searching for other resources, or gaps that they themselves can fill with their own research and arguments. If they have defined a gap to fill with their own work, they should be ready to write an argumentative thesis and an abstract for the research project.

The research project could have a mid-way assessment that evaluates how well the student has defined a topic area, surveyed prior work, and identified a niche for their own work. This assess-

Figure 2. Applying disciplinary taxonomy and extending it into related areas of research (© 2008, Blackboard Inc. Used with permission.)

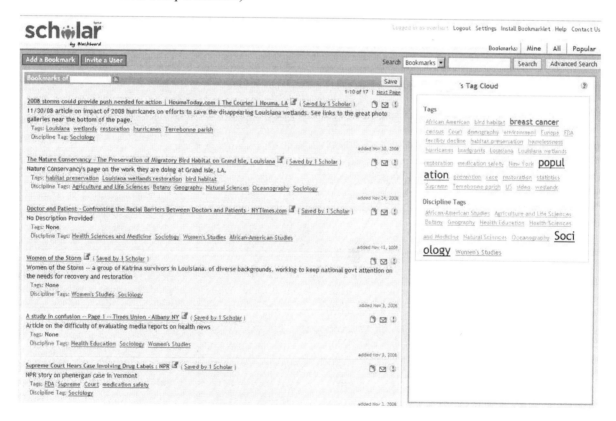

ment check-point provides the instructor with an opportunity to intervene and provide guidance before the student proceeds to the next stage.

As students progress in their research projects, they should be able to articulate their own extensions to the disciplinary taxonomy. By studying the field of research and how it has been professionally and informally tagged, they will have acquired a thorough understanding of the knowledge area and how their work fits in. They should be ready to apply to their work appropriate terminology that is logically related to the controlled vocabulary of the disciplinary taxonomy. The strength of their arguments and their ability to have their work accepted in scholarly communities will determine whether this terminology becomes a standard part of the disciplinary taxonomy.

Students' research projects can be assessed not only on the strength of their original argument, but also on their survey of the field, positioning of their own work, and articulation of exactly how their work appropriately extends the prior taxonomy and disciplinary knowledge.

Example: Participating in Scholarly Communities

Whether or not graduate students have successfully articulated new knowledge in their subject areas, they can benefit from engaging with scholarly communities. An initial, non-threatening way for instructors to enable this is to set up online discussion forums for students who are in the same class or program. Ideally, these forums are in the same context where professionals in the field discuss and communicate ideas, with options for the students to keep their discussions private among themselves or shared with others outside the class or program. These options allow students to try out ideas and share informally with their graduate student peers without being intimidated by more advanced professionals, while on the other hand acclimating students to the professional arena and making it easy to share their ideas in broader circles when

they are ready. No scholarly discipline is fixed, and exposure to debates, disagreements, and new discoveries discussed in professional forums helps graduate students recognize this fact.

The same online scholarly contexts that provide discussion forums also usually provide social bookmarking and commentary on bookmarked resources. As students become more familiar with the work of professionals in their own areas of specialization, they can learn a great deal by following these professionals bookmarking habits. What are they reading? How are they tagging resources? What is in their tag clouds? Can these resources and tag clouds lead the student to other professionals whose work is engaging and worth following? Scholars can set up RSS feeds so that they are notified of changes, enabling them to follow other's research in very specific and immediate ways.

Graduate students will probably want to "lurk" and not directly engage with professional scholars until they are confident of their own work and expertise. Participation in discussion forums with their peers and mentoring by instructors can help them determine when and how to engage. A useful set of activities in preparation for exposing one's professional identity online includes a thorough review of one's own bookmarks. What's there? Are there inappropriate items that should be cleaned up, either among the resources or their tags? Which bookmarks should be public and which should be kept private? As students are exploring the tag clouds of professionals, they should be forming their own sense of how one's tag cloud provides a definition of one's professional identity and shape their own tag clouds accordingly.

As a step toward engaging with professional scholars, graduate students benefit from engaging with their peers at other institutions. Using online profiles to find these peers, they can add them to their online social networks. These peers then use online tools to form their own private or semi-private discussions, exchange of resources, ideas, and advice. They review each others' tag clouds and offer suggestions for both further research and for polishing online identity. The more advanced and mature the graduate students, the more they benefit from these online interactions, as peer-review gradually takes the place of instructors' assessment of their work.

Pedagogical Value

Socialization into the profession takes place gradually over several years of graduate school. Students can start this process in simple, non-threatening ways by deciding how and with whom to share their bookmarks and other aspects of their online identity. Because bookmarks are so closely tied to a student's research areas and interests, sharing them is a natural bridge to academic discussion on these topics and eventually research collaboration.

Instructors can provide mentoring in the socialization process online that is much more immediate and ongoing than prior methods; graduate students may have the opportunity for face-to-face discussions at conferences only once or twice per year, for example, but the students, their mentors, graduate students at other institutions, and professionals in the field can have ongoing online discussions anytime. In the past, these discussions could not easily reference the in-progress research of the students or the professionals, but with the easy availability of social bookmarks, both emerging and experienced scholars can see a "cloud" of research take shape literally as it happens.

Pedagogical Strategies

In all of these examples, students are learning new research methods suitable to their level of expertise, and most of these examples have the added advantage of helping students learn from their peers and other scholars. By comparing their own research and collections of resources to those of others who are more established in the area of expertise, students grow in their understanding of the topic. As students' social bookmark tagging

and annotation skills evolve, they are contributing to collective intelligence on these topics, and the collections they produce can be used by other, subsequent and/or evolving communities of learners.

Social bookmarking tools and other Web 2.0 online knowledge sharing systems are generally free, easy to use, and straightforward to adapt to pedagogical strategies. Like other changes in online teaching and learning, instructors may take the opportunity of using these new tools as an incentive to re-think and adjust their strategies, but even if they do not, social bookmarking can be a very effective "bolt-on" technology added to existing research assignments. Students will welcome the opportunity to collect, tag, and annotate their research resources online, and they will probably take advantage of the ability to share and discuss the value of resources even if instructors do not scaffold these activities.

A note on privacy: Clearly social bookmarking tools would not be "social" if they did not involve sharing. However, instructors should be cognizant of the fact that students' research is part of their academic work and therefore protected by national laws and usually local/institutional policies. Students should not be forced to share their work and should be offered alternative assignments if they do not wish to disclose their research to others besides the instructor. Fortunately, most social bookmarking systems provide different levels of sharing: private to the individual, shared with other named individuals, shared with a specific group, community, or class, and/or public, for example. The instructor should utilize these mechanisms when designing assignments in order to offer the greatest privacy for those students who want it, combined with options for students to disclose their work to specific audiences or the general public if they choose to do so.

For instructors who are new to adopting Web 2.0 practices in their teaching, and also for instructors who want a straightforward way of thinking through how and why they would use

Table 1.

Strategy	What	How	Why
Thematic Organization	An interesting thematic or topic-oriented structure for online course resources, organized using a specific set of tags.	Define tags that represent the topics of the course. Create thematic bookmark streams based on these tags, including useful tag combinations. Teach students to use the tags consistently so that their bookmarks become part of the thematic streams.	Themes provide a sense of the interrelationship of resources, piquing students' interest and inviting interactive learning within and between the topics of the course. This simple but conceptually useful structure supplies part of the cognitive scaffolding necessary for students to build their own meaning from the course materials and activities.
Diverse and Frequently Updated Resources	A variety of different types of resources that can be used to learn the course concepts and achieve the learning objectives. Also, a wealth of supplementary materials for exploration, changing as new bookmarks are added.	Search for, bookmark, and tag a variety of valuable online resources in different formats. Whenever possible, include audio, video, interactive simulations, and images, as well as textual materials. Continue to add bookmarks throughout the term and encourage students to do the same.	Different students learn differently. For example, visual learners benefit from maps, images, charts, etc. Provide choices so that students can take ownership of the course content and become more actively engaged, constructing their own learning paths and contributing to a growing body of resources.
Critical Questions	Questions that trigger student thinking.	Include relevant questions with the resource streams to prompt students to investigate the materials in ways that are relevant for the course.	Challenge students to start thinking about the significance of the resources before they even start using them. Transform "flat" materials to be "covered" into "deep" materials to be actively explored.
Rich Connections	Ties from the course content to resources outside the course.	Provide resource streams from within the syllabus and/or other parts of the course structure. Use these streams to connect course materials and activities (such as discussion forums and assignments), to outside resources. Explain the purpose of the streams.	Providing access to resources outside the course builds a rich, interactive context for understanding. Repeated contact with the connected resources, especially in light of new concepts, reinforces learning.
Social Learning Opportunities	Opportunities for students to communicate with each other, demonstrate their expertise, and work together for richer understanding of course materials.	Teach students to evaluate each others' bookmarks and collaboratively collect and tag resources. Include analysis of bookmarked resources in thematic discussion forums.	Engaging with other students brings diverse perspectives to the resources and provides opportunities for students to learn from each other. Social behaviors such as collaboration, competition, and peer pressure make students' engagement with the course materials and activities more dynamic and provide additional motivations for learning.
Learner Contributions to Course Materials	Resources that are selected and added to the course by the students.	When students tag resources in a way that matches the bookmark streams in the course, these resources instantly become part of the course materials.	Students take greater ownership in the course if they are helping to construct a valuable set of course materials. Knowing that their peers will also be using these resources can instill a sense of pride and encourage responsible contributions.
Learning Objectives Clearly Tied to Activities	Statements of the goals of the course as they pertain to bookmarking activities.	Design bookmarking activities to help students achieve specific learning objectives, such as understanding how to compile an appropriate bibliography for a research project. State the objectives clearly and explicitly.	Help students understand the relationships between course activities and learning objectives. Provide them with the opportunity to shape their interaction with the resources in a way that most effectively addresses one or more specific learning goals. Demonstrate why the activities are relevant to specific outcomes.

continued on following page

Table 1. continued

Strategy	What	How	Why
Assessments and Assignments that Focus the Learning Materials	Quizzes, self-tests, assignments, and other activities that require the student to demonstrate understanding of the resources.	Create meaningful learning activities tied to bookmarked resources, including the activities of compiling and evaluating. Provide students with opportunities to demonstrate their engagement with these resources, such as incorporating them in writing assignments.	Focus the student's engagement with the resources through activities that measure and/or demonstrate what they've learned. Course materials or activities that appear to be random or do not have a clear purpose are more likely to be ignored. When students set their own priorities, they need to have an understanding of exactly which resources and activities will help them most efficiently and effectively address their learning goals.

social bookmarking, the table below provides a framework. The strategies represent general pedagogical values for learner-centered course design. The "What," "How," and "Why" succinctly state simple, fundamental ways of meeting these strategies. Instructors can decide which of these strategies are applicable to their courses and which ones to implement. The table also provides a way of thinking about pedagogical change in "bite-size chunks," since instructors can easily implement one or two of these strategies and consider others later. (Note that this table is available online as a "one-pager" that can easily be adapted and reproduced for distribution to instructors; see Everhart under Academic Resources below.)

CONCLUSION

Berger (2007) asserts that social bookmarking tools "support 21st Century learning skills; they offer a structure that is intellectually engaging, encouraging students to not only locate but also to collaboratively tag, organize and evaluate resources-- thinking more deeply about the process" (p. 3). For students and educators, these innovative research tools allow us to "keep things found, identify new communities, discover new web sites, make us more productive and allow us to create new tools to push the frontiers of the web's utility" (Gordon-Murnane, 2006, p. 27). With the

pedagogical strategies presented, students have the opportunity to gain greater competencies within their own disciplinary vocabulary as well as informal and formal research while engaging in communities of practice. The possibilities are endless.

However, further inquiry is called for in faculty research use of social bookmarking. The immediacy of social bookmarking, RSS feeds, and other Web 2.0 ways of sharing scholarly information online is rapidly changing research practices. Gone are the days of finding out about new research in one's field by thumbing through publishers' catalogs, and even the new ideas presented at conferences might be anticipated if the scholar has shared the research process online. Instructors do a disservice to students if they are not teaching and themselves modeling Web 2.0 practices. Instructors are also missing opportunities for easier, more efficient, more scalable, and more cost-effective graduate student mentoring if they are not helping their students take advantage of peer-to-peer, cross-institution, and emerging/experienced scholarly online collaboration. But perhaps most importantly, instructors can themselves participate in these opportunities and continue to evolve their own research practices and scholarly communities, while at the same time developing further pedagogical strategies for social bookmarking and the possibilities Web 2.0 has to offer.

REFERENCES

Alexander, B. (2006, March/April). Web 2.0: A new wave of innovation for teaching and learning? *EDUCAUSE Review, 41*(2), 32-44. Retrieved from http://connect.educause.edu/Library/EDUCAUSE+Review/Web20ANew-WaveofInnovation/40615

Berger, P. (2007). Social bookmarking: Locate, tag and collaborate. *Information Searcher, 17*(3), 3–6.

Bull, G. (2005). Folk taxonomies. *Learning & Leading with Technology, 33*(1), 22–23.

Everhart, D., Kunnen, E., & Shelton, K. (2007, October). *From information literacy to scholarly identity: Effective pedagogical strategies for social bookmarking*. Paper presented at the annual meeting of EDUCUASE, Seattle, WA. Retrieved from http://net.educause.edu/E07/Program/11073?PRODUCT_CODE=E07/SESS057

Everhart, D., & Morrison, J. (2007, June). *Teaching with social bookmarking: Lessons from early experiences of social bookmarking integrated with an online course environment*. Paper presented at annual meeting of EDEN Conference, Naples, Italy.

Garshol, L. M. (2004, September). Metadata? Thesauri? Taxonomies? Topic maps! [Retrieved from http://www.ontopia.net/topicmaps/materials/tm-vs-thesauri.html]. *Interchange, 10*(3), 17–30.

Golder, S. A., & Huberman, B. A. (2006). The structure of collaborative tagging systems. *Journal of Information Science 32*(2), 198-208. Retrieved from http://arxiv.org/pdf/ cs.DL/0508082

Gordon-Murnane, L. (2006, October). Social bookmarking, folksonomies, and Web 2.0 tools. *Searcher: The Magazine for Database Professionals, 14*(9), 26–28.

Gotta, M. (2008). *Deciphering social networks* (Version 1). Midvale, UT: The Burton Group. Retrieved from http://connect.educause.edu/Library/ECAR/DecipheringSocialNetworks/47253

Guy, M., & Tonkin, E. (2006, January). Folksonomies: Tidying up tags? *D-Lib Magazine, 12*(1). Retrieved from http://www.dlib.org/dlib/january06/guy/01guy.html

Hargadon, S. (2007). Best of social bookmarking. *School Library Journal, 16*(12), 20. Retrieved from http://www.schoollibraryjournal.com/article/CA6505695

Leslie, S., & Landon, B. (2008). Social software for learning: What is it, why use it? *The Observatory on Borderless Higher Education,* 1-27. Retrieved April 29, 2008, from http://www.obhe.ac.uk/products/reports/pdf/2008-01-01.pdf

Lomas, C. (2005). *7 things you should know about...social bookmarking*. Retrieved July 23, 2008, from http://connect.educause.edu/Library/ELI/7ThingsYouShouldKnowAbout/39378

MacGregor, G., & McCulloch, E. (2006). Collaborative tagging as a knowledge organisation and resource discovery tool. *Library Review, 55*(5), 291–300. doi:10.1108/00242530610667558

Muir, D. (2005). *Simply Del.icio.us: Online social bookmarking, or: Tagging for teachers*. Retrieved July 23, 2008 from http://personal.strath.ac.uk/d.d.muir/Delicious_Guide.pdf

Noruzi, A. (2007, June). Folksonomies: Why do we need controlled vocabulary? *Webology, 4*(2). Retrieved from http://www.webology.ir/2007/v4n2/editorial12.html

Richardson, W. (2007, March). Taming the beast: Finding good stuff online isn't a problem, making sense of it is. Thank goodness for social bookmarking. *School Library Journal,* 50–51.

The New Media Consortium & the EDUCAUSE Learning Initiative. (2007). *The 2007 horizon report.* Retrieved July 23, 2008, from http://www.nmc.org/pdf/2007_Horizon_Report.pdf

Trexler, S. (2007). The best of social bookmarking: Diigo. *Information Searcher, 17*(3), 34–36.

Vander Wal, T. (2007). *Folksonomy.* Retrieved August 10, 2008, from http://www.vanderwal.net/folksonomy.html

Watwood, B. (2007, December). Instructional uses of social bookmarking: Reflections and questions. *Romanian Journal of Social Informatics, 8.* Retrieved from http://www.ris.uvt.ro/Publications/Decembrie%202007/Watwood.pdf

ADDITIONAL READING

Academic Social Bookmarking Technologies:

Assignments, G. Faculty Development Resources: Allen, L., & Winkler, M. (n.d.). *Creating and using social bookmarking in a university library.* Retrieved from http://connect.educause.edu/blog/Carie417/e2006podcastcreatingandus/16719

Blackboard Scholar. (n.d.). Retrieved from http://www.scholar.com

Blackboard Scholar quick tutorials. (n.d.). Retrieved from http://wiki.scholar.com/display/SCLR/Scholar+Quick+Tutorials

Churches, A. (2007). *Social bookmarking rubric based upon Bloom's taxonomy.* Retrieved from http://h226.lskysd.ca/pd/files/u2/bookmarking_rubric.pdf

CiteULike. (n.d.). Retrieved from http://www.citeulike.org

Connotea. (2009). Retrieved from http://www.connotea.org/

DesRoches, D. (2007). *Social bookmarking offers a new way to store and share Web sites.* Retrieved from http://www.schoollibraryjournal.com/article/CA6403269.html

DesRoches, D. (n.d.). *Resource Website and k-12 example.* The Living Sky School Division, Saskatchewan, Canada. Retrieved from http://h226.lskysd.ca/pd/social_bookmarking

Everhart, D. (n.d.). *Social bookmarking strategies for interactive learning.* Retrieved from http://www.educause.edu/upload/presentations/E07/SESS057/SocialBookmarkingStrategies.doc

Everhart, D., Kunnen, E., & Shelton, K. (2007). *Practical classroom examples.* Retrieved from http://connect.educause.edu/Library/Abstract/FromInformationLiteracyto/45394

Georgetown University Library. (2009). *Evaluating Internet resources.* Retrieved from http://www.library.georgetown.edu/internet/eval.htm

Kunnen, E., Brand, G., & Morrison, J. (n.d.). *From tagging to teaching: Practical examples of leveraging social bookmarking in teaching and learning.* Retrieved from http://www.slideshare.net/gbrand/tagging-to-teaching

LeFeever, L. (2009). *Social bookmarking in plain English.* Retrieved from http://www.commoncraft.com/bookmarking-plain-english

Northern Illinois University Faculty Development and Instructional Design Center. (2007). *Introduction to social bookmarking.* Retrieved from http://www.facdev.niu.edu/facdev/programs/handouts/socialbookmarking.shtml

PennTags. (2005). Retrieved from http://tags.library.upenn.edu/

Zotero. (2009). Retrieved from http://www.zotero.org/

Chapter 11
VISOLE:
A Constructivist Pedagogical Approach to Game-Based Learning

Morris S. Y. Jong
The Chinese University of Hong Kong, Hong Kong

Junjie Shang
Peking University, China

Fong-Lok Lee
The Chinese University of Hong Kong, Hong Kong

Jimmy H. M. Lee
The Chinese University of Hong Kong, Hong Kong

ABSTRACT

VISOLE (Virtual Interactive Student-Oriented Learning Environment) is a constructivist pedagogical approach to empower computer game-based learning. This approach encompasses the creation of a near real-life online interactive world modeled upon a set of multi-disciplinary domains, in which each student plays a role in this "virtual world" and shapes its development. All missions, tasks and problems therein are generative and open-ended with neither prescribed strategies nor solutions. With sophisticated multi-player simulation contexts and teacher facilitation (scaffolding and debriefing), VISOLE provides opportunities for students to acquire both subject-specific knowledge and problem-solving skills through their near real-life gaming experience. This chapter aims to delineate the theoretical foundation and pedagogical implementation of VISOLE. Apart from that, the authors also introduce their game-pedagogy co-design strategy adopted in developing the first VISOLE instance—FARMTASIA.

INTRODUCTION

The young generation loves computer games (Prensky, 2006). Even if computer gaming is prohibited at school or at home, youngsters will make all attempts

to conduct this beloved activity somewhere else, such as game arcades, cyber cafés, or even game sellers' free demo machines on the streets. This "addiction" has been one of the common premises of various studies on harnessing games[1] in education in recent decades (e.g., Adam, 1998; Bisson &

DOI: 10.4018/978-1-60566-729-4.ch011

Copyright © 2010, IGI Global. Copying or distributing in print or electronic forms without written permission of IGI Global is prohibited.

Lunckner, 1996; Bowman, 1982; Buckingham & Burn, 2007; Cameron, 2008; Crookall & Saunders, 1989; Gredler, 2004; Hub, 2008; Malone, 1980, 1981; Squire, 2005).

Most of the early research of game-based learning focused on investigating what, why, and how gaming can make the process of learning more interesting (e.g., Bowman, 1982; Malone, 1980, 1981). The basis of those studies was the ability of games to let players have fun and enjoyable experiences. Fun and enjoyment are essential elements in the process of learning as students can be more relaxed and motivated to learn (Bisson and Luncker, 1996). Players always undergo hard but engaging, challenging but pleasurable, and risk-taking but rewarding experiences in gaming (Prensky, 2001). All these are the experiences of fun and enjoyment.

In recent years, along with the advancement of gaming technology, the focus on game-based learning has shifted onto the issue of how to harness the ability of games to sustain spontaneous players' engagement and exploit proactive players' communities for students' constructivist learning (e.g., Aylett, 2006; Egenfeldt-Nielsen, 2007; Lee, Lee & Lau, 2006; Gee, 2003, 2005; Prensky, 2001, 2006; Shaffer, 2006; Squire, 2005). For example, Adam (1998) and Squire (2005) studied the opportunities to utilize some prevalent recreational games in the commercial market for activity-based learning at school. Shaffer (2006) and his colleagues developed a number of *epistemic games* for students to participate in simulations of various professional communities in a self-directed manner. Lee, Lee, and Lau (2006) proposed *Folklore-based learning* which portrays a new design paradigm of educational games. Apart from that, in this chapter, we introduce *VISOLE* (Virtual Interactive Student-Oriented Learning Environment)—a constructivist pedagogical approach to game-based learning. In VISOLE, we adopt a game-pedagogy co-design strategy for facilitating students' multi-disciplinary knowledge acquisition and problem-solving skill enhance-

ment. We also emphasize the importance of teachers and their roles therein.

After the introduction, the rest of the chapter is organized as follows. Firstly, we discuss the background of game-based learning and some recent research foci in the domain. After that, we delineate the theoretical foundation and pedagogical tactic of VISOLE, followed by a description of FARMTASIA—the first instance of VISOLE. Further, we discuss some emerging issues of game-based learning, before our concluding remarks are given.

BACKGROUND

The discussion of harnessing games for teaching and learning has started since the widespread popularity of Pac-Man in the early 1980s (Squire, 2003). Without doubt, the "games" discussed in most of today's game-based learning research are quite different from the ones that were used in education in the last few decades. The differences are not only in games' technical enhancement (e.g., more sophisticated 3D user interfaces, dynamic synchronous players' interaction, etc.) brought by the advancement of technology, but also their underpinning learning philosophy, shifting from behaviourism (Rachlin, 1991; Skinner, 1938) to constructivism (Bruner, 1960; Papert, 1993; Piaget, 1964, 1970).

Behaviourist Game-Based Learning

Behaviourism was the dominating learning philosophy adopted in the design of so-called "educational games," when games were introduced to education initially (Egenfeldt-Nielsen, 2007). The behaviourist conception in education advocates that a human's mind can be treated as a black box (Skinner, 1938). The workings inside this black box need not be uncovered. The study of learning should focus only on observable events (i.e., stimuli and responses). Through practice students will learn the correct response to a certain stimulus. Learning can be imposed by conditioning and reinforcement.

One of the typical genres of "behaviourist" educational games is drill-and-practice games. This type of games usually has a clear reward structure that is used as a way to push students' learning forwards. It is assumed that students can be put in front of computers, and then learn content and skills with drill-and-practice games, without teachers' help or involvement. For example, in *Math Blaster!*[2], students have to shoot down the right answer to the mathematics question shown on the screen. On each success, the player's balloon will move towards a needle. A student who can pop his/her balloon eventually will win the game. Egenfeldt-Nielsen (2007) criticized that drill-and-practice games lack integration of learning experience into gaming experience. These games rely only on extrinsic motivation (Malone, 1980, 1981) through arbitrary rewards. "Parrot-like" learning will result in weak transfer and application of knowledge and skills (Gee, 2003; Jonassen & Howland, 2003).

Constructivist Game-Based Learning

Constructivism is a common underlying learning philosophy in most contemporary game-based learning research (e.g., Aylett, 2006; DiPetro, Ferdig, Boyer & Black, 2007; Gee, 2003, 2005; Lee et al.'s 2006; Shaffer, 2006; Squire, 2005). In direct contrast to behaviourist learning, constructivist learning emphasizes that students should construct knowledge on their own. Students' learning is not imposed simply by conditioning and reinforcement, but rather a *cognitive* and *socio-cultural* interaction in a rich and authentic learning environment (Otting & Zwaal, 2007). A gaming environment is a possible room for constructivist learning to take place (Gee, 2003; 2005; Prensky, 2001, 2006; Shaffer, 2006).

When discussing the potential of game-based learning in the cognitive and socio-cultural aspects,

we should first classify today's games (either educational games or recreational games) into *mini-games* or *complex-games* (Prensky, 2006). In general, playing mini-games takes around several minutes to an hour. Usually, these games contain simple challenges and content, with neither ethical dilemma nor human players' interaction. In contrast to mini-games, complex-games require players' dozens of hours (or even more) of concentrated attention to master. Most tasks therein are generative and open-ended without prescribed gaming strategies. Players have to analyze the perceived information and context in complex games cognitively. It is also necessary for them to acquire new and multiple skills, and interact (compete, cooperate or collaborate) with other *human* players, or *NPCs* (non-player characters) in the games social-culturally. This sort of gaming experience coincides with Lave and Wenger's (1991) conception of *situated learning*.

Complex-games create new cognitive and socio-cultural learning opportunities for students to acquire knowledge and skills in a constructivist fashion. Contemporary game-based learning researchers (e.g., Aylett, 2006; Ip, Luk, Cheung, Lee & Lee, 2007; Shaffer 2006; Squire, 2005) have been endeavouring to study how complex-games (hereafter referred as games) can be harnessed in education. In general, their work can be categorized into two research foci, namely, *education in games*, and *games in education*.

Education in Games

Gee (2003, 2005) has been advocating the exploration of the possibility of adopting recreational games in the commercial market for educational use. He argued that many bestselling recreational games (e.g., *Full Spectrum Warrior*[3]) are already "state-of-the-art" learning games as they are hard but fun, time-consuming but enjoyable, and complex but "learnable." As one of proponents of Gee, Squire (2005) studied how to integrate a prevalent recreational game, *Civilization III*[4], into US high-school classrooms for World History teaching. This game allows players to lead a civilization from 4000 BC to the present, with a mission to compete for political, scientific, military, cultural, and economic victories. In this game, each player has to seek out geographical resources, manage economics, plan the growth of his/her own civilization, and engage in diplomacy with other players competitively and collaboratively. Some other research of education in games includes Adams's (1998), Betz's (1995), and Prensky's (2001) studies examining the educational potential of *SimCity 2000*[5].

Some researchers (e.g., Rice, 2007) realize that the education-in-game approach is more appropriate for informal learning than school education. It is because recreational games in the commercial market are designed originally for entertainment purpose, rather than education purpose. Teachers will have difficulties in finding recreational games in which the content and context are compatible with school curricular (Mishra & Foster, 2007). Apart from that, most recreational games offer only little or even no degree of "pedagogical adjustment" (Deubal, 2002) for teachers when integrating the games into their teaching practice.

Games in Education

Instead of utilizing existing recreational games, some game-based learning researchers design their educational games based on different constructivist beliefs. For example, Shaffer (2006) realized that members of a profession have an *epistemic frame*—a particular way of thinking and working. Thus, developing individuals to be members of a particular profession is a matter of equipping them with a right epistemic frame. Shaffer and his colleagues developed a number of *epistemic games* which allow students to participate in simulations of various professional communities that they might someday inhabit. Lee et al. (2006) proposed

a design paradigm of educational games, namely, *Folklore-based learning*. This paradigm suggests that learning takes place in an interactive adventure highlighted by problem-solving tasks which are situated in a folklore-based story plot. It is not only aimed at enabling students to learn in an authentic environment, but also offering interesting story episodes as a motivating agent for less initiated students. As prototype work, Lee et al. developed a game to realize this learning paradigm, namely, *Tong Pak Fu and Chou Heung*[6], based on the topic of probability in the Mathematics curriculum. In addition, other examples of games in education include Aylett's (2006)*narrative games* and Ip et al.'s (2007)*game-based collaborative learning platform*.

Ferdig (2006) argued that, similar to other educational tools, the ultimate impact of educational games on learning depends on the pedagogical strategies and teachers' involvement in utilizing the games in real practice. Nevertheless, not much discussion on the pedagogical framework or teachers' facilitation tactics is found in the current concerned research. We want to draw attention to this area that has been ignored in most of the game-in-education studies, and that is why we propose VISOLE (*Virtual Interactive Student-Oriented Learning Environment*)—a new pedagogical approach to game-based learning. In the following sections, we will delineate the theoretical foundation and praxis of the VISOLE pedagogy.

THEORETICAL FOUNDATION OF VISOLE

The constructivist view in education emphasizes that learning is an active process in which students construct knowledge on their own by interacting in rich and authentic learning environments (Otting & Zwaal, 2007). Hein (1998) proposed a set of principles for constructivist learning design:

Figure 1. The conceptual framework of VISOLE

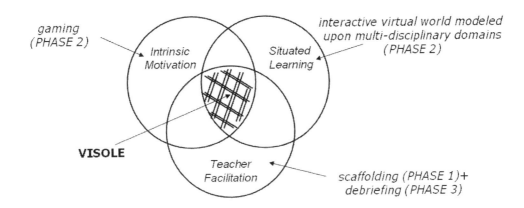

- motivation is essential for learning;
- previous knowledge is a prerequisite to learning;
- learning is contextual and an active process of meaning construction;
- learning is a social activity and happens with other learners;
- experience plus reflection equals learning.

In the theoretical context of constructivist learning, (1) *intrinsic motivation*, (2) *situated learning*, as well as (3) *teacher facilitation* are united to construct the conceptual framework of VISOLE (see Figure 1). Based on this framework, VISOLE is concretized further into three operable pedagogical phases, namely *Multi-disciplinary Scaffolding* (Phase 1*), Game-based Situated Learning* (Phase 2), and *Reflection and Debriefing* (Phase 3). We will focus on discussing the conceptual framework of VISOLE in the current section, while the pedagogical phases will be presented in the next section.

Intrinsic Motivation

Constructivist learning theorists (e.g., Papert, 1993; Piaget, 1964, 1970) realize that intrinsically motivated play-like activities can foster students' deep learning. It is because, in those activities,

students are willing to spend more time and effort on learning. They also feel better about what they learn, and will try to apply the acquired knowledge and skills in the future.

According to Malone's (1980, 1981) theory of intrinsic motivation in learning, students are said to be motivated intrinsically if they engage in a learning activity for its own sake, rather than some external rewards. Malone argued that learning through gaming is an effective means for triggering students' intrinsic motivation because of the three intrinsic motivating elements of computer games: (1) *challenge*, (2) *fantasy*, and (3) *curiosity*. Apart from that, Bowman (1982) tied his intrinsic motivation study on gaming and learning, with Csikszentmihalyi's (1975, 1990) psychological conception—*flow*. Flow is a state of experience of "*intense concentration and enjoyment*." Under the flow state, a person will engage in a complex, goal-directed challenge not for external rewards, but simply for the exhilaration of dealing the challenge. Bowman believed that learning through gaming is a spontaneous way to bring students to the flow state of learning. Although Bowman's work was done more than two decades ago, recent empirical evidence (e.g., DeLisi & Wolford, 2002) still accord with his assertion.

The issue of how to get students motivated intrinsically and with the feeling of immersion is one of the essential considerations in constructivist learning design (Cordova & Lepper; 1996; Martens, Gulikers & Bastiaens, 2004). Thus, we use a gaming strategy to trigger students' intrinsic motivation in VISOLE.

Situated Learning

Papert (1993) observed that knowledge is often fragmented into small and disconnected pieces of learning content in traditional classrooms. The original intention of this act is to make learning easier. However, it usually ends up neglecting the rationale behind the knowledge itself, creating unrealistic learning contexts, and rendering the whole learning process boring.

Lave (1988) argued that, learning is neither an individual nor impersonal process, but a course of *situated cognition*. The premise underlying situated cognition is that all knowledge, skills, and ability are dependent on the contextual and social-cultural situations in which they are acquired. Thus, the issue of education is not seen as how to build representations in each student's head, but how to engage them in near real-life situations through contextual and socio-cultural interactions (Wenger, 1998). This is so-called *situated learning* (Lave & Wenger, 1991), in which learning takes place unintentionally rather than deliberately. CTGV—*Cognition and Technology Group at Vanderbilt* (1993) applied situated learning in the area of technology-based learning activities focusing on the enhancement of students' problem-solving skills.

With today's advanced gaming technology, game-based learning is recognized as an appropriate embodiment of situated learning that Lave and Wenger (1991) delineated (Egenfeldt-Nielsen, 2007; Huh, 2007; Prensky, 2001, 2006; Shaffer, 2006). An interactive gaming environment modeled upon multi-disciplinary domains can facilitate students' contextual and socio-cultural learning in near real-life situations that entwine *practice, participation, community,* and *identity*

(Wenger, 1998). Most tasks in this environment are open-ended. In order to accomplish the tasks, students have to interact (compete, cooperate or collaborate) with other *human* players or *NPCs* (non-player characters) therein social-culturally. In other words, they are involved in a community of practice which embodies certain beliefs and behaviour to be acquired, i.e., knowledge construction. We term the process of students' gaming in VISOLE as *game-based situated learning*.

Teacher Facilitation

Egenfeldt-Nielsen (2007) and Ferdig (2007) realized that it is not sufficient to look at students' intrinsic motivation in gaming, or games as a sophisticated contextual and socio-cultural learning device, and then assert knowledge can flow and be transferred automatically among students in game-based learning. DiPetro et al. (2007) argued that leaving students to float amidst rich experience without teachers' help in the process of game-based learning may not work effectively. According to other constructivist learning approaches, such as problem-based learning (Barrows, 1996), and project-based learning (Krajcik & Blumenfeld, 2006), teachers' facilitation of the activation of students' *prior knowledge* (Hein, 1998), and formulation of students' *reflective habits* (Dewey, 1938) are always of primary importance. There is no exception in game-based learning. Scaffolding (Vygotsky, 1978) and debriefing (Thiagarajan, 1998) are the conceptual bases framing the teacher facilitation design in the VISOLE pedagogy.

Scaffolding

Every new and meaningful learning starts from students' prior knowledge (Wellington, 2006). Vygotsky's (1978) *scaffolding* conception offers clues to frame what, how, and how much teachers should activate students' prior knowledge. Scaffolding refers to a process by which a teacher assists students so that they can solve problems or perform tasks that would otherwise be out of reach. The teacher scaffolds should be removed gradually as the students begin to take on more control and responsibility about the problems or the tasks. For the scaffolding to be effective, the teacher scaffolds should be set inside the so-called *zone of proximal development* (ZPD). The ZPD is the area between *the level at which a student knows something or can do something on his/her own* (namely, Zone A), and *the level of performance or skill he/she could reach if the right intervention is offered* (namely, Zone B). The teacher scaffolds function as a "bridge" so as to assist students in "walking across" the ZPD, from Zone A to Zone B.

Debriefing

Besides the issue of how to activate students' prior knowledge, in the process of game-based learning, students often have difficulties in making connections between the scenarios happening in a game and the corresponding real-world system that the game intends to represent (Clegg, 1991). Moreover, games make assumptions and inevitably contain bias (Thiagarajan, 1998); even

a game designed with high-fidelity simulations cannot represent reality.

Learning is experience plus reflection (Dewey, 1938). Thus, gamers become learners if they can often reflect on their experience in gaming (Salen, 2007; Schon, D, 1983). *Debriefing* (Thiagarajan,1988) is a process to help students reflect on their gaming experience.

Usually, debriefing is conducted by a teacher, which allows students to engage in reflective and meta-cognitive thinking that transforms their gaming experience into learning experience. One of the crucial aims of debriefing is to let students correspond the things happening in games to real-life context, so as to correct the misconceptions in their minds. In fact, a number of researchers (e.g., Garris, Ahlers & Driskell, 2002; Mayer, Mautone & Prothero, 2002; Prensky, 2001) believe that debriefing is one of the most critical components in game-based learning. Furthermore, Thiagarajan (1988) proposed a set of strategies for game-based learning teachers to apply in their debriefing lessons, such as *role dropping, insight sharing, real-world transfer, what-if analysis,* and *second thoughts.*

Figure 2. Three pedagogical phases of VISOLE

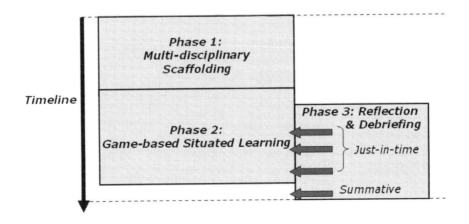

A CLOSE LOOK AT VISOLE

Based on the theoretical foundation, we frame VISOLE as three operable pedagogical phases, namely *Multi-disciplinary Scaffolding* (Phase 1*)*, *Game-based Situated Learning* (Phase 2), and *Reflection and Debriefing* (Phase 3), as diagrammatically shown in Figure 2. Please note that Phase 2 and Phase 3 take place in an interlacing fashion, but Phase 2 starts a bit earlier than Phase 3.

Phase 1: Multi-Disciplinary Scaffolding

VISOLE teachers act as cognitive coaches to activate VISOLE students' learning motive, and assist them in gaining some preliminary high-level abstract knowledge (prior knowledge) based upon a selected multi-disciplinary framework. In this phase, students are equipped with "just enough" knowledge, and given only some initial "knowledge pointers." They have to acquire the necessitated knowledge and skills on their own in the next learning phase, not only from the designated learning resources but also a wider repertoire of non-designated learning resources, such as the Internet.

Phase 2: Game-Based Situated Learning

This phase deploys an online multi-player interactive game portraying a virtual world. The scenarios therein become the dominant motivator driving students to go on to pursue the inter-related understandings of the multi-disciplinary abstractions encountered in Phase 1. The game encompasses the creation of a virtual interactive world in which each student plays a role to shape the development of this world for a period of time. The missions, tasks and problems therein are generative, and there is no prescribed solution. Since every single action can affect the whole virtual world, students have to take account of the overall effects associated with their strategies and decisions on others contextually and socio-culturally. "Being situated" in this virtual world, not only do students have to acquire the subject-specific knowledge in a multi-disciplinary fashion, but they also need the generic skills of problem analysis, strategy composition, decision making, etc.

Phase 3: Reflection and Debriefing

This phase interlaces with the activities in Phase 2. After each gaming session, students are required to write their own reflective journal to internalize their learning experience in the virtual world in a just-in-time fashion. Moreover, at the end of this phase, they are required to write their own report in a summative fashion to reflect on their overall learning experience. In addition, teachers monitor closely the progress of students' development of the virtual world at the backend, and look for and try to act on "debriefable" moments to "lift" students out of particular situations in the game. Respectively during the course and at the end of this phase, teachers extract problematic and critical scenarios arising in the virtual world, and then conduct just-in-time and summative case studies with their students in face-to-face debriefing classes.

FARMTASIA: AN INSTANCE OF VISOLE

FARMTASIA[7] is the first instance of VISOLE. The multi-disciplinary content of FARMTASIA was designed based on the Hong Kong senior secondary curriculum. It involves subject areas of *geography*, *bio*logy, *economics*, and *technol*ogy, while the "virtual world" is composed of interacting farming systems. Figure 3 shows the five components (*the game platform*, *teacher console*, *online knowledge manual*, *online discussion forum*, and *blog platform*) implemented in FARMTASIA. In this section we will delineate how these components support the VISOLE pedagogy.

Game Platform

FARMTASIA's game platform enables Phase 2 of VISOLE *(Game-based Situated Learning)*. It deploys interacting farming systems, covering the domains of *cultivation, horticulture,* and *pasturage.* The "virtual world" therein is modeled upon the multi-disciplinary knowledge of *geography* (natural environment and hazards, as well as environmental problems), *biology, economics* (including government and production system), and *technology.* In this world, each player *(the term "player(s)" and "student(s)" are interchangeable hereafter)* acts as a *farm manager* to run a farm which is composed of *a cropland, an orchard,* and *a rangeland.* Each player competes for financial gain and reputation with three other farm managers who are also at the same time running their own farm somewhere nearby in the same virtual world. Throughout the gaming period, players have to formulate various investment and operational strategies to yield both quality and abundant farm products for making a profit in the market. They should always keep an eye on the contextual factors *(e.g., temperature, rainfall, wind-speed, etc.)* of the virtual world so as to perform some just-in-time actions, such as cultivating and reaping crops at appropriate time. Scheduling tasks for farm workers to conduct fertilization, irrigation and grazing is another critical issue that players should also pay attention to. In spite of the competition for financial gain, the richest may not be the final winner, because players' final reputation in the virtual world is another crucial judging criterion. The reputation index is governed by good public policies and is determined by players' practice on sustainable development and environmental protection. *Wise Genie,* who is an NPC (non-player character), will appear in the virtual world for giving advice or hints to players in some critical moments. Figure 4 shows the gaming interface of FARMTASIA.

In this virtual world, players can fall into di-

Figure 3. Five components implemented in FARMTASIA

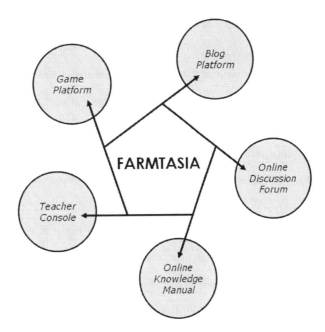

lemmas easily. For example, buying machinery needs large initial investment, but may be able to boost the quantity of the farm outputs. Keeping more livestock will increase the daily operational cost of the farm, but livestock's excrement can be used as a sort of organic fertilizer for nurturing the cropland and the orchard so as to achieve sustainable development. Apart from that, as in real-life, hard work does not guarantee rewards, and sagacity may not come along with fortune. Catastrophes from the nature, and disasters caused by other farm managers can ruin one's achievement in a single day. Nevertheless, by setting a range of precaution measures, "wise" players can often minimize their loss in the catastrophes and disasters.

Scientific Models

FARMTASIA's game context is based on real data simulation articulating sophisticated scientific models. For example, both botanical and biological models are adopted to simulate how crops and livestock evolve in a near real-world way. In the virtual world, players can experience how their crops sprout, flourish and wither, and witness how their livestock grow and propagate themselves. Figure 5 shows a crop's sowing-harvesting relationship against time. In addition, a geographical model is adopted to create the four-seasoned climate, which alternates wind-speed, temperature and rainfall in the virtual world. (see Figure 6) Concerning the economics in the virtual world, an economic model is adopted to deal with the exchange of labour, farm products, and revenues.

Figure 4. The gaming interface

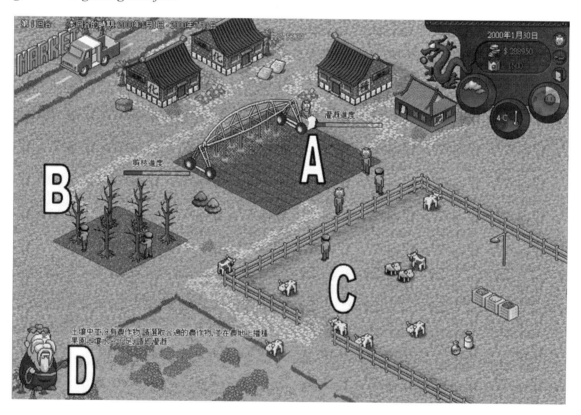

(A) Cropland, (B) Orchard, (C) Rangeland, & (D) Wise Genie

Unforeseen Events

The game system will generate various *unforeseen events* in the virtual world on a random basis. Framing a workable solution to cope with an unforeseen event requires players to analyze every current happening in the virtual world in a contextual and socio-cultural fashion. The unforeseen events will emerge in the form of *local*, *market*, and *mass* issues:

- *Local Issues*. These issues may lead to the risk of a farm closure but without causing inter-farm consequential effects in the virtual world. Examples include fire accidents, workers' strikes, invitations to debit bank loan, etc. See Figure 7.
- *Market Issues*. These issues arise in either the provincial or global market, and will cause consequential effects on all farms in the virtual world. Examples include market-price fluctuations in farm products, outbreaks of bovine spongiform encephalopathy (mad-cow disease), etc. See Figure 8.

- *Mass Issues*. These events involve cooperation and collaboration among players in the virtual world, and will cause interactive effects therein. Examples include raising funds to build a dam, accusing an entrepreneur of plastic industry whose factories pollute the water sources, etc. See Figure 9.

Situating players in these unforeseen events can provide them with opportunities to sharpen their ability to deal with contingency and emergency.

Mini-Games

Besides the main game, players will be assigned to play a mini-game in every round of gaming. One of the key purposes of the mini-game inclusion is to motivate players to pursue their learning in the virtual world.

A set of mini-games are designed corresponding to the routine but essential activities that have to be conducted in a real-life farm, such as cutting off rotting fruits in the orchard (see Figure 10 and 11). These mini-games are competitive in nature, and players compete for better scores therein.

Figure 5. Botanical model: Sowing-harvesting relationship against 12 months

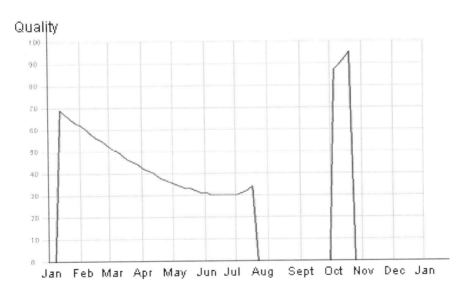

Figure 6. Geographical model: Wind-speed, temperature and rainfall against 12 months

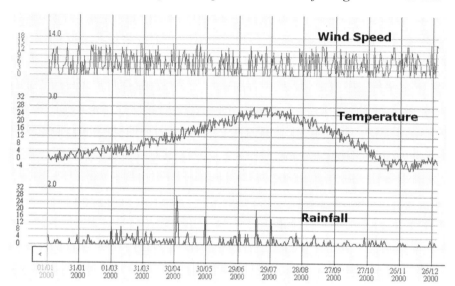

Their performance in the mini-games will affect how well the relevant activities are carried out in their own farm. This is because players' good performance in the mini-games will be rewarded with better overall managerial and financial abilities in the virtual world.

Teacher Console

In Phase 3 of VISOLE *(Reflection and Debriefing)*, teachers need to monitor the progress of students' development of the virtual world, and then give debriefing for facilitating students' reflection on their gaming experience. One of the key functions of the *teacher console* of FARMTASIA is to assist teachers in preparing and conducting their debriefing classes.

While students run their farm in the virtual world, the game server *records* their every single gaming action. Teachers can review all students' gaming histories through the teacher console. The console interface presents the histories in Gantt chart format (see Figure 12. Every rectangular block in a Gantt chart represents the proceedings of a student in a particular timeslot. By clicking the block, teachers can *replay* the proceedings

in a form of *video playback* (see Figure 13. This function is termed *record-and-replay* function of the teacher console.

With the record-and-replay function, teacher can look for and extract interesting, problematic, or

Figure 7. Unforeseen events: Do you need more money for investing in your farm?

Figure 8. Unforeseen events: Market-price fluctuations in farm products

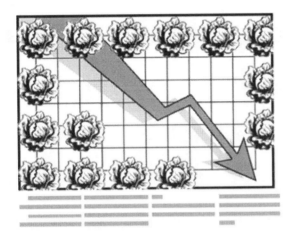

ies with their students. Since all these scenarios come from students' actual gaming experiences, it is easier for them to recognize, empathize, and understand the constructive and destructive occurrences therein, and the corresponding enhancement and corrective actions. Teachers can also ask students to perform *what-if analysis* or have *second thoughts* (Thiagarajan, 1988) based on these scenarios so that students can have deeper reflection on the differences between their current outcomes and other possible outcomes with respect to other possible acts.

Apart from the *record-and-replay* function, the teacher console can also allow teachers to inject "artificial" catastrophes, such as twisters and tsunamis into the virtual world (see Figure 14 and Figure 15). Like the unforeseen events, situating players in these artificial catastrophes provides them with opportunities to sharpen their ability to deal with contingency and emergency.

critical scenarios taking place in the virtual world to conduct just-in-time and summative case stud-

Figure 9. Unforeseen events: Accusing a polluting factory cooperatively

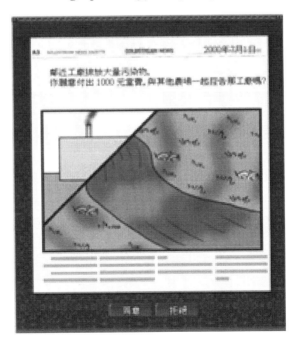

Figure 10. Example of mini-games: Scare-crowing birds

Figure 11. Example of mini-games: Cutting off rotting apples

Online Knowledge Manual

As mentioned in the previous sections, FARMTA-SIA's "virtual world" is modeled upon the multi-disciplinary knowledge of *geography* (natural environment and hazards as well as environmental problems), *biology*, *economics* (including government and production system) and *technology*. In parallel with the development of the game platform, we also created an *online knowledge* *manual* (see Figure 16) which covers all underlying multi-disciplinary knowledge employed to model the virtual world.

This manual serves two proposes. Firstly, it is a reference guide for teachers to prepare and frame their scaffolding lessons in Phase 1 of VISOLE *(Multi-disciplinary Scaffolding)* for equipping students with high-level abstract knowledge required in FARMTASIA. Secondly, this manual is a learning resource bank for students to look

Figure 12. Student's gaming history: Gantt chart

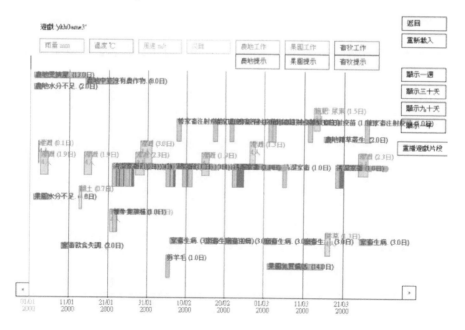

Figure 13. Student's gaming history: Student's gaming proceedings as video playback

up when they meet some unsolvable problems or difficulties arising in the virtual world in Phase 2 of VISOLE *(Game-based Situated Learning)*.

Online Discussion Forum and Blog Platform

An online discussion forum (See Figure 16) is provided as an off-the-game collaborative learning platform for students to discuss both gaming and learning issues arising in Phase 2 of VISOLE *(Game-based Situated Learning)*. Furthermore, in

order to motivate students to write their daily game-based learning journal to reflect on their learning experience, a *blogging* approach is harnessed in Phase 3 of VISOLE *(Reflection and Debriefing)*. Students are required to "blog" their reflection after each round of gaming (see Figure 17). They can also view and reply to other students' blog without restriction. Three reflective questions are provided on the blog platform so as to scaffold students to conduct their reflection on their learning experience in a more focused manner,

Figure 14. "Artificial" catastrophes

Figure 15. "Artificial" catastrophes

Figure 16. The online knowledge manual

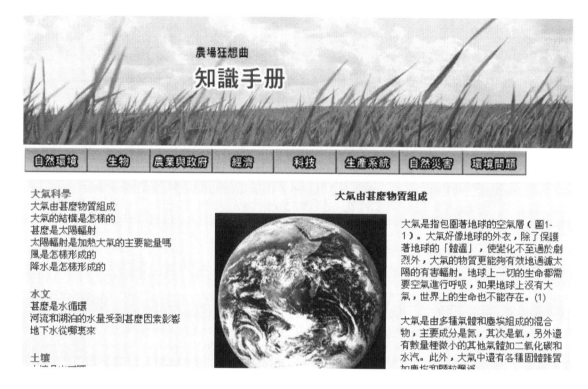

rather than some superficial gaming experience. The questions are:

• How is the current condition of your farm?
•   What have you learned in this round?
•   Based on the new knowledge and skills you learnt in this round, will you adjust your strategies in the next round of gaming? How?

Both online discussion and blogging in the VISOLE process offer additional opportunities for students to interact with one another socio-culturally. This favours situated learning to take place (Lave, 1988; Lave and Wenger, 1991). Besides, the artefacts on the discussion forum and blog platform provide extra information for teachers to frame and conduct their debriefing classes.

FURTHER DISCUSSION

Some recent empirical studies (Jong, Shang, Lee & Lee, 2007a; Jong et al., 2007b; Shang, Jong, Lee & Lee, 2008) investigating the educational realization and accomplishment of the VISOLE pedagogy have been carried out in Hong Kong. In those studies, the participants were secondary-4 (K-10 equivalent) students and their teachers, while FARMTASIA was adopted as the VISOLE instance[8]. Results showed, after the VISOLE process, there was a significant enhancement in the students' multi-disciplinary knowledge, and problem-solving skills in terms of "self," "information," "collaboration," and "task" management (Bennett, Dunne & Carre, 1999). Apart from that, the majority of the teachers were positive towards the use of this pedagogical approach to harness games in education. However, the insufficiency of time for reviewing the students' gaming histories and preparing the debriefing classes was one of

Figure 17. The online discussion forum and the blog platform

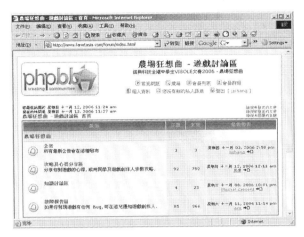 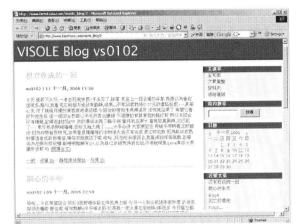

the main difficulties that the teachers encountered during the implementation process. They commented that it was rather time-consuming in selecting suitable case-study scenarios from the gaming proceedings with the teacher console. Notwithstanding this, they did suggest some possible ways to improve the existing console. For instance:

Like sports games ... it would be great if the teacher console can analyze students' gaming data automatically, and then generate a set of possible case-study scenarios, like the highlights in soccer games ... for example, a student suddenly earns a lot of money or there is a dramatic drop of his reputation in the game. We can use these scenarios to conduct debriefing classes.

Improving the existing teacher console is of critical importance to the further development of our game system; otherwise, the inefficient use of the console will become a barrier to teachers implementing the VISOLE pedagogy in practice.

In fact, similar to other tools or media when they were first introduced to schools, studying barriers to the educational use of games has become one of the interests in this research domain. For example, Rice (2007) in his empirical study argued that *stakeholders' (e.g., school principals,*

teachers, and parents) negative perceptions of gaming, unattractive educational games to students, and *insufficient computing hardware for gaming at school* are the dominating barriers to harnessing games in education. Rice's study focused mainly on the entrance barriers to the introduction of games into schools. However, little light was shed on the actual emerging barriers which impede the effectiveness of students' learning and teachers' facilitation in the process of game-based learning at the classroom level. In the current research context, there is still a lack of comprehensive understanding of the barriers that might obstruct the successful implementation of game-based learning in school education.

CONCLUSION

Ferdig (2007), in the preface of a journal's special issue—*Learning and Teaching with Electronic Games,* called for answers to the question of how educational gaming in constructivist fashion will look like. DiPietro et al. (2007), Egenfeld-Nielsen (2007), and Mishra and Foster (2007) argued that although the educational potential of game-based learning has been discussed widely and with strong theoretical arguments, there is still a distance to put it in place, particularly regarding the pedagogical consideration. We have attempted to address the issue by introducing the VISOLE pedagogy—one of the possible ways to harness games in education.

In this chapter, we have introduced the background of game-based learning, from the behavourist learning paradigm in the early 1980s to the recent constructivist learning paradigm, and from its original purpose of "sugaring the pills" to today's purpose of sustaining learners' intrinsic engagement and exploiting cognitive and socio-cultural learning environments. Furthermore, we have elaborated two recent genres of research in the domain—*education in games,* and *games in education.* VISOLE is an instance of games in education. However, the educational paradigm is a bit different from some other work in the same genre.

Despite a great promotion of the shift in education from a traditional, didactic model of instruction to a learner-centered model that emphasizes a more active learner role, the educational paradigm of VISOLE advocates strongly that teachers are always the best at seeing when, what and why learners have difficulties and assisting them in looking for possible solutions in the process of learning (Howard, 2002; Jonassen, 1998; Lee, 2002). We believe even a well-designed educational game per se is unlikely to facilitate learning effectively, unless opportunities of initial enablement, reflection and generalization of abstraction are embedded in the whole gaming process in an appropriate way. This needs human-medication therein, and that is why we propose VISOLE.

VISOLE is a three-phase constructivist pedagogical approach to game-based learning, in which, the importance of teachers' roles are emphasized. FARMTASIA is the first illustration of VISOLE. In this chapter, we have also discussed briefly some VISOLE empirical research findings that were presented in some recent international conferences (Jong et al., 2007a, 2007b; Shang et al., 2008).

By introducing VISOLE, we hope we can generate a flash of inspiration for other game-based learning researchers, educators, school teachers, game designers, as well as game companies, when reflecting on the questions of what, why, how, and when gaming can be educational. More mature and comprehensive frameworks for the educational use of games (*either the education-in-games approach or games-in-education approach)* will emerge soon, provided that we continue to pursue an open-discussion and conversation within multiple fields and disciplines.

ACKNOWLEDGMENT

The work described in this paper was substantially supported by a grant from the Research Grants Council of Hong Kong SAR (CUHK4200/02H).

REFERENCES

Adams, P. C. (1998). Teaching and learning with SimCity 2000. *The Journal of Geography, 97,* 47–55. doi:10.1080/00221349808978827

Aylett, R. (2006). And they both lived happily ever after? Digital stories and learning. In G. Dettori, T. Giannetti, A. Paiva, & A. Vaz (Eds.), *Technology-mediated narrative environments for learning.* Amsterdam: Sense Publishers. Retrieved July 28, 2008, from http://www.macs.hw.ac.uk/~ruth/Papers/narrative/Kal-Lisbon.pdf

Barrows, H. S. (1996). Problem-based learning in medicine and beyond: A brief overview. *New Directions for Teaching and Learning, 68,* 3–12. doi:10.1002/tl.37219966804

Bennett, N., Dunne, E., & Carre, C. (1999). Patterns of core and generic skill provision in higher education. *Higher Education, 37*(1), 71–93. doi:10.1023/A:1003451727126

Betz, J. A. (1995). Computer games: Increase learning in an interactive multidisciplinary environment. *Journal of Educational Technology Systems, 24*(2), 195–205. doi:10.2190/119M-BRMU-J8HC-XM6F

Bisson, C., & Lunckner, J. (1996). Fun in learning: The pedagogical role of fun in adventure education. *Journal of Experimental Education, 9*(2), 109–110.

Bowman, R. F. (1982). A Pac-Man theory of motivation. Tactical implications for classroom instruction. *Educational Technology, 22*(9), 14–17.

Bruner, J. S. (1960). *The process of education.* Cambridge, MA: Harvard University Press.

Buckingham, D., & Burn, A. (2007). Game literacy in theory and practice. *Journal of Educational Multimedia and Hypermedia, 16*(3), 323–349.

Cameron, B. (2008). Gaming, cognitive style, and feedback in the achievement of learning objectives. In T. T. Kidd & H. Song (Eds.), *Handbook of research on instructional systems and technology* (pp. 416-448). Hershey, PA: Information Science Reference.

Cheung, K. K. F., Jong, M. S. Y., Lee, F. L., Lee, J. H. M., Luk, E. T. H., Shang, J. J., & Wong, M. K. H. (2008). FARMTASIA: An online game-based learning environment based on the VISOLE pedagogy. *Virtual Reality (Waltham Cross), 12*(1), 17–25. doi:10.1007/s10055-008-0084-z

Clegg, A. A. (1991). Games and simulations in social studies education. In J. P. Shaver (Ed.), *Handbook of research on social studies teaching and learning* (pp. 523-528). New York: Macmillan.

Cognition and Technology Group at Vanderbilt. (1993). Anchored instruction and situated cognition revisited. *Educational Technology, 33*(3), 52–70.

Cordova, D. I., & Lepper, M. R. (1996). Intrinsic motivation and the process of learning: Beneficial effects of contextualization, personalization, and choice. *Journal of Educational Psychology, 88*, 715–730. doi:10.1037/0022-0663.88.4.715

Crookall, D., & Saunders, D. (1989). Towards an integration of communication and simulation. In *Communication and simulation: From two fields to one theme.* Clevedon, UK: Multilingual Matters.

Csikszentmihalyi, M. (1975). *Beyond boredom and anxiety.* San Francisco: Jossey-Bass.

Csikszentmihalyi, M. (1990). *Flow: The psychology of optimal experience.* New York: Harper & Row.

DeLisi, R., & Wolford, J. L. (2002). Improving children's mental rotation accuracy with computer game playing. *The Journal of Genetic Psychology, 163*(3), 272–282.

Deubel, P. (2002). Selecting curriculum-based software: Valuable educational software can help students rise to the challenge of standardized testing and assessment. *Learning and Leading with Technology, 29*(5), 10–16.

Dewey, J. (1938). *Experience and education.* New York: Macmillan.

DiPietro, M., Ferdig, R. E., Boyer, J., & Black, E. W. (2007). Towards a framework for understanding electronic educational gaming. *Journal of Educational Multimedia and Hypermedia, 16*(3), 225–248.

Egenfeldt-Nielsen, S. (2007). Third generation educational use of computer games. *Journal of Educational Multimedia and Hypermedia, 16*(3), 263–281.

Ferdig, R. E. (2006). Assessing technologies for teaching and learning: Understanding the importance of technological-pedagogical content knowledge. *British Journal of Educational Technology, 37*(5), 749–760. doi:10.1111/j.1467-8535.2006.00559.x

Ferdig, R. E. (2007). Learning and teaching with electronic games. *Journal of Educational Multimedia and Hypermedia, 16*(3), 217–223.

Garris, R., Ahlers, R., & Driskell, J. E. (2002). Games, motivation, and learning: A research and practice model. *Simulation & Gaming, 33*(4), 441–467. doi:10.1177/1046878102238607

Gee, J. P. (2003). *What video games have to teach us about learning.* New York: Palgrave.

Gee, J. P. (2005). *What would be a state of the art instructional video game look like?* Retrieved July 28, 2008, from http://www.innovateonline.info/index.php?view=article&id=80

Gredler, M. (2004). Game and simulations and their relationships to learning. In D. Jonassen (Ed.), *Handbook of research on educational communications and technology* (2ⁿᵈ ed.) (pp. 571-581). Mahway, NJ: Lawrence Erlbaum Associates.

Hein, G. (1998). *Learning in the museum.* London: Routledge.

Howard, J. (2002). Technology-enhanced project-based learning in teacher education: Addressing the goals of transfer. *Journal of Technology and Teacher Education, 10*(3), 343–364.

Huh, J. (2008). Adoption and dissemination of digital game-based learning. In T. T. Kidd & H. Song (Eds.), *Handbook of research on instructional systems and technology* (pp. 409-415). Hershey, PA: Information Science Reference.

Ip, C. W. H., Luk, E. T. H., Cheung, K. K. F., Lee, J. H. M., & Lee, F. L. (2007). A game-based computer supported collaborative learning environment: Learning villages (LV). In *Proceedings of the 11ᵗʰ Annual Global Chinese Conference on Computers in Education,* Guangzhou, China (pp. 289-292).

Jonassen, D. H. (1988). Integrating learning strategies into courseware to facilitate deeper processing. In D. H. Jonassen (Ed.), *Instructional designs for microcomputer courseware* (pp. 151-181). Hillsdale, NJ: Erlbaum.

Jonassen, D. H., & Howland, J. (2003). *Learning to solve problems with technology: A constructivist perspective.* Upper Saddle River, NJ: Merrill Prentice Hall.

Jong, M. S. Y., Shang, J. J., Lee, F. L., & Lee, J. H. M. (2007a). *An exploratory study on VISOLE – a new game-based constructivist online learning paradigm.* Paper presented at the America Educational Research Association Annual Convention 2007 (AERA 2007), Chicago, IL.

Jong, M. S. Y., Shang, J. J., Luk, E. T. H., Cheung, K. K. F., Ng, F. K. Y., Lee, F. L., & Lee, J. H. M. (2007b). Teachers' perceptions of harnessing VISOLE for learning and teaching. In *Proceedings of the 11ᵗʰ Annual Global Chinese Conference on Computers in Education,* Guangzhou, China (pp. 392-399).

Krajcik, J. S., & Blumenfeld, P. (2006). Project-based learning. In R. K. Sawyer (Ed.), *The Cambridge handbook of the learning sciences* (pp. 317-334). Cambridge, UK: Cambridge University Press.

Lave, J. (1988). *Cognition in practice: Mind, mathematics, and culture in everyday life.* Cambridge, UK: Cambridge University Press.

Lave, J., & Wenger, E. (1991). *Situated learning: Legitimate peripheral participation.* Cambridge, UK: Cambridge University Press.

Lee, J. H. M., Lee, F. L., & Lau, T. S. (2006). Folklore-based learning on the Web—pedagogy, case study, and evaluation. *Journal of Educational Computing Research, 34*(1), 1–27. doi:10.2190/3HFM-D9NQ-G7Y7-QC1G

Lee, K. T. (2002). Effective teaching in the information era: Fostering and ICT-based integrated learning environment in schools. *Asia-Pacific Journal for Teacher Education and Development, 5*(1), 21–45.

Malone, T. W. (1980). *What makes things fun to learn? A study of intrinsically motivating computer games.* Palo Alto: Xerox.

Malone, T. W. (1981). Toward a theory of intrinsically motivating instruction. *Cognitive Science, 4*, 333–369.

Martens, R. L., Gulikers, J., & Bastiaens, T. (2004). The impact of intrinsic motivation on e-learning in authentic computer tasks. *Journal of Computer Assisted Learning, 20*, 368–376. doi:10.1111/j.1365-2729.2004.00096.x

Mayer, R. E., Mautone, P., & Prothero, W. (2002). Pictorial aids for learning by doing in multimedia geology game. *Journal of Educational Psychology, 94*, 171–185. doi:10.1037/0022-0663.94.1.171

Mishra, P., & Foster, A. N. (2007). The claims of games: A comprehensive review and directions for future research. In . *Proceedings of the Society for Information Technology and Teacher Education Interactional Conference, 2007*, 2227–2232.

Otting, H., & Zwaal, W. (2007). The identification of constructivist pedagogy in different learning environments. In M. K. McCuddy, H. van-den-Bosch, W. B. Martz, A. V. Alexei, & K. O. Morseb (Eds.), *The challenges of educating people to lead in a challenging world* (pp. 171-196). The Netherlands: Springer.

Papert, S. (1993). *The children's machine: Rethinking school in the age of the computers.* New York: Basis Books.

Piaget, J. (1964). Development and learning. *Journal of Research in Science Teaching, 2*, 176–186. doi:10.1002/tea.3660020306

Piaget, J. (1970). *Science of education and psychology of the child.* New York: Oxford University Press.

Prensky, M. (2001). *Digital game-based learning.* New York: McGraw Hill.

Prensky, M. (2006). *Don't bother me mom – I'm learning.* St. Paul, MN: Paragon House.

Rachlin, H. (1991) *Introduction to modern behaviorism* (3rd ed.). New York: Freeman.

Rice, J. W. (2007). New media resistance: Barriers to implementation of computer video games in the classroom. *Journal of Educational Multimedia and Hypermedia, 16*(3), 249–261.

Salen, K. (2007). Gaming literacies: A game design study in action. *Journal of Educational Multimedia and Hypermedia, 16*(3), 301–322.

Schon, D. (1983). *The reflective practitioner: How professionals think in action.* New York: Basic Books.

Shaffer, D. W. (2006). *How computer games help children to learn.* New York: Palgrave Macmillan.

Shang, J. J., Jong, M. S. Y., Lee, F. L., & Lee, J. H. M. (2008). VISOLE: An example of hybrid learning. In *Proceedings of the International Conference on Hybrid Learning and Education 2008*, HKSAR, China (pp. 348-358). Heidelberg, Germany: Springer.

Skinner, B. F. (1938). *The behavior of organisms.* New York: Appleton-Century-Crofts.

Squire, K. R. (2003). Video games in education. *International Journal of Intelligent Games & Simulation, 2*(1). Retrieved July 30, 2008, from www.cyberfest.us/Education/Video_Games_in_Education-MIT_Study.pdf

Squire, K. R. (2005). Changing the game: What happens when video games enter the classroom? *Innovate, 1*(6). Retrieved July 28, 2008, from http://www.innovateonline.info/index.php?view=article&id=82

Thiagarajan, S. (1998). The myths and realities of simulations in performance technology. *Educational Technology, 38*(5), 35–41.

Vygotsky, L. (1978). *Mind and society.* Cambridge, MA: MIT Press.

Wellington, J. (2006). *Secondary education: The key concepts.* London: Routledge.

Wenger, E. (1998). *Communities of practice: Learning, meaning, and identity.* Cambridge, UK: Cambridge University Press.

ENDNOTES

[1] Unless otherwise specified, the term "game(s)" refers to "computer game(s)."

[2] *Math Blaster* is an educational game for children aged 6-9 to assist them in learning the criteria for Key Stage 1 and 2 mathematics skills. http://www.smartkidssoftware.com/nddav31.htm (Retrieved on August 28, 2008)

[3] http://www.fullspectrumwarrior.com/ (Retrieved on July 28, 2008)

[4] http://www.civ3.com/ (Retrieved on July 28, 2008)

[5] http://www.sc3000.com/sc2000/ (Retrieve July 28, 2008)

[6] http://www.cse.cuhk.edu.hk/~mhp/ (Retrieved on July 30, 2008)

[7] FARMTASIA is a collaborative project conducted by Centre for the Advancement of Information Technology in Education, and Department of Geography and Resource Management at The Chinese University of Hong Kong. The system design and other technical aspects of FARMTASIA have been documented in Cheung, Jong, Lee, Lee, Luk, Shang, and Wong's (2008) recent publication.

[8] For the details of the research design and findings of those empirical studies mentioned in this section, please refer to the work of Jong et al. (2007a, 2007b) and Shang et al. (2008).

Chapter 12
Second Language E-Learning and Professional Training with Second Life®

Patricia Edwards
University of Extremadura, Spain

Mercedes Rico
University of Extremadura, Spain

Eva Dominguez
University of Extremadura, Spain

J. Enrique Agudo
University of Extremadura, Spain

ABSTRACT

Web 2.0 technologies are described as new and emerging for all fields of knowledge, including academia. Innovative e-learning formats like on-demand video, file sharing, blogs, Wikis, podcasting and virtual worlds are gaining increasing popularity among educators and students due to their emphasis on flexible, collaborative and community-building features, a promising natural channel for the social constructivist learning theory. This chapter addresses the application of e-learning in university degree programs based on exploiting the practical, intensive and holistic aspects of Second Life® (SL™). Although the specific framework dealt with is English as a foreign language, it seems feasible to assume that the learning processes are equally transferable to other disciplines. In light of the aforementioned premises, the outlook of e-learning 2.0 approaches require action research and shared experiences in order to back up or challenge the claims and expectations of the academic community concerned with best practices in education.

DOI: 10.4018/978-1-60566-729-4.ch012

Copyright © 2010, IGI Global. Copying or distributing in print or electronic forms without written permission of IGI Global is prohibited.

INTRODUCTION: WELCOME TO WEB 2.0

With the arrival of the so-called Web 2.0, a term coined by Tim O'Reilly (2003), windows of opportunity have burst wide open for internet users to participate, share, communicate and collaborate with one another in order to spread knowledge and learning experiences. The second generation web, coupled with a significant increase in users, has been favored by the appearance on the scene of new technologies such as AJAX, FLASH or RUBY, and standards like XML, XHTML, RSS, RDF and CSS. The combination of these new support systems, plus the fact that internet access has reached even the most remote corners of the globe, has generated the development of innovative Web applications. Unlike their predecessors, the latest developments are not merely limited to displaying multimedia information. They also allow users to interact, modify or create more dynamic and enriched information by means of the integration of social networks (nodes where users interact and share knowledge) as well as encourage initiatives in collaborative web projects.

Regardless of the degree of acceptance and use made of Web 2.0 thus far, the availability of a continuum of tools, applications and platforms is progressively leading higher education towards making virtual learning activity a viable option. Although a minority of teachers and learners has adopted interactive learning models to date, these can alter current educational practices. For instance, by substituting teacher-oriented linear learning processes for a methodological approach where students choose their own resources, manage their learning, collaborate with co-learners, communicate and socialize through blogs, wikis, postcasting, chats, learning and knowledge communities, and learning management systems (LMS) like Moodle™ (Modular Object-Oriented Dynamic Learning Environment is a trademark of Open Source Initiative). Worthy of mention is the birth of Sloodle™ (Second Life Object-Oriented

Distance Learning Environment), an Open Source Initiative Project application which allows Second Life® and Moodle™-users to share certain tools in this brave new virtual world for educational purposes.

This study is centered on the analysis of user-learner capacity to engage and interact in English as a foreign language for the future professional purposes of engineering students. Total immersion in the specific learning scenario of virtual worlds offers the global experience of exposure to elements of interaction rarely present in the teaching-learning of isolated items of knowledge. Three-dimensional interaction provides the means to create motivating environments for students to learn in context, such as foreign language sessions held in a monumental setting of the target language country (Stevens, 2008). In this type of environment the central and the periphery components of any topic are presented as a whole to learn from. Computer Assisted Language-Learning (CALL) specialists are particularly interested in the emerging concept of the second generation Web. The second language learning prospects it can offer regard students collaboratively constructing knowledge on topics of common interest while using the target language and publishing pupil-authored reflections throughout the entire creative process. Thus, the interactivity promoted by these new technologies is bound to have a profound impact on how CALL is approached. Nonetheless, a crucial question remains – Just how effective is a virtual world for second language learning and professional training?

In order to unfold this desideratum, the aim of the work herein presented lies in examining the potential of various pedagogical aspects and second language learning strategies for professional training purposes with the 3D virtual platform Second Life®, a.k.a. SL™ (an unregistered trademark of Linden Research, Inc.). Of the many motivational resources included in this social networking environment, first is virtual role play represented by the individual learner's avatar (Figure 1).

Figure 1. Student avatar prototype

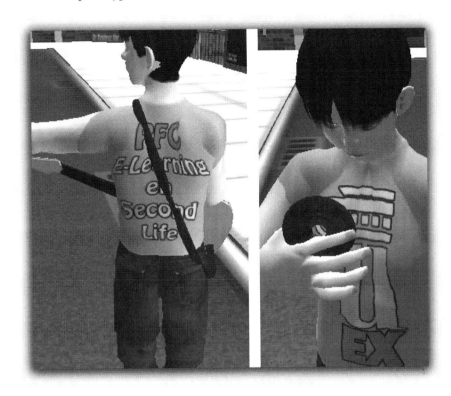

Figure 2. Pilot group at a virtual conference. Graphic compositions from & about the Second Life® world.

Secondly, preferences in engaging activities and interrelationships with other **avatars** are analyzed once immersed in the simulated setting (Figure 2). Finally, the effectiveness of the methodological domain for learning foreign languages for professional applications is scrutinized with research instruments, namely, a learner questionnaire and follow-up interviews, Web 2.0 tools and sites in the case study of a target group of participating university students.

VIRTUAL WORLDS AND THE ROLE OF AVATARS

The process for diving into participation in a virtual world is an extension of a well-known, classical learning technique called role-play. Role-play has always been a teacher-exploited strategy for getting students to assume a given situation and then act it out. However, in virtual worlds, role-play pushes far beyond traditional uses and takes on dimensions simulating reality and fantasy from a holistic perspective, "when the deepest identity change is possible with a single mouse click, the opportunities to…play are endless" (Au, 2008, p. 79). In other words, a role is played out with attention paid to every possible detail, starting with student design of his/her avatar's personalized physical appearance to owning possessions, to acting and reacting to multiple forms of situational context with other avatar-learners for as long a period of time as required. For the purposes of second language learning, the application of role-play can carry avatar-residents towards horizons capable of heightening student motivation levels through intensive, all-encompassing simulation exercises.

Another feature of virtual worlds is 3D browsing, a creative source of fun with role-playing for users "in-world". Since avatars can move about the virtual world at will, interactions can vary and role-play can change according to situations and contexts. Successful role-play demands knowl-

edge of a new virtual environment which modifies the ways people socialize and communicate, ergo, for CALL purposes, the way students learn. Avatar-students can interact at any time, anywhere and with anyone they encounter, so conventional classroom scheduled barriers like limited time, restricted space, and authentic identity fade into the background. For these reasons, a virtual world houses the potential of opening up a wide range of development for variable kinds of e-learning activities.

The complete role-play experience is due to several factors most of which are learner rather than teacher oriented (Edwards et al, 2008):

1) there is a certain amount of personal investment on the part of the learner involved in creating an avatar and in carrying out his/her actions,

2) role-play is not limited to class hours, but rather, can be prolonged over time allowing for really getting into the part,

3) avatar behavior is directed by the protagonist, that is, the learner, who encounters and creates numerous variables in simulated settings,

4) avatar actions can become progressively more complex as s/he accumulates a past, lives out a present and makes plans for a future,

5) both the physical characteristics and behavior of avatars can change, be true to life, or materialize into "want to be" aspirations,

6) the status of anonymity may increase the participation of shyer and more introverted types of students who often find it too challenging to speak up and speak out in traditional classes where one is literally on the spot. However, some scholars argue that **avatars** are not completely anonymous as the avatar name becomes known in-world. Bruckman (1996) discusses this type of middle ground identity and claims that people come to the net to participate, to construct and push new

identity limits. Others suggest that inform- ing students that they are not completely anonymous may encourage inappropriate behavior (Haynes, 1998),

7) Edwards et al (2008) contend however that the identity of the real life learner is fun- damentally wrapped in a protective bubble behind the concealing shield of his/her avatar which may be a particularly attractive feature for motivating students into taking learning risks.

Building an identity in SL™ is relatively easy and it is also free of cost, although with certain limitations like the buying and selling of objects, allowed only in the premium membership. For the goals of the case study, free membership was a satisfactory solution for getting students to develop their **avatars** with imagination and to represent their motivations, decisions and desires while communicating in English. In this respect, each student becomes a creative designer as well as a participating agent (Figure 3). Identities can be made to the image and likeness of the creator, - or not, meaning that one's avatar can be a realistic or an imaginary representation of oneself, as well as a combination of both (see Turkle, 1995 for a psychological perspective of avatars, role-play and identity).

In the event that the reader should prefer a wider range of options for designing and building avatar identities, for a nominal fee, subscribers are provided with a budget to spend as they please in-world. The Linden™ dollar (a trademark of Linden Lab) fluctuates like any other official currency on the virtual financial market, and therefore, so does the avatar's buying power. As monetary transactions occur in any profession as well as in one's personal (first) life, the academic applications and implications of budgeting one's salary could provide yet another experimental tool for learners to manage in pre-work role-play, that is, doing virtual business and making a virtual living (Craig, 2006). Residents can own a home,

Figure 3. Avatar appearances. Adapted from & about the Second Life® world.

shop, go to work, attend college, interact with others, enjoy leisure activities, and in essence, get a (second) life and live it. Time and money can be spent on dining out, at sporting events, the supermarket and the mall, all with corresponding prices. It is even possible to take in a *machinima* movie, a medium in a real-time 3D virtual world created by combining film-making, animation and game development.

Nonetheless, should the free membership be the only choice available in a particular academic setting, there are plenty of role-playing circumstances valid for the educational purposes pursued. Typical examples can be found in social events and cultural activities like those held in museums, parks, exhibit halls and libraries, available to avatar-internet users through innovative techniques in virtual reality and 3D interaction (figure 4).

Thus, avatars play a vital role in a virtual world. The visual composition will be a reflection of oneself, realistic or otherwise, so the creation of a personal avatar should be addressed with care. The e-motional behavior will be remote-controlled by its creator as h/she interacts in-world. For CALL purposes, students will be communicating in English as a foreign language via their avatar, a point which brings us to the question of considering virtual worlds as a second language e-learning tool.

CALL AND WEB 2.0 LANGUAGE LEARNING

Background

Where has CALL methodology and Web 2.0 language learning come from, where are they going, and where will they go from here?

Virtual world methodology is based on Social Constructivist Learning Theory which originally stems from a trio of renowned classical development perspectives on motivation, problem-solving and collaboration. These consist of Piaget's Theory of Cognitive Acquisition (1950), wherein knowledge is acquired through self-motivated experience in the world; Vygotsky's Zone of Proximal Development Theory (ZDP), "the distance between the actual developmental level as determined by independent problem solving and the level of potential development as determined through problem solving under adult guidance, or in collaboration with more capable peers" (1978, p.86); and Wood, Bruner & Ross' Theory of Instructional Scaffolding (1976), providing a temporary structural support system for the learner, like a scaffold, where building knowledge is facilitated by sharing with others until independence is reached. Today's scholars have embraced and expanded on aspects of these important concepts to adapt them to social constructivist theory in virtual worlds.

The concept of Second Life® is not entirely new. It may be likened to a modernized version

Figure 4. Free cultural spaces. Adapted from & about the Second Life® world.

of multi-user text-based virtual environments developed decades ago (e.g., MUDs, MOOs), early 3D games, and precursor virtual worlds used over the years in education to simulate applications rich in learning opportunities. Reminiscent environments include the no longer available *InterZone* site created by Gordon Wilson (Stevens, 2003), which featured voice chat in a text-based 3D environment and encouraged students to participate in building up the world. Current developments include language learning in a game-based multi-user virtual environment, such as the Quest Atlantis project to immerse children, ages 9 to 12, in educational tasks (http://atlantis.crlt.indiana.edu/), presented by Zheng, Brewer & Young at the 2005 WiAOC Conference. A 24-hour online event, SLanguages 2008, provided a forum for practitioners, researchers and consultants in the field of language education to exchange methods, experiences, tools and materials on Second Life at EduNation I & II (http://www.slanguages.net/home.php).

CONTROVERSIAL RESEARCH

There are multiple studies promoting language learning through virtual worlds and online chats. Peterson's (2006) research on Active Worlds for language learning found that participants were able to undertake a variety of tasks in the target language, communicate effectively and use interactive strategies. The study claimed that **avatars** (the role-play vehicle) facilitated learner engagement during computer-mediated communication. This research concluded that interaction was influenced by a number of variables like task type, sociolinguistic factors and context, mixed with the potential provided in-world. In light of such experiences, and the conception that Second Life® might be a creative place to visit and explore, countless institutions are setting up sites, even purchasing islands, for educational purposes, entertainment, conference venues, professional meetings and so on.

Not all scholars however consider Second Life® a universally suitable e-learning environment. Downes (2007) critiques the lack of open standards, interoperability, or data portability of the environment. O'Donnell (2006) raises some critical points and lists reasons to seriously question its use, like the lack of context, a void in guidance, an over-emphasis on escapism encouraging membership supposedly far outpacing the active use of the site. Second Life® claims to have reached a million users in October 2006, and, enrollment is continuously on the rise. (http://blog.secondlife.com/2006/10/18/1000000-residents-happy-crushing-signup-load-sad/) Other reports question such successful statistics as simply the rapid spread of a "Try Me" virus, whose one time users drop out and become immune (Shirky, 2006). A similar opinion is backed by Rose (2007) who suggests that 85% of the avatars have been orphaned once the novelty has diminished.

Interim stances include scholars such as Scott (2007) whose approach recommends an open-minded trial period for interested educators. Her standpoint is seconded by Macleod (2007) who recognizes value in virtual spaces for teaching and learning, but, qualifies his statement by observing that its instructional strengths are by no means unique to virtual reality alone.

PROSPECTS

Regardless of the divided opinions on the educational potential of virtual worlds, the success of Web 2.0 lies in the ability to provide tools for sharing, communicating, collaborating and enhancing creativity among users, and to apply these advantages to improving on-line learning with blogs, podcast, social networks, wikis, folksonomys, and so on. Likewise, multimedia environments allow users to share text, images, videos and audio files, thus enabling learners to communicate in oral chats, audio recordings, on-line audio-video conferences and similar applications.

As previously stated, Sloodle™ combines Moodle™ and Second Life® learning objects to offer teachers and students the benefit of sharing the mutual advantages of both sites. While LMS provide activities, chats, wikis, forums, podcasting, the possibility to share longer documents etc. (Kemp and Haycock, 2008), SL™ enables users to talk to people outside the traditional classroom, visit far away destinations, attend conferences and hold meetings. Availability of oral/aural tools is an important requirement of online language learning in order to provide for the practice and perfection of speaking and listening skills. SL™ virtual environment supplies the communicative context, reveals simulated real world situations and offers valid options for collaborative work to be evaluated in the e-learning classroom. With all these tools integrated in one site, the resources should be capable of the functionality needed to develop an optimal environment for on-line language learning.

Expectations regarding instructional methods and strategies for foreign language e-learning with this virtual channel include:

- Classroom simulation - re-creating traditional classrooms within the 3D world, both in small and large groups of avatars where the instructor teaches with virtual slides, or gives lectures through voice and text chats.
- Role-play - a construed situation to be interpreted in the virtual environment.
- Treasure hunts - hidden clues followed by learners to complete an activity, task or game for educational purposes.
- Guided tours - used to show learners the location of products, services or events by helping them understand relationships between locations/features within an area.
- Virtual cooperation - challenging learners to apply rules and learn by collaborative doing. **Avatars** work on creating in-world through teamwork.

- Critical thinking and problem solving - presenting avatar-learners with simulations in which they must draw on prior knowledge to find answers to thought-provoking pretexts.

Although alternatives exist, Second Life® is one of the largest and most mature platforms available for social interaction (EDUCAUSE Learning Initiative, 2008), making it a prospective place to carry out educational projects which allow for building knowledge in an attractive and social constructivist way. Can it be an ideal tool for the open source nature of the Web and social networking online, or is it just a banal promise which consumes resources, wastes time, and is far removed from educational aims? Gaining insight into the adequacy of the virtual world for collaboration and productivity on the aforementioned challenge is the purpose of the empirical study developed in the next section.

EMPIRICAL CASE STUDY

Aims and Scope

The feasibility of using virtual worlds for second language learning and professional training is developed with an in-depth analysis of the results of the qualitative study undertaken at the University of Extremadura in south-western Spain on Web 2.0 tools and selected Second Life® sites. The general research questions can be summarized as: 1- Is there a motivating and engaging learning life beyond the 4 walls of the traditional classroom space, and to what degree? 2- What are the learning preferences and acquisition goals of the participating target group of students? 3- How effective do students with presumed common interests feel Web 2.0 and virtual worlds for second language learning really is?

The situational context and technical specifications of the research sampling are as follows:

- Participants: 66 first /second life inhabitants
- Course type: elective for undergraduate level engineering students
- Course content: English as a Foreign Language for ICT (Information and Communication Technology)
- Tools for data analysis: questionnaire /follow-up interview /statistical data packages
- Realization date: late spring semester (3 months), 2008.

The data collected has provided evidence for course design and content in the development of virtual worlds and indications requisite to achieving specific learning objectives. It has also supplied a series of warning signals that need be heeded when enthusiasm for innovation can at times blur a clearer vision of the actual state of affairs. In short, analysis, discussion and concluding comments from the results obtained in the current empirical study propose to shed some meaning on the issue of using a virtual world as an instrument for second language e-learning and professional training.

TEST INSTRUMENTS

As previously pointed out, the learner questionnaire (see Table 1 for detailed results) and follow-up interviews were expected to provide practical insight into the issues under study. The questionnaire was anonymous and answers/comments were noted down in the post survey interviews void the identification of authorship to allow students to speak freely.

The twenty-two question survey is structured into three major sections of interest: student motivation (Q 1-8), learner preferences (Q 9-14), and the effectiveness (Q 15-22) of exploiting virtual worlds for second language acquisition and professional training in technical university degree programs. A four-item Likert scale was chosen

(e.g. none/a little/some/a lot) in the motivation and effectiveness sections in order to encourage the 66 participants into evaluating the probes to a greater or lesser degree of commitment, rather than a five point itemization which might lend itself to choosing a middle of the road variable. In this sense, students had to decide between leaning towards either a more or less favorable option in order to state their opinions. The preference section, on the contrary, contains yes/no variables, open responses and check lists, allowing for a certain amount of flexibility.

The follow-up interviews supplied further information regarding the responses received in the questionnaire. Moreover, students commented on the positive and negative aspects of the program, made suggestions, and/or recommendations for future improvement of the methodology carried out. A sampling of 22 volunteers, representing one third of the group, openly spoke about their motivation, preferences and the program effectiveness for learning English. The researchers clarified questions or doubts regarding apparent contradictions and unexpected answers during the dialogue, while comments made with respect to this academic experience were recorded. Throughout the analysis of the pilot program questionnaire, applicable data obtained in the follow-up interviews will be highlighted for the purposes of illustrating the results and identifying specific avenues of future research.

DISCUSSION AND RESULTS

Student Motivation: Is there a motivating and engaging learning life beyond the 4 walls of the traditional classroom space, and to what degree?

Motivation is considered prerequisite for performance and the driving force behind the entire experience, for without it, there would be little acceptance of SL™ at all. Therefore, student receptivity to using a virtual world and their dedication to making the system work constitute an

Table 1. Learner Questionnaire Annex - Sampling = 66

MOTIVATION			
1. I have had previous experience with SL™			
No 84.85%	a little 9.09%	some 6.06%	a lot 0%
2. For me to feel integrated, become involved and participate in the activities is			
Very difficult 12.12%	a little difficult 36.36%	somewhat easy 51.52%	very easy 0%
3. My personal attitude towards learning English through computer support has increased			
No 6.06%	a little 24.24%	some 36.36%	a lot 27.27%
4. This course has contributed to my learning experience			
No 12.12%	a little 18.18%	some 57.58%	a lot 12.12%
5. I have contributed to my learning by taking advantage of my time during this experience			
No 3.03%	a little 21.21%	some 69.70%	a lot 6.06%
6. I was able to solve the problems I encountered in my interactions			
No 9.09%	mostly not 21.21%	mostly yes 54.55%	yes 15.15%
7. I feel more confident about my role in a future job			
No 33.33%	a little 33.33%	some 24.24%	a lot 6.06%
8. I would like to repeat this way of learning			
No 21.21%		Yes 78.79%	
PREFERENCES			
9. I prefer learning English			
In virtual worlds 12.12%		In a traditional classroom 27.27%	A combination of both 60.61%
10. What I want to learn in English is (mark as many options as pertinent)			
72.73%	To speak with confidence		
81.82%	To understand when I am spoken to		
48.48%	To be able to read well		
57.58%	To be able to write correctly		
69.70%	To translate		
11. The language skill I have practiced the most is			
Speaking 12.12%	Listening 12.12%	Reading 48.48%	Writing 78.79%
12. I consider the sites listed useful –YES- or not useful –NO-			
Help Island Public		YES 87.88%	NO 12.12%
Education (Online Conferences)		YES 51.52%	NO 33.33%
Edunation Help you Learn - Educational Consultants		YES 54.55%	NO 30.30%
Knightsbridge 170, 157, 22 (PG) - London Community		YES 81.82%	NO 18.18%
Statue of Liberty (Historic Boat Trip)		YES 78.79%	NO 21.21%
Avignon 140, 180, 490 (PG) - Art Centre		YES 54.55%	NO 27.27%
Waterhead 36, 75, 25 (PG) - Waterhead welcome area		YES 63.64%	NO 24.24%
International Spaceflight Museum, Spaceport Alpha (37, 70, 22)		YES 57.58%	NO 21.21%
13. My favorite sites in SL™ are / The SL™ sites I feel most comfortable at are: (please list):			
Help Island Public, Knightsbridge 170, 157, 22 (PG) - London Community, Statue of Liberty (Historic Boat Trip)			
14. What I enjoy the most about my favorite SL™ sites (mark as many options as pertinent)			

continued on following page

Table 1. continued

MOTIVATION	
75.76%	Entertainment; It's fun
45.45%	The design of the site
45.45%	The cultural information available
69.70%	The language skills I can practice
39.39%	The in-world inhabitants I meet
21.21%	Usefulness for my future job
33.33%	Relevance to my studies
42.42%	The wide variety of environments to learn from
42.42%	Socializing around the globe
63.64%	Talking to people in English outside of classroom situations
45.45%	Finding it easier to learn English words in context
42.42%	Discovering how people use language in virtual worlds
30.30%	Setting up scenarios where I can create the need to learn words
0%	Other (please specify)
0%	I have not enjoyed any SL™ sites

EFFECTIVENESS			
15. I learned English with SL™			
No 6.06%	a little 39.39%	some 42.42%	a lot 12.12%
16. My speaking skills have improved			
No 24.24%	a little 48.48%	some 18.18%	a lot 9.09%
17. My listening skills have improved			
No 27.27%	a little 42.42%	some 24.24%	a lot 3.03%
18. My reading skills have improved			
No 6.06%	a little 33.33%	some 42.42%	a lot 15.15%
19. My writing skills have improved			
No 6.06%	a little 33.33%	some 33.33%	a lot 24.24%
20. My vocabulary has increased			
No 12.12%	a little 39.39%	some 30.30%	a lot 15.15%
21. My communicative capacity with others has improved			
No 9.09%	a little 24.24%	some 39.39%	a lot 27.27%
22. I feel more confident about using my English in a future job			
No 21.21%	a little 39.39%	some 36.36%	a lot 3.03%

important source of information. In this regard, the increase in their personal attitudes towards learning English through computer support (Q 3) varies equally from "a little", to "some", to "a lot", thus presumably showing no clear evidence that the setting in itself motivates in excess.

However, when directly questioned if SL™ has contributed to their learning experience (Q4), the overwhelming majority have responded affirmatively. This apparent contradiction was pursued in the follow-up interviews where participants clarified that as computer engineering students, they are already favorably inclined towards learning through technology, and a virtual world is but one more strategy within the realm of operation they are quite used to handling. However, the vast majority of participants confess to having no prior experience with SL™ (Q1), with minor percentages having "a little" or "some" previous contact in-world. At a first glance, this fact might prove excessively challenging, however, when asked if they were able to solve the problems they encountered in their interactions (Q 6), again the majority answered either that they could, or that most of the time they were able to overcome the difficulties.

Specifically, slightly more than half of the students found it easy to feel integrated, become involved and participate in the required activities (Q 2), wherein the other half considered it somewhat difficult to do so. Further inspection with the half experiencing participation difficulties revealed that at times there was no one at the site to interact with, and others said their home computers were so slow at handling the applications that boredom and frustration set in. Thus, for at least some of these students, obstacles regarding timing with other participants at certain sites and the appropriate conditions of their computer system temporarily jeopardized involvement in English **language learning**. Remedies implemented for 70% of the half encountering problems (Q2) include visitation of more frequented sites (Q12),

and, working from the multimedia computer labs on campus.

Student input is vital to the success of the proposal, and in this regard, three-quarters of the learners claim they have contributed to their own learning by taking advantage of their time during the course (Q5). It is interesting to observe however, that in comparing student input (Q 5) and the input of the virtual program towards their learning experience (Q 4), the most notable differences occur at the extreme ends of the scale (Figure 5). That is, the students who did not feel that their input was sufficient, and, those who said they invested considerable effort in the course, both claim that SL™ has contributed more to their learning than they themselves put into it. In contrast, the students in the mid-range majority state they have worked harder in the program than the benefits rendered. Discussion on this point in the interviews revealed that the novelty of virtual worlds required dedication in order for most of the participants to become familiarized with the tasks and activities. This result does not seem to be particularly detrimental as a first time experience, because four-fifths of the participants say they would like to repeat this way of learning (Q 8) and the majority state that they were able to solve their problems (Q6).

An unexpected result was that only a third of the participants felt that the experience signifi-

Figure 5. Virtual world input & Student input.

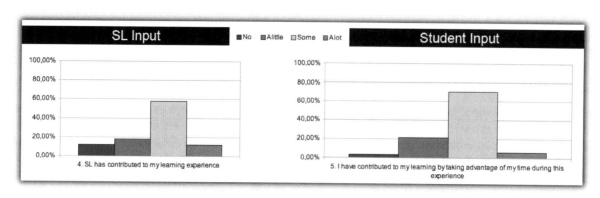

cantly boosted their confidence in their role in a future job (Q 7). Another third said it did not help towards inspiring professional confidence at all, and the rest stated just "a little". This means that further research and testing is required for fulfilling this objective. Nonetheless, discussion of this point during the follow-up interviews revealed that the students, in general immersed at present in an academic environment, feel far removed from the world of work. They have not yet held down jobs in their field, nor carried out work internships, making future job roles an intangible reality for the time being. Some also expressed a great deal of insecurity regarding their on-the-job capacity due to the unknown aspects it holds for them at this time. In addition, recalling their affirmative answer to the contribution of the SL™ world to learning (Q 4), and cross referencing the check list stating SL™ is relevant to their studies (Q 14), it seems safe to confirm that most participant perspectives remain based on an academic environment rather than on future professional employment at this formative stage. Lastly, the response that almost all the students would like to repeat this way of learning (Q 8), seems indicative that the process has somewhat enhanced second language e-learning, and perhaps professional training to be determined as useful to them at a later date.

To conclude the analysis of the motivation section, the experimental group of learners has not had previous exposure to virtual learning environments but they have found it relatively simple to adapt to and participate in the activities. Technical problems aside, mainly when working with their home computers (Q 2), students' personal attitudes towards CALL are favorable. SL™ seems to have contributed to their language learning experience. The students claim to have dedicated time and effort towards acquiring greater skill in English, but confidence as professionals has not been transferable to their projected potential role on the job. Especially encouraging, as well as opening the door towards future pursuits, is that the experience

has motivated the target group enough to want to attend this type of course again.

Learner Preferences: What are the learning preferences and acquisition goals of the participating target group of students?

One of the principles of education rests on a respect for learning styles, so every attempt is made to provide conditions for learner preferences and critical examination of emerging points of conflict. The target group of students has studied English as a foreign language in high school and has taken this college level course as an elective within the Computer Engineering Program syllabus. Given these circumstances, the learners possess an intermediate to advanced level of English and have freely chosen to enroll. Although they have stated that this is a first time experience, they are computer literate and technologically prepared to deal with it.

Curiously enough, the majority of students state that they prefer to learn English with SL™ combined with traditional classroom learning (Q 9). Noteworthy is the statement made by about a quarter of the group preferring only the traditional type classroom, while an eighth of the group prefers learning English exclusively with SL™. Not only do most students prefer a combined learning methodology of ICT and class, but they also want to improve the full range of language skills (Q10) in the following order of preference: listening, speaking, translation, writing and reading. It is of interest to see that the language skills participants have most practiced are writing and reading respectively (Q11) when in fact their priorities lie in speaking and listening. This result is a potential trouble spot for the pilot program. For this reason, as expressed in the interviews, students have a preference in also learning English in a traditional classroom setup in order to fill the gap in aural/oral skills. This data serves as a useful indicator for researchers and program designers for covering the void by devising activities that promote and exploit the learning preferences to a greater degree than has been developed in the project.

Initial plans were made for students to choose from an ample list of 18 sites at which to work in-world (Q 12). These were eventually reduced to eight for several reasons, some of which were beyond the control of the researchers. The main objective was for students to improve their English language capacity, so time efficiency, content management and free public access were major considerations. On the one hand, too many resources complicated the processes involved in preparing the equipment for application and the students for orientation, and on the other hand, some of the most interesting sections of a few sites switched to private payment membership which was not a viable option. As a result, the eight sites listed in Q 12 were finally selected as meeting the conditions needed in conjunction with students' interests. All of these were rated as useful to a high degree by the participants for the language skills they were able to practice in-world. The most preferred sites (Q13) are: *Help Island Public, Knightsbridge* 170, 157, 22 (PG) – *London Community,* and *Statue of Liberty* (historic boat trip). The reasons expressed for the preferences do not differ much from the justifications that might be given in a conventional classroom setting, such as, feeling welcome, interacting and getting feedback from others, being able to understand the content and carry out the tasks.

Q 14 was set up as a check list (see annex for details) in order to ascertain what exactly was attractive to the learners at the sites they participated in. In addition to the specific 14 items we offered, there was also an open space for comments. All the items contain a contributing value with the exception of the last one stating that no site was considered beneficial. The participants were invited to mark as many items as they deemed appropriate to their individual learning styles and tastes. Interpretation of the results corresponding to the percentage of responses received on each item is illustrated in (Figure 6).

Two items were not marked at all, those being the "other" open item option, and, the "I have not enjoyed any SL™ sites" option. A discreet value is applied to "usefulness for my future job" as only about one fifth of the students contemplated this advantage with the program. Most of the items fall into the category of significant relevance: "the design of the site," "the cultural information available," "the wide variety of environments to learn from," "socializing around the globe," "finding it easier to learn English words in context," and, "discovering how people use language in virtual contexts," all nearly reaching a marked status by half of the participants. Meanwhile, "the SL™ inhabitants I meet," "relevance to my studies," and, "setting up scenarios where I can create the need to learn words," obtain percentages marked by roughly one third of the group of learners. A

Figure 6. Preferences

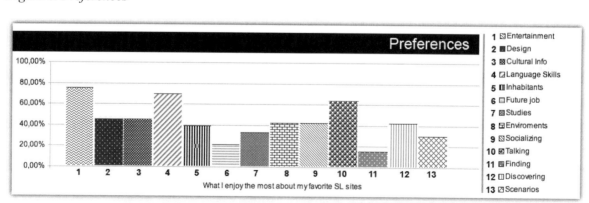

very significant level is reached by "the language skills I can practice," and, "talking to people in English outside of classroom situations" as well above half of the students have so valued both features. The highest percentage received pertains to the ludic aspect denoted as "entertainment, it's fun" marked by over three-quarters of the target group.

A number of deductions can be formulated with the analysis and cross-referencing of these preference-based items. First is the enjoyment factor which has paved the way towards a positive disposition towards learning and is closely linked to motivation. In addition, the option "I have not enjoyed any SL™ sites" was not marked by any participant, and is therefore presumed a solid confirmation of the high rating received by the entertainment variable. This result is not to be taken lightly as its very nature offers educators an attractive way in to using virtual worlds for learning purposes.

The subject matter for the pilot course consists of learning English as a foreign language so a favorable grading of linguistic aspects by the students holds importance. They seem to have adequately focused on the subject material by expressing the desire to perfect all their English language skills, as well as considering features of the sites like "finding it easier to learn English words in context," "discovering how people use language in virtual worlds," "setting up scenarios where I can create the need to learn words," and, "the language skills I can practice." All the aforementioned are essential ingredients to the field, but linguistic capacity encompasses a much larger sphere of influence. Comprehensive language learning pushes far beyond the correct use of grammar and acquisition of an extensive vocabulary.

Language is society's form of communication and the target group of participants appears to have captured this vital premise. They have awarded recognition of several items that may be classified as socio-cultural supporting the foundations of learning theories on social constructivism. In this regard, specific concepts like sharing knowledge with others and collaborative tasking in online interaction seem apparent to the participants in responses such as "the wide variety of environments to learn from," "socializing around the globe," "the SL™ inhabitants I meet," "the cultural information available," "the design of the site," and "talking to people outside of classroom situations." It is here, language in use, where the communicative role of virtual worlds can potentially contribute the most to learners.

One of the original objectives targeted was establishing a threshold for professional training. Most students did not perceive their in-world activities accordingly. The item marked "usefulness

Figure 7. Effectiveness

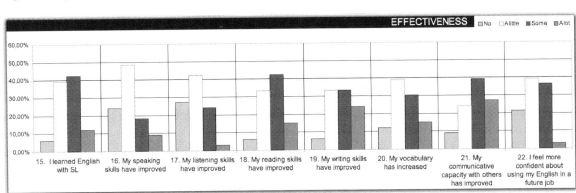

for my future job" not only received the lowest rating, but a weak rating of the concept was corroborated in both the motivation and effectiveness sections. Perhaps the goal is unrealistic, depending on maturity and experience in the world of work before it can be seriously considered by the students. Extended follow-up of the target group a few years after they have obtained a job would provide some direct answers, but obviously goes beyond the intentions of this chapter. Nonetheless, case research of former students in working environments in order to determine the relevance of study programs in professional applications could prove to be an enlightening one.

To highlight what has been learned about the preferences of the target group of students, the empirical data indicates they are favorably inclined towards English language acquisition with SL™ activities complemented by conventional classroom tasks. Linguistic competence is desirable in all the traditional language skills, including translation. The skill most practiced has been writing, and reading to a somewhat lesser degree. On the down side, speaking and listening skills have not quite received attention to the extent the learners would have liked. Some participants commented that they would have preferred a longer duration of the pilot course further removed from the end of the semester due to distraction from studying for final exams. Site selection seems to have been appropriate for in-world learning applicable to their studies. Specifically, *Education* (Online Conferences) and *Edunation Help you Learn - Educational Consultants* have been considered useful for improving the participants' language skills; *International Spaceflight Museum, Spaceport Alpha* (37, 70, 22) and *Waterhead 36, 75, 25 (PG) - Waterhead welcome area* for providing high quotas of enjoyment and moving around in-world; *Avignon 140, 180, 490 (PG) - Art Centre, and Statue of Liberty* (historic boat trip) for cultural discovery; and, *Help Island Public* or *Knightsbridge 170, 157, 22 (PG) - London Community* for visiting and worldwide socialization.

Effectiveness: How effective do students with presumed common interests feel Web 2.0 and second language learning in a virtual world really is?

Thus far, participants in the pilot program claim to have been motivated and have expressed their preferences for learning. Now, the evaluation of effectiveness brings us to the crux of the whole matter. In other words, has the program been successful, and if so, to what degree? To find out let us examine what the target group has to say and proceed to an evaluation of their responses.

The global evaluation of learning English with SL™ is basically a positive one (Q 15), distributed as illustrated in Figure 7. Most of the item ratings fall into the center zone between a little effective and somewhat so. On the extreme ends of both poles, an insignificant percentage states the virtual world has not been effective for them, and, a small percentage claims it has been extremely such. As with any kind of learning methodology, there is a small representation of students who do not favorably respond. There are also a number of students whose response is over-enthusiastic. Although the attitude of the latter is well-received, objective evaluation and caution remind educators that some students adapt and prosper no matter what type of learning situation they are faced with. Likewise, some students do not. For these reasons, logic indicates paying the closest attention to the majority ruling on effectiveness in order to evaluate the proposal for the entire group. In this sense, the program has been effective to a certain degree for over 80% of the participants.

The breakdown of the results on specific language skills varies, with oral production and reception lagging behind more affirmative results scored in writing and reading. The speaking skill has improved "a little" by this method according to about half of the participants (Q 16). Nearly one quarter of them have said their speaking ability has not improved, while one-fifth have claimed oral capacity has improved somewhat. Only a mere tenth of the group rate oral skills as increasing "a lot". Regarding the listening skill (Q 17), most students say aural capacity has improved "a little". About a quarter of them qualify improvement in listening comprehension as "some", whereas a similar rating is claimed as no increase. An insignificant number of students say their comprehension has improved "a lot".

According to about half of the participants they have bettered their reading skill 'somewhat", and another third of them say they have noticed "a little" improvement in this regard (Q 18). Very few students say reading ability has not increased, while for a fair number of learners, their reading skill has improved "a lot". Writing skill improvement (Q 19) is recorded in equal proportions to the reading skill on the lower variables of the scale. A difference is marked on the higher variables, being that a more ample margin of students claims their writing skill has improved "a lot". These scores cross reference and confirm those rendered in Q 11 of the preferences section.

Slightly less than half of the group states an increase in the acquisition of vocabulary (Q 20) ranging from "some" to "a lot". The majority say it has increased "a little", with the remaining minority denying any vocabulary acquisition. Also, and in keeping with the results obtained in Q 7 of the motivation section, practically identical percentages have been derived regarding the feeling of a lack of confidence about using English in a future job (Q 22).

Finally, about a quarter of the students feel their overall communicative capacity in the use of English has improved "a little", and a small percentage say it has not (Q 21). On the contrary, a significant two thirds of the target group has claimed a favorable "some" to large improvement regarding their communication skills. Communicative competence is a term originally coined by the anthropological linguist Hymes (1971). For language learning, the Communicative Approach has developed into a philosophy advocating the ability the get the message across, as well as to understand meaning even though some lexis and/

or syntactical structures are missing or faulty. The underlying principles behind communication theory reject a perfectionist perspective on language and language use. This linguistic point of view is extremely flexible in that it tolerates mistakes and allows for language lapses as long as the flow of conversation is not indefinitely interrupted or completely broken. Effective communication breaks away from traditional correction methods of language teaching simply because unimportant errors are permitted (Larsen-Freeman, 1986). In contrast, the participating students received a grammatical approach to learning English prior to university. Therefore, these results are considered an important step in the right direction towards learning by doing, and a favorable contribution of the pilot program to the target group's English language competence.

To sum up the data analyzed for effectiveness, the experimental group claim to have learned English with SL™ though their speaking and listening skills have not undergone as much improvement as their reading, writing and vocabulary acquisition. Particularly important is the improved ability to communicate with others in English despite imperfections. However, confidence in their communicative capacity does not extend much beyond academia and into the world of work at present.

CONCLUSION

At the start of this chapter, uncertainty regarding the implementation of a virtual world like Second Life® as a viable tool for second language learning and professional training in university degree programs was presented. The main thrust of the empirical study has demonstrated that in fact it can be, notwithstanding certain limitations, modifications and considerations.

From the observable data collected in the pilot study implementing virtual worlds a series of recommendations can be derived, in addition to suggestions for future hands-on research and improvement. For the sake of organization, a three-part division of the conclusions drawn will be offered in these closing remarks, namely, 1- preliminary preparation for the course, 2- intra-program actions, and 3- post-program tasks.

Preliminary Prep: Logistics- Needs Analysis - Task Design & Site Selection- Training

Logistics- For web 2.0-based learning to happen, first and foremost adequate preparation is required of both human and material resources. The core skills needed to get started, as well as approaches, tools and content for in-world learning demand a focus on language teaching and up to date language teacher training in online environments. Advancements regarding support for teaching staff, investments in equipment and technical maintenance cannot be taken for granted. So, where and when participants are learning, who is teaching them, and the efficiency of installations and communications are without a doubt essential. *Needs Analysis* - Needs Analysis (Munby, 1978) is the process by which teachers find out what exactly it is that learners wish to know about a subject. This information is taken into account by the teacher who combines its relevance to the requisites of the course material and goals. *Task Design & Site Selection* - Needs analysis regarding the motivation of the participants towards web 2.0-based learning can be helpful for a more expedient selection of the specific sites to be included in the course, while careful scrutiny of learner preferences conducive to reaching objectives of knowledge in the discipline being studied can aid in designing specialized tasks. Task design and site selection should be anchored on the ultimate aim, namely, professional preparation. *Training*- Finally, before initiating any in-world activity, prior training for skill enhancement on a trial basis would be highly advisable, especially for students with limited computer skills.

Intra-Program Action: Observation- Availability- Combo Format- Target Tasking

Observation

While the program is in process, close observation of in-world activity at all the sites listed can head off problems such as changes in membership status, levels of participation, difficulties in completion of tasks, questions to be answered or confusion easily clarified, among other glitches that may crop up. In essence, this means checking in regularly on the operational functioning at the sites.

Availability

Teacher availability guarantees addressing problems in their initial stages as well as providing relatively immediate feedback for learners. Teachers may find themselves dedicating much more time than the structured number of conventional class time hours. However, any new project requires a maiden voyage, and the rewards can be worth it.

Combo Format

There is really no reason to be exclusive about teaching-learning methods and tools. If the student group and/or facilitator feel the best practice is to combine web 2.0-based learning and traditional classes, this currently seems to be a justifiable transitional way to go about it. *Target Tasking*- Last but not least, targeting appropriate tasks to meet the expectations of Needs Analysis should be sought. In the case in point, speaking and listening skills claim greater presence, whereas, for any degree program, provision for professional apprenticeship activities can provide specialized simulation and realistic role-play. In general terms, further development with Sloodle™ can provide solutions to the former, while a likely measure for the latter could be to design simulations like seeking jobs, preparing resumes and practicing interview techniques, followed by simple introductory on-the-job tasking characteristic of the area of expertise.

Post Program: Student Evaluation- Course Evaluation- Follow-Up

Student Evaluation

The final exam, upon which education traditionally rests its case for student grades, should contain a format familiar to the test-takers in order to assess not only what has been taught, but also the fundamental way knowledge has been acquired in the course processes.

Based on this perspective, evaluation tasks should present a similar activity pattern to that followed during the program in order to contain face validity. If there has been a combination of class and e-formats, these should also be inherent to the final evaluation procedures.

Course Evaluation

Innovative processes can highly benefit from the input of the students with respect to their participation. Evaluation of the positive and negative aspects of the course is a welcomed contribution to further editions and future users.

Follow-Up

If at all feasible, extended follow-up of student success in the world of work specifically regarding the practical applications of the course matter learned at university could be undertaken. If indeed the desired outcome of a college education is preparation for future professional practice in a field, then it stands to reason that the fruits of learning efforts in former students should become apparent in on-the-job experience.

To conclude, the bottom line indicates a favorable academic scenario in store for the use of 3D virtual worlds like SL™ as long as all the parties involved are willing and able to make amends in customizing the educational uses to which they are put. As learning institutions join the state of the art means and ways, invest in the technological support to implement them, and a wider variety of versatile, user-friendly e-learning formats, programs and sites become increasingly available, both teachers and students will become more adept at exploiting the exciting world of web 2.0 and beyond for academic purposes.

NOTICE AND DISCLAIMER

Second Life® is a trademark of Linden Research, Inc. This chapter, "Second Language E-Learning and Professional Training with Second Life®" and its authors are not affiliated with or sponsored by Linden Research.

URL RESOURCES

Avignon Art Center (140,180,491): http://slurl.com/secondlife/Avignon/140/180/491
EDUCAUSE: http://www.educause.edu/
Edunation I (140, 136, 24): http://slurl.com/secondlife/EduNation/140/136/25
Edunation II (128, 128, 23): http://slurl.com/secondlife/EduNation%20II/128/128/23
Edunation III (128, 128, 31): http://slurl.com/secondlife/EduNation%20III/128/128/31
Help Island Public (124, 124, 26): http://slurl.com/secondlife/Help%20Island%20Public/124/124/26
International Spaceflight Museum (137,127,451): http://slurl.com/secondlife/Spaceport%20Alpha/137/127/451
Knightsbridge, London (170,158,22): http://slurl.com/secondlife/Knightsbridge/170/158/22

Second Language E-Learning and Professional Training with Second Life®

Linden Lab®: http://lindenlab.com/

Machinima: http://www.machinima.org/

Moodle™: http://moodle.org/

Papers and Presentations by Vance Stevens: http://www.vancestevens.com/papers

River City Project: http://atlantis.crlt.indiana.edu/

Second Life®: http://secondlife.com/

Sloodle™: http://www.sloodle.org/

Statue of Liberty (90, 154, 40): http://slurl.com/secondlife/Statue%20of%20Liberty/90/154/40

Waterhead (36, 76, 25): http://slurl.com/secondlife/Waterhead/36/76/25

REFERENCES

Au, W. J. (2008). *The making of Second Life. Notes from the New World.* New York: HarperCollins Publishers.

Bruckman, A. (1996). Finding one's own space in cyberspace. *Technology Review*, (January): 48–54.

Craig, K. (2006). Making a LIving in Second Life. *Wired*. Retrieved August 5, 2008, from http://www.wired.com/gaming/virtualworlds/news/2006/02/70153

Downes, S. (2007, May). *Virtual worlds in context.* Paper presented at the Eduserv Foundation Symposium: Virtual worlds, real learning? London. Retrieved October 13, 2008, from http://www.downes.ca/presentation/148

EDUCAUSE learning initiative. (2008). Retrieved from http://www.educause.edu/eli/16086

Edwards, P., Domínguez, E., & Rico, M. (2008). A second look at Second Life: Virtual role-play as a motivational factor in higher education. In K. McFerrin et al. (Eds.), *Proceedings of Society for Information Technology and Teacher Education International Conference 2008* (pp. 2566-2571). Chesapeake, VA: AACE.

Haynes, S. N. (1998). The changing nature of behavioral assessment. In A. S. Bellack & M. Hersen (Eds.), *Behavioral assessment: A practical handbook* (4th ed., pp. 1-21). Boston, MA: Allyn & Bacon.

Hymes, D. (1971). *On communicative competence.* Philadelphia, PA: University of Pennsylvania Press.

Kemp, J. W., & Haycock, K. (2008). Immersive learning environments in parallel universes: Learning through Second Life. *School Libraries Worldwide, 14*(2), 89-97. Retrieved from http://Asselindoiron.pbwiki.com

Larsen-Freeman, D. (1986). *Techniques and principles in language teaching.* Oxford, UK: Oxford University Press.

Macleod, H. (2007, May). *Holyrood Park: A virtual campus for Edinburgh.* Paper presented at the Eduserv Foundation Symposium: Virtual worlds, real learning? London. Retrieved October 13, 2008, from http://www.slideshare.net/efsym/holyrood-park-a-virtual-campus-for-edinburgh/

Munby, J. (1978). *Communicative syllabus design.* Cambridge, UK: Cambridge University Press.

O'Donnell, C. (2006). 10 reasons to go short on Second Life. *This is going to be big.* Retrieved August 13, 2008, from http://www.thisisgoingtobebig.com/2006/11/10_reasons_to_g.html

O'Reilly, T. (2003). The software paradigm shift. *IT Conversations*. Retrieved August 13, 2008, from http://itc.conversationsnetwork.org/shows/detail50.html

Peterson, M. (2006, February). Learner interaction management in an avatar and chat-based virtual world. *Computer Assisted Language Learning, 19*(1), 79–103. doi:10.1080/09588220600804087

Piaget, J. (1950). *Introduction à l'épistémologie génétique.* Paris: Presses Universitaires de France.

226

Rose, F. (2007, July). How Madison Avenue is wasting millions on a deserted Second Life. *Wired Magazine*. Retrieved October 13, 2008 from http://www.wired.com/techbiz/media/magazine/15-08/ff_sheep

Scott, J. (2007, May). *Second nature: Nature publishing group in Second Life*. Paper presented at the Eduserv Foundation Symposium: Virtual worlds, real learning? London. Retrieved October 13, 2008, from http://www.eduserv.org.uk/foundation/symposium/2007/presentations/scott

Shirky, C. (2006, December). Second Life: What are the real numbers? *Many 2 Many*. Retrieved October 13, 2008 from http://many.corante.com/archives/2006/12/12/second_life_what_are_the_real_numbers.php

Slanguages. (2008, May). The conference for language education in virtual worlds. Retrieved October 23, 2008, from http://www.slanguages.net/es/index.php

Stevens, V. (2003). *Some CMC clients promoting language learning through chatting online. ESL_Home A Web Resource for CALL Lab Managers & for Teachers & Learners of Languages Online*. Retrieved August 8, 2008, from http://www.geocities.com/vance_stevens/findbuds.htm

Stevens, V. (2008, June/July). Class of the future. *The Linguist*, 18-20. Retrieved from http://sl2ndchance.pbwiki.com/f/linguist18-21_2ndLife_lores.pdf

Turkle, S. (1995). *Life on the screen: Identity in the age of the Internet*. New York: Simon and Schuster.

Vygotsky, L. S. (1978). *Mind in society: The development of higher psychological processes*. Cambridge, MA: Harvard University Press.

Wood, D. J., Bruner, J. S., & Ross, G. (1976). The role of tutoring in problem solving. *Journal of Child Psychiatry and Psychology, 17*(2), 89–100. doi:10.1111/j.1469-7610.1976.tb00381.x

Zheng, D., Brewer, R. A., & Young, M. F. (2005, November). *English language learning in a game-based Multi-User Virtual environment: Quest Atlantis connects middle school students in China to the world*. Paper presented at Webheads in Action Online Convergence.

Chapter 13
Empirical Evidence and Practical Cases for Using Virtual Worlds in Educational Contexts

Hyungsung Park
Korea National University of Education, South Korea

Youngkyun Baek
Korea National University of Education, South Korea

ABSTRACT

The purpose of this chapter is to offer practical ideas and cases for educational use of the Second Life® virtual world with Web 2.0 based technology. Virtual worlds with Web 2.0 technologies have many methods for testing users' experiences about and mutual understanding of other people, extending limited human capacities, and improving valuable skills in educational contexts. Through these activities, learners may receive positive feedback and beneficial learning experiences. In this chapter, the authors introduce three cases and provide empirical evidence for effective usage within three educational contexts: 1, offering a field trip in virtual space, 2 switching gender roles in the Second Life® virtual world to understand opposite genders, and 3. Object-making and manipulation activities to improve spatial reasoning.

INTRODUCTION

In the past, classroom pedagogy for teaching and learning was characterized by one-way communication, teacher-centered instruction, and textbook-centered delivery of single-media information to students whose role was that of a passive receptor. The evolving nexus of Internet communication and classroom pedagogy is now being altered by two primary foci (Becker & Henriksen, 2006): the rise of social software with social networking power

based on Internet communication technology and the move towards collaborative, constructivist-based teaching and learning methods (Barsky & Purdon, 2006). Interactive technologies through the Internet provide opportunities to create rich learning environments that actively involve students in problem solving and exploring based on motivated attitude. The future learning culture will include toys, games (Kafai, 2005; Prensky, 2001), virtual worlds and activities influenced by the advent of information technology (Park, Jung, & Collins, 2008).

The world is changing rapidly from an information society to a knowledge one as the amount

DOI: 10.4018/978-1-60566-729-4.ch013

Copyright © 2010, IGI Global. Copying or distributing in print or electronic forms without written permission of IGI Global is prohibited.

of knowledge explodes through development of information communication technology (Park & Baek, 2007). Accordingly, technology based on Web 2.0 is offering the opportunity to lead each individual and group to effective learning in the knowledge society. Web 2.0 is a supporting tool that combines ease of content-creation, web delivery, and integrated collaboration activity. Web 2.0 supports sharing, engagement, and collaboration. Learning becomes an organic action that is directed and driven by the learner as a perspective of constructive learning. Also for the teacher and trainer, the Web 2.0 phenomenon has meant a widespread move toward new teaching methods to supplement or replace traditional ones.

Web 2.0 is a set of economic, social, and technology trends that collectively form the basis for the next generation of the Internet - a more mature, distinctive medium characterized by user participation, accessibility, and network effects (O'reilly & Musser, 2006). There are a number of Web-based services and applications that demonstrate the foundations of the Web 2.0 concept, and they are already being used to a certain extent in education. These services include blogs, wikis, multimedia sharing services, content syndication, podcasting and content-tagging services. Many of these applications of Web technology are relatively mature, having been in use for a number of years, although new features and capabilities are being added on a regular basis (Anderson, 2007).

A virtual world based on Web 2.0, including participants, sharing, and collaborating, has brought interactive technologies into learners' homes and they have been received enthusiastically. They are tools for supporting human needs. Computer technologies such as games, simulations, virtual worlds, and computer-assisted design programs all enhance the productivity of their users. A great deal of active research (Aldrich, 2004; Garris, et al., 2002; Malone, 1981; Morales & Patton, 2005; Park, et al., 2008; Prensky, 2001, 2004; Sanders & McKewon, 2007; Sanders & McKeown, 2007; Shaffer, 2006; Slater, et al.,

2000; Squire, 2007) about virtual worlds, computer games and simulations has been conducted examining the educational effects and availability in such situations, which influence the entire society in terms of lifestyle, as well as the play culture of children. A virtual world based on the Web 2.0 in education offers highly immersive, interactive, colorful, visually oriented, fun and generally exciting features. We need to change our teaching methods to enhance the skills that future citizens will need in a digital society. Children and young people are introduced to virtual worlds via videogames, and the ways that they interact with technology may be changing ways of learning and the production of knowledge (Gros, 2007). Garau (2003) comments about the role of virtual worlds recent works of cyber fiction have depicted; in a not-so-distant future, the Internet will develop into a fully three dimensional and immersive data-scope, simultaneously accessible by millions of networked users. This future virtual world is described as having spatial properties similar to the physical world and its virtual cities will be populated by digital proxies of people.

Slater et al. (2000) argue that practical applications of virtual worlds are normally in the realms of engineering, product design, and skill rehearsal. Users can enter into a virtual environment such as Second Life® world in order to learn something new about a real situation, to which the simulation corresponds, or to improve or learn a skill set. Learners can learn by creating their avatar and exploring, meeting other people, owning land, playing games, playing sports, having discussions, dancing, creating, running a business, enhancing their education, along with other activities, through a virtual reality such as the Second Life® virtual world. They can perform actions they do in real life as well as actions that are impossible in real life.

In sum, virtual worlds based on Web 2.0 have the potential to provide teaching and learning opportunities. They can also provide rich interactions and communication environments to improve communication skills and problem-solving skills. To both the teacher and learner, they can provide an engaging environment. Finally, they can provide a low risk environment as an alternative to the real world.

Based on the advantages of virtual worlds, we need to explore several theories and activity practices able to contribute to educational purposes. In this context, we introduce practical evidence and cases in Second Life®, a 3-D virtual world entirely built and owned by its residents based on Web 2.0 technology. Second Life® has the capacity to contain game content, but it is not a game - rather it is a virtual social world within itself. Unlike games, it is a virtual environment without a back story and educators and users have the opportunity to write their own narratives in a virtual social world.

EMPIRICAL EVIDENCE AND PRACTICAL ACTIVITIES IN VIRTUAL WORLDS

Wilson (2006) argues that the next generation learning environment should be learner-centered. Sanders and McKeown(2007) suggest in their research that 3D immersive environments can be used to support communication and collaboration among the learners.

McGivney (1999) argues that informal learning is learning that takes place outside a standardized learning environment and which arises from the activities and interests of individuals and groups. Virtual world-based learning environments, with immersive structures focus on the user as the learner who obtains and creates information, providing more flexible ways of learning to fulfill learners' individual needs. Next generation online learning environment, such as virtual worlds, would be built on a vast, shared library of learning items and educational resource materials.

In this section, we introduce three sets of empirical evidence and cases for benefiting from

the educational potential of virtual worlds: first, experiential learning. Second, learning through interaction, and finally, construction activity. In this context, the aim of using a virtual world is to facilitate creativity, self-directed learning, information making and then sharing field trip activities among learners.

EXPERIENTIAL LEARNING

Introduction

Virtual field trip learning can apply to various teaching and learning models to improve higher-order thinking and skills beyond the classroom. Of the higher-order thinking, problem solving ability in learning is considered an important competence in students' educational environment (Ken & Kevin, 1995). According to Jonassen et al. (2008), the roles for technologies such as virtual reality in supporting meaningful learning are as follows: as a tool to support knowledge construction; as an information vehicle for exploring knowledge to support learning by constructing; as an authentic context to support learning by doing; and as a social medium to support learning through dialogue.

Learners learn in various ways, including seeing and hearing; reflecting and acting; reasoning logically and intuitively; memorizing and visualizing; and drawing analogies and building.

The necessary structures and practical activities in the Second Life® virtual world support teaching and learning. Experiential learning related to cultural assets, field trips, cross-cultural understanding, among others, is also important. In Korea, field trips for experiential learning include learning methods that unfold through observation and investigation. In virtual reality, teachers could set a time and place for all the students to meet, such as at a museum, cultural asset, or national treasure, and then plan other activities and discuss them together.

In this section, we introduce several activities that can be applied in Second Life® world based on the suggested model.

Activity for Teaching and Learning

Virtual field trips for experiential learning can apply various teaching and learning models to improve higher-order thinking and other learning skills that, in turn, support classroom learning and other important areas of students' educational environments. Experiential learning is highly suited to the acquisition of practical skills, where trial and error is essential. Experimental learning focuses on the learning for the individual, while simultaneously focusing learning on the direct process for the individual (Itin, 1999). In Dewey's experiential learning model, learners must recognize a problem through the impulse phase, observe conditions and situations, obtain knowledge, make judgments according to the

response, and finally achieve the purpose.

We suggest an extended model of virtual field trips for experiential learning based on Dewey's experiential learning model (see Figure 1). In the planning phase of a virtual field trip, the teacher should guide and provide learners with the goals, topics, activity methods, activity content, and lists of suitable locations for virtual field trips. In turn, Learners can then choose an appropriate place to explore for learning. As the next goal of the prior learning phase, learners are to investigate materials related to the topic to achieve the learning objective in virtual reality. For this, we can relate the content to the topic and provide it in the Second Life® world.

In addition, Internet content through hyperlinks in WebPages in the Second Life® world can also be used to disseminate content. The virtual field trip phase is a practical activity that features investigation, observation, recording, discussion,

Figure 1. Virtual field trip model based on Dewey's experiential learning model

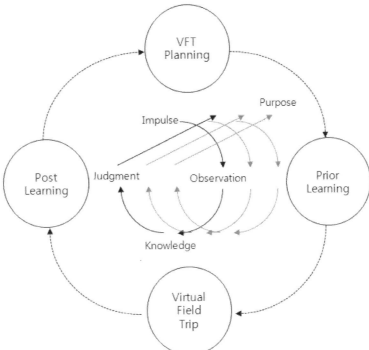

and capturing using Second Life® virtual world functionalities. Finally, in the post learning phase, learners were asked to arrange the materials and to produce two post learning papers: a final paper and a reflection paper.

Results and Implications

We can conceive of some activities that relate field experiential learning in Second Life® virtual world through procedures based on virtual field experiential learning and based on the potential possibilities of virtual reality, as stated above. First, the land in Second Life® world provides an interesting learning environment that can pique learners' curiosity and assist student learning. The virtual learning environment has emerged as a viable alternative to traditional methods of creating spaces for teachers and learners to teach to and to learn from one another, embed themselves in an environment where, in learning about that environment, they are also learning about themselves. (Figure 2 and Figure 3)

For example, Science School land is a place where elementary, middle, and high school learners can learn about the solar system through three-dimensional (3D) environments in Second Life®. Second Nature is another example, where students can learn about cellular structure, stellar evolution, human mitochondrial DNA, a gallery of human chromosomes, and other similar science-related items.

The second item related to experiential field learning in Second Life® virtual world is that it is possible make objects, like cultural assets consisting of Prims, to use virtual fields for experiential learning. In the Second Life® virtual world, residents can make virtual cultural heritage sites by using their mouse and keyboard to navigate their avatars through the multiplayer online environment. There are many places of historical interest that have been duplicated in Second Life virtual world such as China's Forbidden City and Japan's Osaka Castle. (Figure 4)

Students get involved in these vivid virtual

Figure 2. Solar systems from Science School

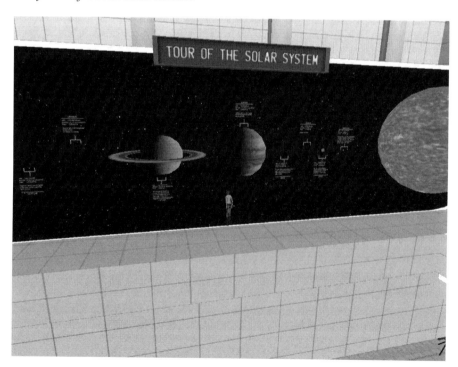

Figure 3. Second Nature

Figure 4. Forbidden City, China

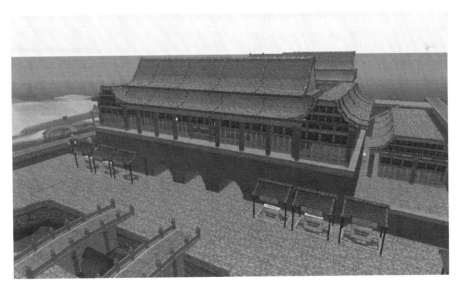

environments, and have unique abilities, such as the ability to fly through the virtual world, to occupy any object as a virtual body, to observe the environment from many perspectives, and, in some places, to creatively build new objects. Through this "learning-by-doing" experience, participants can access get a wealth of information and gain an understanding of the place they have visited.

In addition, the Second Life® virtual world can provide sites for cross-cultural exchange and understanding. A more extensive approach to cross-cultural experiential learning, which is now utilized in many schools, is foreign field-based travel, in which students are immersed for a short period in a foreign culture. The primary reason for the increased popularity of such courses is that the richness of such an experience is difficult to

Figure 5. Tornado Island

duplicate in the classroom. Students can experience culture shock first hand, see the pervasive influence of culture on business and social practices, and preview expatriate life. These elements can also be replicated in the Second Life® virtual world. (Figure 5)

The third element of experiential learning in the Second Life® world is allowing students to experience, through, virtual field trips, those things that cannot be done in the real world. Field trips are a powerful method of learning in any science, especially in the geosciences. Virtual field trips based on technology make it possible to experience natural phenomenon, especially natural disasters, which are too dangerous or impossible to experience first-hand, such as lighting, earthquakes, tsunami, and the like. While virtual worlds can change learning styles, which make the trip interactive and provide students with a virtual experience allowing them to make unique discoveries, students become involved in the processes of natural phenomenon by observing, setting parameters and experience, and become engaged in these vivid environments, which results in high learning efficiency. As shown Figure 5, Tornado Island is a place in the Second Life®

world that allows people to experience tornados in the virtual world.

LEARNING THROUGH INTERACTION

Introduction

In this section, we introduce an empirical result of study demonstrating that virtual world interactions promote mutual understanding between opposite genders. Through activities in the Second Life® world, and especially through playing a gender role other than one's own, individuals can develop a deeper understanding of the special characteristics and advantages of their own gender, as well as increasing recognition of characteristics of the opposite gender. Also, in this context, virtual worlds can become important communication spaces and tools for developing increased understanding, respect, and comfort with the opposite gender.

All social-cultures have special and peculiar expectations and rules for males and females. Because of socio-cultural factors, performance of gender roles have a tremendous influence on an individual's lives. Gender roles are internalized through the socialization processes, often unconsciously. Gender roles also determine social expectations of males and females, such as family and occupational roles, political roles, self-efficacy, and psychological factors. As social customs change, conventional gender roles are being re-examined, and require a deeper understanding of these roles, by both men and women. The current understanding of gender roles is far less dependent on physiological and anatomical differences than previously believed. This permits individuals to utilize interactive social technology within a controlled environment to explore the complicated patterns of behavior that modern society expects in terms of traditional male and female gender roles.

Nood and Attema (2001) contend that the Second Life® world is a virtual reality where one can interact with an environment that is made up of increasingly realistic graphic representations of our physical world. It may also provide new safe places where learners can interact and socialize, without worrying about "stranger danger" and other physical dangers (Alvarez, 2001). The other main appeal of the Second Life® virtual world is that all these issues can be explored in a more risk-free environment. This can encourage experimentation in a way not possible in the real world. There can be some very real, human aspects to this, such as people with social disorders practicing talking to people behind the safety of a computer screen (Johnson, 2006).

Activity for Teaching and Learning

New visitors use the Second Life® world as a modifiable puppet, called an 'avatar' that enables the user to move through the virtual world. With this avatar the user can fly, teleport, or walk to practically any place within the Second Life® virtual world. Players can also perform the following activities while switching gender roles

in the Second Life® world to use the avatar to understand the opposite gender through communication activity

Friend invitation, visiting several lands for male/female and general: Added and invited friends can use the teleport function to visit friends around the world and teleport to a location transmitted to the viewer from a web browser (SLURL). The teleport function summons players into a place for communication and discussion with ease and quickness. A meeting place can be transmitted to other players without any difficulty. In addition, avatars, representing real players of both genders, commonly visit "male only" places and common places in the Second Life® virtual world during the session as cyber characters.

Sharing system via give and take items: Knowledge and information can be delivered and shared though this sharing system in the Second Life® world. This feature facilitates delivery and sharing of items, making the personal networks, and interaction activities among learners. In the future this will likely contribute to interactivity and communication among players.

Communication and discussion via IM, voice, and text chatting: Exchanging opinions is essential for discussion and communication. Several debate topics on social topics take place among players, including, gender equality and male/female employment issues in Korean society. In the Second Life® virtual world, Group IM allows players to send messages to all the members of a given group. The player must also be a member of the said group. This feature permits messages to be sent to all or selected members of a group. Thus, they can share a special affinity with the group. As depicted in Figure 6, Chat allows voice and message communications among players. This facilitates dialogue as well as knowledge sharing. Interaction in chat is open to everyone. Only instant messaging between two students is hidden. These features reinforce intimacy and a strong sense of group identification; furthermore, they experience and participate in a democratic process of decision- making.

Reflection: Reflection is a crucial element of any learning which can form an interrelationships between previous and acquired knowledge based on evolving understanding. Sanders and McKeown (2007) explain that reflection is a learned skill and that students often experience initial challenges and anxieties related to the reflective process; this is especially true for learners who are unfamiliar with the techniques used to generate reflective thoughts and ideas. Kolb (1984) argues that the empirical cycle of learning should be observed reflectively in order to lead to abstract conceptualization or concrete experience, which requires reflection. Reflection should be supported by written composition after discussing social or gender issues. In this study, we employed a reflection activity to debrief the process by having participants write reflection papers after their gaming activities. Peters and

Vissers(2004), Garris et al. (2002) claim that debriefing is an important phase in using gaming activities for educational purposes. Learners are invited to make a connection between experiences gained during gaming activities and experiences in problem-solving situations in the real world. These activities encourage learning from virtual world activity.

Results and Implications

We conducted an experiment based on the above activities to examine the topic of mutual understanding of gender roles in the Second Life® world (Park, Jung, & Collins, 2008). One hundred and twenty female students from a university in Korea, based on a pre-test, were divided into three experimental groups. Each group consisted of thirty participants. Participants did not meet prior to the experiment in the off-line environment, to avoid the possibility of any first impressions influencing their thoughts on gender in their conversations in

Figure 6. Communication through voice chatting in the Second Life® world on a topic

the virtual world. The experiment took place 2 hours per day for twelve weeks to give participants ample opportunity to develop an awareness of gender roles in the virtual environment.

The first group served as a control group, performing as female in the real world. The other groups were performed as male and female in the Second Life® virtual world. During the experimental session, participants performed the above activity through an avatar of switched gender; for instance, the group that was female of the real world was created and used male avatars in the virtual world.

After the experimental session, groups that chose a male avatar in the virtual world increased their posttest mean square of masculine adjectives (M=5.18) compared with their pretest mean square (M=4.49); there were also significant differences among masculine adjectives in relation to the mean square (F=6.320, p<.01, N=86). In addition, the mean of post-feminine adjectives for this group decreased after experiencing activities in the virtual world as a male avatar (M=3.89) compared to the pre-feminine adjectives mean (M=4.76). There were significant differences among masculine adjectives in relation to the mean square (F=5.773, p<.01, N=86). Groups that preferred to maintain female activities in the virtual world and remained were females in the real world showed no significant difference between masculine adjectives and feminine adjectives. As we can see by the results, studying the recognition of gender roles demonstrates that virtual worlds offer mutual understanding among those who choose another gender role for their avatar. Virtual worlds like Second Life® offer meaningful and potentially beneficial sites from explorations of gender roles and issues.

Overall, the results demonstrate that virtual reality interactions can be an important environment for developing a mutual understanding of gender roles. Through activities in virtual worlds, and especially through playing a gender role other than one's own, individuals can develop a deeper understanding of the special characteristics and advantages of their own gender, as well as increased recognition of characteristics of the opposite gender. Virtual worlds could become an important learning environment and tool for developing increased understanding, respect, and comfort with the opposite gender.

LEARNING BY MAKING

Introduction

Learning settings of virtual worlds have significant educational potential in respect to providing learners with experience-based learning conditions. Spatial reasoning allows people to use concepts of shape, features, and relationships in both concrete and abstract ways (Cohen, et al., 2003; Newcombe & Huttenlocher, 2000; Turos & Ervin, 2000). Several recent studies (Battista, 1990; Bryant, 1991; Marusan, et al., 2006; Mayer & Sims, 1994; Mayer, et al., 2002; Waller, 2000) have already shown that spatial ability is positively correlated with learning achievement through multimedia. Considering the recent increase of learning in virtual worlds, spatial abilities are one of the most important elements for learners. The Second Life® virtual world could be employed as a useful tool for improving learners' spatial abilities by providing more spatial experiences.

A number of studies have demonstrated the usefulness of virtual reality in training spatial ability (Barab, et al., 2000; Durlach, et al., 2000; Marusan, et al., 2006; Rizzo, et al., 1998). Oman et al. (2002) conclude that virtual reality is an excellent tool for spatial training in their studies. Passing and Eden (2001) found that mental rotation ability can be developed in 3D-stimuli virtual reality. These studies explore changes in spatial abilities of players through 3-dimensional virtual reality activities and enumerate the individual variables affecting these changes. More importantly, these studies demonstrate the necessity of serious research related to spatial reasoning in virtual reality from the perspective of cognitive processes. However, little to no work has been done towards the development of virtual reality applications for spatial reasoning.

The purpose of this section is to explore the improving of spatial ability of players through Second Life® world activities and to discover the individual variables affecting these changes. For example, as shown in the figures below, several activities improve spatial ability in the Second Life® virtual world. These activities include Figure-ground perception (distinguishing forms of a background) and Perceptual constancy (spatial reasoning).

Activity for Teaching and Learning

Second Life® virtual world activities' improvements of spatial reasoning occur in five domains: analysis and synthesis, deductive reasoning, development and application of visualization methods, systematic approaches, and transforma-tion. These activities, based on study by de Moor (1990), aim to improve spatial reasoning through block building. Instead of wooden block-building, prims supported in the Second Life® world were used while the learning content remained the same. To improve spatial reasoning, each of the activities in the Second Life® virtual world is described below:

Analysis and Synthesis: As depicted in Figure 7, this activity consists of locating the same prim when presented only a top view, side view, or front view; flowed by building the prim after top view, side view, and front view presented; draw-ing the top, the side, and the front shape of the prim; and then assembling the prim after it had been disassembled.

Deductive Reasoning: As depicted in Figure 8, this activity involves building an object after viewing it in one direction; guessing the number of Prims after viewing it from one direction; and then building the Prims and drawing the top, the side, and the front shape of the Prims after view-ing the whole building.

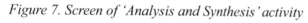

Figure 7. Screen of 'Analysis and Synthesis' activity

Figure 8. Screen of 'Deductive Reasoning' activity

Development and Application of Visualization Methods: As depicted in Figure 9, this activity consists of making various shapes with the same number of prims by moving, turning over, and twisting; drawing a sketch of the top, the side, the front of the shapes.

Systematic Approach: As depicted in Figure 10, this activity consists of building various shapes with four Prims, connected side to side; building various objects with three, four, five, and six prisms.

Transformation: As depicted in Figure 11, this activity consists of building objects in real life with Prims such as a house and an office; drawing the plane figure and the plan.

Results and Implications

We conducted an experiment based on the above activities examining the topic of how building activities in the Second Life® virtual world affect players' spatial reasoning (Hwang, Park, Cha, & Shin, 2008).

In this research, the experiment group included 74 university students. The Learning Style Inventory (LSI) by Kolb was employed and administered to measure learners' information-perception styles. Based on this test, the participants were divided into two groups in terms of information perception styles: a concrete experience group and an abstract conceptualization group. A pretest for spatial reasoning test was then administered to each group. After Second Life® world activities, learners were also given the SRT2 (Spatial Reasoning Test 2; Psytech International) posttest, which is a spatial reasoning test. Each group participated in the Second Life® world activity to improve spatial reasoning for a total of 18 hours; 6 hours per day for 3 weeks.

Results of the increase by the concrete experience group demonstrate a significant difference between the pretest and the posttest mean scores, indicating a significant difference between the pretest and the posttest after completing the planned activities in the Second Life® virtual world (t= -6.58, p<.001). The concrete experience group's posttest results (M=15.92, SD=8.07, N=37) indicate a test mean score that is significantly higher than the pretest's (M=10.97, SD=5.83, N=37). The resulting computation of Cohen's effect size

Figure 9. Screen of 'Development and Application of Visualization' activity

was d=0.7(r=0.33), implying a significant conclusion: that the activities undertaken in this study were effective for the concrete experience group. Furthermore, the improved results by the abstract conceptualization group demonstrate a significant difference between the pretest and the posttest mean scores, indicating a significant difference between the pretest and the posttest upon completion of the experimental activities in the Second Life® virtual world (t= -11.27, p<.001). In other words, the abstract conceptualization group's posttest results (M=21.77, SD=7.01, N=26) showed a test mean score that is significantly higher than the pretest's (M=12.81, SD=4.86, N=26). According to the result of Cohen computation, the effect size was d=1.49(r=0.60); implying that the Second Life® virtual world activities in the study were also effective for the abstract conceptualization group. Moreover, comparing the abstract conceptualization group's effect size with the concrete experience groups, Second Life®

virtual world activities were more effective for the abstract conceptualization group than the concrete experience group.

Overall, the results demonstrate that Second Life® virtual world activities are effective to improve players' spatial reasoning. Support of the activities for spatial reasoning, the interaction between learner's cognition and the Second Life® virtual world may enhance the creation of the cognitive processes related to spatial ability. Through experience building objects in the Second Life® virtual world participants expressed themselves and created objects in space using their minds, not necessarily with real objects.

CONCLUSION AND IMPLICATIONS

Use of virtual worlds in education as a new tutoring and communication medium can be very useful. Virvou and Alepis (2005) asserts that

Figure 10. Screen of 'Systematic Approach' activity

many design and usage issues within educational contexts have to be seriously taken into account so that the resulting applications can be educationally beneficial to students and be included in the educational process.

In recent years, there has been a rapid increase in the capabilities of virtual world technologies. That technology has been widely proposed as a major technological advance that can offer significant support for education. As such, there

Figure 11. Screen of 'Transformation' activity

are several ways in which VR technology can be facilitate learning. One of its unique capabilities is the ability to allow students to visit environments, and to interact with events that distance, time, or safety factors make unavailable. The type of activities supported by this capability facilitate current educational thinking that such students are better able to master, retain, and generalize new knowledge when they are actively involved in constructing knowledge through learning by doing (Park, Jung & Collins, 2008).

In this chapter, we introduced three cases and the results of empirical activity that include mutual understanding of opposite genders, activities improving of spatial reasoning abilities, and activities through process of virtual field trips within educational context in order to use the Second Life® virtual world.

In the first case, we have introduced an extended virtual field trip model based on Dewey's experiential learning model and introduced a variety of activities that can be applied to virtual field trips for experiential learning. If virtual reality is used for learning to support the classroom, instructional design and other educational objectives, there appear to be ample opportunities and the potential to offer experiences for effective teaching and learning environments. There is also ample theoretical and empirically-supported support for positive learning outcomes that virtual worlds can provide encouraging and low risk environments as an alternative to the real world. Virtual worlds provide the potential for various learning activities which may expand on humans' limited capacities in reality.

In the second case, analysis of our statistical results indicates that virtual world environments offer insights and potentially new understandings of gender roles, and their social functions and contexts. These results provide criteria for such information to become the building blocks for further educational processing research. Educational research provides hard and useful data demonstrating the functionality of gender

role impacts and variations significant for formal educational values, strategies, methods, measurable results and treatments. This research data provides opportunities for gender recognition, according to users' various activity experiences within the context of a virtual world educational context. Furthermore, this research demonstrates the capability and capacity for educational virtual worlds to be accurate instruments to promote practical and theoretical data-based knowledge when it comes to conventional understandings of male/female social and educational positions within a given social context.

In the third case, virtual worlds were effective in improving spatial reasoning. By employing activities for spatial reasoning, the interaction between learners' cognition and the Second Life® virtual world may enhance cognitive processes related to spatial ability. Experiences of object-building in the Second Life® world make it possible for participants to conceive and create objects in space with their minds. In this context, Basham(2007) argues that spatial reasoning as a cognitive process has high transferability and is important for generating and conceptualizing solutions to multi-step problems in areas such as architecture, engineering, science, mathematics, art, computer games, robotics and everyday life.

Virtual worlds recreate social systems that parallel the real world. We can employ these systems for educational purposes in many ways. Teachers and learners should consider the educational context and the multiple possible perspectives to use this new media based on Web 2.0.

The function and use of media based on information technology is to support achievement of educational goals. Virtual worlds are also tools that enable easy communication between tutors, teachers and students within a limitless environment.

Virtual worlds allow learners and teachers to have experiences that are impossible in the real world. They also support teaching and learning beyond the classroom. Wen et al. (2004) assert that learning environments should provide students with opportunities to negotiate ideas, conduct inquiry, and conduct self-reflection, thus enhancing cognitive and meta-cognitive outcomes. Learners in virtual worlds engage in meaningful learning, learning processes and higher-order thinking. We should construct such learning environments for learner-centered learning.

In the future, using Web 2.0 technology in the educational context may develop interactional methods between learners to learners, learners to systems, tutors to learners in virtual worlds. In integrating the process to include educational goals and communication technologies such as the Second Life® virtual world, we should consider the following:

First, strengthen the storage of knowledge gained along with information resources based on sharing, participation, and collaboration. Internet-based learning environments should not only offer an abundance of information or knowledge, but also help students deeply elaborate on or evaluate the nature of knowledge (Tsai, 2007). Lim and Chai (2004) argues that informative tools are applications that provide vast amounts of information in various formats such as text, sound, graphics or video, and any other newly-developed media. Examples of informative tools include multimedia encyclopedias or resources available on the Web. Situating tools are systems that situate students in an environment where they may 'experience' the context and happenings include such as games, simulations, and virtual worlds.

Second, offer a learner-centered learning environment focused on easy functionality in order to integrate various learning methods and models. For this, we can use the Second Life® virtual world's open-ended environment for activities for digital storytelling. Virtual environments for storytelling are a digital media in which more and more stories are told with the purpose of teaching, training, entertaining, or communicating something to learners. This dimension allows stimulating more performance from the efforts of

authors at while ensuring coherence and narrative rhythm, and also adapting each generated story to the user profile and the decisions she makes during the execution. Virtual worlds, such a Second Life® virtual world, can provide the opportunity for a rich learning environment analogous to the real world.

Third, consider matters of communication ethics, copyright and personality in virtual world. Today, development of information technology and the wide use of the Internet provide an environment with convenience, enhancing our day to day lives. However, cyber crime poses a challenge. Virtual worlds as cyber spaces allow the development of behaviors, patterns of behavior, social systems and rules like the real world. Accordingly, a virtual world as a virtual society is not able to separate fully from the real world. In this space, we can have experiences that affect our day to day life, through various political, economic, artistic endeavors and behaviors.

Fourth, test item development to evaluate the learning process and outcomes in virtual worlds. Learning activities in virtual worlds can offer an opportunity for a wide variety of students to experience geology in the field without having to leave the classroom. An effective and valuable virtual world learning should be functional and interactive, motivating a student to learn, provide them with enough information to be comfortable in the field and give them the opportunity to develop similar skills and knowledge as in traditional learning (Edelson, 2001; Orion, 1993).

Fifth, there exists a problem of fidelity. Fidelity in this article can be explained as the extent to which the virtual environment emulates the real world. Physical fidelity is defined as the degree to which the physical simulation looks, sounds, and feels like the operational environment in terms of the visual displays, controls, and audio as well as the physics models driving each of these variables (Baum, et al., 1982). Functional fidelity is defined as the degree to which the simulation acts like the operational equipment in reacting to the tasks executed by the trainee (Allen, et al., 1986; Alexander, et al., 2005). For virtual field experiential learning in the Second Life® virtual world, the issue of fidelity is crucial. In this case, fidelity refers to how closely a simulation imitates reality, and is an overarching issue that affects all aspects of a simulation (Alessi & Trollip, 2001). Fidelity affects both initial learning (the learner's performance during the simulation) and transfer of learning (how well one applies new knowledge or skills to new situations).

REFERENCES

Aldrich, C. (2004). *Simulation and the future of learning*. CA: Pfeiffer.

Alessi, S. M., & Trollip, S. R. (2001). *Multimedia for learning: Methods and development* (3rd ed.). Needham Height MA: Allyn and Bacon.

Alexander, A. L., Brunyé, T., Sidman, J., & Weil. S. A. (2005). *From gaming to training: A review of studies on fidelity, immersion, presence, and buy-in and their effects on transfer in PC-based simulations and Games.* DARWARS Training Impact Group.

Allen, J. A., Hays, R. T., & Buffordi, L. C. (1986). Maintenance training, simulator fidelity, and individual differences in transfer of training. *Human Factors, 28*, 497–509.

Alvarez, M. (2001). *Second Life and school: The use of virtual worlds in high school education.* Retrieved July 31, 2008, from http://www.trinity.edu/adelwich/worlds/articles/trinity.manny.alvarez.pdf

Anderson, P. (2007). What is Web 2.0? Ideas, technologies and implications for education. *JISC Technology and Standards Watch*, 2-64.

Barab, S. A., Hay, K. E., Barnett, M. G., & Keating, T. (2000). Virtual solar system project: Building understanding through model building. *Journal of Research in Science Teaching, 37*(7), 719–756. doi:10.1002/1098-2736(200009)37:7<719::AID-TEA6>3.0.CO;2-V

Barsky, E., & Purdon, M. (2006). Introducing Web 2.0: Social networking and social bookmarking for health librarians. *Journal of the Canadian Health Libraries Association, 27*(2), 33–34.

Basham, K. L. (2007). *The effects of 3-dimensional CADD modeling software on the development of the spatial ability of ninth grade technology discovery student.* Unpublished doctoral dissertation, Louisiana State University, USA.

Battista, M. T. (1990). Spatial visualization and gender differences in high school geometry. *Journal for Research in Mathematics Education, 21*(1), 47–60. doi:10.2307/749456

Baum, D. R., Riedel, S., Hays, R. T., & Mirabella, A. (1982). *Training effectiveness as a function of training device fidelity: Current ARI research* (Tech. Rep. 593), Alexandria, VA: US Army Research Institute for the Behavioral and Social Sciences (Defense Technical Information Center No. ADA133104).

Becker, S. W., & Henriksen, T. K. (2006). *In search of the next generation online learning environment* [white paper]. Ecto, LLC.

Bryant, K. J. (1991). Geographical/spatial orientation ability within real-world and simulated large-scale environments. *Multivariate Behavioral Research, 26*, 109–136. doi:10.1207/s15327906mbr2601_6

Cohen, C. A., Hegarty, M., Keehner, M., & Montello, D. R. (2003). *Spatial ability in the representation of cross sections.* Poster presented at the Annual Conference of the Cognitive Science Society, Boston, MA.

De Moor, E. (1990). Geometry instruction in the Netherlands (ages 4-14): The realistic approach. In L. Streefland (Ed.), *Realistic mathematics education in primary school* (pp. 119-138). Culemborg, The Netherlands: Technipress.

Durlach, N., Allen, G., Darken, R., Garnett, R. L., Loomis, J., Templeman, J., & Wiegand, T. E. (2000). Virtual environments and the enhancement of spatial behavior: Towards a comprehensive research agenda. *Presence: Virtual Environments and Teleoperators, 9*, 593–615. doi:10.1162/105474600300040402

Edelson, D. C. (2001). Learning-for-use: A framework for the design of technology supported inquiry activities. *Journal of Research in Science Teaching, 38*(3), 355–385. doi:10.1002/1098-2736(200103)38:3<355::AID-TEA1010>3.0.CO;2-M

Elleven, R., Wircenski, M., Wircenski, J., & Nimon, K. (2006). Curriculum-based virtual field trips: Career development opportunities for students with disabilities. *The Journal for Vocational Special Needs Education, 28*(3), 4–11.

Garau, M. (2003). *The impact of avatar fidelity on social interaction in virtual environments.* Unpublished doctoral dissertation, University College London, UK.

Garris, R., Ahlers, R., & Driskell, J. E. (2002). Games, motivation, and learning: A research and practice model. *Simulation & Gaming, 33*(4), 441–467. doi:10.1177/1046878102238607

Gros, B. (2007). Digital games in education: The design of games-based learning environments. *Journal of Research on Technology in Education, 40*(1), 23–38.

Hwang, J. H., Park, H. S., Cha, J. S., & Shin, B. J. (2008). Effects of the objects building activities in Second Life on players' spatial reasoning. In *Proceeding in the 2nd IEEE International Conference on Digital Game and Intelligent Toy Enhanced Learning*, Banff, Canada.

Itin, C. M. (1999). Reasserting the philosophy of experiential education as a vehicle for change in the 21st century. *Journal of Experiential Education, 22*(2), 91–98.

Johnson, N. (2006). *The educational potential of Second Life*. Columbus, OH: Ohio State University, Digital Union.

Jonassen, D. H., Howland, J., Marra, R. M., & Crismond, D. (2008). *Meaningful learning with technology* (3rd ed.). NJ: Merrill/Prentice Hall.

Kafai, Y. B. (2006). Playing and making games for learning: Instructionist and constructionist perspectives for game studies. *Games and Culture, 1*(1), 36–40. doi:10.1177/1555412005281767

Ken, P., & Kevin, T. (1995). *Virtual reality: Through the new looking glass* (2nd ed.). Windcrest Books.

Kolb, D. A. (1984). *Experiential learning: Experience as the source of learning and development.* Upper Saddle River, NJ: Prentice-Hall.

Lim, C. P., & Chai, C. S. (2003). An activity-theoretical approach to research of ICT integration in Singapore schools: Orienting activities and learner autonomy. *Computers & Education, 43*, 215–236. doi:10.1016/j.compedu.2003.10.005

Malone, T. W. (1981). Toward a theory of intrinsically motivating instruction. *Cognitive Science, 5*(4), 333–369.

Mayer, R. E., Mautone, P., & Prothero, W. (2002). Pictorial aids for learning by doing in a multimedia geology simulation game. *Journal of Educational Psychology, 94*, 171–185. doi:10.1037/0022-0663.94.1.171

Mayer, R. E., & Sims, V. K. (1994). For whom is a picture worth a thousand words? Extensions of a dual coding theory of multimedia learning. *Journal of Educational Psychology, 86*, 389–401. doi:10.1037/0022-0663.86.3.389

McGivney, V. (1999). *Informal learning in the community: A trigger for change and development*. Leicester, UK: National Institute of Adult and Continuing Education.

Morales, E. D., & Patton, J. Q. (2005). Gender bias in a virtual world. *WSU McNair Journal, 3*, 81–89.

Newcombe, N. S., & Huttenlocher, J. (2000). *Making space: The development of spatial representation and reasoning*. Cambridge, MA: MIT Press.

Nood, D., & Attema, J. (2006). *The Second Life of virtual reality* (EPN Report). Retrieved August 19, 2008, from http://www.epn.net/interrealiteit/ EPN-REPORT-The_Second_Life_of_VR.pdf

O'Reilly, T., & Musser, J. (2006). *Web 2.0 principles and best practices*. Retrieved August 19, 2008, from http://oreilly.com/catalog/web2report/ chapter/web20_report_excerpt.pdf

Oman, C. M., Shebilske, W. L., Richards, J. T., Tubré, T. C., Beall, A. C., & Natapoff, A. (2002). Three dimensional spatial memory and learning in real and virtual environments. *Spatial Cognition and Computation, 2*, 355–372. doi:10.1023/A:1015548105563

Orion, N. (1993). A model for the development and implementation of field trips as an integral part of the science curriculum. *School Science and Mathematics, 93*(6), 325–331.

Park, H. S., & Baek, Y. K. (2007). Design of learning contents focus on game to support the mobile learning. *Journal of the Korea Association of Information Education, 11*(2), 167–176.

Park, H. S., Jung, J. Y., & Collins, C. M. (2008). Effect of the activities in the Second Life® as tool for mutual understanding of gender role. In *Proceedings of the Society for information Technology and Teacher Education*, USA (pp. 1778-1783).

Passig, D., & Eden, S. (2001). Virtual reality as a tool for improving spatial rotation among deaf and hard-of-hearing children. *Cyberpsychology & Behavior, 4*(6), 681–686. doi:10.1089/109493101753376623

Perters, V. M., & Vissers, G. N. (2004). A simple classification model for simulation games. *Simulation & Gaming, 35*(1), 70–84. doi:10.1177/1046878103253719

Prensky, M. (2001). *Digital game-based learning*. New York: McGraw-Hill.

Prensky, M. (2004). *The emerging online life of the digital native*. New York: games2train. Retrieved August 07, 2008, from http://www. marcprensky.com/writing/Prensky-The_Emerging_Online_Life_of_the_Digital_Native-03.pdf

Psytech International. (2004). *Technical test battery: The technical manual*. Retrieved March 25, 2008, from http://www.psytech.co.uk/downloads/ manuals/ttbman.pdf

Rizzo, A. A., Buckwalter, J. G., Neumann, U., Kesselman, C., Thiebaux, M., Larson, P., & Rooyen, V. A. (1998). The virtual reality mental rotation spatial skills project. *Cyberpsychology & Behavior, 1*(2), 107–113. doi:10.1089/cpb.1998.1.113

Sanders, R. L., & McKeown, L. (2007). Promoting reflection through action learning in a 3D virtual world. *International Journal of Social Sciences, 2*(1), 50–55.

Shaffer, D. W. (2006). *How computer games help children learn*. New York: Palgrave Macmillan.

Slater, M., Howell, J., Steed, A., Pertaub, D.-P., & Garau, M. (2000). Acting in virtual reality. In *Proceedings of the third international conference on Collaborative virtual environments*, San Francisco, CA, U.S. (pp. 103-110).

Squire, K. (2007). Games, learning, and society: Building a field. *Educational Technology, 4*(5), 51–54.

Tsai, C. C. (2008). The preferences toward constructivist Internet-based learning environments among university students in Taiwan. *Computers in Human Behavior, 24*, 16–31. doi:10.1016/j.chb.2006.12.002

Turos, J. M., & Ervin, A. I. (2000). Training and gender differences on a Web-based mental rotation task. *The Penn State Behrend Psychology Journal, 4*(2), 3–12.

Virvou, M., & Alepis, E. (2005). Mobile educational features in authoring tools for personalized tutoring. *Computers & Education, 44*, 53–68. doi:10.1016/j.compedu.2003.12.020

Waller, D. (2000). Individual differences in spatial learning from computer-simulated environments. *Journal of Experimental Psychology. Applied, 6*, 307–321. doi:10.1037/1076-898X.6.4.307

Wen, M. L., Tsai, C. C., Lin, H. M., & Chuang, S. C. (2004). Cognitive-metacognitvie and content-technical aspects of constructivist Internet-based learning environment: A LISREL analysis. *Computers & Education, 43*, 237–248. doi:10.1016/j.compedu.2003.10.006

Williamson, B., & Facer, K. (2004). More than 'just a game': The implications for schools of children's computer games communities. *Education Communication and Information, 4*, 255–270. doi:10.1080/14636310412331304708

Wilson, S. (2006). *The personal learning environment blog*. Retrieved July 31, 2008, from http://www.cetis.ac.uk/members/ple

Chapter 14
A Pedagogical Odyssey in Three-Dimensional Virtual Worlds:
The SECOND LIFE® Model

Sharon Stoerger
Indiana University, USA

ABSTRACT

Schools based in the United States are trapped in a Henry Ford factory model of education that is focused on high-stakes testing. This model was effective when factories needed workers who possessed the same skill set. But the world has changed and societal demands on student learning have increased. Moreover, millions of students are failing to graduate from high school, which is a problem that continues to escalate. In an attempt to prepare students for work in the 21st century and to address the dropout crisis, educators are examining ways to integrate virtual worlds, including digital games, into the curriculum. This chapter begins by summarizing some of the theories that commonly frame the discussions about these worlds. Next an examination of the issues surrounding virtual worlds is presented. The concluding sections outline and describe the pedagogical mnemonic known as the "SECOND LIFE" model.

INTRODUCTION

The demand for education is on the rise. Between 2006 and 2015, the National Center for Educational Statistics (2006) anticipates a 13% increase in college enrollment alone. But for the most part, our academic institutions continue to follow a trajectory put forth in the 19th century (Herz cited in Foreman, 2004)—a path based on rote learning and high-stakes testing. While the Henry Ford model of education may have been effective when factories needed workers, today's world is different and the societal demands on student learning are higher. Students in the 21st century are tech-savvy and claim that they are bored with school (Prensky, 2001). At the same time, school dropout rates in the United States have risen to crisis levels (e.g., Spellings, 2008). For students who do graduate from high school and college, the reports about their on-the-job performance are not positive. In fact, many employers note dissatisfaction with the young people that they hire (Cassner-Lotto & Wright Benner, 2006).

DOI: 10.4018/978-1-60566-729-4.ch014

Copyright © 2010, IGI Global. Copying or distributing in print or electronic forms without written permission of IGI Global is prohibited.

In an attempt to rectify this situation, individuals are investigating ways to make education more appealing and relevant to students by integrating fun into the curriculum (Barab et al., 2005; Quinn, 2005). To do this, educators are exploring a variety of technological options including virtual worlds such as *Second Life* (SL). This chapter begins by acknowledging the theoretical perspectives that inform teaching and learning initiatives that take place in virtual worlds. Constructivist, situated learning, and digital game-based learning theories will serve as the framework for this discussion. Next, the discussion explores the educational possibilities afforded by these spaces and the challenges teachers and students may face in-world. And finally, the chapter concludes with an outline of a pedagogical structure to support teaching and learning in virtual worlds - the SECOND LIFE model.

BACKGROUND

The Move Toward Student-Centered Education

There are different schools of thought associated with the concept of learning. According to the behaviorist perspective, learning is viewed as an activity that takes place inside the head of a person: an inaccessible black box. The assumption put forth by philosophers John Locke and David Hume is that the child's mind is like a blank slate waiting to be written on or an empty container ready to be filled. Drill and skill techniques and the standardized tests that accompany them often underlie this theory, yet they may not be able to account for higher-order thinking found in society.

Currently, there are a number of individuals who recognize that Americans need different skills to compete in the global marketplace. School reform advocates claim that it is time to cross the "yawning chasm" that separates the classroom from the real world (Wallis & Steptoe, 2006). They

believe that what is needed is a "renewal and reconsideration" of "school culture" (Bruner, 1997, p. 84). In this participatory learning age (Brown & Adler, 2008), the focus is shifting toward more student-centered approaches. The use of emerging Web 2.0 technologies like three-dimensional virtual worlds is often part of this discussion. Frameworks used to support the incorporation of virtual worlds into these teaching and learning models draw from constructivist (e.g., Vygotsky, 1978) and situated learning theories (e.g., Brown, Collins, & Duguid, 1989).

Starting with constructivist theory, this approach argues that students construct their own learning. In other words, students take an active role in their learning. Papert (1993) describes the difference between behaviorism, or "traditional" education, and constructionism in the following manner:

Traditional education codifies what it thinks citizens need to know and sets out to feed children this 'fish.' Constructionism is built on the assumption that children will do the best by finding ('fishing') for themselves the specific knowledge they need…The kind of knowledge children most need is the knowledge that will help them get more knowledge. (p. 139)

Because learning and intelligence are distributed in a person's world (Brown, Collins, & Duguid, 1989; Bruner, 1997; Cole & Engeström, 1993), students must find meaning within a cultural context (Bruner, 1997). It is through these interactions with others that that children learn about the world around them (Bruner, 1997). For example, educational activities such as learning to read do not reside solely with the individual; rather, the process of learning to read is distributed among the teacher, other students, and cultural artifacts (Cole & Engeström, 1993). It is through this course of exploration and interaction that students attempt to reproduce what they observe (Bruner, 1997; Piaget, 1952) and may even imitate behaviors that are well-beyond their own capabilities (Vygotsky, 1978).

Researchers have argued that the incorporation of technology into the teaching and learning process is complementary to the constructivist approach to education. In independent and joint efforts, Meredith and William Bricken have examined virtual reality from a constructivist perspective. In their research, which is aligned with the work put forth by Dewey (1997/1938) and Piaget (1952), the Brickens found that "virtual reality is a powerful educational tool for constructivist learning" (McLellan, 2004, p. 479); it fosters experiential learning where learners actively become part of the virtual environment and are able to interact with the information (Bricken, 1990). Also, their research shows that in this flexible and multidisciplinary environment, learners control the time and scale attributes.

Computer technologies are attractive because they provide students the opportunity to engage in complex thinking through active learning and autonomy. One example is Papert's Logo project and the creation of "microworlds." The Logo microworld was a computer-based environment where students could explore the concepts they learned by using programming languages to create and build creatures, as well as directing the movements of their design in this space. Technology advocates believe that this is the beauty of environments created through Logo; understanding surfaces from meaningful activities rather than memorizing the correct solution. There is no one right way. This approach is in direct opposition to the current educational system that "insists on the student being precisely right" (Papert, 1993, p. 167). The use of technology also enables the teaching and learning to happen anytime, anyplace. These ubiquitous learning opportunities also encourage more independent learning because the teacher and the student are not physically co-present (Wedemeyer, 1981).

Situating the Learning

One way to effectively develop knowledge or skill in a topic area is through experience and learning in a rich, authentic context (Lave, 1988; Vygotsky, 1978). Students come to the classroom with conceptual competencies, which can be quite advanced even early in their educational careers (Vygotsky, 1978). By taking these resources and reorganizing them, learners are able to make sense of their world. However, this process of making sense of the world is not always a smooth one, and learners may face a number of obstacles while attempting to develop their own knowledge skills.

To reduce the effect of these barriers, educators can encourage the development of higher order thinking skills by creating communities of practice (Lave & Wenger, 1991). For learning to be valuable and for knowledge to emerge, there must be a combination and interaction of activity, culture, and concept (Brown, Collins, & Duguid, 1989). Lave and Wenger (1991) refer to this dynamic interaction with these elements as legitimate peripheral participation (LPP). According to these scholars, LPP is where "learners inevitably participate in communities of practitioners and that the mastery of knowledge and skill requires newcomers to move toward full participation in the sociocultural practices of a community" (p. 29).

Anchored instruction methods also permit learners to find ways to use elements that are available in the environment to assist them in solving problems. Students are given the opportunity to identify the problems on their own rather than being told what the problems are. This type of design also supplies the details needed for learners to solve the problems they uncover. Through teacher-guided discovery and coaching, learners can develop a basis for their understanding. Once learners have gained self-confidence and understanding of the material, they can rely less on the teacher and more on collaborative activities with their peers.

Overall, in order to be effective, learning and knowledge should be situated within a triangle of meaningful activities, culture, and concept (Brown, Collins, & Duguid, 1989). Taken out of its indexical context, the learning loses its use value and becomes opaque. However, the concern over transferability has created a learning environment within the culture of schools that emphasizes the regurgitation of facts rather than the development of deep understanding. While it is true that the acquisition of facts can be valuable in certain situations, there is the possibility that this type of knowledge will be meaningless outside the confines of the classroom. In order for learners to take ownership for their learning and develop tools they can use in the world, learning and the development of knowledge must move out of the academic factory and into a more authentic environment. Based on McLellan's (2004) assessment, virtual environments can support this type of situated learning and foster the acquisition of knowledge within a realistic context.

Text-Based Virtual Worlds

MUDs. Before the development of three-dimensional virtual worlds, educators were investigating the use of text- based MUDs (Multi-User Dungeons) for teaching and learning. Bruckman, Fanderclai, Haynes, and Holmevik are just a few of the individuals who have used these spaces for educational purposes. One of the first individuals to show that these text-based virtual worlds could be used for serious purposes was Amy Bruckman, the founder of MediaMOO – a shared online space where media researchers could meet one another, as well as consume and create content via text (Bruckman & Resnick, 1995). Bruckman not only designed MUDs for adults but for young students as well. MOOSE Crossing (MOO Scripting Environment) is one creation that was popular with

children between the ages of 8 and 13 (Bruckman, 1998). In this environment, children could create and show off their projects.

Educators also investigated the use of MUDs with older students. Fanderclai (1995), for example, worked with college-age composition students in a MUD environment and argues that MUDs were places for self-directed learning that blends together work and play. While this often appeared to be a chaotic approach to learning, it could be an effective one as well (Fanderclai, 1995, 1996). In the MUD, Fanderclai's composition students had to work out their own methods and schedules for meeting goals. In addition, the students were responsible to people outside their own on-site classes, which appeared to contribute to their willingness to work out the difficulties. Moreover, because individuals communicated through text, MUDs were effective educational spaces for writing. While there is evidence to suggest that educational MUDs were successful, at least in some cases, they had a limited life span. Today, educators are beginning to investigate the use of graphical virtual environments such as digital games.

Digital Game-Based Theory

There are scholars who believe that today's students obtain knowledge differently from those in previous generations (e.g., Dede, 2005; Prensky, 2001). These new students tend to be experiential learners who prefer finding solutions via multiple paths and through interactions with others. In an attempt to better meet the needs of these new students or "digital natives" (Prensky, 2001), educators are investigating the use of games in the classroom. Certain digital games have also been found to have positive effects on academic performance (Subrahmanyam, Kraut, Greenfield, & Gross, 2000). In fact, these games may serve as a "head start" program that enable young people to acquire a variety of experiences, which may ultimately expand their interest in computers

(Cassell & Jenkins, 1998). Moreover, these game spaces can open up new opportunities for learning – ones that are fun in ways that differ from standard pedagogies (Thomas & Brown, 2007).

In addition to fostering an enjoyable experience, games teach students how to be problem solvers (Gee, 2003; Johnson, 2005). Digital games can also support teamwork, practical experimentation, critical thinking, and other information literacy skills. Aptitude in these areas is important in today's technology-focused world, and "educators must work together to ensure students have these skills" (Jenkins et al., 2008, p. 3). Howard Rheingold is one educator who is taking steps in this direction by bringing emerging technologies into the college classroom. His project, which is referred to as the "Social Media Virtual Classroom," is designed to expose students to "participatory media" (Rheingold, 2008).

As a result of this informal peer learning process and gameplay activities, the roles of the teachers and students change. It is in these environments that "children take on the role of teachers, providing advice, support, hints, tips, and models of learning to other children" (Kirriemuir & McFarlane, 2004, p. 18). While cooperation and collaboration are part of these places and are key components to successful gameplay, these features are not typically found in a school setting. Also, the "expert" versus "novice" delineation that is commonly used in more accepted educational practices is not applicable in a game environment. In these virtual environments, "what 'counts' as hard for students and teachers may be very different" (Facer et al., 2007, p. 50).

What is the Connection Between Games and Virtual Worlds?

The lines that separate games, particularly the massively multiplayer online games (MMOGs) and virtual worlds are blurred. There are scholars who argue that environments such as Second Life are not games (e.g. Robbins, Indiana University

School of Education presentation, November 26, 2007; Steinkuehler, 2008) but rather "virtual frontier[s]" (Steinkuehler, 2008, p. 3). Bartle (2004) refers to these environments as venues – locations much like the Pasadena Rose Bowl. But not everyone agrees with these perspectives (de Freitas, 2007; Delwiche, 2006; Horizon Report, 2007). Even Bartle (2004) acknowledges that virtual worlds did originate from video games. Linden Lab (LL), the creator of Second Life, has addressed this debate, but the response merely adds to the confusion in that LL claims that this world is and is not a MMOG. To the developers at LL, the interface is similar to many MMOGs; however, the features that distinguish SL from other popular MMOGs are that it allows players to express their creativity through the creation of this three-dimensional virtual world and own the items they create in this space (Second Life: FAQ, n.d.).

Moreover, digital games are beginning to adopt the features of virtual worlds, particularly their social immersion characteristics (e.g., Bainbridge, 2007; Ducheneaut & Moore, 2004). Individuals who venture into these virtual worlds for the first time may be surprised to find that the experience is not an individual and isolating one; the image of young boys playing computer games alone in their parents' basement is no longer accurate. Moreover, virtual interactions go beyond simple exchanges. Formal social rituals such as in-world weddings and funerals are common (e.g., Boellstorff, 2008; Kolbert, 2001). In some worlds, visitors can engage in snowboarding and horseback riding as well as other sporting activities (Dremann, 2008). Due to these similarities and the common trajectories, digital games will continue to inform the future study of virtual worlds (Boellstorff, 2008).

The Virtual World Experience

Virtual worlds are visually rich, computer-based simulated environments that are intended for their users to inhabit and interact with through avatars (Electric Sheep Company, n.d.). One virtual world that has caught the attention of many individuals, including educators, is Second Life. SL was released to the public by Linden Lab in 2003, and is the largest three-dimensional virtual world (EDUCAUSE Learning Initiative, 2008). Basic membership is free, and in the past 60 days, more than one million residents have logged into this world. (Second Life: Economic Statistics, 2008). According to Pathfinder Linden (2008), over 60% of the residents are from areas outside the United States.

It is worth noting that individuals in SL are referred to by Linden Lab as "residents" (Au, 2008). All residents begin their SL as an adult. When individuals log in for the first time, they are asked to select an avatar name and create an appearance for their avatar. Many residents begin their in-world life on Orientation Island, which is the default starting location. It is in this space where residents can learn how to navigate the space (e.g., walking, flying, picking up artifacts) through the manipulation of the computer's arrow keys and mouse, change their appearance, and meet others who are new to this virtual world.

In this persistent and diverse environment, individuals communicate through synchronous and asynchronous modes. Text chat is one way residents communicate with others. Instant messaging (IM) is also available for more private conversations. The text chat and IM are recorded for free and these transcripts are available for individuals to review and reflect upon at a later time. In early 2007, SL introduced a voice chat option, which is a common feature included in many MMOGs such as *World of Warcraft* (WoW). In both communication modes, residents can chat with each other in real time, and they can "see" each other while doing so (Boulos et al., 2007).

In addition to the social interactions, virtual worlds are appealing because residents are able to be anyone they want to be. While this option is also possible in the fantastical environments of *EverQuest* or WoW, one feature that makes SL unique (Table 1) is that the users create the content and own the intellectual property rights to it. Interestingly, the ability to create was not the original focus of SL but evolved as residents began experimenting with the space (Au, 2008). Another aspect of SL that sets it apart from other MMOGs is that the goals and the rules are less defined. Instead, the concentration is on play and the social aspects of the space, as well as hands-on collaborative activities that transcend physical world constraints. Roush (2007) makes a distinction between these gaming and social worlds by noting that the main difference is that "they are at the opposite ends of what might be called the Axis of Upheaval" – in comparison to World of Warcraft, SL is an "eternal garden party" (n.p.).

Table 1. Distinguishing characteristics between MMOGs and SL

Virtual World Characteristics	MMOGs	SL
Avatar options	Yes	Yes
Competition	Yes	No
Content creation (creativity)	No	Yes
Goals and rules	More defined	Less defined
Hands-on collaboration	Secondary activity	Primary activity
Intellectual property ownership	No	Yes
Play and social interactions	Secondary activity	Primary activity

TEACHING, LEARNING, AND THE SECOND LIFE EXPERIENCE

Concerns about Education in Virtual Worlds

While there are scholars who tout the effectiveness of these new spaces for educational purposes, it is important to remember that they are not without their problems. First, the power of play is motivating for some students (e.g., Squire, 2005); however, not everyone prefers to learn in a visual manner, which is privileged in virtual worlds. Additionally, there is a significant commitment by both instructors and students. In an examination of learning with commercially available video games in the classroom, the amount of time needed for students and teachers to become adjusted to the virtual environment was one of the main disadvantages (Kirriemuir & McFarlane, 2004).

In addition, banishment from the world for violations of community standards or Terms of Service (TOS) agreements is possible. One example is the situation experienced by Woodbury University whose campus vanished from the SL grid following violations to the TOS agreement (Cheal, 2007). Other disruptions may include encounters with griefers (i.e., players who cause grief to others in world through harassment) and "drive-by shoutings" during class (Haynes and Holmevik, 1998, p. 6).

The proliferation of sexual content is yet another fact of life in this virtual world. As the teaching and learning opportunities conducted in Second Life expand, educators will have to address issues regarding the proliferation of sexually explicit content (Hayes, 2006). When it comes to these environments, the technology itself may distract from the learning process. For instance, this world can be difficult to navigate, especially for those with physical disabilities. Some scholars speculate that the navigational complexities may be minimized if the rumored partnership between Wii – a game space that is navigated through a remote device – and SL is actualized (Boulos et al., 2007).

However, even if the learning curve becomes less steep, the issue of the digital divide will still remain. Because the technical requirements to operate SL are high, only those who can afford powerful computers with graphics cards will have access to this world. The cost of creating a presence in SL is another factor that educators need to consider. For example, the Annenberg School of Communication at the University of Southern California has built structures that cost thousands of dollars to set up. Monthly in-world land fees also add to the financial burden. But the money alone is not the problem. Rather, what this school has achieved in-world is not an improvement in comparison to the educational initiatives that take place on campus (Livingstone & Kemp, 2006).

A Pedagogical Approach: The SECOND LIFE Model

The literature suggests that there are benefits associated with virtual worlds; however, Second Life and other virtual worlds alone cannot foster effective teaching and learning experiences. To create effective learning environments that empower students and motivate them to learn, educators must take into account pedagogical approaches that will enable them to effectively incorporate virtual world initiatives into the curriculum. I developed a model that I refer to by the mnemonic "SECOND LIFE" (Table 2). In this model, there are 10 pedagogical dimensions that are central to the delivery of content in virtual spaces as well as their and corresponding outcomes.

Support Experimentation

In virtual worlds, students are able to experiment with identity, explore online role playing, and develop shared values. As they navigate these visually rich and socially engaging virtual domains, students can experientially develop higher-order

Table 2. The SECOND LIFE Model

Pedagogical Dimensions	Outcomes
Support experimentation	Construct identity, play with roles, develop shared values
Encourage play	Increase student motivation through "fun" activities
Construct scaffolded spaces	Engage in practical experimentation with minimal risk
Opt out of lecture and passive approaches	Actively learn through seeing, knowing, and doing
Nurture player choices and decision-making	Control and own the learning process
Design "realistic" environments (special effects/graphics)	Participate in immersive and authentic experiences
Lead students toward a sense of space	Build and create identities, backstories, and environments
Increase student learning	Complete hands-on, authentic activities; learn more than through reading text alone
Foster the formation of a learning culture	Collaborate, create new knowledge, and promote greater understanding
Enhance technology-focused skills	Develop and enhance visual skills, information literacy, critical thinking

thinking skills. Identity experimentation can be educational as well. Building an identity through trial and error is an important part of the learning process, and online worlds can play a key role in this development (Turkle, 1997). In virtual worlds, individuals construct their identity through their avatars. These digital, graphical characters can be used in a variety of ways – to greet, signal group identification, interact, and even create feelings of closeness. And, students may be motivated to learn simply by selecting an avatar (Lee & Hoadley, 2007).

Role playing through an avatar is another popular form of experimentation among virtual world residents. In SL, for example, individuals can virtually travel back in time to the 1850s and become a member of a small mining town in the Northwest Territory known as Steelhead City. It is in this community that residents can participate in "Gaslamp Fantasy" role play activities that involve magic and science. Through this playful process of what-if experimentation, students are able to learn new practices (Halverson et al., 2006). Moreover, Jenkins et al. (2008) argue that experimentation and risk-taking are encouraged through play.

Encourage Play

Scholars, like Vygotsky and Piaget, believe that play is an important part of the learning process. In fact, Vygotsky (1978) insists that play creates a zone of proximal development for the child. The non-competitive nature of many virtual worlds is thought to contribute to the playfulness of the environment (Brown & Bell, 2006). However, there are a number of other ways that virtual worlds encourage play. For example, in Second Life, it is not uncommon for residents to have multiple avatars or "alts," which also adds to the playful and carnivalesque flavor of the environment (Jenkins, 2004; Turner 1982). Not only is it possible to have multiple avatars, but residents can also alter their appearance with ease. With the click of the mouse, the SL instructor may change her appearance from a woman in a conservative business suit to the sun with rotating planets to a flying monkey monster, all in a single class session. Moreover, educational tasks that occur in virtual worlds often involve role playing, quests, and treasure hunts, just to name a few. Interestingly, many students do not view these activities as work, but rather something that is "fun" and playful.

Construct Scaffolded Spaces

Virtual worlds are powerful in that they enable students to experiment, play, and learn through experiences that occur within mentally engaging scaffolded spaces. There are different types of scaffolding (Table 3), which include conceptual (supportive), procedural, strategic (intrinsic), and metacognitive (reflective) coaching (e.g., Cagiltay, 2006). One example that illustrates scaffolding in SL is the Idaho State University (ISU) Play2Train program for health care professionals and emergency responders (Briggs, 2008). In SL, these emergency professionals work together to respond to large scale bioterrorism attacks and infectious disease epidemics. As an added benefit, these students can participate in these SL scenarios from anywhere – they are not required to physically travel to one central training location. While the likelihood of failure is high in these spaces without prior instruction, virtual worlds are far more likely to be a safe environment with minimal risk of failure or embarrassment (Delwiche, 2003; Steinkuehler, 2004). In contrast, failure in school carries much more weight and tends to matter more (Gee, 2008; Squire, 2005).

Opt Out of Lecture and Passive Approaches

Today's new students are not passive consumers. They are experiential learners who prefer to acquire knowledge by actively doing rather than idly listening. They are also community-oriented and favor collaborative and interactive learning experiences. Web 2.0 technologies are enabling students to be more than passive consumers; they are active producers as well. SL, for one, allows residents to create their own content and engage in experiential learning experiences. In virtual worlds, familiar ways of delivering content (e.g., lectures, rote learning) may not be as effective as in the physical classroom. Thus, instructors must learn how to create greater levels of interactivity between students and the virtual worlds.

An example can be seen in the popularity associated with language learning in SL. Islands devoted to these activities (e.g., Second Life English, The English Village) and a plethora of language resources are available in-world. What makes learning a language in a virtual world powerful is that students are able to practice what they learn in real time with others. Some SL educators are even experimenting with in-world language trips

Table 3. Scaffolding in Virtual Worlds

Type of Scaffolding	Scaffolding Activity	SL Scaffolding Examples
Conceptual	Providing cues, hints, feedback and advice	English as a Second Language learners practice their newly acquired speaking and writing skills with others on the "Second Life English" island.
Procedural	Learning how to use tools and resources available in the learning environment	Residents begin their SL life on Orientation Island where they learn how to change their appearance, fly, and navigate the virtual environment.
Strategic	Guiding students in assessing the task and encouraging alternative approaches	Students receive SL notecards from the instructor that can contain information such as text, textures, URLs, and landmarks.
Metacognitive coaching	Thinking about a task and asking questions (e.g., What have I done up to this point? What do I do next?)	Healthcare professionals and emergency responders work together in the SL Play2Train environment to solve a hypothetical event such as an infectious disease epidemic.

and treasure hunts, which encourage exploration, playful interactions, and decision-making.

Nurture Player Choices and Decision-Making

In contrast to the current system of school, which insists on one "right" way to solve a problem, virtual worlds allow for and encourage multiple ways of knowing. Video games and their virtual world settings are fun spaces, but they are also effective learning tools because players are the ones who set their achievement standards and use those to judge their performance accordingly (Gee, 2003). Because these worlds are complex, offer many options and respond to player choices, students often feel as if they are in control of their learning and, as a result, own their learning process (Herz, 2001). Squire and Barab (2004) also discovered that underserved students in an urban school acquired knowledge about geographical facts, as well as ways to ask sincere questions, through their interactions with the three-dimensional game, *Civilization III*. However, these spaces are not effective learning environments just because they are fun; it is also because players are required to make important decisions (Oblinger, 2006).

Design "Realistic" Environments

Even though it is not always easy to do (e.g., Elliott et al., 2002), instructors must find ways to utilize the affordances of virtual worlds to create entertaining, interactive, and "realistic" experiences in fictional universes. Currently, there are several institutions in virtual worlds that are explaining their presence through physical world metaphors. For instance, colleges and universities such as Ohio University are building replicas of their campuses in SL. These entities are also creating models of museums and even science laboratories (de Freitas, 2008). Vassar College's rendition of the Sistine Chapel in SL is a recreation that exemplifies this type of activity. The Cleveland Public Library, which is known in the physical world for its chess collection, has created colossal chess boards in this virtual space. But why are these residents merely mimicking what can be found in face-to-face environments? One explanation is that these entities are attempting to reach individuals who may not be early technology adopters and attract them to this space (de Freitas, 2008).

Lead Students Toward a Sense of Space

Students are able to create a sense of space in virtual worlds through a process that is a "combination of context, activities, and action" (Kalay, 2004, p. 196); they employ intellectual decision-making in this environment to accomplish both personal and in-game goals. In addition, Kalay (2004) proposes a framework that includes the best of the traditional model but stresses that effective learning environments do more than replicate physical spaces. Instead, it is within these collaboratively constructed spaces that players "generate social capital," create "rituals and practices," "generate in-game antics and adventures," and master these practices through "scaffolded and supported interactions" (Steinkuehler, 2005, p. 12). Moreover, it is in these spaces that the players construct their identities (e.g., Steinkuehler, 2005; Turkle, 1997), create their own backstory, and build their own environments.

Increase Student Learning

The perception that virtual world environments are always fun is an inaccurate one. Students may be frustrated, and in some cases even "confused or disoriented" (Johnson, 2005, p. 25). But, this feeling of being stuck can be valuable in that "frustration during the learning program and then the feeling of resolution afterward is the most reliable sign that learning is going on" (Aldrich, 2005, p. 243). Paivio (1986), an emeritus psychology professor at the University of Western Ontario, put forth the concept of dual coding cognitive models. In other words, individuals process verbal (i.e., language) and non-verbal (i.e., images) information in two different systems. In addition, this process has implications for problem solving and other cognitive domains. Mayer (1999) extended Paivio's work by investigating the ways multimedia can support constructivist ideals and showed that multiple forms of media can be an effective learning tool. Some students may feel frustrated as they learn how to be in virtual worlds. But, as Paivio and Mayer would expect, students often assert that they learned more in these spaces than if they had only read the text (Van, 2007).

Foster the Formation of a Learning Culture

As Nardi, Ly, and Harris (2007) found in their research on the game World of Warcraft, which is set in a three-dimensional virtual world, players often acquired facts through informal chat discussions among players who are excited about the game. Moreover, "learning in conversation" (Nardi et al., 2007, p. 4) – a process that involved answering questions in a friendly manner and volunteering advice to less experienced peers – was part of the WoW learning culture. In WoW, players work collaboratively to solve problems, and as part of the learning culture in this environment, players answer questions quickly and courteously. As Vygotsky would predict, the learners in WoW that Nardi et al. observed accomplished more through the peer-to-peer learning process than they could independently. It is within these communities that "knowledge, skills, identities, and values are shaped by a particular way of thinking into a coherent epistemic frame," which ultimately becomes the "grammar of the culture" (Shaffer et al., 2005, p. 107). In a learning culture, "everyone is involved in a collective effort of understanding" (Oblinger, 2006, p. 3).

Enhance Technology-Focused Skills

There are many advocates who claim that today's young people are technologically savvy (e.g., Howe & Strauss, 2000; Oblinger, 2003; Prensky, 2001); however, questions about their information and computer literacy skills have started to surface. As Oblinger and Oblinger (2005) state, the critical thinking and information skills possessed by these students may be "less well developed than previous cohorts" (p. 2.5). Because of these concerns, educators are beginning to investigate ways to teach information literacy, visual literacy, new media literacy, information fluency, and information competence skills to this new group of students. SL and other virtual worlds provide students scaffolded spaces that can support the acquisition of many of these and other literacy skills. Once acquired, it is likely that many of the proficiencies developed in-world will transfer to other virtual worlds (Au, 2008). There is also evidence to suggest that proficiency in skills acquired in virtual worlds may pay off in the physical world. For example, Brown and Thomas (2006) describe the experiences of Stephen Gillett, an individual who applied for a job at Yahoo!. Because of Gillett's experience as one of the top guild masters in World of Warcraft, which has been described as a "total immersion course in leadership" (Brown & Thomas, 2006, n.p.), he got the job.

FUTURE RESEARCH DIRECTIONS

Students want more opportunities to learn anytime, anywhere; in other words, they want more "learning-on-the-go" options (Oblinger, 2008, p. 24). While the technical demands of many of these worlds make it difficult to be mobile, this situation may be changing. In April 2008, Samsung displayed a new application that will run the SL client on mobile phones. The company hopes to make this item available to individuals in the United States by the end of 2008 (Sweeney, 2008).

But because of the high technical requirements, educators who are interested in the instructional potential of SL and similar worlds indicate that initiatives conducted in this space will likely have classroom-based components as well. Stated another way, teaching and learning will adopt a blended learning approach (e.g., Bonk & Graham, 2006; de Freitas, 2008; Dziuban et al., 2005). To support and guide these new educational initiatives, a pedagogical approach such as the SECOND LIFE model is needed.

Also on the horizon is the development of new forms of virtual worlds. On July 8, 2008, Google introduced a public beta of *Lively*, a three-dimensional virtual chat room that can be accessed through a web browser and integrated into blogs or other websites (Ricknäs, 2008; Stone, 2008). At the time of this writing, visitors to this virtual world can use text chat and animated actions to communicate with others. While Google plans to discontinue its support of Lively at the end of 2008, this company has recently launched a new venture – Ancient Rome 3D on Google Earth. Google is not the only entity exploring ways to create alternative virtual worlds. *Vivaty Scenes*, created by Vivaty, is another space that is similar to Lively. At this time, however, a beta version is only available on Facebook and AOL instant messenger (AIM). In addition, Linden Lab and IBM are experimenting with universal avatars that can move from SL to another virtual world (Linden, H. 2008). These are merely a few examples of the work that is being done to expand the possibilities of these environments. Further, it appears that investments in these types of innovations are on the rise. In Q2, $161 million was contributed to 14 virtual world investments (Virtual Worlds Management, 2008).

Currently, teachers, students, administrator, and software developers are exploring the potential of virtual worlds for educational purposes, but there are also those who remain skeptical. Despite research on earlier versions of virtual worlds (e.g., MUDs, two-dimensional worlds), answers to the questions that surround the new and ever-evolving graphical worlds are lacking. Thus, more research is needed for educators to better understand and fully utilize these spaces. While opinions differ regarding the outcomes of teaching and learning activities in virtual worlds, there appears to be agreement that technology alone will not save education. In a debate with Dr. Robert Kozma, Sir John Daniel (2007), President and CEO of the Commonwealth of Learning, asserted that "there is no magic medium and never will be. Each technology has its strengths" (n.p.). In the end, virtual worlds, and Second Life specifically, may not completely replace educational activities that take place in the first life; but educators who incorporate the SECOND LIFE model concepts into their technology-based initiatives may find that virtual worlds enable them to move away from the factory model of education and rote learning.

CONCLUSION

Interest in informal learning approaches is on the rise (Oblinger, 2004). Educators are beginning to examine ways to integrate virtual worlds into the curriculum and foster student collaboration worldwide. There are also signs to suggest that the application of these virtual worlds is underway: there are conferences and workshops on this topic; groups like the New Media Consortium rent space in SL for educational use; and consumer health information is available at Health InfoIsland (Boulos et al., 2007). Also, recent reports claim that the adoption rates of virtual worlds for educational purposes are growing (Horizon Report, 2007). The approval of the application of law in virtual worlds for continuing education credits by the California Bar Association (Foster, 2008) is an example of this trend. At present, creating virtual worlds is a popular and lucrative (Virtual Worlds Management, 2008) endeavor. Therefore, now is the time for educators to consider pedagogical approaches such as those outlined in the SECOND LIFE model in order to fully utilize the teaching and learning potential of virtual world environments.

REFERENCES

Aldrich, C. (2005). *Learning by doing: A comprehensive guide to simulations, computer games, and pedagogy in e-learning and other educational experiences.* San Francisco: Pfeiffer.

Au, W. J. (2008). *The making of Second Life: Notes from the new world.* New York: Collins.

Bainbridge, W. S. (2007, July 27). The scientific research potential of virtual worlds. *Science, 317,* 472–476. doi:10.1126/science.1146930

Barab, S. A., Thomas, M., Dodge, T., Carteaux, R., & Tuzun, H. (2005). Making learning fun: Quest Atlantis, a game without guns. *Educational Technology Research and Development, 53*(1), 86–107. doi:10.1007/BF02504859

Bartle, R. A. (2004). *Designing virtual worlds.* Berkeley, CA: New Riders.

Boellstorff, T. (2008). *Coming of age in Second Life: An anthropologist explores the virtually human.* Princeton, NJ: Princeton University Press.

Bonk, C. J., & Graham, C. R. (Eds.). (2006). *The handbook of blended learning: Global perspective, local designs.* San Francisco: Pfeiffer.

Boulos, M. N. K., Hetherington, L., & Wheeler, S. (2007). Second Life: An overview of the potential of 3-D virtual worlds in medical and health education. *Health Information and Libraries Journal, 24,* 233–245. doi:10.1111/j.1471-1842.2007.00733.x

Bricken, W. (1990). *Learning in virtual reality* (Memorandum HITL-M-90-5). Seattle, WA: University of Washington, Human Interface Technology Laboratory.

Briggs, L. L. (2008, May 1). Idaho State simulates emergency response in Second Life. *Campus Technology.* Retrieved May 2, 2008, from http://campustechnology.com/articles/61150/

Brown, B., & Bell, M. (2006). Play and sociability in there: Some lessons from online games for collaborative virtual environments. In R. Schroeder & A.-S. Axelsson (Eds.), *Avatars at work and play: Collaboration and interaction in shared virtual environments* (pp. 227-246). The Netherlands: Springer.

Brown, J. S., & Adler, R. P. (2008, January/February). Minds on fire: Open education, the long tail, and learning 2.0. *EDUCAUSE,* 17-32. Retrieved January 29, 2008, from http://www.educause.edu/ir/library/pdf/ERM0811.pdf

Brown, J. S., Collins, A., & Duguid, P. (1998). Situated cognition and the culture of learning. *Educational Researcher, 18,* 32–42.

Brown, J. S., & Thomas, D. (2006, April). You play World of Warcraft? You're hired! *Wired, 14*(4). Retrieved March 1, 2008, from http://www.wired.com/wired/archive/14.04/learn.html

Bruckman, A. (1998). Community support for constructionist learning. *Computer Supported Cooperative Work: The Journal of Collaborative Computing, 7,* 47–86. doi:10.1023/A:1008684120893

Bruckman, A., & Resnick, M. (1995). The MediaMOO project: Constructionism and professional community. *Convergence, 1*(1). Retrieved April 10, 2008, from http://www.cc.gatech.edu/~asb/papers/convergence.html

Bruner, J. (1997). *The culture of education* (2nd ed.). Cambridge, MA: Harvard University Press.

Cagiltay, K. (2006). Scaffolding strategies in electronic performance support systems: Types and challenges. *Innovations in Education and Teaching International, 43*(1), 93–103. doi:10.1080/14703290500467673

Cassell, J., & Jenkins, H. (1998). Feminism and computer games. In J. Cassell & H. Jenkins (Eds.), *From Barbie to Mortal Kombat: Gender and computer games* (pp. 2-45). Cambridge, MA: MIT Press.

Cassner-Lotto, J., & Wright Benner, M. (2006). *Are they really ready to work? Employers perspectives on the basic knowledge and applied skills of new entrants to the 21st century U.S. workforce.* The Partnership for 21st Century. Retrieved March 23, 2008, from http://www.21stcenturyskills.org/documents/FINAL_REPORT_PDF9-29-06.pdf

Cheal, C. (2007). Second Life: Hype or hyperlearning? *Horizon, 15*(4), 204–210. doi:10.1108/10748120710836228

Cole, M., & Engeström, Y. (1993). A cultural-historical approach to distributed cognition. In G. Salomon (Ed.), *Distributed cognitions* (pp. 1-46). Cambridge, UK: Cambridge University Press.

Daniel, J. (2007, October 15). *Technology and the media have transformed all aspects of human life-except education* (The Economist Debate Series). Retrieved July 19, 2008, from http://www.economist.com/debate/index.cfm?action=article&debate_id=1&story_id=9968827de de Freitas, S. (2007). Learning in immersive worlds: A review of game-based learning. Retrieved October 8, 2007, from http://www.jisc.ac.uk/media/documents/programmes/elearning_innovation/gaming%20report_v3.3.pdf de Freitas, S. (2008). Emerging trends in serious games and virtual worlds. *Becta: Emerging Technologies for Learning, 3,* 57-72. Retrieved April 10, 2008, from http://partners.becta.org.uk/upload-dir/downloads/page_documents/research/emerging_technologies08_chapter4.pdf

Dede, C. (2005). Planning for neomillennial learning styles. *EDUCAUSE Quarterly, 28*(1), 7-12. Retrieved October 31, 2007, from http://www.educause.edu/ir/library/pdf/eqm0511.pdf

Delwiche, A. (2003). *MMORPG's in the college classroom. The state of play: Law, games, and virtual worlds.* New York: New York Law School. Retrieved May 1, 2008, from http://www.nyls.edu/docs/delwiche.pdf

Delwiche, A. (2006). Massively multiplayer online games (MMOs) in the new media classroom. *Educational Technology & Society, 9*(3), 160-172. Retrieved May 7, 2008, from http://www.ifets.info/journals/9_3/14.pdf

Dewey, J. (1997/1938). *Experience and education* (1st Touchstone ed.). New York: Touchstone.

Dremann, S. (2008, July 22). Businesses, universities get Second Life. *Palo Alto Online.* Retrieved July 22, 2008, from http://www.paloaltoonline.com/news/show_story.php?id=8781

Ducheneaut, N., & Moore, R. J. (2004). The social side of gaming: A study of interaction patterns in a massively multiplayer online game. In *Proceedings of the 2004 ACM conference on Computer Supportive Cooperative Work* (pp. 360-369). Retrieved January 18, 2008, from http://doi.acm.org/10.1145/1031607.1031667

Dziuban, C. D., Moskal, P. D., & Hartman, J. (2005). Higher education, blended learning, and the generations: Knowledge is power: No more. In J. Bourne & J. C. Moore (Eds.), *Elements of quality online education: Engaging communities* (pp. 85-100). Needham, MA: Sloan Center for Online Education.

EDUCAUSE Learning Initiative. (2008, June 11). 7 things you should know about Second Life. *EDUCAUSE.* Retrieved June 13, 2008, from http://www.educause.edu/ir/library/pdf/ELI7038.pdf

Electric Sheep Company. (n.d.). *Solutions FAQ: What is a virtual world?* Retrieved April 4, 2008, from http://www.electricsheepcompany.com/core/services/faq/

Elliott, J., Adams, L., & Bruckman, A. (2002). No magic bullet: 3D video games in education. In *Proceedings of the ICLS 2002,* Seattle, WA. Retrieved September 27, 2007, from http://www.cc.gatech.edu/~asb/papers/aquamoose-icls02.pdf

Facer, K., Ulicsek, M., & Sandford, R. (2007). Can computer games go to school? *Becta: Emerging Technologies for Learning, 2,* 46-54. Retrieved April 10, 2008, from http://partners.becta.org.uk/page_documents/research/emerging_technologies07_chapter5.pdf

Fanderclai, T. L. (1995, January 1). MUDs in education: New environments, new pedagogies. *Computer-mediated Communication Magazine, 2*(1). Retrieved April 23, 2008, from http://www.ibiblio.org/cmc/mag/1995/jan/fanderclai.html

Fanderclai, T. L. (1996). Like magic, only real. In L. Cherny & E. Weise (Eds.), *Wired women: Gender and new realities in cyberspace* (pp. 224-241). Seattle, WA: Seal Press.

Foreman, J. (2004, October). Game-based learning: How to delight and instruct in the 21st Century. *EDUCAUSE Review.* Retrieved November 15, 2007, from http://www.educause.edu/ir/library/pdf/erm0454.pdf

Foster, A. (2008, July 18). California Bar Association sanctions legal training in virtual world. *The Chronicle of Higher Education.* Retrieved July 18, 2008, from http://chronicle.com/wiredcampus/index.php?id=3175

Gee, J. P. (2003). *What video games have to teach us about learning and literacy.* New York: Palgrave/St. Martin's.

Gee, J. P. (2008). Learning and games. In K. Salen (Ed.), *The ecology of games: Connecting youth, games, and learning* (pp. 21-40). Cambridge, MA: MIT Press. Retrieved April 3, 2008, from http://www.mitpressjournals.org/doi/pdf/10.1162/dmal.9780262693646.021

Halverson, R., Shaffer, D., Squire, K., & Steinkuehler, C. (2006). Theorizing games in/and education. In *Proceedings of the Seventh International Conference on Learning Sciences ICLS '06.*

Hayes, E. (2006). Situated learning in virtual worlds: The learning ecology of Second Life. In *Proceedings of the Adult Education Research Conference 2006.* Retrieved November 13, 2007, from http://www.adulterc.org/Proceedings/2006/Proceedings/Hayes.pdf

Haynes, C., & Holmevik, J. R. (Eds.). (1998). *High wired: On the design, use, and theory of educational MOOs.* Ann Arbor, MI: University of Michigan Press.

Herz, J. C. (2001). Gaming the system: What higher education can learn from multiplayer online worlds. *EDUCAUSE, 169-191.* Retrieved October 7, 2007, from http://www.educause.edu/ir/library/pdf/ffpiu019.pdf

Howe, N., & Strauss, W. (2000). *Millennials rising: The next great generation.* New York: Vintage Books.

Jenkins, C. A. (2004). The virtual classroom as ludic space. In C. A. Haythornthwaite & M. M. Kazmer (Eds.), *Learning, culture and community in online education* (pp. 163-176). New York: Peter Lang.

Jenkins, H., Purushotma, R., Clinton, K., Weigel, M., & Robison, A. J. (2008). *Confronting the challenges of participatory culture: Media education for the 21st century.* Chicago, IL: The John D. and Catherine T. MacArthur Foundation. Retrieved from http://digitallearning.macfound.org/atf/cf/%7B7E45C7E0-A3E0-4B89-AC9C-E807E1B0AE4E%7D/JENKINS_WHITE_PAPER.PDF

Johnson, S. (2005). *Everything bad is good for you* (2nd ed.). New York: Riverhead Books.

Kalay, Y. E. (2004). Virtual learning environments [Special issue]. *Journal of Information Technology in Construction, 9*, 195-207. Retrieved October 8, 2007, from http://www.itcon.org/data/works/att/2004_13.content.04009.pdf

Kirriemuir, J., & McFarlane, A. (2004). *Literature review in games and learning. A report of NESTA Futurelab.* Retrieved November 15, 2007, from http://www.futurelab.org.uk/resources/documents/lit_reviews/Games_Review.pdf

Kolbert, E. (2001, May 28). Pimps and dragons. *New Yorker (New York, N.Y.)*, 88–98.

Lave, J. (1988). The practice of learning: The problem with "context." In S. Chaiklin & J. Lave (Eds.), *Understanding practice: Perspectives on activity and context* (pp. 3-32). Boston, MA: Cambridge University Press.

Lave, J., & Wenger, E. (1991). *Situated learning: Legitimate peripheral participation.* New York: Cambridge University Press.

Lee, J. L., & Hoadley, C. M. (2007). Leveraging identity to make learning fun: Possible selves and experiential learning in massively multiplayer online games (MMOGs). *Innovate, 6*(3). Retrieved January 10, 2008, from http://innovateonline.info/index.php?view=article&id=348

Life, S. *Economic statistics.* (2008, August 29). Retrieved August 30, 2008, from http://secondlife.com/whatis/economy_stats.php

Life, S. *FAQ.* (n.d.). Retrieved August 6, 2008, from http://secondlife.com/whatis/faq.php

Linden, H. (2008, July 8). IBM and Linden Lab interoperability announcement. *Second Life Blog.* Retrieved July 23, 2008, from http://blog.secondlife.com/2008/07/08/ibm-linden-lab-interoperability-announcement/#

Linden, P. (2008, May 29). Inside the lab podcast: Education in Second Life [podcast transcript of an interview with Claudia and Pathfinder Linden]. Retrieved June 3, 2008, from http://static-secondlife-com.s3.amazonaws.com/media/Inside%20the%20Lab%20podcast-transcript-Education.htm

Livingstone, D., & Kemp, J. (2006). Massively multi-learner: Recent advances in 3D social environments. *Computing and Information Systems Journal, 10*(2). Retrieved July 11, 2007, from http://www.cis.paisley.ac.uk/research/journal/v10n2/LivingstoneKemp.doc

Mayer, R. E. (1999). Multimedia aids to problem-solving transfer. *International Journal of Educational Research, 31*, 611–632. doi:10.1016/S0883-0355(99)00027-0

McLellan, H. (2004). Virtual realities. In D. H. Jonassen (Ed.), *Handbook of research for educational communications and technology* (pp. 461-497). Manwah, NJ: Lawrence Erlbaum Associates. Retrieved March 29, 2008, from http://www.aect.org/edtech/17.pdf

Nardi, B. A., Ly, S., & Harris, J. (2007). Learning conversations in World of Warcraft. In *Proceedings of the 40th Hawaii International Conference on Systems Sciences.* Retrieved October 3, 2007, from http://darrouzet-nardi.net/bonnie/pdf/Nardi-HICSS.pdf

National Center for Educational Statistics. (2006). *Digest of educational statistics: 2006.* Retrieved February 10, 2008, from http://nces.ed.gov/programs/digest/d06/index.asp

Oblinger, D. (2003, July/August). Boomers, Gen-Xers, & Millennials: Understanding the "new students." *EDUCAUSE*, 36-47. Retrieved November 12, 2007, from http://www.educause.edu/ir/library/pdf/erm0342.pdf

Oblinger, D. (2004). The next generation of educational engagement. *Journal of Interactive Media in Education, 8,* 1-18. Retrieved October 3, 2007, from http://www-jime.open.ac.uk/2004/8/oblinger-2004-8.pdf

Oblinger, D. G. (2006). Simulations, games and learning. *EDUCAUSE Learning Initiative.* Retrieved February 5, 2008, from http://www.educause.edu/ir/library/pdf/ELI3004.pdf

Oblinger, D. G. (2008). Growing up with Google: What it means to education. *Becta: Emerging Technologies for Learning, 3,* 10-29. Retrieved April 10, 2008, from http://partners.becta.org.uk/upload-dir/downloads/page_documents/research/emerging_technologies08_chapter1.pdf

Oblinger, D. G., & Oblinger, J. L. (2005). Is it age or IT: First steps toward understanding the Net generation. In D. G. Oblinger & J. L. Oblinger (Eds.), *Educating the Net generation* (pp. 2.1-2.20). Retrieved March 1, 2008, from http://www.educause.edu/ir/library/pdf/pub7101c.pdf

Paivio, A. (1986). *Mental representations: A dual coding approach.* New York: Oxford University Press.

Papert, S. (1993). *The children's machine: Rethinking school in the age of the computer.* New York: Basic Books.

Piaget, J. (1952). *The origins of intelligence in children* (M. Cook, Trans.). New York: International Universities Press.

Prensky, M. (2001). *Digital game-based learning.* New York: McGraw-Hill.

Quinn, C. (2005). *Engaging learning: Designing e-learning simulation games.* San Francisco: Pfeiffer.

Report, H. (2007). *The horizon report: 2007 edition.* Retrieved September 20, 2007, from http://www.nmc.org/pdf/2007_Horizon_Report.pdf

Rheingold, H. (2008, February 23). Howard Rheingold one of 17 winners of HASTAC/MacArthur Foundation Competition. Message posted to http://www.smartmobs.com/2008/02/23/howard-rheingold-one-of-17-winners-of-hastac-macarthur-foundation-competition/

Ricknäs, M. (2008, July 9). Google adds third dimension to online social relationships. *Network World.* Retrieved July 9, 2008, from http://www.networkworld.com/news/2008/070908-google-adds-third-dimension-to.html

Roush. W. (2007, July/August). Second earth. *Technology Review.* Retrieved March 19, 2008, from https://www.technologyreview.com/Infotech/18911/

Shaffer, D. W., Squire, K. R., Halverson, R., & Gee, J. P. (2005). Video games and the future of learning. *Phi Delta Kappan, 87*(2), 104–111.

Spellings, M. (2008, April 1). *U.S. Secretary of Education Margaret Spellings announces department will move to a uniform graduation rate, require disaggregation of data.* U.S. Department of Education. Retrieved August 16, 2008, from http://www.ed.gov/news/pressreleases/2008/04/04012008.html

Squire, K. (2005). Changing the game: What happens when video games enter the classroom? *Innovate, 1*(6). Retrieved September 14, 2007, from http://www.innovateonline.info/index.php?view=article&id=82

Squire, K., & Barab, S. (2004). Replaying history: Engaging urban underserved students in learning world history through computer simulation games. In Y. B. Kafai, W. A. Sandoval, N. Enyedy, A. S. Nixon, & F. Herrera (Eds.). *Proceedings of the Sixth International Conference of the Learning Sciences: Embracing Diversity in the Learning Sciences* (pp. 505-512). Mahwah, NJ: Lawrence Erlbaum Associates.

Steinkuehler, C. A. (2004). Learning in massively multiplayer online games. In Y. B. Kafai, W. A. Sandoval, N. Enyedy, A. S. Nixon, & F. Herrera (Eds.), *Proceedings of the Sixth International Conference of the Learning Sciences: Embracing Diversity in the Learning Sciences* (pp. 521-528). Mahwah, NJ: Lawrence Erlbaum Associates. Retrieved September 20, 2007, from http://website.education.wisc.edu/steinkuehler/papers/SteinkuehlerICLS2004.pdf

Steinkuehler, C. A. (2005). Cognition and literacy in massively multiplayer online games. In D. Leu, J. Coiro, C. Lankshear, & K. Knobel (Eds.), *Handbook of research on new literacies*. Mahwah, NJ: Erlbaum. Retrieved September 15, 2007, from http://labweb.education.wisc.edu/curric606/readings/Steinkuehler2005.pdf

Steinkuehler, C. A. (2008). Massively multiplayer online games as educational technology: An outline for research. *Educational Technology, 48*(1), 10–21.

Stone, B. (2008, July 9). Google introduces a cartoonlike method for talking in chat rooms. *The New York Times*. Retrieved July 9, 2008, from http://www.nytimes.com/2008/07/09/technology/09google.html?ex=1216267200&en=68ad9e88cd355b9b&ei=5070&emc=eta1

Subrahmanyam, K., Kraut, R., Greenfield, P., & Gross, E. (2000). The impact of home computer use on children's activities and development. *Children and Computer Technology, 10*(2), 123–144.

Sweeney, T. (2008, April 2). CTIA: Samsung showcases Second Life apps. *Information Week*. Retrieved April 4, 2008, from http://www.informationweek.com/news/mobility/messaging/showArticle.jhtml;jsessionid=CIDWAOZ1DBOGOQSNDLPSKHSCJUNN2JVN?articleID=207001367&_requestid=643783

Thomas, D., & Brown, J. S. (2007, October 21). *Why virtual worlds can matter* [Working Paper]. Retrieved February 7, 2008, from http://www.johnseelybrown.com/needvirtualworlds.pdf

Turkle, S. (1997). *Life on the screen: Identity in the age of the Internet* (1st Touchstone ed.). New York: Touchstone.

Turner, V. (1982). *From ritual to theatre: The human seriousness of play.* New York: PAJ Publications.

Van, J. (2007, August 12). Training for the poor moves into computer age. *The Chicago Tribune*, pp. 5.1, 5.4.

Virtual Worlds Management. (2008, July 8). $161 million invested in 16 virtual worlds-related companies in 2Q 2008, $345 million invested in first half of 2008. *Virtual Worlds News*. Retrieved July 23, 2008, from http://www.virtualworldsnews.com/2008/07/161-million-inv.html

Vygotsky, L. S. (1978). *Mind in society: The development of higher psychological processes.* Cambridge, MA: Harvard University Press.

Wallis, C., & Steptoe, S. (2006, December 10). How to bring out schools out of the 20th century. *Time Magazine*. Retrieved March 23, 2008, from http://www.time.com/time/printout/0,8816,1568480,00.html

Wedemeyer, C. A. (1981). *Learning at the back door: Reflections on non-traditional learning in the lifespan.* Madison, WI: University of Wisconsin Press.

ADDITIONAL READING

Alexander, B. (2008, July/August). Games for education: 2008. *EDUCAUSE Review, 43*(4), 64-65. Retrieved July 10, 2008, from http://www.educause.edu/ir/library/pdf/ERM0849.pdf

Calongne, C. M. (2008). Educational frontiers: Learning in a virtual world. *EDUCAUSE Review, 43*(5), 36-48. Retrieved September 27, 2008, from http://connect.educause.edu/Library/EDUCAUSE+Review/EducationalFrontiersLearn/47221

Coffman, T., & Klinger, M. B. (2008). Utilizing virtual worlds in education: The implications for practice. *International Journal of Social Sciences, 2*(1), 29-33. Retrieved November 2, 2007, from http://www.waset.org/ijss/v2/v2-1-5.pdf

de Freitas, S. (2008). Emerging trends in serious games and virtual worlds. *Becta: Emerging Technologies for Learning, 3,* 57-72. Retrieved April 10, 2008, from http://partners.becta.org.uk/upload-dir/downloads/page_documents/research/emerging_technologies08_chapter4.pdf

de Freitas, S., & Griffiths, M. (2008). The convergence of gaming practices with other media forms: What potential for learning? A review of the literature. *Learning, Media and Technology, 33*(1), 11–20. doi:10.1080/17439880701868796

de Fretias, S. (2008, November). *Serious virtual worlds: A scoping study.* Bristol, UK: JISC. Retrieved November 11, 2008, from http://www.jisc.ac.uk/media/documents/publications/seriousvirtualworldsv1.pdf

Dede, C. (2008, May/June). New horizons: A seismic shift in epistemology. *EDUCAUSE Review, 43*(3), 80-81. Retrieved May 1, 2008, from http://connect.educause.edu/Library/EDUCAUSE+Review/ASeismicShiftinEpistemolo/46613

Dumbleton, T. (2007). Games to entertain or games to teach? *Becta: Emerging Technologies for Learning, 2,* 55-63. Retrieved April 10, 2008, from http://partners.becta.org.uk/page_documents/research/emerging_technologies07_chapter5.pdf

Guest, T. (2007). *Second lives: A journey through virtual worlds.* New York: Random House.

Ito, M., Horst, H. A., Bittanti, M., Boyd, D., Herr-Stephenson, B., Lange, P. G., et al. (2008, November). *Living and learning with new media: Summary of findings from the Digital Youth Project.* Retrieved November 20, 2008, from http://digitalyouth.ischool.berkeley.edu/files/report/digitalyouth-WhitePaper.pdf

Jennings, N., & Collins, C. (2008). Virtual or virtually U: Educational institutions in Second Life. *International Journal of Social Sciences, 2*(3), 180-186. Retrieved March 20, 2008, from http://www.waset.org/ijss/v2/v2-3-28.pdf

Jones, G., & Warren, S. (2008). The time factor: Leveraging intelligent agents and directed narratives in online learning environments. *Innovate, 5*(2). Retrieved December 6, 2008, from http://www.innovateonline.info/index.php?view=article&id=576

Jones, J. G., & Bronack, S. C. (2007). Rethinking cognition, representations, and process in 3D online social learning environments. In D. Gibson, C. Aldrich, & M. Prensky (Eds.), *Games and simulations in online learning: Research and development frameworks* (pp. 89-114). Hershey, PA: Information Science Publishing.

Kelton, A. J. (2007, April 14). Second Life: Reaching into the virtual world for real-world learning. *EDUCAUSE Research Bulletin, 2007*(17), 1-13. Retrieved February 28, 2008, from http://www.educause.edu/ir/library/pdf/ecar_so/erb/ERB0717.pdf

Kemp, J. W., & Haycock, K. (2008). Immersive learning environments in parallel universes: Learning through Second Life. *School Libraries Worldwide, 14*(2), 89-97. Retrieved September 26, 2008, from http://asselindoiron.pbwiki.com/f/RevisedKEMPhaycock.Sept08.pdf

Lenhart, A., Kahne, J., Middaugh, E., Macgill, A. R., Evans, C., & Vitak, J. (2008, September 16). *Teens, video games, and civics.* Washington, DC: Pew Internet & American Life Project. Retrieved September 27, 2008, from http://www.pewinternet.org/pdfs/PIP_Teens_Games_and_Civics_Report_FINAL.pdf

Ludlow, P., & Wallace, M. (2007). *The Second Life Herald: The virtual tabloid that witnessed the dawn of the metaverse.* Cambridge, MA: MIT Press.

Nesson, R., & Nesson, C. (in press). In the virtual classroom: An ethnographic argument for education in virtual worlds. *Space and Culture.* Retrieved April 27, 2008 from http://www.eecs.harvard.edu/~nesson/ed-vw-1.3.pdf

New Media Consortium. (2008). *Spring 2008 NMC survey: Educators in Second Life.* Austin, TX: The New Media Consortium. Retrieved November 30, 2008, from http://www.nmc.org/pdf/2008-sl-survey.pdf

Ondrejka, C. (2008). Education unleashed: Participatory culture, education, and innovation in Second Life. In K. Salen (Ed.), *The ecology of games: Connecting youth, games, and learning* (pp. 229-252). Cambridge, MA: MIT Press. Retrieved April 3, 2008, from http://www.mitpressjournals.org/doi/pdfplus/10.1162/dmal.9780262693646.229

Open University. (2007, May). The schome-NAGTY Teen Second Life pilot final report: A summary of key findings and lessons learnt. *SCHOME: The Education System for the Information Age.* Retrieved March 8, 2008, from http://mediax.stanford.edu/seminars/schomeNAGTY.pdf

Reeves, B., Malone, T. W., & O'Driscoll, T. (2008, May). Leadership's online labs. *Harvard Business Review,* 59–66.

Report, H. (2008). *The horizon report: 2008 edition.* Retrieved September 20, 2008, from http://www.nmc.org/pdf/2008-Horizon-Report.pdf

Rice, K., Pauley, L., Gasell, C., & Florez, C. (2008, October). *Going virtual! Unique needs and challenges of K-12 online teachers.* Vienna, VA: The International Association for K-12 Online Learning (iNACOL). Retrieved November 19, 2008, from http://edtech.boisestate.edu/goingvirtual/goingvirtual2.pdf

Royle, K. (2008, April/May). Game-based learning: A different perspective. *Innovate, 4*(4). Retrieved April 11, 2008, from http://innovateonline.info/?view=article&id=433

Salaway, G., & Caruso, J. B. (2008). *The ECAR study of undergrad students and information technology, 2008.* EDUCAUSE Center for Applied Research. Retrieved October 25, 2008, from http://net.educause.edu/ir/library/pdf/ERS0808/RS/ERS0808w.pdf

Squire, K. (2008). Open-ended video games: A model for developing learning for the interactive age. In K. Salen (Ed.), *The ecology of games: Connecting youth, games, and learning* (pp. 167-196). Cambridge, MA: MIT Press. Retrieved April 3, 2008, from http://www.mitpressjournals.org/doi/pdf/10.1162/dmal.9780262693646.167

Steinkuehler, C., & Duncan, S. (2008). Scientific habits of mind in virtual worlds. *Journal of Science Education and Technology, 17*(6), 530-543. Retrieved October 20, 2008, from http://website.education.wisc.edu/steinkuehler/papers/SteinkuehlerDuncan2008.pdf

Williams, D., Yee, N., & Caplan, S. E. (2008). Who plays, how much, and why? Debunking the stereotypical gamer profile. *Journal of Computer-mediated Communication, 13*(4), 993-1018. Retrieved November 10, 2008, from http://www3.interscience.wiley.com/cgi-bin/fulltext/121394419/HTMLSTART

Ziegler, S. G. (2007). The (mis)education of Generation M. *Learning, Media and Technology, 32*(1), 69–81. doi:10.1080/17439880601141302

Chapter 15
Podcasting:
A Flexible E-Learning Tool

Youmei Liu
University of Houston, USA

Shawn W. McCombs
University of Houston, USA

ABSTRACT

E-Learning has undergone an amazing metamorphosis: it has changed from the delivery of individualized, static curricular information to the consumption and sharing of social knowledge. While Web 2.0 provides the best tools to achieve this goal, podcasting – as one of the Web 2.0 technologies - is one of the most flexible teaching and learning tool used today. It has been used increasingly in higher educational institutions. This chapter will discuss the uniqueness of podcasting technology in promoting e-learning in following aspects: 1) podcasting addressing the needs of a dynamic e-learning environment, 2) research results indicating the educational efficacy of podcasting in e-learning, and 3) podcasting best practice in e-learning design and delivery.

INTRODUCTION

With recent advancements in modern technologies – especially Web 2.0, e-learning has adopted new meanings in both educational experiences and media-rich content delivery. Social networking has become an important component in e-learning interaction and collaboration; and the computer is no longer the dominant medium for content delivery. People's dynamic lifestyles have imposed new learning challenges – e-learners need to access educational content at any time and location available to them. Podcasting can be a very effective tool to address the needs from the flexible e-learning.

Podcasting has become a common, well-known and ubiquitous tool: it has made its way gracefully into our modern lexicon, transcends many of the inherent barriers of the traditional characteristics of mass media (Kaye, 2001), and even enjoys moderate

DOI: 10.4018/978-1-60566-729-4.ch015

Copyright © 2010, IGI Global. Copying or distributing in print or electronic forms without written permission of IGI Global is prohibited.

visibility from most of today's prominent media outlets. In fact, tuning to your favorite news program will inevitably find the anchorperson or disc jockey reminding us of the availability of podcasts from their respective websites.

Higher educational institutions have formed a huge e-learning delivery network under Apple Computer's iTunes U initiative. Only a few years old, the widespread popularity – in terms of creation and dissemination, as well as use and consumption – has grown exponentially in terms of both available podcasts and podcast subscriptions or downloads (Farkas, 2006). This alone suggests that podcasting as a medium satisfies a previously unfulfilled niche. Given the power of Web 2.0 technologies, podcasting is an easy to use tool that empowers all users to be dynamic information creators/generators rather than just static consumers.

This chapter has three sections: Section I will discuss podcasting, as one of the Web 2.0 technologies, is used to address the dynamic e-learning environment from the perspectives of technology change, social change and people's lifestyle change, which changes e-learning environment. E-learning is no longer a simple process of information transfer; e-learners are empowered by Web 2.0 technologies to form strong social bounding to enhance their learning experiences. Section II will discuss the educational efficacy of podcasting when used as a content delivery channel, addressing specific e-learning challenges by providing flexible learning and to enhance student learning experiences. Section III will present podcasting best practices in e-learning design and delivery based on the research data collected during five consecutive research studies on content analysis, selection of best podcasting delivery format, providing students with clear instructions and effective integration of activities in combination with podcasting delivery to improve learning quality.

A DYNAMIC E-LEARNING ENVIRONMENT

Technology Change

The emergence of Web 2.0 is not just a technical revolution: it is also a social revolution (Downes, 2006), and – in addition to its role as an information channel – Web 2.0 technologies help bring people closer together. And the term Web 2.0 is a misnomer, perhaps it is a cultural phenomenon (it is common in today's society to gauge newer iterations by labeling them "new and improved," or "version 2," etc.; or, a need by modern society to differentiate between newer and legacy versions).

Web 2.0 is really about giving power back to the people and Podcasting is a major component to this end. With Web 2.0 technologies, users really do play an equal role in information sharing and consumption. And podcasting is a great example of just how individuals are leveraging the power of Web 2.0 with legacy technologies in order to promote their respective causes. In the case of education, podcasting is seen as a new tool with which educators can easily share their lecture materials with their students. In reality, it is also a way for students to create and share content with peers and educators alike. Some in academe have begun offering their students the choice of a variety of tangible, electronic formats for submitting their class work. For example, a tenth grader in history class may choose to present her findings in the traditional manner (paper), a digital story, or even a video podcast.

Again, perhaps the greatest contribution of Web 2.0 is that it empowers all users of the Web to be equal participants (contributors, consumers, critical reviews, etc.) in online communities. A unique but necessary byproduct of this level playing field is that it changes the relationships we have with those we interact with online. We are able to share files, keep track of our friends, and provide original content (such as videos on YouTube) to the masses. This relationship-changing technology is responsible for modifying our behavior with others online by changing our own perceptions of the Web as a viable channel for sharing information. Ultimately, where once we were very passive in the way we behave when online, we are no longer submissive – rather, we celebrate our ability to be more dynamic and outspoken on this global information sharing system.

But for whatever reason, we have identified the World Wide Web of today as version 2.0 of its legacy counterpart, a counterpart that offered very little in the way of dynamic self-expression or an equal voice: Web 2.0 is seen as a major improvement over Web 1.0 because Web 2.0 empowers everyone in society an equal voice. When we think of the early days of the World Wide Web, we recall how powerful it was in terms of content and organization. It was not just an online encyclopedia, but it was an immediate connection with information that would otherwise have been too difficult to track down or locate; it was structured early on as a UNIX directory system, a document storage system, which remains true today. But whether or not you see a difference between Web 1.0 and 2.0, one thing is certainly true: because of increased bandwidth and technology power, using the Web today is very different from what it was just a decade ago.

For example, viewing streaming media on the Web in 1999 was a very different activity than viewing a YouTube video today; and in 1999, you would have needed access to a technologist, a video camera, and a computer that was capable of editing video; you also would have needed bandwidth (in 1999, a majority of folks were still using dial-up and a phone modem to connect, whereas nearly 80% of folks have broadband or better today) (Kaye, 2001). Regardless of how it got this way, Web 2.0 is really all about putting the power of the Internet and World Wide Web into the hands of the people; it is not just a static electronic document delivery system any longer.

While we focus on Web 2.0 in this chapter, it is important to note the Web continues to advance. Some have even labeled the next generation of Web as Web 3.0 or Web Next. But however you identify with the Web of tomorrow, Web 3 can easily be differentiated from legacy versions of the Web by the Virtual Reality capabilities (such as Second Life), among other new technologies.

Another important factor regarding Web 2.0 and Podcasting deal with user perception and identity; many see the advanced versions of Web Technologies as ultra-modern, re-engineering, a new medium altogether. This designation, however, could not be further from the truth: Web 2, Web 3, or Web Next all rely heavily on the legacy technologies of Web 1 (HTML is still alive and doing well). Advanced Web technologies, however, take advantage of new, integrated technologies that might not have been possible a decade ago. Again, these newer technologies are available today because of increased bandwidth, faster processing, and increased RAM (Random Access Memory) in our computing hardware.

Social Change

Technology has become a major pillar of societal change, and the Internet and related technologies help drive this new change. Sclove (1995) claims that technologies qualify as social structures, which can enhance opportunities when appropriately designed. Where once certain characteristics of communication and learning were dependent upon one or more physical constraints or barriers, these constraints are alleviated by our ability to communicate with hypertext and other electronic communication protocols. And it seems as though it is always been this way; that innovation (from the Industrial Revolution to the Internet) is intended to make life simpler, allowing us to live productive lives while finding more time to enjoy the pleasures of each other's company. "This revolution has transformed the conduct of our daily lives, but in somewhat unexpected ways." (Cowan, 1976, p.1)

So it seems as though technological determinism does indeed shape society, in both positive and negative ways. One of the most obvious areas impacted by technology is its effect on socialization and the manner of time that we spend with one another in person, or "real time" as it is now been dubbed. One way of identifying these technological pillars is through various interpretations and definitions. The term, "Social structure" refers to the background features that help define or regulate patterns of human interaction (Sclove, 1995, p. 11).

The computer has become our portal to the rest of the world, and the iPod the ear and/or eyes of the world. Whether that world is the next cubicle over – or on another continent, we now spend so much time online, in front of the computer, which we now chose to stay connected in this comfortable environment. "Apart from materially influencing social experiences, technologies also exert symbolic and other cultural influences. This is true not only of technologies explicitly called communication devices, but of all technologies" (Sclove, 1995, p.15). Kaye and Medoff (2001) recapitulate that we chose this method of communicating because it is more comfortable to communicate online than it sometime is in person. "Technologies qualify as social structures because they function politically and culturally in a manner comparable to these other, more commonly recognized kinds of social structures"(Sclove, 1995, p. 11).

There is also the question of related consequences for too much time spent online: poor posture, weight gain, anti-social behavior, vision problems, Carpal Tunnel Syndrome… the list goes on and one. While there are many benefits to using technology to advance the human agenda and social experience, we cannot ignore the potential risk that comes along with such power (Kaye & Medoff, 2001). Awareness is key here, and making no mistake: technologies enhance learning, and Podcasting is one such technology. But we have a social obligation to our neighbors and to ourselves. These technologies aid in the communication process, help us to reach our students in different (even unique) ways. And there are many opportunities for this type of technology to help us grow and develop. "Technologies also reconfigure opportunities and constraints for psychological development" (Sclove, 1995, p.16). Harnessing the power for good may indeed present other challenges that will be debated for some time to come.

No matter how you see technology's impact on learning and social living constructs, one truth remains: that we are the masters of our own destinies, and that people must come together en masse to decide upon or create standards for living in the online world. Business and Media now force us to adopt new technologies at an unprecedented rate. "Citizens ought to be empowered to participate in shaping their society's basic circumstances and technologies profoundly affect and partly constitute those circumstances, and technological design and practice should be democratized" (Sclove, 1995, p. ix).

One does not need to travel far today before coming across the path of a modern web and Podcast user: telltale signs can easily be seen by counting the number of little white ear bud sets that seem now to have taken over the world. But all kidding aside, we must recognize the incredible innovation and design that has gone into the making of the mobile media device (MMD). When Apple Computer, Inc. released the first iPod in 2000, no one could have predicted just how popular these little devices would become.

By the Fall of 2004, iPods and other MMDs had clearly staked their claim in this modern day, virtual manifest-destiny with the versatility and social collaboration which now includes the ubiquity of information sharing (music and otherwise). Making matters more interesting is the unanticipated uses for MMDs, which have become commonplace; from voice recorder to portable gaming system, the iPod (and now iPhone) has already begun to impact the way in which people communicate and learn. This presents a major challenge to traditional pedagogy as we embrace new expectations brought to campus by our students. "Technology [is] helping to structure social relations and human behavior" (Sclove, 1995, p. 12). This, coupled with new paradigms in teaching and the high number of broadband users in the Houston metropolitan area – now approaching 75% Nationwide, and nearly 90% in Houston – has created several new and exciting opportunities in mobile learning (Pew, 2007).

One of the greatest components of Podcasting is the mobility factor; another is the timeshifting capability. Mobility is important because it allows for the consumption of content wherever the user is geographically, provided that the necessary media or resource has been downloaded to the device for future playback.

Timeshifting is loosely described as cramming 36 hours of social interactivity into a 24-hour period. More carefully defined, Timeshifting can be seen as the practice of coordinating several multi-tasking events simultaneously in order to maximize available time allotments. In other words, we have given the term "timeshifting" to young people today who are masters at sitting in front of the computer with the TV on, Instant Messaging, watching YouTube, updating MySpace, and writing a paper – all at the same time. Taken individually, these tasks would historically be done sequentially. But with Timeshifting, we are able to exercise at the gym on the treadmill while listening to a class lecture. Combining Podcasting with Timeshifting, then, is just one way that students are taking advantage of the incredible e-learning potential that this new channel of delivery can offer.

Lifestyle Change

One often overlooked attribute of Web 2.0 is the centrality concept regarding applications. Today we see a migration of sorts with respect to new applications and the way in which they are delivered/

sold. With increased bandwidth and faster connection speed, more powerful computing power, software developers are anxious to develop and deliver various wares in an online setting. This has many consequences (some wanted, some not), chief among them is the difficulty this presents software piracy. Though it may take some time for users to accept the idea of web-based applications for sensitive data, it is likely that most of the applications we use and are comfortable with today will eventually be dynamically delivered through the web browser. And with new mobile technologies, like Apple's iPhone, software developers are already porting existing applications to web-based delivery for multiple web clients. Given that we are a mobile society, this new connection fits very nicely with the mobile lifestyles that dominate today's users.

Technology advancement and lifestyle change are mutually affecting each other and depending on each other. Technology innovation is happening to meet the needs of people's daily life; at the same time, people's lifestyle drives technology for new innovation. In this case, we complete the circle of Sclove's technology theory that "technology helping to structure social relations and human behavior" and human behaviors validate technology for its usability and modified behaviors push for new technological innovation. "Technologies seem almost daily to make, unmake, and remake our world" (Sclove, 1995, p. ix). Technology broke community and rebuild community in a very different way. In the process of education, because the advent of internet technology, which promotes the distance and e-learning, it brought convenience and flexibility to learners, but the face-to-face interaction and classroom atmosphere were lost in the wire. With new technologies available to us, people started to form new social networks and connections via powerful communication tools, which rebuild the community once lost. Podcasting bring students the experiences similar to face-to-face classroom experiences at a distance without sacrificing the convenience from life.

EDUCATIONAL EFFICACY OF PODCASTING IN E-LEARNING

Podcasting Research Project

Instructional delivery via podcasting technology provides a dynamic and flexible e-learning environment. Students can carry their learning content wherever they go and whenever they need to access. The mobility and timeshifting afforded by podcasting enables learners and instructors to expand the boundaries of the classroom and bring together course content and the world outside the campus (The Regents of the University of Minnesota, 2006). The flexibility of mobile learning can take advantage of the otherwise wasted time that students use to get to classes, regardless of whether they are driving, using a wheelchair, traveling by bus or walking (Ball State University libraries, 2005). Students are using their free time or multi-tasking for learning wherever and whenever they can. The time-rewarding e-learning has been manifested by the data collected in the research projects at the University of Houston for five consecutive semesters from spring of 2006 to spring of 2008.

The University of Houston (hence UH) is located near the downtown area of Houston, which is the fourth largest metropolitan city in the United States. It is a typical large urban commute campus. A majority of students are non-traditional students. They are either employed part-time or full-time. Spring 2008 survey demographic data indicate that more than 50% (N=537) of the surveyed students work over 20 hours a week. About 84% of them commute by car to school. More than 45% of the car-commuters spent over 30 minutes on the road for each single trip. It is not uncommon that the unexpected traffic accidents prevent students from coming to class on time. Besides, UH has limited student parking space. Sometimes, students were waiting in the parking lot for a parking space longer than the time they spent on the road. Time is wasted on the road and in the parking lot. "Provide more podcasts for core courses on missed lectures. This would

Figure 1. Student podcast use and commute distance

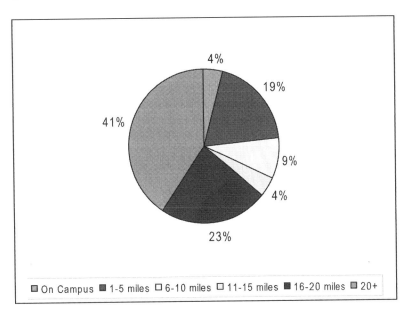

be fantastic in other courses, especially for the thousands of students who have long commutes and children" commented by one student.

The dynamic and flexible learning provided by Podcasting technology is the just-in-time e-learning solution to those issues. One student commented that "I loved having the ability of not carrying so much material whenever I had free time to study." Students who live far away from school are benefiting more from podcasting. *Figure 1* shows that the percentage of students using podcasts rises with the increased distance from where they live. The most valuable feature of podcasting, according to students' report, is to review material at their own pace and at their available time.

From *Figure 1* we can see that there were 23% of students who consumed podcasts during the semester whose travel distance was between 16 to 20 miles. There is a big jump of increase to 41% for the podcast use when students' travel distance was more than 20 miles. The data provide very important information on student need for more flexible and convenient access to learning content to cater to their lifestyle.

Addressing Technical Issues

One of the challenges of e-learning discussed in the article in EDUCAUSE (Vol. 3, 2003), *Supporting E-Learning in Higher Education*, is student technical issue. Due to the discrepancy between teacher's use of technology to deliver e-learning and student's ability to access it, sometimes the e-learning will not achieve expected results. For example, instructor would use the application that students are not familiar with, the large size monitor that students do not have, and high internet connection that students miss, etc. Podcasting technology alleviates most of technical issues of this kind.

Podcasting is not something totally new to students. The audio podcasts use the format of MP3, which is the most popular music format that students are familiar with. Before podcasts became popular, a lot of students were already listening to music on MP3 player, which is the most popular portable device to access podcasts for the students who do not own iPods. Our research data indicate that more than 24% of students used different brand of MP3 players to access course podcasts. Students have increased awareness of podcasts that promote the use of podcasts among students. See *Figure 2* the podcast awareness increases among

Figure 2. Podcast awareness increase among students

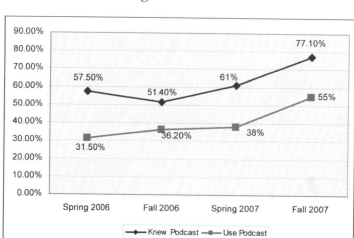

students from spring 2006 to fall 2007.

The data in spring 2006 shows 57.7% (N=161) of surveyed students knew what podcast was and only 31.5% of respondents listened to podcasts before they took the course. In a short period of 3 semesters, the data in fall 2007 show that more than 77% (N=109) of students knew about podcasts and 55% of them listened to podcasts before they took the course. Overall, there is about 20% increase in student awareness of podcast and an increase of 23.5% of podcast use from spring 2006 to fall 2007.

Podcast has three different delivery formats, regular podcast (audio only), enhanced podcast (voice over still images), and vodcast (video podcast). These different formats can assist students' consumption of podcasts with different devices. Our latest data show that Internet connection speed imposed less issue for students to access podcasts since only 1% (Spring 2008, *N*=537) of students use phone line dial-up connection. More than 90% of students reported that they have high-speed internet connection speed. Podcasting used as an e-learning tool is taking advantage of student existing knowledge and resources, which accounts for the fast growth of podcast technology use in education. It is easy to create by faculty and it is simple to consume by students.

Podcasting and Student Learning Styles

Rapid advances in technology are reshaping the learning styles of many students in higher education (Dede, 2005). Geddes (2004) also states that the knowledge acquired through mobile technologies results in behavioral change. Our research data reverberate both of the statements – learning styles and learning habit change. Traditional learning styles have been categorized as auditory, visual and kinesthetic & tactile. Figure 3 shows students self-reported learning styles. Almost half of the students claimed that they are kinesthetic & tactile learners.

Podcasting offers three delivery formats that only cater two learning styles (enhanced podcast and vodcast are grouped into visual): auditory and visual. This big group of tactile learners had to select a different learning format due to podcasting delivery limits.

Figure 4 indicates that a majority of tactile learners selected visual learning, and fewer students changed to auditory learning. The auditory group of students still preferred audio podcasts.

Technology is changing the way students learn. Of course, this is only a simple indication that technology affects student learning style, there are many more other factors, such as social, psychological and physiological, that can cause learning style change. In technology rich environment, "our personal way of selecting can be described as our style" (O'Connor, n. d. para. 2). Student self-selected podcasting learning format provide us with a very vital information, which is visual learners are almost four times as many as auditory learners. "The aim of learning style research is to find out clusters of people who use similar patterns for perceiving and interpreting situation" (O'Connor, n. d. para. 4). Instructors should provide an instructional delivery channel to make learning more efficient. Many students suggested in their comments that more quality video

Figure 3. Student self-reported learning styles

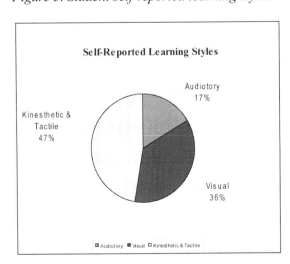

Figure 4. Students self-report preferred podcasting format

podcasts should be made to enhance learning. "The lectures provided through podcasts should include video/still images. It is quite hard to follow along with the professor when there is only audio." "Provide many more videos. The videos for this course were not sufficient to cover all expected chapters," etc. Students learn best when they can address knowledge in the ways that they trust (O'Connor, n. d.).

The research study conducted by Schrum and Hong (2002) identified seven significant dimensions for successful online learners. One of them is study habits and skills. Lackmore (1996) suggested that one of the first things educators can do to aid in the learning process is to simply be aware that there are diverse learning styles in the student population. Podcasting technology can help teachers respond to students' diverse learning styles by creating rich an environment that engages students' visual and auditory senses. The latest generation of iPod is capable of everything; you can listen to audio materials, browse photo slideshows, watch video podcasts, and even TV shows. Gahran (2005) found out from her personal experiences that audio podcasting can improve the learning quality for auditory learners. She

also found out that her retention of the content through listening is better than reading. Our research study also indicates that more than 60% of students perceived that podcasting helped them better retain the course content information.

Addressing Flexible e-Learning and Enhancing Learning Experiences

One of the benefits of e-learning, as summarized by WorldWideLearn, is convenience and portability. Students have full control of location and time to access course content. Students are "unbound by time and place and learning is self-paced" (WorldWideLearn, n. d. para. 3). The best tool to achieve this flexible e-learning is podcasting. One student commented that "I am actually able to access podcasts on my Blackberry and this really helps when I am not able to be at my computer, so if mobile podcast could become available to all the smart phones and Pads, it would definitely prove to be revolutionary for college students." All kind of portable devices capable of podcast playback allows students to carry their learning with them wherever they go, which provides them extra learning opportunity beyond desktop computers.

One of the six learning principles based on cognitive theory outline by Svinicki (1991) is that students continually check understanding, which results in refinement and revision of what is retained. The top reason that students use podcasts is for reviewing class for better understating and retention of knowledge.

Student enjoyment of the course is positively related to their learning attitudes and to their perceived value of the course they take (Patti & Saroja, 2005). iPods and MP3 players are used by students mostly for entertainment, listening to music or watch movies. Spring 2008 data show that about 72% (*N*=537) of students spent less than 5 hours to access course podcasts. Will the entertaining experience transferable to their learning process? More than 50% of students stated that podcast course delivery format made their learning more enjoyable and about 65% of students reported that podcast delivery format enhanced their learning experiences.

PODCAST BEST PRACTICE IN E-LEARNING DESIGN & DELIVERY

Needs Assessment

Conducting a thorough needs assessment is a critical first step in the podcasting process. Needs assessment includes identifying the nature of course content and the portable devices available to students. The assessment of course content will help instructors determine the most appropriate content and format for podcasting delivery, which directly affects the accessibility to the content and overall student learning. Not all the content is suitable for podcasting. However, the materials that are proper for podcasting can be delivered in different podcasting formats. The correct choice of format can optimize the effectiveness of podcasts. So, we need to carefully go through the content, deciding which is best suited for podcasting.

Our research data indicate that students use different types of devices to access podcasts, iPods of different models, and MP3 players by various manufactures; and we see the increased use of mobile phones and PDAs. In spring 2006, only two (N=161) students used mobile phones to access podcasts. Two years later, more than 5% (N=293) of students used mobile phones. Those portable devices are available in a variety of storage capacities and display or playback features. It is important to take full advantage of the devices by considering both length and file size of the podcasts in addition to correct selection of format.

Another possibility is to deliver the same content on all three types of podcasts and let the students determine which type they find most useful based on their devices. From a technology support standpoint, delivery in multiple podcast formats is quite easy (repurposing the content can even be automated) and inexpensive. But more importantly, from the pedagogical point of view, this option provides the most compelling method for making content available to students because it offers the possibility that students will use all three formats at some point and will therefore triple their exposure.

Provide Clear Instructions

Podcasts can be delivered through different venues. You can create a site to upload your podcasts and use RSS to include the descriptions of your podcasts, or you can use Apple's iTunes Store to publish your podcasts. More and more higher educational institutions have signed up with Apple to establish iTunes U accounts to upload content to iTunes U Site. The latest count of iTunes U Site is 79 universities and colleges. iTunes U Site can be set to privately publish your podcasts, which means only your students can access the course podcasts or to publicly publish your podcasts to everyone. Whichever way you prefer to deliver your podcasts, it is very important to provide your students with clear and easy-to-follow instructions on how to locate and subscribe to your podcasts. Five percent of surveyed students (N=537) in spring 2008 reported that they did not use podcasts because the instructions were not clear enough to follow, and they could not get it to work. This group of students never accessed any podcasts before they took the course. Fortunately, the instructors provided alternative delivery formats (streaming, and or voice over PowerPoint) besides podcasting, which is another podcasting best practices – do not use podcasting as the only content delivery format. So, the instructions for those who did not have any prior experiences need to be detailed to every single step. Communication is the key to the success. After podcasts are posted, instructor needs to check with students to see if they have any problems accessing them. The earlier you detect the problem, the sooner the students can benefit from e-learning.

Clearly labeling each podcast to synchronize it with the course content materials or lectures is another important aspect that an instructor needs to pay attention to before upload podcasts. Only use numbering to order podcasts will be very confusing to students. "Make the titles of the podcast much clearer instead of just numbers that doesn't really match the chapters" commented by a student.

Notify students with each new release. Podcast is using RSS feed, which automatically push the newly published podcasts to students after they connect the devices to the computer. Some instructors naturally assume that there is no need to notify students of the new releases. Our data indicate that more than 70% (*N*=322 podcast users, Spring 2008) of respondents would find an email reminder useful whenever a new podcast was available for each course that they were working on. Quite a few students made comments in survey that it would be a very good idea to send email reminder to tell students when new podcasts are released.

Effective Podcasting Delivery

Keep your podcast short, especially a video podcast (Vodcast). For an audio podcast, it should be under 30 minutes, for an enhanced podcast, under 20 minutes, and for Vodcast under 15 minutes. Several issues arise when using long podcasts. It takes longer time to download the content; it takes up more space to store it, and some MP3 players have limited battery power. You need to re-structure the content, and "cut" it to meaningful segments for effective delivery. There are no accurate data indicating how long our memory retention span is, but good design and presentation of the information can improve the development of long-term memory of the material.

Students suggested that making meaningful break points of long podcast for easy review.

"Since some podcasts are longer than others, if they could have a break point, somehow split into chapters, instead of having to listen from the beginning." Besides, the data indicate that more than 71% (*N*=322 podcast users, Spring 2008) of students use less than 5 hours to listen/view course podcasts. Some students had limited storage space on their MP3 players for a full-length lecture podcast. By splitting long podcasts to meaningful segments, students can resourcefully use their storage space to download the podcasts based on their needs, and they will also use their time more efficiently to target on the points for effective learning.

CONCLUSION

As Farkas (2005) notes, with the proliferation and ubiquity of iPods and other digital media players, it is clear that podcasting is here to stay. It is educators' responsibility to use this technology to benefit student learning (McCombs & Liu, 2007). Technology has helped shape the education process since the beginning of time – and will likely continue at an unprecedented rate. This is even more prevalent in e-learning scenarios because we expect and use the technology to provide easy channels of curriculum delivery between our students and us. And Podcasting is a relatively modern phenomenon, invented by accident, which found a home in education and is an inexpensive, additional channel of information sharing that broadens the e-learning horizons by adding new, innovative ways to the teaching toolchest.

Podcasting and technology is a major influence upon the human experience. We know very little today of the effects of modern technology (Internet, iPhone, MMDs, etc.) on humans in terms of physiology and psychology. While there are definitely pros and cons to the ubiquity and prevalence of technology in our daily lives, most of the advances serve to benefit the living experience. To many young people and/or early adopters of technology, Podcasting (and related technologies) represents a new and useful method for Timeshifting, the practice of combining two or more tasks, and working on said tasks simultaneously. This allows humans to multitask, or do more at the same time in order to maximize efficiency and time. While Timeshifting presents some challenges of its own, one can see the incredible opportunities that Podcasting brings to the Timeshifting arena.

As society continues to experience exponential population expansion while governments continue to trim operating budgets and lowering allotments for teaching, Podcasting can be seen as a low-cost method of curriculum delivery that is easy to use, and that most young people today have already embraced. Pew estimates a population spike in August of 2010; we are still experiencing exponential growth, and Podcasting is a powerful, inexpensive tool that can be used in order to meet curriculum needs.

We, as a people, are facing new challenges in the way we teach and our students learn (receive) information. These issues notwithstanding, we need to champion new learning strategies in order to effectively meet the needs of the modern learners. The Pew Internet and American Life Survey, conducted in early 2007, produced telling results about our willingness to adopt new technologies faster than ever before. Putting this in perspective, we can compare mass adoption of other related technologies throughout history. It took Radio 33 years to attain critical mass, the process where 16% of a population adopts a new communication channel. It took 11 years for Television. The Internet attained critical mass in only five years, and Podcasting became an overnight success story. In November of 2004, there were less than 50 available podcasts for download. It did not take long for Podcasting to catch on either: By 2007, Podcasting had surpassed TV and Internet as being the quickest attainers of critical mass. "Podcasting"-type technologies are just now being realized and invented. With podcasting technology available now, learning will happen whenever and wherever learners are. Education evolves around the students instead of students evolving around the teachers (McCombs & Liu, 2007). The revolution is under way, and it is gaining steam (Farkas, 2005).

REFERENCES

Cowan, R. S. (1976). Industrial revolution in the home: Household technology and social change in the 20th century. *Technology and Culture, 17*(1), 1–23. doi:10.2307/3103251

Dede, C. (2005). Planning for neo-millennial learning styles. *EDUCAUSE Quarterly*, (1): 8–12.

Downes, P. (2006). *E-learning 2.0.* Retrieved May 5, 2008, from http://www.elearnmag.org/subpage.cfm?section=articles&article=29-1

Farkas, B. (2006). *What is podcasting? In secretes of podcasting: Audio blogging for the masses.* Berkley, CA: Peachpit Press.

Geddes, S. J. (2004). Mobile learning in the 21st century: Benefit for learners. *The Knowledge Tree: An ejournal of flexible learning in VET*, (6).

Kaye, B., & Medoff, N. (2001). *The World Wide Web: A mass communication perspective.* Mountain View, CA: McGraw-Hill/Mayfield Publishing Company

McCombs, S., & Liu, Y. (2007). Podcasting in education – learning on the go. In T. Kidd & H. Song (Eds.), *Handbook of research on instructional systems and technology.* Hershey, PA: IGI Global.

O'Connor, T. (n. d.). *Using learning styles to adapt technology for higher education.* Retrieved August 28, 2008, from http://iod.unh.edu/EE/articles/learning-styles.html

PewInternet & American Life – 2007 survey. (n.d.). Retrieved May 20, 2008, from http://www.pewinternet.org/pdfs/PIP_Teens_Social_Media_Final.pdf

Sclove, R. E. (1995). *Democracy and technology.* New York: Guilford Press.

Svinicki, M. D. (1991). Practical implications of cognitive theories. In R. Mengis & M. Savinki, (Eds.), *College teaching: From theory to practice.* San Francisco: Jossey Bass.

WorldWideLearn. (n.d.). *New dimension of education - benefits of e-learning.* Retrieved August 25, 2008, from http://www.worldwidelearn.com/e-learning-essentials/e-learning-benefits.htm

Chapter 16
Using Social Networking to Enhance Sense of Community in E-Learning Courses

Steve Chi-Yin Yuen
The University of Southern Mississippi, USA

Harrison Hao Yang
State University of New York at Oswego, USA

ABSTRACT

This chapter provides an overview and development of sense of community and social networking; discusses the potential uses of social networking in education; and presents a case study that integrates social networking into two graduate courses for the purpose of building a sense of community, improving communications and interactions, and promoting student-centered collaboration. The construction of class social networking sites, the implementation of these networks, and their effects on the students' learning experience are examined. In addition, an analysis of feedback from students on the value of social networking in learning is included.

INTRODUCTION

The rapid technological change and proliferation of information resources are lineaments of our contemporary society. Online information and communication are changing the way instructors and learners interact within the teaching/learning process. Online teaching and learning represents a new educational paradigm. The "anytime, anywhere" accessibility of e-learning courses provide students and teachers the opportunities to work at

their own pace and at locations they are able to control (Berge, 1995; Edelson, 1998; Spiceland & Hawkins, 2002). Furthermore, as Richardson and Swan (2003) indicated, "[e-learning] allows students to reflect upon the materials and their responses before responding, unlike traditional classrooms" (p. 69). Currently, there are two main types of e-learning applications within higher education courses: (a) fully online applications in which teaching and learning activities take place entirely at an online computer-mediated communication (CMC) setting; (b) hybrid applications in which

DOI: 10.4018/978-1-60566-729-4.ch016

Copyright © 2010, IGI Global. Copying or distributing in print or electronic forms without written permission of IGI Global is prohibited.

both traditional classroom instruction and online CMC are blended (Yang & Liu, 2008). In either online or hybrid applications, online learning content is typically provided by courseware authors/instructors, structured into courses by a learning management system (LMS), and consumed by students. This approach is often driven by the needs of the institution/corporation rather than the individual learner.

While online and hybrid courses are expanding and the numbers of participants are increasing, questions are being raised on conventional LMS based e-learning. For example, researchers are asking how best to foster community among learners and their instructors who are physically separated from each other, as well as separated in time (Palloff & Pratt, 1999; Rovai, 2002a, 2002b). Such separation may increase social insecurities, communication anxieties, and feelings of disconnectedness (Jonassen, 2000; Kerka, 1996). As a result of such separations, Sherry (1996) stated that "the student becomes autonomous and isolated, procrastinates, and eventually drops out" (¶ 27). Previous studies suggest that a sense of community, which is related to connectedness and learning, is essential for an e-learning course to occur (Yang & Liu, 2008).

With the emerging Web 2.0 technologies, more opportunities and possibilities to enhance existing e-learning courses are provided. For instance, social networks are collections of Web 2.0 technologies combined in a way that help build online communities. Social networking sites are on the rise globally and are developing rapidly as technology changes with new mobile dimensions and features. These sites are changing the ways people use and engage each other utilizing the Internet (Childnet International, 2008). Today's technology enhanced students have shown growing interest in social networking sites because of the community, the content, and the activities in which they can engage in the sites. Students can share their profile information, find out what their

peers think about topics of interest, share music and playlists, and exchange messages with friends. Students use social networking sites to connect daily or even hourly for social as well as educational activities. They get to know their classmates through Facebook and share their lives with others on MySpace. Students use other social networking sites like RateMyProfessors and PickAProfessor to learn about their professors and choose their classes. In addition, they share their photos on Flickr and their videos on YouTube (The New Media Consortium, 2008).

Social networking sites are changing the social fabric of colleges and universities. In its fifth study of undergraduate students and information technology, the EDUCAUSE Center for Applied Research (ECAR) investigated the use of technology by undergraduate students in American colleges and universities. The *ECAR Study of Undergraduate Students and Information Technology, 2008* analyzed the Web-based survey responses of over 27,000 freshmen and seniors at 90 four-year institutions and eight two-year institutions, as well as findings from focus group discussions. The key findings of the Social Networking Sites section of the study included:

- Over 85 percent of respondents reported using social networking sites. The striking change over the last two years was in how many respondents now use social networking sites on a daily basis, from 32.8 percent in 2006 to 58.8 percent in 2008.
- Facebook was the most commonly used social networking site (SNS) (89.3% of SNS users), with MySpace as the second choice (48.3% of SNS users). Traditional college-age respondents (18 to 24 years old) used Facebook more than MySpace. However, older respondents used MySpace more than Facebook.
- Over 55 percent of SNS users spent 5 hours or less per week on SNSs, and about

27 percent spent 6 to 10 hours per week. Younger respondents reported spending more time than older respondents.

- Half of SNS users used social networking sites to communicate with classmates about course-related topics, but only less than 6 percent of them used social networking sites to communicate with instructors about course-related topics (Educause Center for Applied Research, 2008).

Social networking is already second nature to many students. Social networking sites not only attract students but also hold their attention, impel them to contribute, and bring them back time and again. Because of students' tremendous interest in social networking, many educational institutions are now evaluating existing social networking tools and even developing new ones, experimenting with social networking tools to support learning, and examining the effects of social networking in education (Educause Center for Applied Research, 2008; The New Media Consortium, 2008). Consequently, educators are beginning to recognize the popularity of social networking, to understand the importance and appeal of social networking among young people, and to explore the possibility of using social networking to enhance the sense of community in e-learning courses. This chapter provides an overview and development of sense of community and social networking. It then discusses the potential uses of social networking in education, and presents a case study that integrated social networking into two graduate courses for the purpose of building a sense of community, improving communications and interactions, and promoting student-centered collaboration. The construction of class social networks, the implementation of these networks, and their effects on the students' learning experience are examined. Also, an analysis of feedback from students on the value of social networking in learning is included.

DEVELOPMENT OF SENSE OF COMMUNITY AND SOCIAL NETWORKING

Sense of Community

The early research concerning community can be traced back over 30 years (Sarason, 1974). Sarason (1974) defined psychological sense of community as "the perception of similarity to others, an acknowledged interdependence with others, a willingness to maintain this interdependence by giving to or doing for others what one expects from them, and the feeling that one is part of a larger dependable and stable structure" (p. 157). Since then there have been various studies that attempt to describe and measure the sense of community (Buckner, 1988; Chavis, Hogge, McMillan, & Wandersman, 1986; Davidson & Cotter, 1986; Doolittle & MacDonald, 1978; Glynn, 1981; McMillan & Chavis, 1986; Pretty, 1990). The most influential and frequently quoted study is probably McMillan and Chavis (1986), who defined the concept as "a feeling that members have of belonging, a feeling that members matter to one another and to the group, and a shared faith that members' needs will be met through their commitment to be together" (p. 9). They proposed that a sense of community was composed of four elements: (a) membership; (b) influence; (c) integration and fulfillment of needs; and (d) shared emotional connection. The dynamics among these four elements were demonstrated by McMillan and Chavis in the following example:

Someone puts an announcement on the dormitory bulletin board about the formation of an intramural dormitory basketball team. People attend the organizational meeting as strangers out of their individual needs (integration and fulfillment of needs). The team is bound by place of residence (membership boundaries are set) and spends time together in practice (the contact hypothesis). They play a game and win (successful shared valued event). While playing, members exert energy on behalf of the team (personal investment in the group). As the team continues to win, team members become recognized and congratulated (gaining honor and status for being members). Someone suggests that they all buy matching shirts and shoes (common symbols) and they do so (influence). (McMillan and Chavis, 1986, p. 16)

McMillan and Chavis's view of sense of community has been well supported and documented (Yang & Liu, 2008). Previous research studies indicated that spirit, trust, sense of belonging, interactivity, common goals, shared values and beliefs, and common expectations were the most essential elements of community (McMillan, 1996; Rovai, 2002a; Royal & Rossi, 1997; Shaffer & Anundsen, 1993; Strike, 2004). Rheingold (1991) and Hill (1996) suggested that the sense of community differed from setting to setting. Rovai (2002a) noted, "one such setting is the classroom where learning is the goal" (p. 201). Tebben (1995) found that student satisfaction and success were mainly attributed to the caring attitude of the instructor and the supportive environment created by classmates. McKinney, McKinney, Franiuk, and Schweitzer (2006) investigated the sense of community in a college classroom and found that six variables could significantly predict students' classroom attitudes, perception of learning, and actual performance on course exams: connection, participation, safety, support, belonging, and empowerment.

Wighting (2006) found that using computers in the classroom positively affected students' senses of learning in a community, and that students believed the connectedness with their peers was the most important variable in developing a sense of community. Bellah, Madsen, Sullivan, Swidler, and Tipton (1985), Rheingold (1991), and Wellman (1999) pointed out that the communities most important to people might not be defined within a geographical sense but instead consisted of groups of people who had common interests and may never physically meet each other. Accordingly, as Rovai (2001) noted, "community can be examined in virtual learning environments used by distance education programs" (p. 34). Studies on online environments have indicated that the sense of community could be created and supported through various interactive electronic media (Baym, 1995; Dede, 1996; Reid, 1995; Rheingold, 1993). Rovai (2001) explored the community of students in an asynchronous learning network course and found that the sense of classroom community grew significantly during the course in terms of spirit, trust, interaction, and learning. Rovai (2002a) refined the Classroom Community Scale focusing on: (a) connectedness, which represented the feelings of students regarding their cohesion, community spirit, trust, and interdependence; and (b) learning, which represented the feelings of community members regarding the degree to which they shared educational goals and experienced educational benefits by interacting with other members of the course.

Using the Classroom Community Scale, Rovai and Jordan (2004) examined the relationship of sense of community among traditional classroom, blended/hybrid, and fully online higher education learning environments, and found that blended courses produced a stronger sense of community among students than in either traditional or fully online courses. However, a large body of literature was somewhat limited in that it only assessed and reported the sense of community in CMC environments. Wilson (2001) pointed out that this type of research could be a useful component in tracking and assessing group cohesiveness, "while a reported sense of community does not itself establish effective community" (¶ 15). Rovai (2002a) argued:

Proper attention must be given to community building in distance education programs because it is a "sense of community" that attracts and retains learners. Educators who perceive the value of community must conceptualize how sense of community can be nurtured in distant learning environments. (p. 199)

Accordingly, there are a growing number of research studies on the sense of community through a complex interplay of social, instructional, and technological variables. Yang and Liu (2008) found that sense of community could be enhanced among students in e-learning courses through pedagogical, social, managerial, and technical functions.

Social Networks

Social networks are a social structure of nodes (individuals or organizations) and the relationships between the members. Social networks are usually built based on the strength of relationships and trust between the members (Liccardi, Ounnas, Pau, Massey, Kinnumen, Lewthwaite, Midy, and Sakar, 2007). Boyd and Ellison (2007) define social network sites as Web-based services that allow individuals to: (a) construct a public or semi-public profile within a bounded system, (b) articulate other users with whom they share a connection, and (c) view and traverse their list of connections and those made by others within the system. Social networking is when individuals or organizations are tied together through a similar objective or interest. There are many ways to participate in a social network. The most common is through the Web-based social network services that provide a variety of ways for users to interact, such as chat, messaging, email, video, voice chat, file sharing, blogging, discussion groups, and so on. Social networking sites focus on building online communities of people who share interests and activities, or who are interested in exploring the interests and activities of others (Wikipedia, 2008). Social networking sites allow users to create, develop, and manage their online presence.

Social networking sites have created powerful new ways to communicate and share information.

Social networking sites are being used regularly by millions of people; and they keep people connected through a fast, free, simple, and an accessible way. Social networking sites play a role in social life, business, health care, and charity. People from all walks of life participate in social networking. Social networking sites are used not only for people to communicate on a local and global scale, but also to advertise their products and services, to network other business and industry professionals (e.g., LinkedIn), to highlight individual physicians and institutions in the medical field, to connect with other patients dealing with similar issues and research patient data related to their condition (e.g., PatientsLikeMe), to locate pedophiles by many police investigations/trials using MySpace and Facebook pages as evidence, and to locate college students participating in illegal activities. Businesses and entrepreneurs have joined the young adults who connect through social networking sites. Also, companies use the sites to communicate with customers, promote themselves, recruit employees and conduct market research. (Wikipedia, 2008).

Childnet International (2008) reviewed the current range of social networking services available and grouped the social networking services into two main formats: sites that are primarily organized around users' profiles, and those that are organized around collections of content. In addition, social networking sites are classified into 6 categories: (a) Profile-based services (e.g., Bebo, Facebook, MySpace); (b) Content-focused services (e.g., Flickr, YouTube); (c) White-label networks (e.g., PeopleAggregator, Ning); (d) Multi-User Virtual Environments (e.g., Second Life, World of Warcraft); (e) Mobile services (e.g., Twitter); and (f) Microblogging/Presence update services (e.g., Jaiku, Twitter). Young people use social networking sites for various activities: (a) communicate with their contacts and develop friendships, (b) create and develop an online presence, (c) search information, (d) create and customize personal profiles to show their online identities, (e) create and upload their own digital media content, (f) add and share third-party content on their pages, (g) post public and private messages through message boards or internal email, and (h) collaborate with other users (Childnet International, 2008).

In the United Kingdom (U.K.), Ofcom's *International Communications Market 2007* report indicated that more adults use social networking sites than in any other of the European countries included in the survey (Childnet International, 2008). Also, a report published by ComScore (2007) revealed the European social networking community stood at 127.3 million unique visitors in August 2007 – reaching 56 percent of the European online population. The usage of social networking sites in the U.K. were heavier than the European average in terms of hours spent, pages viewed, and the number of visits per month. The average visitor to social networking sites in the U.K. spent 5.8 hours per month on those sites and made 23.3 visits. Ofcom reported that 39% of all U.K. Internet users use social networking sites, while the ComScore figures show 24.9 million individual social networking site visitors in August 2007 (Childnet International, 2008; ComScore, 2007). The most popular dedicated social networking sites in the U.K. and Europe are Bebo, Facebook Hi5, MySpace, Tagged, and Xing (Childnet International, 2008; Wikipedia, 2008). MySpace and Facebook are the most widely used in North America; Friendster, Orkut, Xiaonei and Cyword in Asia while Orkut and Hi5 in South America and Central America (Wikipedia, 2008).

Social networking sites such as Bebo, Facebook and MySpace facilitate informal communications and information sharing across the Internet. Many social networking sites target teenagers and young adults. Most of the social networking sites have a minimum membership age of 13 or 14, and may explicitly state that they are designed for individual 18 years or older. Services aimed at younger children typically have stricter privacy settings, greater levels of moderation

and more limited user interactions. Some even require parental permissions for signing up and setting communication preferences (Childnet International, 2008). A research study by the Pew Internet and American Life Project (2007) indicates that 55% of teens between the ages of 12-17 use social networking sites. According to the study, older female teens use sites, such as Facebook and MySpace, primarily to reinforce pre-existing friendships, while male teens use them to flirt and create new friendships.

SOCIAL NETWORKING IN E-LEARNING

Digital Natives and Social Networking

According to Wolfe (2008), the worldwide generation Y population is nearly 2 billion strong and outnumbers the baby boomers, the previously largest generation. Generation Y is also known as boomlets, echo boomers, millennials, or net generation. Generation Y is born after 1980 and some of the older millennials already graduated and entered the workforce. Prensky (2001a) described the generation Y as digital natives and their predecessors as digital immigrants. Digital natives have been reared with technology, and most have had the Internet at their disposal during their younger years. So, this generation of digital natives is unique in that it is the first to grow up with digital and Web technologies and have had online and digital media access all their lives. They have made websites like YouTube and Facebook a massive phenomenon. Social networking sites like Facebook and MySpace are the backbone of their relationships with friends and family. Digital natives are comfortable with technology and the idea of sharing information via the Internet. By age 21, digital natives will have spent 10,000 hours on a cell phone, 10,000 hours playing video games, sent 200,000 emails, watched 20,000 hours of television, watched over 500,000 TV commercials, but spent less than 5,000 hours reading (Prensky, 2001b). Computer games, email, cell phones, mp3, flickr, Facebook, YouTube, and the Internet are integral parts of their lives.

As digital natives raised in an age of media saturation and convenient access to digital technologies, they have distinctive ways of thinking, communicating, and learning. Digital natives are highly connected, increasing mobile, interactive, and electronically social. They are visually-oriented, technologically savvy, and they see technology as an essential part of their lives. In addition, digital natives rely heavily on communications technologies to access information and to carry out social and professional interactions. They prefer multi-tasking and quick, non-linear access to information. Although they value education highly, digital natives learn differently from their predecessors. Digital natives prefer active learning rather than passive learning and have a low tolerance for lectures (Prensky 2001a, 2001b; Oblinger, 2003).

Social networking is deeply embedded in the lifestyles of digital natives. One of the popular technology tools the digital natives use to interact with others outside of school is the social networking sites such as Facebook and MySpace. Results of a 2007 national study conducted by the Pew Internet and American Life Project show that 55% all online American youths between the ages of 12 and 17 use social networking sites for communication. Forty eight percent of teens visit social networking sites daily or more often. Furthermore, 91% of all social networking teens say they use the sites to stay in touch with friends they see frequently, while 82% use the sites to stay in touch with friends they rarely see in person (Pew Internet & American Life Project, 2007).

The Office of Communications (2008) report, *Social networking: A quantitative and qualitative research report into attitudes, behaviours and us,* draws on numerous qualitative and quantitative research studies conducted in U.K. in 2007. The

key findings of the report include:

- Social networking sites are most popular with teenagers and young adults.
- The average adult social networking users have profiles on 1.6 sites, and most users check their profile at least every other day.
- Two-thirds of parents claim to set rules about their child's use of social networking sites, although only 53% of children said that their parents set such rules.
- Social networking users fall into five distinct groups based on their behaviors and attitudes: a) Alpha socialisers, b) Attention seekers, c) Followers, d) Faithfuls, and e) Functionals.
- Non-users of social networking sites fall into three distinct groups: a) Concerned about safety, b) Technically inexperienced, and c) Intellectual rejecters.
- Only a few users highlighted negative aspects of social networking.
- Seventeen percent of adults used their profile to communicate with people they do not know. This increases among younger adults. Thirty-five percent of adults spoke to people who were 'friends of friends'.
- Facebook is the most popular site with adults followed by MySpace and then Bebo. For children aged between 8 and 17, Bebo was the most used social networking site.
- Some teenagers and adults in their early twenties reported feeling 'addicted' to social networking sites and were aware that their use was squeezing their study time.

Another study, *Creating and connecting: Research and guidelines on online social- and educational-networking,* conducted by the National School Boards Association (NSBA) indicates that American children are spending almost as much time using social networking sites as they spend watching television – around nine hours online, compared with 10 hours of TV. The report is based on online surveys of approximately 1,300 American children from 9 to 17 years old and over 1,000 parents. Additionally, telephone interviews were conducted with more than 250 school district officials. The findings of the study indicate that 96% of students with Internet access engage in social networking. Almost 60% of students said they use the social networking tools to discuss classes, learning outside school, and planning for college. Students also reported using chatting, text messaging, blogging, and online communities such as Facebook and MySpace for educational activities, including collaboration on school projects (National School Boards Association, 2007).

Digital native students are the most avid users of social networking sites, but older students are joining the social networking users ranks as well. Students typically join one or two social networking sites and do not change their profile often. They use social networking sites to keep in touch with their friends – most of whom they have already met in person – and to communicate with their classmates. These digital natives are not very concerned about privacy and security issues (Educause Center for Applied Research, 2008).

Social Networking for Teaching and Learning

Social networking has great potentials in education and will likely impact the teaching and learning process. The *2007 Horizon Report* described six areas of emerging technologies that will have significant impact on college and university campuses within three adoption horizons over the next one to five years. These areas are presented in priority order: (a) user-created content, (b) social networking, (c) mobile phones, (d) virtual worlds, (e) the new scholarship and emerging forms of publication, and (f) massively multiplayer educational gaming. The report further suggested that user-created content and social networking are the nearest adoption horizon. Social networking

is already a fact of life on campuses across the world and examples are readily available. Social networking may be an important way to increase student access to and participation in educational activities (The New Media Consortium, 2007). Also, social operating systems are identified as one of six emerging technologies as likely being of increasing relevance to educators in the *2008 Horizon Report*. The time-to-adoption horizon of social operating systems is four to five years (The New Media Consortium, 2007). According to the *2008 Horizon Report*,

The essential ingredient of next generation social networking, social operating systems, is that they will base the organization of the network around people, rather than around content. This simple conceptual shift promises profound implications for the academy and for the ways in which we think about knowledge and learning. Social operating systems will support whole new categories of applications that weave through the implicit connections and clues we leave everywhere as we go about our lives, and use them to organize our work and our thinking around the people we know. (The New Media Consortium, 2008, p. 4)

Many of today's learners use technology primarily for social networking, and they are quite familiar with using social networking sites (JISC, 2007). Social networking sites have the capability to deliver a platform for learning where the student is potentially at the center of activities. (Oradini & Saunders, 2008). Students are far more ready and comfortable using social networking sites than their teachers. Cengage Leaning (2007) conducted a survey of 677 professors teaching at two- and four-year colleges to examine faculty views on social networking sites and new media tools. The survey results revealed that 65% of the respondents are not familiar with social networking sites and those who used social networking sites used them for both personal and work purposes. Nearly 50 percent of faculty respondents who are familiar with social networking sites felt such sites have or will change the way students learn. Furthermore, nearly 90% of respondents who are familiar with social networking sites said they know about sites that allow students to grade or rate professors, and 67% have checked if they have been rated.

In recent years, social networking sites have received significant attention in higher education as increasing numbers of digital native students have made use of public systems such as Facebook and MySpace. Such sites, along with other Web 2.0 tools (e.g. social bookmarking and syndication technologies), help students find information, create work, and share knowledge (Oradini & Saunders, 2008). Many educators and researchers are now developing their own social networking system and exploring the uses of social networking in teaching and learning (e.g., Marsh & Panckhurst, 2007; Oradini & Saunders, 2008). According to Oradini and Saunders (2008), several universities in the U.K. have recently experimented with the provision of institutionally owned social networking (e.g. the University of Brighton's Community System, University of Westminister) or blogging systems (e.g. the University of Leeds). Marsh & Panckhurst (2007) conducted a pilot study to explore the opportunities for a more flexible learner-centered approach through the provision of an online social network. They set up a private community eLEN (eLearning Exchange Network) using Ning (www.ning.com) to provide virtual space with a social network environment. Two groups of graduate students from France and the U.K. were invited into the eLEN. Their study showed that collaborative learning could take place in a social network. Their social network (eLEN) gave the students a sense of belonging, a sense of freedom, and a sense of pedagogical innovation. Also, the social network provided a learning community for knowledge sharing.

Childnet International (2008) offers many ideas for school administrators to explore the use of social networking sites in education. Educators may use social networking sites for delivering staff development and digital literacy; providing information about a school, college, or organization; supporting e-learning; and developing ICT provision planning and personal learning environment planning. Also, there are many potential educational benefits to students using social networking sites: (a) allowing learners as social participants and active citizens to discuss issues and causes that affect and interest them; (b) developing a voice and building trust in a community; (c) allowing students to become content creators, managers, and distributors of their work; (d) supporting students to work, think, and act together as collaborators and team players; (e) encouraging discovery learning and helping students develop their interests and find other people who share their interests; (f) becoming independent and building resilience; and (g) developing key and real-world skills (Childnet International, 2008).

Social networking offers many potential uses in education. Social networking can be used in education for: (a) providing a casual place of learning; (b) developing literacy and communication skills; (c) providing effective communication and collaboration; (d) enhancing students' learning experiences; (e) building an online learning community; (f) offering immersion in a foreign language environment; (g) developing e-portfolios; (h) learning about data protection and copyright issues; (i) learning about self-representation and presentation; (j) learning about e-safety issues; (k) producing public showcases for work, events, or organizations; (l) forming communities of practice; (m) organizing and scheduling educational timetables; and (n) being where learners are (Childnet International, 2008).

While social networking shows great potentials for e-learning in general, little is yet known about how to integrate social networking focusing on building a sense of community, particularly in e-learning courses. As Wilson (2001) suggested, "[w]e need continuing development and publishing of specific teaching models and frameworks that can be studied and shared through research—

the profession thus emulates the community behaviors we are talking about" (¶ 14).

CASE STUDY: INTEGRATING SOCIAL NETWORKING IN E-LEARNING COURSES

To obtain specific information about the process of the social network instructional approach and participants' perceptions on the use of social networking on the sense of community in e-learning, two courses in a blended learning or hybrid format were selected for this study. It should be noted that the participants were selected by the way of convenience sampling since one of the researchers for this study was the instructor of both courses. Furthermore, the sample size was relatively small. Therefore, instead of any strict inferential attempts, a descriptive research design was utilized in the study. The following questions guided this study:

- How could the researchers design and implement a social networking site for teaching an online or hybrid course?
- How did students feel regarding the use of a social networking site in learning?
- What were the effects of using a social networking site in a course on the sense of community among learners?
- Were there differences in the use of a social networking site and the sense of community among different learners (age and gender)?

Design of Social Networking Sites

A social networking site was created for each course using Ning (www.ning.com). The unique feature of Ning is that anyone can create their own customized social network for a particular topic or need, catering to specific audiences. Also, minimum technical skills are required to set up a social network, and there are no limits to the

Figure 1. The social network main page for Course A

Figure 2. A personal page on a social network

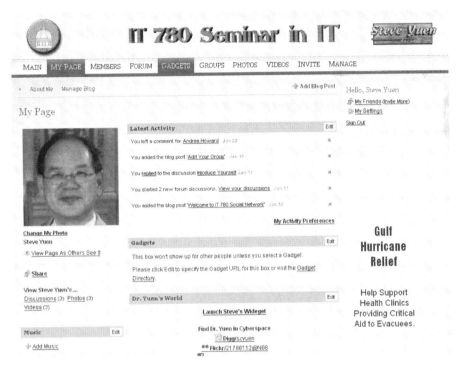

Figure 3. The forum page

Figure 4. The videos page

Figure 5. The social network main page for Course B

number of networks a user can join. Ning has a very good user-friendly interface that allows even novice Web users to create his/her own highly customized social network free of charge. Also, Ning has excellent functionality similar to that of more well-known social networking sites, such as Facebook and MySpace. Various features allow Ning users to read news or learn about related events, join groups, read and comment on blog entries, view photos and videos, and participate in forum activities. Other social network sites such as Facebook, MySpace, etc. were not chosen to use in the study despite the popularity of these social networking sites. Facebook and MySpace tend to be used by many students for personal or social extra-curricula networking tools. It was the belief of the researchers that a personal social networking site created with Ning seemed more appropriate and provided an exclusive and personalized learning environment for the students.

Each site allowed students to create their own profiles; upload photos, audio, podcasts, and videos; create and join discussion groups; send messages; and publish blogs and presentations. Each social networking site was designed for private use. Only class members in each course were invited to join the class social network. No guest or outsider was allowed to join or participate in the social network. Figures 1 to 5 show the main features of a class social network.

Participants

The participants were 30 students enrolled in educational technology classes from two universities during the spring semester in 2008. Specifically, the participants were enrolled in the course *Seminar in Instructional Technology* (Course A) at a state university in the southern region of the United States and the course *IT Management in School* (Course B) at a public university in Hong Kong. Both of these courses were graduate level courses in educational technology and were offered in blended learning or

hybrid format, where approximately one-half of the course learning activities was scheduled in an online environment. Furthermore, the course *Seminar in Instructional Technology* was offered in a regular 15-week semester while the course *IT Management in School* was taught in an intensive 4 weeks format. The majority of participants in both courses were part-time in-service teachers who were pursuing a master's degree or a graduate minor in educational technology. In addition, one of the researchers of this study served as the instructor for both courses.

Implementation

Two social networking sites were designed and tested prior to the beginning of class with each having a similar layout and identical features and components. Both courses were taught by the same instructor/researcher in spring 2008. In the beginning of the semester, social networking concepts and the social networking sites were introduced in the courses. Also, the instructor/ researcher gave a hands-on demonstration on using the social network site and explained how the social network could be used in the course.

Students in each course were invited to join the respective social network. No outside-of-class students nor the general public were allowed to join the class' social network. Each student was required to create a personal profile that included a personal introduction, current status, e-mail address, city of residence, personal Web site, instant messaging accounts, and interests. Also, each student was encouraged to post personal media (digital photos, music, and videos) as well as personal blog, podcasts, and videos related to the course content to the social networking site. Class information such as the course syllabus, schedule, assignments, instructor's blog, the links to the lecture notes and resource materials were provided by the instructor on the social networking site. Bi-weekly class discussions were facilitated by the forum on the social networking site. Each student was required to participate in the class discussions and shared their opinions on the current class topic. In addition, students were encouraged to form groups and initiate and moderate a forum for other personal or class activities. At the end of semester, students in both courses were requested to complete a survey designed by the researchers.

Data Collection and Instrumentation

A questionnaire was developed to evaluate the use of social networking in teaching and learning and assess its effectiveness on the sense of community among learners. The questionnaire consisted of three major parts. Part A consisted of 8 items to collect background information such as age, sex, types of Internet connections, Internet access locations, years of using computers, social network memberships, frequency of access to a social network, and numbers of friends in a social network. Part B consisted of 18 items which were designed to obtain students' feedback regarding the use of a social networking site in teaching and learning. A five-point Likert scale was used for the 18 items, with 4 representing a strong agreement and 0 representing a strong disagreement. In addition, two categorical types of questions regarding the access and profile and one open-end question were included. Part C consisted of a 20 item Classroom Community Scale (CCS) developed by Rovai (2002a). CCS was adopted to measure the sense of community for students on two factors: connectedness and learning. A five-point Likert scale was used for items 1, 2, 3, 6, 7, 11, 13, 15, 16, and 19, with 4 representing strong agreement and 0 representing strong disagreement. A five-point Likert scale was also used for items 4, 5, 8, 9, 10, 12, 14, 17, 18, and 20; but for these items, 0 represented strong agreement and 4 represented strong disagreement. The scores of odd items (1, 3, 5, 7, 9, 11, 13, 15, 17, and 19) were added together for the connectedness

subscale score. The scores of the even items (2, 4, 6, 8, 10, 12, 14, 16, 18, and 20) were added for the learning subscale score. Scores on each subscale ranged from 0 to 40, with higher scores reflecting a stronger sense of classroom community (Rovai & Jordan, 2004).

To ensure the reliability and content validity of the instrument, the questionnaire was sent to a jury of experts to determine the appropriateness and content validity of the Part A and Part B of the questionnaire. Their comments and feedback were used to refine Part A and Part B of the questionnaire. Also, a reliability test was conducted for the 18 items of Part B, and a Cronbach's coefficient α was 0.93 indicating excellent reliability. According to Rovai (2002a), Cronbach's coefficient α for the full Classroom Community Scale was .93 and the equal-length split-half coefficient was .91, indicating excellent reliability. Cronbach's coefficient α and the equal-length split-half coefficient for the connectedness subscale were .92 each, and for the learning subscale were .87 and .80, respectively.

All students from both courses were requested to complete the questionnaire at the end of the spring semester. Thirteen out of 13 students' responses (100%) from Course A, and 17 out of 18 students' responses (94.4%) from Course B were completed and usable.

Findings

This section reports on an analysis of the use of social networking site by participants in two graduate courses at two different universities. Quantitative data was collected via questionnaires in the spring semester of 2008. Table 1 shows the demographic profile of the participants. Seventy-seven percent of participants were between the ages of 25 to 39. Sixty percent of them were female. Ninety-four percent accessed the Internet with high speed connections (cable, DSL, T1 and etc). Almost 90% of the participants had over 7

Table 1. Frequency distributions of demographic variables

Variable	Category	N	Percentage
Age	Under 20	0	0.0
	20-24	1	3.3
	25-30	10	33.3
	31-34	6	20.0
	35-39	7	23.3
	40 and above	6	20.0
Gender	Female	12	40.0
	Male	18	60.0
Internet Connection	High speed (Cable, DSL)	20	66.7
	T1/LAN/WAN	8	26.7
	Other	2	6.6
Internet Access Location	Campus	8	29.6
	Home	9	33.3
	Workplace	10	37.0
Computing Experience	<2 years	1	3.4
	5-7 years	2	6.9
	7+ years	26	89.7
Social Network Member	Bebo	1	3.3
	Classmate	6	20.0
	Facebook	17	56.7
	Friendster	3	10.0
	Linkedin	3	10.0
	Myspace	10	33.3
	Tagged	1	3.3
	Xanga	7	23.3
	Ning	7	23.3
	No social network	5	16.7
Access Social Network	Everyday	8	26.7
	Every week	9	30.0
	Every 2 weeks	4	13.3
	Every month	3	10.0
	Less Frequently	6	20.0
Number of Friends on Social Network	<10	11	36.7
	11-20	3	10.0
	21-30	3	10.0
	31-40	2	6.7
	50+	11	36.7

years of computing experience. The majority of them (57%) had a Facebook account while only 33% used MySpace and 23% had a Xang or Ning account.

Students' Perceptions of the Use of a Social Network

Most students indicated positive and favorable feelings of using a social networking site in both courses. Among the respondents on the Part B of the survey, 100% of them agreed/strongly agreed on items 2, 3, 4, 5, 6, 7, 8, 10, 13, 14, 15, 17, 18, and 19. Ninety-seven percent of the students agreed/strongly agreed on items 9, 11, 12, and 16: "My class social networking site allows me to communicate with classmates about course-

related topics;" "My class social networking site provides collaborative learning opportunities;" "My class social networking site gives me a sense of belonging, and "Social networking can be used for professional development." Ninety percent of the students agreed/strongly agreed on item 1 "I feel comfortable using the class social networking site." In comparison of the two courses, as indicated in Table 2, the mean score on each item in Course A was higher than that in Course B. Furthermore, t-test analysis showed nine significant differences were found between respondents in Course A and Course B on items 2, 3, 3, 7, 8, 10, 13, 18, and 19 ($p<.005$). This indicated the students in Course A felt much stronger about the use of social networking in learning than students from Course B.

In addition to the 19 survey items, participants

Table 2. Means and standard deviations of the class social network items

Item		Course A	
		(n=13)	
		M	SD
1.	I feel comfortable using the class social networking site.	3.08	0.76
2.	My class social networking site allows me to interact and build a learning community.	3.46	0.51
3.	My class social networking site allows me to personalize pages to express individuality and creativity.	3.62	0.51
4.	My class social networking site allows me to pose questions to the community.	3.54	0.52
5.	My class social networking site allows me to share photos, music, and videos.	3.62	0.51
6.	My class social networking site allows me to hold forums to discuss topics of interest.	3.62	0.51
7.	My class social networking site allows me to find and share educational resources.	3.62	0.51
8.	My class social networking site allows me to create study groups.	3.62	0.51
9.	My class social networking site allows me to communicate with classmates about course-related topics.	3.62	0.51
10.	My class social networking site encourages learner-centered activities.	3.46	0.52
11.	My class social networking site provides collaborative learning opportunities.	3.38	0.51
12,	My class social networking site gives me a sense of belonging.	3.08	0.76
13.	My class social networking site promotes knowledge sharing.	3.38	0.51
14.	My class social networking site is user-friendly.	3.54	0.52
15.	Social networking is a great tool for class communications.	3.69	0.48
16.	Social networking can be used for professional development.	3.62	0.51
17.	I will become more actively involved in courses that use social networking.	3.77	0.44
18.	I would like to see more social networking class sites used in other classes.		3.65
	Overall	3.51	0.35

indicated they accessed the class social networking site every day (13.3%), every week (73.3%), or less frequently (13.3%). They changed their profile in the class social networking site daily (3.3%), several times per week (13.3%), monthly (23.3%), or once a semester (60%). Also, all participants (100%) in both courses indicated that their overall experience using the class social networking site were positive or very positive. Furthermore, participants were also encouraged to provide their personal feedback and comments on the survey. Here are their written comments regarding their class social network:

[Student 1 in Course A]

The more I used the class social network – the better I became at it. And we did share information. I enjoyed everything.

[Student 2 in Course A]

It is really a great experience. I like this experience to be communicating with others and this gives me more knowledge about the social networking, so I can set up my own social network.

[Student 3 in Course A]

I enjoyed using the social networking. There was almost never a moment of uncertainty. I could be in touch with anyone from class. Very good! Might very well be the BEST class I've taken! Very helpful and I honestly learned a lot!

[Student 4 in Course A]

This was the first course that incorporated a social network with the activities. The social network encouraged a laid back atmosphere that one could personalize and share with other classmates. It was different from the normal learning environment and I felt more apt to access the site than I would with your typical online course site (WebCT).

[Student 5 in Course A]

The class social networking site was very fun and meaningful. I enjoyed using Ning and creating anything I want. This was truly a remarkable project. I will use Ning continuously.

[Student 6 in Course A]

I had a great experience using the social network and the site is easy to navigate through and user friendly. I enjoyed reading other people's view on different technology issues from reading and writing on different topics under the site. I have gained much knowledge on new technology.

[Student 7 in Course A]

I enjoyed using the site, working with peers using the forum was the most valuable. I wish the social networking site allowed a little more "personality." I would have liked to have a Wordpress plug-in for Ning.

[Student 8 in Course A]

Using a social networking site has helped me stay in touch with friends and classmates. The ability to share ideas with people worldwide is one of the best benefits I have experienced. I believe social networking sites have great potentials for teaching students in K-12 and college and for connecting teachers with each other in professional development.

[Student 1 in Course B]

It is useful to share experiences with classmates and get information from others.

[Student 2 in Course B]

The feeling of the site is rather formal making it less attractive compared with famous sites, like Facebook.

[Student 3 in Course B]

I started my class social networking recently and already loved it because it provides a good platform for students and colleagues to share their experience and post topics for discussion.

[Student 4 in Course B]

I liked using the class social networking site. I thought it was a great way to discuss topics and I could have used even more.

Connectedness

Most of the students indicated positive and favorable feelings of their cohesion, community spirit, trust, and interdependence from both courses. Among the respondents on the connectedness subscale of the CCS, eighty-seven percent of them agreed/strongly agreed on item 3 "I feel connected to others in this course;" approximately 83% of the students agreed/strongly agreed on item 1 and 11: " I feel that students in this course care about each other;" "I trust others in this course;" about 83% disagreed/strongly disagreed on item 9 "I feel isolated in this course;" about 80% agreed/strongly agreed on item 7 " I feel that this course is like a family;" about 77% disagreed/strongly disagreed on item 5 "I do not feel a spirit of community;" about 73% agreed/strongly agreed on item 19 "I feel confident that others will support me, " about 70% agreed/strongly agreed on item 13 "I feel that I rely others in this course;" about 53% disagreed/strongly disagreed on item 17 "I feel uncertain about others in this course." In the comparison of the two courses, as indicated in Table 3, the mean scores on all items in Course A are higher than those items in Course B. The students in Course A felt much stronger in connecting with their classmates than students from Course B.

Most students indicated positive and favorable feelings of community members regarding the degree to which they shared their learning experiences by interacting with other members in both

Table 3. Means and standard deviations of connectedness subscale by courses learning

Item	Course A	Course B	Combined				
	(n=13)	(n=17)	(n=30)				
		M	SD	M	SD	M	SD
1.	I feel that students in this course care about each other.	3.38	0.50	2.82	0.64	3.07	0.64
3.	I feel connected to others in this course.	3.23	0.60	3.06	0.66	3.13	0.63
5.	I do not feel a spirit of community.	3.23	1.01	2.53	0.94	2.83	1.02
7.	I feel that this course is like a family.	3.23	0.83	2.77	0.75	2.97	0.81
9.	I feel isolated in this course.	3.15	0.90	2.83	0.88	2.97	0.89
11.	I trust others in this course.	3.31	0.86	2.88	0.60	3.07	0.74
13.	I feel that I can rely on others in this course.	3.23	0.93	2.59	0.71	2.87	0.86
15.	I feel that members of this course depend on me.	2.23	1.01	1.71	0.84	1.93	0.94
17.	I feel uncertain about others in this course.	3.00	0.71	2.24	0.75	2.57	0.82
19.	I feel confident that others will support me.	3.31	0.63	2.59	0.71	2.90	0.76
	Overall	3.13	0.65	2.60	0.29	2.83	0.54

Table 4. Means and standards deviations of learning subscale by courses

Item	Course A	Course B	Combined				
	(n=13)	(n=17)	(n=30)				
		M	SD	M	SD	M	SD
2.	I feel I am encouraged to ask questions.	3.31	0.48	2.88	0.78	3.07	0.69
4.	I feel that it is hard to get help when I have a question.	3.46	0.66	2.41	1.18	2.87	1.10
6.	I feel that I receive timely feedback.	3.15	0.90	2.65	0.70	2.87	0.82
8.	I feel uneasy exposing gaps in my understanding.	2.92	0.95	2.00	0.94	2.40	1.04
10.	I feel reluctant to speak openly	3.08	0.95	2.18	0.95	2.57	1.04
12.	I feel that this course results in only modest learning.	3.15	0.99	1.59	0.87	2.27	1.20
14.	I feel that other students do not help me learn.	3.08	0.86	2.53	1.00	2.77	0.97
16.	I feel that I am given ample opportunities to learn.	3.38	0.65	2.42	0.71	2.83	0.84
18.	I feel that my educational needs are not being met.	3.23	1.17	2.53	0.87	2.93	1.05
20.	I feel that this course does not promote a desire to learn.	3.61	0.51	2.53	0.80	3.00	0.87
Overall		3.23	0.54	2.37	0.44	2.75	0.65

courses. Among the respondents on the learning subscale of the CCS, eighty-seven percent of them agreed/strongly agreed on items 2 "I feel that I am encouraged to ask questions;" approximately 80% of the students disagreed/strongly disagreed on item 20 "I feel that this course does not promote a desire to learn;" approximately 77% disagreed/ strongly disagreed on item 14 "I feel that other students do not help me learn" approximately 73% disagreed/strongly disagreed on item 4 "I feel that it is hard to get help when I have a question;" approximately 73% agreed/strongly agreed on item 6 "I feel that I receive timely feedback;" approximately 70% disagreed/strongly disagreed on item 18 "I feel that my educational needs are not being met;" about 63% agreed/strongly agreed on item 16 "I feel that I am given ample opportunity to learn;" and approximately 53% disagreed/ strongly disagreed on item 10 "I feel reluctant to speak openly." As indicated in Table 4, the mean scores on all items in Course A are also higher than those items in Course B. The students in Course A felt much stronger about sharing their learning experiences by interacting with other members than students from Course B.

Age and Gender Differences on Social Networking and the Sense of Community

A one-factor analysis of variance was used to investigate the differences in students' age and gender on their social networking experiences as well as their sense of community. The results showed that no significant differences were found in students' age and gender on their social networking experiences as well as their sense of community in terms of connectedness and learning.

DISCUSSION AND CONCLUSION

With the recent advances of Web 2.0 technologies, the role of social software has become increasingly popular in recent years. Social network applications have great potential in education because of their open nature, ease of use, and support for effective collaboration and communication. Today, social networking is very popular and digital natives already found social networking tools integral to daily life. Social networks could be used in education to enhance students' learning experiences. This chapter yields findings of previous research related to sense of community and social networking in the e-learning environment and indicates the social networking approach should be considered, designed and implemented for e-learning courses.

The findings of the case study indicated that the approach of designing and integrating a class social networking site into two courses were fun, worthwhile, and positive. Students in both courses welcomed the opportunity to experience and explore the use of a social network in teaching and learning. They had positive experiences using a social networking site in learning. They found the class social networking site was user-friendly and gave them a sense of belonging. All participants in both courses felt comfortable using the class social networking site, and they felt more actively involved in the courses that use social networking. Participants in both courses felt that social networking is a great tool for class communications and can be used for professional development. They used their class social networking site to pose questions to the community, share digital media, hold forums to discuss topics of interest, share educational resources, create study groups, and communicate with classmates. Furthermore, they indicated the class social networking site can encourage learner-center activities, provide collaborative learning opportunities, and promote knowledge sharing.

The study revealed that using a social networking site in a class could build a sense of community among learners. All items in CCS received moderate high means except item 15 "I feel that I can rely on others in this course." Perhaps, students who rely more on self-regulation have stronger sense of community. It was interesting to note that participants in Course A had more positive and favorable feelings about the use of a social networking site in learning than participants in Course B. Also, participants in Course A had a stronger sense of community in both connectedness and learning than participants in Course B. Although both courses were taught by the same instructor and used a very similar social networking site with identical features, design and layout, Course A and Course B were offered in different countries and in different formats (regular 15 weeks for Course A versus intensive 4 weeks for Course B).

It appeared that the length of time using a social networking site in a class could be an important factor. As compared to participants in Course B, participants in Course A had a much longer time to explore, learn, communicate in a social network and develop a stronger sense of community. Also, it is possible that culture plays a role in social networking since Course A was taught in the United States while Course B was taught in Hong Kong. It appeared that students in the United States in general are more open and more acceptable for online culture and socializing. It is recommended that culture issues be investigated for further research.

REFERENCES

Baym, N. K. (1995). The emergence of community in computer-mediated communication. In S. Jones (Ed.), *CyberSociety: Computer-mediated communication and community* (pp. 138-163). Thousand Oaks, CA: Sage.

Bellah, R., Madsen, R., Sullivan, W., Swidler, A., & Tipton, S. (1985). *Habits of the heart: Individualism and commitment in American life.* New York: Harper & Row.

Berge, Z. L. (1995). Facilitating computer conferencing: Recommendations from the field. *Educational Technology, 35*(1), 22–30.

Boyd, D. M., & Ellison, N. B. (2007). Social network sites: Definition, history, and scholarship. *Journal of Computer-Mediated Communication, 13*(1), 11. http://jcmc.indiana.edu/vol13/issue1/boyd.ellison.html.

Buckner, J. C. (1988). The development of an instrument to measure neighborhood cohesion. *American Journal of Community Psychology*, *16*(6), 771–791. doi:10.1007/BF00930892

Cengage Learning. (2007). *Many college professors see podcasts, blogs and social networking sites as a potential teaching tool.* Retrieved March 1, 2008, from http://www.cengage.com/press/release/20070507.html

Chavis, D., Hogge, J., McMillan, D., & Wandersman, A. (1986). Sense of community through Burnswick's lens: A first look. *Journal of Community Psychology*, *14*(1), 24–40. doi:10.1002/1520-6629(198601)14:1<24::AID-JCOP2290140104>3.0.CO;2-P

Childnet International. (2008). *Young people and social networking services: A Childnet International research report.* Retrieved December 2, 2008, from http://www.digizen.org/downloads/fullReport.pdf

ComScore. (2007). *U.K. social networking site usage highest in Europe* [Press release]. Retrieved December 2, 2008, from http://www.comscore.com/press/release.asp?press=1801

Davidson, W. B., & Cotter, P. R. (1986). Measurement of sense of community within the sphere of city. *Journal of Applied Social Psychology*, *16*(7), 608–619. doi:10.1111/j.1559-1816.1986.tb01162.x

Dede, C. (1996). The evolution of distance education: Emerging technologies and distributed learning. *American Journal of Distance Education*, *10*(2), 4–36.

Doolittle, R., & MacDonald, D. (1978). Communication and a sense of community in metropolitan neighborhood: A factor analytic examination. *Communication Quarterly*, *26*, 2–7.

Edelson, P. J. (1998). *The organization of courses via the Internet, academic aspects, interaction, evaluation, and accreditation.* Educational Resources Information Center, 2-15. U.S. Department of Education, Office of Educational Research and Improvement. (ERIC Document Reproduction Service No. ED422 879)

Educause Center for Applied Research. (2008). *ECAR study of undergraduate students and information technology, 2008.* Retrieved December 1, 2008, from http://www.educause.edu/ir/library/pdf/ers0808/rs/ers0808w.pdf

Glynn, T. (1981). Psychological sense of community: Measurement and application. *Human Relations*, *34*(7), 789–818. doi:10.1177/001872678103400904

Hill, J. L. (1996). Psychological sense of community: Suggestions for future research. *Journal of Community Psychology*, *24*(4), 431–438. doi:10.1002/(SICI)1520-6629(199610)24:4<431::AID-JCOP10>3.0.CO;2-T

JISC. (2007). *Design courses and activities for e-learners.* Retrieved May 6, 2008, from http://www.jisc.ac.uk/media/documents/programmes/elearningpedagogy/guide3_designing_activities.pdf

Jonassen, D. H. (2000). *Computers as mind tools for schools: Engaging critical thinking* (2nd ed.). Upper Saddle River, NJ: Merrill.

Kerka, S. (1996). *Distance learning, the Internet, and the World Wide Web.* (ERIC Document Reproduction Service No. ED 395 214, 1996)

Liccardi, I., Ounnas, A., Pau, R., Massey, E., Kinnumen, P., Lewthwaite, S., et al. (2007). The role of social networks in students' learning experiences. *ACM SIGCSE Bulletin* (December Issue). pp. 224-237.

Marsh, D., & Panckhurst, R. (2007). *eLEN – eLearning Exchange Networks: Reaching out to effective bilingual and multicultural university collaboration.* Retrieved June 10, 2008, from http://www.eadtu.nl/conference-2007/files/CC4.pdf

McKinney, J. P., McKinney, K. G., Franiuk, R., & Schweitzer, J. (2006). The college classroom as a community: Impact on student attitudes and learning. *College Teaching, 54*(3), 281–284. doi:10.3200/CTCH.54.3.281-284

McMillan, D. W. (1996). Sense of community. *Journal of Community Psychology, 24*(4), 315–325. doi:10.1002/(SICI)1520-6629(199610)24:4<315::AID-JCOP2>3.0.CO;2-T

McMillan, D. W., & Chavis, D. M. (1986). Sense of community: A definition and theory. *Journal of Community Psychology, 14*(1), 6–23. doi:10.1002/1520-6629(198601)14:1<6::AID-JCOP2290140103>3.0.CO;2-I

National School Boards Association. (2007). *Creating and connecting: Research and guidelines on online social- and educational-networking.* Alexandria, VA: National School Boards Association.

Oblinger, D. (2003). The name assigned to the document by the author. This field may also contain sub-titles, series names, and report numbers. Boomers, gen-Xers, and millennials: Understanding the new students. *Educause Review, 38*(3), 378-47. Retrieved March 12, 2008 from http://net.educause.edu/ir/library/pdf/ERM0342.pdf

Office of Communications. (2008). *Social networking: A quantitative and qualitative research report into attitudes, behaviours and use.* Retrieved April 13, 2008, from http://www.wwww.radioauthority.org.uk/advice/media_literacy/medlitpub/medlitpubrss/socialnetworking/report.pdf

Oradini, F., & Saunders, G. (2008). *The use of social networking by students and staff in higher education.* Retrieved August 18, 2008, from http://www.eife-l.org/publications/proceedings/ilf08/contributions/improving-quality-of-learning-with-technologies/Oradini_Saunders.pdf

Palloff, R. M., & Pratt, K. (1999). *Building learning communities in cyberspace.* San Francisco: Jossey-Bass Publishers.

Pew Internet & American Life Project. (2007). *Social networking Websites and teens: An overview.* Retrieved September 10, 2007, from http://www.pewinternet.org/pdfs/PIP_SNS_Data_Memo_Jan_2007.pdf

Prensky, M. (2001a, September/October). Digital natives, digital immigrants. *Horizon, 9*(5), 1–6. doi:10.1108/10748120110424816

Prensky, M. (2001b, November/December). Digital natives, digital immigrants, part 2: Do they really think differently? *Horizon, 9*(6), 1–6. doi:10.1108/10748120110424843

Pretty, G. (1990). Relating psychological sense of community to social climate characteristics. *Journal of Community Psychology, 18*(1), 60–65. doi:10.1002/1520-6629(199001)18:1<60::AID-JCOP2290180109>3.0.CO;2-J

Reid, E. (1995). Virtual worlds: Culture and imagination. In S. Jones (Ed.), *CyberSociety: Computer-mediated communication and community* (pp. 164-183). Thousand Oaks: Sage.

Rheingold, H. (1991). *The virtual community.* New York: Summit.

Rheingold, H. (1993). *The virtual community: Homesteading on the electronic frontier.* Reading, MA: Addison-Wesley.

Richardson, J. C., & Swan, K. S. (2003). Examining social presence in online courses in relation to students' perceived learning and satisfaction. *Journal of Asynchronous Learning Networks, 7*(1), 68–88.

Rovai, A., & Jordan, H. (2004). Blended learning and sense of community: A comparative analysis with traditional and fully online graduate courses. *The International Review of Research in Open and Distance Learning, 5*(2). Retrieved August 1, 2007 from http://www.irrodl.org/index.php/irrodl/article/view/192

Rovai, A. P. (2001). Building classroom community at a distance: A case study. *Educational Technology Research and Development, 49*(4), 33–48. doi:10.1007/BF02504946

Rovai, A. P. (2002a). Development of an instrument to measure classroom community. *The Internet and Higher Education, 5*(3), 197–211. doi:10.1016/S1096-7516(02)00102-1

Rovai, A. P. (2002b). A preliminary look at the structural differences of higher education classroom communities in traditional an ALN courses. *Journal of Asynchronous Learning Networks, 6*(1), 41–56.

Royal, M. A., & Rossi, R. J. (1997). *Schools as communities*. Eugene, OR: ERIC Clearinghouse on Educational Management. (ERIC Document Reproduction Service No. ED405641).

Sarason, S. B. (1974). *The psychological sense of community: Prospects for a community psychology*. San Francisco: Jossey-Bass.

Shaffer, C., & Anundsen, K. (1993). *Creating community anywhere*. New York: Perigee.

Sherry, L. (1996). Issues in distance learning. [from http://carbon.cudenver.edu/~lsherry/pubs/issues.html]. *International Journal of Educational Telecommunications, 1*(4), 337–365. Retrieved July 11, 2008.

Spiceland, J. D., & Hawkins, C. P. (2002). The impact on learning of an asynchronous active learning course format. *Journal of Asynchronous Learning Networks, 6*(1), 68–75.

Strike, K. A. (2004). Community, the missing element of school reform: Why schools should be more like congregations than banks. *American Journal of Education, 110*, 215–232. doi:10.1086/383072

Tebben, S. L. (1995). Community and caring in a college classroom. *Journal for a Just and Caring Education, 1*(3), 335–344.

The New Media Consortium. (2007). *The 2007 horizon report*. Retrieved January 12, 2008 from http://www.nmc.org/pdf/2007_Horizon_Report.pdf

The New Media Consortium. (2008). *The 2008 horizon report*. Retrieved November 12, 2008 from http://www.nmc.org/pdf/2008-Horizon-Report.pdf

Wellman, B. (1999). The network community: An introduction to networks in the global village. In B. Wellman (Ed.), *Networks in the global village* (pp. 1-48). Boulder, CO: Westview Press.

Wighting, M. J. (2006). Effects of computer use on high school students' sense of community. *The Journal of Educational Research, 99*(6), 371–379. doi:10.3200/JOER.99.6.371-380

Wikipedia. (n.d.). *Social network services*. Retrieved December 1, 2008 from http://en.wikipedia.org/wiki/Social_networking

Wilson, B. G. (2001, July). *Sense of community as a valued outcome for electronic courses, cohorts, and programs*. Paper presented at the VisionQuest PT3 Conference, Denver, CO. Retrieved July 11, 2008, from http://carbon.cudenver.edu/~bwilson/SenseOfCommunity.html

Wolfe, I. (2008). *Basic survival skills for managing Gen Y*. Retrieved December 1, 2008 from http://www.articlesbase.com/business-articles/basic-survival-skills-for-managing-gen-y-500456.html

Yang, H., & Liu, Y. (2008). Building a sense of community for text-based computer-mediated communication courses. *Journal of Educational Technology Systems, 36*(4), 393–413. doi:10.2190/ET.36.4.d

Compilation of References

A. B. v. State of Indiana, 885 N.E. 2d 1223 (Ind., 2008).

Abel, R. (2007). Innovation, adoption, and learning impact creating the future of IT. *EDUCAUSE Review, 42*(2), 12–30.

Adobe Systems, Inc. (2008). *Flash player penetration.* Retrieved July 12, 2008, from http://www.adobe.com/products/player_census/flashplayer/

Akbulut, Y., & Kiyici, M. (2007). Instructional use of Weblogs. *Turkish Online Journal of Distance Education, 8*(3), 6–15.

Aldrich, C. (2004). *Simulation and the future of learning.* CA: Pfeiffer.

Aldrich, C. (2005). *Learning by doing: A comprehensive guide to simulations, computer games, and pedagogy in e-learning and other educational experiences.* San Francisco: Pfeiffer.

Alessi, S. M., & Trollip, S. R. (2001). *Multimedia for learning: Methods and development* (3rd ed.). Needham Height MA: Allyn and Bacon.

Alexa. (2008). Traffic rankings for MySpace.com. *Alexa.com.* Retrieved April 25, 2008 from http://www.alexa.com/data/details/traffic_details/myspace.com

Alexander, A. L., Brunyé, T., Sidman, J., & Weil. S. A. (2005). *From gaming to training: A review of studies on fidelity, immersion, presence, and buy-in and their effects on transfer in PC-based simulations and Games.* DARWARS Training Impact Group.

Alexander, B. (2006, March/April). Web 2.0: A new wave of innovation for teaching and learning? *EDUCAUSE Review, 41*(2), 32-44. Retrieved July 9, 2007, from http://www.educause.edu/apps/er/erm06/erm0621.asp

Alexander, B. (2008, July/August). Games for education: 2008. *EDUCAUSE Review, 43*(4), 64-65. Retrieved July 10, 2008, from http://www.educause.edu/ir/library/pdf/ERM0849.pdf

Alexander, S. (1999). An evaluation of innovative projects involving communication and information technology in higher education. *Higher Education Research & Development, 18*(2), 173–183. doi:10.1080/0729436990180202

Allen, E. I., & Seaman, J. (2007). *Online nation: Five years of growth in online learning.* Needham, MA: Sloan Consortium. Retrieved from http://sloanconsortium.org/publications/survey/pdf/online_nation.pdf

Allen, I. E., & Seaman, J. (2007). *Online nation: Five years of growth in online learning.* Retrieved August 5, 2008, from http://www.sloan-c.org/publications/survey/pdf/online_nation.pdf

Allen, J. A., Hays, R. T., & Buffordi, L. C. (1986). Maintenance training, simulator fidelity, and individual differences in transfer of training. *Human Factors, 28,* 497–509.

Allen, N. (2008). *Course correction: How digital textbooks are off track and how to set them straight.* Needham, MA: Sloan Consortium. Retrieved November 1, 2008, from http://www.maketextbooksaffordable.org/course_correction.pdf

Copyright © 2010, IGI Global, distributing in print or electronic forms without written permission of IGI Global is prohibited.

Altman, I. (1977). Privacy regulation: Culturally universal or culturally specific? *The Journal of Social Issues, 33*(3), 66–84.

Alvarez, M. (2001). *Second Life and school: The use of virtual worlds in high school education.* Retrieved July 31, 2008, from http://www.trinity.edu/adelwich/worlds/articles/trinity.manny.alvarez.pdf

Anastasi, A. (1965). *Individual differences.* New York: Wiley.

Anderson, P. (2007). What is Web 2.0? Ideas, technologies and implications for education. *JISC Technology and Standards Watch*, 2-64.

Andrews, A. S. (1999). When is a threat "truly" a threat lacking first amendment protection? A proposed true threats test to safeguard free speech rights in the age of the Internet. *The UCLA Online Institute for Cyberspace Law and Policy.* Retrieved on May 19, 2008 from http://www.gseis.ucla.edu/iclp/aandrews2.htm

Andrews, D. H., & Goodson, L. A. (1980). A comparative analysis of models of instructional design. *Journal of Instructional Development, 3*(4), 2–14. doi:10.1007/BF02904348

Assignments, G. Faculty Development Resources: Allen, L., & Winkler, M. (n.d.). *Creating and using social bookmarking in a university library.* Retrieved from http://connect.educause.edu/blog/Carie417/e2006podcastcreatingandus/16719

Associated Press. (2005, July 11). *Arizona school won't use textbooks: Vail's new Empire High to be all-wireless, all-laptop.* Retrieved August 5, 2008, from http://www.msnbc.msn.com/id/8540381/

Associated Press. (2008). Mississippi school district bars teacher-student texting. *Yahoo News.* retrieved August 13, 2008 from http://news.yahoo.com/s/ap/20080721/ap_on_bi_ge/text_ban

Attwell, G. (2006). *Personal learning environments.* Retrieved November 23, 2008, from http://www.knownet.com/writing/weblogs/Graham_Attwell/entries/6521819364

Au, W. J. (2008). *The making of Second Life. Notes from the New World.* New York: HarperCollins Publishers.

Au, W. J. (2008). *The making of Second Life: Notes from the new world.* New York: Collins.

Aucoin, D. (2007). MySpace or the workplace? *Boston Globe.* Retrieved April 25, 2008 from http://www.boston.com/news/globe/living/articles/2007/05/29/myspace_vs_workplace/

Aufderheide, P., & Jaszi, P. (2008). *Recut, reframe, recycle: Quoting copyrighted material in user-generated video.* Washington, DC: Center for Social Media. Retrieved July 19, 2008 from http://www.centerforsocialmedia.org/resources/publications/recut_reframe_recycle

Bach, M. (2003). Critical view on a concept to present learning material using different didactical theories in a learning environment. In *Computers and advanced technology in education.*

Bainbridge, W. S. (2007, July 27). The scientific research potential of virtual worlds. *Science, 317*, 472–476. doi:10.1126/science.1146930

Barab, S. A., Hay, K. E., Barnett, M. G., & Keating, T. (2000). Virtual solar system project: Building understanding through model building. *Journal of Research in Science Teaching, 37*(7), 719–756. doi:10.1002/1098-2736(200009)37:7<719::AID-TEA6>3.0.CO;2-V

Barab, S. A., Thomas, M., Dodge, T., Carteaux, R., & Tuzun, H. (2005). Making learning fun: Quest Atlantis, a game without guns. *Educational Technology Research and Development, 53*(1), 86–107. doi:10.1007/BF02504859

Barnes, C., & Tynan, B. (2007). The adventures of Miranda in the brave new world: Learning in a Web 2.0 millennium. ALT-J. *Research in Learning Technology, 15*(3), 189–200.

Barsky, E., & Purdon, M. (2006). Introducing Web 2.0: Social networking and social bookmarking for health librarians. *Journal of the Canadian Health Libraries Association, 27*(2), 33–34.

Bartle, R. A. (2004). *Designing virtual worlds.* Berkeley, CA: New Riders.

Basham, K. L. (2007). *The effects of 3-dimensional CADD modeling software on the development of the spatial ability of ninth grade technology discovery student.* Unpublished doctoral dissertation, Louisiana State University, USA.

Battista, M. T. (1990). Spatial visualization and gender differences in high school geometry. *Journal for Research in Mathematics Education, 21*(1), 47–60. doi:10.2307/749456

Baum, D. R., Riedel, S., Hays, R. T., & Mirabella, A. (1982). *Training effectiveness as a function of training device fidelity: Current ARI research* (Tech. Rep. 593), Alexandria, VA: US Army Research Institute for the Behavioral and Social Sciences (Defense Technical Information Center No. ADA133104).

Baym, N. K. (1995). The emergence of community in computer-mediated communication. In S. Jones (Ed.), *CyberSociety: Computer-mediated communication and community* (pp. 138-163). Thousand Oaks, CA: Sage.

Beaudoin, M. F. (2006). The impact of distance education on the academy in the digital age. In M. F. Beaudoin (Ed.), *Perspectives on higher education in the digital age* (pp. 1-20). Hauppauge, NY: Nova Science Publishers.

Becker, S. W., & Henriksen, T. K. (2006). *In search of the next generation online learning environment* [white paper]. Ecto, LLC.

Beldarrain, Y. (2006). Distance education trends: Integrating new technologies to foster student interaction and collaboration. *Distance Education, 27*(2), 139–153. doi:10.1080/01587910600789498

Bellah, R., Madsen, R., Sullivan, W., Swidler, A., & Tipton, S. (1985). *Habits of the heart: Individualism and commitment in American life.* New York: Harper & Row.

Berg, J., Berquam, L., & Christoph, K. (2007). Social networking technologies: A "poke" for campus services. *EDUCAUSE Review, 42*(2), 32–44.

Berge, Z. L. (1995). Facilitating computer conferencing: Recommendations from the field. *Educational Technology, 35*(1), 22–30.

Berger, P. (2007). Social bookmarking: Locate, tag and collaborate. *Information Searcher, 17*(3), 3–6.

Blackboard Scholar quick tutorials. (n.d.). Retrieved from http://wiki.scholar.com/display/SCLR/Scholar+Quick+Tutorials

Blackboard Scholar. (n.d.). Retrieved from http://www.scholar.com

Blin, F., & Munro, M. (2008). Why hasn't technology disrupted academics' teaching practices? Understanding resistance to change through the lens of activity theory. *Computers & Education, 50,* 475–490. doi:10.1016/j.compedu.2007.09.017

Boellstorff, T. (2008). *Coming of age in Second Life: An anthropologist explores the virtually human.* Princeton, NJ: Princeton University Press.

Boettcher, J. V. (2008). 'Socializing' the CMS. *Campus Technology, 21*(11), 20–23.

Bonk, C. J., & Graham, C. R. (Eds.). (2006). *The handbook of blended learning: Global perspective, local designs.* San Francisco: Pfeiffer.

Bonk, C. J., & Kim, K. A. (1998). Extending sociocultural theory to adult learning. In M. C. Smith & T. Pourchot (Eds.), *Adult learning and development: Perspectives from educational psychology* (pp. 67-88). Mahwah, NJ: Lawrence Erlbaum Associates.

Bonk, C. J., Lee, M., Kim, N., & Lin, G. (2008, March). *The tensions of transformation in cross-institutional Wikibook projects: Looking back twenty years to today.* Paper presented at the American Educational Research Association 2008 Annual Meeting, New York, NY.

Boulos, M. N. K., Hetherington, L., & Wheeler, S. (2007). Second Life: An overview of the potential of 3-D virtual worlds in medical and health education. *Health Information and Libraries Journal, 24,* 233–245. doi:10.1111/j.1471-1842.2007.00733.x

Boyd, D. (2008). Why youth (heart) social network sites: The role of networked publics in teenage social life. In D. Buckingham (Ed.), *Youth, identity, and digital media*. Cambridge, MA: The MIT Press.

Boyd, D. M., & Ellison, N. B. (2007). Social network sites: Definition, history, and scholarship. *Journal of Computer-Mediated Communication, 13*(1), 11. http://jcmc.indiana.edu/vol13/issue1/boyd.ellison.html.

Bransford, J. D., Sherwood, R. D., Hasselbring, T. S., Kinzer, C. K., & Williams, S. M. (Eds.). (1990). *Anchored instruction: Why we need it and how technology can help*. Hillsdale, NJ: Lawrence Erlbaum.

Breeding, M. (2006). Web 2.0? Let's get to Web 1.0 first. *Computers in Libraries, 26*(5), 30–33.

Brewer, S., & Milam, P. (2006, June). New technologies-like blogs and Wikis-are taking their place in the school media center. *School Library Journal, •••*, 46–50.

Bricken, W. (1990). *Learning in virtual reality* (Memorandum HITL-M-90-5). Seattle, WA: University of Washington, Human Interface Technology Laboratory.

Briggs, L. L. (2008, May 1). Idaho State simulates emergency response in Second Life. *Campus Technology*. Retrieved May 2, 2008, from http://campustechnology.com/articles/61150/

Brown, A. L., & Palincsar, A. S. (1989). Guided, cooperative learning and individual knowledge acquisition. In L. Resnick (Ed.), *Cognition and instruction: Issues and agendas* (pp. 393-451). Hillsdale, NJ: Erlbaum.

Brown, B., & Bell, M. (2006). Play and sociability in there: Some lessons from online games for collaborative virtual environments. In R. Schroeder & A.-S. Axelsson (Eds.), *Avatars at work and play: Collaboration and interaction in shared virtual environments* (pp. 227-246). The Netherlands: Springer.

Brown, J. S. (1989, March 29). Situated cognition---a view of learning [keynote address]. In *Proceedings of the Annual American Education Research Association Conference*, San Francisco, California.

Brown, J. S. (2006, December 1). *Relearning learning—applying the long tail to learning*. Retrieved February 9, 2007, from http://www.mitworld.mit.edu/video/419

Brown, J. S., & Adler, R. P. (2008). Minds on fire: Open education, the long tail, and learning 2.0. *EDUCAUSE Review, 43*(1), 16-32. Retrieved November 1, 2008 from http://connect.educause.edu/Library/EDUCAUSE+Review/MindsonFireOpenEducationt/45823?time=1225579636

Brown, J. S., & Thomas, D. (2006, April). You play World of Warcraft? You're hired! *Wired, 14*(4). Retrieved March 1, 2008, from http://www.wired.com/wired/archive/14.04/learn.html

Brown, J. S., Collins, A., & Duguid, P. (1988). *Cognitive apprenticeship, situated cognition, and social interaction* (Tech. Rep. No. 6886). Bolt, Beranek, and Newman, Inc.

Brown, J. S., Collins, A., & Duguid, P. (1989). Situated cognition and the culture of learning. *Educational Researcher, 18*(1), 32–42.

Bruckman, A. (1996). Finding one's own space in cyberspace. *Technology Review*, (January): 48–54.

Bruckman, A. (1998). Community support for constructionist learning. *Computer Supported Cooperative Work: The Journal of Collaborative Computing, 7*, 47–86. doi:10.1023/A:1008684120893

Bruckman, A., & Resnick, M. (1995). The MediaMOO project: Constructionism and professional community. *Convergence, 1*(1). Retrieved April 10, 2008, from http://www.cc.gatech.edu/~asb/papers/convergence.html

Bruner, J. (1997). *The culture of education* (2nd ed.). Cambridge, MA: Harvard University Press.

Brunstetter, M. R. (1937). *How to use educational sound film*. Chicago, IL: The University of Chicago Press. Retrieved June 11, 2008, from http://www.archive.org/details/howtouseeducatio00brunrich

Bryant, K. J. (1991). Geographical/spatial orientation ability within real-world and simulated large-scale environments. *Multivariate Behavioral Research, 26,* 109–136. doi:10.1207/s15327906mbr2601_6

Buchanan, M. (2002). *Nexus: Small worlds and the groundbreaking science of networks.* New York: W. W. Norton & Company.

Buckner, J. C. (1988). The development of an instrument to measure neighborhood cohesion. *American Journal of Community Psychology, 16*(6), 771–791. doi:10.1007/BF00930892

Bull, G. (2005). Folk taxonomies. *Learning & Leading with Technology, 33*(1), 22–23.

Burbules, N. C., & Callister, T. A. Jr. (2000). Universities in transition: The promise and the challenge of new technologies. *Teachers College Record, 102*(2), 273–295. doi:10.1111/0161-4681.00056

Burgess, J. R. D., & Russell, J. E. A. (2003). The effectiveness of distance learning initiatives in organizations. *Journal of Vocational Behavior, 63,* 289–303. doi:10.1016/S0001-8791(03)00045-9

Buss, A. R., & Poley, W. (1976). *Individual differences: Traits and factors.* New York: Gardner Press.

Byrnside, I. (2008). Six clicks of separation: The legal ramifications of employers using social networking sites to research applicants. *Vanderbilt Journal of Entertainment and Technology Law, 445.*

Cagiltay, K. (2006). Scaffolding strategies in electronic performance support systems: Types and challenges. *Innovations in Education and Teaching International, 43*(1), 93–103. doi:10.1080/14703290500467673

Calongne, C. M. (2008). Educational frontiers: Learning in a virtual world. *EDUCAUSE Review, 43*(5), 36-48. Retrieved September 27, 2008, from http://connect.educause.edu/Library/EDUCAUSE+Review/EducationalFrontiersLearn/47221

Carlson, P. M., & Fleisher, M. S. (2002). Setting realities in higher education: Today's business model threatens our academic excellence. *International Journal of Public Administration, 25*(9/10), 1097–1111. doi:10.1081/PAD-120006127

Carr, N. (2007, October). YouTube creates cyber nightmare for teachers. *eSchool News, 10,* 41.

Carvin, A. (2006, October 10). Is MySpace your space as well? *Learning.now.* Retrieved July 21, 2008 from http://www.pbs.org/teachers/learning.now/2006/10/is_myspace_your_space_as_well.html

Cassell, J., & Jenkins, H. (1998). Feminism and computer games. In J. Cassell & H. Jenkins (Eds.), *From Barbie to Mortal Kombat: Gender and computer games* (pp. 2-45). Cambridge, MA: MIT Press.

Cassner-Lotto, J., & Wright Benner, M. (2006). *Are they really ready to work? Employers perspectives on the basic knowledge and applied skills of new entrants to the 21ˢᵗ century U.S. workforce.* The Partnership for 21st Century. Retrieved March 23, 2008, from http://www.21stcenturyskills.org/documents/FINAL_REPORT_PDF9-29-06.pdf

Castro, M. (1922). Some psychological and pedagogical aspects of visual education. *The Educational Screen, 1*(3), 6-9. Retrieved June 6, 2008, from http://www.archive.org/details/educationalscree01chicrich

Cengage Learning. (2007). *Many college professors see podcasts, blogs and social networking sites as a potential teaching tool.* Retrieved March 1, 2008, from http://www.cengage.com/press/release/20070507.html

Chavis, D., Hogge, J., McMillan, D., & Wandersman, A. (1986). Sense of community through Burnswick's lens: A first look. *Journal of Community Psychology, 14*(1), 24–40. doi:10.1002/1520-6629(198601)14:1<24::AID-JCOP2290140104>3.0.CO;2-P

Cheal, C. (2007). Second Life: Hype or hyperlearning? *Horizon, 15*(4), 204–210. doi:10.1108/10748120710836228

Cheng-Chang, S. P., & Sullivan, M. (2005). Promoting synchronous interaction in an elearning environment. *T.H.E. Journal,* (September). Retrieved from http://www.thejournal.com/articles/17377

Childnet International. (2008). *Young people and social networking services: A Childnet International research report.* Retrieved December 2, 2008, from http://www.digizen.org/downloads/fullReport.pdf

Christenson, C. M., Horn, M. B., & Johnson, C. W. (2008). *Disrupting class: How disruptive innovation will change the way the world learns.* New York: McGraw-Hill.

Churches, A. (2007). *Social bookmarking rubric based upon Bloom's taxonomy.* Retrieved from http://h226.lskysd.ca/pd/files/u2/bookmarking_rubric.pdf

Churchland, P. S. (1986). *Neurophilosophy: Toward a unified science of the mind-brain.* Cambridge, MA: MIT Press.

Churchland, P. S., & Sejnowski, T. J. (1992). Computation in the age of neuroscience. In D. Hillis (Ed.), *The new computation.* Cambridge, MA: MIT Press

CiteULike. (n.d.). Retrieved from http://www.citeulike.org

Clark, R. (1994). Media will never influence learning. *Educational Technology Research and Development, 42*(2), 21–29. doi:10.1007/BF02299088

Clark, R. E. (1983). Reconsidering research on learning from media. *Review of Educational Research, 53*(4), 445–459.

Clark, R. E., & Feldon, D. E. (2005). Five common but questionable principles of multimedia learning. In R. E. Mayer (Ed.), *The Cambridge handbook of multimedia learning* (pp. 97-115). New York: Cambridge University Press.

Coffman, T., & Klinger, M. B. (2008). Utilizing virtual worlds in education: The implications for practice. *International Journal of Social Sciences, 2*(1), 29-33. Retrieved November 2, 2007, from http://www.waset.org/ijss/v2/v2-1-5.pdf

Cognition and Technology Group at Vanderbilt. (1990). Anchored instruction and its relationship to situated cognition. *Educational Researcher, 19*(6), 2–10.

Cohen, C. A., Hegarty, M., Keehner, M., & Montello, D. R. (2003). *Spatial ability in the representation of cross sections.* Poster presented at the Annual Conference of the Cognitive Science Society, Boston, MA.

Cohen, E. G. (1994). *Designing groupwork: Strategies for the heterogeneous classroom.* New York: Teachers College Press.

Cole, M., & Engeström, Y. (1993). A cultural-historical approach to distributed cognition. In G. Salomon (Ed.), *Distributed cognitions* (pp. 1-46). Cambridge, UK: Cambridge University Press.

Collins, A. (1990). Cognitive apprenticeship and instructional technology. In L. Idol & B. F. Jones (Eds.), *Educational values and cognitive instruction: Implications for reform.* Hillsdale, NJ: Lawrence Erlbaum Associates.

Collins, A., Brown, J. S., & Newman, S. (1989). Cognitive apprenticeship: Teaching the crafts of reading, writing, and mathematics. In L. Resnick, (Ed.), *Knowing, learning, and instruction: Essays in honor of Robert Glaser* (pp. 453-494). Hillsdale, NJ: Erlbaum.

Collis, B., & Moonen, J. (2008). Web 2.0 tools and processes in higher education: Quality perspectives. *Educational Media International, 45*(2), 93–106. doi:10.1080/09523980802107179

Communication Workers of America. (2008). *Speed matters: A report on Internet speeds in all 50 states.* Retrieved August 23, 2008, from http://www.speedmatters.org/document-library/sourcematerials/cwa_report_on_internet_speeds_2008.pdf

Compare them all. (n.d.). Retrieved June 30, 2008 from http://www.wikimatrix.org/

Comparison of Wiki software. (n.d.). Retrieved June 30, 2008 http://en.wikipedia.org/wiki/Comparison_of_wiki_software

ComScore. (2007). *U.K. social networking site usage highest in Europe* [Press release]. Retrieved December 2, 2008, from http://www.comscore.com/press/release.asp?press=1801

Comscore. (2007). *YouTube continues to lead U.S. online video market with 28 percent market share.* Retrieved October, 6, 2008, from http://www.comscore.com/press/release.asp?press=1929

Connotea. (2009). Retrieved from http://www.connotea. org/

Cox, R. D. (2005). Online education as institutional myth: Rituals and realities at community colleges. *Teachers College Record, 107*(8), 1754–1787. doi:10.1111/j.1467-9620.2005.00541.x

Craig, E. M. (2007). Changing paradigms: Managed learning environments and Web 2.0. *Campus-wide Information Systems, 24*(3), 152-161. Retrieved from http://www.emeraldinsight.com/1065-0741.htm

Craig, K. (2006). Making a LIving in Second Life. *Wired.* Retrieved August 5, 2008, from http://www.wired.com/ gaming/virtualworlds/news/2006/02/70153

Crawford, J. (2007, January 25). Teacher fired over MySpace page. January 25, 2007. *Tallahassee.com.* Retrieved December 3, 2007 from http://tallahassee. com/legacy/special/blogs/2007/01/teacher-fired-over-myspace-page_25.html

Cross, J. (2007). *Informal learning: Rediscovering natural pathways that inspire innovation and performance.* San Francisco, CA: Pfeiffer Publishing.

Dalsgaard, C. (2006). Social software: E-learning beyond learning management systems. *European Journal of Open, Distance and E-Learning.* Retrieved from http://www.eurodl.org/materials/contrib/2006/Christian_Dalsgaard.htm

Daniel, J. (2007, October 15). *Technology and the media have transformed all aspects of human life-except education* (The Economist Debate Series). Retrieved July 19, 2008, from http://www.economist.com/debate/index.cfm?action=article&debate_id=1&story_id=9968827de

Davidson, W. B., & Cotter, P. R. (1986). Measurement of sense of community within the sphere of city. *Journal of Applied Social Psychology, 16*(7), 608–619. doi:10.1111/j.1559-1816.1986.tb01162.x

de Freitas, S. (2007). Learning in immersive worlds: A review of game-based learning. Retrieved October 8, 2007, from http://www.jisc.ac.uk/media/documents/

programmes/elearning_innovation/gaming%20report_v3.3.pdf de Freitas, S. (2008). Emerging trends in serious games and virtual worlds. *Becta: Emerging Technologies for Learning, 3,* 57-72. Retrieved April 10, 2008, from http://partners.becta.org.uk/upload-dir/ downloads/page_documents/research/emerging_technologies08_chapter4.pdf

de Freitas, S. (2008). Emerging trends in serious games and virtual worlds. *Becta: Emerging Technologies for Learning, 3,* 57-72. Retrieved April 10, 2008, from http:// partners.becta.org.uk/upload-dir/downloads/page_documents/research/emerging_technologies08_chapter4. pdf

de Freitas, S., & Griffiths, M. (2008). The convergence of gaming practices with other media forms: What potential for learning? A review of the literature. *Learning, Media and Technology, 33*(1), 11–20. doi:10.1080/17439880701868796

de Fretias, S. (2008, November). *Serious virtual worlds: A scoping study.* Bristol, UK: JISC. Retrieved November 11, 2008, from http://www.jisc.ac.uk/media/documents/ publications/seriousvirtualworldsv1.pdf

De Moor, E. (1990). Geometry instruction in the Netherlands (ages 4-14): The realistic approach. In L. Streefland (Ed.), *Realistic mathematics education in primary school* (pp. 119-138). Culemborg, The Netherlands: Technipress.

Dede, C. (1996). The evolution of distance education: Emerging technologies and distributed learning. *American Journal of Distance Education, 10*(2), 4–36.

Dede, C. (2005). Planning for neomillennial learning styles. *EDUCAUSE Quarterly, 28*(1), 7-12. Retrieved October 31, 2007, from http://www.educause.edu/ir/ library/pdf/eqm0511.pdf

Dede, C. (2008). New horizons: A seismic shift in epistemology. *EDUCAUSE Review, 43*(3), 80–81.

Dede, C. (2008, May/June). New horizons: A seismic shift in epistemology. *EDUCAUSE Review, 43*(3), 80-81. Retrieved May 1, 2008, from http://connect.educause.

edu/Library/EDUCAUSE+Review/ASeismicShift-inEpistemolo/46613

Delwiche, A. (2003). *MMORPG's in the college classroom. The state of play: Law, games, and virtual worlds.* New York: New York Law School. Retrieved May 1, 2008, from http://www.nyls.edu/docs/delwiche.pdf

Delwiche, A. (2006). Massively multiplayer online games (MMOs) in the new media classroom. *Educational Technology & Society, 9*(3), 160-172. Retrieved May 7, 2008, from http://www.ifets.info/journals/9_3/14.pdf

DeNigris, J., & Witchel, A. (2000). *How to teach and train online.* Needham Heights, MA: Pearson.

Derouin, R. E., Fritzsche, B. A., & Salas, E. (2005). E-learning in organizations. *Journal of Management, 31,* 920–940. doi:10.1177/0149206305279815

DeSchryver, M., & Spiro, R. (2008). New forms of deep learning on the Web: Meeting the challenge of cognitive load in conditions of unfettered exploration in online multimedia environments. In R. Zheng (Ed.), *Cognitive effects of multimedia learning* (pp. 134-152). Hershey, PA: IGI Global Publishing.

DesRoches, D. (2007). *Social bookmarking offers a new way to store and share Web sites.* Retrieved from http://www.schoollibraryjournal.com/article/CA6403269.html

DesRoches, D. (n.d.). *Resource Website and k-12 example.* The Living Sky School Division, Saskatchewan, Canada. Retrieved from http://h226.lskysd.ca/pd/social_bookmarking

Dewey, J. (1884, January). The new psychology. *Andover Review, 2,* 278-289. Retrieved May 30, 2008, from http://psychclassics.yorku.ca/Dewey/newpsych.htm

Dewey, J. (1897, January). My pedagogic creed. *School Journal, 54,* 77-80. Retrieved May 30, 2008, from http://dewey.pragmatism.org/creed.htm

Dewey, J. (1910). *How we think.* Boston, MA: D. C. Heath.

Dewey, J. (1916). *Democracy and education: An introduction to the philosophy of education.* New York: Macmillan.

Dewey, J. (1997/1938). *Experience and education* (1st Touchstone ed.). New York: Touchstone.

Dick, J. T. (1999). DVD the next big (digital) thing? *Library Journal, 124*(9), 50–51.

Dick, W., & Johnson, R. B. (2007). Evaluation in instructional design: The impact of Kirkpatrick's four-level model. In R. A. Reiser & J. V. Dempsey (Eds.), Trends and issues in instructional design and technology (2nd ed.) (pp. 94-103). Upper Saddle River, NJ: Pearson Educational.

Dick, W., Carey, L., & Carey, J. O. (2005). *The systematic design of instruction* (6th ed.). Boston, MA: Pearson/Allyn & Bacon.

Dickson, W. K. L., & Dickson, A. (1970). *History of the kinetograph, kinetoscope & kinetophonograph.* New York: Arno Press & The New York Times.

Doolittle, R., & MacDonald, D. (1978). Communication and a sense of community in metropolitan neighborhood: A factor analytic examination. *Communication Quarterly, 26,* 2–7.

Downes, S. (2002). *Aggregators, assimilators, analysts and advisors.* Retrieved November 23, 2008, from http://www.downes.ca/cgi-bin/page.cgi?post=84

Downes, S. (2003). Public policy, research and online learning. *ACM Ubiquity Views, 4*(25). Retrieved November 23, 2008, from http://www.acm.org/ubiquity/views/v4i25_downes.html

Downes, S. (2004). The Buntine oration: Learning networks. *International Journal of Instructional Technology and Distance Learning, 1*(11), 3-14. Retrieved February 2, 2009, from http://www.itdl.org/Journal/Nov_04/Nov_04.pdf

Downes, S. (2005). *E-learning 2.0.* Retrieved November 23, 2008, from http://www.elearnmag.org/subpage.cfm?section=articles&article=29-1

Downes, S. (2005). Understanding PISA. *Turkish Online Journal of Distance Education-TOJDE, 6*(2). Retrieved November 23, 2008, from http://tojde.anadolu.edu.tr/tojde18/articles/article10.htm

Downes, S. (2005, October). E-learning 2.0. *E-Learn Magazine.* Retrieved October 26, 2006, from http://elearn-mag.org/subpage.cfm?section=articles&article=29-1

Downes, S. (2007, May). *Virtual worlds in context.* Paper presented at the Eduserv Foundation Symposium: Virtual worlds, real learning? London. Retrieved October 13, 2008, from http://www.downes.ca/presentation/148

Dremann, S. (2008, July 22). Businesses, universities get Second Life. *Palo Alto Online.* Retrieved July 22, 2008, from http://www.paloaltoonline.com/news/show_story.php?id=8781

Dretske, F. (1999). *Knowledge and the flow of information.* Stanford, CA: Center for the Study of Language and Inf.

Drews vs. Joint School District, Not Reported in F.Supp.2d, 2006 WL 1308565 (D. Idaho).

Dreyfus, H., & Dreyfus, S. (1986). *Mind over machine: The power of human intuition and expertise in the era of the computer.* Oxford, UK: Blackwell.

Ducheneaut, N., & Moore, R. J. (2004). The social side of gaming: A study of interaction patterns in a massively multiplayer online game. In *Proceedings of the 2004 ACM conference on Computer Supportive Cooperative Work* (pp. 360-369). Retrieved January 18, 2008, from http://doi.acm.org/10.1145/1031607.1031667

Dumbleton, T. (2007). Games to entertain or games to teach? *Becta: Emerging Technologies for Learning, 2,* 55-63. Retrieved April 10, 2008, from http://partners.becta.org.uk/page_documents/research/emerging_technologies07_chapter5.pdf

Durlach, N., Allen, G., Darken, R., Garnett, R. L., Loomis, J., Templeman, J., & Wiegand, T. E. (2000). Virtual environments and the enhancement of spatial behavior: Towards a comprehensive research agenda. *Presence: Virtual Environments and Teleoperators, 9,* 593–615. doi:10.1162/105474600300040402

Dyck, B. (2007). *Using YouTube in the classroom.* Retrieved August 3, 2008, from http://www.education-world.com/a_tech/columnists/dyck/dyck016.shtml

Dye, S. (2006, May 15). Text messages to help students study by phone. *The New Zealand Herald.* Retrieved August 22, 2006, from http://subs.nzherald.co.nz/topic/story.cfm?c_id=186&objectid=10381845

Dziuban, C. D., Moskal, P. D., & Hartman, J. (2005). Higher education, blended learning, and the generations: Knowledge is power--no more. In J. Bourne & J. C. Moore (Eds.), *Elements of quality online education: Engaging communities.* Needham, MA: Sloan Center for Online Education.

Dziuban, C. D., Moskal, P. D., & Hartman, J. (2005). Higher education, blended learning, and the generations: Knowledge is power: No more. In J. Bourne & J. C. Moore (Eds.), *Elements of quality online education: Engaging communities* (pp. 85-100). Needham, MA: Sloan Center for Online Education.

Edelson, D. C. (2001). Learning-for-use: A framework for the design of technology supported inquiry activities. *Journal of Research in Science Teaching, 38*(3), 355–385. doi:10.1002/1098-2736(200103)38:3<355::AID-TEA1010>3.0.CO;2-M

Edelson, P. J. (1998). *The organization of courses via the Internet, academic aspects, interaction, evaluation, and accreditation.* Educational Resources Information Center, 2-15. U.S. Department of Education, Office of Educational Research and Improvement. (ERIC Document Reproduction Service No. ED422 879)

Educause Center for Applied Research. (2008). *ECAR study of undergraduate students and information technology, 2008.* Retrieved December 1, 2008, from http://www.educause.edu/ir/library/pdf/ers0808/rs/ers0808w.pdf

EDUCAUSE learning initiative. (2008). Retrieved from http://www.educause.edu/eli/16086

EDUCAUSE Learning Initiative. (2008, June 11). 7 things you should know about Second Life. *EDUCAUSE.* Retrieved June 13, 2008, from http://www.educause.edu/ir/library/pdf/ELI7038.pdf

Edwards, P. N. (2003). Infrastructure and modernity: Force, time, and social organization in the history of sociotechnical systems. In T.J. Misa, P. Brey, & A. Feenberg (Eds.), Modernity and technology (pp. 185-226). Cambridge, MA: MIT Press.

Edwards, P., Domínguez, E., & Rico, M. (2008). A second look at Second Life: Virtual role-play as a motivational factor in higher education. In K. McFerrin et al. (Eds.), *Proceedings of Society for Information Technology and Teacher Education International Conference 2008* (pp. 2566-2571). Chesapeake, VA: AACE.

Electric Sheep Company. (n.d.). *Solutions FAQ: What is a virtual world?* Retrieved April 4, 2008, from http://www.electricsheepcompany.com/core/services/faq/

Elleven, R., Wircenski, M., Wircenski, J., & Nimon, K. (2006). Curriculum-based virtual field trips: Career development opportunities for students with disabilities. *The Journal for Vocational Special Needs Education, 28*(3), 4–11.

Elliott, J., Adams, L., & Bruckman, A. (2002). No magic bullet: 3D video games in education. In *Proceedings of the ICLS 2002,* Seattle, WA. Retrieved September 27, 2007, from http://www.cc.gatech.edu/~asb/papers/aquamoose-icls02.pdf

Ellis, D. C., & Thornborough, L. (1923). *Motion pictures in education: A practical handbook for users of visual aids.* New York: Thomas Y. Crowell Company. Retrieved June 4, 2008, from http://www.archive.org/details/motionpicturesin00ellirich

Ellison, N. B., & Wu, Y. H. (2008). Blogging in the classroom: A preliminary exploration of student attitudes and impact on comprehension. *Journal of Educational Multimedia and Hypermedia, 17*(1), 99–122.

Ellul, J. (1967). The technological society. New York: Knopf

Ely, D. P. (1999). Conditions that facilitate the implementation of educational technology innovations. *Educational Technology, 34*(6), 23–27.

e-Marketer. (2008). *Online video viewing still rising.* Retrieved May 29, 2008, from http://www.emarketer.com/Article.aspx?id=1006291&src=article_head_sitesearch

Ensminger, D. C. (2005). The conditions that facilitate the implementation of technology and process innovations: A comparison of K-12, higher education, and business/industry using the implementation profile inventory (DAI-A 66/02).

E-School News Staff. (2007). Teachers warned about MySpace profiles. *e-School News.* Retrieved July 17, 2008 from http://www.eschoolnews.com/news/top-news/related-top-news/?i=50557;_hbguid=49a1babb-b469-4a85-a273-292a0514d91d

Evans, P. (2006, January/February). The Wiki factor. *BizEd,* 28-32. Retrieved February 11, 2007, from http://www.aacsb.edu/publications/Archives/JanFeb06/p28-33.pdf

Everhart, D. (n.d.). *Social bookmarking strategies for interactive learning.* Retrieved from http://www.educause.edu/upload/presentations/E07/SESS057/SocialBookmarkingStrategies.doc

Everhart, D., & Morrison, J. (2007, June). *Teaching with social bookmarking: Lessons from early experiences of social bookmarking integrated with an online course environment.* Paper presented at annual meeting of EDEN Conference, Naples, Italy.

Everhart, D., Kunnen, E., & Shelton, K. (2007). *Practical classroom examples.* Retrieved from http://connect.educause.edu/Library/Abstract/FromInformationLiteracyto/45394

Everhart, D., Kunnen, E., & Shelton, K. (2007, October). *From information literacy to scholarly identity: Effective pedagogical strategies for social bookmarking.* Paper presented at the annual meeting of EDUCUASE, Seattle, WA. Retrieved from http://net.educause.edu/E07/Program/11073?PRODUCT_CODE=E07/SESS057

Eynon, R. (2008). The use of the World Wide Web in learning and teaching in higher education: Reality and rhetoric. *Innovations in Education and Teaching International, 45*(1), 15–23. doi:10.1080/14703290701757401

Facebook statistics. (2008). Retrieved August 15, 2008 from http://www.facebook.com/press/info.php?statistics

Facer, K., Ulicsek, M., & Sandford, R. (2007). Can computer games go to school? *Becta: Emerging Technologies for Learning, 2,* 46-54. Retrieved April 10, 2008, from http://partners.becta.org.uk/page_documents/research/emerging_technologies07_chapter5.pdf

Fahs, C. (2008). *How to do everything with YouTube.* New York: McGraw-Hill.

Fanderclai, T. L. (1995, January 1). MUDs in education: New environments, new pedagogies. *Computer-mediated Communication Magazine, 2*(1). Retrieved April 23, 2008, from http://www.ibiblio.org/cmc/mag/1995/jan/fanderclai.html

Fanderclai, T. L. (1996). Like magic, only real. In L. Cherny & E. Weise (Eds.), *Wired women: Gender and new realities in cyberspace* (pp. 224-241). Seattle, WA: Seal Press.

Federal Trade Commission. (2004). *The fair credit reporting act.* Retrieved August 13, 2008 from http://www.ftc.gov/os/statutes/031224fcra.pdf

Ferris, S. P., & Wilder, H. (2006). Uses and potentials of Wikis in the classroom. *Innovate, 2*(5). Retrieved May 23, 2008, from http://www.innovateonline.info/index.php?view=article&id=258

Finn, J. (2004). A survey of online harassment at a university campus. *Journal of Interpersonal Violence, 19*(4), 468–483. doi:10.1177/0886260503262083

Fodor, J. (1983). *RePresentations: Philosophical essays on the foundations of cognitive science.* Cambridge, MA: The MIT Press

Fodor, J. (1989). *Psychosemantics: The problem of meaning in the philosophy of mind.* Cambridge, MA: The MIT Press.

Fodor, J. (2005). *The language of thought.* Cambridge, MA: Harvard University Press

Follett, J. (2008). *The rules of digital engagement.* Retrieved June 23, 2008, from http://alistapart.com/articles/rulesofdigitalengagement

Foreman, J. (2003). Distance learning and synchronous interaction. *The Technology Source,* (July/August). Retrieved from http://ts.mivu.org/default.asp?show=article&id=1034

Foreman, J. (2004, October). Game-based learning: How to delight and instruct in the 21st Century. *EDUCAUSE Review.* Retrieved November 15, 2007, from http://www.educause.edu/ir/library/pdf/erm0454.pdf

Foster, A. (2008, July 18). California Bar Association sanctions legal training in virtual world. *The Chronicle of Higher Education.* Retrieved July 18, 2008, from http://chronicle.com/wiredcampus/index.php?id=3175

Foulger, T., Ewbank, A., & Kay, A. Osborn Popp, S., & Carter, H. (2008). *Moral spaces in MySpace: Preservice teachers' perspectives about ethical issues in social networking* (Manuscript in progress).

Fox, E. J. (2006). Constructing a pragmatic science of learning and instruction with functional contextualism. *Educational Technology Research and Development, 54*(1), 5–36. doi:10.1007/s11423-006-6491-5

Friedman, B. (1997). Social judgments and technological innovation: Adolescents' understanding of property, privacy, and electronic information. *Computers in Human Behavior, 13*(3), 327–351. doi:10.1016/S0747-5632(97)00013-7

Friedman, B., Kahn, P. H. Jr, Hagman, J., Severson, R. L., & Gill, B. (2006). The watcher and the watched: Social judgments about privacy in a public place. *Human-Computer Interaction, 21*(2), 235–272. doi:10.1207/s15327051hci2102_3

Fulmer, J. (2002). Dismissing the 'immoral' teacher for conduct outside the workplace-do current laws protect the interests of both school authorities and teachers? *Journal of Law and Education, 31,* 271–290.

Gagne, R. (1965). *The conditions of learning.* New York: Holt, Rinehart and Winston.

Gallimore, R., & Tharp, R. (1990). Teaching mind in society: Teaching, schooling, and literate *discourse*. In L. C. Moll (Ed.), *Vygotsky in education: Instructional implications of sociohistorical psychology* (pp. 175-205). New York: Cambridge University Press.

Garau, M. (2003). *The impact of avatar fidelity on social interaction in virtual environments*. Unpublished doctoral dissertation, University College London, UK.

Garris, R., Ahlers, R., & Driskell, J. E. (2002). Games, motivation, and learning: A research and practice model. *Simulation & Gaming, 33*(4), 441–467. doi:10.1177/1046878102238607

Garrobo, A. (2007). No borders: Global text project digitizes third world. *Redandblack.com*. Retrieved January 30, 2007, from http://www.redandblack.com/news/2007/01/30/

Garshol, L. M. (2004, September). Metadata? Thesauri? Taxonomies? Topic maps! [Retrieved from http://www.ontopia.net/topicmaps/materials/tm-vs-thesauri.html]. *Interchange, 10*(3), 17–30.

Garson, J. (2007). *Connectionism*. Retrieved November 17, 2008, from http://plato.stanford.edu/entries/connectionism/

Gee, J. P. (2003). *What video games have to teach us about learning and literacy*. New York: Palgrave/St. Martin's.

Gee, J. P. (2008). Learning and games. In K. Salen (Ed.), *The ecology of games: Connecting youth, games, and learning* (pp. 21-40). Cambridge, MA: MIT Press. Retrieved April 3, 2008, from http://www.mitpressjournals.org/doi/pdf/10.1162/dmal.9780262693646.021

Georgetown University Library. (2009). *Evaluating Internet resources*. Retrieved from http://www.library.georgetown.edu/internet/eval.htm

Gibson, J. J. (1977). The theory of affordances. In R. Shaw & J. Bransford (Eds.), *Perceiving, acting, and knowing*. Hillsdale, NJ: Erlbaum.

Gibson, S. G., Harris, M. L., & Colaric, S. M. (2008). Technology acceptance in an academic context: Faculty acceptance of online education. *Journal of Education for Business, 83*(6), 355–359. doi:10.3200/JOEB.83.6.355-359

Glaser, B. G., & Strauss, A. L. (1967). *The discovery of grounded theory: Strategies for qualitative research*. New York: Aldine.

Glass, R., & Spiegelman, M. (2007). Incorporating blogs into the syllabus: Making their space a learning space. *Journal of Educational Technology Systems, 36*(2), 145–155. doi:10.2190/ET.36.2.c

Glogoff, S. (2005). Instructional blogging: Promoting interactivity, student-centered learning, and peer input. *Innovate, 1*(5). Retrieved May 23, 2008, from http://www.innovateonline.info/index.php?view=article&id=126

Glynn, T. (1981). Psychological sense of community: Measurement and application. *Human Relations, 34*(7), 789–818. doi:10.1177/001872678103400904

Golder, S. A., & Huberman, B. A. (2006). The structure of collaborative tagging systems. *Journal of Information Science 32*(2), 198-208. Retrieved from http://arxiv.org/pdf/ cs.DL/0508082

Gonzales, T. (2008). *Facebook, Myspace, and online communities: What your college must know* (CD recording). Retrieved August 28, 2008 from https://www.highered-hero.com/audio/main.asp?G=2&E=1317&I=1

Google Press Center. (2006). *Google to acquire YouTube for $1.65 billion in stock*. Retrieved May 29, 2008, from http://www.google.com/press/pressrel/google_youtube.html

Gordon-Murnane, L. (2006, October). Social bookmarking, folksonomies, and Web 2.0 tools. *Searcher: The Magazine for Database Professionals, 14*(9), 26–28.

Gotta, M. (2008). *Deciphering social networks* (Version 1). Midvale, UT: The Burton Group. Retrieved from http://connect.educause.edu/Library/ECAR/DecipheringSocialNetworks/47253

Greene, N. L. (1926). Motion pictures in the classroom. *The Annals of the American Academy of Political and Social Science, 128*, 122–130. doi:10.1177/000271622612800120

Greening, A. (1998). WWW support of student learning: A case study. *Australian Journal of Educational Technology, 14*(1), 49–59.

Griffin, E. (2002). *A first look at communication theory* (5th ed.). New York: McGraw-Hill.

Griffiths, M. (2002). Occupational health issues concerning Internet use in the workplace. *Work and Stress, 16*(4), 283–286. doi:10.1080/0267837031000071438

Gros, B. (2007). Digital games in education: The design of games-based learning environments. *Journal of Research on Technology in Education, 40*(1), 23–38.

Grush, M. (2008). The future of Web 2.0. *Campus Technology, 21*(7), 20–23.

Guess, A. (2008, August 26). Next steps for e-texts. *Inside Higher Ed.* Retrieved November 1, 2008 from http://www.insidehighered.com/news/2008/08/26/etextbooks

Guest, T. (2007). *Second lives: A journey through virtual worlds.* New York: Random House.

Gunawardena, C. N., Ortegano-Layne, L., Carabajal, K., Frechette, C., Lindemann, K., & Jennings, B. (2006). New model, new strategies: Instructional design for building online wisdom communities. *Distance Education, 27*(2), 217–232. doi:10.1080/01587910600789613

Guri-Rosenblit, S. (2001). Virtual universities: Current models and future trends. *Higher Education in Europe, 26*(4), 487–499. doi:10.1080/03797720220141807

Guri-Rosenblit, S. (2005). Eight paradoxes in the implementation process of e-learning in higher education. *Higher Education Policy, 18,* 5–29. doi:10.1057/palgrave.hep.8300069

Guy, M., & Tonkin, E. (2006, January). Folksonomies: Tidying up tags? *D-Lib Magazine, 12*(1). Retrieved from http://www.dlib.org/dlib/january06/guy/01guy.html

Haber, J., & Mills, M. (2008). Perceptions of barriers concerning effective online teaching and policies: Florida community college faculty. *Community College Journal of Research and Practice, 32,* 266–283. doi:10.1080/10668920701884505

Halverson, R., Shaffer, D., Squire, K., & Steinkuehler, C. (2006). Theorizing games in/and education. In *Proceedings of the Seventh International Conference on Learning Sciences ICLS '06.*

Hanson, N. R. (1958). *Patterns of discovery: An inquiry into the conceptual foundations of science.* Cambridge, UK: Cambridge University Press.

Hargadon, S. (2007). Best of social bookmarking. *School Library Journal, 16*(12), 20. Retrieved from http://www.schoollibraryjournal.com/article/CA6505695

Hargittai, E. (2007). Whose space? Differences among users and non-users of social network sites. *Journal of Computer-Mediated Communication, 13*(1), 14.

Harmon, S. W., & Jones, M. G. (1999). The five levels of Web use in education: Factors to consider in planning an online course. *Educational Technology, 39*(6), 28–32.

Harmon, S. W., & Jones, M. G. (2001). An analysis of situated Web-based instruction. *Educational Media International, 38*(4), 271–280. doi:10.1080/09523980110105123

Hartman, J., Dziuban, C., & Moskal, P. (2007). Strategic initiatives in the online environment: Opportunities and challenges. *Horizon, 15*(3), 157–168. doi:10.1108/10748120710825040

Hayes, E. (2006). Situated learning in virtual worlds: The learning ecology of Second Life. In *Proceedings of the Adult Education Research Conference 2006.* Retrieved November 13, 2007, from http://www.adulterc.org/Proceedings/2006/Proceedings/Hayes.pdf

Haynes, C., & Holmevik, J. R. (Eds.). (1998). *High wired: On the design, use, and theory of educational MOOs.* Ann Arbor, MI: University of Michigan Press.

Haynes, S. N. (1998). The changing nature of behavioral assessment. In A. S. Bellack & M. Hersen (Eds.), *Behavioral assessment: A practical handbook* (4th ed., pp. 1-21). Boston, MA: Allyn & Bacon.

Hebb, D. O. (2002). *The organization of behavior: A neuropsychological theory.* Mahwah, NJ: Lawrence Erlbaum.

Hermes, J. (2008). Colleges create Facebook-style social networks to reach alumni. *The Chronicle of Higher Education, 54*(33), A18.

Herz, J. C. (2001). Gaming the system: What higher education can learn from multiplayer online worlds. *EDUCAUSE,* 169-191. Retrieved October 7, 2007, from http://www.educause.edu/ir/library/pdf/ffpiu019.pdf

Hill, J. L. (1996). Psychological sense of community: Suggestions for future research. *Journal of Community Psychology, 24*(4), 431–438. doi:10.1002/(SICI)1520-6629(199610)24:4<431::AID-JCOP10>3.0.CO;2-T

Hiltz, S. R., & Turoff, M. (2005). Education goes digital: The evolution of online learning and the revolution in higher education. *Communications of the ACM, 48*(10), 60–64. doi:10.1145/1089107.1089139

Hiltz, S. R., Kim, E., & Shea, P. (2007). Faculty motivators and de-motivators for teaching online: Results of focus group interviews at one university. In *Proceedings of the 40th Hawaii International Conference on System Sciences.* Retrieved from http://doi.ieeecomputersociety.org/10.1109/HICSS.2007.226

Hinton, G. E. (1986). Learning distributed representations of concepts. In *Proc. of the Ann. Conf. of the Cognitive Science Society, volume 1.*

Hoover, T. (2008). *MySpace profile.* Retrieved August 26, 2008 from http://myspace.com/mshoover.

Houghton, W. (2004). *Learning and teaching theory for engineering academics.* Retrieved October 23, 2008, from http://www.engsc.ac.uk/downloads/resources/theory.pdf

Howe, N., & Strauss, W. (2000). *Millennials rising: The next great generation.* New York: Vintage Books.

Huff, D. (1993). *How to lie with statistics.* New York: W. W. Norton & Company.

Hutchins, E. (1991). The social organization of distributed cognition. In L.B. Resnick, J.M. Levine, & S.D. Teasley (Eds.), *Perspectives on socially shared cognition* (pp. 283-306). Pittsburgh, PA: Learning Research and De-velopment Center, University of Pittsburgh, American Psychological Association.

Hwang, J. H., Park, H. S., Cha, J. S., & Shin, B. J. (2008). Effects of the objects building activities in Second Life on players' spatial reasoning. In *Proceeding in the 2nd IEEE International Conference on Digital Game and Intelligent Toy Enhanced Learning,* Banff, Canada.

Hymes, D. (1971). *On communicative competence.* Philadelphia, PA: University of Pennsylvania Press.

Irlbeck, S., Kays, E., Jones, D., & Sims, R. (2006). The Phoenix rising: Emergent models of instructional design. *Distance Education, 27*(2), 171–185. doi:10.1080/01587910600789514

Itin, C. M. (1999). Reasserting the philosophy of experiential education as a vehicle for change in the 21st century. *Journal of Experiential Education, 22*(2), 91–98.

Ito, M., Horst, H. A., Bittanti, M., Boyd, D., Herr-Stephenson, B., Lange, P. G., et al. (2008, November). *Living and learning with new media: Summary of findings from the Digital Youth Project.* Retrieved November 20, 2008, from http://digitalyouth.ischool.berkeley.edu/files/report/digitalyouth-WhitePaper.pdf

J.S. v. Blue Mountain School District, 2007 WL 954245 (M.D.Pa.).

Jaszi, P., & Aufderheide, P. (2008). *Code of best practices in fair use for online video.* Washington, DC: Center for Social Media. Retrieved August 10, 2008 from http://www.centerforsocialmedia.org/resources/publications/fair_use_in_online_video/

Jenkins, C. A. (2004). The virtual classroom as ludic space. In C. A. Haythornthwaite & M. M. Kazmer (Eds.), *Learning, culture and community in online education* (pp. 163-176). New York: Peter Lang.

Jenkins, H., Purushotma, R., Clinton, K., Weigel, M., & Robison, A. J. (2008). *Confronting the challenges of participatory culture: Media education for the 21st century.* Chicago, IL: The John D. and Catherine T. MacArthur Foundation. Retrieved from http://digitallearning.macfound.org/atf/cf/%7B7E45C7E0-A3E0-4B89-AC9C-

E807E1B0AE4E%7D/JENKINS_WHITE_PAPER. PDF

Jennings, N., & Collins, C. (2008). Virtual or virtually U: Educational institutions in Second Life. *International Journal of Social Sciences, 2*(3), 180-186. Retrieved March 20, 2008, from http://www.waset.org/ijss/v2/v2-3-28.pdf

Jha, A. (2005). *Where belief is born.* Retrieved November 20, 2008, from http://www.guardian.co.uk/science/2005/jun/30/psychology.neuroscience

JISC. (2007). *Design courses and activities for e-learners.* Retrieved May 6, 2008, from http://www.jisc.ac.uk/media/documents/programmes/elearningpedagogy/guide3_designing_activities.pdf

Johnson, D. W., Johnson, R. T., & Smith, K. A. (1998). Cooperative learning returns to college: What evidence is there that it works? *Change,* (July/August): 27–35.

Johnson, E. (2001). *Emergence: The connected lives of ants, brains, and software.* New York: Simon & Schuster.

Johnson, M., & Liber, O. (2008). The personal learning environment and the human condition: From theory to teaching practice. *Interactive Learning Environments, 16*(1), 3–15. doi:10.1080/10494820701772652

Johnson, N. (2006). *The educational potential of Second Life.* Columbus, OH: Ohio State University, Digital Union.

Johnson, S. (2005). *Everything bad is good for you* (2nd ed.). New York: Riverhead Books.

Jonassen, D. (1999). Designing constructivist learning environments. In C. M. Reigeluth (Ed.), *Instructional-design theories and models: A new paradigm of instructional theory* (Vol. 2, pp. 215-239). Mahwah, NJ: Lawrence Erlbaum Associates, Inc.

Jonassen, D. H. (1999). Designing constructivist learning environments. In C. M. Reigeluth (Ed.), *Instructional design theories and models: Their current state of the art* (2nd ed.). Mahwah, NJ: Lawrence Erlbaum Associates.

Jonassen, D. H. (2000). *Computers as mind tools for schools: Engaging critical thinking* (2nd ed.). Upper Saddle River, NJ: Merrill.

Jonassen, D. H., Howland, J., Marra, R. M., & Crismond, D. (2008). *Meaningful learning with technology* (3rd ed.). NJ: Merrill/Prentice Hall.

Jones, G., & Warren, S. (2008). The time factor: Leveraging intelligent agents and directed narratives in online learning environments. *Innovate, 5*(2). Retrieved December 6, 2008, from http://www.innovateonline.info/index.php?view=article&id=576

Jones, J. G., & Bronack, S. C. (2007). Rethinking cognition, representations, and process in 3D online social learning environments. In D. Gibson, C. Aldrich, & M. Prensky (Eds.), *Games and simulations in online learning: Research and development frameworks* (pp. 89-114). Hershey, PA: Information Science Publishing.

Jones, M. G., & Harmon, S. W. (2002). What professors need to know about technology to assess online student learning. *New Directions for Teaching and Learning, Fall*(91), 19-30.

Jones, M. G., & Harmon, S. W. (2006). Ancillary communication as an intentional instructional strategy in online learning environments. In M. Simonson & M. Crawford (Eds.), *Proceedings of the 2006 international conference of the Association of Educational Communications and Technology* (Vol. 2, pp. 194-199).

Kafai, Y. B. (2006). Playing and making games for learning: Instructionist and constructionist perspectives for game studies. *Games and Culture, 1*(1), 36–40. doi:10.1177/1555412005281767

Kalay, Y. E. (2004). Virtual learning environments [Special issue]. *Journal of Information Technology in Construction, 9,* 195-207. Retrieved October 8, 2007, from http://www.itcon.org/data/works/att/2004_13.content.04009.pdf

Kauffman, D. F. (2004). Self-regulated learning in Web-based environments: instructional tools designed to facilitate cognitive strategy use, metacognitive processing, and motivational beliefs. *Journal of Educational Computing Research, 30*(1), 139–161. doi:10.2190/AX2D-Y9VM-V7PX-0TAD

Kawachi, P. (2003). Initiating intrinsic motivation in online education: Review of the current state of the art. *Interactive Learning Environments, 11*(1), 59–82. doi:10.1076/ilee.11.1.59.13685

Keller, J. M. (1987). The systematic process of motivational design. *Performance and Instruction, 26*(9/10), 1–8.

Kelton, A. J. (2007, April 14). Second Life: Reaching into the virtual world for real-world learning. *EDUCAUSE Research Bulletin, 2007*(17), 1-13. Retrieved February 28, 2008, from http://www.educause.edu/ir/library/pdf/ecar_so/erb/ERB0717.pdf

Kemp, J. W., & Haycock, K. (2008). Immersive learning environments in parallel universes: Learning through Second Life. *School Libraries Worldwide, 14*(2), 89-97. Retrieved from http://Asselindoiron.pbwiki.com

Kemp, J. W., & Haycock, K. (2008). Immersive learning environments in parallel universes: Learning through Second Life. *School Libraries Worldwide, 14*(2), 89-97. Retrieved September 26, 2008, from http://asselindoiron.pbwiki.com/f/RevisedKEMPhaycock.Sept08.pdf

Ken, P., & Kevin, T. (1995). *Virtual reality: Through the new looking glass* (2nd ed.). Windcrest Books.

Kerka, S. (1996). *Distance learning, the Internet, and the World Wide Web.* (ERIC Document Reproduction Service No. ED 395 214, 1996)

Kesim, E., & Agaoglu, E. (2007). A paradigm shift in distance education: Web 2.0 and social software. *Turkish Online Journal of Distance Education, 8*(3), 66–75.

Kidney, G., Cummings, L., & Boehm, A. (2007). Toward a quality assurance approach to e-learning courses. *International Journal on E-Learning, 6*(1), 17–30.

Kim, H. N. (2008). The phenomenon of blogs and theoretical model of blog use in educational contexts. *Computers & Education, 51*(3), 1342–1352. doi:10.1016/j.compedu.2007.12.005

Kim, S., Phillips, W. R., Pinsky, L., Brock, D., Phillips, K., & Keary, J. (2006). A conceptual framework for developing teaching cases: A review and synthesis of the literature across disciplines. *Medical Education, 40,* 867–876. doi:10.1111/j.1365-2929.2006.02544.x

Kirkpatrick, D. (2006). *Life in a connected world.* Retrieved November 20, 2008, from http://money.cnn.com/2006/06/23/technology/brainstormintro.fortune/index.htm

Kirkpatrick, D. L. (1994). Evaluating training programs: The four levels. San Francisco: Berrett-Koehler.

Kirriemuir, J., & McFarlane, A. (2004). *Literature review in games and learning. A report of NESTA Futurelab.* Retrieved November 15, 2007, from http://www.futurelab.org.uk/resources/documents/lit_reviews/Games_Review.pdf

Kleeman, M. (2007). *Point of disconnect: Internet traffic and the US communications infrastructure.* San Diego, CA: University of California. Retrieved November 1, 2008, from http://cpe.ucsd.edu/assets/013/6535.pdf

Knowles, M. (1984). *Andragogy in action.* San Francisco: Jossey-Bass.

Kolb, D. A. (1984). *Experiential learning: Experience as the source of learning and development.* Upper Saddle River, NJ: Prentice-Hall.

Kolbert, E. (2001, May 28). Pimps and dragons. *New Yorker (New York, N.Y.),* 88–98.

Kolodner, J. (1993). *Case-based reasoning.* San Mateo, CA: Morgan Kaufmann.

Kosslyn, S. M. (2002). *Image and mind* (Reprint ed.). Cambridge, MA: Harvard University Press.

Kozma, R. B. (1994). Will media influence learning? Reframing the debate. *Educational Technology Research and Development, 42*(2), 7–19. doi:10.1007/BF02299087

Kunnen, E., Brand, G., & Morrison, J. (n.d.). *From tagging to teaching: Practical examples of leveraging social bookmarking in teaching and learning.* Retrieved from http://www.slideshare.net/gbrand/tagging-to-teaching

Lakoff, G. (1990). *Women, fire, and dangerous things.* Chicago, IL: University Of Chicago Press.

Land, S., & Hannafin, M. (2001). Student-centered learning environments. In D. Jonassen & S. Land (Eds.), *Theoretical foundations of learning environments* (pp. 1-23). Mahwah, NJ: Lawrence Erlbaum Associates.

Langer, J. A., & Applebee, A. A. (1987). *How writing shapes thinking.* Urbana, IL: National Council of Teachers of English.

Larreamendy, J., & Leinhardt, G. (2006). Going the distance with online education. *Review of Educational Research, 76,* 567–606. doi:10.3102/00346543076004567

Larsen-Freeman, D. (1986). *Techniques and principles in language teaching.* Oxford, UK: Oxford University Press.

Laupa, M. (1991). Children's reasoning about three authority attributes: Adult status, knowledge, and social position. *Developmental Psychology, 27*(2), 321–329. doi:10.1037/0012-1649.27.2.321

Laupa, M. (1995). Children's reasoning about authority in home and school contexts. *Social Development, 4*(1), 1–16. doi:10.1111/j.1467-9507.1995.tb00047.x

Laupa, M., & Turiel, E. (1993). Children's concepts of authority and social contexts. *Journal of Educational Psychology, 85*(1), 191–197. doi:10.1037/0022-0663.85.1.191

Lave, J. (1988). The practice of learning: The problem with "context." In S. Chaiklin & J. Lave (Eds.), *Understanding practice: Perspectives on activity and context* (pp. 3-32). Boston, MA: Cambridge University Press.

Lave, J., & Wenger, E. (1991). *Situated learning: Legitimate peripheral participation.* New York: Cambridge University Press.

Layshock v. Hermitage School District, 496 F.Supp.2d 587 (W.D.Pa., 2007).

LeDoux, J. (2002). *Synaptic self: How our brains become who we are.* New York: Viking Adult.

Lee, J. L., & Hoadley, C. M. (2007). Leveraging identity to make learning fun: Possible selves and experiential learning in massively multiplayer online games (MMOGs). *Innovate, 6*(3). Retrieved January 10, 2008, from http://innovateonline.info/index.php?view=article&id=348

Lee, Y. J. (2004). The effect of creating external representations on the efficiency of Web search. *Interactive Learning Environments, 12*(3), 227–250. doi:10.1080/10494820512331383439

LeFeever, L. (2009). *Social bookmarking in plain English.* Retrieved from http://www.commoncraft.com/bookmarking-plain-english

Lenhart, A. (2007). Cyberbullying and online teens. *Pew Internet & American Life Project.* Retrieved July 21, 2008 from http://www.pewInternet.org/pdfs/PIP%20Cyberbullying%20Memo.pdf

Lenhart, A., & Fox, S. (2006, July 19). *Bloggers: Portrait of America's new storytellers.* Washington, DC: Pew Internet & American Life Report. Retrieved on July 9, 2007, from http://www.pewinternet.org/pdfs/PIP%20Bloggers%20Report%20July%2019%202006.pdf

Lenhart, A., Kahne, J., Middaugh, E., Macgill, A. R., Evans, C., & Vitak, J. (2008, September 16). *Teens, video games, and civics.* Washington, DC: Pew Internet & American Life Project. Retrieved September 27, 2008, from http://www.pewinternet.org/pdfs/PIP_Teens_Games_and_Civics_Report_FINAL.pdf

Lenhart, A., Madden, M., & Hitlin, P. (2005). *Teens and technology: Youth are leading the transition to a fully wired and mobile nation.* Washington, DC: Pew Internet & American Life Report. Retrieved on November 3rd, 2006 from http://www.pewinternet.org/pdfs/PIP_Teens_Tech_July2005web.pdf

Lenhart, A., Madden, M., Macgill, A., & Smith, A. (2007). Teens and social media. *Pew Internet & American Life Project.* Retrieved July 18, 2008 from http://www.pewInternet.org/pdfs/PIP_Teens_Social_Media_Final.pdf

Leskovec, J., & Horvitz, E. (2007). *Planetary-scale views on an instant-messaging network* (Microsoft Research Technical Report MSR-TR-2006-186). Retrieved August 26, 2008 from http://arxiv.org/PS_cache/arxiv/pdf/0803/0803.0939v1.pdf

Leslie, S., & Landon, B. (2008). Social software for learning: What is it, why use it? *The Observatory on Borderless Higher Education,* 1-27. Retrieved April 29, 2008, from http://www.obhe.ac.uk/products/reports/pdf/2008-01-01.pdf

Levin, J. (2004). Functionlism. In *Stanford encyclopedia of philosophy.* Retrieved February 2, 2009 from http://plato.stanford.edu/entries/functionalism/

Levy, S. (2003). Six factors to consider when planning online distance learning programs in higher education. *Online Journal of Distance Learning Administration, 6*(2). Retrieved August 25, 2008, from http://www.westga.edu/~distance/ojdla/spring61/levy61.htm

Lewis, D. K. (2001). *Counterfactuals* (2nd ed.). New York: Wiley-Blackwell.

Liccardi, I., Ounnas, A., Pau, R., Massey, E., Kinnumen, P., Lewthwaite, S., et al. (2007). The role of social networks in students' learning experiences. *ACM SIGCSE Bulletin* (December Issue). pp. 224-237.

Life, S. *Economic statistics.* (2008, August 29). Retrieved August 30, 2008, from http://secondlife.com/whatis/economy_stats.php

Life, S. *FAQ.* (n.d.). Retrieved August 6, 2008, from http://secondlife.com/whatis/faq.php

Lim, C. P., & Chai, C. S. (2003). An activity-theoretical approach to research of ICT integration in Singapore schools: Orienting activities and learner autonomy. *Computers & Education, 43,* 215–236. doi:10.1016/j.compedu.2003.10.005

Linden, A., & Fenn, J. (2003). *Strategic analysis report R-20-1971: Understanding Gartner's hype cycles.* Stamford, CT: Gartner Inc.

Linden, H. (2008, July 8). IBM and Linden Lab interoperability announcement. *Second Life Blog.* Retrieved July 23, 2008, from http://blog.secondlife.com/2008/07/08/ibm-linden-lab-interoperability-announcement/#

Linden, P. (2008, May 29). Inside the lab podcast: Education in Second Life [podcast transcript of an interview with Claudia and Pathfinder Linden]. Retrieved June 3, 2008, from http://static-secondlife-com.s3.amazonaws.com/media/Inside%20the%20Lab%20podcast-transcript-Education.htm

Lindenberger, M. (2006). Questions of conduct. *Diverse Issues in Higher Education, 23*(21), 36–37.

Lipka, S. (2008). The digital limits of "in loco parentis." . *The Chronicle of Higher Education, 54*(26), 1.

Livingstone, D., & Kemp, J. (2006). Massively multi-learner: Recent advances in 3D social environments. *Computing and Information Systems Journal, 10*(2). Retrieved July 11, 2007, from http://www.cis.paisley.ac.uk/research/journal/v10n2/LinvingstoneKemp.doc

Löfström, E., & Nevgi, A. (2007). From strategic planning to meaningful learning: Diverse perspectives on the development of Web-based teaching and learning in higher education. *British Journal of Educational Technology, 38*(2), 312–324. doi:10.1111/j.1467-8535.2006.00625.x

Lomas, C. (2005). *7 things you should know about... social bookmarking.* Retrieved July 23, 2008, from http://connect.educause.edu/Library/ELI/7ThingsYouShouldKnowAbout/39378

Lorenzo, G. (2006). Business models for online education. *Educational Pathways, 10*(2), 69–95.

Low, R., & Sweller, J. (2005). The modality principle in multimedia learning. In R. E. Mayer (Ed.), *The Cambridge handbook of multimedia learning* (pp. 147-158). New York: Cambridge University Press.

Ludlow, P., & Wallace, M. (2007). *The Second Life Herald: The virtual tabloid that witnessed the dawn of the metaverse.* Cambridge, MA: MIT Press.

Mabrito, M., & Medley, R. (2008). Why Professor Johnny can't read: Understanding the Nt generation's texts. *Innovate, 4*(6). Retrieved from http://www.innovateonline.info/index.php?view-article&id=510

MacGregor, G., & McCulloch, E. (2006). Collaborative tagging as a knowledge organisation and resource discovery tool. *Library Review*, *55*(5), 291–300. doi:10.1108/00242530610667558

Mackintosh, W. (2006). Modelling alternatives for tomorrow's university: Has the future already happened? In M. F. Beaudoin (Ed.), *Perspectives on higher education in the digital age* (pp. 1-20). Hauppauge, NY: Nova Science Publishers.

Macleod, H. (2007, May). *Holyrood Park: A virtual campus for Edinburgh*. Paper presented at the Eduserv Foundation Symposium: Virtual worlds, real learning? London. Retrieved October 13, 2008, from http://www.slideshare.net/efsym/holyrood-park-a-virtual-campus-for-edinburgh/

Madden, M. (2007). *Online video*. Washington, DC: Pew Internet & American Life Project. Retrieved from http://www.pewinternet.org/PPF/r/219/report_display.asp

Madden, M., & Fox, S. (2006). *Riding the waves of "Web 2.0": More than a buzzword, but still not easily defined.* Retrieved November 23, 2008, from http://www.pewinternet.org/pdfs/PIP_Web_2.0.pdf

Malone, T. W. (1981). Toward a theory of intrinsically motivating instruction. *Cognitive Science*, *5*(4), 333–369.

Maloney, E. J. (2007, January). What Web 2.0 can teach us about learning. *The Chronicle of Higher Education*, *53*(18), B26.

Malpas, J. (2005). *Donald Davidson*. Retrieved November 17, 2008, from http://plato.stanford.edu/entries/davidson/

Marr, D. (1982). Vision. *Times*.

Marsh, D., & Panckhurst, R. (2007). *eLEN – eLearning Exchange Networks: Reaching out to effective bilingual and multicultural university collaboration.* Retrieved June 10, 2008, from http://www.eadtu.nl/conference-2007/files/CC4.pdf

Marshall, M. (2005). *Wiki war born out of deal with Walt Disney*. Retrieved October 23, 2008, from http://www.mickeynews.com/News/DisplayPressRelease.asp_Q_id_E_1195Wiki

Mashhadi, A. (1998). *Instructional design for the 21st century: Towards a new conceptual framework*. Paper presented at the International Conference on Computers in Education, Beijing, China. (ERIC Document Reproduction Service No. ED429583)

May, M. (2006, June 23). Hoover: Caught in the flash. *Austin Chronicle*. Retrieved December 3, 2007 from http://www.austinchronicle.com/gyrobase/Issue/story?oid=oid%3A378611

Mayer, R. E. (1999). Multimedia aids to problem-solving transfer. *International Journal of Educational Research*, *31*, 611–632. doi:10.1016/S0883-0355(99)00027-0

Mayer, R. E. (2001). *Multimedia learning*. New York: Cambridge University Press.

Mayer, R. E., & Chandler, P. (2001). When learning is just a click away: Does simple user interaction foster deeper understanding of multimedia messages? *Journal of Educational Psychology*, *93*(2), 390–397. doi:10.1037/0022-0663.93.2.390

Mayer, R. E., & Moreno, R. (2003). Nine ways to reduce cognitive load in multimedia learning. *Educational Psychologist*, *38*(1), 43–52. doi:10.1207/S15326985EP3801_6

Mayer, R. E., & Sims, V. K. (1994). For whom is a picture worth a thousand words? Extensions of a dual coding theory of multimedia learning. *Journal of Educational Psychology*, *86*, 389–401. doi:10.1037/0022-0663.86.3.389

Mayer, R. E., Mautone, P., & Prothero, W. (2002). Pictorial aids for learning by doing in a multimedia geology simulation game. *Journal of Educational Psychology*, *94*, 171–185. doi:10.1037/0022-0663.94.1.171

McCoy, S. (2006). Evaluating group projects: A Web-based assessment. In *Proceedings of the 2006 Midwest Instruction and Computing Symposium*. Retrieved June 27, 2008, from http://www.micsymposium.org/mics_2006/papers/McCoy.pdf

McGee, P., & Diaz, V. (2007). Wikis and podcasts and blogs! Oh, my! What is a faculty member supposed to do? *EDUCAUSE Review*, *42*(5), 28–40.

McGivney, V. (1999). *Informal learning in the community: A trigger for change and development.* Leicester, UK: National Institute of Adult and Continuing Education.

McKinney, J. P., McKinney, K. G., Franiuk, R., & Schweitzer, J. (2006). The college classroom as a community: Impact on student attitudes and learning. *College Teaching, 54*(3), 281–284. doi:10.3200/CTCH.54.3.281-284

Mcklin, T., Harmon, S. W., Jones, M. G., & Evans, W. (2002). Cognitive engagement in Web-based learning: A content analysis of student's online discussions. In M. Crawford & M. Simonson (Eds.), *Proceedings of the 2001 international conference of the Association of Educational Communications and Technology* (Vol. 1, pp. 272-277).

McLellan, H. (2004). Virtual realities. In D. H. Jonassen (Ed.), *Handbook of research for educational communications and technology* (pp. 461-497). Manwah, NJ: Lawrence Erlbaum Associates. Retrieved March 29, 2008, from http://www.aect.org/edtech/17.pdf

McLoughlin, C., & Lee, M. J. W. (2008). Future learning landscapes: Transforming pedagogy through social software. *Innovate, 4*(5). Retrieved from http://www.innovateonline.info/index.php?view=article&id=539

McMillan, D. W. (1996). Sense of community. *Journal of Community Psychology, 24*(4), 315–325. doi:10.1002/(SICI)1520-6629(199610)24:4<315::AID-JCOP2>3.0.CO;2-T

McMillan, D. W., & Chavis, D. M. (1986). Sense of community: A definition and theory. *Journal of Community Psychology, 14*(1), 6–23. doi:10.1002/1520-6629(198601)14:1<6::AID-JCOP2290140103>3.0.CO;2-I

McNeilly, D. P. (2008). YouTube and the emerging worlds of video-sharing for behavioral science education. *Annals of Behavioral Science and Medical Education, 14*(1), 25–30.

McQuiggan, C. A. (2007). The role of faculty development in online teaching's potential to question teaching beliefs and assumptions. *Online Journal of Distance Learning Administration, 10*(3). Available online at http://www.westga.edu/~distance/ojdla/fall103/mcquiggan103.htm

Mesthene, E. G. (2003). The role of technology in modern society. In E. Katz, A. Light, & W. Thompson (Eds.), Controlling technology: Contemporary issues (2nd ed.) (pp. 117-138). Amherst, NY: Prometheus Books.

Metallidou, P., & Platsidou, M. (2008). Kolb's learning style inventory-1985: Validity issues and relations with metacognitive knowledge about problem-solving strategies. *Learning and Individual Differences, 18*(1), 114–119. doi:10.1016/j.lindif.2007.11.001

Mezirow, J. (1991). *Transformative dimensions of adult learning.* San Francisco, CA: Jossey-Bass.

Miller, G. E., & Schiffman, S. (2006). ALN business models and the transformation of higher education. *Journal of Asynchronous Learning Networks, 10*(2), 15–21.

Milligan, C. (2006). *What is a PLE? The future or just another buzz word?* Retrieved November 23, 2008, from http://www.elearning.ac.uk/news_folder/ple%20event

Millis, B. J. (2006). *Using new technologies to support cooperative learning, collaborative services, and unique resources.* Retrieved June 23, 2008, from http://www.tltgroup.org/resources/rmillis3.html

Miltiadou, M., & Savenye, W. C. (2003). Applying social cognitive constructs of motivation to enhance student success in online distance education. *Educational Technology Review, 11*(1), 78–95.

Minsky, M., & Papert, S. (1969). *Perceptrons: An introduction to computational geometry.* Cambridge, MA: The MIT Press.

Moore, A. H., Fowler, S. B., & Watson, C. E. (2007). Active learning and technology: Designing change for faculty, students, and institutions. *EDUCAUSE Review, 42*(5), 43–60.

Moore, D. M., Burton, J. K., & Myers, R. J. (2004). Multiple-channel communication: The theoretical and research foundations of multimedia. In D. H. Jonassen (Ed.), *Handbook of research on educational communica-*

tions and technology (2nd ed.) (pp. 981-1005). Mahwah, NJ: Lawrence Erlbaum Associates.

Moore, M. G. (1973). Towards a theory of independent learning and teaching. *The Journal of Higher Education, 44*(9), 661–679. doi:10.2307/1980599

Moore, M. G. (1989). Editorial: Three types of interaction. *American Journal of Distance Education, 4*(2), 1–6.

Moore, M. G. (1993). Three types of interaction. In K. Harry, M. John, & D. Keegan (Eds.), *Distance education: New perspective*. London: Routledge.

Morales, E. D., & Patton, J. Q. (2005). Gender bias in a virtual world. *WSU McNair Journal, 3*, 81–89.

Moran, J. (2007). *Battling the upstream bottleneck of broadband connections: How fast does your data swim upstream?* Retrieved August 29, 2008, from http://cws.internet.com/article/3541-.htm

Morrison, G., Ross, S., & Kemp, J. (2004). *Designing effective instruction* (4th ed.). Hoboken, NJ: John Wiley.

Muir, D. (2005). *Simply Del.icio.us: Online social bookmarking, or: Tagging for teachers.* Retrieved July 23, 2008 from http://personal.strath.ac.uk/d.d.muir/Delicious_Guide.pdf

Muis, K. R. (2008). Epistemic profiles and self-regulated learning: examining relations in the context of mathematics problem solving. *Contemporary Educational Psychology, 33*(2), 177–208. doi:10.1016/j.cedpsych.2006.10.012

Munby, J. (1978). *Communicative syllabus design*. Cambridge, UK: Cambridge University Press.

Myspace.com. (2008). Myspace.com safety and security. *Myspace.com*. Retrieved August 26, 2008 from http://www.myspace.com/safety

Nagel, T. (1974). What is it like to be a bat? [from http://www.clarku.edu/students/philosophyclub/docs/nagel.pdf]. *The Philosophical Review*, 435–450. Retrieved November 3, 2008. doi:10.2307/2183914

Nakashima, E. (2007, March 7). Harsh words die hard on the Web. *Washingtonpost.com*. Retrieved July 21, 2008 from http://www.washingtonpost.com/wp-dyn/content/article/2007/03/06/AR2007030602705.html

Nardi, B. A., Ly, S., & Harris, J. (2007). Learning conversations in World of Warcraft. In *Proceedings of the 40th Hawaii International Conference on Systems Sciences.* Retrieved October 3, 2007, from http://darrouzet-nardi.net/bonnie/pdf/Nardi-HICSS.pdf

Nathan, M., & Robinson, C. (2001). Considerations of learning and learning research: Revisiting the "media effects" debate. *Journal of Interactive Learning Research, 12*(1), 69–88.

National Center for Educational Statistics. (2006). *Digest of educational statistics: 2006*. Retrieved February 10, 2008, from http://nces.ed.gov/programs/digest/d06/index.asp

National Education Association & American Federation of Teachers. (2008). *Access, adequacy, and equity in education technology: Results of a survey of America's teachers and support professionals on technology in public schools and classrooms*. Washington, DC: National Education Association. Retrieved June 11, 2008, from http://www.nea.org/research/images/08gainsandgapsedtech.pdf

National School Boards Association. (2007). *Creating and connecting: Research and guidelines on online social- and educational-networking*. Alexandria, VA: National School Boards Association.

Natriello, G. (2005). Modest changes, revolutionary possibilities: Distance learning and the future of education. *Teachers College Record, 107*, 1885–1904. doi:10.1111/j.1467-9620.2005.00545.x

Nesson, R., & Nesson, C. (in press). In the virtual classroom: An ethnographic argument for education in virtual worlds. *Space and Culture*. Retrieved April 27, 2008 from http://www.eecs.harvard.edu/~nesson/ed-vw-1.3.pdf

New Media Consortium & EDUCAUSE Learning Initiative. (2008). *The horizon report*. Retrieved from http://www.nmc.org/pdf/2008-Horizon-Report.pdf

New Media Consortium & EDUCAUSE Learning Initiative. (2008). *The horizon report: 2008 edition.*

Retrieved May 18, 2008, from http://www.nmc.org/publications/2008-horizon-report

New Media Consortium. (2008). *Spring 2008 NMC survey: Educators in Second Life*. Austin, TX: The New Media Consortium. Retrieved November 30, 2008, from http://www.nmc.org/pdf/2008-sl-survey.pdf

Newcombe, N. S., & Huttenlocher, J. (2000). *Making space: The development of spatial representation and reasoning*. Cambridge, MA: MIT Press.

Newell, A., & Simon, H. A. (1963). GPS, a program that simulates human thought. In E. A. Feigenbaum & J. Feldman (Eds.), *Computers and thought* (pp. 279-293). New York: McGraw-Hill. Retrieved November 18, 2008, from http://www.math.grinnell.edu/~stone/events/scheme-workshop/gps.html

Nielsen Online. (2008). *The video generation: Kids and teens consuming more online video content than adults at home*. Retrieved October, 6, 2008, from http://www.nielsen-netratings.com/pr/pr_080609.pdf

Noel, J. (2008, May 17). Cicero town president wants MySpace poser's identity revealed. *Chicagotribune.com*. Retrieved August 13, 2008 from http://www.chicagotribune.com/news/local/chi-myspaceimposters_bd-may18,0,3460074.story?page=1

Nood, D., & Attema, J. (2006). *The Second Life of virtual reality* (EPN Report). Retrieved August 19, 2008, from http://www.epn.net/interrealiteit/EPN-REPORT-The_Second_Life_of_VR.pdf

Norman, D. (1988). *The design of everyday things*. New York: Doubleday.

Northern Illinois University Faculty Development and Instructional Design Center. (2007). *Introduction to social bookmarking*. Retrieved from http://www.facdev.niu.edu/facdev/programs/handouts/socialbookmarking.shtml

Noruzi, A. (2007, June). Folksonomies: Why do we need controlled vocabulary? *Webology, 4*(2). Retrieved from http://www.webology.ir/2007/v4n2/editorial12.html

O'Donnell, C. (2006). 10 reasons to go short on Second Life. *This is going to be big*. Retrieved August 13, 2008, from http://www.thisisgoingtobebig.com/2006/11/10_reasons_to_g.html

O'Hanlon, C. (2007). If you can't beat 'em, join 'em. *T.H.E. Journal, 34*(8), 39–40, 42, 44.

O'Hear, S. (2006). *E-learning 2.0: How Web technologies are shaping education*. Retrieved November 23, 2008, from http://www.readwriteweb.com/archives/e-learning_20.php

O'Neil, R. (2008). It's not easy to stand up to cyberbullies, but we must. *The Chronicle of Higher Education, 54*(44), A23.

O'Reilly, R. C. (2006). Modeling integration and dissociation in brain and cognitive development. In Y. Munakata & M. H. Johnson (Eds.), *Processes of change in brain and cognitive development: Attention and performance XXI*. New York: Oxford University Press. Retrieved February 2, 2009, from http://psych-www.colorado.edu/~oreilly/papers/OReillyIPap.pdf

O'Reilly, R. C. (2006). *Part of human brain functions like a digital computer, professor says*. Retrieved February 2, 2009 from http://www.physorg.com/news79289076.html

O'Reilly, T. (2003). The software paradigm shift. *IT Conversations*. Retrieved August 13, 2008, from http://itc.conversationsnetwork.org/shows/detail50.html

O'Reilly, T. (2005). *What is Web 2.0: Design patterns and business models for the next generation of software*. Retrieved November 23, 2008, from http://www.oreillynet.com/pub/a/oreilly/tim/news/2005/09/30/what-is-web-20.html

O'Reilly, T., & Musser, J. (2006). *Web 2.0 principles and best practices*. Retrieved August 19, 2008, from http://oreilly.com/catalog/web2report/chapter/web20_report_excerpt.pdf

Oblinger, D. (2003). The name assigned to the document by the author. This field may also contain sub-titles, series names, and report numbers. Boomers, gen-Xers, and millennials: Understanding the new students. *Educause Review, 38*(3), 378-47. Retrieved March 12, 2008 from http://net.educause.edu/ir/library/pdf/ERM0342.pdf

Oblinger, D. (2003, July/August). Boomers, Gen-Xers, & Millennials: Understanding the "new students." *EDUCAUSE*, 36-47. Retrieved November 12, 2007, from http://www.educause.edu/ir/library/pdf/erm0342.pdf

Oblinger, D. (2004). The next generation of educational engagement. *Journal of Interactive Media in Education, 8*, 1-18. Retrieved October 3, 2007, from http://www-jime.open.ac.uk/2004/8/oblinger-2004-8.pdf

Oblinger, D. G. (2006). Simulations, games and learning. *EDUCAUSE Learning Initiative*. Retrieved February 5, 2008, from http://www.educause.edu/ir/library/pdf/ELI3004.pdf

Oblinger, D. G. (2008). Growing up with Google: What it means to education. *Becta: Emerging technologies for learning, 3*, 10-29. Retrieved April 10, 2008, from http://partners.becta.org.uk/upload-dir/downloads/page_documents/research/emerging_technologies08_chapter1.pdf

Oblinger, D. G. (2008). Growing up with Google: What it means to education. *Becta: Emerging Technologies for Learning, 3*, 10-29. Retrieved April 10, 2008, from http://partners.becta.org.uk/upload-dir/downloads/page_documents/research/emerging_technologies08_chapter1.pdf

Oblinger, D. G., & Hawkins, B. L. (2006). The myth about online course development. *EDUCAUSE Review, 41*(1), 14–15.

Oblinger, D. G., & Oblinger, J. L. (2005). Is it age or IT: First steps toward understanding the Net generation. In D. G. Oblinger & J. L. Oblinger (Eds.), *Educating the Net generation*. Retrieved August 26, 2008, from http://www.educause.edu/books/educatingthenetgen/5989

Office of Communications. (2008). *Social networking: A quantitative and qualitative research report into attitudes, behaviours and use*. Retrieved April 13, 2008, from http://www.wwww.radioauthority.org.uk/advice/media_literacy/medlitpub/medlitpubrss/socialnetworking/report.pdf

Oh, C. H. (2003). Information communication technology and the new university: A view on elearning. *THE ANNALS, 585*, 134–153. doi:10.1177/0002716202238572

Ohland, M. W., Layton, R. A., Loughry, M. L., & Yuhasz, A. G. (2005). Effects of behavioral anchors on peer evaluation reliability. *Journal of Engineering Education*, (July). 319-326.

Oliver, R., & Herrington, J. (2003). Exploring technology-mediate learning from a pedagogical perspective. *Interactive Learning Environments, 11*(2), 111–126. doi:10.1076/ilee.11.2.111.14136

Oman, C. M., Shebilske, W. L., Richards, J. T., Tubré, T. C., Beall, A. C., & Natapoff, A. (2002). Three dimensional spatial memory and learning in real and virtual environments. *Spatial Cognition and Computation, 2*, 355–372. doi:10.1023/A:1015548105563

Ondrejka, C. (2008). Education unleashed: Participatory culture, education, and innovation in Second Life. In K. Salen (Ed.), *The ecology of games: Connecting youth, games, and learning* (pp. 229-252). Cambridge, MA: MIT Press. Retrieved April 3, 2008, from http://www.mitpressjournals.org/doi/pdfplus/10.1162/dmal.9780262693646.229

Open University. (2007, May). The schome-NAGTY Teen Second Life pilot final report: A summary of key findings and lessons learnt. *SCHOME: The Education System for the Information Age*. Retrieved March 8, 2008, from http://mediax.stanford.edu/seminars/schomeNAGTY.pdf

Oradini, F., & Saunders, G. (2008). *The use of social networking by students and staff in higher education*. Retrieved August 18, 2008, from http://www.eife-l.org/publications/proceedings/ilf08/contributions/improving-quality-of-learning-with-technologies/Oradini_Saunders.pdf

Orion, N. (1993). A model for the development and implementation of field trips as an integral part of the science curriculum. *School Science and Mathematics, 93*(6), 325–331.

Otte, G., & Benke, M. (2006). Online learning: New models for leadership and organization in higher education. *Journal of Asynchronous Learning Networks, 10*(2), 23–31.

Oudshoorn, N., & Pinch, T. (2005). Introduction: How users and non-users matter. In N. Oudshoorn & T. Pinch (Eds.), How users matter: The co-construction of users and technology (pp. 1-25). Cambridge, MA: The MIT Press.

Paivio, A. (1986). *Mental representations: A dual coding approach.* New York: Oxford University Press.

Paivio, A. (1990). *Mental representations: A dual coding approach* (Vol. 9). New York: Oxford University Press.

Palen, L., & Dourish, P. (2003). Unpacking "privacy" for a networked world. In *Proceedings of the ACM Conference on Human Factors in Computing Systems CHI 2003,* Fort Lauderdale, FL (pp. 129-136). New York: ACM.

Palincsar, A. S. (1986). The role of dialogue in providing scaffolded instruction. *Educational Psychologist, 21*(1 & 2), 73–98. doi:10.1207/s15326985ep2101&2_5

Palloff, R. M., & Pratt, K. (1999). *Building learning communities in cyberspace.* San Francisco: Jossey-Bass Publishers.

Panda, S., & Mishra, S. (2007). E-learning in a mega open university: Faculty attitude, barriers and motivators. *Educational Media International, 44*(4), 323–338. doi:10.1080/09523980701680854

Papastergiou, M. (2006). Course management systems as tools for the creation of online learning environments: Evaluation from a social constructivist perspective and implications for their design. *International Journal on E-Learning, 5,* 593–622.

Papert, S. (1980). *Mindstorms.* New York: Basic Books.

Papert, S. (1993). *The children's machine: Rethinking school in the age of the computer.* New York: Basic Books.

Papert, S. A., & Harel, I. (1991). *Constructionism.* Norword, NJ: Ablex Publishing

Park, H. S., & Baek, Y. K. (2007). Design of learning contents focus on game to support the mobile learning. *Journal of the Korea Association of Information Education, 11*(2), 167–176.

Park, H. S., Jung, J. Y., & Collins, C. M. (2008). Effect of the activities in the Second Life® as tool for mutual understanding of gender role. In *Proceedings of the Society for information Technology and Teacher Education,* USA (pp. 1778-1783).

Passig, D., & Eden, S. (2001). Virtual reality as a tool for improving spatial rotation among deaf and hard-of-hearing children. *Cyberpsychology & Behavior, 4*(6), 681–686. doi:10.1089/109493101753376623

Patchin, J., & Hinduja, S. (2006). Bullies move beyond the schoolyard: A preliminary look at cyberbullying. *Youth Violence and Juvenile Justice, 4*(2), 148–169. doi:10.1177/1541204006286288

Patten, L. (2007). Successful integration of WebCT into a small business school. Developments in Business Simulation and Experiential Learning, 34.

Patton, M. Q. (1990). *Qualitative evaluation and research.* Beverly Hills, CA: Sage.

Payne, B. K., & Monk-Turner, E. (2006). *Students' perceptions of group projects: The role of race, age, and slacking.* Retrieved October 22, 2008, from http://findarticles.com/p/articles/mi_m0FCR/is_/ai_n26844266?tag=artBody;col1

Pea, R. (1993). Practices of distributed intelligence and design for education. In G. Salomon (Ed.), *Distributed cognition: Psychological and educational considerations* (pp. 47-86). Cambridge, MA: Cambridge University Press.

PennTags. (2005). Retrieved from http://tags.library.upenn.edu/

Perters, V. M., & Vissers, G. N. (2004). A simple classification model for simulation games. *Simulation & Gaming, 35*(1), 70–84. doi:10.1177/1046878103253719

Peterson, M. (2006, February). Learner interaction management in an avatar and chat-based virtual world. *Computer Assisted Language Learning, 19*(1), 79–103. doi:10.1080/09588220600804087

Pew Internet & American Life Project. (2007). *Social networking Websites and teens: An overview*. Retrieved September 10, 2007, from http://www.pewinternet.org/pdfs/PIP_SNS_Data_Memo_Jan_2007.pdf

Pfeil, U., Zaphiris, P., & Ang, C. S. (2006). Cultural differences in collaborative authoring of Wikipedia. *Journal of Computer-Mediated Communication, 12*(1), article 5. Retrieved October 23, 2008, from http://jcmc.indiana.edu/vol12/issue1/pfeil.html

Phillips, G. (2007, June 6). Teacher's blog draws probe from the system. *Southern Maryland Newspapers Online*. Retrieved December 3, 2007 from http://www.somdnews.com/stories/060607/rectop180341_32082.shtml

Piaget, J. (1950). *Introduction à l'épistémologie génétique*. Paris: Presses Universitaires de France.

Piaget, J. (1952). *The origins of intelligence in children* (M. Cook, Trans.). New York: International Universities Press.

Pinch, T. J., & Bijker, W. E. (2003). The social construction of facts and artifacts. In R. C. Scharff & V. Dusek (Eds.), The philosophy of technology: The technological condition: An anthology (pp. 221-232). Malden, MA: Blackwell.

Polanyi, M. (1974). *Personal knowledge: Towards a post-critical philosophy*. Chicago, IL: University Of Chicago Press.

Prensky, M. (2001). *Digital game-based learning*. New York: McGraw-Hill.

Prensky, M. (2001, September/October). Digital natives, digital immigrants. *Horizon, 9*(5), 1–6. doi:10.1108/10748120110424816

Prensky, M. (2001, November/December). Digital natives, digital immigrants, part 2: Do they really think differently? *Horizon, 9*(6), 1–6. doi:10.1108/10748120110424843

Prensky, M. (2004). *The emerging online life of the digital native*. New York: games2train. Retrieved August 07, 2008, from http://www.marcprensky.com/writing/Prensky-The_Emerging_Online_Life_of_the_Digital_Native-03.pdf

Prensky, M. (2005). "Engage me or engage me": What today's learners demand. *EDUCAUSE Review, 40*(5), 60–64.

Prensky, M. (2008). Turning on the lights. *Educational Leadership, 65*(6), 40–45.

Pretty, G. (1990). Relating psychological sense of community to social climate characteristics. *Journal of Community Psychology, 18*(1), 60–65. doi:10.1002/1520-6629(199001)18:1<60::AID-JCOP2290180109>3.0.CO;2-J

Psytech International. (2004). *Technical test battery: The technical manual*. Retrieved March 25, 2008, from http://www.psytech.co.uk/downloads/manuals/ttbman.pdf

Pursula, M., Warsta, M., & Laaksonen, I. (2005). Virtual university – a vehicle for development, cooperation and internationalisation in teaching and learning. *European Journal of Engineering Education, 30*(4), 439–446. doi:10.1080/03043790500213201

Quine, W. V. O. (1951). Two dogmas of empiricism. [from http://www.ditext.com/quine/quine.html]. *The Philosophical Review, 60*, 20–43. Retrieved November 20, 2008. doi:10.2307/2181906

Quine, W. V. O. (1964). *Word and object*. Cambridge, MA: The MIT Press.

Quinn, C. (2005). *Engaging learning: Designing e-learning simulation games*. San Francisco: Pfeiffer.

Rantanen, T. (2007). University 2.0: Enhancing communication and collaboration in universities. Helsinki, Finalnd: Helsinki University of Technology.

Ravenscroft, I. (2004). *Folk psychology as a theory*. Retrieved November 3, 2008, from http://plato.stanford.edu/entries/folkpsych-theory/

Rees, J. (2008). Teaching history with YouTube. *Perspectives on History, 46*(5). Retrieved June 11, 2008, from http://www.historians.org/Perspectives/issues/2008/0805/0805tec2.cfm

Reeve, R. A., & Brown, A. L. (1984). *Metacognition reconsidered: Implications for intervention research.* Cambridge, MA: Bolt Beranek and Newman.

Reeves, B., Malone, T. W., & O'Driscoll, T. (2008, May). Leadership's online labs. *Harvard Business Review,* 59–66.

Reid, E. (1995). Virtual worlds: Culture and imagination. In S. Jones (Ed.), *CyberSociety: Computer-mediated communication and community* (pp. 164-183). Thousand Oaks: Sage.

Reigeluth, C. M., & Stein, F. S. (1983). The elaboration theory of instruction In W. Schramm (Ed.), *The process and effects of mass communication* (pp. 5-6). Urbana, IL: The University of Illinois Press.

Report, H. (2007). *The horizon report: 2007 edition.* Retrieved September 20, 2007, from http://www.nmc.org/pdf/2007_Horizon_Report.pdf

Report, H. (2008). *The horizon report: 2008 edition.* Retrieved September 20, 2008, from http://www.nmc.org/pdf/2008-Horizon-Report.pdf

Requa v. Kent School District, 492 F.Supp.2d 1272 (W.D.Wash., 2007).

Rheingold, H. (1991). *The virtual community.* New York: Summit.

Rheingold, H. (1993). *The virtual community: Homesteading on the electronic frontier.* Reading, MA: Addison-Wesley.

Rheingold, H. (2008, February 23). Howard Rheingold one of 17 winners of HASTAC/MacArthur Foundation Competition. Message posted to http://www.smartmobs.com/2008/02/23/howard-rheingold-one-of-17-winners-of-hastacmacarthur-foundation-competition/

Rice, K., Pauley, L., Gasell, C., & Florez, C. (2008, October). *Going virtual! Unique needs and challenges of K-12 online teachers.* Vienna, VA: The International Association for K-12 Online Learning (iNACOL). Retrieved November 19, 2008, from http://edtech.boisestate.edu/goingvirtual/goingvirtual2.pdf

Richardson, J. C., & Swan, K. S. (2003). Examining social presence in online courses in relation to students' perceived learning and satisfaction. *Journal of Asynchronous Learning Networks, 7*(1), 68–88.

Richardson, W. (2006). *Blogs, wikis, podcasts, and other powerful Web tools for classrooms.* Thousand Oaks, CA: Corwin Press.

Richardson, W. (2007, March). Taming the beast: Finding good stuff online isn't a problem, making sense of it is. Thank goodness for social bookmarking. *School Library Journal,* 50–51.

Richardson, W. (2007, March). The seven C's of learning. *District administration.* Retrieved from http://www.districtadministration.com.

Ricknäs, M. (2008, July 9). Google adds third dimension to online social relationships. *Network World.* Retrieved July 9, 2008, from http://www.networkworld.com/news/2008/070908-google-adds-third-dimension-to.html

Rizzo, A. A., Buckwalter, J. G., Neumann, U., Kesselman, C., Thiebaux, M., Larson, P., & Rooyen, V. A. (1998). The virtual reality mental rotation spatial skills project. *Cyberpsychology & Behavior, 1*(2), 107–113. doi:10.1089/cpb.1998.1.113

Rogers, C. R. (1983). *Freedom to learn for the 80s.* Columbus, OH: Charles E. Merrill Publishing Company.

Rogers, E. M. (1995). *Diffusion of innovations* (4th ed.). New York: The Free Press.

Rogers, P. C., Liddle, S. W., Chan, P., Doxey, A., & Isom, B. (2007). Web 2.0 learning platform: Harnessing collective intelligence. *Turkish Online Journal of Distance Education, 8*(3), 16–33.

Rose, F. (2007, July). How Madison Avenue is wasting millions on a deserted Second Life. *Wired Magazine.*

Retrieved October 13, 2008 from http://www.wired.com/techbiz/media/magazine/15-08/ff_sheep

Roush. W. (2007, July/August). Second earth. *Technology Review.* Retrieved March 19, 2008, from https://www.technologyreview.com/Infotech/18911/

Rovai, A. P. (2001). Building classroom community at a distance: A case study. *Educational Technology Research and Development, 49*(4), 33–48. doi:10.1007/BF02504946

Rovai, A. P. (2002). Development of an instrument to measure classroom community. *The Internet and Higher Education, 5*(3), 197–211. doi:10.1016/S1096-7516(02)00102-1

Rovai, A. P. (2002). A preliminary look at the structural differences of higher education classroom communities in traditional an ALN courses. *Journal of Asynchronous Learning Networks, 6*(1), 41–56.

Rovai, A., & Jordan, H. (2004). Blended learning and sense of community: A comparative analysis with traditional and fully online graduate courses. *The International Review of Research in Open and Distance Learning, 5*(2). Retrieved August 1, 2007 from http://www.irrodl.org/index.php/irrodl/article/view/192

Rowley, D. J., & Sherman, H. (2004). Academic planning: The heart and soul of the academic strategic plan. Lanham, MD: University Press of America.

Royal, M. A., & Rossi, R. J. (1997). *Schools as communities.* Eugene, OR: ERIC Clearinghouse on Educational Management. (ERIC Document Reproduction Service No. ED405641).

Royle, K. (2008, April/May). Game-based learning: A different perspective. *Innovate, 4*(4). Retrieved April 11, 2008, from http://innovateonline.info/?view=article&id=433

Rumelhart, D. E., & McClelland, J. L., & the PDP Research Group. (1987). *Parallel distributed processing: Foundations.* Cambridge, MA: The MIT Press.

Rummler, G., & Brache, A. (1995). *Improving performance: How to manage the white space in the organization chart.* San Francisco: Jossey-Bass.

Saettler, P. (2004). *The evolution of American educational technology.* Greenwich, CT: Information Age Publishing.

Salaway, G., & Caruso, J. B. (2008). *The ECAR study of undergrad students and information technology, 2008.* EDUCAUSE Center for Applied Research. Retrieved October 25, 2008, from http://net.educause.edu/ir/library/pdf/ERS0808/RS/ERS0808w.pdf

Salomon, G. (1993). No distribution without individual's cognition: A dynamic interactional view. In G. Salomon (Ed.), *Distributed cognition: Psychological and educational considerations* (pp. 111-138). Cambridge, MA: Cambridge University Press.

Salter, D., Richards, L., & Carey, T. (2004). The "T5" design model: An instructional model and learning environment to support the integration of online and campus-based courses. *Educational Media International, 41*(3), 207–218. doi:10.1080/09523980410001680824

Samarawickrema, G., & Stacey, E. (2007). Adopting Web-based learning and teaching: A case study in higher education. *Distance Education, 28*(3), 313–333. doi:10.1080/01587910701611344

Sanders, R. L., & McKeown, L. (2007). Promoting reflection through action learning in a 3D virtual world. *International Journal of Social Sciences, 2*(1), 50–55.

Sarason, S. B. (1974). *The psychological sense of community: Prospects for a community psychology.* San Francisco: Jossey-Bass.

Scardamalia, M., & Bereiter, C. (1986). Research on written composition. In M. C. Wittrock (Ed.), *Handbook of research on teaching.* (3rd ed., pp. 778-803). New York: Macmillan Education Ltd.

Schank, R. C. (2007). The story-centered curriculum. *eLearn, 4*(April).

Schiffman, S., Vignare, K., & Geith, C. (2007). Why do higher-education institutions pursue online education? *Journal of Asynchronous Learning Networks, 11*(2), 61–71.

Schoetz, D., Canning, A., & Brady, J. (2008). Teens in video beating case charged as adults. *ABC News.* Retrieved August 1, 2008, from http://abcnews.go.com/GMA/Story?id=4609528&page=1

Schon, D. A. (1983). *The reflective practitioner: How professional think in action.* New York: Basic Books.

Schonefeld, E. (2008). Facebook is not only the world's largest social network, it is also the fastest growing. *Techcrunch.com.* Retrieved August 13, 2008 from http://www.techcrunch.com/2008/08/12/facebook-is-not-only-the-worlds-largest-social-network-it-is-also-the-fastest-growing/

Schramm, W. (1964). *Mass media and national development.* Stanford, CA: Stanford University Press.

Schramm, W. (1997). *The beginnings of communication study in America: A personal memoir.* Thousand Oaks, CA: Sage.

Schweitzer, H. (2008). Extending the online classroom with Wikis. In *Proceedings of the 2008 Conference of the Society for Information Technology & Teacher Education* (pp. 2826-2830).

Sclater, N. (2008, July 6). *Are open source VLEs/LMSs taking off in UK universities?* Retrieved from http://sclater.com/blog/?p=114

Scott, J. (2007, May). *Second nature: Nature publishing group in Second Life.* Paper presented at the Eduserv Foundation Symposium: Virtual worlds, real learning? London. Retrieved October 13, 2008, from http://www.eduserv.org.uk/foundation/symposium/2007/presentations/scott

Scott, W., Oleg, L., Phil, B., Colin, M., Mark, J., & Paul, S. (2006). *Personal learning environments: Challenging the dominant design of educational systems.* Retrieved November 23, 2008, from http://hdl.handle.net/1820/727

Searle, J. R. (1980). Minds, brains, and programs. *Behavioral and Brain Sciences 3*(3), 417-457. Retrieved November 3, 2008, from http://www.bbsonline.org/Preprints/OldArchive/bbs.searle2.html

Shaffer, C., & Anundsen, K. (1993). *Creating community anywhere.* New York: Perigee.

Shaffer, D. W. (2006). *How computer games help children learn.* New York: Palgrave Macmillan.

Shaffer, D. W., Squire, K. R., Halverson, R., & Gee, J. P. (2005). Video games and the future of learning. *Phi Delta Kappan, 87*(2), 104–111.

Shannon, C. F., & Weaver, W. (1964). *The mathematical theory of communication.* Urbana, IL: The University of Illinois Press. Torrance, E. P. (1985). *Creative motivation scale: Norms technical manual.* Bensenville, IL: Scholastic Testing Service.

Sherry, L. (1996). Issues in distance learning. [from http://carbon.cudenver.edu/~lsherry/pubs/issues.html]. *International Journal of Educational Telecommunications, 1*(4), 337–365. Retrieved July 11, 2008.

Shin, N., Jonassen, D. H., & McGee, S. (2003). Predictors of well-structured and ill-structured problem solving in an astronomy simulation. *Journal of Research in Science Teaching, 40*(1), 6–33. doi:10.1002/tea.10058

Shirky, C. (2006, December). Second Life: What are the real numbers? *Many 2 Many.* Retrieved October 13, 2008 from http://many.corante.com/archives/2006/12/12/second_life_what_are_the_real_numbers.php

Siemens, G. (2004). *Connectivism: A learning theory for the digital age.* Retrieved November 23, 2008, from http://www.elearnspace.org/Articles/connectivism.htm

Skiba, D. J. (2007). Nursing education 2.0: YouTube. *Nursing Education Perspectives, 28*(2), 100–102.

Slanguages. (2008, May). The conference for language education in virtual worlds. Retrieved October 23, 2008, from http://www.slanguages.net/es/index.php

Slater, M., Howell, J., Steed, A., Pertaub, D.-P., & Garau, M. (2000). Acting in virtual reality. In *Proceedings of the third international conference on Collaborative virtual environments*, San Francisco, CA, U.S. (pp. 103-110).

Smetana, J. G. (2006). *Social-cognitive domain theory: Consistencies and variations in children's moral and social judgments*. Mahwah, NJ: Lawrence Erlbaum Associates.

Smith, D. E., & Mitry, D. J. (2008). Investigation of higher education: The real costs and quality of online programs. *Journal of Education for Business, 83*(3), 147–152. doi:10.3200/JOEB.83.3.147-152

Snelbecker, G., Miller, S., & Zheng, R. (2007). Functional relevance and online instructional design. In R. Zheng & S. P. Ferris (Eds.), *Understanding online instructional modeling: Theories and practices* (pp. 1-17). Hershey, PA: IGI Global.

Snelson, C. (2006). Virtual design based research. *Academic Exchange Quarterly, 10*(4), 107–110.

Snelson, C. (2008). Web-based video in education: Possibilities and pitfalls. In *Proceedings of the Technology, Colleges & Community Worldwide Online Conference* (pp. 214-221). Retrieved August 23, 2008, from http://etec.hawaii.edu/proceedings/2008/Snelson2008.pdf

Snelson, C. (2008). YouTube and beyond: Integrating Web-based video into online education. In K. McFerrin, R. Weber, R. Carlsen, & D. A. Willis (Eds.), *Proceedings of Society for Information Technology and Teacher Education International Conference 2008* (pp. 732-737). Chesapeake, VA: AACE.

Sorensen, E. K., Takle, E. S., & Moser, H. M. (2006). Knowledge-building quality in online communities of practice: Focusing on learning dialogue. *Studies in Continuing Education, 28*(3), 241–257. doi:10.1080/01580370600947470

Spellings, M. (2008, April 1). *U.S. Secretary of Education Margaret Spellings announces department will move to a uniform graduation rate, require disaggregation of data*. U.S. Department of Education. Retrieved August 16, 2008, from http://www.ed.gov/news/pressreleases/2008/04/04012008.html

Spiceland, J. D., & Hawkins, C. P. (2002). The impact on learning of an asynchronous active learning course format. *Journal of Asynchronous Learning Networks, 6*(1), 68–75.

Squire, K. (2005). Changing the game: What happens when video games enter the classroom? *Innovate, 1*(6). Retrieved September 14, 2007, from http://www.innovateonline.info/index.php?view=article&id=82

Squire, K. (2007). Games, learning, and society: Building a field. *Educational Technology, 4*(5), 51–54.

Squire, K. (2008). Open-ended video games: A model for developing learning for the interactive age. In K. Salen (Ed.), *The ecology of games: Connecting youth, games, and learning* (pp. 167-196). Cambridge, MA: MIT Press. Retrieved April 3, 2008, from http://www.mitpressjournals.org/doi/pdf/10.1162/dmal.9780262693646.167

Squire, K., & Barab, S. (2004). Replaying history: Engaging urban underserved students in learning world history through computer simulation games. In Y. B. Kafai, W. A. Sandoval, N. Enyedy, A. S. Nixon, & F. Herrera (Eds.). *Proceedings of the Sixth International Conference of the Learning Sciences: Embracing Diversity in the Learning Sciences* (pp. 505-512). Mahwah, NJ: Lawrence Erlbaum Associates.

Stalnaker, R. C. (1987). *Inquiry*. Cambridge, MA: The MIT Press.

Steiner, E. (2007, May 1). MySpace photo costs teacher education degree. *Washington Post.com*. Retrieved April 25, 2008 from http://blog.washingtonpost.com/offbeat/2007/05/myspace_photo_costs_teacher_ed.html

Steinkuehler, C. A. (2004). Learning in massively multiplayer online games. In Y. B. Kafai, W. A. Sandoval, N. Enyedy, A. S. Nixon, & F. Herrera (Eds.), *Proceedings of the Sixth International Conference of the Learning Sciences: Embracing Diversity in the Learning Sciences* (pp. 521-528). Mahwah, NJ: Lawrence Erlbaum Associates. Retrieved September 20, 2007, from http://website.education.wisc.edu/steinkuehler/papers/SteinkuehlerICLS2004.pdf

Steinkuehler, C. A. (2005). Cognition and literacy in massively multiplayer online games. In D. Leu, J. Coiro, C. Lankshear, & K. Knobel (Eds.), *Handbook of research on new literacies*. Mahwah, NJ: Erlbaum. Retrieved September 15, 2007, from http://labweb.education.wisc.edu/curric606/readings/Steinkuehler2005.pdf

Steinkuehler, C. A. (2008). Massively multiplayer online games as educational technology: An outline for research. *Educational Technology, 48*(1), 10–21.

Steinkuehler, C., & Duncan, S. (2008). Scientific habits of mind in virtual worlds. *Journal of Science Education and Technology, 17*(6), 530-543. Retrieved October 20, 2008, from http://website.education.wisc.edu/steinkuehler/papers/SteinkuehlerDuncan2008.pdf

Stephenson, K. (1998). What knowledge tears apart, networks make whole. *Internal Communication Focus, 36.* Retrieved November 23, 2008, from http://www.netform.com/html/icf.pdf

Stevens, V. (2003). *Some CMC clients promoting language learning through chatting online. ESL_Home A Web Resource for CALL Lab Managers & for Teachers & Learners of Languages Online.* Retrieved August 8, 2008, from http://www.geocities.com/vance_stevens/findbuds.htm

Stevens, V. (2008, June/July). Class of the future. *The Linguist,* 18-20. Retrieved from http://sl2ndchance.pbwiki.com/f/linguist18-21_2ndLife_lo-res.pdf

Stone, B. (2008, July 9). Google introduces a cartoon-like method for talking in chat rooms. *The New York Times.* Retrieved July 9, 2008, from http://www.nytimes.com/2008/07/09/technology/09google.html?ex=1216267200&en=68ad9e88cd355b9b&ei=5070&emc=eta1

Strike, K. A. (2004). Community, the missing element of school reform: Why schools should be more like congregations than banks. *American Journal of Education, 110,* 215–232. doi:10.1086/383072

Subrahmanyam, K., Kraut, R., Greenfield, P., & Gross, E. (2000). The impact of home computer use on children's activities and development. *Children and Computer Technology, 10*(2), 123–144.

Surowiecki, J. (2004). *The wisdom of crowds.* New York: Doubleday.

Surry, D. W. (2002, April). A model for integrating instructional technology into higher education. Paper presented at the meeting of the American Educational Research Association (AERA), New Orleans, LA.

Surry, D. W. (2008). Technology and the future of higher education: An Ellulian perspective. In J. Luca & E. R. Weippl (Eds.), Proceedings of the ED-MEDIA 2008-World Conference on Educational Multimedia, Hypermedia & Telecommunications (pp. 4901-4906). Chesapeake, VA: Association for Advancement of Computing in Education.

Surry, D. W., & Ely, D. P. (2006). Adoption, diffusion, implementation, and institutionalization of educational innovations. In R. Reiser & J. V. Dempsey (Eds.), Trends & issues in instructional design and technology (2nd ed.) (pp. 104-111). Upper Saddle River, NJ: Prentice-Hall.

Surry, D. W., Porter, B., & Jackson, M. K. (2005, April). A comparison of technology implementation factors for three adopter groups. Presentation at the annual meeting of the American Educational Research Association, Montreal, Quebec, Canada.

Sweeney, T. (2008, April 2). CTIA: Samsung showcases Second Life apps. *Information Week.* Retrieved April 4, 2008, from http://www.informationweek.com/news/mobility/messaging/showArticle.jhtml;jsessionid=CIDWAOZ1DBOGOQSNDLPSKHSCJUNN2JVN?articleID=207001367&_requestid=643783

Sweller, J. (1988). Cognitive load during problem solving: Effects on learning. *Cognitive Science, 12,* 257–285.

Sweller, J. (2006). How the human cognitive system deals with complexity. In J. Elen & R.E. Clark (Eds.), *Handling complexity in learning environments: Theory and research* (pp. 13-25). Amsterdam: Elsevier.

Sweller, J., & Chandler, P. (1991). Evidence for cognitive load theory. *Cognition and Instruction, 8*(4), 351–362. doi:10.1207/s1532690xci0804_5

Sweller, J., & Chandler, P. (1994). Why some material is difficult to learn. *Cognition and Instruction, 12*(3), 185–233. doi:10.1207/s1532690xci1203_1

Sweller, J., van Merrienboer, J. J. G., & Paas, F. (1998). Cognitive architecture and instructional design. *Educational Psychology Review, 10*(3), 251–296. doi:10.1023/A:1022193728205

Tahmincioglu, E. (2008, September 7). Online colleges earning respect to a degree: Many hiring managers still skeptical, but distance learning hard to ignore. *MSNBC*. Retrieved November 1, 2008 from http://www.msnbc. msn.com/id/26458424/

Tamim, R., Shaikh, K., & Bethel, E. (2007). EDyoutube: Why not? In G. Richards (Ed.), *Proceedings of World Conference on E-Learning in Corporate, Government, Healthcare, and Higher Education 2007* (pp. 1302-1307). Chesapeake, VA: AACE.

Tapscott, D., & Williams, A. D. (2007, March 26). The Wiki workplace. *BusinessWeek*. Retrieved May 30, 2008, from http://www.businessweek.com/innovate/content/ mar2007/id20070326_237620.htm?chan=search

Tebben, S. L. (1995). Community and caring in a college classroom. *Journal for a Just and Caring Education, 1*(3), 335–344.

Technorati. (2006). *State of the blogosphere*. Retrieved November 20, 2008, from http://www.sifry.com/alerts/ archives/000436.html van Fraassen, B. C. (1980). *The scientific image*. New York: Oxford University Press.

Tharp, R. (1993). Institutional and social context of educational reform: Practice and reform. In E. A. Forman, N. Minnick, & C. A. Stone (Eds.), *Contexts for learning: Sociocultural dynamics in children's development* (pp. 269-282). New York: Oxford University Press.

Tharp, R., & Gallimore, R. (1988). *Rousing minds to life: Teaching, learning, and schooling in social context*. New York: Cambridge University Press.

The Design Based Research Collective. (2003). Design-based research: An emerging paradigm for educational inquiry. *Educational Researcher, 32*(1), 5–8. doi:10.3102/0013189X032001005

The New Media Consortium & the EDUCAUSE Learning Initiative. (2007). *The 2007 horizon report*. Retrieved July 23, 2008, from http://www.nmc.org/pdf/2007_Ho- rizon_Report.pdf

The New Media Consortium. (2007). *The 2007 horizon report*. Retrieved January 12, 2008 from http://www. nmc.org/pdf/2007_Horizon_Report.pdf

The New Media Consortium. (2008). *The 2008 horizon report*. Retrieved November 12, 2008 from http://www. nmc.org/pdf/2008-Horizon-Report.pdf

The Pennsylvania State University. (2007). *Student teaching handbook: The Pennsylvania State University college of education*. Retrieved July 17, 2008 from http://www.ed.psu.edu/preservice/things%20to%20 update/2007-2008%20ST_HANDBOOK_August%20 2007.pdf

Thomas, D., & Brown, J. S. (2007, October 21). *Why virtual worlds can matter* [Working Paper]. Retrieved February 7, 2008, from http://www.johnseelybrown.com/ needvirtualworlds.pdf

Thompson, J. (2007). Is education 1.0 ready for Web 2.0 students? *Innovate, 3*(4). Retrieved from http://www.in- novateonline.info/index.php?view-article&id=393

USA Today (2006, July 16). *YouTube serves up 100 million videos a day*. Retrieved May 29, 2008, from http:// www.usatoday.com/tech/news/2006-07-16-youtube- views_x.htm

Torrance, M., Fidalgo, R., & Garcia, J. (2007). The teach-ability and effectiveness of cognitive self-regulation in sixth-grade writers. *Learning and Instruction, 17*(3), 265–285. doi:10.1016/j.learninstruc.2007.02.003

Trentin, G. (2008). Learning and knowledge sharing within online communities of professionals: An approach to the evaluation of virtual community environments. *Educational Technology, 48*(3), 32–38.

Trexler, S. (2007). The best of social bookmarking: Diigo. *Information Searcher, 17*(3), 34–36.

Tsai, C. C. (2008). The preferences toward constructivist Internet-based learning environments among university students in Taiwan. *Computers in Human Behavior, 24*, 16–31. doi:10.1016/j.chb.2006.12.002

Turiel, E. (1983). *The development of social knowledge: Morality and convention*. Cambridge, UK: Cambridge University Press.

Turiel, E. (2002). *The culture of morality: Social development, context, and conflict*. New York: Cambridge University Press.

Turkle, S. (1995). *Life on the screen: Identity in the age of the Internet*. New York: Simon and Schuster.

Turkle, S. (1997). *Life on the screen: Identity in the age of the Internet* (1st Touchstone ed.). New York: Touchstone.

Turner, V. (1982). *From ritual to theatre: The human seriousness of play*. New York: PAJ Publications.

Turos, J. M., & Ervin, A. I. (2000). Training and gender differences on a Web-based mental rotation task. *The Penn State Behrend Psychology Journal, 4*(2), 3–12.

Tyler, L. E. (1974). *Individual differences: Abilities and motivational directions*. New York: Appleton-Century-Crofts.

U.S. Department of Education, National Center for Education Statistics. (2003).Web-related legal issues and policies. In *Weaving a secure Web around education: A guide to technology standards and security*. Retrieved from http://nces.ed.gov/pubs2003/secureweb/ch_3.asp#H9

Universal Service Administration Company. (2008). *Step 10: Children's Internet Protection Act (CIPA)*. Retrieved June 11, 2008, from http://www.usac.org/sl/applicants/step10/cipa.aspx

University of Colorado at Boulder. (2006, October 6). Human brain region functions like digital computer. *ScienceDaily*. Retrieved November 23, 2008, from http://www.sciencedaily.com/releases/2006/10/061005222628.htm

van der Stel, M., & Veenman, M. V. J. (2008). Relation between intellectual ability and metacognitive skillfulness as predictors of learning performance of young students performing tasks in different domains. *Learning and Individual Differences, 18*(1), 128–134. doi:10.1016/j.lindif.2007.08.003

van Merrienboer, J. J. G., & Sweller, J. (2005). Cognitive load theory and complex learning: Recent developments and future directions. *Educational Psychology Review, 17*(2), 147–177. doi:10.1007/s10648-005-3951-0

Van, J. (2007, August 12). Training for the poor moves into computer age. *The Chicago Tribune*, pp. 5.1, 5.4.

Vander Wal, T. (2007). *Folksonomy*. Retrieved August 10, 2008, from http://www.vanderwal.net/folksonomy.html

Vaughan, N. D. (2008). Supporting deep approaches to learning through the use of Wikis and weblogs. In *Proceedings of the 2008 Conference of the Society for Information Technology & Teacher Education* (pp. 2857-2864).

Venners, B. (2003). *Exploring with Wiki: A conversation with Ward Cunningham, part I*. Retrieved July 2, 2008, from http://www.artima.com/intv/wiki.html

Viégas, F. B. (2005). Bloggers' expectations of privacy and accountability: An initial survey. *Journal of Computer-Mediated Communication, 10*(3). doi:. doi:10.1111/j.1083-6101.2005.tb00260.x

Vignare, K., Geith, C., & Schiffman, S. (2006). *Business models for online learning: An exploratory survey*. Retrieved August 25, 2008, from http://www.sloan-c.org/publications/jaln/v10n2/pdf/v10n2_5vignare.pdf

Villano, M. (2008). Wikis, blogs, & more, oh my! *Campus Technology, 21*(8), 42–50.

Virtual Worlds Management. (2008, July 8). $161 million invested in 16 virtual worlds-related companies in 2Q 2008, $345 million invested in first half of 2008. *Virtual Worlds News*. Retrieved July 23, 2008, from http://www.virtualworldsnews.com/2008/07/161-million-inv.html

Virvou, M., & Alepis, E. (2005). Mobile educational features in authoring tools for personalized tutoring. *Computers & Education, 44*, 53–68. doi:10.1016/j.compedu.2003.12.020

Vivanco, H. (2007, March 29). Teacher still posting on MySpace. *Inland Valley Daily Bulletin*. Retrieved on December 3, 2007 from http://www.dailybulletin.com/news/ci_5553720

Volti, R. (2006). Society and technological change (5th ed.). New York: Worth.

Vygotsky, L. (1986). *Thought and language* (rev. ed.). Cambridge, MA: MIT Press.

Vygotsky, L. S. (1978). *Mind in society: The development of higher psychological process.* Cambridge, MA: Harvard University Press.

Wallace, L. (2007). Online teaching and university policy: Investigating the disconnect. *Journal of Distance Education, 22*(1). Retrieved August 26, 2008, from http://www.jofde.ca/index.php/jde/article/viewArticle/58/494

Waller, D. (2000). Individual differences in spatial learning from computer-simulated environments. *Journal of Experimental Psychology. Applied, 6,* 307–321. doi:10.1037/1076-898X.6.4.307

Wallis, C., & Steptoe, S. (2006, December 10). How to bring out schools out of the 20th century. *Time Magazine.* Retrieved March 23, 2008, from http://www.time.com/time/printout/0,8816,1568480,00.html

Wang, Q. (2006). Quality assurance: Best practices for assessing online programs. *International Journal on E-Learning, 5*(2), 265–274.

Wang, S. K., & Hsua, H. Y. (2008). Reflections on using blogs to expand in-class discussion. *TechTrends, 52*(3), 81–85. doi:10.1007/s11528-008-0160-y

Warnick, B. R., & Burbules, N. C. (2007). Media comparison studies: Problems and possibilities. *Teachers College Record, 109*(11), 2483–2510.

Wassell, B., & Crouch, C. (2008). Fostering critical engagement in preservice teachers: Incorporating Weblogs into multicultural education. *Journal of Technology and Teacher Education, 16*(2), 211–232.

Watson, P. (2005). Ideas: A history of thought and invention from fire to Freud. New York: HarperCollins.

Watts, D. J. (2004). *Six degrees: The science of a connected age.* New York: W. W. Norton & Company.

Watwood, B. (2007, December). Instructional uses of social bookmarking: Reflections and questions. *Romanian Journal of Social Informatics, 8.* Retrieved from http://www.ris.uvt.ro/Publications/Decembrie%202007/Watwood.pdf

Web 3.0. (2008, August 25). In *Wikipedia, the free encyclopedia.* Retrieved August 25, 2008, from http://en.wikipedia.org/w/index.php?title=Web_3.0&oldid=234152612

Webber, C. (2005). *Making collaboration work.* Retrieved June 16, 2008, from http://www.projectsatwork.com/content/articles/222381.cfm

Wedemeyer, C. A. (1981). *Learning at the back door: Reflections on non-traditional learning in the lifespan.* Madison, WI: University of Wisconsin Press.

Wedemeyer, C. A. (1981). *Learning at the back door: Reflections on non-traditional learning in the lifespan.* Madison, WI: University of Wisconsin Press.

Weinberger, D. (2002). *Small pieces loosely joined.* Cambridge, MA: Perseus Books.

Welcome to Technorati. (n.d.). Retrieved from http://technorati.com/about/

Wellman, B. (1999). The network community: An introduction to networks in the global village. In B. Wellman (Ed.), *Networks in the global village* (pp. 1-48). Boulder, CO: Westview Press.

Wells, J., Lewis, L., & Greene, B. (2006). *Internet access in U.S. public schools and classrooms: 1994-2005* (No. NCES 2007-020). Washington, DC: U.S. Department of Education, National Center for Education Statistics. Retrieved November 4, 2008, from http://nces.ed.gov/pubsearch/pubsinfo.asp?pubid=2007020

Wen, M. L., Tsai, C. C., Lin, H. M., & Chuang, S. C. (2004). Cognitive-metacognitvie and content-technical aspects of constructivist Internet-based learning environment: A LISREL analysis. *Computers & Education, 43,* 237–248. doi:10.1016/j.compedu.2003.10.006

Wenger, E. (1998). *Communities of practice: Learning, meaning, and identity.* Cambridge, UK: Cambridge University Press.

Wenger, E. (1998). *Communities of practice: Learning, meaning, and identity.* Cambridge, UK: Cambridge University Press.

Wertheim, E. (n.d.). *Surviving the group project: A note on working in teams.* Retrieved June 23, 2008, from http://web.cba.neu.edu/~ewertheim/teams/ovrvw2.htm

Wertsch, J. V. (1991). *Voices of the mind: A socialcultural approach to mediated action.* Cambridge, MA: Harvard University Press.

Wesch, M. (2007). *Web 2.0...the machine is us/ing us* [Video file]. Video posted to http://www.youtube.com/watch?v=6gmP4nk0EOE

Wheeler, T. (2007). Personnel pitfalls in the cyberworld. *School Administrator, 64*(9), 22–24.

Wighting, M. J. (2006). Effects of computer use on high school students' sense of community. *The Journal of Educational Research, 99*(6), 371–379. doi:10.3200/JOER.99.6.371-380

Wikipedia. (2008). *Social networking.* Retrieved August 13, 2008 from http://en.wikipedia.org/wiki/Social_networking

Wikipedia. (n.d.). *Social network services.* Retrieved December 1, 2008 from http://en.wikipedia.org/wiki/Social_networking

Wiley, D. (2006). Open source, openness, and higher education. *Innovate, 3*(1). Retrieved from http://www.innovateonline.info/index.php?view-article&id-354.

Williams, D., Yee, N., & Caplan, S. E. (2008). Who plays, how much, and why? Debunking the stereotypical gamer profile. *Journal of Computer-mediated Communication, 13*(4), 993-1018. Retrieved November 10, 2008, from http://www3.interscience.wiley.com/cgi-bin/fulltext/121394419/HTMLSTART

Williamson, B., & Facer, K. (2004). More than 'just a game': The implications for schools of children's computer games communities. *Education Communication and Information, 4,* 255–270. doi:10.1080/14636310412331304708

Wilson, B. G. (2001, July). *Sense of community as a valued outcome for electronic courses, cohorts, and programs.* Paper presented at the VisionQuest PT3 Conference,

Denver, CO. Retrieved July 11, 2008, from http://carbon.cudenver.edu/~bwilson/SenseOfCommunity.html

Wilson, B. G., Parrish, P., Balasubramanian, N., & Switzer, S. (2007). Contrasting forces affecting the practice of distance education. In R. Luppicini (Ed.), *Online learning communities* (pp. 333-346). Charlotte, NC: IAP-Information Age Publishing.

Wilson, B., & Ryder, M. (1996). Dynamic learning communities: An alternative to designed instructional systems. In M. Crawford & M. Simonson (Eds.), *Proceedings of the 1996 international conference of the Association of Educational Communications and Technology.*

Wilson, S. (2006). *The personal learning environment blog.* Retrieved July 31, 2008, from http://www.cetis.ac.uk/members/ple

Winn, W. (2006). Functional contextualism in context: A reply to Fox. *Educational Technology Research and Development, 54*(1), 55–59. doi:10.1007/s11423-006-6495-1

Winslow, K. (1970). *The adoption and distribution of videotape materials for educational use.* Washington, DC: Academy for Educational Development, Inc. (Eric Document Reproduction Service No. ED039716)

Wisniewski v. Board of Education, Weedsport Central School District, 494 F. 3d 34, (2nd Cir. 2007).

Wittgenstein, L. (1973). *Philosophical investigations* (3rd ed.). Upper Saddle River, NJ: Prentice Hall.

Wolfe, I. (2008). *Basic survival skills for managing Gen Y.* Retrieved December 1, 2008 from http://www.articlesbase.com/business-articles/basic-survival-skills-for-managing-gen-y-500456.html

Wood, D. J., Bruner, J. S., & Ross, G. (1976). The role of tutoring in problem solving. *Journal of Child Psychiatry and Psychology, 17*(2), 89–100. doi:10.1111/j.1469-7610.1976.tb00381.x

Woolcock, N. (2008). Soaring number of teachers say they are 'cyberbully' vicitms. *The Times.* Retrieved July 21, 2008 from http://www.timesonline.co.uk/tol/life_and_style/education/article3213130.ece

WSBTV.com. (2006, May 16). Student faces criminal charges for teacher jokes. *WSBTV.com*. Retrieved July 21, 2008 from http://www.wsbtv.com/education/9223824/detail.html

Wyatt, S. (2005). Non-users also matter. In N. Oudshoorn & T. Pinch (Eds.), How users matter: The co-construction of users and technology (pp. 67-79). Cambridge, MA: The MIT Press.

Xie, Y., Ke, F., & Sharma, P. (2008). The effect of peer feedback for blogging on college students' reflective learning processes. *The Internet and Higher Education*, *11*(1), 18–25. doi:10.1016/j.iheduc.2007.11.001

Yang, H., & Liu, Y. (2008). Building a sense of community for text-based computer-mediated communication courses. *Journal of Educational Technology Systems*, *36*(4), 393–413. doi:10.2190/ET.36.4.d

Yates, J., & Orlikowski, W. J. (1992). Genres of organizational communication: A structurational approach to studying communication and media. *Academy of Management Review*, *17*(2), 299–326. doi:10.2307/258774

Young, J. R. (2008, February). Blog comments vs. peer review: Which way makes a book better? *The Chronicle of Higher Education*, *54*(21), A20.

Young, J. R. (2008a, February 28). Abilene U. to give iPhones or iPods to all freshman. *Chronicle of Higher Education*. Retrieved February 28, 2008, from http://chronicle.com/wiredcampus/article/2782/university-to-give-iphones-or-ipods-to-all-incoming-freshmen?utm_source=at&utm_medium=en

Young, J. R. (2008b, February 29). Forget e-mail: New messaging service has students and professors atwitter. *Chronicle of Higher Education*, A15. Retrieved February 26, 2008, from http://chronicle.com/free/v54/i25/25a01501.htm

YouTube Help Center. (2008). *What is YouTube's video identification tool?* Retrieved July 30, 2008, from http://www.google.com/support/youtube/bin/answer.py?answer=83766&topic=13656

YouTube. (2008). *YouTube fact sheet: Overview and features*. Retrieved October, 08, 2008 from http://www.youtube.com/t/fact_sheet

Zhang, D., Zhou, L., Briggs, R. O., & Nunamaker, J. F. (2006). Instructional video in e-learning: Assessing the impact of interactive video on learning effectiveness. *Information & Management*, *43*(1), 15–27. doi:10.1016/j.im.2005.01.004

Zheng, D., Brewer, R. A., & Young, M. F. (2005, November). *English language learning in a game-based Multi-User Virtual environment: Quest Atlantis connects middle school students in China to the world*. Paper presented at Webheads in Action Online Convergence.

Zheng, R. (2007). Understanding the underlying constructs of Webquests. In T. Kidd & H. Song (Eds.), *Handbook of research on instructional systems and technology* (pp. 752-767). Hershey, PA: IGI Global.

Zheng, R., Flygare, J. A., Dahl, L. B., & Hoffman, R. (in press). The impact of individual differences on social communication pattern in online learning. In C. Mourlas, N. Tsianos, & P. Germanakos (Eds.), *Cognitive and emotional processes in Web-based education: Integrating human factors and personalization*. Hershey, PA: IGI Global.

Ziegler, S. G. (2007). The (mis)education of Generation M. *Learning, Media and Technology*, *32*(1), 69–81. doi:10.1080/17439880601141302

Zimmerman, B. J. (2008). Investigating self-regulation and motivation: Historical background, methodological developments, and future prospects. *American Educational Research Journal*, *45*(1), 166–183. doi:10.3102/0002831207312909

Zotero. (2009). Retrieved from http://www.zotero.org/

About the Contributors

Harrison Hao Yang (Ed.D., Florida International Univeristy, 1996) is a professor in the Department of Curriculum and Instruction at Stae University of New York at Oswego, USA. His research specialties include assessment and e-folios, distance/flexible education, information literacy, information technology diffusion/integration, learning theories, issues and trends on vocational-technical education, Web/learning communities, etc. Dr. Yang is the recipient of SUNY Oswego President Award of Teaching Excellence in 2006.

Steve Chi-Yin Yuen (Ph.D., The Pennsylvania State University, 1984) is a professor in the Department of Technology Education at The University of Southern Mississippi (USM), USA. His research specialties include electronic performance support system, e-learning 2.0, handheld technology in teaching and learning, mobile learning, multimedia instruction, semantic Web, social networking in education, technology planning and implementation in the classrooms, Web 2.0, Web accessibility, Web-based instruction, etc. Dr. Yuen is the recipient of USM Excellence in Teaching Award in 1997 and 2004, Mississippi Technology Educator of the Year in 2002, and Fulbright Scholar Lecturing Award in 1992.

* * *

J. Enrique Agudo, from Zafra in south western Spain, is an engineering specialist in Hypermedia applied to educational contexts. He holds a PhD in Computer Science from the University of Extremadura. At present, he works as a full-time Assistant Lecturer in the Telecom and Information Systems Technology Department of the same academic institution. His most recent research involves work on educational ICT applications, adaptive hypermedia systems, e-learning and computer assisted language learning. He is an active participant in various regional projects on e-learning in professional contexts, mobile learning for young children, and, machine translation.

Jay Alden is a Professor of Systems Management at the Information Resources Management (IRM) College of National Defense University in Washington DC. He conducts courses on performance measurement. Dr. Alden served as the founding Director of Distance Education for the IRM College when it first established a distance education program in 1994. Besides his faculty duties, he is the administrator for a community of practice website for the College that keeps alumni aware of new developments in the management of information technology. He previously was the Director of Executive Programs at the University of Maryland University College and Manager of Evaluation and Research at Xerox Corporation. Dr. Alden is author of *A Trainer's guide to Web-based Instruction.*

Copyright © 2010, IGI Global, distributing in print or electronic forms without written permission of IGI Global is prohibited.

Youngkyun Baek has been teaching at Korea National University of Education since 1991. His research interests are on educational games, simulation, and mobile devices in education. Dr. Baek has presented several papers at SITE and NECC on gaming and simulations. He published three books on educational games and wrote two books chapters: "Design of an adaptive mobile learning management system based on student learning styles" in Handbook of Research on User Interface Design and Evaluation For Mobile Technology; "Revealing New Hidden Curriculum of Digital Games" in *Handbook of Research on Effective Electronic Gaming in Education* (IGI Global). He is co-author of the book entitled *"Digital Simulations for Improving Education: Learning Through Artificial Teaching Environments"* by IGI Global. Now he is authoring the book, *"Gaming for Classroom-Based Learning: Digital Role Playing as a Motivator of Study"*.

Curt Bonk is Professor of Instructional Systems Technology at Indiana University and adjunct in the School of Informatics. He has received several distance learning awards and recognitions. His new book, *"Empowering Online Learning: 100+ Activities for Reading, Reflecting, Displaying, and Doing,"* was published by Jossey Bass in 2008. Dr. Bonk is currently researching blended learning, the Web 2.0 including YouTube, wikibooks, blogs, and online language learning, and other emerging learning technologies. He may be contacted at cjbonk@indiana.edu and his homepage is at http://mypage. iu.edu/~cjbonk/.

Heather Lynn Carter, Associate Clinical Professor and Director of Education Downtown at Arizona State University's College of Teacher Education and Leadership, currently oversees the college's masters and certification program for non-traditional teacher candidates. Her research interests include new technologies and non-traditional methods for teacher professional development.

Eva Dominguez is a Lecturer at the University of Extremadura and member of the Department of Music Education, Applied Visual Arts and Corporal Expression. Born in Caceres (Spain) in 1971, she got her first degree in Fine Arts, BA, majoring in Design and Visual Communication at Salamanca University. Her PhD from Extremadura University verses on the History of Graphic Design. Most of her research covers the field of graphic design for visual communication, specifically the creation and design of interfaces in multimedia / hypermedia environments. She recently spent a year at the University of South Alabama in the Department of Visual Arts sponsored by the Ministry of Education of Spain. As a designer and artist, she has held various national and international exhibitions as well as received awards for her work.

Stephen Downes works for the National Research Council of Canada where he has served as a Senior Research, based in Moncton, New Brunswick, since 2001. Affiliated with the Learning and Collaborative Technologies Group, Institute for Information Technology, Downes specializes in the fields of online learning, new media, pedagogy and philosophy. Downes is perhaps best known for his daily newsletter, OLDaily, which is distributed by web, email and RSS to thousands of subscribers around the world. He has published numerous articles both online and in print, including The Future of Online Learning (1998), Learning Objects (2000), Resource Profiles (2003), and E-Learning 2.0 (2005). He is a popular speaker, appearing at hundreds of events around the world over the last fifteen years.

Elizabeth Downs is a Professor in the Instructional Technology program at Georgia Southern University. She received her B.S. in Elementary Education from Florida State University and an M.Ed. in Educational Psychology and Ph.D. in Instructional Technology from the University of Florida. Dr. Downs taught 3rd and 4th grade for seven years in Palm Beach County, Florida. She has been on the faculty of Georgia Southern University for 18 years. Her research interests include analyzing the characteristics of Generation "Y" learners and studying the impact of emerging technology applications on instruction.

Patricia Edwards, originally from Syracuse, New York, has lived abroad and worked in private and public sectors of Education since the 1970s. She holds a PhD in Applied Linguistics from Zaragoza University, specializing in discourse analysis in professional contexts. Currently, as a senior lecturer at the University of Extremadura in south-western Spain, she teaches English for Specific Purposes at the School of Business Science and Hospitality Studies on both the undergraduate and post-graduate levels. Her main research interests lie in language learning through ICT with a particular emphasis on sociolinguistics. In addition to active participation in national and international research projects, she is often commissioned to partake in regional and European academic initiatives. Collaboration on the advisory boards of several scientific committees for academic excellence and university management positions complement her background.

David C. Ensminger is a Clinical Assistant Professor at Loyola University Chicago. He has worked as an evaluation and instructional design consultant and was Director of the Instructional Media Center (IMC) and Coordinator of the Program for the Enhancement of Teaching and Learning (PETAL) at the University of South Alabama. He has also worked for the U.S. Navy in the areas of performance technology and evaluation. A Nationally Certified Psychologist, he holds a Doctor of Philosophy in Instructional Design & Development from the University of South Alabama, a Master of Arts in Psychology from Stephen F. Austin University and a Bachelor of Science in Psychology from the University of Utah. He has also worked as a school mental health counselor and in the areas of substance abuse counseling and drug prevention.

Deborah Everhart teaches as an Adjunct Assistant Professor in Georgetown University's Medieval Studies program. She received her Ph.D. in English from the University of California, Irvine. Dr. Everhart has been using computers in the classroom since 1985. She served for six years as the Sr. Internet Development Coordinator in University Information Services at Georgetown University. Since 2000 she has been an architect at Blackboard, now Principal Architect, providing leadership in product strategy and development. Her responsibilities include researching, analyzing, and designing features and functionality for Blackboard products. Dr. Everhart has written numerous articles and presented papers and seminars on medieval literature, pedagogical technologies, and the future of online teaching and learning.

Ann Dutton Ewbank is the Education Liaison Librarian at Arizona State University's Fletcher Library. She teaches future and current classroom teachers how to effectively find and use information in technology rich environments. Her research interests include school library advocacy and aspects of teacher professional development.

Teresa S. Foulger, is an Assistant Professor of Educational Technology in the College of Teacher Education and Leadership at Arizona State University, where she teaches undergraduate and graduate courses in educational technology, innovations in teaching and learning, and professional development. Her research interests focus on technology-rich environments where collaboration, communities of practice, and innovative professional development models support organizational change.

Stephen W. Harmon is the Director of Learning Technologies at Georgia State University and an Associate Professor of Learning Technologies at Georgia State University in Atlanta, GA. Dr. Harmon teaches graduate courses in Instructional Design and Technology. His research interests and consulting experience includes project evaluation, elearning, Instructional Technology in Developing Countries and hypermedia. Dr. Harmon can be reached at swharmon@gsu.edu or his website at http://swharmon.gsu.edu/.

Marshall G. Jones is an Associate Professor of Educational Technology at Winthrop University in Rock Hill, SC. Dr. Jones teaches graduate courses in Educational Technology and undergraduate courses in technology integration. He was awarded the inaugural Bank of America Professorship of Education in 2004 at Winthrop University to study mobile, ubiquitous learning environments. His research interests and consulting experience includes project evaluation, instructional design, mobile learning, elearning, the design and development of constructivist learning environments, emerging technologies and new media. Dr. Jones can be reached at jonesmg@winthrop.edu, or through his website, http://marshallgjones.com.

Morris S. Y. Jong, is a instructor at Centre for the Advancement of Information Technology in Education, The Chinese University of Hong Kong. Motivated by his keen interest in education and information technology, Mr. Jong has been teaching teacher education programmes specializing in IT in education, at undergraduate, postgraduate, and master levels, for over 7 years. He became a member of Centre for the Advancement of Information Technology in Education, The Chinese University of Hong Kong in 2007. Apart from teaching, Mr. Jong has been active in diverse international, global Chinese, and local scholarly activities which promote the integration of IT into teaching and learning. Besides assisting in the organization of these activities, he has published more 30 international and global Chinese journal and conference papers, given presentations in conferences, as well as invited talks in seminars and scholarly visits. Currently, he is pursuing a PhD degree in the area of computer game-based learning at The Chinese University of Hong Kong.

Adam Kay, Lecturer in Teacher Preparation, teaches graduate and undergraduate courses in child and adolescent development and learning and motivation in the College of Teacher Education and Leadership at Arizona State University. His research interests include social and moral development and ethical reasoning in educational contexts.

Nari Kim is a doctoral candidate in Instructional Systems Technology at Indiana University, Bloomington. Her major research interests are designing inquiry-based learning environments, Web 2.0 technology integration in education, wikibooks, and computer-mediated communication and learning. She may be contacted at narkim@indiana.edu.

Fong-Lok Lee is the Director of Centre for the Advancement of Information Technology in Education, The Chinese University of Hong Kong. Apart from being the Centre Director, Dr. Lee is also the Programme Director of the Advanced Postgraduate Diploma in Education (Information Technology in Education) Programme and the Master of Arts Programme in Information Technology in Education since 2001 and 2003, respectively. He has fifteen years of working experience in his specialist field, twenty-two years of teaching experience in local secondary schools and more than eleven years in conducting teacher training courses for local secondary school teachers. He served as a secondary school teacher, extra-curricular activities master and mathematics panel chairman. Presently he is a member of the executive committee of the Global Chinese Association on Computers in Education, co-chief Editor of Global Chinese Journal of Computers in Education; past-president of Asia-Pacific Society for Computers in Education; Chair of the HK & Macau Chapter, Global Chinese Society on Computers in Education. His research interests include Educational Technology Cognitive Processes, Artificial Intelligence, Mathematics Learning, and Application of Information Technologies in Education.

Jimmy H. M. Lee is Professor of Department of Computer Science and Engineering, The Chinese University of Hong Kong. Dr. Lee read both his BMath (Hons) degree and MMath degree from the University of Waterloo in 1987 and 1988, respectively, and his PhD from the University of Victoria in 1992. Immediately upon graduation, he joined The Chinese University of Hong Kong. His research focuses on the theory and practice of constraint satisfaction and optimization with applications in scheduling, resource allocation, and combinatorial problems. In recent years, Professor Lee has also been conducting research on novel Web-based learning platforms and the accompanying pedagogies, particularly in the development of educational games. He is currently the Associate Director (Research and Development) of the Centre for the Advancement of Information Technology in Education under the Hong Kong Institute of Educational Research, CUHK. Professor Lee has 100 refereed technical publications in international journals and conferences, and has obtained over $11 million in competitive research funding. He is on the editorial boards of the Journal of Discrete Algorithms, the CONTRAINTS journal, and the Constraint Programming Newsletter. Professor Lee is active in extramural educational activities. He has taught for the Programs for the Gifted and Talented, and was the Chief Examiner of Paper II of the HK A-Level Computer Studies subject from 1995 to 2001. Inspired by his many former good teachers from elementary school to universities, Jimmy's passion for teaching garnered him the Vice-Chancellor's Exemplary Teaching Award in 2005, and the Faculty of Engineering Exemplary Teaching Award in 1999, 2000, 2001, and 2003.

Mimi Miyoung Lee is an Assistant Professor in the Department of Curriculum and Instruction at University of Houston. She received her Ph.D. in Instructional Systems Technology from Indiana University at Bloomington in 2004. Her research interests include theories of identity formation, sociological examination of online communities, issues of representation, and critical ethnography. She may be contacted at mlee7@uh.edu.

Meng-Fen Grace Lin is an Assistant Professor in the Educational Technology department at the University of Hawaii at Manoa. Prior to moving to Hawaii, Dr. Lin was an adjunct faculty for University of Houston in Texas and National Taitung University in Taiwan. Her research interests include educational use of Web 2.0 tools such as wikibooks and YouTube, social learning, and open education resources. She may be contacted at gracelin@hawaii.edu.

Youmei Liu earned her Ed. D at the College of Education of University of Houston. She currently works as an Educational Production Specialist in the Office of Educational Technology and University Outreach at UH. She collaborates with faculty on the projects of innovative use of technologies; and conducts research studies to evaluate instructional technology use, such as Second Life, podcasting, and Classroom Performance System, etc. She has published broadly in the areas of instructional technology and e-learning. Her research interests cover faculty development, academic assessment, instructional technology evaluation, cross-cultural online learning, development of learning communities, and the integration of multimedia technologies in teaching and learning. She can be reached at yliu5@uh.edu.

Shawn W. McCombs is a Clinical Professor and Manager, Communication Technology Center at the Jack J. Valenti School of Communication. He earned his M.Ed. in Instructional Technology from the University of Houston in 2003. He teaches Communication Web Technologies I and II, as well as both undergraduate and graduate courses in E-Health & Telemedicine. He has worked in the Information Systems field for a number of years. His formal training includes two years as a computing consultant for Enron, Corp., one year in Systems Analysis and Design for Houston Community College System, and one year as a media services technician for MD Anderson Library. E-mail: shawn@uh.edu.

Hyungsung Park has been teaching at Korea National University of Education and Chungbuk National University since 2006. His research interests are on educational games and mobile learning in educational context. Dr. Park has recently published two articles entitled "Development of learning contents in game to support a mobile learning" and "Research for the simulation development to improve teacher's questioning skill" in Korea, and published two books on educational games and mobile learning entitled chapters: "Design of an adaptive mobile learning management system based on student learning styles" in *Handbook of Research on User Interface Design and Evaluation For Mobile Technology*; "Learning by doing via game making" in *Digital Simulations for Improving Education: Learning Through Artificial Teaching Environments* by IGI Global.

Judi Repman is a Professor of Instructional Technology and Coordinator of the Instructional Technology Program in the Department of Leadership, Technology, and Human Development at Georgia Southern University. She received a Ph.D. from Louisiana State University in Educational Media in 1989. Dr. Repman's first faculty position was at Texas Tech University and she has been on the faculty at Georgia Southern since 1997. She began teaching using distance learning technologies in 1990 and the Instructional Technology Program at Georgia Southern is offered completely online. In addition to serving as a faculty member, Dr. Repman is active in a variety of professional organizations and has served as a consultant with the Department of Defense for post-secondary military education. Her research interests include school library media centers, information literacy, Web 2.0, and online learning.

Mercedes Rico, a native of Merida, Spain, holds a PhD in English Language and is a senior lecturer at the University of Extremadura. She teaches English applied to science and technology on a full-time basis in a diverse number of engineering degrees, Masters and doctorate programs. Being *involved in a great deal* of applied linguistics & ICT *projects*, her research is focused on English for Specific Purposes and computer assisted language learning / assessment. She coordinates the interdisciplinary research group, GexCALL, dedicated to computer assisted language learning and its evaluation at all educational levels. In addition, she has served as Head of the Department of English Language and Literature, as well as on other college commissions at home and abroad.

Junjie Shang is Associate Professor, Department of Educational Technology, Peking University. Dr. Shang read both his BSc Degree and MPhil degree from Peking University in 1996 and 1999, respectively, and his PhD from The Chinese University of Hong Kong in 2007. He is currently an associate professor of the Department of Educational Technology under the Graduate School of Education, Peking University. His research focuses on computer game-based learning and virtual reality in education. Dr. Shang has published more than 35 papers in international and global Chinese journals and conferences.

Kaye Shelton is the dean of online education at Dallas Baptist University, whose Online Education program now offers thirty-five fully online degree programs, maintains a 92% course completion rate and has been a model program for many peer institutions. Ms. Shelton is a certified online instructor and winner of the 2005 Blackboard Bbionic course contest and the Instructional Technology Council's (ITC) e-Learning 2006 Outstanding Online Course award. She co-authored the book *An Administrator's Guide of Online Education* as well as writing other recent journal articles and book chapters related to online education and also practices as an online education consultant and peer reviewer. Ms. Shelton is currently a mentor for Sloan-C exemplary online course development workshops, and is now a member of a Sloan-C oversight board for quality online faculty development. She also speaks at numerous workshops and conferences regarding online faculty development and the possibilities online education provides institutions.

Chareen Snelson received her doctorate in curriculum and instruction at Boise State University where she later became an assistant professor in the Department of Educational Technology. Since 2003 she has designed and taught online courses in the master's program and has integrated Web-based video into most of them. In the fall 2008 semester, she developed and taught an online course called "YouTube for Educators." She maintains an active YouTube channel and a blog called *Web-Based Video in Education.* Dr. Snelson serves as an advisory board member for WatchKnow, a video aggregation site designed to provide children with easy access to of safe educational video content that has been reviewed for quality.

Sharon Stoerger is a doctoral student in the School of Library and Information Science at Indiana University, Bloomington. Her research interests include computer-mediated communication in learning environments and communities of practice. More specifically, she has been investigating virtual worlds, their use in formal and informal educational settings, and the ways in which visitors to these Web 2.0 spaces communicate with each other. Her current work examines continuing education courses in *Second Life* (SL) through an ethnographic approach, including participant observation and informal interviews. In addition, she has been using discourse analysis methods to better understand the interactions between students and instructors in virtual environments, as well as the learning potential of these worlds.

Daniel W. Surry is Associate Professor of Instructional Design & Development at the University of South Alabama in Mobile. He holds a Doctor of Education in Instructional Technology from the University of Georgia, a Master of Science in Instructional Design from the University of South Alabama, and a Bachelor of Arts in Mass Communication from the University of Alabama. Prior to his current position, he served on the faculty of the University of Alabama and the University of Southern Mississippi and as Instructional Technologist at California State University, Fresno. Dan's research and consulting interests are related to the adoption, diffusion, and implementation of innovations. He is the author of numerous papers on the topic and has presented at local, regional, national, and international conferences.

Robert Z. Zheng is a faculty member and director of instructional design and educational technology (IDET) program in the Department of Educational Psychology at the University of Utah. His research interests include online instructional design, cognition and multimedia learning, and human-computer interaction. He is the editor and co-editor of *Cognitive Effects on Multimedia Learning*; *Online Instructional Modeling: Theories and Practices*; and *Adolescent Online Social Communication and Behavior: Relationship Formation on the Internet*. He has published widely in the areas of multimedia, online learning, and cognition. He is also an active presenter at numerous national and international conferences on issues related to educational technology and learning.

Cordelia D. Zinskie is a Professor of Educational Research and Chair of the Department of Curriculum, Foundations, and Reading at Georgia Southern University. She received her Ed.D. in 1988 from Memphis State University with a major in Foundations of Education with an emphasis in Research Methodology and Statistics. At Georgia Southern since 1993, Dr. Zinskie teaches online graduate courses in quantitative and qualitative research methods. Prior to assuming an administrative role in 2006, Dr. Zinskie served as an evaluator on several funded projects. Her recent research interests include effective instructional design and delivery in the online environment and growth of the business model of online learning in higher education.

Index

A

ancillary communication 79, 81, 83, 84, 85, 86, 87, 88, 92
artificial intelligence (AI) 3
avatars 208, 210, 211, 212, 214, 226, 229, 235, 237, 245, 253, 255, 259

B

behaviourist educational games 187. *See* drill-and-practice games
behaviourist theory 1, 186, 187
Blackboard 12, 78, 167, 175, 178, 184. *See also* learning management systems (LMS)
Blackboard Scholar 167, 184. *See also* social bookmarking websites
browser software 11, 150, 151, 162, 163, 235, 259, 272. *See* Firefox; *See* Internet Explorer; *See* Safari

C

CiteULike 167, 184. *See* social bookmarking websites
co-construction of technology theory 98, 107, 108
cognitive demand 64
cognitive load 64, 68, 70, 73, 74, 76, 149, 156, 165
cognitive strategies 64, 65, 72, 73
cognitivist theory 1, 6, 9
collaboration, classroom 110
collaboration, online 62, 110, 121, 131, 182
communication, asynchronous 45, 51, 63, 78, 81, 82, 86, 91, 155, 158, 253, 284, 303

communications theory 2, 80
communication, synchronous 11, 45, 51, 63, 78, 81, 82, 86, 88, 91, 92, 149, 186, 253
communities of practice, E-Learning 2.0 45
community, sense of 45, 86, 127, 138, 141, 281, 282, 283, 284, 285, 289, 290, 294, 299, 300, 301, 302, 303, 304
complex-games 187. *See* constructivist educational games
computer assisted language-learning (CALL) 208, 210, 212, 219, 227
computer-mediated communication (CMC) 63, 227, 281, 282, 284
connectivist theory 1, 3, 4, 9, 25, 52
Connotea 167, 184. *See also* social bookmarking websites
constructivist educational games 187, 188, 189. *See* complex games; *See* mini-games
constructivist theory 7, 52, 59, 63, 67, 69, 72, 79, 80, 84, 85, 92, 137, 141, 157, 164, 185, 186, 187, 188, 189, 190, 201, 202, 204, 205, 207, 212, 214, 228, 247, 248, 249, 250, 258
continuity of thought 149
CourseInfo™ 78, 82. *See also* e-learning portals
course management systems 45, 46, 49, 51, 52, 84, 122, 123, 124, 158
crowds, wisdom of 11, 111, 112, 126

D

Delicious 167, 183. *See also* social bookmarking websites
Diigo 167, 184. *See also* social bookmarking websites
drill-and-practice games 187

Copyright © 2010, IGI Global, distributing in print or electronic forms without written permission of IGI Global is prohibited.